CIMA Official
Learning System

Relevant for
Computer-Based Assessments

C5 – Fundamentals of Ethics, Corporate Governance and Business law

CIMA Certificate in Business Accounting

**David Sagar,
Larry Mead and
Kevin Bampton**

ELSEVIER

AMSTERDAM BOSTON HEIDELBERG LONDON NEW YORK OXFORD
PARIS SAN DIEGO SAN FRANCISCO SINGAPORE SYDNEY TOKYO

CIMA Publishing is an imprint of Elsevier
Linacre House, Jordan Hill, Oxford OX2 8DP, UK
30 Corporate Drive, Suite 400, Burlington, MA 01803, USA

First edition 2008

British Library Cataloguing in Publication Data
A catalogue record for this book is available from the British Library

Library of Congress Cataloguing in Publication Data
A catalogue record for this book is available from the Library of Congress

978-1-85617-787-0

For information on all CIMA publications
visit our website at www.elsevierdirect.com

Typeset by Macmillan Publishing Solutions
(www.macmillansolutions.com)

Printed and bound in Italy

09 10 11 11 10 9 8 7 6 5 4 3 2 1

Contents

The CIMA *Learning System*

Acknowledgements

Every effort has been made to contact the holders of copyright material, but if any here have been inadvertently overlooked the publishers will be pleased to make the necessary arrangements at the first opportunity.

How to use your CIMA *Learning System*

This *Fundamentals of Ethics, Corporate governance amd Business Law Learning System* has been devised as a resource for students attempting to pass their CIMA computer-based assessments, and provides:

- A detailed explanation of all syllabus areas;
- extensive 'practical' materials, including readings from relevant journals;
- generous question practice, together with full solutions;
- an exam preparation section, complete with exam standard questions and solutions.

This Learning System has been designed with the needs of home-study and distance-learning candidates in mind. Such students require very full coverage of the syllabus topics, and also the facility to undertake extensive question practice. However, the Learning System is also ideal for fully taught courses.

The main body of the text is divided into a number of chapters, each of which is organised on the following pattern:

- *Detailed learning outcomes*. Expected after your studies of the chapter are complete. You should assimilate these before beginning detailed work on the chapter, so that you can appreciate where your studies are leading.
- *Step-by-step topic coverage*. This is the heart of each chapter, containing detailed explanatory text supported where appropriate by worked examples and exercises. You should work carefully through this section, ensuring that you understand the material being explained and can tackle the examples and exercises successfully. Remember that in many cases knowledge is cumulative: if you fail to digest earlier material thoroughly, you may struggle to understand later chapters.

- *Readings and activities.* Some chapters are illustrated by more practical elements, such as relevant journal articles or other readings, together with comments and questions designed to stimulate discussion.
- *Question practice.* The test of how well you have learned the material is your ability to tackle exam-standard questions. Make a serious attempt at producing your own answers, but at this stage do not be too concerned about attempting the questions in exam conditions. In particular, it is more important to absorb the material thoroughly by completing a full solution than to observe the time limits that would apply in the actual assessment.
- *Solutions.* Avoid the temptation merely to 'audit' the solutions provided. It is an illusion to think that this provides the same benefits as you would gain from a serious attempt of your own. However, if you are struggling to get started on a question you should read the introductory guidance provided at the beginning of the solution, and then make your own attempt before referring back to the full solution.

You will note that the topics covered in this Learning System do not appear in the same order as they are listed in the CIMA syllabus. The syllabus contains a list of appropriate topics in the following order:

1. Ethics and Business.
2. Ethical Conflict.
3. Corporate Governance
4. Comparison of English Law and Alternative Legal Systems.
5. Law of Contract.
6. Law of Employment.
7. Company Administration and Finance.

The syllabus is not intended as a teaching/learning programme and Ethics and Corporate Governance appear first as evidence that CIMA regard these issues as of prime importance.

The topics have been arranged and presented in this Learning System in a manner best suited to teaching/learning. Thus Company Administration, which is the largest topic in the syllabus, has been divided into two chapters i.e. Company Administration (Chapter 4) and Company Finance and Management (Chapter 5). In addition these topics are studied before Corporate Governance so that students first learn the essentials of company law before going on to learn how corporate governance impacts on companies.

Students who use this Learning System will cover all topics within the CIMA syllabus and will be extremely well prepared for the examination.

Having worked through the chapters you are ready to begin your final preparations for the examination. The final section of this CIMA *Learning System* provides you with the guidance you need. It includes the following features:

- A brief guide to revision technique.
- A note on the format of the assessment. You should know what to expect when you tackle the real exam, and in particular the number of questions to attempt, which questions are compulsory and which optional, and so on.
- Guidance on how to tackle the assessment itself.
- A table mapping revision questions to the syllabus learning outcomes allowing you to quickly identify questions by subject area.
- Revision questions. These are of exam standard and should be tackled in exam conditions, especially as regards the time allocation.

- Solutions to the revision questions. As before, these indicate the length and the quality of solution that would be expected of a well-prepared candidate.

If you work conscientiously through this CIMA *Learning System* according to the guidelines above you will be giving yourself an excellent chance of exam success. Good luck with your studies!

Guide to the Icons used within this Text

Key term or definition

Equation to learn

Exam tip to topic likely to appear in the exam

Exercise

Question

Solution

Comment or Note

Study technique

Passing exams is partly a matter of intellectual ability, but however accomplished you are in that respect you can improve your chances significantly by the use of appropriate study and revision techniques. In this section we briefly outline some tips for effective study during the earlier stages of your approach to the exam. Later in the text we mention some techniques that you will find useful at the revision stage.

Planning

To begin with, formal planning is essential to get the best return from the time you spend studying. Estimate how much time in total you are going to need for each subject that you face. Remember that you need to allow time for revision as well as for initial study of the material. The amount of notional study time for any subject is the minimum estimated time that students will need to achieve the specified learning outcomes set out earlier in this chapter. This time includes all appropriate learning activities, for example, face-to-face tuition, private study, directed home study, learning in the workplace, revision time, etc. You may find it helpful to read CIMA pass first time by David Harris, CIMA publishing, ISBN: 9780750683968. This book will provide you with proven study techniques and is packed with useful hints and tips on how to pass your exam.

The notional study time for Certificate level *Fundamentals of Ethics, Corporate Governance and Business Law* is 130 hours. Note that the standard amount of notional learning hours attributed to one full-time academic year of approximately 30 weeks is 1,200 hours.

By way of example, the notional study time might be made up as follows:

	Hours
Face-to-face study: up to	40
Personal study: up to	65
'Other' study – e.g. learning in the workplace, revision, etc.: up to	25
	130

Note that all study and learning-time recommendations should be used only as a guideline and are intended as minimum amounts. The amount of time recommended for face-to-face tuition, personal study and/or additional learning will vary according to the type of course undertaken, prior learning of the student, and the pace at which different students learn.

Now split your total time requirement over the weeks between now and the assessment. This will give you an idea of how much time you need to devote to study each week. Remember to allow for holidays or other periods during which you will not be able to study (e.g. because of seasonal workloads).

With your study material before you, decide which chapters you are going to study in each week, and which weeks you will devote to revision and final question practice.

Prepare a written schedule summarising the above – and stick to it!

The amount of space allocated to a topic in the study material is not a very good guide as to how long it will take you.

It is essential to know your syllabus. As your course progresses you will become more familiar with how long it takes to cover topics in sufficient depth. Your timetable may need to be adapted to allocate enough time for the whole syllabus.

Tips for effective studying

1. Aim to find a quiet and undisturbed location for your study, and plan as far as possible to use the same period of time each day. Getting into a routine helps to avoid wasting time. Make sure that you have all the materials you need before you begin so as to minimise interruptions.
2. Store all your materials in one place, so that you do not waste time searching for items around the house. If you have to pack everything away after each study period, keep them in a box, or even a suitcase, which will not be disturbed until the next time.
3. Limit distractions. To make the most effective use of your study periods you should be able to apply total concentration, so turn off the TV, set your phones to message mode, and put up your 'do not disturb' sign.
4. Your timetable will tell you which topic to study. However, before diving in and becoming engrossed in the finer points, make sure you have an overall picture of all the areas that need to be covered by the end of that session. After an hour, allow yourself a short break and move away from your books. With experience, you will learn to assess the pace you need to work at. You should also allow enough time to read relevant articles from newspapers and journals, which will supplement your knowledge and demonstrate a wider perspective.
5. Work carefully through a chapter, making notes as you go. When you have covered a suitable amount of material, vary the pattern by attempting a practice question. Preparing an answer plan is a good habit to get into, while you are both studying and revising, and also in the examination room. It helps to impose a structure on your solutions, and avoids

rambling. When you have finished your attempt, make notes of any mistakes you made, or any areas that you failed to cover or covered only skimpily.

6. Make notes as you study, and discover the techniques that work best for you. Your notes may be in the form of lists, bullet points, diagrams, summaries, 'mind maps', or the written word, but remember that you will need to refer back to them at a later date, so they must be intelligible. If you are on a taught course, make sure you highlight any issues you would like to follow up with your lecturer.
7. Organise your paperwork. There are now numerous paper storage systems available to ensure that all your notes, calculations and articles can be effectively filed and easily retrieved later.

Computer-based assessments

CIMA has introduced computer-based assessments (CBAs) for all subjects at Certificate level. The website says

> Objective questions are used. The most common type is 'multiple choice', where you have to choose the correct answer from a list of possible answers, but there are a variety of other objective question types that can be used within the system. These include true/false questions, matching pairs of text and graphic, sequencing and ranking, labelling diagrams and single and multiple numeric entry.
>
> Candidates answer the questions by either pointing and clicking the mouse, moving objects around the screen, typing numbers, or a combination of these responses. Try the online demo at http://www.cimaglobal.com to see how the technology works.
>
> The CBA system can ensure that a wide range of the syllabus is assessed, as a pre-determined number of questions from each syllabus area (dependent upon the syllabus weighting for that particular area) are selected in each assessment.

In every chapter of this Learning system we have introduced these types of questions but obviously we have to label answers A, B, C etc. rather than using click boxes. For convenience we have retained quite a lot of questions where an initial scenario leads to a number of sub-questions. There will be questions of this type in the CBA but they will rarely have more than three sub-questions. In all such cases examiners will ensure that the answer to one part does not hinge upon a prior answer.

There are two types of questions which were previously involved in objective testing in paper-based exams and which are not at present possible in a CBA. The actual drawing of graphs and charts is not yet possible. Equally there will be no questions calling for comments to be written by students. Charts and interpretations remain on many syllabi and will be examined at Certificate level but using other methods.

For further CBA practice, CIMA Publishing has produced CIMA E-success CD-ROMs for all certificate level subjects. These products are available at www.cimapublishing.com or go online at www.cimapublishing.com/esuccess for a free demo.

Fundamentals of Ethics, Corporate Governance and Business Law, and computer-based assessments

The examination for Fundamentals of Ethics, Corporate Governance and Business Law syllabus, is a two hour computer-based assessments comprising 75 compulsory questions, with one or more parts. Single part questions are generally worth 1–2 marks each, but two and three part questions may be worth 4 or 6 marks. There will be no choice and all questions should be attempted if time permits. CIMA are continuously developing the question styles within the CBA system and you are advised to try the on-line website demo at www.cimaglobal.com, to both gain familiarity with assessment software and examine the latest style of questions being used.

Fundamentals of ethics, corporate governance and business law syllabus

Syllabus outline:

The syllabus comprises:

Topic and Study Weighting		
1.	Comparison of English Law with Alternative Legal Systems	10%
2.	The Law of Contract	20%
3.	The Law of Employment	10%
4&5.	Company Administration and Finance	25%
6.	Ethics and Business	15%
7.	Ethical Conflict	10%
8.	Corporate Governance	10%

Learning aims

Students should be able to:

- discuss the framework of professional values, ethics and attitudes for exercising professional judgement and acting in an ethical manner, that is in the best interests of society and the profession;
- explain the need to comply with the CIMA and IFAC 'Codes of Ethics for Professional Accountants';
- explain the importance of good corporate goverance and the evolution of good practice;
- explain fundamental aspects of the organisation and operation of the English legal system and compare with other legal systems;
- explain the elements of the tort of negligence and the manner in which the tort impacts upon professional advisers;
- explain the essential elements of simple contract, what is regarded as adequate performance of the simple contract, and the remedies available to the innocent party in the event of a breach;
- explain the essential differences between sole traderships, partnerships and companies limited by shares;
- explain the way in which companies are administered, financed and managed;
- apply legal knowledge to solve business problems.

Unless specifically mentioned, the English legal system will be the context for those parts of this syllabus that relate to the study of business law.

Assessment strategy

There will be a computer-based assessments of 2 hours duration, comprising 75 compulsory questions, each with one or more parts.

A variety of objective test question styles and types will be used within the assessment.

Learning outcomes and indicative syllabus content

1. Comparison of English Law with Alternative Legal System – 10%

Learning outcomes

On completion of their studies students should be able to:

(i) explain the manner in which behaviour within society is regulated by the civil and the criminal law;
(ii) identify and explain the sources of English law;
(iii) illustrate the operation of the doctrine of precedent by reference to the essential elements of the tort of negligence and its application to professional advisers;
(iv) compare the elements of alternative legal systems, Sharia Law and the role of international legal regulations.

Indicative syllabus content

- The sources of English law.
- The system of judicial precedent.
- The essential elements of the tort of negligence, including duty, breach and damage/loss/injury and the liability of professionals in respect of negligent advice.
- Alternative legal systems, including codified (civil law) systems, Sharia Law and international legal regulations.

2. The Law of Contract – 20%

Learning outcomes

On completion of their studies students should be able to:

(i) identify the essential elements of a valid simple contract and situations where the law requires the contract to be in a particular form;
(ii) explain how the law determines whether negotiating parties have reached agreement and the role of consideration in making that agreement enforceable;
(iii) explain when the parties will be regarded as intending the agreement to be legally binding and how an agreement may be avoided because of misrepresentations;
(iv) explain how the contents and the terms of a contract are established and the possible repercussions of non-performance;
(v) explain how the law controls the use of unfair terms in respect of both consumer and non-consumer business agreements;
(vi) explain what the law regards as performance of the contract, and valid and invalid reasons for non-performance;
(vii) explain the type of breach necessary to cause contractual breakdown and the remedies which are available for serious and minor breaches of contract.

Indicative syllabus content

- The essential elements of a valid simple contract.
- The legal status of statements made by negotiating parties. Enforceable offers and acceptances, and the application of the rules to standard form contracts using modern forms of communication and the role of consideration.

- The principles for establishing that the parties intend their agreement to have contractual force and how a contract is affected by a misrepresentation.
- Incorporation of express and implied terms, conditions and warranties.
- The main provisions of sale of goods and supply of services legislation.
- The manner in which the law controls the use of exclusion clauses and unfair terms in consumer and non-consumer transactions.
- The level of performance sufficient to discharge contractual obligations.
- Valid reasons for non-performance by way of agreement, breach by the other party and frustration.
- The remedies of specific performance, injunction, rescission and requiring a contract party to pay the agreed price.
- Causation and remoteness of damages, and their quantification.

3. The Law of Employment – 10%

Learning outcomes

On completion of their studies students should be able to:

(i) explain the difference between employees and independent contractors and how the contents of a contract of employment are established;
(ii) explain the distinction between unfair and wrongful dismissal;
(iii) demonstrate an awareness of how employers and employees are affected by health and safety legislation, including the consequences of a failure to comply.

Indicative syllabus content

- The tests used to distinguish an employee from an independent contractor.
- The express and implied terms of a contract of employment.
- Unfair and wrongful dismissal.
- An outline of the main rules relating to health and safety at work, sanctions on employers for non-compliance and remedies for employees.

4 & 5. Company Administration and Finance – 25%

Learning outcomes

On completion of their studies students should be able to:

(i) explain the essential characteristics of the different forms of business organisations and the implications of corporate personality;
(ii) explain the differences between public and private companies and establishing a company by registration or purchasing 'off the shelf';
(iii) explain the purpose and legal status of the memorandum and articles of association;
(iv) explain the ability of a company to contract;
(v) explain the main advantages and disadvantages of carrying on business through the medium of a company limited by shares.
(vi) explain the use and procedure of board meetings and general meetings of shareholders;
(vii) explain the voting rights of directors and shareholders and identify the various types of shareholder resolutions;
(viii) explain the nature of different types of share, the procedure for the issue of shares and acceptable forms of payment;

(ix) explain the maintenance of capital principle and the procedure to increase and reduce share capital, including the repercussions of issuing shares for an improper purpose;
(x) explain the ability of a company to take secured and unsecured loans, the different types of security and the registration procedure.
(xi) explain the procedure for the appointment, retirement, disqualification and removal of directors and their power and duties during office;
(xii) explain the rules dealing with the possible imposition of personal liability upon the directors of insolvent companies;
(xiii) identify and contrast the rights of shareholders with the board of a company.
(xiv) explain the qualifications, powers and duties of the company secretary.

Indicative syllabus content

- The essential characteristics of sole traderships/practitionerships, partnerships, companies limited by shares and corporate personality.
- 'Lifting the corporate veil' both at common law and by statute.
- The distinction between public and private companies.
- The procedure for registering a company, the advantages of purchasing a company 'off the shelf', and the purpose and contents of the memorandum and articles of association.
- Corporate capacity to contract.
- Board meetings: when used and the procedure at the meeting.
- Annual and Extraordinary General Meetings: when used and the procedure at the meeting including company resolutions and the uses of each type of resolution;
- The rights attaching to the different types of shares and the purposes and procedures for issuing shares.
- The maintenance of capital principle, the purposes and rules for which shares may be issued, redeemed, or purchased and the provision of financial assistance for the purchase of its own shares.
- The ability of a company to borrow money, and the procedure to be followed.
- Unsecured loans, and the nature and effect of fixed and floating charges.
- The appointment, retirement and removal of directors and their power and duties during office.
- Fraudulent and wrongful trading, preferences and transactions at an under-value.
- The division of powers between the board and the shareholders.
- The rights of majority and minority shareholders.
- The qualifications, powers and duties of the company secretary.

6. Ethics and Business – 15%

Learning outcomes

On completion of their studies students should be able to:

(i) apply the values and attitudes that provide professional accountants with a commitment to act in the public interest and with social responsibility.
(ii) explain the need for a framework of laws, regulations and standards in business and their application;
(iii) explain the nature of ethics and its application to business and the accountancy profession;
(iv) identify the difference between detailed rules-based and framework approaches to ethics;

(v) identify the need for continual personal improvement and life-long learning;
(vi) identify the need to develop the virtues of reliability, responsibility, timeliness, courtesy and respect;
(vii) explain the ethical priciples of integrity, objectivity, professional competence, due care and confidentiality;
(viii) identify concepts of independence, scepticism, accountability and social responsibility;
(ix) explain the reasons why CIMA and IFAC each have a 'Code of Ethics for Professional Accountants'.

Indicative syllabus content

- Values and attitudes for professional accountants.
- Legal frameworks, regulations and standards for business.
- Nature of ethics and its relevance to business and the accountancy profession.
- Rules-based and framework approaches to ethics.
- Personal development and life-long learning.
- Personal qualities of reliability, responsibility, timeliness, courtesy and respect.
- Ethical principles of integrity, objectivity, professional competence, due care and confidentiality.
- Concepts of independence, scepticism, accountability and social responsibility.
- The CIMA and IFAC 'Codes of Ethics for Professional Accountants'.

7. Ethical Conflict – 10%

Learning outcomes

On completion of their studies students should be able to:

(i) explain the relationship between ethics, governance, the law and social responsibility;
(ii) describe the consequences of unethical behaviour to the individual, the profession and the society;
(iii) identify situations where ethical dilemmas and conflicts of interest occur;
(iv) explain how ethical dilemmas and conflicts of interest can be resolved.

Indicative syllabus content

- Relationship between ethics, governance, the law and social responsibility.
- Unethical behaviour.
- Ethical dilemmas and conflicts of interst.

8. Corporate Governance – 10%

Learning outcomes

On completion of their studies students should be able to:

(i) define corporate governance;
(ii) explain the interaction of corporate governance with business ethics and company law;
(iii) describe the history of corporate governance internationally;
(iv) explain the effect of corporate governance on directors' behaviour and their duties of skill and care;

(v) explain different board structures, the role of the board and corporate governance issues;
(vi) describe the types of policies and procedures that best-practice companies introduce;
(vii) explain the regulatory governance framework for companies.

Indicative syllabus content

- The role and key objectives of corporate governance in relation to ethics and the law.
- Development of corporate governance internationally.
- The behaviour of directors in relation to corporate governance and duty of care towards their stakeholders.
- The role of the board in establishing corporate governance standards.
- Types of board structures and corporate governance issues.
- Policies and procedures for *best-practice* companies.
- Rules- and principles-based approaches to governance.
- The regulatory governance framework.

1

Comparison of English Law with Alternative Legal Systems

Comparison of English Law with Alternative Legal Systems

1

Learning Outcomes

After completing this chapter you should be able to:

- explain the manner in which behaviour within society is regulated by the civil and the criminal law;
- identify and explain the sources of English law;
- explain and illustrate the operation of the doctrine of judicial precedent by reference to the essential elements of the tort of negligence, and its application to professional advisers.
- compare the elements of alternative legal systems, Sharia law and the role of international legal regulations.

The chapter has been arranged into sections based on the learning outcomes as above.

1.1 Law: criminal and civil

Learning Outcome: To explain the manner in which behaviour within society is regulated by the civil and the criminal law.

Law is necessary in every society, to help the relationships between its members. As the population expands, as people live more closely together in towns and cities, and as technology becomes more powerful, law has to become more detailed. Freedom for one person means that the freedom of another must be limited. To protect your right to drive along a motorway, my freedom to park my car in the middle of it must be taken away.

In all modern societies, legal rules fall into two main categories:

1. criminal;
2. civil.

Criminal law. A crime is regarded as an offence against all of us, and the state, on our behalf, steps in to punish those who transgress. It is because the action is brought not by an individual, but rather by the state that it falls within the body of law known as Public Law. It follows that the purpose of the criminal law is to regulate behaviour within society by outlawing certain types of behaviour. People cannot live together unless murder is forbidden. The same applies to other forms of personal violence. Similarly, it is felt that people should not be able to take the property of others dishonestly. Therefore, theft and various forms of fraud are forbidden. Offenders are punished, partly as retribution, and partly to deter them and others from such conduct in the future. The same approach applies to all offences, right down to car-parking ones.

Civil law. It has a different but complementary approach. It exists to enable disputes between citizens to be resolved peacefully, without turbulent feuds. Civil law sets out the rights and duties of citizens as between themselves. If one party acts in breach of these rules, the person whose rights have been infringed can claim compensation ('damages') from the wrongdoer. Because here the action is between two private individuals or bodies, such actions fall within the body of law known as Private Law.

It can be seen that indirectly the civil law also serves to regulate behaviour within society. Thus for example, if a man's driving causes him to accidentally damage another motorist's car, the civil law makes it possible for the other to obtain compensation. The fact that we know that if we cause damage we may be called upon to pay for it must cause us to think twice as to how we conduct ourselves. This is so, even if there is no possibility of any fine, imprisonment or other form of punishment.

In most countries the criminal courts are separate from the civil courts. The parties and the terms used are different. In the criminal courts in England and Wales, the prosecution is started by public officers, such as the Crown Prosecution Service. The decision to prosecute is not taken by the victim (if any). A criminal conviction is very serious, and the case against the accused must normally be proved beyond reasonable doubt. In the civil courts, the action is started by the claimant (the victim). Liability in a civil action can usually be proved merely on a balance of probabilities, that is, that the claimant's case is marginally more probable than the defendant's. The types of proceeding can be contrasted.

In a criminal prosecution	*In a civil action*
the state	the claimant
prosecutes	sues
the accused	the defendant
to punish the offender	for a remedy
by imprisonment or a fine to the government	e.g. damages payable to the claimant
(if the accused is found guilty)	(if the defendant is held liable)

In criminal cases, there need not even be a direct victim. In an unsuccessful theft, no property need have been taken. In an unsuccessful attempted murder, or in a speeding or car-parking offence, no one need have been hurt. Nevertheless, there has been a criminal offence. In civil cases, there must normally be a claimant who has suffered loss.

Finally, the same events are often both a criminal offence and a civil wrong. Most types of physical assault and serious fraud are criminal offences by the wrongdoers. However, the fact that the wrongdoers have been fined or imprisoned following conviction for assault or fraud does not provide the victim with any compensation. It follows that assault and fraud are also breaches of the civil law thereby providing the victim with a means of obtaining compensation. It must be said, however, that this is generally only true if the wrongdoer has sufficient funds available to meet any claims for compensation.

1.2 The sources of English law

Learning Outcome: To identify and explain the sources of English law.

The sources of English law are:

- custom/common law;
- equity;
- legislation;
- European law;
- other sources.

1.2.1 Custom/common law

Custom was an important source of law historically, but is of less practical importance today. Prior to the Norman Conquest in 1066, there was no single body of law applicable to the whole country. After 1066, the Normans attempted to rule the country through the application of local customs. Over time, customs considered capable of general application were absorbed and made common to all areas of the country so that there was one law common to all the country; hence the term, the common law. The common law today is made up of past cases which are recorded in law reports. It is still of considerable importance, and develops from case to case in order to reflect the changing times. In order to ensure certainty, the legal principles which are pronounced by the higher courts are binding on the lower courts under the doctrine of judicial precedent.

The organic common law

The common law is an organic and dynamic body of rules. It has grown and evolved over centuries. It has not ossified. It continues to grow and to adapt to social change. In a case in 1954 (about child custody and illegitimacy), Lord Denning refuted the idea that the law could not adapt and modernise itself.

'What is the argument on the other side? Only this, that no case has been found in which it has been done before. That argument does not appeal to me in the least. If we never do anything which has not been done before, we shall never get anywhere. The law will stand still whilst the rest of the world goes on: and that will be bad for both.' Denning LJ, *Packer* v. *Packer* [1954] P 15 at 22

See also Article content on page 20, 'Legal traditions'.

1.2.2 Equity

Again historically, the common law was incomplete, for example the main remedy available was restricted to monetary compensation. Equity was developed by the Court of Chancery to fill in gaps in the common law, for example by the development of non-monetary remedies such as injunctions and orders of specific performance. An injunction is prohibitory whereas a specific performance order imposes an obligation to act. Both of these types of equitable remedy are used in the area of contract law, and can assist to ensure that requirements under the contract are satisfied. Equitable remedies are discretionary, and, in the event of a conflict between equity and the common law, equity prevails. Equity has also been responsible for the development of the law of trusts.

1.2.3 Legislation

Acts of Parliament

Legislation is the formal enactment of rules by a body having the constitutional right and power to do so. In the United Kingdom, the only body with this inherent power is the UK Parliament. Its legislation takes the form of Acts of Parliament, also known as statutes. The process of passing an Act can be a long one. It must pass through long proceedings in both – the House of Commons and the House of Lords, and then receive the (purely formal) Royal Assent. The normal procedure followed requires:

1. a green paper – outline proposal
2. a white paper – more detailed content

It is usually the House of Commons that considers the 'Bill' initially. If approved in the House of Commons, the Bill will pass to the House of Lords where a similar procedure is followed.

This procedure involves:

1. first reading – merely the title is read out
2. second reading – a vote is taken
3. committee stage – detailed consideration of the bill
4. report stage – the committee report back to the House.
5. third reading – final vote.

Exceptions to this procedure exist e.g. in relation to the introduction of the Finance Acts following the budget speech. Many Acts contain a section delaying direct effect for a short time to give those affected time to adapt.

Once enacted and in force, a statute remains law unless and until it is repealed or amended by another Act of Parliament. If the government dislikes an earlier Act, the full parliamentary procedure must be used in order to change or repeal the Act into a new one. This can always be done, however, because an Act cannot make itself unrepealable.

The courts cannot generally question the validity of an Act of Parliament. They must obey and apply the words of the statute, because Parliament has 'legislative sovereignty'. Where the words of a statute are unclear or ambiguous, the courts must interpret the words as best they can. The courts will not ask the government what an Act means because a government might give whatever answer is most helpful to it at the time. The courts will, however, try to achieve the purpose for which the statute was enacted, and can look at what the government said in the Parliamentary proceedings *before* the Act was passed.

In one exceptional respect the courts can challenge the validity of a provision in an Act. The European Communities Act 1972 made changes required by UK membership of (what is now) the European Union. The United Kingdom agreed to be bound by EC law. Therefore, if a provision in a UK Act contravenes EU law, the UK court can suspend the operation of the provision.

Delegated legislation

For many reasons, Parliament has delegated some of its legislative powers to other bodies. Usually, Parliament passes an 'enabling' Act setting out the policy involved and the objectives it wishes to achieve. The Act then delegates to some other body the task of filling in the details. Such a delegation of powers saves parliament time which can then be devoted to more far-ranging and important issues. Also, expertise and where appropriate, specialist local knowledge can be used. Rules enacted under such powers are called delegated legislation, and the following are examples:

- The Parliaments of Scotland and Wales have been given *some* legislative powers on matters that affect their own regions.
- In the United Kingdom, the government cannot make law without the authority of Parliament. However, Parliament has delegated wide powers to government ministers within their own departments. Many rules are too detailed and technical to undergo the full Parliamentary process, and they may need to be changed too frequently. The detailed rules on motor vehicle construction and use are a good example. Therefore, individual ministers and their civil service departments are given the task of making rules within the guidelines set out in the enabling Acts. These regulations are usually in the form of *statutory instruments*.
- Local authorities have been given wide powers to make *by-laws* within their own boundaries. Certain public bodies likewise have this power e.g. the London Underground.
- The Crown and Privy Council have the power to introduce delegated legislation in times of emergency in the form of orders in council. Such orders can be introduced quickly. Of further significance is the value of this means of law creation where circumstances demand that measures be introduced, but at a time when parliament is not sitting.

Many controls exist to prevent abuse of delegated powers. Parliament itself exercises the main supervision, and it can always take away delegated powers by a new Act. A Scrutiny Committee exists to oversee delegated legislation introduced. However, the volume of delegated legislation introduced annually, and the fact that it can be introduced speedily and revoked quickly, makes thorough consideration of content impossible.

The courts also have supervisory powers over delegated legislation (unlike over statutes). If a delegated body exceeds or abuses its powers, the courts can hold that the regulations, by-laws, and so on are *ultra vires* (outside of the powers given) and therefore void.

1.2.4 Judicial interpretation of legislation

After parliament has created law through legislation it is then the role of the judiciary to interpret and apply this law. A number of rules and aids exist that can be used by the judiciary to assist them in this task.

The rules are:

The Literal rule
The Golden rule
The Mischief rule
The Rules of language
(Also the purposive approach can be used)

The aids to interpretation fall into two categories:

The internal aids
The external aids.

The Literal rule

Where words in a statute have only one possible meaning then that ordinary dictionary meaning must be applied even though it may result in an absurd outcome. With this rule the supremacy of parliament is recognised, alongside the role of the judiciary as that of applying rather than creating law. Where an error is found in legislation it is for parliament to introduce new law to rectify the error.

In *Fisher* v. *Bell* (1960), the court had to consider the meaning of the wording 'offer for sale'. It was an offence to 'offer for sale' offensive weapons. A shopkeeper had flick-knives with price tags attached on display in his shop window. The court applied the principles of contract law accepting that the display of flick-knives was an invitation to treat. It was the customer who made an offer to buy. In consequence the shopkeeper was found not to be acting illegally. The aim of parliament, however, had been to prevent sales in this way of offensive weapons.

The Golden rule

Where words in a statute have more than one meaning the judiciary can apply the meaning that avoids an absurd consequence.

In *Re: Sigworth* (1935), a man murdered his mother and being the only heir on the literal interpretation of legislation was entitled to inherit. The court, however, interpreted the wording of the relevant Administration of Estates Act 1925 content, applying the golden rule, in order to prevent the murderer form benefiting.

The Mischief rule

Where legislation is introduced to remedy a defect or 'mischief' in the law then the judiciary should interpret the legislation to achieve this objective. The rule has origins in Heydon's Case 1584 in which judges were guided to consider:

- Relevant law prior to the legislation
- The mischief that the existing law failed to address
- The intended remedy for the mischief that parliament sought to introduce.

In *Gorris* v. *Scott* (1874) the court had to interpret the wording of the Contagious Diseases (Animals) Act 1869. The relevant content of the Act required animals being transported by ship to be in pens. The aim of this was to prevent the spread of contagios diseases. On the case facts animals on board ship were not housed in pens and some were washed overboard. The claim against the defendant failed as the basis for the claim varied from the 'mischief' that parliament was looking to address.

In more recent times the *Purposive approach* has become recognised. Here the judiciary are guide to look at the purpose for the introduction of the legislation and reach decisions on that basis. This approach can be seen as a development on from and being closely associated with the mischief rule.

The Rules of Language offer assistance to judges through

1. *Eiusdem generic* – where general words follow particular words in a statute, the meaning of the general words should be taken from the meaning of the particular words.

   In *Powell* v. *Kempton Racecourse Co.* (1899) the court had to consider where it was unlawful for betting to take place. The relevant legislation provided that betting was illegal in any 'house, office, room or other place'. The problem related to the wording 'or other place'. The court decided that the wording related to any enclosed place. This being based on the meaning to be attributed to the particular words in the term.
2. *Expressio unius exclusion alterius* – where legislation specifically identifies that which is to be affected, by implication anything else is to be excluded.

3. *Noscitur a sociis* – where the meaning to be attributed to a word can be determined from other words around it.
4. *In pari material* – where courts can look at previous legislation dealing with the same subject matter to discover the appropriate interpretation.

Internal aids (Intrinsic aids)

These are found within the statute and include:

- The long title
- The preamble identifying the intentions and objectives of the legislation
- The interpretation section
- Headings
- Marginal notes.

External aids (extrinsic aids)

These are found outside the statute and include:

- Dictionaries
- Hansard which provides information of what was said in parliament when the Bill was being considered
- The Interpretation Act 1978
- The judiciary are also assisted by a number of Presumptions. These include:
  - An Act will not bind the Crown
  - The Act will apply to the whole of the UK Legislation may however, provide that it is only to apply to an identified area within the UK
  - The Act will not have retrospective effect
  - An Act is not intended to deprive a person of their liberty.

1.2.5 European Union law

In 1972, the United Kingdom joined the European Community (EC), now called the European Union (EU). Accession meant that the United Kingdom agreed to conform with existing and future EC law, and the United Kingdom complied by passing the European Communities Act 1972. There are several sources of EU law:

- *The Treaties*. They are the primary source: the Treaties of Paris and Rome (2) that created the first EU bodies, and all subsequent Treaties. The provisions (e.g. on competition) are directly applicable, and have, basically, legislative effect. They automatically become law in the member states, with no need for further legislation.
- *Regulations*. The regulations by the Commission and Council are similarly directly applicable, with no need for further legislation.
- *Directives*. The directives by the Commission and Council are generally addressed to the member states, and require that the *states* take action within an identified time period to change their own law so as to comply. In the United Kingdom, this may be done by ministerial regulations. Sometimes, a full Act of Parliament is used.
- *Decisions*. These are addressed to individuals or companies, or to member states, and are directly binding on those to whom they are addressed. They have no effect on anyone else, however (unlike legislation). The Commission has power to give decisions on various issues.

- *Recommendations.* These are self-explanatory; they have no formal legal effect, but have considerable persuasive force.
- *The European Court of Justice.* It gives decisions and rulings in disputes involving EU law, and its decisions are binding on the parties themselves in the United Kingdom. They also form precedents and are influential in building up EU law.
- *The European Parliament.* Differs significantly from the English Parliament in the roles it fulfils. The European Parliament is not directly a law-maker in the way in which the English Parliament creates legislation. It is the Commission and the Council of Ministers also known as the Council of the European Union that have a more direct role in law creation, with the European Parliament providing them with supervision and advice.

It should be borne in mind that the United Kingdom plays an active role in proposing, creating and drafting EU law.

1.2.6 Other sources

It may be that there is no English precedent to apply to a case being decided by the court. In that event, the barristers arguing the case may seek to rely on a precedent decided by a court in another common law jurisdiction, such as Australia, Canada, Singapore and other Commonwealth countries. Although cases decided in foreign courts are not binding upon English judges, the court may be persuaded to follow the case on the ground that it is an accurate reflection of English law. Again, in the absence of an English precedent, the court may be persuaded that the hypothesis of a textbook writer accurately states how the law should be applied. Such an event is rare, however, and lawyers will resort to other sources of law only in the absence of the above sources.

1.3 Judicial precedent and the tort of negligence

Learning Outcome: To explain and illustrate the operation of the doctrine of judicial precedent by reference to the essential elements of the tort of negligence, and its application to professional advisers.

A tort is a civil wrong. Action is brought by the victim of wrongful conduct (the 'claimant') against the wrongdoer (the 'defendant'). For most torts – particularly the tort of negligence – the main remedy sought is damages (monetary compensation).

Negligence is the most important of all torts, and occurs when one person causes harm to another by failing to take the care that is legally required. It gives some excellent examples of the doctrine of judicial precedent in operation.

A tort must be distinguished from a breach of contract. A contract is a voluntary agreement. The parties may agree upon a number of stringent obligations which each party promises to observe. In the event of default, the claimant will be entitled to sue for breach of contract (see Chapter 2). In the tort of negligence, however, obligations are not accepted by voluntary agreement but are imposed upon the persons concerned, by the state.

1.3.1 Judicial precedent

Essentially the doctrine of judicial precedent means that the decisions of the higher courts are binding on the lower courts. It follows that the doctrine of judicial precedent is intricately tied up with the fact that there is a hierarchy of courts, that is some courts are superior to others.

An overview of the hierarchy of the courts

The civil courts. In practice most civil cases start in the County Court. If a significant amount of money is involved, the case may start in the High Court which in effect has three branches or divisions: the Queen's Bench Division, the Family Division and the Chancery Division. Each division specialises in particular areas of law. For example, the Queen's Bench Division hears cases involving disputes in contract and tort. Appeals may be made from the County and the High Court to the Court of Appeal (Civil Division), and from the Court of Appeal and the High Court to the House of Lords, but only where the appeal involves a point of law of general public importance. If the dispute involves issues of European law then any court below the House of Lords may, and the House of Lords must, refer the matter to the European Court of Justice for a 'preliminary ruling' as to how European law should be interpreted and applied.

The criminal courts. All criminal cases start in the Magistrates Court. The court has a dual role. First, it may try less serious offences by itself, and in practice, most criminal cases are dealt with by the Magistrates Court. Second, so far as the more serious offences are concerned, the court decides whether the accused has a case to answer and, if so, will send the case to the Crown Court to be tried by a judge and jury. Appeal by way of 'case stated' from the Magistrates and Crown Court lies to the Divisional Court of the Queen's Bench Division. In this type of appeal, the findings of fact and law made by the Magistrates and Crown Courts are stated in writing and sent to the Divisional Court which decides whether the law has been correctly applied. If it hasn't, the case will be sent back to the Magistrates or Crown Court which will be obliged to apply the interpretation of the law specified by the Divisional Court. The Court of Appeal (Criminal Division) hears appeals from the Crown Court, and the House of Lords hears appeals from the Court of Appeal or the Divisional Court involving points of law of general public importance.

When a court reaches a decision, the judge does three things:

1. He/she examines the facts and states which facts he/she regards as 'material', that is, essential to his/her decision.
2. He/she considers the law relating to facts such as these.
3. He/she applies the law to the facts and gives his/her decision.

The *ratio decidendi* and *obiter dicta* are part of this process.

- The *ratio decidendi* of a judge is the reasoning vital to his decision: what facts are material and how the law applies to them.
- *Obiter dicta* are other comments that he will make, for example regarding general principles of law or hypothetical situations.

The importance of a previous case can depend to a substantial extent upon whether it becomes a *binding* or merely a *persuasive* precedent. A binding precedent is one which a later court *must* follow. The court is legally bound to do so. A later court *may* (and usually will) follow a persuasive precedent, but it is not bound to do so. The rule today basically is that previous decisions of a higher court are binding on lower courts in future cases. Therefore:

- House of Lords' decisions are binding on all lower courts in future cases on the same material facts. The House is free to deviate from its own earlier decisions, but in practice rarely does so. A Practice Statement in 1966 established that this court did not have to follow its own previous decisions (Note that the House of Lords as a court is very different from the political/legislative House of Lords chamber of Parliament.).

The House of Lords Overruling Itself

Introduction

One expected quality of the court at the apex of the pyramidal system is finality of judgment. What is laid down as the law by such a court will be certain and reliable because there is no court above it to which a dissatisfied side can appeal for another decision on the law. The House of Lords for a long time would not overrule its earlier decisions even if they later seemed wrong. Since 1966, it has been able to overrule its earlier rulings. It seldom does so but has this year, and has thereby conduced greater justice for litigants.

Background

House of Lords' decisions are binding on all other courts in the legal system, except the House of Lords itself. The historical practice of always sticking faithfully to whatever it ruled was the law had been established in the 19th century and was re-affirmed in a famous case in 1898 – *London Tramways Co Ltd v London County Council.*

However, this approach did not appear to create certainty and had become very rigid by the end of the 19th century. Several areas of law fossilised because rules laid down by the Lords remained fixed, while social developments rendered them archaic and Parliament did nothing to modernise them using legislation. The practice was eventually changed in July 1966 when Lord Gardiner, the Lord Chancellor, made a statement on behalf of himself and his fellow Law Lords. This *Practice Statement* [1966] 3 All ER 77 says:

> Their Lordships regard the use of precedent as an indispensable foundation upon which to decide what is the law and its application to individual cases. It provides at least some degree of certainty upon which individuals can rely in the conduct of their affairs as well as a basis for orderly development of legal rules.
>
> Their Lordships nevertheless recognise that too rigid adherence to precedent may lead to injustice in a particular case and also unduly restrict the proper development of the law. They propose, therefore, to modify their present practice and, while treating former decisions of this House as normally binding, to depart from a previous decision when it appears right to do so. In this connection they will bear in mind the danger of disturbing retrospectively the basis on which contracts, settlements of property, and fiscal arrangements have been entered into and also the special need for certainty as to the criminal law. This announcement is not intended to affect the use of precedent elsewhere than in this house.

The current practice enables the House of Lords to adapt English law to meet changing social conditions. It was also regarded as important at the time that the House of Lords' practice be brought into line with that of superior courts in other countries, like the United States Supreme Court and State supreme courts elsewhere which are not bound by their own previous decisions.

The possibility of the House of Lords changing its previous decisions is a recognition that law, whether expressed in statutes or cases, is a living, and therefore changing, institution which must adapt to the circumstances in which and to which it applies if it is to retain practical relevance.

Since 1966, the House has used this power quite sparingly. It will not refuse to follow its earlier decision merely because that decision was technically wrong. A material change of circumstances will usually have to be shown.

- The Court of Appeal is bound by decisions of the House of Lords. Generally, it is bound by its own decisions also. However, if a decision has been reached per incuriam (without due care), or there are contradictory previous decisions, then the court will not be bound.
- The High Court is bound by the House of Lords and the Court of Appeal, but *not* by its own previous decisions.
- A County Court is bound by all previous decisions of higher courts, but not by previous County Court decisions. If a previous case went on appeal to the Court of Appeal (etc.), the County Court is bound by the decision of the highest court that earlier heard the case.

Notice, however, that not all of a previous judgment – even that of a much higher court – will be binding. In a later case, a judge will only be bound by the *ratio decidendi* of the earlier judge(s). *Obiter dicta* in the earlier case can only have persuasive influence.

A case can cease to be a precedent in various ways. In the same case, a higher court can reverse the decision of a lower one if one party appeals. The lower decision then ceases to have any effect as a precedent. In a later case between different parties, a higher court can overrule an earlier lower decision; the lower court judgment remains valid between the parties to it, but it ceases to be a precedent. Most importantly, a later court can always *distinguish* the material facts from those of the earlier decision, so that the later court is not bound. Examples of judicial precedent in action can be seen in the following sections dealing with the tort of negligence.

Stare decisis and the court of appeal

Nicholas Mercer, Barrister, Student News & Case Summaries, from *The Daily Law Notes*, 18th Edition, Autumn 2004, pp. 7, 8. Reproduced with permission from the author

Stare Decisis and the Court of Appeal

This year marks the sixtieth anniversary of *Young* v. *Bristol Aeroplane Co Ltd* [1944] KB 718. In that case Lord Greene MR held that, subject to three exceptions, the Court of Appeal was bound to follow its own previous decisions. Those exceptions were as follows. First, where the court is faced by previous conflicting decisions of the Court of Appeal, it could choose which to follow. Second, where a previous decision of the Court of Appeal, although not expressly overruled, cannot stand with a subsequent decision of the House of Lords, the decision in the House of Lords must be followed. Third, a decision of the Court of Appeal given *per incuriam* need not be followed.

Lord Greene MR expressed surprise that so fundamental a matter as the application of *stare decisis* in the Court of Appeal had been a matter of doubt. However, if it was the court's intention to remove that doubt permanently, then it patently failed. In the years since, the extent of the three exceptions and whether additional examples subsist are matters which have exercised numerous judicial minds. In this article I want to draw your attention to *Great Peace Shipping Ltd* v. *Tsavliris Salvage (International) Ltd* [2003] QB 679; *Starmark Enterprises Ltd* v. *CPL Distribution Ltd* [2002] Ch 306; *R* v. *Simpson* [2004] QB 118; *Cave* v. *Robinson Jarvis & Rolf* [2002] 1 WLR 581 and *In re Spectrum plus Ltd* [2004] 3 WLR 503, five relatively recent cases in which the Court of Appeal has considered the extent to which it is at liberty to depart from its previous decisions.

In *Great Peace Shipping Ltd* v. *Tsavliris Salvage (International) Ltd* [2003] QB 679, the Court of Appeal applied a modified version of the first exception in refusing to follow its decision in *Solle* v. *Butcher* [1950] 1 KB 671. *Solle's* case was inconsistent with the earlier decision of the House of Lords in *Bell* v. *Lever Bros Ltd* [1932] AC 161. It was not *per incuriam* since the Court of Appeal had plainly been aware of *Bell's* case. Although the implications of *Great Peace Shipping* for *stare decisis* attracted little attention, the decision was of considerable significance to the doctrine. Until *Great Peace Shipping*, the weight of authority strongly indicated that the first exception enunciated in *Young's* case applied only to *subsequent* decisions of the House of Lords. Clearly, Lord Greene MR was of that view in *Young*, a point which he later reiterated. In *Williams* v. *Glasbrook Bros* [1947] 2 All ER 884, his Lordship asserted that if the Court of Appeal misinterpreted an earlier decision of the House of Lords, 'nobody but the House of Lords can put that mistake right'. The court, in *Miliangos* v. *George Franks (Textiles) Ltd* [1975] QB 487, 499, took the same view, holding that it was bound by its decision in *Schorsch Meier GmbH* v. *Hennin* [1975] QB 416, notwithstanding that it was inconsistent with the prior decision of the House of Lords in *United Railways of Havana and Regia Warehouses Ltd* [1961] AC 1007. On appeal, only Lord Cross of Chelsea expressed the view that the Court of Appeal ought not to have considered itself bound by *Schorsch Meier*. Accordingly, in *Great Peace Shipping*, there must have been considerable doubt as to whether the Court of Appeal had power to depart from its decision in *Solle* v. *Butcher*. It was surprising therefore that the point was disposed of cursorily and without reference to the leading authorities.

There is some academic opinion to the effect that where there are inconsistent decisions of the Court of Appeal then the court should follow the later. However, in *Starmark Enterprises Ltd* v. *CPL Distribution Ltd* [2002] Ch 306, the Court of Appeal expressly reaffirmed its right to apply the earlier decision. It held that its decisions in *Mecca Leisure Ltd* v. *Renown Investment (Holdings) Ltd* (1984) 49 P & CR 12 and *Trustees of Henry Smith's Charity* v. *AWADA Trading and Promotion Services Ltd* (1983) 47 P & CR 607 were indistinguishable and irreconcilable and concluded that it should follow the *Henry Smith* case, the earlier of the two decisions.

The Criminal Division's approach to *stare decisis* was recently considered by a five-judge court, including the Lord Chief Justice, in *R* v. *Simpson* [2004] QB 118. In principle, there is no difference in the application of *stare decisis* as between the civil and criminal divisions of the Court of Appeal: see *R* v. *Spencer* [1985] QB 771. However, since it is desirable that justice should take precedence over certainty where the liberty and reputation of the appellant are at stake, the Criminal Division has tended to adopt a more relaxed practice in respect of *stare decisis*. In *R* v. *Gould* [1968] 2 QB 65, 68 Lord Diplock said:

> 'In its criminal jurisdiction . . . the Court of Appeal does not apply the doctrine of stare decisis with the same rigidity as in its civil jurisdiction. If upon due consideration we were to be of opinion that the law had been either misapplied or misunderstood in an earlier decision of this court . . . we should be entitled to depart from the view as to the law expressed in the earlier decision notwithstanding that the case could not be brought within any of the exceptions laid down in *Young* v. *Bristol Aeroplane Co Ltd* . . .'

1.3.2 The tort of negligence

Torts of negligence were recognised in many separate and individual situations in the nineteenth and early-twentieth centuries, but the leading case which tried to pull these separate strands together into principles which could apply in all situations was the House of Lords' decision in *Donoghue* v. *Stevenson* (1932).

In *Donoghue* v. *Stevenson*, the claimant, Mrs Donoghue, went into a café with a friend, who bought a bottle of ginger beer and gave it to Mrs Donoghue. The ginger beer was in an opaque bottle which had been sealed by the manufacturer. Mrs D drank half of the contents. When she poured the other half, it was found to contain what appeared to be the remains of a decomposed snail. Mrs D suffered shock and stomach pains.

Mrs D did not buy the bottle, otherwise she could have sued the café for breach of contract, and recovered full damages even though the café was not at fault. Instead, she had to claim that Stevenson, the manufacturer of the drink, was liable to her for negligence. The House of Lords held that a manufacturer of goods owed a duty not only to the buyer, but also to anyone else who should reasonably be foreseen as likely to suffer physical injury from defects in them. The duty was to take reasonable care.

As a wider guideline for the future, Lord Atkin also suggested his famous 'neighbour' principle:

> You must take reasonable care to avoid acts or omissions which you can reasonably foresee would be likely to injure your neighbour. Who then in law is my neighbour? The answer seems to be persons who are so closely and directly affected by my act that I ought reasonably to have them in contemplation as being so affected when I am directing my mind to the acts or omissions which are called in question.

In other words, everyone must take reasonable care not to cause foreseeable harm to foreseeable victims.

The House of Lords is the highest court in the United Kingdom. It is quite separate from the political chamber. Cases are usually heard by five Law Lords, and decisions can be by a majority, if need be. *Donoghue* v. *Stevenson* was only decided by a 3 to 2 majority. Lord Atkin's statement was much wider than required for the actual case, and could be regarded as only an *obiter dictum*. Nevertheless, it had enormous influence in future cases.

Lord Macmillan, another judge in the case, set out the essential features of the tort. It applies where 'there is a *duty of care* and where *failure* in that duty has caused *damage*' to the claimant. These, then, are the three essential elements.

1.3.3 Duty to take care

How do you know whether you owe someone a duty of care? The answer is that if it is reasonably foreseeable that your actions are likely to affect someone, then it is likely that you owe that person a duty of care. (In other words, the so-called 'neighbour test' set out in *Donoghue* v. *Stevenson*.)

The duty of care was extended in many cases after *Donoghue* v. *Stevenson*. One example is *Home Office* v. *Dorset Yacht Co Ltd* (1970), where some 'Borstal' boys (youngsters who had been criminally convicted) were working on an island under Home Office supervision. Some boys escaped and damaged the claimant's yacht. The House of Lords said that the Home Office could be liable for negligence. Lord Reid said: 'The time has come when we can and should say that [Lord Atkin's neighbour rule] ought to apply unless there is some justification or valid explanation for its exclusion.'

It had already been made clear in *Bourhill* v. *Young* (1942) (see below) that the rule could apply to cases where the claimant only suffered nervous shock as opposed to other physical harm, and in *Hedley Byrne* v. *Heller and Partners* (1963), the House of Lords said in *obiter dicta* that the rule could apply to statements (as opposed to acts) and to purely financial loss (as opposed to physical harm); see also Section 1.4 later.

Nevertheless, it was always made clear in later cases that there are limits to the neighbour rule.

- *First, there must be sufficient proximity* between the person who was careless and the person suffering harm. The duty cannot be owed over a limitless physical area, or to a limitless number of people.

Examples

In *Bourhill* v. *Young* (1942), a lady heard a motor accident some 45 feet away. She did not see it because it was on the other side of a stationary vehicle. Nevertheless, she saw blood on the road, suffered severe shock, and lost her unborn child. Her claim for damage failed because she was too far from the accident and not within the foreseeable range of harm.

In *Alcock* v. *Chief Constable of South Yorkshire Police* (1991), one of a number of cases arising from the Sheffield football disaster where many spectators were killed, an action was brought by relatives of the victims, who saw the tragedy from a distance or on live television. They all suffered nervous shock, and sued the police for negligence. These actions failed.

In *Sutradhar* v. *Natural Environment Research Council* (2004), the claimant, along with numerous other persons, had been poisoned as a result of drinking contaminated water. It was alleged that a duty of care was owed to the claimant by the party who had carried out a water survey and produced a report on findings. It was decided that there was insufficient proximity between the claimant and defendant and so no realistic prospect of establishing that a duty of care was owed.

In *London Borough of Islington* v. *University College London NHS Trust* (2004), a local authority failed in its claim to recover the costs of providing care to a person who suffered a stroke as a result of receiving negligent medical advice from the defendant. It was decided that no duty of care was owed, as first the loss suffered by the claimant was not reasonably foreseeable, secondly there was not sufficient proximity between the claimant local authority and the defendant. Further, the loss suffered was due to compliance with a statutory obligation.

- *Second, there may be public policy grounds* for refusing to apply the neighbour principle. For example, the rule might cause absurdity or otherwise be grossly undesirable.

Example

In *Mulcahy* v. *Ministry of Defence* (1996), it was held that an officer does not owe a legally actionable duty of care to a soldier during hostilities.

1.3.4 Breach of duty

The victim only has a valid claim for damages if the person who owes the duty is shown to have broken it. The standard required is that of the reasonable person. Higher duties in the law of tort are placed on those who are in a position of responsibility. Similarly, the more serious the consequences are likely to be, the more care is expected. Greater care is expected towards especially vulnerable victims, such as children. Conversely, normally, a lower duty of care is expected *from* children.

It may, of course, sometimes be difficult to discover why and how an accident occurred. Since it is for the claimant to prove that his injury or loss was due to the defendant's breach of duty, this can defeat his claim. Exceptionally, therefore, the courts may reverse the normal burden of proof, and call upon the defendant to prove that he has not been careless. This is contrary to the normal rules of evidence, and it will only be done where:

- the harm would not normally happen if proper care were taken;
- there is no (other) explanation for what has occurred – the phrase *res ipsa loquitur* (the thing speaks for itself) – is often used 'This serves to highlight the belief that the breach does not have to be proved. The very existence of the damage caused by the defendant is seen by the plaintiff as establishing that the defendant must have been in breach of duty;
- the defendant was in control of the situation, and the victim was not.

Example

In *Mahon* v. *Osborne* (1939), a patient awoke from an abdominal operation to discover (eventually) that swabs had been left inside him. The normal burden of proof was reversed so that the surgeon was required to prove that this was not due to his negligence. This case can be compared with *Fish* v. *Kapur* where a patient, when having a tooth removed, suffered a broken jaw. The logical explanation for the injury was negligence on the part of the dental surgeon, so *res ipso loquitur* was relevant. The defence, having therefore the burden of proof, brought in evidence of the likelihood of such injury resulting where the plaintiff had a weak jaw. In consequence, the court rejected the negligence claim.

1.3.5 Damage caused by negligence

The claimant cannot recover damages for negligence unless he has suffered damage. This can include some or any of the following:

- Personal injury claims, particularly from accidents on the road or at work, constitute a large proportion of all negligence claims – to such an extent that potential wrongdoers are required by statute to insure against possible liability, so as to ensure that victims will get any damages awarded. Personal injury can include illness from nervous shock if this is clearly caused by the defendant's negligence.
- Damage to property can be recovered (a wrecked car for instance).
- Financial loss directly connected with personal injury or to property is recoverable (loss of earnings, repair costs for instance).
- *Purely* financial loss is only recoverable in exceptional situations, such as for professional liability to an identified person to whom responsibility was undertaken, as in the cases which followed the *Hedley Byrne dicta*; see *Smith* v. *Eric S Bush* in Section 1.3.7 later. Otherwise, purely economic loss is unlikely to count.

Example

In *Murphy* v. *Brentwood DC* (1990), a local authority's negligent approval of a site as suitable for house building was *not* actionable by an eventual owner whose home subsided. The loss was held to be essentially economic/financial.

The harm must also have been clearly caused by the negligence, and only damage which should have been reasonably foreseen at the time of the negligence will be included.

Example

In *Boardman* v. *Sanderson* (1964), a driver negligently backed his car from a garage, and injured a young boy. The father, who was known to be nearby, heard the scream and ran to the scene. He recovered damages for his nervous shock. This harm was not too remote, because he was a relative of the main victim and was known to be in the close vicinity. (Compare this case with *Bourhill* v. *Young* earlier.)

1.3.6 Contributory negligence

The most important (partial) defence to a claim for negligence also involves causation. The defence of *contributory negligence* arises if the claimant was partly the author of his own misfortune, so that the accident was partly caused by the claimant himself. In these circumstances, the courts have a discretion to reduce the damages awarded by any percentage which they consider appropriate.

Example

In *Sayers v. Harlow UDC* (1958), the door of a public toilet had a defective pay-lock. A lady found herself locked in. She tried to climb out, allowing her weight to rest on the toilet roll, which rotated. She fell and was injured. The court (which described her plight as an 'inconvenience') held that her injuries were 75 per cent the fault of the local authority and 25 per cent her own fault. Damages were reduced accordingly.

1.3.7 Negligence and professional advisers

Despite an initial reluctance, the courts have extended the 'neighbour' principle to negligent *advice* and to purely financial loss. This has had a profound effect on situations arising when a professional person's advice is relied upon by a non-client.

The *Donoghue* v. *Stevenson* principle was extended dramatically in the case of *Hedley Byrne* v. *Heller and Partners* (1963). A firm of advertising agents had a client who sought credit from them. The agents, therefore, sought a credit reference *from the client's bank*. The reference was favourable but the bank, which knew the purpose of the reference, expressly disclaimed liability for any error. Nevertheless, relying on the reference, the agents gave credit to their client, and lost a large sum of money when the client became insolvent. The agents sued the bank. They had no contract with the bank, so they relied on *Donoghue* v. *Stevenson* and similar cases. The House of Lords held that the bank was not liable because of the disclaimer which it had made.

However, the judges also said that, contrary to what had previously been believed, the duty of care in Donoghue v. Stevenson could apply to statements as well as to acts or omissions, and could extend to purely financial loss as well as to physical injury (plus the monetary consequences of that physical injury).

These *obiter dicta* in the *Hedley Byrne* case influenced the courts in the following years to hold several times that a professional person can owe a duty of care not only to the client who employs and pays him, but also to any other specific person whom he knows to be relying on his advice, and for whose benefit he knows that the advice will be used. In *Smith* v. *Eric S Bush* (1989), for example, a surveyor was engaged by a building society to value a house. The surveyor knew that the society would show his valuation to a specific potential buyer, who would rely on it. The valuation was negligent, and the buyer lost money. The House of Lords held that the surveyor was liable for his negligent statement, for the purely financial loss caused to the buyer.

However, the limits on these decisions were shown by the very important case of *Caparo Industries plc* v. *Dickman* (1990), which was an action by a shareholder against the auditors of a company. The shareholder claimed that the annual audit was negligent and incorrect. In reliance on it, the shareholder had bought more shares and had suffered financial loss as a result. When the auditors make their annual report to members, they know that their statements will be relied upon by *all* of the shareholders (possibly hundreds of thousands in number) as well as by possible future investors (equally numerous). The House of Lords held that the auditors' duty of care could not practicably be owed to so many people, otherwise there might be no end to claims.

(Note that the House of Lords in this case was not bound by the *obiter dicta* in the *Hedley Byrne* case; and the previous decisions of the House of Lords in cases like *Smith* v. *Eric S Bush* were *distinguished*, because in the earlier cases the statement was made solely to one identified person who the defendant knew would rely on it.)

Caparo Industries v. Dickman was itself distinguished by the High Court in the later case of *ADT Ltd* v. *Binder Hamlyn* (1995). In this case, ADT was bidding to take over a company whose accounts were audited by Binder Hamlyn. At a 'serious' business meeting with ADT, the auditors expressly said, without any disclaimer, that the 'target' company's accounts were accurate. The auditors made this statement specifically to ADT, knowing that ADT would rely on it without further enquiry. The accounts were not in fact reliable, and ADT suffered loss. These facts were much more like the cases prior to *Caparo* and, indeed, similar to the facts of *Hedley Byrne* itself but without any disclaimer. The auditors were therefore held liable. The need to establish all three elements of negligence – duty, breach of duty and damage resulting in order to succeed with a claim arose recently where a professional adviser was involved. Negligence in the process of valuing shares was exhibited, but the final valuation could have been arrived at by a reasonably competent valuer not displaying negligence. It was decided in *Goldstein* v. *Levy Gee (a firm) (2003)* that if the final valuation identified was within the range that a reasonably competent valuer would have arrived at, then no liability would attach.

'The potential extent of auditor liability for negligence can be reduced under the provisions of the Companies Act 2006. Section 534 introduces a 'liability limitation agreement'. This is an agreement between a company and its auditors under which the amount of liability owed by the auditor is limited '. . . in respect of any negligence, default, breach of duty or breach of trust, occurring in the course of the audit of accounts, . . .'. Section 537 provides that the agreement will not be effective in limiting auditor liability beyond that which '. . . . . . is fair and reasonable in all the circumstances . . .'. This legislation comes at a time when negligence actions against large audit firms, have reduced significantly. Reforms in accounting and auditing standards are included in the reasons put forward for this reduction'.

1.4 English Legal System

Note at this stage the main sources, classifications and court structure applicable to the English Legal System. Further, when studying the legal systems applicable in other countries note these elements.

Sources (see 1.2)
Case law or 'judge – made law' has historically been an important source of law and remains important today. However, much law is now created by Parliament through legislation. The history of a country will invariably have an influence on the development of its legal system. Many countries do have sources of law likened to those in England with a similar scope for change and development through the application of precedent in judicial law making in the courts, and through the legislature.

Classifications (see 1.1)
The English Legal System can be classified into 'civil law' and 'criminal law'. The former includes areas of law that have developed to enable disputes between individuals to be resolved, for example contract law, tort, and company law (all important in this syllabus). Criminal law matters are seen as relevant to the state, and actions will be brought in the name of the Crown. An alternative classification of the legal system is as 'private law' and 'public law'. 'Private law' can be likened to the civil law. 'Public law' relates to matters involving the state and includes criminal law, but would also extend to constitutional and administrative law.

Court Structure (see 1.3.1)
Separate civil and criminal court structures exist.

Civil Court Structure

House of Lords
Court of Appeal (Civil Division)
High Court (Queen's Bench Division, Chancery Division and Family Division)
County Court.

(Civil disputes are also dealt with in tribunals or through arbitration, mediation and conciliation)

Criminal Court Structure

House of Lords
Court of Appeal (Criminal Division)
Crown Court
Magistrates Court.

1.4.1 European Union and Member States

Whilst England and other states that are members of the European Union retain their domestic law, as we have seen (see 1.2.4), the primary source of European Law – Treaties, and the secondary sources, for example regulations and directives, influence the law applicable within the domestic law of each member state. The European Union now has a membership of twenty seven independent states. Of these, ten joined on the 1 May 2004.

Most recently, Bulgaria and Rumania joined the European Union on 1 January 2007. The European Union is unique in being made up of independent sovereign nations that recognise a collective sovereignty of the European Union. As such it can be distinguished from the United Nations which serves as an organisation for cooperation between governments. It also differs significantly from a federation, such as the United States.

The supremacy of parliament can be questioned on the basis that power is surrendered to Institutions of the European Union to create laws binding on individual member states. It could be argued, however, that parliament retains its supremacy in the power of the United Kingdom to cease being a member of the European Union.

The Institutions of the European Union are:

The European Parliament
The Council of Ministers (The Council) also known as the Council of the European Union
The European Commission
The Court of Justice of the European Communities (The Court).

EU INSTITUTIONS

The Commission is the *executive* arm of the European Union, initiating and implementing EU legislations and decisions. The Commission is independent and Commissioners do not represent the interests of their respective Member States. However, the Commission is guided by broad guidelines and general political priorities agreed by the European Council. The Commission comprises a number of departmental Directorates-General (DGs), each responsible for one or more specific areas of policy-making.

Council of Ministers ('The Council') is the main *legislative and decision-taking* arm of the European Union, acting on the basis of proposals initiated by the Commission. The Council consists of a representative minister from each of the Member States. The membership is not fixed but is formulated according to the issue. For example, transport ministers will attend on transport issues, finance ministers on finance issues, and so on. The General Affairs Council ensures consistency and coordination in the work of different Council configurations. The Council is served by a permanent body of national representative known as COREPER (**C**omitedes **r**eprésentants **pé**rmanents).

European Parliament (EP) exercises a *supervisory* role over EU institutions. Importantly, since the Maastricht Treaty, it has had an increasing role in the passage of legislation under the 'co-decision' procedure. Essentially, this procedure requires the Council to consult and reach agreement with the EP over its legislative proposals, with the EP holding an ultimate right of veto. The continuing expansion of the use of the co-decision procedure under recent treaties reflects the importance of the EP's democratic mandate. The EP also has important powers over the Commission, such as the ability to pass a 'motion of censure' which, if carried, obliges the Commission to resign and no budget can be adopted without its approval. The EP consists of directly elected Members of the European Parliament (MEPs) serving five year terms. The number of MEPs from each Member State reflects its population size and there are broad political groupings.

European Council is not, as such, an institution but is the name given to the twice-yearly meetings (or summits) of the heads of state or government and the President of the Commission. Foreign ministers are also entitled to attend. These meetings decide the overall strategies and policies for the European Union. The Council usually expresses itself by way of Conclusions, Resolutions or Declarations, though these have no status in law. The European Council would be formally made an institution under the draft Constitution.

European Court of Justice (ECJ) is the *judicial arm* of the European Union; it is the final arbiter on all questions of EU law and operates on the principle of the supremacy of EU law over national law. The court comprises judges from Member States. The ECJ adjudicates upon failures of Member States to fulfil treaty obligations or to implement community law and to decide the compatibility of national legislation. It also adjudicates upon 'failures to act' by EU institutions, as well as the legality of legal instruments adopted or actions taken by them. Where questions of EU law interpretation arise before a national court, a 'preliminary ruling' may be sought from the ECJ in order to resolve the issue.

The responsibilities and powers of these Institutions are contained in Treaties. 'Changes relating to the Institutions of the European Union will be introduced if and when the Lisbon Treaty is ratified. 'Ireland is the only country to hold a referendum on the Treaty, and it was rejected. All European Union member states must give approval before it can become effective. Without a referendum, ratification can be achieved in member states through national parliaments rather than vote of the people.' Some of these changes repeat changes identified under the previously proposed Constitution. Proposals under the new Treaty include bringing an end to the system of having rotating presidents of the European Council. Instead a long-term appointment to the position of president would be made. Further, the two positions existing at present which relate to foreign affairs and that of the external affairs minister will be combined.' It is the European Commission that proposes legislation. Different procedures exist for the creation of law. The main procedures adopted are – 'consultation', 'assent' and 'co-decision'. The 'co-decision' procedure is now the most commonly used. The European Parliament and the Council are the Institutions that pass the law.

'The Court' has the role of ensuring that European Law is applied and interpreted in the same way by all member states. 'The court' will give rulings on matters brought before it through either:

1. the preliminary ruling procedure under which countries can ask for advice on interpretation of law;
2. actions brought by the Commission based on a failure to fulfil an obligation;
3. actions for annulment where it is believed that an EU law is illegal;
4. actions for failure to act where a complaint is made that the Parliament, the Council or the Commission have not acted in compliance with obligations under a Treaty.

The Lisbon Treaty

Work on drafting a Constitution began in early 2002. The Constitution was to stand in place of all earlier European Union Treaties but did not come into force. The Lisbon

Treaty, originally called the Reform Treaty, was prepared with the intention that it should replace the draft Constitution. All 27 EU countries must ratify this Treaty. If it is ever implemented different parts of the Treaty would be implemented at different times with the full implementation process possibly not being completed for 10 years.

Whilst the aim of the Constitution was to replace all previous Treaties, the Lisbon Treaty would amend only the Maastricht Treaty and the Treaty of Rome.

Learning Outcome: To compare the elements of alternative legal systems, sharia law and the role of international legal regulations.

The European Union and Domestic Legal Systems

The European Union at present is made up of 27 states. A significant number of these states have a codified system of law. In other words, a collection of comprehensive laws which can be found in constitutions, legislation, rules and regulations. The *Code de Napoleon (1804)* introduced in France provides an early example. Statutes which contain, in a systematic and comprehensive way, all case law and existing legislation on a particular area or aspect of law are described as codifying statutes. Although in England much law is contained in legislation, we do not have a codified system.

States of the European Union predominantly adopt civil law systems. However, origins of law sometimes differ significantly and countries invariably have some unique features in their legal systems. Austria and Greece have Roman Law influence, whilst Finland has a legal system based on Swedish law and Belgium has a system showing clear application of English constitutional theory.

The French Legal System

History often has a significant effect on the legal system that develops in a country and France is a clear example of this, with the monarch, demands of the people and outside influences playing a part in the development and formulation of its legal system. In 1904, the Code *Civile* was created. This was a law made for the people and to be accessible by them. Today, France's law is in the main created by the legislative body and so codified. Tort law is not codified, but is created by the judiciary.

The judicial system is in two parts. First, private law or law of the people, including Criminal Law (the judicial order), and second, public law or the law applicable to government, branches of government as well as private citizens (the administrative order).

The court structure is very similar to that in England. In the judicial order, there is a trial court level where matters are dealt with at first instance. This level is made up of six sections which distinguish between specialised jurisdictions, for example commerce, labour law and social security and the ordinary jurisdiction and criminal jurisdiction. Above the trial level is the appeal level. The appeal courts include chambers which specialise and deal with commercial, social, criminal and civil matters, for example. The courts of appeal effectively hear the whole case again and consider both issues of fact and law. A similar court structure is found at the highest level or supreme court level. If the supreme court disagrees with the decision of the lower court, the matter is sent back for the lower court to consider amending its decision. The decision of the supreme court will ultimately prevail.

Under French Law, everyone is entitled to legal representation. The advocates will make a verbal plea before the court but it is the judge who will carry out questioning in the court room. Both adversarial and inquisitorial principles apply. In English Law, an adversarial approach is taken. A further interesting distinction between French and English Law is found in the fact that in France individuals are appointed judges at the beginning of their legal careers. In England, appointment to the Judiciary will follow on from a successful career as a lawyer.

The German Legal System

The Federal Republic of Germany is a democratic and social federal state. A Constitution gives authority for the creation of legislation.

As in France, codified law established by Parliament exists. This codified law acknowledges that everyone is equal before the law. Customary law based on long-term practice must be followed by the judiciary also. Further, ordinances or statutory instruments exist. These can be likened to delegated legislation under English Law with the right to create an ordinance given under codified law, just as in England an Enabling Act or Parent Act would give such power. Also, 'statutes' can be created by public corporations. Under these statutes, the corporation can create laws to regulate its own affairs. Again, authority to create such law must be found in the constitution.

Whilst the codified law has to be interpreted through the judgments of the courts, such judgments only bind the parties to the relevant action. The decisions do not constitute a precedent and thereby law. In reality, though, the lower courts will respect decisions of higher courts to prevent the obvious consequence if they didn't so act as causing matters to be taken to appeal.

The Polish Legal System

Poland is a democratic republic and has a Constitution which is the supreme law of the land. A legal system is based on the continental legal system (codified civil law). The parliament, made up of the lower house 'the Sejm' and the upper house 'Senate', has the power of creating legislation. Further sources of law are regulations, which, as in Germany, require specific authorisation under statute by bodies permitted under the Constitution. Ratified international agreements provide a further source of law as do local laws created by authorised bodies within limits prescribed.

The court structure is made up of the supreme court, that is, the highest court of appeal; also provincial courts and district courts. Both courts have jurisdiction to hear civil and criminal law matters. A high administrative court which sits in ten distinct centers deals with public sector matters of administration.

The Italian Legal System

Italy is a democratic republic. The republic is made up of the state which has state law. Also, municipalities, provinces, metropolitan cities and regions which are autonomous are recognised and have their own statutes. Creation of legislation must be in accordance with that provided in the Constitution. Further, it is limited by constraints imposed under EU law and existing international obligations. It has a parliament made up of two chambers, the first, a House of Representatives (630 representatives) and second, the Senate (315 senators). The chambers act jointly in the creation of legislation. The parliamentary process for the creation of legislation is similar to that of England, with a bill being introduced and considered by committee and both chambers. The representatives are elected on a national basis, whereas the senators are in the main elected on a regional basis.

Delegated legislation can be created by government, but clear criteria on the subject area and the time allowed for its creation must be determined by the parliament.

Jurisdiction of the courts is broken down into specific areas. These are civil and criminal law, accounting, taxation, military and administrative. A hierarchy of courts exists which deals with the civil and criminal law matters.

The Legal System of Denmark

Denmark provides a good example of a legal system that has its roots in history with the fundamental principles being traced back to the Middle Ages. Provincial laws originally existed which were integrated into a unified system in 1683. Outside influences, particularly German jurisprudence and the cooperation between the Nordic countries, have contributed to the development of the legal system. Denmark does not have a civil code. Civil law is found in established practices and legislation. Danish law can be classified into:

1. Public Law
   (This includes constitutional and administrative law, international law and criminal law.)
2. Civil Law
   (This area regulates the interests of individuals and legal persons, for example companies.)

The classification can be likened to what we find in English Law, even though these classifications are open to different interpretation.

The sources of law are:

(A) The Constitutional Act
This regulates the relationships between the organs of state. It also determines the requirements for the creation of legislation. This process, as with the classification of law, which can be compared with the English procedure involves approval within Parliament and finally Royal Assent.

(B) Acts of Parliament

(C) Case Law
The courts do create law through decision-making where no legislation exists. However, compared to countries that have Anglo-Saxon origins, the court's role as law maker is somewhat limited.

(D) Custom
Legislation can be introduced to override a custom. Also, the courts can refuse to recognise a custom on the basis that it is unreasonable.

Denmark and International Law. The Danish government has the power to commit the country to international agreements. A Treaty will be created to incorporate the agreement into Danish Law. In some instances, it is necessary to hold a referendum before agreement to an international agreement of major significance can be approved.

Denmark and the European Union. As with all other member states, European Treaties and regulations are automatically binding, and directives must be implemented and become incorporated within the law.

A hierarchy of courts exists with the most senior being the Supreme Court. Below is the High Court, and the lowest courts are the city courts. Denmark does differ from France, Spain and Germany in not having a constitutional court or administrative court.

The Legal System of Greece

Greece was established as a presidential parliamentary republic in 1975. The Greek law is influenced by various sources including nineteenth-century continental codifications, French and Roman traditions. Its Constitution is the supreme law.

The main sources of law are:

(A) Legislation
All legislation must be published and comes into force 10 days after publication.

(B) Codes
These include:
- a civil code;
- a code of civil procedure;
- a code of criminal procedure;
- a code of law tribune (this contains statute law).

(C) Case Law

The Legal System of Cyprus

Historical events have brought about significant changes in the politics and legal system of the country. In 1925, Cyprus became a Crown colony, and 10 years later, English common law was established in the legal system. In 1959, Cyprus became an independent republic and a Constitution was introduced which remains the supreme law. The extent to which non-compliance with the Constitution is found following the withdrawal of the Turkish Cypriots has resulted in a doctrine of necessity being applicable and the law under the Constitution being qualified. The situation is somewhat problematic, however, following the invasion by Turkey and the northern part of the island being recognised by Turkey as the Turkish Republic of Northern Cyprus. The Republic of Cyprus joined the European Union in 2004.

The sources of law repeat to a notable extent that found in other countries, as might be expected with certain additions. These sources include:

The Constitution
Legislation
Common Law
Muslim Law
Ecclesiastical Greek Orthodox Law
European Union Law
International Treaties.

1.4.2 Legal systems around the world

Historic events have shaped the development of legal systems in many countries. English, Roman and French laws have provided the basis for the development of legal systems to a significant extent.

Australia, Bangladesh, Canada, Egypt, Hong Kong, India, Malaysia, New Zealand and Nigeria are examples of countries that have a legal system based on English Law. Many smaller countries also have systems based on English Common Law. It would be inappropriate to try to classify the dominant influences on the establishing of legal systems around the world. Whilst, in some instances, a common basis for legal development can be found due to the historical influence of a country in a specific part of the world, often, the features that contributed to the establishing of a legal system are complex and unique. Chile has a legal system that derives from Spanish Law, but has also been influenced by French and Austrian Laws. Egypt, whilst having a legal system based on English Common Law, has also been influenced by Islamic Law and Napoleonic codes.

The shaping of, and the content of, legal systems around the world invariably differ greatly. Equally, common features can be identified, sometimes in relation to the present sources of law, court hierarchy and classification of law.

The Malaysian Legal System

The legal system is based on English Common Law. As is so often found around the world, law primarily has its origins in the legislation or decisions of the courts. Federal and state legislatures have legislative power. The federal government has authority over the administration of justice. However, Islamic and other traditional laws apply to Muslims and other indigenous people. The court structure and hierarchy is similar to that found in England. The court structure consists of:

1. Subordinate courts
   (Magistrates courts and Sessions Courts)
2. Superior Courts
   (Two High Courts with the same jurisdiction and status. First, for the states of Sabah and Sarawak, the second, for Peninsular Malaysia.)
3. A Court of Appeal
   (The Federal Court has the highest judicial authority and is the final court of appeal.)

A Special Court was formed in 1993 to deal with any offences committed by the monarchical heads of the states. Malaysia has a constitutional monarch, a 'paramount ruler' who would also appear before this court.

The Legal System of the United States of America

Again, we find the government and the judiciary effective in establishing law with a broadly similar internal structure of government and courts. However, some significant differences lie within this broad structure.

The United States has a national government. And each state has its own government. Both national and state governments have the separate branches of the executive, legislative and judicial. The United States has a federal system and where any conflict between state and federal legislation is found, the federal legislation will apply.

It is the Constitution of the United States which is recognised as the 'supreme law of the land'. It is the Constitution which guarantees rights and freedoms of all citizens of the United States. The Constitution prevails over all other laws and regulations. Interpretation of the Constitution is a role of the federal courts.

International Treaties under the Constitution which are made by the United States are also regarded as 'supreme laws' of the land.

Federal Statutes are likewise regarded as 'supreme laws'. Federal legislation is introduced by the United States' Congress. The process of creating legislation starts with a Bill which is then considered by committee. The two chambers of Congress will also consider the Bill. In many respects the procedure follows that of the United Kingdom, without of course ultimately Royal Assent being provided. If such Statutes and Treaties conflict, the more recent or more specific will normally prevail.

What can be likened to delegated legislation in the United Kingdom can be found in the United States. Executive Orders and Agency Rules can be created by administrative bodies so long as the authority is given under statute by Congress.

Law is developed in the United States through the Common Law. All states except Louisiana have a common law system, with decisions of the courts establishing precedents. Decisions of the United States' Supreme Court and the majority of states' appellate courts are reported, again very much in line with the role and process of precedent in England.

The Legal System of China

The law of China developed in the past through the teachings of Confucius which highlighted social control and social order. Whilst codified law was seen as inadequate to address the range of human activity, laws did evolve to regulate the behaviour of the people. Early in the legal development, a criminal code was established as were statutes dealing with areas of civil law. The early belief that law was secondary to self-discipline and morality was heavily criticised. Attitudes and opinions regarding the traditional Chinese legal system have varied. Some thought it backward and barbaric. Recent research, however, likens the eighteenth-century legal system to European legal systems of the same period.

In identifying the Chinese legal system of today, 1979 can be seen as a point in time when notable progress began. Since then, in excess of 300 laws have been introduced along with the development of a system for administering justice. Mediation committees are used to address legal issues and deal with disputes. There are in excess of 800,000 such committees in rural and urban areas and these have dealt with over 90 percent of civil disputes in the People's Republic of China and minor criminal matters at no cost to the litigants. Many of the judges have had no legal training.

Law has been created piecemeal with specific areas of activity and dealings often serving as the basis for new law. An approach has often been adopted whereby new laws go through a trial period and then a redrafting takes place. There was opposition to simply adopting that found within an already existing legal system. An adverse consequence of this piecemeal development of law has been the discovery of contradictions and notable omissions.

With significant progress made since 1979 in the establishing of the legal system, law reform became a government priority in the 1990s. Criminal law, procedures applicable with criminal law administration, and also human rights have been areas where significant reforms have been made.

Hong Kong and Macau, on transferring sovereignty to China, did not change their legal systems. They continue to adopt the English Common Law and Portuguese legal systems, respectively.

The Legal system of Sri Lanka

Sri Lanka became independent in 1948 and is now a republic within the commonwealth of nations. The Sri Lankan Parliament is the law-making body. Parliament is made up of 168 members who are elected by the public. Within Parliament is a cabinet made up of 49 ministers which is led by the prime minister.

Originally, British Laws were applied. These were replaced by a Penal Code which was seen as based on existing Indian Law. This Penal Code is retained today with amendments. As is commonly found in jurisdictions around the world, a hierarchy of courts exists.

Minor matters will be dealt with in the lowest courts, for example criminal matters are dealt in the Magistrates Court. Above this court is the High Court, then the Court of Appeal, with the final appellate jurisdiction being exercised by the Supreme court.

1.4.3 Sharia Law (Islamic Law)

Sharia has been connected to the idea of 'spiritual law' and a system of 'divine law'. Social, economic and political issues as well as religious rituals are covered by Sharia. Some laws within Sharia are treated as divinely ordained and can never be altered. Other laws within Sharia are created by lawyers and judges. Lawmakers are seen as establishing what is a human approximation of that which is seen as divine. The Islamic lawmakers are endeavouring to interpret divine principles. Whilst the specific opinions and laws created by lawyers and judges are not considered divine, Sharia law in general is considered to be divine. In recognising that the lawmakers are attempting an interpretation of divine principles, that created is not beyond question, but is said to be 'ruling by Sharia'.

Through the application of Sharia law, the allowing of people to live in harmony and the maintaining of a just society is sought.

Primary sources of Sharia law are:

1. The Qur'an.
2. The Sunnah (the Way) recognising that approved by directions of the Prophet Muhammad.
3. For some Muslims, the unanimity of the disciples of Muhammad on certain issues.

A secondary source of Sharia law is found where no rules exist, by reasoning, possibly through analogy, and thereby law is applied to new situations. Beyond this, a further secondary source is found through consensus of the people or community, and where the public interest is seen to be served.

Today, Sharia relates also to practices which have their origins in custom, and most of the law has been codified.

In Muslim societies, the interpretation and implementation of Sharia law differs significantly. Seen as a significant cause of this is colonialisation. The relevance of Sharia law has been questioned. Today, some of the countries with the largest Muslim populations have only a few Sharia law provisions in the area of family law, and beyond this, have mainly secular constitutions and laws. These countries include Pakistan, Indonesia and Bangladesh.

A system made up of secular courts and religious courts is found in most North African and Middle East countries.

It is believed that Sharia law must provide fully for a person's spiritual and physical well-being. On this basis, it must be comprehensive.

Five categories of action are identified. The Five Pillars of Islam. These are:

1. obligatory
2. meritorious
3. permissible
4. reprehensible and
5. forbidden.

Just as the interpretation of Sharia law differs in different societies, this can also be seen when considering people, places and the passing of time. In this regard, it can clearly be likened to Christian canon law and Jewish law. Where fundamentalists have influence, the law will effectively be binding on people of the relevant faith. Where moderates or philosophers look to its role, theology can be recognised as distinct from laws that specifically regulate society.

Rules relating to evidence, testimony and burdens of proof differ where Sharia law is applied, and the nature and severity of punishments do not always align with the level of strictness observed in the court procedural demands. Amputation of hands and stoning are punishments recognised and seen as harsh in many Western countries. However, those who would defend the using of such measures provide justification in the deterrent factor.

Sharia law can be seen as divided principally into two parts.

1. The first relates to religion and worship. This includes prayers, pilgrimage to Mecca and fasting.
2. The second part includes court process and the judiciary. This includes the admissibility of forms of evidence and rules relating to witnesses.

Areas that have been distinctly identified within Sharia law are:

(A) Family law matters
(Within this area, marriage, divorce and child care are included. Also, the laws of inheritance and endowments.)
(B) Financial/commercial transactions
(C) Peace and warfare
(D) Penal punishments
(E) Obligations related to food and drinks.

Features of Sharia law are noteworthy acknowledging that interpretations can vary. These include:

Freedom of speech

Examples of a denial of freedom of speech can be found. On strict interpretation, criticism of the Prophet Muhammad is not allowed. Individual countries also provide examples of limitations to this freedom. One example is Egypt where public authorities tried to annul the marriage of a professor without his consent. The basis of this attempted annulment of marriage was because his reading of the Qur'an was condemned as being against the acknowledged orthodox interpretation.

Muslim apostates

Apostasy is likened to the crime of treason in Muslim theology. Conversion of Muslims to another religion is one some interpret as forbidden. Consequences of a person converting to another religion depends notably on the country in which they live. If a person lives in a Western country or indeed in a significant number of Muslim countries, they will suffer no penalty or no significant penalty.

Dietary laws

Obligations exist in relation to the eating of meat. Stringent dietary requirements and a need for animals to be killed in the name of God apply on a strict interpretation. Also, the eating of pork is prohibited.

The role of women

Restrictions can be found in relation to the right to work, becoming a cleric or religious scholar, and marriage. Again, bearing in mind differing interpretations and attitudes we can see numerous examples of where any such limitations are minimal or do not exist. The non-Sharia Muslim countries of Turkey, Bangladesh and Pakistan provide good examples of where women have held the position of head of government or head of state. The post of head of Pakistan's Central Bank has been held by a woman. Also, the Pakistan army appointed a woman to the position of General and in so doing, made her the first woman in the world to hold such a position.

1.4.4 International legal relations

Whilst countries have their own domestic laws and legal systems, international law has developed which relates to the dealings between nations. Public International Law relates to the dealings of states between each other and the subjects and citizens of the states. Private International Law relates to issues involving private individuals where the relevant situation relates to more than one state. Public and private international law can overlap. International law requires the recognition and acceptance by the relevant states. The primary sources of International Law are customs and convention laws. Where a number of states follow practices and procedures consistently out of a recognised obligation, customary international law will emerge. International law can then be found in the formal recognition and adoption of such common practices. The Vienna Convention on the Law of Treaties is an example of codifying, and so formalising, customary law. International agreements can take whatever form the participating parties wish to. Such agreements establish law binding on the parties to such agreements.

Just as individual countries or states can be parties to international agreements dealing with, for example, rights of the individual and standards of justice, so organisations can develop agreements that are binding on an international scale. Commercial dealings and professional practice can justify the need for cooperation within particular fields, and areas of activity can demand collective agreements on an international scale. Numerous international bodies have been formed which serve to address the need for uniformity in the practices, procedures and demands of particular professional practices as well as the regulation of dealings.

Through international cooperation and agreement on collective regulations regarding terminology, standards, procedures and technical demands, application can be simplified. Where countries harmonise regulations applicable and so eliminate the differences that would otherwise be found in the various countries, domestic laws, fairness in obligations and rights are achieved.

We do not have to consider merely the domestic and international regulations. Numerous bodies exist that look to establishing collective agreements within difined areas of the world. The European Union provides an obvious example. Within the European Union, the United Nations Economic Commission for Europe (UNECE) has implemented regulations which have served to establish harmonisation on matters such as technical details and standards. UNECE provides a forum for governments to pursue the creation of policies and internationally accepted regulations. The International Standardisation Organisation (ISO) and the International Electrotechnical Commission (IEC) emerged out of the facility for standardisation provided by the UNECE.

The Chartered Institute of Management Accountants is a body active in promoting the international dimension.

The following is an extract from online CIMA material:

'CIMA is a member of the International Federation of Accountants (IFAC), which is the global organization for the accountancy profession. The aim of IFAC's Professional Accountants in Business (PAIB) Committee is to evolve the global development and exchange of knowledge and best practice. PAIB also build public awareness of the value of professional accountants. Bill Connell, Chairman of CIMA's Technical Committee, chairs the PAIB, and Charles Tilley, CIMA's Chief Executive is a member of the chief IFAC Board.

CIMA is also a member of the European Federation of Accountants (FEE), which gives us an influence on the developments of the European Commission, the European Financial Reporting Advisory Group and other key bodies at the European Union. CIMA has quarterly meetings with the Department of Trade and Industry. We are currently promoting the public affairs content of our research and development more heavily, and we will continue to increase our contact with ministers and MPs to raise the profile of our work as a membership body.

International legal regulations applicable within areas of professional activity serve to remove barriers for individuals wishing to move from one country to another and work using their expertise. Recognition of qualifications not only in the field of accounting but also in the field of law, medicine and engineering assist the individuals and countries in achieving progress and high standards comparable around the world. Such regulations are also necessary to aid commercial activity. Many companies trade on a global scale and are aided by the uniformity in rights and obligations that emerge through the establishing of regulations applicable within particular fields of activity as well as aspects of trade such as banking and insurance.

1.5 Summary

At the end of this chapter, students should make sure that they are familiar with the following material:

- the differences between civil law and criminal law;
- the sources of English Law – in particular:
  - judicial precedent
  - legislation
  - European Union law.
- the hierarchy and jurisdiction of courts should be noted. (This relates to study of judicial precedent and its application.)
- elements of the tort of negligence and how judicial precedent applies to this area. Negligence can often be the subject of examination questions. Section 1.3.7 is particularly important and shows how the tort can apply to professional advisers.
- the legal systems of other countries including (codified) civil law systems, noting the elements and distinguishing features.
- Sharia law.
- International legal regulations.

Revision Questions

Question 1 Multiple-choice selection

1.1 Which one the following identifies civil proceedings?

(A) A prosecution for murder.
(B) An action by a claimant for £1 million damages for fraudulent misrepresentation.
(C) Proceedings where the accused is tried for the offence of applying a false trade description to goods.
(D) A prosecution by the Inland Revenue for non-payment of tax.

1.2 Which *one* of the following statements is correct?

(A) The aim of the criminal law is to regulate behaviour within society by the threat of punishment.
(B) The aim of the criminal law is to punish offenders.
(C) The aim of the criminal law is to provide a means whereby injured persons may obtain compensation.
(D) The aim of the criminal law is to ensure that the will of the majority is imposed on the minority.

1.3 Which of the following statements is *correct?*

(i) In the event of a conflict between equity and the common law, the common law prevails.
(ii) An Act of Parliament can overrule any common law or equitable rule.

(A) (i) only.
(B) (ii) only.
(C) Neither (i) nor (ii).
(D) Both (i) and (ii).

1.4 All criminal cases commence in

(A) the County Court.
(B) the Crown Court.
(C) the Court of Appeal.
(D) the Magistrates Court.

1.5 Explain which of the following most closely expresses the *ratio decidendi* of *Donoghue* v. *Stevenson*.

(A) A manufacturer of drinks must not deliberately put a snail in the bottle.
(B) Everyone must be nice to his neighbours.
(C) A claimant who only suffers financial loss cannot recover damages for negligence.
(D) A manufacturer owes a duty of care to those who he should reasonably foresee might be physically injured by his products.

1.6 In *Caparo Industries plc* v. *Dickman* (1991) (which was a House of Lords' decision), previous House of Lords' decisions constituting precedents were not followed. The relevant facts of the previous cases involved the making of inaccurate statements to one identified party by a defendant who knew that the statements would be relied upon. What means were used in *Caparo* v. *Dickman* to avoid following the existing House of Lords precedents?

(A) Distinguishing.
(B) Reversing.
(C) Overruling.
(D) Disapproving.

1.7 Which *one* of the following is delegated legislation?

(i) a statutory instrument.
(ii) a civil service memorandum.
(iii) a County Court judgment.
(iv) the Finance Act.
(v) the motor vehicles (Construction and Use) Regulations made under the Road Traffic Acts.
(vi) the articles of association of a company.

(A) (i) (ii) and (iv).
(B) (i) and (iii).
(C) (i) and (v).
(D) (ii) and (vi).

1.8 A passenger in a car is injured in an accident caused by the negligence of the driver of another vehicle. The passenger was not wearing a seatbelt. What effect would this have on any claim which he might have against the other driver for negligence?

(A) No effect because the other driver did not know that the passenger was not wearing his seatbelt.
(B) It defeats his claim; he is the sole author of his own misfortune.
(C) His own driver must bear the loss, because he did not insist that the passenger should wear a seatbelt.
(D) The court will have power to reduce the passenger's damages against the other driver by such amount as the court thinks fit.

1.9 Which *one* of the following does not provide codified law?

(A) A Constitution.
(B) Regulations.
(C) Case Law.
(D) Legislation.

1.10 Which *one* of the following areas of law is not codified in France?

(A) Contract Law.
(B) Employment Law.
(C) Company Law.
(D) Tort.

1.11 Which *one* of the following countries has a legal system based on English Common Law, Islamic Law and Napoleonic codes?

(A) Nigeria.
(B) Egypt.
(C) Pakistan.
(D) Greece.

1.12 Which *one* of the following Institutions of the European Union proposes new legislation that is to apply to its member states?

(A) The European Commission.
(B) The European Parliament.
(C) The Court of Justice of the European Communities.
(D) The Council of the European Union.

Question 2

(a) The most superior domestic court is the ...... (3 words) **(1 mark)**. The ...... (2 words) **(1 mark)** is a court made up of three divisions, the Queen's Bench, Family and Chancery divisions. The ...... (3 words) **(1 mark)** is a court which has a civil division and criminal division. **(3 marks)**

(b) Complete the following:
...... (1 word) **(2 marks)** is the supreme source of English law. However, if its provisions should contradict law of the ...... (2 words) **(2 marks)**, the latter will prevail. **(4 marks)**

(Total marks = 7)

Question 3

(a) In order to succeed in an action for negligence it is necessary to establish a ...... (3 words) **(1 mark)** owed, secondly a ...... (3 words) **(1 mark)** and finally ...... (1 word) **(1 mark)**. **(3 marks)**

(b) Complete the following:
In the tort of negligence, the principle of ...... (3 words) **(2 marks)** means that 'the thing speaks for itself'. Where this principle applies, the ...... (3 words) **(1 mark)** is shifted on to the ...... (1 word) **(1 mark)** who must show that he or she was not negligent in order to avoid liability. **(4 marks)**

(c) Complete the following:
Under the doctrine of judicial precedent, the ...... (2 words) **(2 marks)** of the case is binding upon lower courts whereas the ...... (2 words) **(2 marks)** is not binding and is said to be of persuasive authority only. **(4 marks)**

(Total marks = 11)

Question 4

(a) When judges are interpreting legislation, application of the . . . . . . (1 word) **(1 mark)** rule can result in an absurd outcome. By using the . . . . . . (1 word) **(1 mark)** rule an absurd outcome can be avoided. **(2 marks)**

(b) The Rules of Language include *eiusdem generis* under which judges can identify the meaning of . . . . . . (1 word) **(1 mark)** words in a statute from the meaning of . . . . . . (1 word) **(1 mark)** words found. **(2 marks)**

(c) When interpreting legislation the judiciary can rely on certain presumptions. These include the presumptions that . . . . . . (2 words) **(1 mark)** will not be bound by the relevant legislation and that the legislation will not have . . . . . . (2 words) **(1 mark)**. **(2 marks)**

(Total marks = 6)

Solutions to Revision Questions

1

Solution 1

1.1 Answer: (B)

The prosecution for murder is plainly criminal (A). The terms used in (C) make it plain that this is criminal ('accused', 'tried', 'offence'). Similarly, in (C), the term 'prosecution' makes it plain that this is criminal. In (B), the terms used ('action', 'claimant', 'damages') make it clear that these are the civil proceedings.

1.2 Answer: (A)

(B) is incorrect as the punishment of offenders is a feature of criminal law, but not the sole aim. Compensation identified in (C) is a remedy in civil actions. Further, the majority will being imposed on the minority is not an aim of the criminal law.

1.3 Answer: (B)

Common Law and equity exist side by side today in all courts. Therefore (A) and (D) are incorrect. Common Law or an equitable rule can be overruled by an Act of Parliament. Therefore (C) cannot be correct.

1.4 Answer: (D)

(A) is incorrect as the County Court deals with civil actions. Criminal actions are heard in the Crown Court. However criminal actions do not commence in this court, therefore (B) is incorrect. The Court of Appeal hears matters on appeal from lower courts, so (C) cannot be correct.

1.5 Answer: (D)

(A) is much narrower than the *ratio decidendi* of *Donoghue* v. *Stevenson*. The case is not limited to decomposed snails, or to drinks or to bottles. Moreover, the facts are different; for example, it was never suggested that the manufacturer deliberately placed a snail in the bottle. (B) is very different from the *ratio decidendi* of *Donoghue* v. *Stevenson*. (C) has very little to do with *Donoghue* v. *Stevenson*; it became an important issue in some later cases, but even in these the statement is not wholly accurate.

1.6 Answer: (A)

This was not an appeal from any of the other decisions; it was an entirely separate case. Therefore, the earlier decisions were not 'reversed' (B). 'Disapproving' an earlier decision is a mere expression of opinion by the present court, in *obiter dicta*; it is not a valid reason to disregard a precedent (D). The earlier cases were not 'overruled' (C) (even if they could be); indeed, the House of Lords in the *Caparo* case did not suggest that the earlier decisions were wrong, only that the material facts were different from those before the court now.

1.7 Answer: (C)

Memoranda are not legislation, neither are county court judgments which are judicial decisions. The Finance Act is primary legislation and articles of association are the internal regulations of a limited company agreed by the shareholders. It follows that the correct solution is (C).

1.8 Answer: (C)

(A) is of no effect, because the other driver still owed a duty of care to the passenger. (B) does not alter the fact that the passenger's injury is partly caused by the other driver. (C) is irrelevant to any claim by the passenger against the *other* driver. (D) is an example of probable contributory negligence.

1.9 Answer: (C)

Codified law is found in a comprehensive collection of documents. A Constitution, legislation and regulation can all provide or contribute towards codified law. Case law decisions provide an interpretation of stated law and show the application of law, usually with a hierarchy of courts recognised that is relevant in the application of precedent. Case law is therefore an exception.

1.10 Answer: (D)

Much of French Law is codified but one area that provides a notable exception is Tort.

1.11 Answer: (B)

Nigeria and Pakistan have legal systems based on English Common Law with an influence of Islamic Law, but the Napoleonic codes have not contributed to the development of these systems. (A) and (C) are therefore not the correct answers. Greece has a legal system based principally on codified Roman, Law, so (D) is not the correct answer. It is Egypt that has been influenced by English and Islamic laws as well as the Napoleonic codes, so (B) is the correct answer.

1.12 Answer: (A)

The European Parliament and the Council of the European Union are bodies that pass new laws which are proposed by the European Commission. (A) is therefore the correct answer. The Court of Justice of the European Communities has a role aiding interpretation of the law, but does not propose new law.

Solution 2

(a) The most superior domestic court is the *House of Lords*. The *High Court* is a court made up of three divisions, the Queen's Bench, Family and Chancery divisions. The *Court of Appeal* is a court which has a civil division and a criminal division.

(b) *Legislation* is the supreme source of English law. However, if its provisions should contradict law of the *European union,* the latter will prevail.

Solution 3

(a) In order to succeed in an action for negligence it is necessary first, to establish a *duty of care* owed, second, a *breach of duty* and finally, *damage*.
(b) In the tort of negligence, the principle of *res ipsa loquitur* means that 'the thing speaks for itself'. Where this principle applies the *burden of proof* is shifted on to the *defendant* who must show that he or she was not negligent in order to avoid liability.
(c) Under the doctrine of judicial precedent, the *ratio decidendi* of the case is binding upon lower courts whereas *obiter dicta* is not binding and is said to be of persuasive authority only.

Solution 4

(a) When judges are interpreting legislation, application of the *literal* rule can result in an absurd outcome. By using the *golden* rule an absurd outcome can be avoided.
(b) The Rules of Language include *eiusdem generis* under which judges can identify the meaning of *general* words in a statute from the meaning of the *particular* words found.
(c) When interpreting legislation the judiciary can rely on certain presumptions. These include the presumptions that *the Crown* will not be bound by the relevant legislation and that the legislation will not have *retrospective effect.*

The Law of Contract

The Law of Contract

2

Learning Outcomes

After completing this chapter you should be able to:

- identify the essential elements of a valid simple contract and situations where the law requires the contract to be in a particular form;
- explain how the law determines whether negotiating parties have reached agreement and the role of consideration in making that agreement enforceable;
- explain when the parties will be regarded as intending the agreement to be legally binding and how an agreement may be avoided because of misrepresentations.
- explain how the contents and the terms of a contract are established and the possible repercussions of non-performance;
- explain how the law controls the use of unfair terms in respect of both consumer and non-consumer business agreements;
- explain what the law regards as performance of the contract, and valid and invalid reasons for non-performance;
- explain the type of breach necessary to cause contractual breakdown and the remedies which are available for serious and minor breaches of contract.

The chapter has been arranged into sections based on the learning outcomes as above.

2.1 Contractual obligations

A contract is an agreement which the law will recognise. As will be seen throughout this text, it is of vital importance in business life, and forms the basis of most commercial transactions such as dealings in land and goods, credit, insurance, carriage of goods, the formation and sale of business organisations, and employment. The law of contract is therefore concerned mainly with providing a framework within which business can operate.

2.1.1 The essential elements of a valid simple contract

> *Learning Outcome*: To identify the essential elements of a valid simple contract and situations where the law requires the contract to be in a particular form.

A contract is a legally enforceable agreement. A simple contract is one which does not require the agreement to be in any particular form. It follows that the contract may be entirely oral, it may be in writing or it may even be implied from the conduct of the parties. In fact the vast majority of simple contracts are entirely oral. For example, all of the following everyday transactions are simple contracts: purchasing a newspaper, buying a bus or rail ticket, purchasing a sandwich and a drink at lunchtime, buying a book or a CD, going to the cinema, the theatre or a football game. To amount to a valid simple contract, the following essential elements must be present:

(i) *Agreement.* The parties must be in agreement. Whether they are in agreement is usually determined by the presence of an offer by one party which has been accepted by the other. This is discussed in more detail in Section 2.2.

(ii) *Consideration.* A contract in English law must be a two-sided bargain, each side providing or promising to provide some consideration in return for what the other is to provide. It is discussed in Section 2.2.3. (Only a promise made by deed can be binding if there is no consideration; see Section 2.2.3.)

(iii) *Intention to create legal relations.* The parties must clearly have intended their agreement to be legally binding. For example, a mere social arrangement – such as an agreement with a friend to meet for a meal – will not normally be treated as a contract. This is discussed further in Section 2.3.

(iv) *Reality of the consent.* This element relates back to 'agreement'. The parties must have freely entered into their agreement. If the truth is that the offer or acceptance was brought about by virtue of a 'misrepresentation', that is, an untrue statement of fact which induced the agreement, then the victim of the misrepresentation may be able to avoid the contract as this factor is said to render the contract 'voidable'. (see Section 2.3.1.)

(v) *Capacity to contract.* As a general rule, everyone is capable of entering into contracts. There are, however, some exceptions. Most importantly, some artificially created bodies such as local authorities are entitled only to do the things for which they were created or which have been specially authorised. Anything else is *ultra vires* (outside of its powers) and therefore void. Another example of lack of capacity is that infants (those under 18) may not be bound by some of their contracts.

(vi) *Legality.* Illegality can often invalidate a contract. Certainly some agreements which are *wholly* illegal – such as agreements to commit a murder – will not be recognised as valid contracts.

2.1.2 Form

There is a common misconception that simple contracts must be in writing. In fact, as stated above, most contracts are made by word of mouth. It may be desirable to have a written agreement where a lot is at stake, or where the contract is to last for a long time, but this is only for purposes of proof and is not necessary for validity. Exceptionally, though, certain types of agreement are only valid if made in a particular form.

Certain contracts must be in writing or they will be *void.* These include bills of exchange, cheques and promissory notes, contracts of marine insurance, the transfer of shares in a company, and legal assignment of debts.

Hire purchase and other regulated consumer credit agreements may be *unenforceable* against a borrower unless they are made in writing and include the information required by the Consumer Credit Act 1974. Contracts of guarantee need not be in writing but they are unenforceable in the courts unless there is written evidence of the essential terms and they are signed by or on behalf of the guarantor.

2.1.3 Transactions where a deed is required

Some transactions must be made by a formal document known as a deed. This must be signed, attested by a witness who also signs, and delivered. 'Delivery' means an intention to put the deed into effect rather than physically handing it over. It is no longer necessary for the deed to be 'sealed'. Deeds are required for the validity of promises for no consideration, and some bills of sale (mortgages of goods).

Special rules apply to land where a transfer normally takes place in two stages. The parties will first contract to sell or lease the land. Under the Law of Property (Miscellaneous Provisions) Act 1989, this contract must be made in writing in a signed document which 'incorporates' all the terms which the parties have expressly agreed; the terms can either be set out in the document itself or be included by reference to other documents. In practice, two identical documents are prepared, each signed by one of the parties, and then handed over to the other party with a deposit paid by the purchaser. These formalities do not apply to sales by public auction.

The second stage is the completion of the transaction by conveying the title of the land to the purchaser in return for payment of (the rest of) the price. This conveyance must be by deed if the land is sold or leased for more than 3 years.

2.2 Agreement

Learning Outcome:	To explain how the law determines whether negotiating parties have reached agreement and the role of consideration in making that agreement enforceable.

Agreement is usually shown by the unconditional acceptance of a firm offer. It marks the conclusion of negotiations, and thereafter, any withdrawal will constitute a breach of contract. The rules governing offer and acceptance will be examined in turn.

2.2.1 Offer

This is a statement of the terms on which the offeror (the person making the offer) is willing to be bound and, if the offer is accepted as it stands, agreement is made. An offer may be made to a particular person, to a class of persons (e.g. employees of a company or members of a club), or to the world at large (e.g. a reward for a person returning a lost article or, as in *First Sport Ltd* v. *Barclays Bank plc* (1993), a cheque-guarantee card). Only the person or a member of the class of persons to whom the offer is made may accept it.

Offers must be distinguished from other actions which may appear to be similar. First, an invitation to treat or to make an offer is an indication that a person is willing to enter into or continue *negotiations* but is not yet willing to be bound by the terms mentioned. Advertisements of goods for sale in catalogues or newspapers usually fall into this category; if they were held to be firm offers, there could well be the impossible situation where one offer was followed by ten acceptances. Other examples include goods in a shop window, shares in a company prospectus and inviting tenders for the supply of goods or services. In all of these instances, the other party is being invited to make an offer which may then be accepted or refused. It follows therefore that, in a self-service store, the goods on the shelves are an invitation to treat, the offer is made by the customer when the goods are taken to the checkout and the acceptance is made by the cashier [*Pharmaceutical Society of Great Britain* v. *Boots Cash Chemists* (1953)].

Second, a claim made about goods or services which no one would take too seriously, for example that a particular washing powder washes whitest, is not a firm offer. Care is needed here though, as there may be a narrow borderline between boasts and promises (see *Carlill* case below).

Third, a declaration of intention is not an offer intended to form the basis of a contract. A statement that an auction sale will be held is not actionable if a person travels to the place of sale only to find the auction has been cancelled [*Harrison* v. *Nickerson* (1873)].

Fourth, an answer to a request for information is not an offer. If a person asks for the lowest price that another will accept for a house and that other replies by stating a price, it does not necessarily mean that the house will be sold to that person at that price [*Harvey* v. *Facey* (1893)].

Once it has been established that a firm offer has come into existence, the offer must be communicated to the other party in order to be effective. Until the other party knows of the offer, he cannot accept it. Thus, if a lost article is returned to the owner without the finder being aware that a reward is being offered for its return, he cannot later claim the reward. Similarly, an ex-employee cannot claim for work later performed of which his former employer had no previous knowledge [*Taylor* v. *Laird* (1856): ship's captain resigned abroad and owners had no knowledge in advance that he later worked on homeward voyage].

An offer cannot continue indefinitely. It may come to an end in a number of ways so that it can no longer be accepted. An offeror may revoke or withdraw his offer at any time up to the moment of acceptance [*Routledge* v. *Grant* (1828)], provided that the revocation is communicated to the offeree. Revocation may be expressly made or it may be implied by conduct which clearly shows an intention to revoke, for example, by selling goods elsewhere and the other party learning of the sale. Communication may come directly from the seller or through some other reliable source [*Dickinson* v. *Dodds* (1876): offeree heard from a friend that the offeror had sold the horse elsewhere]. Revocation is possible at any time even though there has been a promise to keep the offer open for a specified period. If, however, an 'option' has been bought, that is the other party has given consideration to keep open the offer for a period of time, an early withdrawal will be a breach of this subsidiary contract.

Likewise, the offeree may reject the offer, again provided that the rejection is communicated to the offeror, since this only becomes effective when the offeror learns of it. Rejection may take the form of a counter-offer or by attempting to introduce new terms into the agreement. For example, in *Neale* v. *Merrett* (1930), M offered to sell land to N for £280. N 'accepted' and promised to pay on *credit* terms. This was not an acceptance. It is important to note that once an offer has been rejected, the offeree cannot later try to revive and accept it [*Hyde* v. *Wrench* (1840)].

An offer will lapse if a time limit is fixed for acceptance and this is not adhered to by the offeree. If no time limit is expressly fixed, the offer will lapse after a reasonable time which will depend upon the circumstances. In *Ramsgate Victoria Hotel Co* v. *Montefiore* (1866), 5 months was held to be too long a delay for the acceptance of an offer to buy shares. With perishable goods, a reasonable time would be much shorter.

Death of either party before acceptance will usually bring the offer to an end and will certainly do so when the other party learns of the death. If the identity of the parties is vital, as in a contract of employment, the offer will lapse at the time of death. The effect of death after acceptance when the contract has been made will be dealt with in Section 2.7.1.

The offer may also be conditional upon other circumstances and will lapse if these conditions are not fulfilled. An offer to buy a car assumes, by implication, that the car will remain in substantially the same state, and if it is subsequently badly damaged before acceptance the offer will thereafter cease to exist [*Financings Ltd* v. *Stimson* (1962)]. The position if this happens *after* acceptance will be dealt with later.

Finally, if an offer is made to a group of persons which can only be accepted by one of them, and one accepts, the offer ceases to exist so far as the rest of the group are concerned.

2.2.2 Acceptance

Acceptance, while the offer is still open, completes the contract. It must be an absolute and unqualified acceptance of the offer as it stands with any terms that may be attached to it. Anything else will amount to rejection. If a 'blanket acceptance' is not provided, the communication will be deemed a counter-offer and will have the effect of terminating the previous offer. The offeree is therefore prevented from subsequently providing an acceptance, and holding the offeror to the original offer. If, however, the response to an offer is a request for information, this will not terminate the original offer. Sometimes, an acceptance may be made *subject to a written agreement* or *subject to contract*. It must then be decided whether the parties intend to be bound immediately and the later document is only for the purpose of recording this, or whether there is no intention to be bound at all until the written agreement is made. If the agreement is one which is not valid until it is embodied in writing, the second of these alternatives will apply; see *Pitt* v. *PHH Asset Management Ltd* (1993). Where a document is described as a 'letter of intent', generally this will denote that no binding contract exists. However, positive content in such a document might cause contractual obligations to arise.

In instances where two organisations are negotiating a contract, each party may have its own 'standard terms and conditions' which appear on relevant documentation provided. Looking at the document content it will be impossible to find a binding contract because, no doubt, the standard terms of each party will differ. In such situations, the term 'battle of the forms' is appropriate. A contract will be found to exist in such situations when one of the parties positively acts in performing obligations under the agreement. The first party who so acts will be deemed to have accepted the terms and conditions put forward by the other party.

Let the buyer beware

Susan Singleton, *Chartered Secretary*, February 2004
Reprinted with permission of ICSA

Work before a contract is signed

It is not prudent as a supplier to start any work before any legal commitment is made as regards payment.

Yet lawyers are regularly asked to advise on when a supplier can be required to pay for work undertaken pre-contract. Typically, the supplier will say that they were given a verbal go-ahead, or that there was a 'handshake' or an oral contract or confirmation in an e-mail, or even that they were told that whatever happened, they would be paid for their time.

The law is very simple. If there was an agreement that the supplier would be paid whatever happens, then the supplier will be able to claim payment, even if the final contract is not signed, and even if the said agreement took verbal, e-mail or short note form. Verbal agreements, however, are hard to prove and require witnesses giving evidence under oath in court. It is much better to have a written agreement from a buyer that he or she will pay for work even if the contract is never signed.

Three phrases need to be considered here: 'Subject to contract', 'letter of intent' and 'heads of agreement'.

Subject to contract

If this phrase is said or written, it is clearly intended to mean that nothing is binding until the contract is signed. It is very hard later to argue otherwise.

A typical dispute might arise where work starts before the contract, and the buyer pulls out – perhaps for some internal or political reason – even though the parties have been working together for some time. The supplier, unsurprisingly, expects to be paid.

If there is no contract, then a law called 'quantum meruit' could possibly apply – that is, a right to payment for benefits or merits received in relation to the quantity or value of those works. If, however, the said works were undertaken as a favour, no claim may be possible. If there were deliverables, however, such as equipment or computer software, the supplier may be able to take them back: without a contract, title or property in them will not have passed to the buyer. If the buyer wants them it must pay. If the supplier has invoiced and been paid for some pre-contract works, then clearly there was some form of binding contract, so further recoveries may be possible.

Letter of intent

A document called a letter of intent is not usually intended to be legally binding, but to offer some comfort to the buyer.

It probably includes phrases such as 'the buyer hopes to enter into a contract with the supplier'. It is, in other words, an expression of wishes. It is possible that a letter of intent can be legally binding if it is sufficiently definite.

Heads of agreement

A supplier wanting authorisation to start work before a contract is formed needs more than a letter of intent or document headed 'subject to contract'.

What the supplier will need instead is an absolutely clear legal statement – something along the lines of 'Whether or not we sign the contract we are currently negotiating, you will be paid £400 a day for the services provided within 30 days of the date of invoice.' In many cases, however, it is much better just to negotiate and sign the main contract itself quickly. A short agreement such as the above omits many important legal details, such as liability and warranty issues.

Since acceptance completes the contract, the place where the acceptance is made is the place of the contract. This may be important if the parties are negotiating from different countries. It may determine which country's law shall apply and which country's courts shall have jurisdiction.

Acceptance may be by words, spoken or written, or it may be implied by conduct by performing an act required by the offer. In *Bryen & Langley Ltd* v. *Boston* (2005), a tender to complete building work was not signed. However, work on the basis of the agreement was commenced and the court held that a binding contract existed. Some positive act is necessary. Mental assent by silence is not enough, nor is it possible to dispense with acceptance. There is no contract if a buyer does nothing after a seller has offered to sell him a horse for a prescribed amount and has said that if he hears nothing to the contrary he will assume that the horse has been bought [*Felthouse* v. *Bindley* (1863)].

An application of this rule today would be unsolicited goods arriving by post with a note saying that unless they are returned within a specified time, the recipient will be bound to pay for them. Provided that the buyer does not treat the goods as his by using them or intentionally destroying them, he will not be bound if he does nothing. Under the Unsolicited Goods and Services Act 1971, the recipient will become the owner of the goods after 30 days. If the seller is a dealer, to demand payment in these circumstances is a criminal offence.

As a general rule, acceptance must be communicated to the person making the offer and no contract will come into being until the offeror knows of the acceptance. Moreover, communication must be carried out by the offeree or his properly authorised agent; unlike revocation, acceptance cannot be communicated by an unauthorised though reliable third party [*Powell* v. *Lee* (1908): school manager not empowered to act on behalf of other managers when offering headship to applicant].

There are two exceptional situations when actual communication of acceptance need not take place. First, the offeror may indicate to the offeree that, if he wishes to accept, he may merely carry out his side of the bargain without first informing the offeror. Thus, an order for goods may be accepted by delivery of the goods. In *Carlill* v. *Carbolic Smoke Ball Co.* (1893), where the defendants advertised that they would pay £100 to anyone who caught influenza after using their product, it was held that the use itself was adequate acceptance without the need for prior communication of this to the defendants. Similarly, a retailer may accept a cheque-guarantee card without telling the issuing bank that it is doing so [*First Sport Ltd* v. *Barclays Bank plc* (1993)]. Note that, while *communication* of acceptance may be dispensed with, acceptance itself cannot be (see *Felthouse* v. *Bindley* above).

The second exception is when the posting rule applies, for a letter of acceptance, properly addressed and stamped, may be effective from the moment of posting, even if it never arrives. The rule only applies though where it is within the contemplation of the parties that the post will be used, either by express agreement or by implication; for example, this would be so if previous negotiations had taken place by post, but not if the telephone had been used. There must also be some evidence of posting in the normal way, and handing the letter to another person to post, even a postman, is not enough. The rule does not apply to almost instantaneous methods of communication, such as fax, telephone or telex, where acceptance is only effective when and where it reaches the other party [*Entores* v. *Miles Far East Corporation* (1955)]. And confirmed in *Brinkibon Ltd* v. *Stahag Stahl and Stahlwarenhandels Gmbh* (1983).

Whether or not the postal rules apply to E-mail communications is not certain. However, in *NBTY Europe Ltd* v. *Nutricia International BV* (2005), where both parties involved communicated by e-mail, the court did hold that a binding contract was created at the time the acceptance was sent. With the use of e-mails so extensive in business activity, it is reasonable to anticipate further judicial consideration on this issue in the near future. The Electronic

Commerce (EC Directive) Regulations 2002 identifies clearly when an offer is deemed to be communicated by e-mail. This is at the point in time when the party to whom the offer is addressed is able to access the communication. (See the article below for an extended consideration of e-mail usage, and in such circumstances, the significance today of the postal rules.)

You've got mail

Deveral Copps, *New Law Journal*, 13 June 2003
Reproduced by permission of Reed Elsevier (UK) Ltd, trading as LexisNexis Butterworths

The postal rule was established in Adams *v.* Lindsell (1818) 1 B & Aid 680, to promote certainty within contractual formation at a time when the principal method of communication – the postal service – was slow. Had there been some alternatives to the postal service at the time, it is doubtful whether an exception to the normal rules of communication of acceptance would have been necessary. However, the postal rule was created almost 20 years before the telegraph system became practically useful in 1837 and some 60 years before Alexander Graham Bell made the first telephone call in 1876.

So without the postal rule, contracting parties who posted letters of acceptance would have been unsure whether their acceptances had been successful. Of course, the law could have required some positive notification of the receipt of the acceptance from the offeror, although it would follow that if notification of the receipt of acceptance was required, then this too would need to be communicated to ensure that the parties knew that they were legally bound. It would have been ludicrous for such a situation to occur; creating contracts by post would have been a lengthy process and this would have unnecessarily hampered business transactions. Parties may have had resources tied up in readiness for agreements that would not have been created and would miss out on alternative business opportunities for fear of being in breach of contract. In short, the postal rule ensures the swift conclusion of an agreement, in that contracts are created when the letter of acceptance is posted.

Should the postal rule apply to e-mail?

It is well-established that the postal rule does not apply to instantaneous forms of communication (Brinkibon Ltd *v.* Stahag Stahl und Stahlwarenhandels GmbH [1983] 2 AC 34 confirmed the decision in Entores Ltd *v.* Miles Far East Corp [1955] 2 QB 327). E-mail, whilst undoubtedly swift and certainly far quicker than the traditional postal service, cannot be said to be instantaneous as hours and even days can elapse between the sending of a message and its receipt. As the postal rule applies to non-instantaneous methods of communication, including telegrams (Bruner *v.* Moore [1904] 1 Ch 305), this would certainly support a claim for the extension of the postal rule to electronic mail.

A further argument which supports the application of the postal rule to e-mail relates to control. Once a letter has been posted, the responsibility of delivery lies with the post office and is outside the control of the sender. As the law appears to favour the person who 'trusts the post' (Household Fire Insurance Co Ltd *v.* Grant (1879) 4 Ex D 216, 223), the same principle should apply to e-mail, as once an e-mail is dispatched, the sender has no control over ensuring that the e-mail drops into the mailbox of the person to whom it was addressed.

The above certainly illustrates that there are some obvious similarities between e-mail and post however, this does not necessarily mean that the postal rule should be extended to e-mail.

The simple reason for this lies with the motive for the postal rule's creation which was to create certainty in contractual formation at a time when the communication system involved unavoidable delay. Whilst e-mail is not instantaneous, it is normally very quick and although there are occasional delays, these are rare and normally last less than a day.

Also, given that the post was the only form of distance communication available in the early nineteenth Century, it would have been difficult to check whether an acceptance had been successful. In the twenty-first Century, an offeree can easily check whether any e-mailed acceptance has been received, possibly using an instantaneous method of communication, such as the telephone or fax. If checking the success of an e-mailed acceptance by telephone or fax is not possible or is undesirable, almost all e-mail software allows for the request of 'delivery' and 'read' receipts at the time when an e-mail is sent. Here, a 'delivery' receipt will inform the sender that an e-mail has been successfully delivered to the addressee's e-mail account and a 'read' receipt will inform the sender that an e-mail has been read. Essentially, these receipts allow the sender of an e-mail to check that an e-mail has been successfully transmitted and operates in a similar way to recorded delivery packages sent via the traditional postal service.

In addition to delivery and read receipts, it is now standard for the sender of an e-mail to be informed if an e-mail is not delivered. This, for example, can occur when a mistake has been made in the recipient's address or when the recipient's e-mail service provider is experiencing problems. If a message is returned, there would be few advocates of a rule that could allow a contract to be created when the offeree knows that acceptance has definitely not been communicated! As it is now possible to confirm whether or not an e-mail has been successfully delivered, is there really a need to stretch the postal rule to encompass e-mail?

The Government could have settled the e-mail/postal rule argument in the recent Electronic Commerce (EC Directive) Regulations 2002 (SI 2002/2013), but unfortunately, failed to do so. Interestingly, the Regulations clearly state the point at which an order – which although not absolute will tend to amount to an offer – is deemed to be communicated. Regulation 11(2)(b) states that where businesses contract, 'the order and the acknowledgement of receipt will be deemed to be received when the parties to whom they are addressed are able to access them'. Where e-mail is concerned, therefore, this would be the time when the e-mail drops into the mailbox of the person or business to whom it is addressed and not when the message is actually read.

Regulation 11(2)(b) makes reference to an 'acknowledgment of receipt', whereby a seller is required by Reg. 11(1)(a) to 'acknowledge receipt of the order . . . without undue delay and by electronic means'. It is worth pointing out that it is completely possible for a carelessly drafted acknowledgement of receipt to amount to an acceptance. For example, a company that acknowledges the receipt of an order with the words 'thank you for your order, your goods should arrive within 4–7 working days' is intimating that they wish to fulfil their part of the contract and would find it difficult to convince a court that the offer had not been accepted. In this situation, Reg. 11(2)(b) suggests that acceptance would be deemed communicated at the time the e-mail is available to be read, although this is probably not how this Regulation was meant to be interpreted.

Since this posting rule only applies to acceptance and not to revocation or rejection, there may be unexpected problems. In *Byrne* v. *Van Tienhoven* (1880), the offeror posted a letter of revocation before the offeree posted his acceptance. Nevertheless there was a contract, because the acceptance was *posted* before the revocation *arrived.* However, it is always possible for the offeror to stipulate that he will not be bound until the acceptance actually reaches him. In *Holwell Securities Ltd* v. *Hughes* (1974), the vendor specified in his offer that acceptance could only be made 'by *notice* in writing to the intending vendor'; the posting rule did not apply, and a letter of acceptance which was posted but never arrived had no effect.

On occasions, pre-contractual negotiations may consist of a series of counter-offers, and it is not easy to determine what terms have eventually been agreed. As in *Butler Machine Tools Ltd* v. *Ex-Cell-O Ltd* (1979), there may be a 'battle of forms', where seller and buyer each sends his own printed standard terms to the other, and the two sets of terms differ. In this case, the buyer's terms were received last; the seller probably did not read them, but he acknowledged receipt and went on with the contract. The buyer's terms prevailed.

Application of the rules relating to offer, revocation of offer, counter-offer, acceptance and acceptance through conduct can be found in *Pickfords Ltd.* v. *Celestica Ltd* (2003). In this case, an offer which had been revoked was ultimately held to be binding on the offeror. Looking a little more closely at the facts, the offeror provided an offer on the 13th September 2001 and then a second offer on the 27th September 2001 which differed in content from the first offer and served to revoke the first offer. On the 15th October 2001, the offeree sent an acceptance of the original offer. This 'acceptance' did not cause a contract to be created. It merely served as a counter-offer to the offer of the 27th September 2001. The party who had provided the original offer then acted on the 'acceptance' of the 15th October 2001. What amounted to a counter-offer to the offer of the 27th September became in effect a fresh offer which was accepted by conduct, and so eventually a binding contract was recognised.

> You are warned against the not uncommon confusion between acceptance of an *offer*, which concludes a contract, and acceptance of *goods*, which may signify performance of the contract and take away the buyer's right to reject the goods as unsatisfactory. The latter is dealt with in Section 2.9.3.

2.2.3 Consideration

The English law of contract is concerned with bargains and not mere promises. If a bare promise to deliver goods is broken, there will be no remedy. If, however, the promise to deliver goods is countered by a promise to do something in return, for example to pay for them, then a contract will come into being. The promised payment is the consideration for the promised goods, and vice versa.

Thus, a contract must be a two-sided affair, each side providing or promising to provide some consideration in exchange for what the other is to provide. This may take the form of an act, a forbearance to act, or a promise. If a promise is to be fulfilled in the future, it is known as executory consideration. When the promise is eventually fulfilled, it is executed consideration.

Vague promises without such value, for example to show natural love and affection or to behave as a good son should, are not sufficient. But a court will not concern itself as to whether the value is adequate in relation to that which is given in exchange. The value of property or services is largely a matter of opinion for the parties to decide and a court will not intervene to substitute its own view of what the bargain should be. The price may be relevant in deciding whether the goods are of a satisfactory quality at that price (see Section 2.4.2) but this does not directly affect the validity of the contract. Goods, services or other things sold at a very high or very low price may be evidence, but only evidence, of fraud.

Past consideration has no value, and therefore is not consideration. No agreement will have been made whereby the two parties are aware of consideration to be provided by each. One party will have provided a benefit (it's in the past). This will then be identified as consideration for a subsequent promise made by another. If a promise is made for work already done, the work cannot constitute consideration for the promise, as its benefit has already been received. In the old case of *Roscorla* v. *Thomas* (1842), promises made about a horse *after* sale simply had no effect; the same would apply today to promises made by a car salesman after the car had been sold. On the other hand, if work is requested or authorised and it is the type of work which is normally paid for, then it may be implied that everyone concerned intended *from the outset* that the work would be paid for this time. The buyer, in effect, is taken to promise at the outset that he will pay the bill – so long as it is reasonable – in due course. In *Stewart* v. *Casey* (1892), the defendant asked the claimant to promote the defendant's patents (work which is normally paid for). The claimant did this work successfully, and after he had done so, the defendant promised him a share in the profits. This promise was binding. The consideration had impliedly been promised at the outset, and was not past. The same would apply today if a builder was asked to do certain repairs, did the work and sent his bill afterwards; the implied promise by the buyer to pay the bill would be binding.

A promise to perform an existing obligation to the promisee similarly has no value. The promisor is only giving what he is already bound to give. This applies particularly if the promisor merely promises again to perform an existing contract with the promisee. Thus, if a debtor promises to pay part of his debt in consideration of the creditor releasing him from the rest, the release is not binding. This is known as the rule in *Pinnel's Case* (1602).

Examples

The following cases show ways in which this rule has been applied and has evolved.

In *Foakes* v. *Beer* (1884), the debtor owed £2,090 to a creditor who had obtained a court judgment for this amount. The debtor could not pay immediately, so the creditor promised him that, if he paid by agreed instalments, she would not charge the interest to which she was entitled. Note that there was no consideration for the creditor's promise not to charge the interest. The debtor was only promising to pay what he already owed. He duly did so. The creditor thereupon went back on her promise, and claimed the interest. Her claim succeeded.

Similarly, in *Re Selectmove* (1994), the company owed arrears of taxes, due immediately. At first, the Inland Revenue promised to let the company pay late, by instalments, but later went back on this and threatened winding-up proceedings unless the company paid in full immediately. The Inland Revenue was entitled to do this. There was no consideration for the earlier promise to allow delayed payments.

In *D & C Builders* v. *Rees* (1966), the building company agreed to take a cheque for £300 in full settlement of a debt of £482. There was no consideration for the promise to forego the right to receive the extra £182. They were later held to be entitled to the remaining £182. In this case, the creditor (D & C) was a small firm which was in difficulties. In his judgment, Lord Denning commented: 'the debtor's wife held the creditor to ransom. The creditor was in need of money to meet his own commitments, and she knew it'. At the time, £300 must have seemed better than nothing. It was understandable that D & C were still entitled to the rest.

However, it has always been accepted that if a debtor gives some new consideration, the promise to forego part of a debt will be binding. This applies if he does or promises to do something he was not already bound to do, for example by paying the debt earlier than it was due, or paying it at a different place; but it is not enough merely to pay by cheque instead of cash, or vice versa. What is sufficient to be new consideration was extended by *Williams* v. *Roffey Bros* (1989). A carpenter who had contracted to do work for builders found that he could not complete on time. The builders, who would lose badly if the carpenter defaulted, promised on their own initiative to pay extra if the carpenter could find some way of doing the work promptly. The promise was held to be binding. The carpenter was carrying out his existing obligations, but in changed circumstances which demanded new, unusual and exceptional effort. The builders would benefit from this. There was no suggestion of fraud or duress by the carpenter. The extra money was offered voluntarily by the builders on their own initiative, unlike in *D & C Builders* v. *Rees* (1966).

Some earlier cases suggest another limit to the consideration rules. Although a promise without consideration cannot be sued upon, it may sometimes be used for a defence known as promissory estoppel. If a promise is intended to be binding and to be acted upon in the future, and is in fact so acted upon by the promisee, the promiser may be estopped (or prevented) from bringing a later action inconsistent with his promise if it would be unfair or inequitable for him to do so. In *Central London Property Trust* v. *High Trees House Ltd* (1947), in a lease which started in 1937, the landlord promised, because of the war, to reduce the rent. The premises were sublet, and people were reluctant to live in London. After the war, the landlord could charge the full rent again for the future, but the court said – in *obiter dicta* – that he would not have been entitled to arrears. It would have been unfair and inequitable for him to claim this for a time when the tenant had relied on the promise of half-rent during the exceptionally dangerous times. This defence is limited, and may apply to even fewer situations now following the decision in *Williams* v. *Roffey* (above). It might be held today that the tenant had given consideration for the landlord's promise, as circumstances had changed since the original lease, the tenant was finding it increasingly difficult to sublet the premises, the landlord did still want a tenant, and the arrangement had been made amicably and without any fraud or duress by the tenant.

It should be noted that a promise to perform an existing obligation *to a third party can* be consideration. Suppose that A owes money to B. C then appears and tells A that, if A makes a further promise *to* C that A will pay the debt, C will give A a guarantee. If A accepts this offer, there is a valid contract between A and C. If A fails to pay the debt, he can be sued by C as well as by B, and this additional obligation is the consideration which he gives to C for the guarantee; see *Pao On* v. *Lau Yiu Long* (1979).

A promise to perform an existing public duty can raise different issues. It will not normally be valid consideration. It would be contrary to public policy to allow a public official to receive extra payment for carrying out his public duties. If, however, the promise is to do *more* than the public duty, this will be sufficient consideration. Thus, the police authority were entitled to payment for providing *extra* officers to guard a coal mine during a strike [*Glasbrook Bros Ltd v. Glamorgan County Council* (1925)] and for providing officers *inside* the football ground during matches [*Harris* v. *Sheffield United Football Club Ltd* (1987)].

Privity of contract (whose contract is it) can depend upon consideration. If A and B exchange promises, there is a contract between A and B. Each has given consideration to the other. Each could sue the other. But, as a general rule, no one else could sue either of them on this contract. The Contract (Rights of Third Parties) Act 1999 provides exceptions to the privity rule.

Under s.1(1) a person who is not a party to a contract is given the right to enforce a term of the contract. This right exists where either the contract expressly provides that the third party can sue, or the contract term purports to confer a benefit on the third party. However, third party rights will not exist if the contracting parties did not intend the contract to be enforceable by a third party and this is apparent on a proper construction of the contract. The presumption that third parties have a right to sue on the contract can therefore be rebutted. It is only when the third party is identified by name in the contract, or is identified as a member of a class, or is identified . . . as answering a particular description – that the right to sue exists. The need for clarity of wording in the contract and identification of the contracting parties, intentions are particularly important.

The right of a third party to recover commission was recognised in *Nissin Shipping Co Ltd* v. *Cleaves & Co Ltd and others* (2003). It was decided that the chartering broker had a direct claim against owners for commission not paid, even though they were a third party to the charterparty. The chartering brokers relied successfully on the rights provided under the Contracts (Rights of Third Parties) Act 1999.

Where a promise is embodied in a deed, it is binding without the need for consideration, and the above rules do not apply. This exception is not used very often, but deeds of gift, to bind the donor to *give to charity for instance*, are examples; see Section 2.1.3.

2.3 Intention that the agreement should be legally binding

Learning Outcome:	To explain when the parties will be regarded as intending the agreement to be legally binding and how an agreement may be avoided because of misrepresentation.

An agreement will only be recognised as a contract if the parties intended that the agreement should be legally binding. With agreements of a friendly, social or domestic nature, this intention is rarely present. In fact, the law presumes that there is no such intention in the absence of strong evidence to the contrary. Therefore, an arrangement between friends to meet for a meal, or between husband and wife for apportioning housekeeping duties, would not be legally binding contracts. In *Balfour* v. *Balfour* (1919), an agreement in an ongoing marriage that the husband should pay a specified amount to the wife as a house keeping allowance, while he was away on career duties, was not held to be binding. However, it might be different if the agreement was made after the marriage had broken up (so long as there was consideration). An agreement made between husband and wife in *Merritt* v. *Merritt* (1970) was held to be legally binding. Here, the husband had left the matrimonial home and under the agreement, the husband was to pay the wife £40 per month and the wife was to use this money in satisfying the outstanding mortgage payments on the house.

With business agreements, on the other hand, there is a strong presumption that legal relations *are* intended. A business agreement would be identified where, for example, one or both contracting parties were a company or business, the agreement was of a clearly commercial nature or the contract involved money and money was factor of significance. If the parties do not wish to be legally bound, they must clearly say so, usually in a written contract for purposes of proof. An agreed statement that an arrangement is 'not to be subject to the jurisdiction of the courts' would show that the parties did not wish to be legally bound; see *Rose and Frank* v. *Crompton Bros Ltd* (1925). *Binding in honour only* clauses on football pool coupons are another example as in *Jones v. Vernons Pools Ltd* (1938).

It is not always easy to distinguish social and business contracts, and so determine whether or not a presumption to be legally bound exists. In *Simpkins* v. *Pays* (1955), three parties were involved; a landlady, her granddaughter and a lodger. On that basis any agreement between the three might reasonably be seen as a social arrangement. However, the issue before the court related to the parties together entering a competition on a regular basis. The aim was clearly to win money, and the arrangement was deemed to be of a business nature. Here the landlady received a prize in her name which she refused to share.

If the parties are still negotiating, then obviously they do not intend to be legally bound yet. Similarly, an 'agreement' where at least one *vital* term is left unsettled is clearly not binding yet. Therefore, an option to renew a lease 'at such rental as may be agreed between the parties' would have no effect, because the parties still have some negotiating to do. However, it might be different if the option was to renew 'at a market rent', because this could be settled by outside evidence and without further negotiation.

Collective agreements between employers and trade unions as to wages and other terms of employment are not normally binding. They are presumed to be intended as working arrangements, and not binding contracts subject to the jurisdiction of the courts.

2.3.1 Misrepresentation

During the negotiations preceding a contract, statements are often made with a view to inducing the other party to enter into a contract. If any such statement is false, the party thereby misled is not agreeing to what is the true state of affairs and the contract may be voidable for misrepresentation. Misrepresentation, therefore, may be defined as a false statement of fact (not of law or a mere expression of opinion), made by one party to the other before the contract, and made with a view to inducing the other party to enter into it. The statement must have been intended to be acted upon, and it must actually have deceived the other party and induced him to make the agreement. Representations made prior to contract creation may differ from the terms of a written contract signed by the parties. Terms of the contract recognised by the courts would be found in the signed agreement. However, pre-contract representations can prevail where the court accepts that no intention existed to have the content of a subsequent written agreement replace earlier communications. It was information provided over the telephone that served to establish contract terms rather than the subsequently prepared written contract in *PeekayIntermark Ltd* v. *Australia and New Zealand Banking Group Ltd* (2005). The claimant who was a regular customer of the banking group was able to rely on statements given over the phone about a product as being contract terms even though he subsequently signed a written contract, which he did not read, containing contradictory information.

Even a misleading half truth can be a misrepresentation as when a person, completing a proposal form for life assurance, stated that he had had two previous proposals accepted but omitted to mention that several other proposals had been rejected [*London Assurance* v. *Mansel* (1879)]. However, as a general rule, silence cannot amount to misrepresentation and there is no duty to disclose facts, even though the silent party knows that the other party is deceiving himself. In contracts for the sale of goods, this rule is known as *caveat emptor* (let the buyer beware).

There are two exceptional instances when there is a duty to disclose. The first is a duty to correct statements which were true when made but, because the facts have changed, they have subsequently become false and it would be unfair to let them stand. In *With* v. *O'Flanagan* (1936), it was held that a true statement about the profits from a doctor's practice should have been corrected when the practice was sold some months later and in the meantime the profits had fallen because of the doctor's illness.

The other exception relates to contracts of the utmost good faith (*uberrimae fidei*), contracts where one party alone possesses full knowledge of the material facts and must disclose them. This applies in contracts of insurance with respect to material facts affecting the decision whether to insure and in fixing the amount of the premium; in contracts for the sale of land with regard to defects in title; in a prospectus inviting subscription for shares as to matters required by statute; and in contracts for family arrangements.

Misrepresentations may later become incorporated as terms in the contract. If so, it will be more advantageous for the party deceived to sue for breach of contract which, if successful, gives an automatic right to damages. Damages will not normally be awarded for misrepresentation if the person liable can prove that he reasonably believed that he was telling the truth. It may not be easy to distinguish between contractual promises and mere representations, but the courts will usually hold that, in contracts of sale, statements made by dealers are contractual terms and statements made by sellers who are not dealers are representations.

In all instances of misrepresentation, the contract is said to be voidable at the option of the party deceived. The contract may be rescinded or ended, and the parties restored to their original positions, for example by returning property transferred and money paid. The right to rescind will be lost if such restoration is not possible as when property has been resold or destroyed. The right will also be lost if the party deceived affirms the contract by going on with it, knowing of the misrepresentation.

The right of rescission is 'equitable', which means that the courts can refuse to grant it when they think that it would be unfair. The courts will insist that rescission be exercised reasonably promptly once the misrepresentation has been or should have been discovered by reasonable diligence; this rule is necessary to avoid uncertainty as to the ownership of property which might or might not have to be returned. What is 'reasonably promptly' is a question of fact. For things that change rapidly in value, the time can be very short – sometimes only weeks or less. Rescission will become effective from the time that it is made public, for example by notifying the other party or, if this is not possible, informing the police [see *Car and Universal Finance Co Ltd* v. *Caldwell* (1965)].

A claim for damages is the other possible remedy for misrepresentation:

- Damages can be awarded if the claimant can prove that the misrepresentation was made deliberately and fraudulently. It is the claimant who must prove that there has been fraud and this is not easy. This is therefore not very common.
- Under the Misrepresentation Act 1967 s. 2(1), damages may also be claimed *unless* the *defendant* can prove that, up to the time of contracting, he believed that the statements were true and had reasonable cause to believe so. This is sometimes referred to as *negligent misrepresentation.* It has the great advantage that negligence is *presumed*, so that the defendant must in effect prove his innocence.
- Under the Misrepresentation Act 1967 s. 2(2), damages may also be awarded at the court's discretion, as an alternative to rescission, even for *innocent misrepresentation.* If the defendant can prove his innocence, however, the claimant has no *right* to damages. He can only ask the court to exercise its discretion in his favour. This is not common.

In addition to these civil remedies for misrepresentation, a false statement of fact may also give rise to criminal liability, for example under the Trade Descriptions Act 1968 or the Property Misdescriptions Act 1991.

Any term in the contract which tries to exclude liability for misrepresentation is void unless it can be shown to be reasonable; see Section 2.5.

Examples

In *Walker v. Boyle* (1982), the wife owned a family house and wished to sell it. Statements for which she was responsible helped to persuade a buyer to make a contract to buy the house, paying a deposit of £10,500. The statements were misrepresentations, although not deliberately so. When the buyer discovered the facts, he:

- rescinded the contract;
- recovered his £10,500 deposit;
- recovered damages under the Misrepresentation Act s.2(1) for the additional expenses which he had incurred. (The statements had been made negligently.)

In *Howard Marine Ltd v. Ogden* (1978), damages were awarded for false statements about the carrying capacity of two barges. The statements were not deliberately false and fraudulent; but the owners should have checked the correct capacity, and therefore the Misrepresentation Act s.2(1) applied.

2.4 The contents of the contract – the agreement and incorporation of terms

Learning Outcome: To explain how the contents and the terms of a contract are established and the possible repercussions of non-performance.

This learning outcome is satisfied by explaining which of the various statements made by negotiating parties become terms of the contract. This in turn requires students to know how the law determines that the parties have reached *agreement*, through the rules of *offer and acceptance*, and how terms come to be *incorporated* into the contract. Students also need to know the categories of contractual terms and the significance of this categorisation, along with how the actual status of contractual terms is determined.

2.4.1 Incorporation of terms

The law on the incorporation of express terms may be summarised in a single sentence. Thus, to be bound by a clause a person must know of that clause, or have been given reasonable notice of it at or before the time when the contract was entered into. More specifically, express terms (see Section 2.4.2) may be incorporated by the following means:

(i) *Incorporation by actual notice*. This applies where terms are known and agreed to by the parties at the time when the contract is entered into.

(ii) *Incorporation by signature*. If a person signs a written agreement, he or she is prima facie deemed to have read the document, in other words to have been given notice of the terms. [See *L'Estrange* v. *Graucob* (1934)].

(iii) *Incorporation by the provision of reasonable notice*. As stated above, even if a contracting party does not actually know of a particular term it will nonetheless be incorporated into the contract if the other party has given reasonable notice of it at or before the time of the contract. In *Olley* v. *Marlborough Court Ltd* (1949), a husband and wife paid for a room in a hotel at the reception desk. They then went up to their room and inside was a notice which stated: 'The proprietors will not hold themselves responsible for articles lost or stolen unless handed to the manageress for safe custody.' The couple left their room key at the reception and when they returned they discovered that due to inadequate supervision, someone had taken the key, entered their room and stolen certain of the wife's furs. The defendants tried to rely on the notice in the claimant's room, but it was held that it was ineffective as it had not been brought to the claimant's attention at or before the time when they contracted, that is, when they paid for their room at the reception desk.

(iv) *Incorporation by a* course of dealings. If, for example, the claimants in the *Olley* v. *Marlborough Court Ltd* (1949) case had been regular visitors to the hotel, so that they could be said to know the contents of the notice inside their hotel rooms, then the defendants may have been able to rely on the notice as being incorporated into the contract by their course of dealings.

In addition to express terms it must be remembered that various statutes imply terms into contracts, irrespective of the express wishes of the contracting parties. Thus, for example, the Sale of Goods Act 1979 contains a number of provisions which are implied into all contracts for the sale of goods. Furthermore, the Unfair Contract Terms Act 1977 prohibits the exclusion of some of those provisions in certain types of contract, in particular those involving the sale of goods by a business to a consumer.

2.4.2 Express terms

Express terms are those specifically mentioned and agreed to by the parties at the time of contracting, either in writing or orally. In a small cash sale, for example, where goods and money are exchanged, such terms may be virtually non-existent. In other cases, where the agreement is complicated, involves valuable subject-matter, or is to last for a long time, it is more usual for detailed terms to be incorporated in a written document even though writing may not be required by law.

2.4.3 Implied terms

Where an issue arises upon which the parties have not made an express provision, it may be necessary for a court to imply a term into the contract to resolve the issue. In other instances, various statutes have provided for implied terms in certain types of contract which will apply either irrespective of the wishes of the parties or only if the parties have failed to cover a particular point.

Terms are implied by the courts to fill omissions and give business effect to the intentions of the parties. Such obligations will be imposed as the court feels the parties would have reasonably agreed to, had they considered the matter. Thus, where the owner of a wharf had agreed to provide a berth for a ship, it was implied that the berth would be suitable [*The Moorcock* (1889)], and in a tenancy agreement for a tower block of flats, it was implied that the landlord had a duty to keep the lifts and stairs in good repair [*Liverpool City Council* v. *Irwin* (1977)].

There are many other examples of implied terms which have become generally acknowledged and are now embodied in the common law. In a tenancy of a furnished house, it is implied that the premises will be reasonably fit for human habitation when the tenancy begins. In a contract for the carriage of goods by sea, it is implied that the ship is seaworthy and will proceed with reasonable despatch without unnecessary deviations. In a contract of employment, it is implied that the employer will provide a safe system of work and that the employee will exercise care and skill in carrying out his or her work.

The Sale of Goods Act 1979 (as amended in 1994) provides a number of examples of terms implied by statute. There are five important terms which can be implied into every contract of sale. These impose obligations upon a seller:

- that the seller has (or will have) the right to sell the goods;
- that the goods shall correspond with any description applied to them;
- that the bulk will correspond with any sample; and
- where the sale is made in the course of business, that the goods shall be both, of satisfactory (formerly 'merchantable') quality and reasonably fit for the required purpose if the seller has been made aware of this.

Most of these obligations are self-explanatory. From the standpoint of consumer protection, the most important is the term requiring satisfactory quality, although the protection may also apply to business customers if not excluded (later). Satisfactory quality will be achieved if the goods meet a standard that a reasonable person would regard as satisfactory, taking account of any description of the goods, the price (if relevant) and all the other relevant circumstances. The Act goes on to give a non-exhaustive list of considerations which it may be appropriate to take into account: fitness for all the purposes for which goods of that kind are commonly supplied, appearance and finish, freedom from minor defects, safety and durability. Excluded are defects which are specifically drawn to the buyer's attention before the sale and, if the buyer has examined the goods before the sale (which he is not required to do), defects which that examination ought to reveal. The obligation, which requires strict compliance, applies to all goods supplied under the contract and hence there will be a breach if the packaging is defective or if dangerous extraneous matter is supplied with the goods.

A number of amendments have been made to the Sale of Goods Act ('SOGA') provisions outlined above by the Sale and Supply of Goods to Consumers Regulations 2002 ('SSGCR'). The Regulations introduce a number of remedies for consumers in addition to those contained in SOGA. Thus, for example, in determining whether goods are of satisfactory quality, the buyer is entitled to take account of any specific claims as to the qualities of the goods made by the seller, the producer or his representative in any public statements, for example in advertisements or on labelling. Again, if the goods fail to conform to the contract of sale at the time of delivery, or in some cases up to 6 months after delivery, the buyer is entitled to require the seller to repair or replace the goods, reduce the price to take account of the defect or rescind the contract. The buyer in *Clegg* v. *Olle Andersson* (2003) retained the right to reject a yacht where there was a failure to supply goods of satisfactory quality. The vessel had an overweight keel which had an adverse effect on its safety. The court held that although communications between the parties took place between August 2000 and March 2001, rejection of the goods still took place within a reasonable time. It was appropriate to look not merely at the time factor but also other factors of relevance which related to the time factor involved.

Examples

The following cases show how these terms implied by the Sale of Goods Act can work in practice.

In *Beale* v. *Taylor* (1967), the buyer bought a car described as a '1961 model'. It later transpired that it had been 'bulkheaded': the front part was from a pre-1961 model and had been welded to the back. The goods did not comply with the description.

In *Grant* v. *Australian Knitting Mills* (1936), a buyer of underpants found, after wearing them, that the material contained a chemical which gave him dermatitis. The goods were not of satisfactory quality, and they were not reasonably fit for the purpose (wearing) which he had impliedly made known to the seller.

In *Bartlett* v. *Sidney Marcus Ltd* (1965), the buyer bought a cheap second-hand car. It was obviously in poor condition, and he was told about a damaged clutch. Repairs cost much more than anticipated, but the buyer's claim for damages failed. The car was not unsatisfactory at that price and in that situation.

In *Rogers* v. *Parish Ltd* (1987), the car was an expensive new Range Rover. At that price, even minor defects made the quality unsatisfactory.

In *Feldaroll Foundry plc* v. *Herries Leasing (London) Ltd* (2004) defects found in a car would have cost relatively little to rectify. Nevertheless the car was found not to be of satisfactory quality as it was potentially unsafe to drive.

In *Frost* v. *Aylesbury Dairy Co Ltd* (1905), the dairy sold milk infected by typhoid germs. A buyer, Mrs Frost, died. The dairy proved that it had taken all reasonable – even possible – precautions.

Mrs Frost's estate recovered damages because the milk was not of satisfactory quality, and not reasonably fit for the purpose impliedly made known.The dairy's precautions were no defence. Liability under these terms is strict. Even an innocent seller is liable.

Note: This last case illustrates an important point. In an action for breach of contract, a defendant can sometimes be liable for damages even if he can prove that he was not at fault. Compare this with damages for misrepresentation (Section 2.3.1).

Buy implication

Richard Lawson, *Solicitors Journal*, 20 June 2003
© Sweet & Maxwell Ltd. Reprinted with permission

The Sale of Goods Act 1979 implies into contracts of sale conditions as to the goods being of satisfactory quality and reasonably fit for their purpose. In the event of breach, the buyer is entitled to rescind the contract and claim damages. This right to rescind is disapplied if, in the circumstances set out in the Act, the buyer can be said to have accepted the goods. Two recent cases have elaborated on the rights of both buyers and sellers where it is claimed there has been a breach of the implied terms.

Leicester Circuits Ltd v. Coates Bros [2003] EWCA Civ 333

The claimants manufactured printed circuit boards, and the defendants manufactured special inks. The process adopted by the claimants was such that the boards had to be prepared with a special ink, hence the contract they made with the defendants. Leicester subsequently claimed that, because blistering occurred in the boards, something the ink was meant to prevent, the ink could not have been reasonably fit for its purpose. They claimed this unfitness caused them financial loss.

The High Court upheld the claim. The court said that while some of the evidence favoured one party, and some the other, it was significant that once a different type of ink replaced that supplied by the defendants, the level of unfit boards dropped to manageable proportions. Accordingly the court held that on the balance of probabilities, the claimants had made out their claim that the ink had not been reasonably fit for its purpose. The defendants appealed.

The Court of Appeal said it was tempting to leave the lower court's ruling, on a matter of fact and made in relation to a complex and largely scientific dispute, undisturbed, but said that would be a 'negation of our appellate responsibilities'. Although the defendants would have a 'substantial mountain to climb' to win their appeal, the question for determination was one of inferential fact, and it was the appellate court's duty to decide if the lower court's ruling was a legitimate inference from the evidence presented in the case.

After hearing copious and detailed evidence from both sides, the Court of Appeal was satisfied the appeal had been made out. The key factors in its reaching this decision were:

- The ink worked adequately for nearly 2 years from the time it was first used.
- Even when the problems began to arise, it was only 'intermittently and to a surprisingly varying degree'.
- The expert evidence could not identify any specific cause for the problems which had arisen, though the processing work undertaken by the claimants was 'more likely to be blamed than the quality of the ink'.
- Given the intermittent and varying nature of the problems encountered by the claimants, the fact that other inks seemed to work well could not of itself mean the ink supplied by the defendants was therefore unfit.
- The alleged experience of other board manufacturers could prove nothing, in the absence of proper allegations and proof that such experience was close enough to the problems met by the claimants to warrant a similar conclusion as to unfitness.

Damages aspect

One element in the claim was for the loss of business with a particular third party. The High Court dismissed this claim on the ground the loss of the business could not be attributed to any problems with the ink. Had the claim been admissible, it would have had to be considered under the principles laid down in *Victoria Industries Ltd* v. *Newnan Ltd* [1949] 2 KB 528. There, boilers had been delivered late, but the claimants could not claim for the loss of a particularly lucrative Government contract, since the defendants were unaware of that contract when their own contract with the claimant was made. The claimants were instead entitled to general loss of business profits arising from the late delivery.

The contract in *Leicester*, which was made pursuant to the defendants' terms and conditions, excluded liability for 'consequential or incidental damage of any kind whatsoever . . . including without limitation any indirect loss or damage such as operating loss, loss of clientele'. The Court of Appeal ruled that, had it been relevant, this clause would not have been held to exclude the claim for loss of profit, since such claims would have been within the reasonable contemplation of the parties if the ink supplied had been unsuitable and hence within the first rule of *Hadley* v. *Baxendale* (1854) 9 Ex 341. This provides that a person in breach of contract is automatically liable for all loss which is the direct and natural consequence of a breach, and so within the reasonable contemplation of the party in breach. For the reasons given above, the particular loss of the third party contract would almost certainly have been consequential loss and hence covered by the exclusion clause.

Clegg v. Olle Andersson [2003] EWCA Civ 320

The contract in issue in this case was for the sale of a yacht. The yacht's keel was about 600 kg overweight (it should have been 5500 kgs). In the light of this, the claimants maintained the yacht was not of satisfactory quality, a claim rejected by the High Court.

The 1979 Act requires a number of factors to be considered when deciding if goods are of satisfactory quality, including freedom from minor defects, durability and safety. The judge concluded there was no evidence that the heavy keel made the yacht unsafe, even though it would reduce the safety factor of the rigging, given that the safety factor was of the order of 2.5 (the rigging being designed to take a load exceeding 40 per cent of its breaking load). The excess weight would, though, reduce the service life of the rigging, which would be around 10 or 20 years if carrying the excess weight.

On appeal, the Court of Appeal drew specific attention to what had been agreed by the experts. In particular:

- The heavy keel would have an adverse effect on speed, fuel efficiency, rig safety, freeboard and safe capacity;
- The increased rig loads were considered unacceptable by the rig designers.

On these findings the Court of Appeal held the High Court was wrong to say there was no evidence that the yacht was unsafe. One witness said the yacht, as built, was quite safe and could have been left even though mast and rigging would have required alteration. The seller accepted that remedial work was necessary, but thought the only problem was the shortening of the life of the rig. At the end of the rig's life, the mast would have been replaced, rather than loving fallen down. The Court of Appeal thought the High Court had attached too much weight to these two views, and underestimated the agreed findings of the experts. It was therefore established that the effect of the overweight keel on the safety of the rig was both adverse and unacceptable to the manufacturers of the rig. Since the rig could not be modified to take account of the heavy keel, it was necessary to reduce the weight of the keel. While the witnesses did not agree on the consequences of the keel being overweight, all accepted that remedial treatment was required.

However, this finding did not mean the yacht was not of satisfactory quality. The sellers pointed out that the increased risk to the rigging was absorbed by the margin of safety built into the rig by the manufacturers. They also pointed out the cost of the remedial work was just £1,680, compared with the purchase price of £236,000. These points did not find favour with the Court of Appeal. As noted above, the experts had agreed the manufacturers had found the increased load unacceptable. There had also been expert evidence that the yacht could not have been fit for its purpose because the increased load was considered unacceptable by the rig manufacturers. The evidence was that, even if the risk factor was only slightly increased, it was significant that the rig designers would still not be prepared to guarantee the rig. The Court of Appeal also said the cost of repairs was no reliable indicator as to whether the defect which needed to be remedied prevented the yacht from being of satisfactory quality. The court saw no reason to consider all the factors listed by the 1979 Act as relevant to the question of satisfactory quality. There was a breach of the implied condition because a reasonable person would conclude that, because the keel was overweight, its adverse effect on rig safety and the need for more than minimal remedial work meant the yacht was not of satisfactory quality.

Very similar obligations are implied by statute into hire-purchase transactions and into contracts for the hire of goods.

These terms cannot be excluded where the goods are supplied to a consumer, and, where the goods are supplied to a business, can only be excluded normally if it is reasonable to do so (see later).

The Sale of Goods Act 1979 impose other duties of a different nature. For example, the payment for goods becomes due on delivery and the buyer is entitled to delivery of all the goods at once. These terms, however, only apply in the absence of express agreement to the contrary, and the parties may vary them to allow the buyer credit or to allow delivery by instalments.

The Supply of Goods and Services Act 1982 (SGSA) applies to contracts which are mainly for services, but in the course of which some goods are provided. The contract with a plumber, or a house painter, or a dentist is mainly for the skilled services of the operator, but in all cases lead, or paint, or tooth fillings might be supplied incidentally. These are not *sales* of goods, but the SGSA 1982 imposes obligations almost identical to those in the Sale of Goods Act 1979 as regards the *materials*. As regards the *services* provided, there is a wider statutory term that 'the supplier will carry out the service with reasonable care and skill'.

In contracts for professional services, the practitioner's primary duty is to his own client, who employs and pays him. In particular, the practitioner owes the following duties as implied terms in the contract with his client:

- The practitioner will obey his client's instructions (but not illegal ones).
- He promises to show such skill as he has professed (this is the meaning of 'profession'). It is generally no excuse to say that mistakes were due to inexperience.
- He must show all such care as it is reasonable to expect, and the standard required can be very high. For breach of this duty (and probably only this one), there can be concurrent liability, both for breach of contract and in tort; if so, damages may sometimes be reduced for contributory negligence by the client.
- The practitioner promises to be honest.
- A professional person always impliedly promises to show good faith. In particular, he must not allow an undisclosed *conflict of interest* with his client. For example, he must not, *without his client's full knowledge and consent*, buy from his own client or allow his relatives or close associate to do so; or sell to his own client; or act for both his client and someone else whose interests are *opposed* to his client's on the same matter.
- The practitioner promises confidentiality as regards information acquired from his client or on his client's behalf. This duty often extends after the contract has ended. He impliedly promises to pass on to his client any information which he has acquired which will relate to his client's instructions and requirements.
- He promises to keep proper records, to keep his client's assets and money separate from his own (e.g. to have separate bank accounts), and to submit full accounts for the work which he is doing.

In addition to these implied duties in the contract, various statutes (such as the Solicitors Acts) may impose detailed special duties.

Examples

In *Armstrong* v. *Jackson* (1917), a stockbroker, engaged to buy specific shares for his client, secretly sold him shares which he himself held. This was breach of contract.

Note: This case is mentioned again in Section 2.9.1.

In *Fullwood* v. *Hurley* (1928), a professional agent was instructed to find a buyer for a hotel. He found someone who wanted to buy a hotel, but did not tell him that he already acted for the seller, and he tried to claim commission from both of them. He could not claim commission from the buyer.

Keppel v. *Wheeler* (1927) concerns an estate agent who was engaged for the sale of a house. He received a bid of £6,150, which he passed on to his client. He later received another bid of £6,750, which he neglected to pass on. His client therefore accepted the lower bid. The estate agent was liable to his client for damages (£600).

A professional practitioner may also, exceptionally, owe duties of care to persons other than his client. Particularly as regards financial loss, however, these duties will usually arise only from the practitioner's assumption of responsibility towards a specific person (other than his client) who was known from the outset to be relying on him in his professional capacity.

> You should refer again to cases such as *Smith* v. *Eric S Bush* and *ADT Ltd* v. *Binder Hamlyn* in Section 1.3.7, and contrast these with the case of *Caparo Industries plc* v. *Dickman.*

2.5 The status of contractual terms

2.5.1 The repercussions of a breach of contract

Once the contents of the contract have been ascertained, the next step is to determine the status of those terms. In essence, terms may be classified as conditions or warranties. If it is not known whether the clause falls into either of these two categories, the clause is said to be 'innominate'.

2.5.2 Conditions

A condition is a fundamental term going to the very root of the contract. In other words conditions are regarded as setting down the primary obligations of the parties. The difference between conditions and warranties may be seen in the following two cases, each arising in 1876 and each involving opera singers.

In *Poussard* v. *Spiers and Pond* (1876), Madame Poussard was under contract to appear in an operetta for the season. In fact she was unavailable because of illness until 1 week after the season had started. It was held that the obligation to perform from the first night was a condition and the producers were entitled to terminate Mrs Poussard's contract.

In *Bettini* v. *Gye* (1876), Bettini was under contract to appear in concert for a season. A term of the contract required him to be in London for rehearsals 6 days before the start of the season. On arrival three days late, Gye refused to accept his services. It was held that Bettini's late arrival was a breach of a warranty so that Gye was himself in breach by terminating Bettini's contract.

A breach of a condition does not automatically cause a contract to be terminated, but causes the innocent party to have a choice as to how to proceed. Thus the innocent party may choose to cancel ('repudiate') the contract and claim damages and rescission, or he/she may choose to carry on with ('affirm') the contract and claim damages. Rescission is an equitable remedy which returns the parties to their pre-contract position.

Example

Tom, a self-employed sales representative, purchased a new car for £10,000. He paid a deposit of £5,000 and agreed to pay the balance by instalments. The very first time Tom drove the car, the engine seized. The manufacturers are prepared to replace the engine which is covered by its guarantee.

It is an implied *condition* under Section 14 of the Sale of Goods Act 1979 that the goods sold are of a 'satisfactory quality'. It follows that Tom has two options:

1. He may repudiate the contract, and claim rescission and damages. Repudiation means that Tom is no longer bound to make any payments on the car. Rescission enables him to recover his deposit of £5,000 and any instalment payments. In addition, Tom may recover damages to compensate him for any additional costs such as having the car towed to a garage, the cost of hiring a car, arranging alternative transport, and so on.
2. He may decide to accept the manufacturers' promise to repair the car, that is, he may affirm the contract and recover damages only, for example compensation as under option 1 above. In this option, Tom has, in effect, chosen to treat the breach as one of warranty rather than condition, see below.

2.5.3 Warranties

A warranty is a term of relatively minor importance. The innocent party is not entitled to repudiate the contract for a mere breach of a warranty, but is restricted to a claim for damages. In fact, if the innocent party should proceed by repudiating the contract following a breach of warranty, the party is no longer innocent but has himself acted in breach of contract (see *Bettini* v. *Gye* above).

Example

Anne, a self-employed sales representative, purchased a new car for £10,000. After 1 week, Anne discovered that the car radio was faulty and needed to be replaced. This is a relatively minor breach and entitles Anne to be compensated for the cost of a replacement radio. However, Anne is not entitled to repudiate the contract to purchase the car.

2.5.4 How to determine the status of contractual terms

Unfortunately, it is not always clear whether a term is a condition or a warranty. In such cases, unclassified terms are known as 'innominate'. Such a lack of classification can create problems, for example where one party has acted in breach of a particular term and the other wishes to know the extent of his/her legal rights. It is the nature and seriousness of a contract breach that can serve to determine whether the relevant term is a condition or a warranty. A contract term in *Hong Kong Fir Shipping Co Ltd* v. *Kawasaki Kisen Kaisha Ltd [1962]* shows the difficulty that can arise in deciding the status of a contract term. The relevant term provided that a ship would be seaworthy and 'in every way fitted for cargo service'. The ship in fact had engine trouble and some staff were incompetent. The Court of Appeal saw the breach as a breach of warranty. Beyond this, the actual consequences of the breach were seen as relevant, and in some instances sufficient to justify discharge of the contract.

In general, the law allows contracting parties freedom of contract in that they are free to classify terms as they choose. What may appear to be a minor issue to one person may be of crucial importance to another. It follows that the overriding task of the courts is to determine the intention of the parties.

The status of terms may be determined by asking the following questions, which can almost be used as a flow chart:

(i) *Does the contract expressly state that breach of a particular term gives the innocent party the right to terminate the contract?*
- If the answer is yes, then the term must be a condition. This is so even if, when looked at objectively, the term appears to be of relatively minor importance.
- If the answer is no, it is necessary to ask additional questions.

(ii) *Does the contract describe a particular term as a condition or a warranty?* Even where the parties use the word condition or warranty to describe a particular term, the courts have stated that this will not in itself be conclusive. In *Schuler AG* v. *Wickman Machine Tools Sales Ltd* (1974), a term described as a 'condition' required Wickman to make weekly visits over a four-and-a-half-year period to six named firms, a total of some 1,400 visits in all. A further clause allowed Schuler to terminate the agreement in the event of a 'material breach'. Wickman failed to make some of the weekly visits so Schuler terminated the contract. It was held that Schuler acted in breach by repudiating the contract. Even though the word 'condition' had been used to describe the term, the House of Lords did not believe that it was the parties' intention that a failure to make a single visit would give Schuler the right to terminate. It follows that even the use of the word condition or warranty by the parties is not conclusive.

(iii) *Does the law state that the term in question is a condition?* For example, suppose that a dispute should arise from the delivery of goods to the buyer which turn out to be different from their description in the seller's catalogue. Is this a breach of a condition or a warranty? The answer lies in Section 13 of the Sale of Goods Act 1979, which provides, 'in contracts for the sale of goods by description there is an implied condition that the goods shall correspond with their description.'

Clearly, the law states that the term is a condition. In this instance there is no room for any argument, and it follows that the innocent party is entitled to the options described above for breach of a condition.

(iv) *Has the innocent party been deprived substantially of what it was intended that he should receive under the contract?* This test has been criticised on the ground that the courts should be attempting to determine the intention of the parties at the time the contract was entered into, rather than looking at the effect of the breach. Consequently, it can be viewed as a test of last resort. Where the other questions have not produced a conclusive answer, and evidence of intention is unclear, a pragmatic way of resolving the dispute is to look at the seriousness or otherwise of the breach. If the effect of breaking a term was to deprive the innocent party of the main benefit of the contract, then that term must have been a condition. If not, it follows that the term must have been a warranty.

2.6 Unfair contract terms

Learning Outcome: To explain how the law controls the use of unfair terms in respect of both consumer and non-consumer business agreements.

The principle of freedom of contract assumes that both parties are able to negotiate freely the terms of a contract but, in practice, this is often not possible. In many instances, one party is in a much stronger bargaining position than the other. Such situations tend to arise when one of the parties is in a monopoly position or is one of the few suppliers of goods or services. Inequality may also stem from a weak bargaining position caused by financial pressure (e.g. a borrower who has no money is likely to be in a weaker position than a lender who has), or where goods are so technically complicated that it is beyond the competence of the average person to judge their quality. In these situations there is no genuine bargaining and a standard form contract is often placed before one of the parties who must accept it as it stands. Such a contract often contains a mass of clauses in small print and in language difficult to understand, and it is almost invariably signed without being read.

The stronger party may abuse his position in various ways. He may impose harsh terms such as an extortionate rate of interest or a harsh penalty clause. In particular, he may include exemption clauses in the contract which attempt to limit or totally exclude his liability. This has posed problems for the courts in deciding whether or not the clause is a valid term of the contract and Parliament has been forced to intervene to protect the weaker parties.

The following notes deal with four topics to do with unfair terms:

- the attitude of the courts to exemption clauses;
- the Unfair Contract Terms Act 1977, which imposes statutory controls over exemption clauses;
- some other Acts controlling unfair terms;
- the Unfair Terms in Consumer Contracts Regulations 1994.

The first two of these deal with exemption clauses, which are probably the best known (and most notorious) of unfair terms. The last two include wider varieties of contractual term.

2.6.1 Exemption clauses and the courts

Before accepting an exemption clause as a contractual term, the courts must first be satisfied that the party other than the one attempting to enforce it agreed to the clause when or before the contract was made. If the contract is made by signing a written document, the signer will normally be bound by the terms included in it, even if he has not read them [*L'Estrange* v. *Graucob* (1934)]. If the document is unsigned, it must be proved that the other party knew or should have known that it was intended to be a contractual document and that everything reasonably possible had been done to bring the terms to the notice of the other party. Many cases on this point have concerned documents such as tickets [*Thompson* v. *LMS Railway Co* (1930)], receipts [*Chapelton* v. *Barry UDC* (1940)], order forms and 'sold notes' [*Roe* v. *R A Naylor Ltd* (1918)].

Any attempt to introduce an exemption clause after the contract has been made will be ineffective, for example, a notice in a hotel bedroom after the room has been booked [*Olley* v. *Marlborough Court Ltd* (1949)] a parking ticket issued after payment had been made [*Thornton* v. *Shoe Lane Parking Ltd* (1971)]. If, however, there has been a course of past dealings between the parties, always on the same basis, the court may assume an intention to continue to deal on the same terms and with the same exemption clauses. It was for this reason that the court upheld an exemption in a contract which was made several days before the document including it was sent to the other party [*Spurling (J) Ltd* v. *Bradshaw* (1956): sale of barrels of orange juice].

In the past, the courts have treated exemption clauses *contra proferentem* by deciding on any ambiguities against the party seeking to rely upon the clauses. Thus, the exclusion of warranties has been held not to exclude also conditions [*Wallis, Sons & Wells* v. *Pratt & Haynes* (1911)], and a term that 'nothing in this agreement' should make the defendants liable was held to cover only liability for breach of contract and not liability in tort [*White* v. *John Warrick & Co Ltd* (1955): injury from faulty hired tricycle]. The courts will also tend to look more favourably upon a clause which limits liability to a particular sum of money rather than one which excludes liability entirely, since the former at least envisages shared responsibility for any loss [*Ailsa Craig Fishing Co Ltd* v. *Malvern Fishing Co* (1983): liability limit of £1,000 for negligence of security guard upheld].

If the contract is between two parties with equal bargaining power, the clause will be examined in the context of the contract as a whole. It may have been accepted in return for a low price, on the assumption that there would be insurance against loss, or in return for some other favourable trading term. If the clause is clear it will be upheld, even if the breach was of a fundamental or serious nature. In *Photo Production Ltd* v. *Securicor Transport Ltd* (1980), a security firm was held to be protected by a clause, even though the loss was caused by a fire deliberately started by one of its employees.

Finally, it must be remembered that the terms of a contract will only affect the parties to that contract. An exemption clause which protected a shipping company did not protect the ship's officer whose negligence caused the loss [*Adler* v. *Dickson* (1955)].

2.6.2 The Unfair Contract Terms Act 1977

The most important statute affecting exemption clauses is the Unfair Contract Terms Act 1977 (UCTA). It is largely restricted to business liability, that is, liability arising from things done in the course of business or from the occupation of premises for business purposes. Certain contracts are excluded, in particular contracts relating to land, insurance, and those affecting the formation or management of companies.

Under the UCTA 1977, it is not possible to exclude in any way business liability in contract or in tort for death or bodily injury arising from negligence. Liability for financial loss or loss of property arising from negligence can be excluded or limited if it is reasonable to do so. (This may be possible where two large businesses with equal bargaining power agree upon a clear exemption clause which is reasonable in the context of the contract as a whole.) Furthermore, an exemption clause can only be included in a written standard form contract if it is reasonable, and, if the other party is a consumer, the test of reasonableness applies irrespective of the form of the contract.

The chairman and managing director of a foundry company signed a contract on behalf of the company in *Feldaroll Foundry plc* v. *Hermes Leasing (London) Ltd* (2004). The contract contained an exclusion clause relating to description, merchantable quality and fitness for purpose. It was acknowledged that the car was purchased for his own business purposes. It was held that the foundry purchased the car as a customer. The exclusion clause was therefore invalid.

Special protection is given to consumers in contracts for the sale of goods, that is, to those who buy, for private use, goods normally sold for such use from those selling in the course of business. The implied terms regarding title, description, sample, quality and fitness for purpose cannot be excluded. There can be exclusion, if the buyer is a non-consumer, if this is reasonable. Similar rules apply to contracts of hire-purchase, hire and for 'work and materials', and for separate guarantees of goods given by manufacturers and distributors where the guarantee is the only contractual relationship with the ultimate buyer.

A schedule to the UCTA 1977 gives guidelines to determine what is reasonable. Account must be taken of the relative bargaining strength of the parties, whether the buyer is given any inducement such as a price reduction, whether the buyer should have known of the exemption clause, whether compliance with any condition such as a time-limit for complaints was reasonable, and whether the goods were made to the buyer's special order. Thus, in *R. W. Green Ltd* v. *Cade Bros* (1978), it was held to be unreasonable to impose a time limit of three days for complaints about seed potatoes since defects might not be discovered until after growth.

> The Unfair Contract Terms Act 1977, had a somewhat misleading title. It was never directly concerned with unfair terms (which later became the purview of the Unfair Terms in Consumer Contracts Regulations 1999, SI 1999 No 2083), but was more directly concerned with clauses which sought to exclude or limit liability for breach of contract. In essence, any such clause was invalid unless its proponent could show that it was, in all the circumstances of the case, a reasonable clause. For the most part, case law under the Act has centred on deciding whether or not a particular clause was a reasonable one. Two recent cases, however, have probed the perhaps no less important point as to just which categories of clause the Act applies.

2.6.3 Other Acts which restrict unfair terms

Other statutes impose restrictions upon contractual terms in general and upon exemption clauses in particular. Under the Misrepresentation Act 1967, any term excluding liability for misrepresentation is void unless it is proved that the exemption was fair and reasonable, having regard to the circumstances which were known or ought reasonably to have been known to the parties when they contracted. This applies also to non-business liability as in *Walker* v. *Boyle* (1982), where an exemption clause in the conditions of private sale of a house was held to be unreasonable and hence did not exclude liability for misrepresentations. (See Section 2.3.1 for the full facts of this case.)

The Consumer Credit Act 1974 includes various provisions to protect the debtor during the credit period. Contractual terms cannot prevent the debtor paying off what he owes at any time, a prescribed procedure must be followed if the debtor is in default and this cannot be excluded. Any 'extortionate' bargain to the debtor's detriment in the past could have been reopened and varied by the court. 'The Consumer Credit Act 2006 contains amendments to the Consumer Credit Act 1974 and updates existing legislation. The new Act is aimed at establishing greater competition and fairness for consumers.' Now under Section 19 of the Consumer Credit Act 2006, he can challenge the credit agreement content on the basis of their being an unfair relationship between the contracting parties.

Section 19 of the Consumer Credit Act 2006 provides that borrowers will be able to challenge credit agreements before a court on the grounds that the relationship between the parties is unfair. This test replaces the present concept of extortionate credit bargains. Enforcement actions will be taken by the Office of Fair Trading. Other consumer bodies will be able to enforce the provisions under Part 8 of the Enterprise Act 2002 where unfair relationships are harming the collective interests of consumers.

The Office of Fair Trading has issued draft guidance on the new unfair relationship provisions, giving advice to consumer organisations and businesses on how the new powers will be used. The draft guidance, *Unfair Relationships*, can be accessed through the consultations section of the OFT's website at www.oft.gov.uk.

Another example is the Fair Trading Act 1973 which empowers the Department of Trade and Industry to make regulations prohibiting certain undesirable consumer trade practices. Exemption clauses which are unaffected by other legislation can thereby be invalidated.

Criminal liability may also be imposed, for example, where a seller of goods uses a void exemption or other clause in a contract with a consumer who is not aware of this invalidity.

2.6.4 The Unfair Terms in Consumer Contracts Regulations 1994

These regulations were made because of an EU directive. They add to the above Acts in several important respects. Unlike the UCTA 1977, they are not limited to exemption clauses. They apply equally, for example, to some 'penalty' clauses, by which a party who breaks the contract will be required to pay exorbitant 'compensation', and to some 'inertia' clauses where obligations can be extended unduly if one party forgets to act.

There are, however, several limits on the regulations. First, unlike the UCTA 1977, they apply only to consumer contracts. These are contracts between a supplier or seller of goods or services in the course of a business, and a customer who is a natural person not acting for business purposes. Thus, companies, trade or professional partnerships, government departments and local authorities can never be consumers. Second, the regulations only apply to terms which have not been individually negotiated, that is, to those contracts or parts of contracts which are drafted in advance in standard form and which are therefore outside the influence of the consumer. Third, certain contracts are specifically excluded – in particular, contracts of employment and those relating to the incorporation and/or organisation of companies and partnerships. However, unlike the UCTA 1977, the regulations do cover insurance and mortgages of land.

Where the Regulations apply, written terms of the contract must be expressed in plain, intelligible language, and any doubts about interpretation must be resolved in favour of the consumer. More importantly, any non-negotiated written term which is *unfair*, because, contrary to the requirement of good faith, it causes a significant imbalance in the parties' rights and obligations to the detriment of the consumer, shall not be binding on the consumer.

This new test of good faith depends on all the circumstances at the time the contract was made, including the nature of the goods and services to be supplied and the other terms of the contract. Regard must also be paid to the strength of the bargaining positions of the parties; whether the consumer had an inducement to agree; whether there was a special order from the customer; and whether the supplier had dealt fairly and equitably with the consumer. In addition, a schedule contains an indicative but non-exhaustive list of terms which may be considered unfair. Many of these guidelines are similar to those in the UCTA 1977 for deciding reasonableness.

An unfair term does not bind a consumer, but the contract may continue if capable of still existing. A complaint may be made to the Director-General of Fair Trading, who may seek an undertaking from the supplier to discontinue the term or, if necessary, an injunction from the court.

Unfair terms in consumer contracts: recent developments

by Robert Duxbury, Principal Lecturer in Law at Nottingham, Law School, Nottingham, Trent University

An area of contract law that students tend to find challenging is the validity of unfair terms, including clauses excluding or restricting liability. It is a multi-layered topic that has developed in a piecemeal fashion and which, in some respects, is in a process of transition. It is governed partly by well-established and developed common law principles and by more recent statutory regulation.

The main instrument of statutory control in domestic law is the Unfair Contract Terms Act 1977 (UCTA) which, inter alia, declares certain types of exclusion or restriction of liability to be invalid, whilst others it subjects to a requirement of reasonableness. In addition, the EC Directive on Unfair Contract Terms (93/13 EEC) has been implemented in domestic law by the Unfair Terms in Consumer Contracts Regulations (UTCCR). The first set of regulations, which appeared in 1994, were replaced by the current regulations, which were made in 1999 (SI 1999/2083).

To an extent the UTCCR overlap with UCTA but in some respects the regulations are significantly broader in that they regulate unfair terms generally and not merely clauses which exclude or restrict liability, or have like effect. In other respects, the regulations are narrower in that they apply only where goods or services are supplied to consumers, as defined in the regulations. The existence of two parallel but different regimes – the Act and the regulations – has done nothing to simplify the law and is one of the more difficult issues with which students have to grapple in contract law. The Law Commission has recommended that a single statute should replace both UCTA and UCCR and has published a draft bill (Law Com No 292 (2005)). Such a development would be most welcome.

2.7 Performance of the contract and reasons for non-performance

Learning Outcome: To explain what the law regards as performance of the contract, and valid and invalid reasons for non-performance.

2.7.1 Performance

This is by far the most common way of discharging a contract (bringing it to an end), since most contracts are made with the intention of performance and are in fact performed. As a general rule, each party must perform *precisely* what he bargained to do. Anything else will be breach.

In *Cutter* v. *Powell* (1795), Mr Cutter had contracted to serve on a ship sailing from Jamaica to Liverpool for 30 guineas (£31.50), payable on completion of the voyage. Mr Cutter died when the ship was some 19 days from Liverpool and his widow sued to recover compensation in respect of the work her husband had carried out prior to his death. It was held that Mr Cutter had been a party to an 'entire' contract. This meant that he was only entitled to payment when he had completed the contract. As he failed to complete it he, and therefore his widow, was entitled to nothing. This decision may appear harsh and the law has changed since then so that today a person in the position of Mrs Cutter would be able to recover some compensation. (See the law relating to 'frustration' in Section 2.7.2.) In deciding whether or not the parties have precisely performed all the terms of the contract, the courts will ignore minor discrepancies under the *de minimis* rule. In *Peter Darlington Partners Ltd* v. *Gosho Ltd* (1964), seed which was 98 per cent pure was sufficient to meet the contractual requirement that it should be 'on a pure basis'. The parties may, of course, expressly provide for less than precise performance by inserting appropriate terms into the contract.

Liability in contract can be strict and it may often be no defence for failure to perform to plead that all reasonable care has been taken. If milk contains typhoid germs, even without any fault on the part of the supplier, the latter will have failed to perform the duty to supply milk which was reasonably fit for drinking [*Frost* v. *Aylesbury Dairy Co Ltd* (1905)].

Performance often takes the form of payment of money. It is then the duty of the debtor to seek out the creditor at a reasonable time of day and offer the correct money in legal tender without any necessity for the creditor to give change. A cheque is not legal tender and is accepted as a conditional payment until it has been honoured. Payment by credit card or charge card, however, does discharge a debt and the supplier must then recover from the card company.

If the creditor refuses the tender, the debt is not discharged but the creditor must then seek out the debtor and claim payment. If money is sent by post, the risk of loss rests upon the sender. If the use of the post has been expressly or impliedly authorised by the creditor, the risk passes to him, always provided that reasonable precautions have been taken for the care of the money in transit.

Where there are several debts and part payment is made, the debtor first has the right to appropriate the money against specific debts. If he does not do so, this right passes to the creditor. Exceptionally, with current accounts, where money is being continually paid in and out and appropriation would be difficult, the rule is that first debts are paid first. This may be important because debts normally become unenforceable after 6 years.

Performance of a contract for the sale of goods is covered by the Sale of Goods Acts 1979/94. It is the duty of the seller to deliver the goods and of the buyer to accept and pay for them and, unless otherwise agreed, delivery and payment must take place at the same time. The obligations of the seller include compliance with the express and implied terms of the contract (see earlier), which are difficult to exclude, and with rules regarding the mechanics of delivery which can be varied easily.

Exceptions

(i) *Divisible contracts*. Although this is not strictly an exception to the general rule requiring precise performance, its relevance to this topic is obvious. Thus, for example, in a contract to build a house for £100,000, the contract may provide for £30,000 to be paid on completion of the foundations; £30,000 on completion of the fabric of the house and the balance of £40,000 to be paid on completion of the house. It should be noted that despite these 'stage payments', there is only one contract and, if the builder should fail to complete the project, he would be liable to compensate the land owner.

(ii) *Substantial performance*. In *Hoenig* v. *Isaacs* (1952), the claimant contracted to decorate and install some furniture into the defendant's flat for £750. The work was completed apart from minor defects which were to cost some £56 to remedy. It was held that the contract had been substantially performed so that the claimant was entitled to payment less £56 for the defects.

Contrast this case with that of *Bolton* v. *Mahadeva* (1972) in which the claimant contracted to install central heating in the defendant's house for £560. The work was badly carried out with the result that the system was inefficient and gave off fumes so that some rooms could not be used. It was estimated that the cost of remedying the defects would be some £179. The defendant refused to pay and the claimant sued arguing that he had substantially performed the contract. It was held that the contract had not been substantially performed so the claimant was not entitled to £560 less £179 to remedy the defects. In fact, he was entitled to nothing as the general rule applied and he had not performed his obligations under the contract.

These two cases seem to suggest that completion of the contract subject to minor defects (in effect, breach of a warranty) amounts to substantial performance, whereas completion of the contract subject to major defects (in effect, breach of a condition) amounts to non-performance.

(iii) *Voluntary acceptance of partial performance.* If a contracting party is able to accept or reject partial performance of a contract and chooses to accept, a reasonable sum must be paid for the performance received. For example, suppose that X has contracted for 30 bottles of wine to be delivered to his house by Y. In breach of contract, Y only delivers 20 bottles. X has an option. First, he may reject the whole delivery on the ground that Y has not performed the contract, and second, he may choose to accept the wine delivered. In the event of the latter, X must pay a reasonable sum to Y on a *quantum meruit* basis ('so much as he deserves').

The case of *Sumpter* v. *Hedges* (1898) provides an example of partial performance which was not voluntarily accepted. The claimant contracted to erect some buildings on the defendant's land for £565. After work valued at £333 had been completed, the claimant told the defendant that he could not finish the job because he had run out of money. As a result, the defendant completed the work using materials left on the site by the claimant. It was held that the claimant was entitled to payment for the materials used by the defendant, but was entitled to nothing in respect of the work done because the defendant had been given no choice but to accept the partially completed buildings. It follows that he had not *voluntarily* agreed to accept the partial performance.

(iv) *Contractual performance prevented by the other party.* In *Planche* v. *Colburn* (1831), P agreed to write a book on costume and ancient armour for the sum of £100. After he had collected materials and written part of the book, the defendant advised him that the book was no longer required. It was held that P was entitled to a reasonable sum on a *quantum meruit* basis for the work he had completed.

(v) *Frustration.* If the contract becomes impossible to perform through no fault of either contracting party, the contract is said to be frustrated and the contract becomes unenforceable. In these circumstances the inability to perform the contracts terms are excused and the provisions of the Law Reform (Frustrated Contracts) Act 1943 seek to provide for justice between the parties (see Section 2.7.2).

2.7.2 Valid reasons for non-performance

Various valid reasons can be used by a party to justify non-performance of his or her own obligations:

- *A new agreement* may have been made which replaces the existing one.
- *Frustration* (and therefore termination) of the existing agreement may occur because of some outside event for which neither party is responsible, which makes nonsense of the existing contract.
- *Serious breach by the other party* may sometimes be a valid reason for the injured party to refuse to perform his or her own obligations.

New agreement

A new agreement may be made which either cancels or replaces the original one. The new contract must be a valid one. In particular it must be supported by consideration. Where obligations are outstanding on both sides there are no problems, for mutual promises to give up these rights constitutes consideration of the one for the other. This form of discharge is sometimes referred to as accord (agreement) and satisfaction (consideration). However, where one party has completed his obligations under the existing contract, there may be difficulties, and there must normally be new consideration to discharge the obligations of the other. Alternatively, one party can release the other without consideration if this is done by deed (of discharge).

Frustration

A contract may validly be discharged, and therefore not performed, if some extraneous event beyond the control of either party destroys the whole basis of the agreement.

Examples

One instance might be subsequent physical impossibility if the subject matter upon which the contract depends is accidentally destroyed or rendered unusable.

In *Taylor* v. *Caldwell* (1886), a music hall hired for a series of concerts was accidentally burnt down beforehand without the fault of either party. This frustrated the hiring contract.

In *Condor* v. *Barron Knights* (1996), the drummer of a pop group became ill and was forbidden by his doctor to perform for more than four nights each week. This frustrated his contract, which required him to perform for seven nights.

Second, there might be some change in the law after the contract was made which rendered it illegal to perform the contract. Thus, an outbreak of war will frustrate a contract if to continue would be illegal as trading with the enemy (*Avery* v. *Bowden* (1855)).

Third, the basis of the contract might be removed when the whole agreement is dependent upon some future event which does not take place. The Coronation of Edward VII was postponed because of his illness and contracts to hire rooms along the route of the procession were frustrated [*Chandler* v. *Webster* (1904)].

Fourth – and exceptionally – some other radical change in circumstances might occur which makes nonsense of the purpose of the existing agreement. What would now have to be performed would bear no relation to what was originally intended. However, the change must be fundamental. Something which merely makes performance more difficult or expensive is no excuse.

In *Metropolitan Water Board* v. *Dick, Kerr & Co.* (1918), construction of a reservoir was stopped by the government for economic reasons throughout the war. It was held that the character and duration of this interruption, and the changed financial environment which affected everyone after the war, made nonsense of the original contract and ended it by frustration.

On the other hand, in *Tsakiroglou & Co. Ltd* v. *Noblee & Thorl GmbH* (1962), the closure of the Suez Canal in 1956, which led to a longer and more costly sea journey for the oil and shipping companies, and which made things more difficult for them, did not frustrate the contract.

At common law, frustration automatically brought the contract to an end. All sums previously paid were recoverable and all sums not yet paid ceased to be due. This could have harsh results which was demonstrated by the *Fibrosa Case* (1943). An English company had agreed to supply machinery to a Polish company when the contract was frustrated by the outbreak of war. Despite the fact that the English company had already incurred expenses in manufacturing the goods, it was obliged to refund money already received on account and was left without any claim on the other party.

As a consequence, the Law Reform (Frustrated Contracts) Act 1943 was enacted. The general common law rule above was restated, but two qualifications were added to mitigate any inequity. If, before the date of discharge, a party has incurred expenses in performing the contract, the court has a discretion to allow him to retain all or part of sums already paid by the other party or to recover all or part of any sums due. If, by reason of anything done by the other party, one party has obtained a valuable benefit under the contract other than the payment of money, then the other party may recover such sum as the court considers just. In brief, the parties are returned to their original positions subject to the power of the court to make adjustments for expenses incurred and benefits received. Excluded from these provisions are contracts where the parties have expressly provided for frustration and contracts for the carriage of goods by sea, or marine insurance, and for the sale of specific goods which perish before risk has passed to the buyer; this last is covered by the Sale of Goods Acts 1979–1994.

Force majeure

David Allen, *Solicitors Journal*, 12 December 2003, p1416/7

Although the millennium bug did not cause the threatened levels of business disruption, the past 3 years have been plagued by other calamities such as the war against Iraq, increasing global terrorism, SARS, and the large-scale blackouts in North America, the United Kingdom and Italy. Such events can impact massively on contracts, rendering performance impossible or imposing financial hardship. So is it possible to tailor a contract so as to allow one party to suspend performance or renegotiate the deal if events such as September 11 make a contract economically onerous?

Frustration of contract

Under English law, contractual liability is strict. The law will not excuse a party from performance merely because some incident prevents or delays performance. The policy behind this is that a contracting party should provide for risks in the contract itself.

Strict liability is mitigated to some extent by the doctrine of 'frustration'. A contract is frustrated if an unforeseeable event renders the item undertaken fundamentally different from the item contracted for. For example, a contract may be frustrated if the subject-matter of the contract is destroyed or rendered illegal by governmental decree. However, frustration will do nothing for parties seeking to get out of a bad bargain. The courts have held that closure of the Suez Canal did not frustrate a shipment contract of goods to Hamburg because the contractor could still have shipped the goods via the Cape of Good Hope, despite the fact that the detour rendered performance considerably more expensive for the supplier.

If a contract really is frustrated then it is terminated; the courts have no flexibility to rewrite the contract to the circumstances.

Contractual solutions

The common law doctrines discussed above can create unsatisfactory results. While certainty is important in any contractual arrangement, commercial parties also have profit margins they expect – and need – to realise. Unforeseen events outside the control of the parties such as war, terrorist attacks or outbreaks of disease can destroy the entire reason for entering into a contract. This is why a 'force majeure clause' is inserted into many contracts. Such clauses are, however, often added with little thought and are considered mere 'boilerplate'. To realise the full benefits of such clauses they must be drafted carefully.

A force majeure clause typically contains the following three components:

- The act of force majeure, which is customarily defined as an 'event, circumstance or occurrence' beyond the reasonable control of the parties – a non-exhaustive list of events of force majeure often follows;
- The force majeure event usually must prevent, hinder or delay performance for the clause to take effect;
- If the force majeure event occurs, the party affected by the event must usually serve notice on the other. This will suspend performance for a defined period and if the event continues past a certain time, the party may terminate the contract.

Serious breach by the other party

Breach of contract by the other side is not necessarily a valid reason for non-performance. Mere breach of *warranty* by the other party (see Section 2.5) is not a valid reason for non-performance. The claimant may recover *damages*, but he must still perform his own side of the bargain.

Even breach of condition by the other party does not *automatically* end the contract. It merely gives a claimant the *right* to end it, and refuse further performance by himself. If he does choose to exercise this right, then he must do so reasonably promptly (as with rescission for misrepresentation – see Section 2.3.1). The right may therefore be lost very soon, particularly with perishable goods. The right may also be lost if the claimant has chosen to 'affirm' the contract, and go on with it knowing of the serious breach.

If a claimant exercises a right to end the contract, then this is a valid reason for no longer performing his own obligations. Otherwise, however, he must still perform his own side of the contract. The effects of breach are fully discussed in Section 2.8.

2.8 Types of breach

Learning Outcome: To explain the type of breach necessary to cause contractual breakdown and the remedies which are available for serious and minor breaches of contract.

There are many ways in which a contract can be broken. In particular, one party can repudiate it in such a way that the contract can no longer be performed. He may do this deliberately (e.g. by destroying the subject-matter). In this event, the breach itself ends the contract by making it impossible to go on. Another form of total breach is if one party repudiates it by refusing to go on. In this event, the injured party has a choice: he can either continue to press for performance, or he can accept the repudiation and treat the contract as ended. Third, the wrongdoer can purport to perform the contract, but do so defectively (e.g. by supplying goods which are not of satisfactory quality, if he is a dealer). If the term broken is a condition, or if the defect is so serious as to amount to a breach of condition, the victim again has a choice: he can either go on with the contract, and simply claim damages; or he can treat the contract as ended (and also claim damages). Fourth, the defective performance can be merely the breach of minor obligation – mere breach of warranty. In this event, the victim cannot choose to end the contract. He is still bound to carry out his obligations. He can only claim for damages.

Exceptionally, even the breach of a statutory condition may not give the right to treat the contract as ended. By the Sale of Goods Act s.15A, where breach of the seller's obligations as to description, quality and sample is so slight that it would be unreasonable for a *business* buyer to reject the goods, then he will not be allowed to do so; he will only be entitled to damages. It is the seller who must show that the breach is so slight. The contract can exclude this provision.

As we have seen, a written contract often makes it plain that some of the terms must be treated as conditions. Moreover, some terms implied by statute are described in the Act (e.g. the Sale of Goods Act 1979) as conditions. Subject to this, however, the courts often find that they cannot classify a term in advance as a condition or a warranty. Instead, therefore, they look at the seriousness of the *breach* to see what remedies should be available (see Section 2.5.4). For example, duties of care in a contract can be broken either in a serious or in a very minor manner.

2.9 Remedies for breach of contract

A breach of condition can result in the contract being terminated. A less serious breach can result in a monetary award or an equitable remedy.

2.9.1 Discharge for breach

The right to treat a contract as discharged for breach is similar in many ways to the right to rescind for misrepresentation (see Section 2.3.1). Indeed, the terms 'rescind' and 'rescission' are often used to describe ending a contract for breach too.

Discharge for breach does not normally mean that the parties must be put back into their original position. The contract might have gone too far for that. For example, a hire contract or a lease might be ended as a result of breach which occurs a long time after the hiring or lease started; so might an agency, partnership or employment contract. The effect of rescission for breach, therefore, will be to end the contract *for the future*. Sums already due must be paid, and obligations already incurred must be honoured; but obligations which have not yet become due are discharged. Moreover, a victim can be discharged from continuing obligations for the future: an employee wrongfully dismissed is no longer bound by a restraint of trade clause in his employment contract.

Where goods are sold by instalments, each to be paid for separately, any defective instalment can be rejected; but the question still remains whether one defective instalment entitles a buyer to treat the contract as repudiated for the future so that he can reject future instalments, good or bad. Unless there is express provision in the contract, this depends upon the ratio which the breach bears to the contract as a whole, and the likelihood or otherwise of its being repeated. In *Maple Flock Co* v. *Universal Furniture Ltd* (1934), one defective instalment, the 16th out of 20, did not entitle the buyer to treat the contract as ended for the future.

Rescission is normally carried out by the victim making known to the wrongdoer that the victim regards the breach as being repudiation, and that he now regards the contract as ended. The contract ends when the wrongdoer knows this. It may be impracticable to do this, however, if the contract breaker is a rogue who has fled. In this event, therefore, it can be sufficient for the victim to do everything reasonable to make public his intention to end the contract, for example by informing the police and any other parties involved; see *Car and Universal Finance Co Ltd* v. *Caldwell* (1965), where the victim parted with his car to a rogue whose cheque was dishonoured. Rescission of the contract at the outset enabled the seller to recover his car when it was eventually found in the hands of an innocent buyer.

Where goods are delivered to a buyer and he rightly rejects them, he need not send them back; it is sufficient if he tells the seller that he rejects.

The right to end the contract as a result of breach may be lost fairly easily, but the rules are flexible. Affirmation of the contract – expressly choosing to go on with it knowing of the breach and its seriousness – will end the right to treat the contract as terminated. In sale of goods contracts, the buyer loses his rights to reject the goods and treat the contract as repudiated if he intimates to the seller that he has accepted the goods. However, returning goods to the seller with a request or agreement that they be repaired does not defeat the buyer's right to rescind if the goods remain faulty afterwards.

The right to end the contract may also be lost if the essential subject-matter is destroyed or consumed, so that it can no longer be returned. Even radically altering goods can have this effect, although discharge on terms, with financial provision for changes, can be ordered for minor alterations. Resale by a buyer can similarly remove his right to end the original contract. However, a buyer of goods is not deemed to have accepted them until he has had a reasonable opportunity of examining the goods to see whether they conform with the contract. Therefore, if a buyer resells prepackaged goods which he could not examine, for example because they were in bottles or cans, and then is told by his own buyer that the goods are faulty, he can still reject against the original seller within a reasonable time.

The option to treat the contract as terminated must always be exercised within a reasonable time, but this in particular must be flexible. For perishable goods, it may be a matter of days or even hours. In cash sales, the courts sometimes want the matter over and done with; there should, whenever possible, be finality in commercial transactions.

On the other hand, this can sometimes be harsh. In *Bernstein* v. *Pamson Motors Ltd* (1987), a *consumer* buyer lost his right to terminate the contract 3 weeks (and 140 miles) after buying a car. This case has been adversely criticised, particularly by consumer protection bodies. However, this does not affect the general rule: if the buyer discovers a defect which entitles him to rescind the contract, he must make up his mind reasonably quickly. What is 'reasonable' depends on the judge's view of the particular facts. If a manufacturer knows that his buyer (a retailer) will keep the goods (e.g. a washing machine or a carpet) for a time with a view to resale, and that the defect would not become apparent until the goods were used after resale, then a reasonable time for the first buyer would take account of this. For mechanical goods, a reasonable time will often make some allowance for attempted repairs or negotiations about repairs. Where credit has been allowed and the price not yet paid, so that the contract is not yet fully performed, the courts will allow termination for much longer. A number of amendments have been made to the Sale of Goods Act ('SOGA') provisions outlined above by the Sale and Supply of Goods to

Consumers Regulations 2002 ('SSGCR') which came into effect on 31 March 2003. The Regulations introduce a number of remedies for consumers in addition to those contained in SOGA. (See Section 2.4.2)

The courts may also, where appropriate, give the victim time to consider his position. In *Marriott* v. *Oxford and District Co-op* (1970), an employee was wrongfully demoted and had his wages reduced. This was a serious breach of contract by the employer. Nevertheless, the employee went back to work under protest for 3 weeks while looking for another job. He was still allowed to treat his contract as ended, and regard himself as dismissed. Going back under protest was not affirmation, and the 3-week delay was not unreasonable in these circumstances.

When there has been fraudulent or dishonest breach of contract, the right to treat the contract as terminated may last for very much longer, probably until the fraud was or should have been discovered. This can be a long time. In *Armstrong* v. *Jackson* (1917), a stockbroker who was engaged to buy shares sold some of his own shares to his client, without disclosing this conflict of interest. The contract was set aside 5 years later, when the client discovered the facts. The shares were returned, and the client recovered what he had paid (even though this was twelve times what the shares were worth now).

2.9.2 Other non-monetary remedies

Specific performance

In some instances, monetary compensation will be an inadequate remedy for breach of contract and justice will only be done if the offending party is ordered to do or refrain from doing some action. Thus, the court may award a decree for specific performance which orders a party to carry out his contractual promises with liability for penalties for contempt of court if the order is not obeyed. This is an equitable remedy and is discretionary, as compared with common law damages which may be claimed as of right.

An order will not be made if damages would be an adequate remedy and it is therefore rarely granted in commercial transactions. A disappointed buyer may buy the goods elsewhere and claim monetary compensation if he has to pay more than the contract price. The same rule applies to shares which may be readily available in the market. If, however, the goods are unique, for example a specific painting, or the shares are not readily available, the contract may be specifically enforceable; so also may be a contract for the sale of land since each piece of land is deemed to be unique.

Before making the decree the court must be sure that it can adequately supervise enforcement. Thus, contracts of a personal nature, particularly of employment, which depend upon good faith, will not be specifically enforced. This also applies to building contracts. The remedy must be 'mutual' and available to both parties and, since it could not be awarded against a minor, it will not be awarded to a minor. In all cases, the court has a discretion and will withhold the remedy if it is not felt just and equitable to grant it. It was refused in *Malins v. Freeman* (1837), as it would have been harsh to compel a buyer to take property he had bought at an auction in the belief that he was bidding for an entirely different lot.

Injunction

The other equitable remedy awarded at the discretion of the court is an injunction, an order of the court directing a person not to break a contract. It may be used to enforce a negative stipulation in a contract and is awarded on the same principles as specific performance, above. Thus, it may be used to enforce a valid restraint of trade clause by preventing a former employee from working for another or setting up in business in breach of his promise not to do so. In *Warner Bros Pictures Inc.* v. *Nelson* (1937), the actress, Bette Davis, was restrained by injunction from working for another film company. On the other hand, if the indirect effect of an award would be to enforce specifically a contract for personal services by leaving the defendant with no alternative except to perform or remain idle, the award will not be made. Other uses for injunctions include the enforcement of negative promises in contracts relating to land, for example a promise not to build on it, and exceptionally to prevent a seller of goods from withholding delivery where other sources of supply are not available [*Sky Petroleum Ltd* v. *VIP Petroleum Ltd* (1974)].

2.9.3 Remedies in sale of goods contracts

The buyer's main remedies are to reject the goods, to treat the contract as repudiated, and/or to claim damages. The seller's main remedies are to sue for the price or damages for non-acceptance. In addition, the Sale of Goods Act 1979 (SGA) gives an unpaid seller certain rights over the goods themselves.

Goods in the seller's possession may be retained under a *lien* or right to withhold delivery until money due is paid. When the buyer becomes insolvent, the right of stoppage in transit can be exercised. Finally, there is a right to rescind the contract and resell the goods where the goods are perishable, where the seller has expressly reserved this right in the contract, or where the buyer is notified of an intention to resell unless the price is paid within a reasonable time.

A seller may seek further protection by including a 'reservation of title' clause in the contract of sale, although this is not a remedy in itself. It is often referred to as a *Romalpa* clause, from the name of the case in which it first became prominent. Such a clause provides that ownership of the goods will pass to the buyer only when they have been paid for, so that in the event of the buyer's insolvency, the seller may recover the goods instead of becoming an unsecured trade creditor. Problems arise when the buyer resells the goods or the goods become altered or mixed with other goods.

2.9.4 Requiring payment of the price

To a very great extent, this depends upon the terms of the contract. Payment in advance may be required: for package holidays, mail-order goods, or rail fares for example. Payment may be at the same time as performance: on cash sales in shops or at the bar in a pub. Payment may be in arrear, after performance by the seller, particularly when credit is allowed; in most contracts to provide work in return for payment, the work must be completed before payment becomes due, but there can be many variations on this. In contracts for work, payments may be made due when a particular part of the task is complete, such as completion of the foundations in a building contract. In long professional assignments, by a solicitor, for example, the practitioner may require payments on account at various stages.

In the absence of specifically agreed terms, the duty to pay the price arises when the seller has completed his side of the bargain. In sales of goods, unless otherwise agreed, delivery of the goods and payment of the price are concurrent conditions, that is to say, the seller must be ready and willing to give possession of the goods to the buyer in exchange for the price and the buyer must be ready and willing to pay the price in exchange for possession of the goods: payment on delivery (SGA s.28). The seller may sue for the price when ownership has passed to the buyer (SGA s.49), and he can claim the full sum without any further duty to mitigate his losses. (Contrast Section 2.9.5. If the seller claims *damages*, he must take reasonable steps to mitigate or minimise his loss. He will, therefore, prefer to sue simply for the price if he can.)

In situations where an injured party is not entitled to the price, he may nevertheless become entitled to compensation on a *quantum meruit* basis (for so much as he has deserved). This may arise if the injured party has been prevented from completing the bargain by the defendant's conduct or repudiation. He may well have done considerable work, and this claim would give him compensation in proportion to what he has done. [See *Planche* v. *Colburn* (1831).]

Compensation on this basis may also be used where work has been done under a void contract, and neither the price nor damages for breach can be recovered because no contract exists. In *British Steel Corporation* v. *Cleveland Bridge & Engineering Co Ltd* (1984), steel was supplied while a contract was being negotiated. The negotiations failed and there was no contract, but a *quantum meruit* claim for the steel supplied and used was upheld.

2.9.5 Damages for breach

As we have seen, the party injured by a breach of contract has a right to claim damages to compensate for loss suffered as a result of the breach. There are five main problems:

- remoteness and causation;
- measure;
- mitigation by claimant;
- contributory negligence;
- possible liquidated damages clauses (and penalty clauses).

Remoteness and causation

The injured party cannot recover damages for all of the consequences which might flow from the breach, otherwise there could be no end to liability. The loss must not be too remote. In the leading case of *Hadley* v. *Baxendale* (1854), a carrier delayed in delivering the broken crankshaft of a mill for repair and the mill stood idle longer than necessary. Damages were awarded to the mill owner but a claim for loss of profits was held to be too remote as the carrier did not know that the mill could not be operated without the crankshaft. Two basic principles regarding remoteness were laid down by the court. First, such damages will be awarded as may fairly and reasonably be considered as arising naturally, that is, according to the usual course of things, from the breach. Second, such other loss may be included as may reasonably be supposed to have been in the contemplation of both parties at the time of contracting so that the defendant in effect accepted responsibility for it. These principles have subsequently been applied in many cases and still form the basis of the tests applied to determine whether a particular item of loss is too remote.

The principles established in *Hadley v. Baxendale* (1854) were considered and applied by the House of Lords in *Transfield Shipping Inc. v. Mercator Shipping Inc. (The Achilleas)* 2008. The House of Lords allowed an appeal by Transfield Shipping Inc. who had chartered a ship and failed to return the vessel by the identified date under the contract. The date for return was 2 May 2004 but the ship was actually returned on 11 May 2004. Transfield Shipping Inc. claimed they should be liable to pay damages on the basis of the market rate for daily hire. Mercator Shipping Inc. had contracted to hire the ship to another party with this charter beginning on 8 May 2004. The original contract price was £39,500 per day. Under the amended contract the daily hire rate was £31,500. Whilst arbitrators and the Court of Appeal had found in favour of Mercator Shipping Inc., the House of Lords decided that the extent of loss claimed was not contemplated by Transfield Shipping Inc.

Examples

In *Victoria Laundry Ltd* v. *Newman Industries Ltd* (1940), the late delivery of a boiler led to an award of compensation for loss of normal profits which the supplier should have anticipated; but a claim for the loss arising from a particularly profitable contract not known to the supplier was struck out.

In *The Heron II* (1969), a cargo of sugar was delivered late and could only be sold at a lower market price. It was held that changing market prices and the need for a quick sale must reasonably have been in the contemplation of the parties when the contract was made. Damages were awarded for the loss suffered.

In *Parsons* v. *Uttley Ingham* (1978), the defendant sold hoppers to a farmer for the storage of animal food. The hoppers were defective; animal food became mouldy and infected, and many animals died. It was held that the possibility of harm to the animals must reasonably have been in the contemplation of the parties when the contract was made, and compensation for the full loss was therefore awarded.

In *Jackson* v. *Royal Bank of Scotland plc* [2005], Jackson imported and sold on dog chews. The bank was in breach of contract in disclosing the profit mark up of Jackson to a party who purchased dog chews from them in an open ended agreement. It was held that the bank should have realised the releasing of this information might result in a loss of business, and so was not too remote. The House of Lords supported the level of damages awarded by the lower court, which were based on profits spanning 4 years. A reduced profit factor with passing of time was built in.

Jackson v. Royal bank of Scotland plc (2005)

Richard Bragg, Student Law Review, Vol. 47, 2006

Comment

It is perhaps surprising that every few years, the courts have to revisit the principles of remoteness of damage. One would have thought that, although not easy to apply, the principles were by now well established. On this occasion, the Court of Appeal seems to have made the basic student error of applying foreseeability from the time of breach of contract. This cannot be correct, because contract is different from tort. In tort, the principle is that the tortfeasor commits the tort and must be responsible for that act. To apply forseeability at the time of the breach makes eminent sense. In contract, one takes on responsibilities at the making of the contract. It is assumed liability. The whole point is that it is the terms of the contract that set out the duties and benefits that the contractor takes on board as part of that contract. A contract is negotiated on the basis that the parties understand exactly what the nature of the risk is. Of course, this depends on the party setting out the correct terms in the first place, but that is not a matter within the contemplation of the law. The court will enforce exactly what the parties have agreed; no more, no less. Thus it is logical that the contracting party must ask himself 'what is the likely consequence if I break this contract?'. The rules of remoteness flow from the answer to that question.

The basic rule of remoteness remains that laid down in *Hadley* v. *Baxendale* (1854) 9 Exch 341 as 'arising naturally, that is, according to the usual course of things, from such breach of contract itself, or such as may reasonably be supposed to have been in the contemplation of both parties at the time they made the contract as the probable result of the breach of it'. Later cases, such as *Victoria Laundry (Windsor)* v. *Newman Industries* [1949] 2 KB 528 and *Koufos* v. *C Czarnikow* (The Heron II) [1969] 1 AC 350, explain that these cases, are really two aspects of a single rule. The answer to the question, 'what happens if I break this contract?', depends on the knowledge of the contracting parties. Certain things will arise as the usual or ordinary consequences. Those things are ordinary enough that any intelligent contractor would contemplate them. Further liability will depend on the knowledge of the contracting parties. If there are special losses, recovery will depend on whether the contract breaker was aware of the facts that might lead to special losses when they made the contract, and therefore must be taken to accept those risks as part of the contractual promises.

In practice, the situation in the current case is an application of the first limb of *Hadley* v. *Baxendale*. Since the Bank knew that it is a basic rule of banking that each customer is entitled to confidentiality, there can be no question that there was a breach of contract and that seems to have been common ground between the parties. The Bank also knew, because it handled the documentary credits, what the arrangements between Samson and Economy Bag were, but it may not have known the details of that relationship. If the Bank had been asked to speculate what was the likely result of the Bank's breach, it is clear that it would have contemplated some potential financial loss, although it may not have been able to say with any precision how that loss would arise or its particular nature. This latter point is of no importance after the decision in *Parsons (Livestock) Ltd* v. *Uttley Ingham & Co Ltd* [1978] QB 791. This case decided that it was the type of loss that was important and not the precise way in which it occurs or its extent. Applying that here, if the Bank could contemplate financial loss, the fact that it arose from the terminating of the contract between Samson and Economy Bag is unimportant. It seems clear on the facts that the loss was not too remote and that is reflected in the decision.

There can also be more direct breaks in the chain of causation between the breach and the harm. In *Lambert* v. *Lewis* (1981), a motor dealer sold a vehicle and trailer with a faulty coupling to a farmer, who noticed the defect but did nothing about it. The coupling broke when the vehicles were on the road, and a car containing the Lambert family was destroyed. The farmer had to pay damages to the Lamberts. He could not recover these from the dealer. The Lamberts' deaths and injuries were caused by the farmer *using* a vehicle known to be dangerous, not directly by the dealer's breach of contract.

It is sufficient to show that the *type* of loss was foreseeable (e.g. *ordinary* profits). If so, it can all be recovered, whatever its extent. In *Brown* v. *KMR Services Ltd* (1995), the agent of a Lloyd's 'name' advised him inadequately. Some investment loss was foreseeable. The fact that the loss was much higher than expected was immaterial. It was all recoverable from the agent.

Measure

Most types of loss can be recovered for breach of contract. Financial loss is normally measured as expenditure which the claimant has incurred in reliance on the contract. The courts may also sometimes include a claimant's loss of profits, but not always. Profits can be included if the claimant has already suffered them when the contract ends. If the vendor of land wrongfully refuses to complete the sale, the buyer can recover the difference between the contract price and the market value of the house when the contract ends (if the value is rising).

Even losing the possibility of future profits may be included if it is fairly certain that they would have been made. If the buyer of goods is a dealer, and it is known that he intends to resell, then foreseeable loss of ordinary profit may be included.

However, the court will not include speculative profits, which might have accrued. On the other hand, if the claimant has definitely suffered some loss, then the courts will try to assess it, even if this is difficult.

The difficulty which the courts had in *Jackson* was that the potential losses were hard to calculate. There is plenty of precedent to the effect that damages can be awarded for loss of opportunity (an example cited by Lord Hope is *Allied Maples Group Ltd* v. *Simmons & Simmons* [1995] 4 All ER 907). However, the losses depended on Samson being able to show that it was more likely than not, that for such period of time as Economy Bag were in ignorance of Samson's mark up, they would continue to contract with Samson and thus repeat orders would continue to flow. If the contract had been of finite duration, that would have settled the issue. However, the contract was one of infinite duration, terminable by notice. Evidence was given at the trial by Economy Bag that they were happy with the arrangement. Using Samson removed all the hassle of importing with which they were not familiar. They received the goods at their Preston store ready for immediate sale. They were selling the goods for a sizeable profit. There was no intention of cutting out the middle man, until they saw the size of the mark up and started to believe that they were being 'ripped off'. This evidence was probably enough to suggest that the loss of repeat orders was real, rather than speculative. However, projecting into the future is always difficult. The judge thought four years was realistic, although on a reducing basis. As the contract went on, the chances of it being terminated increased. The Lords rejected the Court of Appeal's reduction of this to one year. The evidence showed that the judge had made some errors of calculation and his quantification was 'open to some criticism'. Lord Walker took the view that he had 'probably overestimated and certainly did not underestimate'. However, since the events occurred in 1993, the Lords took the view that to send the matter back for recalculation was inappropriate and therefore reinstated the original judgement.

Examples

In *ATV* v. *Reed* (1971), R broke his contract to take the lead in a TV series. ATV recovered their expenses in preparing the series, but could not claim the speculative profits which they might have made from it.

In *McRae* v. *CDC* (1950), the defendant broke his contract to supply a ship for a salvage expedition. The costs of preparing the expedition were recovered, but not the (speculative) vast profits which might have been made if it had been successful.

In *Re Houghton Main Colliery Co.* (1956), the company contracted to pay pensions at an agreed rate to ex-employees (whose ages varied). The company then went into liquidation and broke its contracts. The pensioners had definitely suffered loss. Therefore, the court did try to assess the current value of the pensions, although this was difficult.

Where no actual loss has been suffered, for example where a buyer refuses to accept goods and the seller is able to sell them elsewhere at the same price as in the contract, the courts may award a small nominal sum as damages to mark the breach.

Damages for breach of contract can include compensation for bodily injury, as in *Frost* v. *Aylesbury Dairy Co* (1905) and in many other cases. Even damages for distress or disappointment may be awarded in contracts where the main purpose is to give peace of mind or pleasure, as where a tour operator defaults on his obligations and an expected holiday is spoiled; see *Jarvis* v. *Swans Tours Ltd* (1973). Damages under this head will not be awarded for distress or injured feelings caused by unfair dismissal from employment, however; see *Addis* v. *Gramophone Co Ltd* (1909).

Damages may be awarded for loss of valuable reputation in appropriate cases. In *Kpohraror* v. *Woolwich BS* (1996), the Woolwich wrongly refused to honour the claimant's cheque, and he recovered damages for potential harm to his credit rating; but the damages were not punitive or exemplary.

Mitigation of loss by the claimant

The claimant's duty to (try to) mitigate his loss is another important rule governing the awards of damages. When a contract has come to an end, all reasonable steps must be taken by the victim to minimise the loss. Thus, an employee who has been wrongfully dismissed must seek another job. A seller must attempt to sell rejected goods elsewhere for the best price possible, and a buyer must try to replace goods which were not delivered at the cheapest price possible. Loss arising from failure to mitigate is not recoverable, though it must be emphasised that only reasonable efforts are required from the injured party.

Contributory negligence by the claimant

Where a contract imposes a duty of *care* (as by a professional person to his own client), then a claimant's damages for breach *of this duty* may be reduced if the claimant has shown contributory negligence. In *Platform Home Loans Ltd* v. *Oyston Shipways Ltd* (1999), a valuer negligently overvalued property which his client, a mortgage lender, intended to take as security. The client suffered loss, partly because of the overvaluation, but partly because of his own recklessness in granting the loan which was too risky anyway. Damages against the valuer for breach of contract were reduced by 20 per cent for the client's own contributory negligence.

On the other hand, contributory negligence will be no defence to an action of fraud. Nor will it be a defence if, as is often the case, negligence need not be proved because the obligation is strict. Therefore, it will not be contributory negligence for a person to buy goods from a dealer without checking them first.

Liquidated damages and penalty clauses

Some contracts include a liquidated damages clause which provides in advance for the damages payable in the event of breach. For example, contracts for building and for the sale of goods may provide that a specified amount shall be payable for every day late in completion of the building or delivery of the goods. Such provision for liquidated damages may be useful in limiting the cost of litigation, if a breach should occur. They will be enforced by the court if they are a genuine attempt to pre-estimate the likely loss, even if they do not coincide with the actual loss which later arises. However, if it is not a genuine pre-estimate but inserted *in terrorem* of the offending party by pressuring him into performing the contract, or imposing punitive damages for breach which would not otherwise be awarded, the clause will be void as a penalty. The court will then assess the damages in the normal way. Some guidance on how to distinguish liquidated damages from a penalty is found in *Alfred McAlpine Capital Projects Ltd* v. *Tilebox Ltd* (2005). Where commercial parties adopt a liquidated damages clause, the courts will be inclined to accept this as part of the contract. Even if the actual loss is less than the estimated loss, the courts will look at the actual discrepancy which should be substantial, not merely at the fact that there was a discrepancy. Further, Jackson J. stated that in his opinion, where a pre-estimate of damages was incorrect it could still be deemed reasonable and so enforceable. It must also be noted that some of these clauses may now be invalidated by the Unfair Terms in Consumer Contracts Regulations 1994 (see Section 2.6.4).

Penalty clauses used to be common in hire-purchase contracts so that a hirer who returned the goods after paying perhaps only one instalment could, but for the intervention of the court, incur liability to pay up to one-half or more of the total purchase price. Where the Consumer Credit Act 1974 applies, such penalty clauses are now invalidated by statute.

2.9.6 Limitation of actions

Contractual obligations are not enforceable indefinitely. There must be an end to possible litigation if only because evidence becomes less reliable with the passage of time. After a certain period, therefore, contracts become unenforceable. It is still possible to carry out such contracts and any dispositions of property under them are valid but, in the event of a dispute, the law bars any remedy.

The general periods within which an action must be brought are prescribed under the Limitation Act 1980. Actions based on a simple contract will be barred within 6 years from the date when the cause of action accrued. Where the action is based on a deed or the recovery of land, the period is extended to 12 years. A right 'accrues' when a breach occurs and an action could begin. Thus, if a loan is made for a fixed time, the right will accrue when this time expires. If no time is agreed upon, it will be when a demand for payment is made.

However, if the claimant is under a disability as a minor or through insanity when the cause of action accrues, then time will not start to run until the disability ends or until death, whichever comes first. Once the period has started, though, it will continue and be unaffected by subsequent insanity. Similarly, if the defendant acts fraudulently or conceals material facts, or if the claimant acts under a mistake, the limitation period will not begin until the claimant has discovered or should reasonably have discovered the true state of affairs.

2.10 Summary

At the end of this chapter, students should make sure that they are familiar with the following material:

- The essential features of a valid contract, namely:
  - (i) Agreement – shown by offer and acceptance (Sections 2.2.1 and 2.2.2).
  - (ii) Consideration – the rule that a simple contract is a bargain where each side gives consideration to the other; and the exception that in a specialty contract a promise can be binding without consideration if it is made by deed (Section 2.2.3).
  - (iii) Intention to create legal relations (Section 2.3).

(iv) Reality of the consent.
(v) Capacity of the parties to contract – the rule that, exceptionally, some parties' power to make a valid or/binding contract is limited: particularly (although not in detail):
  – infants.
  – parties whose contracts may be *ultra vires*.
(vi) Legality – (Section 2.1.1) – not in detail.

- The rule that in general there are no requirements that the contract should be in any particular form, but that there are exceptional circumstances where written documents or even a deed may be required (Sections 2.1.2 and 2.1.3).
- The rules of misrepresentation which are required by the syllabus to be included here, and may often be the subject of examination questions. Students should pay particular attention to the Misrepresentation Act 1967.
- The normal terms of contract should be studied very carefully – in particular:
  – conditions and warranties, and the differences between them.
  – express terms and implied terms, particularly implied terms in contracts between a professional person and his client; at this point, students should refer again to the situations where a professional person can also be liable to a non-client.
- Exemption clauses are important, and students should make sure that they know about the attitude of the courts, and the effect of legislation such as the Unfair Contract Terms Act 1977.
- Discharge of a contract by performance and by agreement.
- Discharge by frustration.
- The results of breach of contract (briefly).
- Breach of contract.
- Rescission for breach and rights to treat the contract as repudiated.
- Specific performance.
- Injunctions.
- Requiring payment of the price.
- Damages for breach of contract
  – remoteness and causation.
  – measure.
  – mitigation.
  – exceptional cases where damages can be reduced for contributory negligence
  – liquidated damages and 'penalty' clauses.
- Limitation periods.

Revision Questions

? Question 1 Multiple-choice selection

1.1 The vast majority of contracts are 'simple'. What is the meaning of the word 'simple' in this context?

(A) The terms of the contract are set out in writing.
(B) The contract does not need to be in any particular form to be binding.
(C) The contract contains fewer than ten provisions.
(D) The contract is not supported by consideration.

1.2 A Ltd placed the following advertisement in a local newspaper.

We are able to offer for sale a number of portable colour television sets at the specially reduced price of £5.90. Order now while stocks last.

The advertisement contained a mistake in that the television sets should have been priced at £59.00. B Ltd immediately placed an order for 100 television sets.

Which *one* of the following statements is *correct*?

(A) B Ltd has accepted an offer and is contractually entitled to the 100 television sets.
(B) A Ltd can refuse to supply B Ltd as the advertisement is not an offer, but an invitation to treat.
(C) A Ltd can only refuse to sell the television sets to B Ltd if it has sold all its stock.
(D) As B Ltd has not yet paid for the television sets, the company has no contractual right to them.

1.3 Dennis wrote to Mark, offering to sell him a Renoir painting for £100,000. One week later, Mark wrote back saying he would pay that amount but not for another 2 months. Dennis did not respond and Mark, who decided that he wanted the painting, then heard that Dennis had sold the painting to Tom. Was there a contract between Dennis and Mark?

(A) Yes. Dennis has made a valid offer which Mark has accepted.
(B) Yes. Mark's response was a request for further information and he was able to accept the offer afterwards.
(C) No. Mark's response constitutes a counter-offer which effectively destroyed Dennis's original offer.
(D) No. Dennis's letter to Mark constituted an invitation to treat, not an offer.

1.4 In relation to a valid enforceable contract, which *one* of the following statements is *untrue*?

(A) Consideration must not be past.
(B) Consideration must move from the promisee.
(C) In certain circumstances, a promise may be binding without consideration.
(D) Consideration must be adequate.

1.5 Which *one* of the following statements is *correct*?

(A) If the creditor agrees to accept less than the full amount due, the debt is discharged at common law.
(B) At common law, a creditor who has agreed to accept less than the full amount due may go back on his word and recover the balance.
(C) Payment of less than the full amount due by a third party cannot discharge the whole debt.
(D) Payment of less than the amount due cannot discharge the whole debt, even if made early at the request of the creditor.

1.6 The law of contract is of special importance in providing a legal framework within which businesses can operate. Which *one* of the following statements is *correct*?

(A) A contract need not necessarily be in writing.
(B) A contract is always binding even when the parties do not intend the agreement to be legally binding.
(C) A contract comes under the remit of criminal law rather than civil law.
(D) A contract by a corporate body is always valid.

1.7 X Ltd makes an offer by post to Y Ltd, sending X Ltd's standard written terms. Y Ltd agrees to it, sending Y Ltd's standard terms (which are different from X's). X Ltd starts to perform the contract without writing back to Y Ltd. Which one of the following statements is correct?

(A) There is no contract.
(B) There is a contract on X Ltd's terms.
(C) There is a contract on Y Ltd's terms.
(D) There is a contract on reasonable terms to be settled by the courts.

1.8 Which of the following statements is correct?

(A) Misrepresentation always renders the contract voidable.
(B) Misrepresentation always gives the party deceived an absolute right to damages.
(C) The contract is only voidable if the party deceived can prove that the misrepresentation was negligent.
(D) The contract only gives a right to damages if the party deceived can prove that the misrepresentation was negligent.

1.9 Which *one* of the following is *incorrect*?

(A) A term may be implied into a contract by statute.
(B) A term may be implied into a contract by a court on the ground that the term is customary in the parties' trade.
(C) A term may be implied into a contract by a court on the ground that it would make the contract more equitable.
(D) A term may be implied into a contract by a court on the ground of business efficacy.

1.10 All the following statements relating to contract terms are correct, except one. Which *one* is wrong?

(A) A breach of condition only gives the injured party the right to terminate the contract.
(B) A breach of warranty does not give the injured party a right to rescission.
(C) A breach of condition gives the injured party the right to terminate the contract and claim damages.
(D) A breach of warranty gives the injured party a right to claim damages.

1.11 Which *one* of the following is *incorrect*?

(A) A condition is a term which the parties intend to be of fundamental importance.
(B) A warranty is a term which the parties do not intend to be of fundamental importance.
(C) If a condition is breached, then the contract must be terminated.
(D) If a warranty is breached, then the innocent party cannot terminate the contract.

1.12 Which *one* of the following is not true?

(A) An exclusion clause must be incorporated into a contract at or before the time when the contract is made.
(B) An exclusion clause may be invalidated by the Unfair Contract Terms Act 1977, in a case to which the Act applies.
(C) To be bound by an exclusion clause, the contracting party must have read it.
(D) A contracting party can be bound by an exclusion clause which is incorporated into the contract by reference to an earlier course of dealing.

1.13 Tom and Sarah visited Bath for the first time in their lives, and booked into a hotel for a night. On arriving in their room they noticed that there were many conditions of contract pinned to the back of the door, and that these included clauses purporting to exclude liability by the hotel for personal injuries or loss suffered by guests while at the hotel. Tom and Sarah had never seen these conditions before. Which *one* of the following is true?

(A) Tom and Sarah are not bound by the conditions.
(B) Tom and Sarah are bound by the conditions if they are fair and reasonable.
(C) Tom and Sarah are bound by the conditions relating to loss of property but not those relating to personal injuries.
(D) Tom and Sarah are not bound by the conditions because a hotel is never allowed to exclude its own liability in contract.

1.14 Which *one* of the following statements relating to frustration is inaccurate?

(A) Frustration will arise due to subsequent physical impossibility.
(B) A radical and fundamental change in circumstances can frustrate a contract.
(C) A change in the law can render a contract frustrated.
(D) A change in circumstances can frustrate a contract by making performance very much more costly.

1.15 Builder Ltd was under contract to build an extension for Land Ltd at a price of £40,000. Builder Ltd completed three-quarters of the extension, stopped work, and was then placed in creditors' voluntary liquidation, and failed to complete the extension. Which of the following is *correct*?

(A) Builder Ltd is entitled to nothing.
(B) Builder Ltd has substantially performed the contract and is entitled to a reasonable sum in respect of the work done.
(C) Builder Ltd has completed three-quarters of the work and is, therefore, entitled to £30,000.
(D) The contract between Builder Ltd and Land Ltd is frustrated.

1.16 Which of the following statements is *correct*?

(i) As a general rule, a contract will only be discharged if all its terms have been precisely performed.
(ii) If a contract becomes impossible to perform through no fault of either contracting party, the contract is frustrated and unenforceable, unless its terms provide for the frustrating event.

(A) (i) only.
(B) (ii) only.
(C) Neither (i) nor (ii).
(D) Both (i) and (ii).

1.17 Which *one* of the following contracts might be specifically enforceable?

(A) Alan has contracted to sell his house to Bob but has changed his mind and no longer wishes to sell it.
(B) Chris has contracted to buy a new Ford motor car but the garage is now refusing to honour the contract.
(C) Diane has contracted to purchase a number of tins of fruit for her business but the seller has now stated that he no longer wishes to proceed with the contract.
(D) Eduardo has contracted to sing at a concert organised by Fernando, but Eduardo has withdrawn as he has received a more lucrative offer from Giovanni.

1.18 In the event of a breach of contract, what is the purpose of damages?

(i) To punish the contract breaker.
(ii) To compensate the innocent party.
(iii) To put the innocent party in the same position as if the contract had been carried out correctly.

(A) (i) only.
(B) (ii) and (iii) only.
(C) (ii) only.
(D) (i), (ii) and (iii).

1.19 In breach of contract, C Ltd refused to sell a motor car to D Ltd at the agreed price of £10,000. If the type of motor car is readily available on the market at a price of £9,000 which *one* of the following is *correct*?

(A) D Ltd is entitled to an order of specific performance, forcing C Ltd to carry out its contract.
(B) D Ltd is entitled to damages of £1,000.
(C) D Ltd is entitled to nominal damages only.
(D) D Ltd is not entitled to damages.

1.20 Tee Ltd has broken one of the terms of its contract with Vee Ltd. If that term is a condition, which of the following is *correct*?

(A) Vee Ltd is only entitled to sue for damages.
(B) Vee Ltd may rescind the contract and sue for damages.
(C) The contract is void.
(D) Vee Ltd is only entitled to treat the contract as repudiated.

1.21 In an action for breach of contract, the court will *never* award

(A) unliquidated damages.
(B) nominal damages.
(C) liquidated damages.
(D) exemplary damages.

1.22 Anne was induced to enter into a contract to purchase goods by the negligent misrepresentation of Bob. Anne seeks rescission of the contract. Which of the following is *incorrect*?

(A) Rescission is a court order requiring a contract to be correctly carried out.
(B) Anne will be granted rescission only if she applies within a reasonable time.
(C) The remedy may be refused if Anne herself has acted inequitably.
(D) Anne will lose the right to rescind if an innocent third party buys the goods and uses them.

1.23 Farmer owns some land, part of which is woodland. He sells the land to B, who covenants in the contract that he will not cut down the trees. One year later, B does prepare to cut down the trees. Farmer seeks a remedy immediately. What remedy is appropriate at this stage?

(A) Damages.
(B) Specific performance.
(C) Injunction.
(D) Rescission.

1.24 How soon must the injured party in normal circumstances start an action for damages for breach of a simple contract?

(A) Within a reasonable time.
(B) Within 3 years.
(C) Within 6 years.
(D) There is no time limit unless the contract has imposed one.

Question 2

Beryl enters a shop to purchase a new dress. She tells the shop assistant that she would like to buy the blue dress which is displayed in the shop window and priced at £100. The assistant removes the dress from the window for Beryl, but when she tries to pay for it at the till, the manager informs her that it is not for sale. He tells her that the dress is for display purposes only.

Requirement

Delete as appropriate and complete the following sentences:

Beryl is/is not **(1 mark)** entitled to the dress because the display of the dress in the shop window constitutes an .... (3 words) **(2 marks)** and not an .... (1 word) **(2 marks)**. It follows that Beryl does not have/has **(1 mark)** a contract with the shop owners who have/have not **(1 mark)** acted in breach of contract. **(Total marks = 7)**

Question 3

Vendor owned a factory. He persuaded Mr Purchaser to sign a contract to buy it, and to pay a deposit of £50,000. During negotiations he told Purchaser that the local authority had no plans to build a rumoured road nearby. In fact the local authority had decided to build the road and was about to commence work. This might have been discovered by checking at the Town Hall, but Vendor genuinely believed what he had said.

Requirement

Delete as appropriate and complete the following sentences:

Vendor appears to have made a .... (1 word) **(2 marks)** to Purchaser. This renders the contract .... (1 word) **(2 marks)** and if Purchaser acts quickly, he will be able to .... (1 word) **(1 mark)** the contract which means that Vendor and Purchaser will be returned to their pre-contract position. Purchaser will/will not **(1 mark)** be obliged to pay the rest of the price and he will/will not **(1 mark)** be able to recover his deposit. In addition, Purchaser may be able to recover damages from Vendor unless Vendor can show that he was not negligent under the .... Act 1967 (1 word) **(1 mark).** **(Total marks = 8)**

Question 4

On 1 November 2008, Hirer Ltd contracted to hire a conference suite from Owner Ltd. The suite was to be used on 1 February 2009 as the venue for a presentation by a marketing expert, entitled 'Developing Markets in China: My Experiences in Peking'. The contract required Hirer Ltd to pay £4,000 immediately, and the balance of £6,000 to be paid on or before 14 February 2009.

Owing to the unforeseen and serious illness of the marketing expert, the presentation had to be cancelled, and all those who had purchased tickets were given a refund.

Requirement

Delete as appropriate and complete the following sentences:

If the identity of the expert was not crucial and Owner Ltd was able to obtain the services of another expert, the contract between Hirer Ltd and Owner Ltd would/would not be **(1 mark)** enforceable. If however, the identity of the marketing expert was crucial then the contract between Hirer Ltd and Owner Ltd would appear to have been .... (1 word) **(2 marks)**. Hirer Ltd will/will not **(1 mark)** be able to recover the deposit of £4,000 under the .... Act 1943 (4 words) **(2 marks)**. Hirer Ltd will/will not **(1 mark)** be obliged to pay the balance of £6,000. If Owner Ltd has incurred any expenses as a result of its contract with Hirer Ltd, it may be able to retain a .... (1 word) **(1 mark)** sum to cover those expenses. **(Total marks = 8)**

Question 5

HIJ Ltd contracted with TUV plc for the latter to service the former's industrial machinery. HIJ Ltd agreed to sign a document headed '*TUV plc Service Agreement*', which contained a clause stating *neither TUV plc nor its employees will accept any responsibility for any loss or damage arising from the servicing of customers' machinery, irrespective of the manner in which the loss was caused.*

An employee of TUV plc carelessly failed to replace certain parts of a machine which he had serviced. This error caused the machine to seize up, and HIJ Ltd lost several days' production and had to purchase a replacement machine.

Requirement

Delete as appropriate and complete the following sentences:

The clause was/was not **(1 mark)** incorporated into the contract by the .... (1 word) **(2 marks)** of HIJ Ltd. The term is an .... (1 word) **(1 mark)** clause and, as such, is subject to the provisions of the .... (3 words) **(2 marks)** Act 1977. This Act provides that such a clause is .... (1 word) **(1 mark)** unless it can be shown to be .... (1 word) **(1 mark)**. A schedule to the 1977 Act sets down a .... (1 word) **(1 mark)** test. On balance, it would appear that the clause is/is not **(1 mark)** valid. **(Total marks = 10)**

Question 6

Retailer Ltd contracted to purchase goods from Wholesaler Ltd for £10,000. The goods were to be sold to a customer of Retailer Ltd for £12,000. Retailer Ltd paid £500 to Distributor Ltd in return for its agreement to transport the goods, and paid a deposit of £1,000 to Wholesaler Ltd.

Wholesaler Ltd has now advised Retailer Ltd that it will be unable to supply the goods ordered.

Requirement

Delete as appropriate and complete the following sentences:

Retailer is obliged to .... (1 word) **(2 marks)** its loss by attempting to purchase the goods elsewhere. If they are available elsewhere at a price of £11,000, Retailer will be entitled to damages of .... (state the amount) **(2 marks)**. If they are available elsewhere at a price of £9,000, Retailer Ltd will be entitled to .... (2 words) **(2 marks)**. Retailer will/will not **(1 mark)** be entitled to obtain the equitable remedy of .... (2 words) **(2 marks)** unless the goods were unique or otherwise unavailable elsewhere. Retailer will/will not **(1 mark)** be able to recover its deposit of £1,000. If Retailer is forced to lose its sale to the customer but the profit is considered too .... (1 word) **(2 marks)** because it is not within the contemplation of the parties, Retailer will not be able to recover its lost profit. In the facts of this problem, it is likely/unlikely **(1 mark)** that the sale to a customer was within the contemplation of Wholesaler Ltd with the result that Retailer Ltd will/will not **(1 mark)** be able to recover its lost profit. **(Total marks = 14)**

Question 7

Delete as appropriate and complete the following sentences:

The remedy which requires a person to carry out his contract is known as .... (2 words) **(2 marks)**. The remedy requiring a person not to act in breach of contract is known as an .... (1 word) **(2 marks)**. These are both .... (1 word) **(1 mark)** remedies and, as such, are discretionary. If the contract contains a provision which is designed to frighten the other party into completing the contract by setting down a disproportionate sum payable in the event of a breach, the provision will be regarded as a .... (1 word) **(2 marks)** clause and will be treated as .... (1 word) **(2 marks)**, that is, of no legal effect. If one party has completed his contractual obligations, all that remains is to sue for the price, in which case remoteness of damage and mitigation of loss are relevant/irrelevant **(1 mark)**. **(Total marks = 10)**

Solutions to Revision Questions 2

Solution 1

1.1 Answer: (B)

Most contracts are binding irrespective of their form, and in this respect are described as 'simple', (A) which refers to written contracts is therefore inaccurate. The number of provisions as identified in (C) is of no relevance. Further, a contract is only recognised where consideration is provided by both parties, therefore (D) cannot be correct.

1.2 Answer: (B)

Both (A) and (C) are incorrect as no contract between A Ltd and B Ltd exists. B has merely made an offer. Whether or not B Ltd has paid for the television sets is, on the facts, of no significance. The offer made by B Ltd would have to be accepted by A Ltd for a contract to exist.

1.3 Answer: (C)

(A) is not true, because Mark did not accept Dennis's offer in full, by the fact that he introduced a further term, that is that he would pay in 2 months' time. B is not true, because Mark did not request further information. (C) is the correct answer, because Mark is trying to impose his own terms, and thus is making a counter-offer which is capable in turn of acceptance, and which destroys Dennis's original offer. (See *Hyde* v. *Wrench* (1840)) (D) is not correct, because the language used indicates that a definite offer is being made by Dennis, indicating a definite intention to be bound.

1.4 Answer: (D)

(A) is true: consideration cannot consist of work already done, or goods already delivered, as the benefit has been received. (B) is true: only the person who has given value in relation to the contract may enforce it. (C) is also true: although normally a promise is not enforceable as lacking consideration, it may be enforceable if contained in a deed. (D) is untrue, and therefore the right answer. Consideration need not be adequate, as parties will not be protected by the courts where they make a bad bargain.

1.5 Answer: (B)

A promise to accept less than the full contract price due is unenforceable unless the promise is 'brought', in other words consideration for the promise is provided.

A party can therefore go back on a promise in isolation to accept a lesser sum. (B) is therefore the correct answer.

1.6 Answer: (A)

Many contracts of sale, for example when a small item is bought in a shop or when a passenger pays a bus fare, are unwritten. Statement (A) is therefore the correct answer. But to be valid in law, all contracts, unwritten as well as written, must meet a number of conditions. Intention to form a legal contract must exist, hence statement (B) is incorrect. Statement (D) is also incorrect because the objects clause in the Memorandum of Association of a company may restrict that company's contracted capacity. The law of contract is of course part of the civil law and not the criminal law, which renders statement (C) wrong.

1.7 Answer: (C)

There is a contract: Y Ltd has made a counter-offer, which X Ltd has impliedly accepted by acting on it (A). Y Ltd by his counter-offer has impliedly rejected X Ltd's standard terms (B). There is no need (or right) for a court to settle reasonable terms (D).

1.8 Answer: (A)

The contract is voidable even for innocent misrepresentation (C). Damages are not available as of right if the deceiver can prove that he was innocent (B). The party deceived does not need to prove negligence, however; it is for the deceiver to prove that he was not negligent (D).

1.9 Answer: (C)

(A) is correct. A good example of implied terms found in statute is the Sale of Goods Act 1979 as amended. Contract terms are implied into contracts on the basis of custom, therefore (B) is correct. Also, business efficacy is a basis for contract terms being implied into contracts, as seen in the Moorcock case (1889). (D) is a correct statement.

1.10 Answer: (A)

This question highlights the difference in potential consequences where either a breach of warranty or breach of condition occurs. Answers (B) and (D) relating to warranties correctly identify the limited rights available to the injured party. Answers (A) and (C) give opposing information in relation to conditions, and of the two, it is (C) which identifies the true extent of the injured party's rights.

1.11 Answer: (C)

(C) is the correct answer because whilst a breach of condition can result in the contract being terminated, it is wrong to say the contract must be terminated. A condition is of fundamental importance to a contract and a warranty is not of fundamental importance; therefore (A) and (B) are correct statements. Also, a contract cannot end as a result of a breach of warranty, so (D) is a correct statement.

1.12 Answer: (C)

(A) is true, since an exclusion clause must be incorporated into the contract when the contract is made, in order to form part of the contractual terms. (B) is true, since the Unfair Contract Terms Act 1977 will invalidate certain exclusion clauses which relate to exclusion of liability for personal injuries or death, or where the clause fails the test of being fair and reasonable, where applicable. (C) is untrue, and therefore the right answer, because a person can be bound by an exclusion clause of which he or she was unaware, for example in an unread document signed by the contracting party. (D) is true, since the parties may have already agreed terms for all future contracts on a previous occasion.

1.13 Answer: (A)

The question is concerned with offer and acceptance and also with exclusion of liability. (A) is true, and therefore the correct answer. Tom and Sarah are not bound by the conditions because they were not made aware of them before reaching agreement. Therefore, any questions about the fairness or otherwise of the conditions under the Unfair Contract Terms Act 1977 and the regulations are irrelevant, as in (B) and (C). (D) is untrue: the hotel could have excluded liability by contract or by notice for breach of contract or breach of duty, provided that the exclusion is fair and reasonable, and provided that it did not relate to liability for personal injuries or death.

1.14 Answer: (D)

This question addresses the issue of when a contract will be frustrated, but beyond that deals with the extent to which performance of contract obligations must change before frustration will occur. The change in circumstances must be both radical and fundamental.

1.15 Answer: (A)

Performance must normally be total and precise for any entitlement to payment to arise. If a party *chooses* to accept part performance in circumstances where they are able to make such a choice, then they must pay for what they *choose* to take; but Land Ltd does not seem to have any option but to take the partially completed job here.

1.16 Answer: (D)

Whilst exceptions exist, it is correct to say that as a general rule precise performance is required in order to discharge a contract. Further, as a result of a frustrating event a contract will be terminated and so becomes unenforceable. Parties can however, provide in their contract for the occurrence of a frustrating event and such contract provision would be respected by the courts. (D) is therefore the correct answer.

1.17 Answer: (A)

Where goods such as motor cars and tins of fruit are identified as consideration, then the usual remedy on any breach of contract would be compensation as such items are available from any number of suppliers. (B) and (C) are therefore not the correct answers. Likewise, on the facts of (D), where Eduardo will sing at a concert organised by Giovanni rather than Fernando, compensation is the appropriate remedy. A house is unique in that it cannot be likened to cars or tins of fruit, where effectively the same product can be acquired from various sources. A specific performance order requiring Alan to sell to Bob might therefore be available.

1.18 Answer: (B)

The sanction of punishment relates to criminal actions rather than civil claims, therefore (i) is incorrect. The general aims in providing damages are to compensate the injured party, and to return the injured party to the position they would have enjoyed had there been contract performance. (B) is therefore the correct answer.

1.19 Answer: (C)

As the type of motor car is readily available on the market, a specific performance order would not be the appropriate remedy. (A) therefore is incorrect. (D) is incorrect as a breach of contract has occurred and the innocent party can look to the common law remedy of damages. As D Ltd can purchase the car on the market for less than the original contract price, nominal damages only can be recovered. Damages are provided to restore an injured party to the position they would have enjoyed had the contract been properly performed. (C) and not (B) is therefore the correct answer.

1.20 Answer: (B)

The remedy of damages only would be available on a breach of warranty, therefore (A) is incorrect. (D) is incorrect in that an innocent party on breach of condition can seek more than repudiation alone. (B) rather than (C) is the correct answer. A condition is an important term of a contract and breach of such a nature is a serious breach. Contract law provides the injured party with rights to seek appropriate remedies on that basis.

1.21 Answer: (D)

Exemplary or punitive damages are not now awarded for breach of contract, although they were awarded in the past. Damages for breach of contract should do no more than compensate the plaintiff for his loss. Unliquidated damages (choice (A)) are damages which have not yet been quantified, and once they have been quantified, can be awarded by a court. Nominal damages (choice (B)) are awarded by courts where no actual loss has been suffered but there has been a breach of contract, and are sometimes awarded to recognise that there has been a breach. Liquidated damages (choice (C)) are agreed in advance by the parties as the measure of loss if there is breach of that contract, and are commonly agreed in the case of large construction works.

1.22 Answer: (A)

The definition of rescission in (A) is incorrect. This is an equitable remedy whereby the court looks to, for example ordering a returning of goods/money received under a contract in order to, where possible, restore the parties to the original position they enjoyed. The answers in (B), (C) and (D) identify valid factors that highlight the equitable nature of the remedy and features of fairness that can relate to it.

1.23 Answer: (C)

Not (A) – the farmer has not really suffered any damage yet. It is probably too late to rescind the contract (D). Specific performance (B) is an order to do something;

the farmer wants an order *not* to do something. An injunction (C) is appropriate and it can often be obtained very quickly.

1.24 Answer: (C)

A 'reasonable time' is only the time limit for equitable remedies such as rescission, injunction and so on; therefore not (A). The others (B) and (D) are simply wrong.

Solution 2

Beryl *is not* entitled to the dress because the display of the dress in the shop window with a price tag constitutes an *invitation to treat* and not an *offer to sell*. It follows that Beryl *does not have* a contract with the shop owners, who *have not* acted in breach of contract.

Solution 3

Vendor appears to have made a *misrepresentation* to Purchaser. This renders the contract *voidable* and if Purchaser acts quickly, he will be able to *rescind* the contract which means that Vendor and Purchaser will be returned to their pre-contract position. Purchaser *will not* be obliged to pay the rest of the price and he *will* be able to recover his deposit. In addition, Purchaser may be able to recover damages from Vendor unless Vendor can show that he was not negligent under the *Misrepresentation* Act 1967.

Solution 4

If the identity of the expert was not crucial and Owner Ltd was able to obtain the services of another expert, the contract between Hirer Ltd and Owner Ltd *would* be enforceable. If, however, the identity of the marketing expert was crucial then the contract between Hirer Ltd and Owner Ltd would appear to have been *frustrated*. Hirer Ltd *will* be able to recover the deposit of £4,000 under the *Law Reform (Frustrated Contracts)* Act 1943. Hirer Ltd *will not* be obliged to pay the balance of £6,000. If Owner Ltd has incurred any expenses as a result of its contract with Hirer Ltd, it may be able to retain a *reasonable* sum to cover those expenses.

Solution 5

The clause *was* incorporated into the contract by the *signature* of HIJ Ltd. The term is an *exclusion* clause, and, as such, is subject to the provisions of the *Unfair Contract Terms* Act 1977. This Act provides that such a clause is *void* unless it can be shown to be *reasonable*. A schedule to the 1977 Act provides a *reasonableness* test. On balance, it would appear that the clause *is* valid.

Solution 6

Retailer is obliged to *mitigate* its loss by attempting to purchase the goods elsewhere. If they are available elsewhere at a price of £11,000, Retailer will be entitled to damages of

£1,000. If they are available elsewhere at a price of £9,000, Retailer Ltd will be entitled to *nominal damages*. Retailer *will not* be entitled to obtain the *equitable* remedy of *specific performance* unless the goods were unique or otherwise unavailable elsewhere. Retailer *will* be able to recover its deposit of £1,000. If Retailer is forced to lose its sale to the customer but the profit is considered too *remote* because it is not within the contemplation of the parties, Retailer will not be able to recover its lost profit. In the facts of this problem, it is *likely* that the sale to a customer was within the contemplation of Wholesaler Ltd with the result that Retailer Ltd *will* be able to recover its lost profit.

Solution 7

The remedy which requires a person to carry out his contract is known as *specific performance.* The remedy requiring a person not to act in breach of contract is known as an *injunction.* These are both *equitable* remedies and, as such, are discretionary. If the contract contains a provision which is designed to frighten the other party into completing the contract, by setting down a disproportionate sum payable in the event of a breach, the provision will be regarded as a *penalty* clause and will be treated as *void*, that is, of no legal effect. If one party has completed his contractual obligations, all that remains is to sue for the price, in which case remoteness of damage and mitigation of loss are *irrelevant.Learning Outcome*: To explain the type of breach necessary to cause contractual breakdown and the remedies which are available for serious and minor breaches of contract.

3

The Law of Employment

The Law of Employment

3

Learning Outcomes

After completing this chapter you should be able to:

- distinguish between employees and independent contractors and how the contents of a contract of employment are established;
- explain the distinction between unfair and wrongful dismissal;
- demonstrate an awareness of how employers and employees are affected by health and safety legislation, including the consequences of a failure to comply.

The chapter has been arranged into sections based on the learning outcomes as above.

3.1 The employment relationship

Learning Outcome: To distinguish between employees and independent contractors and how the contents of a contract of employment are established.

The employment relationship arises when one person (the employee) supplies skill and labour to another (the employer) in return for payment; this may be for a fixed or indefinite period or to complete a particular job. Other legal relations may also exist between these persons at the same time, as when the employee is the director of a company or acts as the agent of the employer/principal, but these matters are dealt with elsewhere.

The relationship is primarily contractual and the rules outlined in the first three chapters relating to the formation and discharge of contracts apply equally to contracts of employment as to other types of contract. In addition to the contractual rights enjoyed by an employee, there are a number of rights which are established by statute; for example, Employment Rights Act 1996, Minimum Wage Act, Working Time Regulations and so on. These regulate specific aspects of the employment and often cannot be contracted out of, even with the consent of the employee. A breach of such statutory rights will often give rise to a claim for unfair dismissal, whereas a breach of a contractual right may give rise to a claim for both wrongful and unfair dismissal (see Sections 3.2.2–3.2.4).

The terms of employment detailing the rights and duties of the parties may come from a number of sources. Some terms, for example the wage, hours of attendance and work required, may be expressly negotiated and agreed, either orally or in written correspondence, when the employee is initially offered and accepts the job. Details may be found in a works handbook or in a notice displayed at the place of work or exceptionally, and normally for senior appointments, in one document known as a 'service agreement'. The terms of a collective agreement with a trade union may be expressly incorporated into the contract or may be implied by being observed over a period of time [*Gray, Dunn & Co. Ltd* v. *Edwards* (1980): binding effect of disciplinary procedure negotiated with union]. There are terms implied at common law in the absence of express terms to the contrary which apply generally or only to particular trades or industries, and there are terms imposed by statute which usually may not be excluded. Finally, there is today a strong European influence through EU directives and European Court decisions by which, for example, matters such as discrimination, equal pay, and health and safety have been affected.

The Employment Rights Act 1996 seeks to ensure that an employee knows what his terms are. The employer must give written notification of certain specified matters to both full-time and part-time employees within 2 months of them starting a job; this is known as the written statement of particulars of employment or statement of terms. Later changes must be notified within 1 month of taking place. The particulars must include details regarding the calculation and payment of remuneration, hours and place of work, holidays and holiday pay, incapacity for work, the length of notice which must be given and received, and disciplinary and grievance procedures. It is sufficient if reference is made to other reasonably accessible documents. Missing particulars may, if necessary, be determined by an employment tribunal. While this notification does not constitute a contract of employment, it is evidence of the contractual terms, and a heavy burden is placed upon the party who asserts that the terms differ from the written particulars [*Lee* v. *GEC Plessey Telecommunications* (1993)].

The terms of employment may be varied from time to time as when a new wage is agreed. Difficulties will only arise where one party does not accept the proposed change. An attempt to impose the change unilaterally would be a breach of contract and, if sufficiently serious, bring the contract to an end. An employee may even treat such an attempt as a constructive unfair dismissal (see Section 3.2.3). The employer may terminate the existing contract by proper notice and reissue a new one but this may also give rise to a claim for unfair dismissal. An employee who carries on working under the new terms may be deemed to have impliedly accepted them, but if he or she does so after an immediate protest, he or she may still have a remedy [*Rigby* v. *Ferodo Ltd* (1988)].

3.1.1 Employees and contractors

We have so far been considering the close and continuing relationship which exists under a contract of employment. Another form of employment relationship may arise when an independent contractor is engaged for one particular job. For example, a builder, instead of employing joiners, may engage self-employed joiners as 'labour-only sub-contractors' for the woodwork on each new house.

This practice has advantages for an employer. Income tax and national insurance contributions need not usually be deducted from wages. The independent contractor has no statutory protection in respect of sick pay, required notice period, short-time working, unfair dismissal and redundancy, and has no preferential rights over other creditors if the employer becomes insolvent. Social security provisions are different. Of special importance is the vicarious liability which an employer normally has for wrongful acts committed by employees in the course of employment, but not for those of an independent contractor. Vicarious liability will attach to an employer where an employee acting in the course of his employment commits a civil wrong. The courts will consider the wrongful act alongside the actual contract obligations of the employee, as a wrong committed outside such contract obligations, deemed as arising from 'a frolic of one's own', will not serve as a basis for employer vicarious liability. The scope for employers being so liable was extended recently in the case of *Majrowski* v. *Guy's and St Thomas's NHS Trust* (2005). Here, it was decided that even though a statutory duty was imposed on employees only, the employer could be liable where a breach of this duty occurred. An employer, whilst not generally being vicariously liable for wrongs of independent contractors, can nevertheless be so liable in some albeit few instances, for example where the employer is negligent in the selection of a contractor.

Agency workers: implied contract with end-user reinforced

The court of appeal has reinforced a legal concept which states that, in appropriate circumstances, a tribunal can find an implied contract between an agency worker and the client or end-user, even where the contract between the agency and the worker states that the worker is to be considered as employed by the agency (see *Cable & Wireless plc* v. *Muscat* (2006) 782 IRLB 14).

Mr Muscat was employed by Exodus Internet Ltd (EIL). EIL dismissed Mr Muscat but immediately engaged him as a contractor. He then continued to work for EIL as before, although he did set up a company called E-Nuff Comms Ltd to receive his pay and became responsible for his own tax and national insurance. Mr Muscat was transferred to Cable & wireless under TUPE when the takeover of EIL by Cable & Wireless took place.

After this, he continued to work as a contractor for Cable & Wireless but was later required by them to supply his services through an agency, Abraxas plc, with whom Cable & Wireless had a contract for agency services. Mr Muscat continued to supply his services through his company arrangement and E-Nuff Comms Ltd made a contract with the agency, Abraxas plc, to supply Mr Muscat's services to Cable & Wireless. This set up a triangular situation between the agency, the service provider, and the end-user. Later, Mr Muscat was told by Cable & Wireless that his services would no longer be required and he claimed unfair dismissal, naming Cable & Wireless as his employer. The case eventually reached the Court of Appeal which ruled that:

- tribunals should always consider the possibility of an implied contract of employment between the worker and the end-user where there is this triangular worker, agency, and end-user arrangement;
- on the facts of the case, there was an implied employment contract between Mr Muscat and Cable & Wireless, inferred or implied from their conduct. The fact that the worker's contract with the agency provided, as it did in this case, that the worker could not validly enter into a contract with the end-user did not prevent an implied contract from being construed from the facts of the case.

Comment. This is an important case on the status of agency workers, particularly in the sense that the agency contract specifically precluded a contractual relationship with the end-user. It must be said, however, that the case has unusual facts in that Mr Muscat was found to be an employee of the end-user before making the agency contract. It will be interesting to see how tribunals will apply this ruling in triangular cases that are more typical.

Vicarious liability

Another recent House of Lords decision, in the case of Majrowski *v.* Guy's and St Thomas' NHS Trust [2006] UKHL 34, has confirmed that employers may now be held vicariously liable for breaches of statutory duties as well as other common law duties imposed upon employees.

Mr Majrowski's original action in the Central London County Court argued that he had been harassed and bullied during the course of his employment and that Guy's and St Thomas' had breached its statutory duties under the Protection from Harassment Act 1997. Mr Majrowski had been employed by the Trust as a clinical audit coordinator and, he alleged, had been bullied, harassed and intimidated by his manager. She had been excessively critical of his work, he claimed, strict about his time-keeping and rude and abusive to him even in front of other staff.

The 1997 Act is primarily intended to deal with stalking and other activities which constitute criminal harassment: prior to this case, it was not though that it could be applied in an employment context. This judgemet, however, effectively expands the scope of vicarious liability and confirms that employers can be vicariously liable for breaches of statutory duty, provided that the actions are committed in the course of employment.

The decision in the Lords in mid-July is a worrying development, as employers could now be faced with harassment claims brought in the civil courts. Although the civil courts' costs regime may deter most employees from making such claims, the fact that there is a 6-year limitation period and no need to link the harassment to discrimination may make it an attractive option for some.

For these reasons, the courts have had to distinguish between employees and independent contractors and various tests have been developed for this purpose. The older *control* test provided that a worker was an employee if the employer had control over the manner of performance and could tell the worker not only what to do but also how to do it. The test, by itself, became unsatisfactory and unrealistic with the increase in the size of firms and the technical skills involved, and was replaced by the 'right to control'. An alternative *organisation* or *integration* test has also been used, particularly for professional people where there is no right of control over the method of performance. It is based upon the concept that an employee is an integral part of the organisation, whereas a contractor performs work for the organisation but remains outside it. More generally today, the wider *economic reality* or *multiple* test will be used. This also brings into consideration such matters as the right to engage, suspend and dismiss, the method of payment, whether statutory deductions for tax and social security are made from wages, whether hours of work are fixed and whether the worker provides tools and equipment. What the parties call themselves is relevant but not conclusive. The courts have recently established that an important factor in determining whether a worker is an employee or an independent contractor is the requirement to give personal service. If the worker is permitted to delegate the work to someone else rather than to perform the work personally, this is generally thought to be inconsistent with a contract of employment [*Express and Echo* v. *Tanton* (2000)].

Examples

In *Cassidy* v. *Ministry of Health* (1951), a resident surgeon in a hospital was held to be an employee, so that the hospital was liable for his negligence.

In *Hillyer* v. *St Bartholomew's Hospital* (1909), the claimant chose a consultant, who merely used the facilities of this hospital. The consultant was an independent contractor.

In *Ferguson* v. *John Dawson & Partners Ltd* (1976), a labour-only sub-contractor in the building industry was held to be an employee for occupational safety reasons, so that the builder owed him a duty of care. This could be so even if he claimed to be self-employed for tax purposes. The court emphasised that it was more concerned with reality than with labels.

3.1.2 The terms of employment

3.1.3 Wages

The amount of the wage may be fixed by negotiation, or depend upon a collective agreement, or be implied from custom or practice or stem from a combination of these. Very exceptionally, in the absence of agreement, it will be implied that a reasonable wage will be paid.

The National Minimum Wages Act 1998 imposed minimum levels of pay that have subsequently been amended. Most recently, the National Minimum Wage Regulations 1999 (Amendment) Regulations 2006, which came into force on the 1 October 2006 has increased the previous minimum wage level. The rate was increased from £5.35p to £5.52p. For workers between the ages of 18 and 21 the minimum rate rose from £4.45p to £4.60p. 'The development rate applicable for 16 to 17 year olds is £3.40p, raised from £3.30p. Some classes of persons can be excluded from qualifying for the identified minimum sums. The government looks to provide fair minimum standards of pay. As a result of recommendations of the Low Pay Commission the following are the rates applicable from 1 October 2008,

£5.73p per hour for workers aged 22 and over
£4.77p per hour for workers aged 18–21
£3.53p per hour for workers aged 16–17'.

The Employment Act 2008 will give Enforcement Officers the power to demand employers make good totally any underpayment but also pay a penalty of up to 50% of the underpayment.

The Wages Act 1986, now largely replaced by the Employment Rights Act 1996, contained detailed provisions regarding deductions from wages, which applied to all workers. Deductions for income tax and national insurance must be made and other deductions, for example for a pension scheme, provision of clothing or bad timekeeping, may be made if agreed in the contract of employment or if the employee gives written consent in advance. A unilateral reduction in wages is treated in the same way as a deduction. Complaints of unauthorised deductions may be made to an employment tribunal.

A special provision for retail workers restricts deductions for stock losses and cash shortages to 10 per cent of gross pay in any payment period. Employees generally are entitled to an itemised written pay statement on or before each payment showing the gross amount, the amount and purposes of all deductions and the net amount to be paid. This does not apply to employers with less than twenty employees nor to employees working less than 8 hours per week.

Whether wages must be paid during absence through illness depends upon the facts of each case [*Mears* v. *Safecar Security Ltd* (1982): security guard's particulars did not mention payment and he was held not to be entitled]. This question should now be covered by the written particulars given on engagement but, in any event, there is a right to payment during statutory suspension for an occupational disease and during absence due to pregnancy. More generally, an employer must usually pay statutory sick pay during the first 28 weeks of illness and small employers can recover this from the government; this is paid at two weekly rates depending on average earnings. Longer periods of illness may give an entitlement to incapacity (formerly invalidity) benefit. The contract of employment may provide that these social security benefits shall be deducted from wages paid by the employer.

3.1.4 Other duties of employers

In addition to the payment of wages, an employer owes certain implied common law obligations to his employees in the absence of express agreement to the contrary. Thus, there is a duty to provide work where the employee's remuneration depends upon the work done or if the employee needs work to maintain reputation, skills or familiarity with technical change [*Breach* v. *Epsylon Industries Ltd* (1976): need for senior engineer to keep up to date]. A connected duty is the making of 'guarantee payments' when work is not provided and employees are laid off or on short time. This may be a contractual amount, perhaps under a collective agreement, but this must not be less generous than a statutory minimum which has detailed rules for determining entitlement and calculating the payment.

Employers owe a duty, both as an implied term in the contract and under the tort of negligence, to provide a reasonably safe system of work and to comply with all statutory safety provisions. Failure to do so may lead to criminal liability, and to civil liability, if an employee is thereby injured.

If an employee reasonably and necessarily incurs liabilities and expenses in the performance of the work, it is implied that the employer will indemnify and reimburse him.

An employee is entitled to a minimum 28 days statutory holiday. Further, unless the employee signs a voluntary opt out, the most hours of working cannot exceed 48 per week.

Finally, there is today a more general implied duty upon an employer to behave reasonably and responsibly towards employees. Breach of this duty could take many different forms, for example pressurising an employee to take risks and unreasonable demotion. If such arbitrary and inconsistent action is sufficiently serious, it may constitute constructive unfair dismissal [*Bracebridge Engineering Ltd* v. *Darby* (1990): sexual harassment by supervisor for whose acts employer is vicariously liable].

A corporate duty of care is owed under the Corporate Manslaughter and Corporate Homicide Act 2006. Under this legislation, an organisation can be guilty of corporate manslaughter where a failing by senior management causes death. It must also be established that the organisation failed to satisfy a relevant duty of care owed to the deceased. This duty of care can be owed by an employer to an employee, but can also arise on the basis of the organisation being, e.g. a supplier of goods or services.

It must be mentioned that there is normally no duty to give a testimonial or reference when an employee is seeking another post. An exception exists where the Financial Service Authority requires a reference. If one is given, the employer must be careful and honest. Otherwise, he may be liable to the employee for defamation or negligence and to the prospective new employer for deceit or negligence [*Spring* v. *Guardian Royal Exchange* (1994)]. Likewise, there is no implied contractual right to smoke [*Dryden* v. *Greater Glasgow Health Board* (1992): nurse who resigned after hospital imposed smoking ban was not constructively dismissed].

A duty of a somewhat different type was placed upon employers from 1997. They must now check that potential employees are legally entitled to work and remain in the United Kingdom. The Immigration, Asylum and Nationality Act 2006 introduced provisions aimed at preventing illegal working. A civil penalties scheme under which employers can be liable to a fine of up to £2,000 was established. Also under this Act where an employer knowingly employs persons who are prohibited from working can be subject to a maximum 2 years imprisonment and unlimited fines.

3.1.5 Statutory rights of employees

In addition to the common law duties of employers outlined above, legislation has imposed further statutory duties upon employers in recent years. These tend to apply only to particular types of employee or in special situations. Rights are thereby conferred upon employees, and the more important of these will now be considered. The more general rights relating to dismissal will be considered later.

The provisions of the Sex Discrimination Acts 1975–86, while applying equally to discrimination against men or on grounds of marriage, are designed mainly to protect women and, for convenience, will be considered in these terms. It is generally unlawful for employers to discriminate on grounds of sex in advertising a post, engaging employees, or in the terms offered. During employment, it is unlawful to discriminate in promotion, training, transfer or other benefits, or in selection for dismissal, short-time or other detriments. An employer will discriminate against a woman directly if he treats her less favourably than he would a man, or indirectly, if he applies some requirement or condition that men are more likely to meet, unless the job demands this special requirement [*Bullock* v. *Alice Otley School* (1993)].

The Sex Discrimination (Amendment of Legislation) Regulations 2008 provide further protection for the employee with the elements for employer liability based on sexual harassment identified. Discrimination based on pregnancy or maternity is defined. Also, under the Regulations, the employee on maternity leave will receive more benefits such as pension rights, insurance rights and annual leave entitlements the distinction between ordinary maternity leave and additional maternity leave is removed.

Jobs which demand authentic male characteristics (e.g. actor) are excluded, but this does not extend to jobs demanding physical strength [*Shields* v. *Coomes Ltd* (1979): possible need for male clerk to deal with trouble in betting shop did not justify higher pay]. Decency or privacy might require selection because of physical contact or living together. Constraints may be put upon women of child-bearing age and upon pregnant women with respect to certain jobs. Special rules apply to ministers of religion, police and prison officers. The retirement age and pension rights must not differ in private pension schemes [*Barber* v. *Guardian*

Royal Exchange Assurance (1990), a European Court decision, but this does not yet apply to state provision; however, the government has announced that equalisation of pension provision will be introduced to the state scheme in due course]. A final exception is that minor distinctions may be ignored. [*Peake* v. *Automotive Products Ltd* (1977): women employees allowed to leave 5 minutes early to avoid rush]. Discrimination can occur before or after the employment relationship exists as well as during the period of the employment. Where an applicant claiming sexual discrimination shows there is a case to answer, the employer then has the burden of proving that no discrimination has occurred.

A number of allowable exceptions exist which an employer can rely on to justify an employee receiving less favourable treatment. It is where a 'genuine occupational qualification', as identified in originally s7 Sex Discrimination Act 1975 or s5 Race Relations Act 1976, exists that a discrimination claim will not succeed. Such genuine occupational qualifications include:

The nature of the job requires persons of a particular sex to carry it out because of physiology.

Special care or supervision is needed in a single sex establishment, where it would be unreasonable for an employer to have to build separate premises for members of a particular sex with a live-in job, and in welfare or education where the work involves personal services and can be carried out more effectively by a particular type of person.

Where discrimination is established, remedies available are a declaration that the individual employees' rights have been infringed and/or a compensation payment for pecuniary, physical and/or mental harm.

The Equal Opportunities Commission, with wide powers of investigation, has the task of keeping the legislation under review and promoting equal opportunity. Now, under the Equality Act 2006, the Equal Opportunities Commission has been merged with the Commission for Racial Equality and the Disability Rights Commission to form the Commission for Equality and Human Rights. This body will oversee application of law relating to discrimination on grounds of sex, religion or belief and age. The Commission has a further role in promoting human rights. Complaints are normally heard by employment tribunals which may declare rights, recommend that the cause of the complaint be remedied and/or award compensation (since 1993 without limit). If necessary, a County Court injunction may be obtained against a defaulting employer.

The Equal Pay Act 1970, as amended, seeks to prevent discrimination with remuneration, holidays and sickness pay. Following decisions of the European Court, it is now provided that the contract of a woman employee shall contain an 'equality clause' whereby her terms of employment shall be no less favourable than those of a man doing like work of equal value. Value is to be decided in terms of effort, skill and decision-making, assessed, if necessary, by a job-evaluation study [*Hayward* v. *Cammell Laird Ltd* (1988): work of cook rated as of equal value to that of painter, joiner and heating engineer]. An employer may, however, be able to successfully oppose an equal pay claim where the variation in pay is based on a material factor other than the person's sex. Any claim must be commenced within 6 months, subject to the Equal Pay Act 1970 (Amendment) Regulations 2003.

The Employment Rights Act 1996, as amended, gives minimum rights to women in the event of maternity. These may be extended by contract but not reduced. It is automatically unfair to dismiss a woman because of pregnancy and reasonable time off must be given for antenatal care. There are detailed rules providing for maternity leave, statutory maternity pay, and for later return to work. The Employment Act 2002 built on family-friendly measures introduced under the Employment Relations Act 1999. Changes relating to maternity, paternity and adoption leave and pay were introduced. Sections 17 and 18 of this Act altered the ordinary paid maternity leave to 26 weeks from 18 weeks. This entitlement is available irrespective of the amount of time worked for the employer. A basic entitlement for all is extended for those with continuous employment of 1 year. Both men and women employees are entitled to be absent from work where they have or expect to have responsibility for a child under the Maternity and Parental Leave etc. Regulations 1999. Such employees must have completed at least 1 year continuous service. Further, absence from work is determined by the child fitting one of a number of categories identified. Amendments to these Regulations have been made under the National Minimum Wage Regulations 1999 (Amendment) Regulations 2006. The amendments include extending the notice an employee must give the employer of an intention to return to work after maternity leave. The notice period is extended from 28 days to 8 weeks. Maternity pay is extended to 12 months from April 2010. Also, paternity leave and pay will be extended from this date.

Further rights exist against discrimination for race or trade union membership. It is unlawful under the Race Relations Act 1976 for an employer to discriminate against employees on the grounds of colour, race, ethnic or national origins. The rules and procedure, covered also by a code of practice, are very similar to those applying to sex discrimination. It is also unlawful to discriminate against an employee for joining an independent trade union (one not controlled by the employer), for taking part in its activities or for refusing to join a union. Dismissal for any of these reasons is automatically unfair and compensation may be claimed even if the employer's action falls short of dismissal. The Disability Discrimination Act 1995 makes it unlawful for an employer to treat a disabled person less fairly in the field of employment without a justifiable reason; small employers with less than twenty staff are excluded.

Adding to the existing legislation dealing with discrimination in the workplace is the Employment Equality (Age) Regulations 2006 and Amendment Regulations 2008. These Regulations apply to all employers irrespective of size or type of organisation, and make it unlawful to discriminate against an employee on the basis of age. Direct or indirect discrimination on the basis of age, relating to young and old employees, are prohibited. A number of specific exceptions to the prohibitions are identified in the Regulations. Unlawful discrimination on the basis of age can arise not merely in relation to appointment, but through all aspects of the employment. The Regulations contain information of additional specific aspects of employment where discrimination can arise, and where the employees' rights to fair treatment are protected. These include pay and benefits, training and promotion. An employment tribunal will hear complaints of discrimination on the basis of age. The remedies available do not differ from those applicable for other forms of discrimination.

The Age Discrimination Regulations follow the format of the earlier Religion or Belief and Sexual Orientation Regulations, defining direct and indirect discrimination on the grounds of age (reg. 3), discrimination by way of victimisation (reg. 4), instructions to discriminate against a third party (reg. 5), and harassment on the grounds of age (reg. 6). Regulation 7 makes the above actions by an employer unlawful.

There are a number of exceptions, for example, it is not unlawful to discriminate on the grounds of age 'in the arrangements he (the employer) makes for the purposes of determining to whom he should offer employment' or 'by refusing to offer, or deliberately not offering, . . .employment' if the applicant is either older than the employer's normal retirement age or, if no such age exists, the age of 65, or if the applicant at the time of application is within 6 months of such age.

Regulation 8 concerns 'genuine occupational requirements'; the employment of, the promotion, transfer to or training for, or the dismissal of an employee on the grounds of age is not unlawful in a situation where, 'having regard to the nature of the employment or the context in which it is carried out, the possessing of the characteristic related to age is a genuine and determining occupational requirement'.

An exception is also made, in reg. 28, for positive action (the affording of access to training or the encouragement of particular age groups to take advantage of opportunities) where it reasonably appears to the employer that certain age groups are presently disadvantaged.

As with other similar legislation, the employer will be vicariously liable for unlawful acts or deliberate omissions of his employees carried out in the course of their employment (reg. 25) – and bear in mind that the phrase 'in the course of their employment' is, certainly in discrimination cases, interpreted more broadly than in much of the body of tort case law (following the Court of Appeal ruling in *Jones* v. *Tower Boot Co Ltd* [1997] IRLR 168).

There are various other statutory rights. Thus, employees have a right to time off work for trade union duties, training as a safety representative, to look for new work upon redundancy, and to carry out certain specified public duties, such as magistrate, local councillor or tribunal member. There is a right to full pay for up to 26 weeks if suspended on medical grounds after working with dangerous materials and no suitable alternative work is offered.

If an employee is a willing party to an illegal contract of employment, for example where payment is made to evade tax unlawfully, the contract will be unenforceable. Even if the employee is a reluctant party or does not realise the arrangements are illegal, statutory rights may then be lost.

3.1.6 Implied duties of employees

As well as rights, employees owe implied duties towards the employer. A serious breach may justify summary dismissal (see later).

Thus, the employee must work personally within the terms of the contract and cannot delegate the work to a substitute. Reasonable care must be taken in the performance of the work, and such care and skill as the employee professed to have must be exercised. This duty would extend to care of the employer's property and care towards both fellow workers and third parties. If vicarious liability is imposed upon the employer, the latter may seek an indemnity from the employee. [*Lister* v. *Romford Ice and Cold Storage Co* (1957)].

All reasonable orders which are within the terms of employment must be obeyed. Disobedience is only justified if the order is illegal, likely to prove dangerous or wholly unreasonable [*Morrish* v. *Henlys* (*Folkestone*) *Ltd* (1973): dismissal unjustified when driver refused order to make false expense claims].

It is also said that an employee must give loyal and faithful service, a somewhat vague expression which may apply to many different types of situation, even to conduct in the employee's own time. For example, an employee may be restrained from spare time work for himself or for another if that work competes with and damages his employer. [*Hivac*

Ltd v. *Park Royal Scientific Instruments Ltd* (1946)]; perhaps also, if the work is of a different nature, if it renders the employee less capable for his usual work. An employee also has a duty not to disclose trade secrets or confidential information acquired during the course of employment and, as with an agent, must account for any unauthorised benefit which accrues to him except where it is customary to receive such a benefit or it is of a trivial nature. [*Reading* v. *Attorney General* (1951)].

Patent rights normally belong to the employee/inventor even if the invention is made in the course of employment. By the Patents Act 1977, however, the employer may claim ownership if the invention arose from normal duties, from work which might reasonably be expected to produce an invention or where the employee had a special obligation to further the employer's undertaking. Even then the employee may still claim a fair share of the monies derived from a patent which proves to be of outstanding benefit to the employer. On the other hand, in the absence of agreement, copyright of written work produced during employment normally belongs to the employer. [*Stevenson, Jordan and Harrison Ltd* v. *MacDonald and Evans* (1952)].

Some duties may continue after employment has ended. There may be a valid restraint of trade clause in the contract which restrains the employee from certain future employment. The case of *Countrywide Assured Financial Services Ltd* v. *Pollard* (2004) provides illustration that restrictive covenants are prima facie void. They will, however, be respected to the minimum extent necessary in order to protect a recognised interest of the employer. It was decided in this case that Mr. Pollard, on leaving his employer, an estate agent, was not bound by a restrictive covenant preventing him from working for another estate agent for 3 months. This was because he was subject to a further restrictive covenant that prevented him from soliciting his former employers for 6 months. The duty of secrecy may continue even in the absence of a specific contractual clause but it may be prudent to insert such a clause. As a general rule, an ex-employee can be restrained from using confidential information but not acquired skills. [*Faccenda Chicken Ltd* v. *Fowler* (1986)].

3.2 Notice and dismissal

Learning Outcome: To explain the distinction between unfair and wrongful dismissal.

Many rights and obligations, both common law and statutory, may arise when the contract of employment is brought to an end. It is this aspect of employment law which tends to give rise to the most disputes.

The Employment Act 2002 contained minimum dismissal and disciplinary and grievance procedures to apply to all employers and employees. This legislation identified an obligatory three-step procedure to be followed that is repealed by the Employment Act 2008. Further changes introduced in the 2008 Act include a revised ACAS Code of Practice that extends its role as conciliator. Further, what is deemed 'fair and reasonable' will be the determining factor in the decision-making of employment tribunals. Guidance on principles to apply in disciplinary and grievance procedures will emerge from non-statutory origins.

3.2.1 Termination by notice

While a contract for a fixed time or a particular job will normally end automatically on the expiration of the time or the completion of the job, it is more usual for employment to be for an indefinite period. Either party may then end it by giving notice to the other, and the length of notice required is frequently an express term in the contract. Even in a fixed-term contract, there may be a term entitling either party to terminate earlier by notice.

If there is no prior agreement on the notice period, reasonable notice must be given. At common law, reasonable notice depended upon such matters as trade practice, length of service, and periods by which wages are calculated. Generally, the more important the post, the longer will be a reasonable period.

These rules are now subject to statutory minimum periods of notice under the Employment Rights Act 1996. After 1 month's employment, the employee has a right to at least 1 week's notice. Thereafter, there is entitlement to 1 week for each year of service up to a maximum of 12 weeks. On the other hand, the employer, after 1 month, is always entitled to 1 week's notice if the employee leaves. The employee is safeguarded during the notice period by payment at the normal rate.

Either party may waive the right to notice. Thus, the employer, who has no obligation to provide work, may pay wages in lieu of notice if he no longer wishes to have the employee on the premises and has no grounds for summary dismissal; serving out notice at home is commonly referred to as 'garden leave'. Even if proper notice is given or payment is made in lieu, the employee may still claim for unfair dismissal or redundancy.

3.2.2 Summary dismissal and wrongful dismissal

If the employee commits a sufficiently serious breach of the terms of employment, the employer may dismiss him without notice. The grounds that will justify summary or instant dismissal will depend upon the nature of the misconduct and the nature of the job. In some cases, misconduct in the employee's own time will be sufficient if this is relevant to the position held. The dismissal may be justified by disobedience of a lawful order which the employer is competent to give, provided that it relates to a serious matter and is not perhaps an isolated occurrence, such as a single act of disobedience; likewise, if the employee lacks the competence or qualification he claimed to have on engagement or loses a qualification which is essential for the job. One careless act of negligence will normally be insufficient but if it is very serious, repeated, or follows warnings then dismissal may be justified. In general, any serious misbehaviour which is inconsistent with the position held and the proper performance of the employee's duties will be enough. This may include immorality, persistent drunkenness, physical assault, dishonesty, breach of employer's rules, or a breach of the duty of good faith.

If an employee is dismissed without proper notice or justification, he may sue for wrongful dismissal. This is essentially an action of breach of contract. Damages may be recovered based upon the wages that would have been earned had proper notice been given, subject to the duty to mitigate by seeking other employment (see later).

An employee has a corresponding right to leave employment immediately in the event of serious misconduct on the part of the employer, for example by failure to comply with health and safety provisions. [*British Aircraft Corporation* v. *Austin* (1978): failure to provide suitable safety goggles constituted constructive dismissal as a basis for a claim for unfair dismissal]. Otherwise, the employer has a right of action if the employee leaves without notice but, in practice, such actions are rarely worth bringing.

Examples

Laws v. *London Chronicle Ltd* (1959) illustrates the general point that an isolated act of disobedience will have to be quite serious before it can justify instant dismissal. In the present case, a secretary walked out of an acrimonious meeting in support of her immediate boss, but against the orders of a senior director. This single act of disobedience did not justify her immediate dismissal, which was wrongful.

Morrish v. *Henlys (Folkstone) Ltd* (1973) held that disobedience of an unlawful instruction to falsify his expenses claim did not justify dismissal of the employee concerned.

The duties of competence and skill required can vary immensely depending on the nature of the job. Some issues are fairly straightforward, however, as in *Tayside Regional Council* v. *McIntosh* (1982), where a driver who had lost his licence was rightfully dismissed.

The duties of care required can vary, but are owed by all. An isolated act of negligence will rarely justify instant dismissal, but even here, there can be exceptions: in *Taylor* v. *Alidair Ltd* (1978), a single, very negligent (and therefore very dangerous) landing by the pilot of a passenger aeroplane did justify his instant dismissal.

The standards of honesty and good faith required are high, especially for professionally qualified persons acting as such in employment. The duties are owed by all employees: in *Sinclair* v. *Neighbour* (1967), an employee borrowed secretly from the shop till. He repaid the next day, but he was rightfully dismissed.

3.2.3 Unfair dismissal

This is a wider statutory remedy which may be used whether or not notice is given and which is now governed by the Employment Rights Act 1996 as amended by the Employment Act 2008. As a general rule, it applies only after continuous employment for a qualifying period of 1 year. Part-time employment is now enough since the former 16 and 8 hours per week limits have been abolished.

Continuous employment is an important concept which is also used to determine entitlement to other statutory rights, for example redundancy and notice period. There must be continuity, but this will not be broken in certain specified instances which include absence for maternity up to 40 weeks or for sickness or injury up to 26 weeks, stoppage due to a strike, a temporary stoppage other than a strike, and absence such as sabbatical leave. Stoppage due to a strike will not affect continuity but, unlike in the other instances, the time spent on strike does not count towards the qualifying period. There is normally a presumption in favour of continuity unless the employer can prove otherwise.

Statutory protection is given to preserve continuity when it would otherwise be broken by a change of employer. For example, service with the old owner of a business will count if the new owner buys the business and the same trade or business continues as before, but not if it is merely the premises and other assets which are transferred. [*Dallow Industrial Properties Ltd* v. *Else* (1967): no continuity when employee remained as caretaker for new employer but premises were then empty]. There is no interruption of service when a company is taken over or if an employee is transferred to another associated company in the same group, and it is always possible for a new employer to agree that service with the earlier employer shall count. Since 1993, these rules apply to all undertakings and not to commercial undertakings only.

A person claiming unfair dismissal must obviously have been dismissed, either actually, with or without notice; by failure to renew a fixed-term contract; or constructively, by the employer's misconduct pressurising the employee into leaving. There is no dismissal if the contract is frustrated by illness or military conscription. Whether or not illness will frustrate the contract, depends upon many matters including length of previous employment and expected future length, nature of the job, nature and length of the illness, and any need for a replacement. The essential question to be asked is whether a reasonable employer could be expected to wait any longer for the sick employee to return to work.

An employee who is dismissed after at least 1 year's service may request a written statement of the reasons for dismissal and the employer must supply this within 14 days. This document may then be used as evidence in any proceedings. If the employer unreasonably refuses or gives inadequate or untrue reasons, the employee may complain to an employment tribunal which may declare what it considers to be the true reasons. Further, following a written request by the employee for reasons for their dismissal, if the employer refuses or fails to provide such, the employee will automatically be entitled to 2 weeks' compensation pay.

Certain reasons are deemed to be automatically unfair. This will be so if an employee is dismissed for acting properly in connection with health and safety issues. Also, if the employee is dismissed for joining or refusing to join an independent trade union, for taking part in union activities at an appropriate time or for acting properly in connection with health and safety risks. This will also apply if an employee is selected for redundancy either because of trade union activities or membership, or contrary to a customary or agreed arrangement without good reason. It is automatically unfair to dismiss on the grounds of pregnancy unless the woman is incapable of doing the work or it would be illegal for her to do it, and suitable alternative work, if available, has been offered. A more recent addition is dismissal for bringing proceedings against an employer to enforce a statutory right; an employee who acts in good faith is protected even if no right exists. The importance of all of these situations lies in the fact that a remedy may be sought without a qualifying period of employment being required.

All other reasons are presumed unfair unless the employer can prove otherwise. Two requirements must be satisfied. First, the employer must show that the principal reason falls within one of five categories:

1. the employee was incapable of doing the work through lack of skill, illness, lack of qualifications, and so on;
2. misconduct;
3. genuine redundancy;
4. contravention of a statute (e.g. loss of a driving licence or work permit);
5. some other substantial reason (e.g. marriage to a competitor).

Second, the tribunal must itself decide whether, having regard to equity and the substantial merits of the case, the employer acted reasonably in dismissing the employee. Proceedings can be determined without a hearing under Employment Act 2008 s4 where all parties agree, or a party against whom proceedings are brought does not respond as required in preliminary communications. Such matters as whether the employer has followed prescribed disciplinary procedures and complied with Advisory, Conciliation and Arbitration Service (ACAS) codes of practice by, for example, issuing previous warnings, will be examined. Length of service and disciplinary records, and whether dismissal was a reasonable response by the employer, will also be relevant here. Unless both of these requirements are satisfied, the dismissal will be unfair.

In determining if an employer has acted fairly in the procedure that was followed which led to the dismissal, the tribunal can consider factors that include: generally the fairness of any hearing held, the procedure in relation to the providing of warnings, the use of a common process for all employees, the evidence used at the hearing, the right to have a representative, the suitability of any other form of discipline short of dismissal and the past record of the employee including the length of the employment. The Employment Act 2008 provides for a new ACAS Code of Practice that will come into force in April 2009. Employers who fail to comply with Code recommendations will be liable to pay up to a further 25% compensation.

Under the Employment Act 2002 an obligation is attached to employers requiring a letter containing information of the alleged misconduct to be sent to the employee. The content must identify that which forms the basis of any dismissal or disciplinary action being pursued. The employee must be invited to a meeting to discuss the situation. Any dismissal will automatically be deemed unfair if these requirements are not satisfied. The importance of this procedure in helping both parties to understand relevant issues and the respective views was seen in *Shergold's Fieldway Medical Centre [2006]*. But equally in this case, the need to avoid undue technicality was acknowledged. Case law including *Draper* v. *Mears Ltd [2006]* and *Alexander* v. *Bridgen Enterprises Ltd [2006]* have established that the letter sent by the employer need only identify the relevant issues, giving the grounds for and the basis of the grounds for the desired disciplinary steps. This must, however, be sufficient to allow the employee to provide a positive and informed response.

Special situations are also covered. Thus, if a Minister of the Crown certifies that the dismissal was to safeguard the national interest, the tribunal must dismiss the complaint. Similarly, a tribunal cannot intervene if an employer dismisses *all* of the employees involved in an official strike or other industrial action, nor if there is selective re-engagement, provided that 3 months have elapsed. [*Highland Fabricators Ltd* v. *McLaughin* (1984)]. Temporary workers engaged to cover for an employee absent for pregnancy or for statutory suspension due to occupational illness will also receive no protection if later dismissed, unless for a reason which is automatically unfair, such as pregnancy.

Complaints of unfair dismissal must normally be pursued through an employment tribunal within 3 months, though, exceptionally, this period may be extended. An attempt is first made to reach a settlement with the assistance of a conciliation officer of ACAS. The Employment Act 2008 extends the duty of ACAS to conciliate through until judgment is delivered by the tribunal.

Compensation awarded to a successful employee is assessed in several stages. There is first a *basic award* calculated, as with redundancy, on age and length of service. This may be augmented by a *compensatory award* which was increased under the Employment Rights (Increase of Limits) Order 2008 from a previous maximum of £63,000 to £66,200. There may be a reduction if loss is not mitigated or if the employee's conduct contributed to the dismissal. Section 123(1) of the Employment Rights Act 1996 provides that compensation payable 'shall be such amount as the tribunal considers just and equitable *in all* the circumstances … .' In *Dunnachie* v. *Kingston upon Hull City Council* (2004), the House of Lords held that this did not relate to the range of grounds of heads of loss, but that the award is 'subject to the statutory minimum'; the specific aspect of the claim before the court related to injury to feelings. The tribunal may order reinstatement or re-engagement if this is practicable and, if the employer refuses to comply, further compensation by way of a *special award* or an *additional award* may be added. Appeals from decisions of employment tribunals lie to the Employment Appeal Tribunal.

There are very limited exclusions from the unfair dismissal provisions. They do not apply to employees over the normal retirement age (except where the dismissal is automatically unfair) nor to a few occupations such as police officers. Any attempt to contract out is void except where this is done by written agreement before the expiry of a fixed-term contract for 1 year or more or where an alternative procedure, at least as beneficial, is approved by the Secretary of State.

3.2.4 Which remedy?

As we have seen above, there are now two possible remedies for an employee who has been dismissed. First, there is the older and today's more rare common law remedy for wrongful dismissal, in effect for breach of contract by the employer, which was pursued only through the courts. Second, there is the more recent statutory claim for unfair dismissal which will be heard by an employment tribunal. These remedies must be carefully distinguished.

Unfair dismissal is more commonly used today. It is wider in that it covers dismissal with notice and the failure to renew certain fixed-term contracts. Early attempts at conciliation are prescribed. Employment tribunal proceedings tend to be more simple, quicker, less formal and less expensive. In consequence, tribunals have now been given jurisdiction also to award damages for wrongful dismissal but, unlike in the courts, there is a limit to the amount that may be awarded. On the other hand, actions for wrongful dismissal have not been superseded and may be more appropriate in certain cases. There is no requirement for a 1-year qualifying period of continuous employment which normally applies to unfair dismissal claims, nor are there excluded classes of employees. Actions are only barred after 6 years and not 3 months. The remedy may be more advantageous for those in senior positions who are entitled to lengthy periods of notice, since damages are unlimited and not subject to a maximum amount.

A final difference arises when an employee is dismissed for possibly inadequate reasons and the employer then discovers more serious misconduct. In an action for wrongful dismissal, evidence of these subsequent discoveries would be admissible as part of the employer's defence. [*Boston Deep Sea Fishing & Ice Co* v. *Ansell* (1888): dismissal justified by evidence of later discovery of receipt of secret commissions]. In a claim for unfair dismissal, evidence of such discoveries made after notice has been given or before internal appeal procedures have been exhausted is admissible. However, anything discovered after this when employment has ended may only be used in assessing, and therefore reducing, the award. [*Devis and Sons Ltd* v. *Atkins* (1977): dismissal for disobedience, dishonesty discovered later].

3.3 Occupational safety

Learning Outcome: To demonstrate an awareness of how employers and employees are affected by health and safety legislation, including the consequences of a failure to comply.

3.3.1 Legislative controls

The common law was not directly concerned with preventing occupational accidents, but instead, principally through the tort of negligence, provided compensation for the victims of such occurrences. Preventive measures have come through legislation, slowly at first, and in a piecemeal fashion, with specific statutes directed at particular industries and particular types of industrial premises and processes.

The Health and Safety at Work, Act 1974 (HSWA) marked an important step forward. Additional statutory obligations regarding safety were introduced and applied uniformly for the first time to almost all work situations. Increased use was to be made of codes of practice. Older statutes, notably the Factories Act 1961, have been largely replaced by regulations made under the HSWA 1974. The administrative machinery was improved.

The HSWA 1974 imposed a general duty not only upon employers but also on those in control of premises, manufacturers, suppliers, the self-employed and employees. The duty covers the health and safety of both, employees and other people who may be in the workplace. It is a duty to take such measures with respect to materials, people and methods of working as are reasonably practicable in order to ensure safety. Breach of these duties is a criminal offence only and cannot give rise to a civil action. Maximum penalties that can be imposed by the courts for certain health and safety offences are increased under the Health and Safety (Offences) Act 2008.

More recent changes emanating from an attempt to harmonise health and safety requirements across the European Union means that the law here has been in a state of flux. Six directives became the first six regulations (the 'six-pack') in 1992. Made under the HSWA 1974, and, supplemented by codes of practice, these have come gradually into effect down to 1996 as existing workplaces made any necessary changes. Existing statutes, such as the Factories Act 1961 and the Offices, Shops and Railway Premises Act 1963, have, over the same period, been replaced.

Central to the new structure are the Management of Health and Safety at Work Regulations 1992. A duty is imposed upon employers to make a suitable and sufficient assessment of the risks likely to arise to health and safety. Appropriate measures must then be taken to eliminate or reduce these risks or, as a last resort, issue personal protective equipment. Other provisions cover safety training, the issue of comprehensible and relevant information to employees, and responsibility for shared workplaces – such as when a number of sub-contractors are working on a building site. A duty is also imposed on employees to cooperate and take reasonable care for the safety of themselves and others.

The other five regulations relate to the provision and use of work equipment, personal protective equipment, manual handling operations, display screen equipment, and the workplace. Many of the requirements included already existed, but they have now been consolidated and applied generally. A detailed scheme for health and safety applying to all workplaces has now therefore largely replaced the previous patchwork of assorted enactments.

The general health and safety duties of employers

***Employers Law*, November 2003**
This article is an extract from XpertHR employment law reference manual (www.xperthr.co.uk). Reprinted with permission of Reed Business information

Duties to employees

Health and Safety at Work Act 1974 (HSWA) is the core piece of legislation concerning health and safety, and under it, various health and safety regulations have been enacted.

Some of these regulations, such as the Management of Health and Safety at Work Regulations 1999 (MHSWR), have a general application to all workplaces and work activities. Others may be sector- or work-activity specific.

Regulations may set minimum standards for employers to follow, determined on the basis of what is 'reasonably practicable' or impose absolute duties, such as a requirement to fence off, with a guard or other protective measure, dangerous machinery.

Breaches of health and safety obligations by an employer can lead to occupational injuries, diseases and deaths to employees and even to members of the public who might be affected by the employer's operation. Such breaches can give rise to:

- enforcement action by the Health & Safety Executive;
- civil claims on the part of employees and others;
- employment tribunal claims from employees;
- criminal sanction against individual employees, directors and other senior officers, the owners of the business and, if that business is a body corporate, the body corporate itself.

There is a general duty on every employer under the HSWA, s.2 'to ensure, so far as is reasonably practicable, the health, safety and welfare at work of all his employees'.

What is 'reasonably practicable' in any given situation involves the employer balancing the risk of injury against the sacrifice involved in taking safety measures to eliminate or reduce the risk. If there is a gross disproportion between them, the risk being insignificant compared to the sacrifice, then compliance will not be reasonably practicable. The employer must make a judgment as to whether or not the safety measures should be implemented.

Many factors might be taken into consideration by the employer including the time, trouble or cost of implementing a particular safety measure.

However, cost in itself will not be an attractive or successful defence for not taking a particular measure, where the risk of injury is disproportionately high compared to the cost.

The Health and Safety Commission, acting through the Health and Safety Executive and its inspectorate, is responsible for the enforcement of the HSWA 1974 and its related legislation. The inspectors have wide powers of entry and investigation, and may issue improvement notices requiring a defaulter to remedy the specified contravention of the legislation within a stated period. More serious offences may result in a prohibition notice ordering the cessation of certain activities until the breach has been remedied. As a last resort, the factory occupier may face a criminal prosecution.

Two other duties of the occupier must be mentioned. Records must be kept of such matters as the required testing of equipment and of more serious accidents which must be notified to the inspector. The occupier is also required to set up a safety committee if requested by safety representatives nominated by a trade union.

Risk assessments

The Management of Health and Safety at Work Regulations 1999 (MHSWR) require all employers to carry out a hazard analysis study of their business operation, identify risks through the appointment of competent persons, analyse them as to their degree of seriousness and put in place appropriate protective and preventative measures to guard against them.

There are many other regulations that deal with the requirement to carry out risk assessments and put in place appropriate protective and preventative measures in relation to specified hazards or workplaces.

However, the MHSWR are of fundamental importance in health and safety law. Most of the remaining legislative provisions, including other regulations made pursuant to the EC Framework Directive (known as the six-pack), should be read in conjunction with them. In any event, in many respects, the various sets of regulations overlap.

Each set of regulations will usually have an associated Approved Code of Practice and/or guidance notes provided by the Health and Safety Executive or others.

Vulnerable Employees

Health and safety legislation requires employers to take greater care of the more vulnerable employees, whether that is because:

- they have a pre-existing injury (mental or physical);
- they are more susceptible to dangerous working conditions or processes (such as in the case of pregnant women);
- they cannot appreciate the dangers (because of lack of experience or maturity, such as in the case of young people);
- they have a disability that otherwise puts them at a disadvantage.

The Management of Health and Safety at Work Regulations 1999 specifically require employers to take account of individuals' capabilities when assessing risks, particularly so in the case of pregnant women and young people.

3.3.2 Civil liability for occupational injuries

In addition to any criminal liability for safety breaches, the employer must initially pay statutory sick pay to workers absent through injury caused by a breach. Later, he or she may be obliged to pay compensation following a common law claim for breach of an implied term in the contract of employment. Claims can also be for the torts of negligence or breach of statutory duty. Liability may arise for the employer's own acts or for the acts of other employees for whom he or she is vicariously responsible.

Claims for breach of contract or negligence are based on the principles outlined earlier. It is well established that an employer owes a duty of care to his employees in three respects:

1. With regard to other staff, he must take care with their selection, give proper instructions and training and dismiss those whose behaviour is dangerous. [*Hudson* v. *Ridge Manufacturing Co Ltd* (1957)].
2. He must be careful in providing and maintaining the materials, machinery and other equipment provided. [*Bradford* v. *Robinson Rentals Ltd* (1967): liability for frost-bite by use of unheated van]. By the Employers' Liability (Defective Equipment) Act 1969, he cannot escape liability by showing that the equipment was obtained from a reputable supplier.
3. There is the duty to combine staff and equipment into a reasonably safe system of working.

The test of whether the duty has been broken is based upon what a reasonable and prudent employer would have done in the circumstances. Thus, it would be reasonable to take greater care where the consequences of an accident would be severe or where an employee at risk has a known disability. [*Paris* v. *Stepney Borough Council* (1951): more need to provide goggles where employee has only one eye]. With safety equipment, the mere provision may be enough with experienced workers, but supervision of its use may be reasonable with the less experienced. *Woods* v. *Durable Suites Ltd* (1953): provision of barrier cream against dermatitis.

The third requisite for a successful claim is that the employee's loss was suffered in consequence of the employer's breach and was not too remote. [*Robinson* v. *Post Office* (1974): employee allergic to anti-tetanus injection given later]. The Employers' Liability (Compulsory Insurance) Act 1969 now makes it compulsory for all employers to insure against liability so that any claims for compensation can be paid.

An alternative action for an injured employee is to sue for breach of statutory duty, provided that the statute or regulation, upon interpretation by the court, allows a civil action. For example, the Factories Act 1961 fell into this category; the Health and Safety at Work Act 1974 does not; the Management of Health and Safety at Work Regulations 1999 expressly exclude civil liability but the other five new regulations do not. However, even if the enactment is enforceable by a criminal prosecution only, the fact that such a prosecution took place may be used as evidence in a common law action for negligence.

Whether or not the duty has been broken requires an examination of the words used to ascertain the standard of care required. Thus, 'so far as is reasonably practicable' imposes a standard akin to the reasonable care required at common law. On the other hand, the duty may impose strict liability when it will be no defence that reasonable safety precautions were taken. Guarding dangerous machinery has traditionally been a strict duty and it has been no defence that it would be impossible or impracticable to fence the machine [*John Summers and Sons Ltd* v. *Frost* (1955)].

In the case of both negligence and breach of statutory duty, the employer may reduce the damages payable on the grounds of contributory negligence by proving that the employee was partially to blame for the accident. Where reasonable care only is required, the employer may defeat the claim by delegating the duty to an apparently responsible third party; these defences are not available where the duty is strict.

3.3.3 Social security compensation

More immediate compensation for an injured employee may be obtained through the social security scheme. While absent from work, statutory sick pay and incapacity benefit may be claimed. After return to work or after 6 months, if there are lasting effects of the injury, a claim may be made for disablement benefit – a pension paid on a sliding scale according to a medical assessment of 'loss of faculty'; the loss must be at least 14 per cent. There may also be entitlement to various supplements, for example for dependants, or to other benefits such as a disability living allowance. In order to claim disablement benefit, an employee must prove that loss arose either from personal injury caused by accident arising out of, or in the course of, employment or from a prescribed industrial disease.

An important change introduced by the Social Security Act 1989 allows the Department of Social Security to recoup almost all social security benefits received in the ensuing 5 years from compensation paid in respect of an injury or disease. Before an employer (or insurance company) pays any compensation, including out-of-court settlement, a certificate must be obtained from the Compensation Recovery Unit of the Department stating the amount of benefit to be deducted. This amount must then be deducted and paid over to the Unit and the balance paid to the injured employee.

3.4 Summary

At the end of this chapter, students should make sure that they understand the following:

- the employment relationship, particularly the distinction between employees and independent contractors;
- duties of employers/rights of employees, particularly regarding
  - wages,
  - other general obligations, such as to provide a reasonably safe system of work,
  - sex discrimination and race discrimination;
- duties of employees, such as obedience, care and good faith;
- notice and dismissal;
- summary dismissal and wrongful dismissal;
- unfair dismissal;
- occupational safety:
  - legislative controls,
  - judicial controls,
  - liability and compensation for occupational injuries.

Revision Questions

Question 1 Multiple-choice selection

1.1 Which of the following statements suggests that John is an independent contractor in relation to the work he carries out for Zed Ltd?

(i) He is requied to provide his own tools.
(ii) He is required to carry out his work personally and is not free to send a substitute.
(iii) He is paid in full without any deductin of income tax.

(A) (i) and (ii) only.
(B) (ii) and (iii) only.
(C) (i) and (iii) only.
(D) (i), (ii) and (iii).

1.2 Which *one* of the following statements is *correct*?

(A) An employer is obliged to provide a careful and honest reference.
(B) An employer is obliged to provide a safe system of working.
(C) An employer is obliged to provide employees with smoking facilities during authorised breaks at work.
(D) An employer with fewer than 20 employees is obliged to provide an itemised written pay statement.

1.3 What is the minimum statutory holiday entitlement applicable for full-time employees?

(A) 20 days
(B) 24 days
(C) 28 days
(D) 30 days

1.4 The distinction between ordinary maternity leave and additional maternity leave is removed under the Sex Discrimination Act 1995 (Amendment of Legislation) Regulations 2008. This will be beneficial to the employee, but which *one* of the following correctly identifies the benefit(s) applicable?

(A) Pension rights
(B) Insurance rights
(C) Annual leave entitlement
(D) All of (A),(B) and (C)

1.5 A trade union can expel or refuse membership to an employee on the basis of which *one* of the following grounds?

(A) Any ground
(B) Previous convictions
(C) Past or present membership of a particular political party
(D) Previous anti-trade union behaviour

1.6 Under the Employment Act 2008 Enforcement officers will have the power to demand the making good of any underpayment to an employee. Also, in addition, they can demand a payment as a penalty. Up to what percentage of the underpayment can a penalty be demanded?

(A) 25%
(B) 50%
(C) 80%
(D) 100%

1.7 The role of ACAS as a conciliator is identified in the Employment Act 2008. Under this legislation up to when does the duty to conciliate exist?

(A) Until the tribunal hearing begins
(B) Until the tribunal removes the need for ACAS conciliation
(C) Until both parties agree that the role of ACAS is no longer needed
(D) Until judgment is delivered by the tribunal

1.8 Which *one* of the following can *not* justify the dismissal of an employee?

(A) The employee's incompetence.
(B) The employee's misconduct.
(C) The employee's inability to do the job without contravening a statute.
(D) That the employee proposes to join an independent trade union.

1.9 In which *one* of the following situations is an employee *not* entitled to time off work?

(A) When the employee has given proper notice that he intends to leave, and wants to attend interviews for a new job.
(B) When the employee receives proper redundancy notice from the firm, and wants to attend interviews for a new job.
(C) When the employee is a trade union official, and wants time off to carry out trade union duties.
(D) When the employee who is in training as his company's safety representative seeks time off to attend a course.

1.10 Which *one* of the following is an employer today always bound to do?

(A) Give a testimonial to an employee who asks for one when he or she wishes to leave.
(B) Insure himself against possible occupational safety liability to employees.
(C) Pay wages to an employee during absence for illness.
(D) Prohibit smoking indoors.

1.11 H plc carries on its business using both employees and independent contractors. It is important for H plc to be able to distinguish between its employees and its independent contractors for a number of reasons. Which of the following is *not* correct?

(A) Employees owe statutory occupational safety duties to employees but not to independent contractors.
(B) Employees have a right not to be unfairly dismissed, but this does not apply to independent contractors.
(C) H plc must deduct income tax and national insurance contributions from the wages of its employees, but not from the amounts paid to independent contractors.
(D) H plc must give statutory notice of detailed terms of work to part-time employees but not to independent contractors.

1.12 Three of the following grounds for dismissal are *automatically* unfair. One *might* be unfair, but not automatically. Which one?

(A) The employee proposed in his or her own time to take part in the activities of an independent trade union.
(B) The employee had become pregnant but could still have done her job until antenatal care was needed.
(C) The employee complained to the employer that the latter was breaking a statutory health and safety provision.
(D) The employee was secretly working part-time for another company.

1.13 Various tests have been developed for the purpose of distinguishing between employees and independent contractors. Which one of the following is not an identifiable test applicable?

(A) The control test.
(B) The liability test.
(C) The organisation test.
(D) The economic reality test.

? Question 2

Tom had in the past been employed as a technician by a television production company. He decided to work for himself and offered his services to a number of production companies.

The contracts he obtained never lasted for more than 10 days, and on one or two occasions, he sent a substitute when he was unable to attend personally.

One – Tom submitted invoices, which were paid in full without deduction of tax. He was registered for VAT, and bore the responsibility of dealing with his own accounts and chasing slow payers. Two – Tom provided no tools of his own, contributed no money to the cost of any of the productions, and the companies which employed him determined the time, place and duration of any assignment.

Requirements

Complete the following:

In relation to the work that he undertakes, information provided in the scenario content numbered .... (1 word) **(2 marks)** supports the argument that he is an employee according to the .... test (1 word) **(1 mark)**. However, the fact that the scenario content numbered .... (1 word) **(2 marks)** applied to Tom is more consistent with his status as an independent contractor. That Tom may send along a substitute is more consistent with his status as an .... (2 words) **(1 mark)**. On balance, Tom is likely to be regarded as an .... (2 words) **(1 mark)**. The distinction is particularly important to issues including .... (1 word) **(2 marks)** protection, ... (1 word) **(2 marks)** liability and the payment of .... (4 words) **(3 marks)**.

(Total marks = 14)

Question 3

Nigel is employed by New Bank Limited as a clerk. He has worked for the bank for 3 years, and, until recently, the quality of his work was excellent. In the last few weeks, however, the quality of his work has deteriorated and he is often late for work. His manager, Supreet, has warned him informally on several occasions that his work is unsatisfactory, but to no avail. When Nigel joined the bank he undertook to study to obtain his banking qualifications within 3 years, but so far he has made little progress, passing only the first part of the examinations after several attempts.

Supreet has spoken to the bank's personnel manager about Nigel's poor performance and his failure to obtain the required qualifications within 3 years. He has advised Supreet that Nigel's employment should be terminated unless there is an immediate improvement in his performance and punctuality.

Supreet proposes to hold a formal disciplinary interview with Nigel, but is concerned about its content and structure.

Requirements

(a) Delete as appropriate and complete the following:

Nigel's contract may be determined by giving him either .... **(2 marks)** weeks' notice or the length of notice specified in the contract, whichever is the .... (1 word) **(1 mark)**. Failure to give Nigel the correct period of notice would constitute .... (2 words) **(2 marks)**. A claim may be made before the court or .... (2 words) **(1 mark)** and must be made within .... (2 words) **(1 mark)**. Only if the Bank can show that Nigel was guilty of gross misconduct can .... (1 word) **(1 mark)** dismissal be justified. **(8 marks)**

(b) Nigel could alternatively claim .... (1 word) **(1 mark)** dismissal and he may make a claim within 3 months of his dismissal. **(1 mark)**

(c) The Bank would have to show that the reason for the dismissal was for one of the following.

.... (1 word) **(1 mark)**
.... (1 word) **(1 mark)**
.... (1 word) **(1 mark)**
.... (4 words) **(1 mark)**
.... (3 words) **(1 mark)** **(5 marks)**

Furthermore, the tribunal would have to be satisfied that the Bank acted reasonably in all the circumstances.

(d) The bank would probably rely on .... (1 word) **(1 mark)** as the potentially fair ground for Nigel's dismissal on the basis that his performance has been unsatisfactory and that he was recruited on the understanding that he would gain his banking qualification within 3 years. **(1 mark)**

(Total marks = 15)

Question 4

(a) The Equal Opportunities Commission has now been merged with the .... (4 words) **(1 mark)** and the......................(3 words) **(1 mark)** to form the.................. ....(6 words) **(2 marks)**. This merger was brought about under the............(1 word) (**1 mark**) Act 2006. **(5 marks)**

(b) Legislation introduced in 1995 made it unlawful for an employer to discriminate against a person on the basis of ....(1 mark) **(1 mark)**. Regulations introduced in 2006 made it unlawful for an employer to discriminate against a person on the basis of ....(1 word) **(1 mark)** **(2 marks)**

(Total marks = 7)

Solutions to Revision Questions

Solution 1

1.1 Answer: (C)

Whilst an employee is required to carry out work personally, an independent contractor can use a substitute. A contractor is required however, to provide his own tools and pay income tax personally, having received the full contract price for the services provided. (C) is therefore the correct answer.

1.2 Answer: (B)

An employer does not have an obligation to provide a reference, therefore (A) is not the correct answer. Further, the obligations identified in (C) and (D) do not apply to an employer. Employers are however, required to provide workers with a safe system of working under contract and the tort of negligence. Obligations in statute relating to safety in the workplace also exist.

1.3 Answer: (C)

The statutory minimum holiday entitlement for full-time employees was extended from 20 days to 28 days. This became applicable from 1 April 2009. (C) is therefore the correct answer.

1.4 Answer: (D)

The Sex Discrimination Act 1995 (Amendment of Legislation) Regulations 2008 provide a number of benefits to employees on maternity leave. These include pension rights, insurance rights and annual leave entitlement. The correct answer is therefore (D).

1.5 Answer: (C)

It is the Employment Act 2008 section 19 that identifies the right of trade unions to expel or refuse membership to a person on the basis of a previous or existing membership of a political party. A trade union does not have the right to refuse membership on any ground. Equally, previous convictions or anti-trade union behaviour are not acceptable reasons for refusal of membership. (A), (B) and (D) are therefore incorrect answers.

1.6 Answer: (B)

The right of Enforcement officers to impose a penalty of up to 50% was introduced in the Employment Act 2008. (B) is therefore the correct answer.

1.7 Answer: (D)

Prior to the introduction of the Employment Act 2008 ACAS had a duty to act as a conciliatory body, but this duty did not continue up to the point where the tribunal made a decision. The Employment Act 2008 extended the relevant period up to the point of decision-making. (D) is therefore the correct answer.

1.8 Answer: (D)

(A), (B) and (C) are all stated in the Employment Rights Act 1996 as being categories of potentially fair dismissal. Dismissal in category (D) is an automatically unfair dismissal.

1.9 Answer: (A)

(A) is the correct answer, because resignation is a voluntary act, and not as in (B), where the employee is entitled to time off work under the Employment Rights Act 1996 to look for a new job. In (C), trade union officials are allowed time off work with pay to carry out their official duties. In (D), safety representatives are entitled to time off work with pay to enable them to carry out their safety duties.

1.10 Answer: (B)

An employer *may* agree by contract to do (A), (C) or (D), but he is not bound to do so.

1.11 Answer: (A)

(B), (C) and (D) are all differences between employees (even part-time ones) and independent contractors.

1.12 Answer: (D)

1.13 Answer: (B)

(A), (C) and (D) identify recognised tests applicable in distinguishing the employee from the independent contractor. (B) is false and therefore the correct answer.

Solution 2

In relation to the work that he undertakes, information provided in the scenario content numbered *two* supports the argument that he is an employee, according to the *multiple* test. However, the fact that the scenario content numbered one applied to Tom is more consistent with his status as an independent contractor. That Tom may send along a substitute, is more consistent with his status as an *independent contractor*. On balance, Tom is an *independent contractor*. The distinction is particularly important to issues, including *statutory* protection, *vicarious* liability and the payment of *tax and national insurance*.

Solution 3

(a) Nigel's contract may be determined by giving him either *3* weeks' notice or the length of notice specified in the contract, whichever is the *longer*. Failure to give Nigel the correct period of notice would constitute *wrongful dismissal*. A claim may be made before the court or *Employment Tribunal* and must be made within *6 years*. Only if the Bank can show that Nigel was guilty of gross misconduct can summary dismissal be justified.

(b) Nigel could alternatively claim *unfair* dismissal and he may make a claim within 3 months of the date of his dismissal.

(c) The Bank would have to show that the reason for the dismissal was one among the following: *capability, conduct, redundancy, contravention of statutory provisions, other substantial reason*. Furthermore, the tribunal would have to be satisfied that the Bank acted reasonably in all the circumstances.

(d) The bank would probably rely on capability as the potentially fair ground for Nigel's dismissal on the basis that his performance has been unsatisfactory and that he was recruited on the understanding that he would gain his banking qualification within 3 years.

Solution 4

(a) The Equal Opportunities Commission has now been merged with the *Commission for Racial Equality* and the *Disability Rights Commission* to form the *Commission for Equality and Human Rights*. This merger was brought about under the *Equality* Act 2006.

(b) Legislation introduced in 1995 made it unlawful for an employer to discriminate against a person on the basis of *disability*. Regulations introduced in 2006 made it unlawful for an employer to discriminate against a person on the basis of *age*.

Company Administration

Company Administration

4

Learning Outcomes

On completion of their studies students should be able to:

- explain the essential characteristics of the different forms of business organisations and the implications of corporate personality;
- explain the differences between public and private companies and establishing a company by registration or purchasing 'off the shelf';
- explain the purpose and legal status of the memorandum and articles of association;
- explain the ability of a company to contract;
- explain the main advantages and disadvantages of carrying on business through the medium of a company limited by shares;
- explain the use and procedure of board meetings and general meetings of shareholders;
- explain the voting rights of directors and shareholders and identify the various types of shareholder resolutions.

The chapter has been arranged into sections based on the learning outcomes as above.

4.1 The impact of the Companies Act 2006

For the purposes of the examination, please note that you will be expected to know the changes made by the Companies Act 2006, including those parts of the Act which are not yet in force. Whenever reference is made to the Companies Act 2006, the reference will inform you when the provision is expected to be in force.

Please note that it is therefore essential that you keep up to date on the new law as it is implemented. The best way for you to do this is by accessing the Act itself and supporting secondary legislation and explanatory notes and briefing on latest developments at www .berr.gov.uk/.

The Companies Act 2006 ('CA 2006') received the Royal Assent on November 8 2006. The Act is a major piece of legislation consisting of 1,300 sections and 16 Schedules. The Act both consolidates the Companies Act 1985 and makes important changes to company law and procedure. It is intended that the Act will be fully implemented by Statutory Instrument by October 2009.

4.1.1 The commencement dates of the remaining parts of the Companies Act 2006

	Provisions of the Companies Act 2006	Date of/Expected date of implementation
1	General introductory provisions	
	Section 1	1 October 2009
	Section 2	6 April 2007
	Sections 3–6	1 October 2009
2	Company formation	
	Sections 7–16	1 October 2009
3	A company's constitution	
	Sections 17–28	1 October 2009
	Sections 29–30	1 October 2007
	Sections 31–38	1 October 2009
4	A company's capacity and related matters	
	Sections 39–43	1 October 2009
	Section 44	6 April 2008
	Sections 45–52	1 October 2009
5	A Company's name	
	Sections 53–68	1 October 2009
	Sections 69–74	1 October 2008
	Sections 75–81	1 October 2009
	Sections 82–85	1 October 2008
6	A Company's registered office	
	Sections 86–88	1 October 2009
7	Re-registration as a means of altering a company's status	
	Sections 89–111	1 October 2009
8	A company's members	
	Sections 112–115	1 October 2009
	Sections 116–119	1 October 2007
	Section 120	1 October 2009
	Sections 121–128	6 April 2008
	Sections 129–144	1 October 2009
9	Exercise of members' rights	
	Sections 145–153	1 October 2007
10	A company's directors	
	Sections 154	1 October 2007
	Sections 155–159	1 October 2008
	Sections 160–161	1 October 2007
	Sections 162–167	1 October 2009
	Sections 168–174	1 October 2007
	Sections 175–177	1 October 2008
	Sections 178–179	1 October 2007
	Section 180 (1), (2) (in part) & (4) (b)	1 October 2008
	Section 181 (2) & (3)	1 October 2008
	Sections 182–187	1 October 2008
	Sections 188–239	1 October 2007
	Sections 240–247	1 October 2009
	Sections 248–259	1 October 2007
11	Derivative claims and proceedings by members	
	Sections 260–269	1 October 2007

	Provisions of the Companies Act 2006	Date of/Expected date of implementation
12	Company secretaries	
	Section 270 (3) (b) (ii)	1 October 2009
	Sections 271–274	6 April 2008
	Sections 275–279	1 October 2009
	Section 280	6 April 2008
13	Resolutions and meetings	
	Sections 281–307	1 October 2007
	Sections 308–309	20 January 2007
	Sections 310–332	1 October 2007
	Section 333	20 January 2007
	Sections 334–361	1 October 2007
	Sections 327 (2) (c) & 330 (6) (c) are not being implemented for the time being	
14	Control of political donations and expenditure	
	Sections 362–379	1 October 2007
	Part 14 comes into force in Northern Ireland on 1 November 2007, except for provisions relating to independent election candidates	
15	Accounts and reports	
	Sections 380–416	6 April 2008
	Section 417	1 October 2007
	Section 418–462	6 April 2008
	Section 463: for reports and statements first sent to members and others after that date	20 January 2007
	Sections 464–474	6 April 2008
16	Audit	
	Sections 475–484	6 April 2008
	Sections 485–488	1 October 2007
	Sections 489–539	6 April 2008
17	A company's share capital	
	Sections 540–543	1 October 2009
	Section 544	6 April 2008
	Sections 545–640	1 October 2009
	Section 641 (1) (a) & (2)–(6)–643	1 October 2008
	Sections 644–651	1 October 2009
	Section 652	1 October 2008
	Section 653	1 October 2009
	Section 654	1 October 2008
	Sections 655–657	1 October 2009
18	Acquisition by limited company of its own shares	
	Sections 658–737	1 October 2009
	Repeal of the restrictions under the Companies Act 1985 on financial assistance for acquisition of shares in private companies, including the 'whitewash' procedure	1 October 2008
19	Debentures	
	Sections 738–754	6 April 2008
20	Private and public companies	
	Sections 755–767	6 April 2008
21	Certification and transfer of securities	
	Sections 768–790	6 April 2008

	Provisions of the Companies Act 2006	Date of/Expected date of implementation
22	Information about interests in a company's shares	
	Sections 791–810	20 January 2007
	Sections 811 (4)–812	6 April 2008
	Section 813	20 January 2007
	Section 814	6 April 2008
	Sections 815–828	20 January 2007
23	Distributions	
	Sections 829–853	6 April 2008
24	A company's annual return	
	Sections 854–859	1 October 2009
25	Company charges	
	Sections 860–894	1 October 2009
26	Arrangements and reconstructions	
	Sections 895–901	6 April 2008
27	Mergers and divisions of public companies	
	Sections 902–941	6 April 2008
28	Takeovers etc.	
	Sections 942–992	6 April 2007
29	Fraudulent trading	
	Section 993	1 October 2007
30	Protection of members against unfair prejudice	
	Sections 994–999	1 October 2007
31	Dissolution and restoration to the register	
	Sections 1000–1034	1 October 2009
32	Company investigations: amendments	
	Sections 1035–1039	1 October 2007
33	UK companies not formed under the Companies Act	
	Sections 1040–1042	1 October 2009
	Section 1043	6 April 2007
34	Overseas companies	
	Sections 1044–1059	1 October 2009
35	The registrar of companies	
	Sections 1060–1062	1 October 2009
	Section 1063 (in respect of England, Wales and Scotland)	6 April 2007
	Sections 1064–1067	1 October 2009
	Section 1068 (5)	1 January 2007
	Sections 1069–1076	1 October 2009
	Sections 1077–1080	1 January 2007
	Sections 1081–1084	1 October 2009
	Sections 1085–1092	1 January 2007
	Sections 1093–1101	1 October 2009
	Sections 1102–1107	1 January 2007
	Sections 1108–1110	1 October 2009
	Section 1111	1 January 2007
	Sections 1112–1120	1 October 2009
36	Offences under the Companies Act	
	Sections 1121–1133	With relevant provision
	Section 1124	1 October 2007
37	Companies: supplementary provisions	
	Sections 1134–1136	With relevant provision
	Section 1137 (1), (4), (5) (b) and (6)	30 September 2007
	Sections 1138–1142	With relevant provision
	Sections 1143–1148	20 January 2007
	Sections 1149–1156	With relevant provision
	Section 1157	1 October 2008

	Provisions of the Companies Act 2006	Date of/Expected date of implementation
38	Companies: interpretation	
	Sections 1158–1169	With relevant provision
	Section 1170	6 April 2007
	Section 1171	With relevant provision
	Section 1172	6 April 2008
	Section 1173–1174	With relevant provision
39	Companies: minor amendments	
	Section 1175 (only for Part 1 of Schedule 9)	1 April 2008
	Sections 1176–1179	6 April 2007
	Section 1180	1 October 2009
	Section 1181	1 October 2009
40	Company directors: foreign disqualification, etc.	
	Sections 1182–1191	1 October 2009
41	Business names	
	Sections 1192–1208	1 October 2009
42	Statutory auditors	
	Sections 1209–1264	6 April 2008
43	Transparency obligations and related matters Sections 1265–1273	8 November 2006 (Royal Assent)
44	Miscellaneous provisions	
	Sections 1274 and 1276	Royal Assent
	Sections 1277–1280	1 October 2008
	Section 1281	6 April 2007
	Section 1282	6 April 2008
	Section 1283	1 October 2009
45	Northern Ireland	
	Sections 1284–1287	With relevant provision
46	General supplementary provisions	
	Sections 1288–1294	Royal Assent
	Section 1295	With relevant provision
	Sections 1296–1297	Royal Assent
47	Final Provisions	
	Sections 1298–1300	Royal Assent

4.1.2 General overview of the impact of the Companies Act 2006

Both public and private companies will have to make changes to their administration procedures. The changes will have an impact upon:

- Company names;
- The memorandum of association;
- The articles of association;
- Share capital and the maintenance of capital;
- Meetings;
- Communications with shareholders;
- Directors' duties, breach of duty and derivative actions;
- The company secretary and company records;
- Annual reports and accounts.

4.1.3 Actions to be taken now in order to ensure that the company complies with the provisions which have already come into force

1. *All companies*. Review websites, business letters and order forms and amend as necessary to ensure that they all state:
   - The name of the company;
   - The company's registered number;
   - Place of registration;
   - Address of registered office.
2. *Public limited companies*. Shareholders must disclose voting rights at 3 per cent (and 1 per cent increments). The company must publish the company's total number of voting rights and capital in respect of each class of shares admitted to trading on Official List, AIM and Plus Markets.
3. *All companies*. Review articles of association and consider whether any amendments are necessary to facilitate electronic communications with shareholders. Subject to members' consent in general meeting or a provision in the company's articles, all companies may use electronic communications with members. If they are necessary, draft resolutions should be prepared for presentation to the shareholders at the next general meeting or AGM. In addition, as mentioned above, all shareholders must be contacted individually and asked if they consent to receiving communications in electronic form. If a shareholder fails to respond within 28 days the company can assume that he consents. If a shareholder refuses to agree to e-communication, the company must wait 12 months before asking him again.
4. *All companies*. If the company is or becomes involved in a takeover, it should be aware of the fact that the Takeover Panel now has statutory powers and should comply with the new takeover provisions as appropriate.
5. *All companies*. If it is intended that the company should make political donations, the shareholders are required to authorise the donations in advance.

4.2 Business organisations

Learning Outcome:	To explain the essential characteristics of the different forms of business organisations and the implications of corporate personality.

4.2.1 Individual traders/practitioners

Human beings can trade or practice in a business or profession. Most such practices are small, but this is not necessarily so. Some individuals can operate wealthy and multinational enterprises, whether or not they employ a lot of people.

Under a sole tradership or practionership, as the name suggests, one person is fully responsible for putting in the capital and expertise of the business. If the business should fail, then that person is fully liable for the debts of the business and is subject to the rules of bankruptcy.

Many traders and practitioners prefer to trade under a 'business name' that is in general, a name which does not consist solely of the surname and initials of the trader or professional. For example, a business called 'High Street Fashions' must be operating under a business name. First, this is clearly not the name of a real person, and second, it cannot be the name of a company as it does not end in 'Limited' or 'Ltd', 'public limited company' or 'plc'.

If a trader or a professional chooses to operate under a business name then he or she must comply with the rules contained in Part 41 of the CA 2006, Sections 1192–1208 (which are scheduled to come into force on 1 October 2009). Do not confuse a business name (which is not the name of a person or any legal entity) with a company name which is the name of a legal person. The main controls under the Act are that the name of the owner of the business must be stated on all business letters, written orders, receipts and invoices and so on, and must be stated prominently at all premises from which the business is carried on. The reason for this requirement is that, to use the above example, High Street Fashions does not exist as a legal entity, and cannot therefore sue or be sued. It follows that the name of the owner must be disclosed to facilitate claims being made by and against the business. In addition, the Act contains a number of controls over the use of certain names and words as explained below. Examples of business names are 'Computer 2006', 'Smith and Company (Solicitors)' and 'Indian Palace'. In each of these examples it is impossible to know whether the owner is a sole trader, a partnership, a private or a public limited company merely by looking at the name. A sole trader may use the word 'company' in his or her business name. It follows that the name of the owner must be obtained by looking at business letters or notices displayed on business premises.

A sole practitioner's main duty (like any other business or practice) is to his own client or customer, with whom he has a contract. As seen in Chapter 2, there are implied terms in the contract. The practitioner impliedly promises to use such skill as he has professed, and to exercise such professional care as is reasonable. He or she can be liable to his or her client for all loss, financial and otherwise, which may fairly and reasonably be considered as arising naturally, according to the usual course of things, from the breach; and for any further loss which may reasonably be supposed to have been in the contemplation of the parties when the contract was made, so that the practitioner in effect took responsibility for it; see *Hadley* v. *Baxendale* (1854) in Chapter 2.

A practitioner can also, exceptionally, incur liability to someone other than his client. A claim against a sole practitioner by a person other than his or her client would most commonly be made in tort. As seen in Chapter 1, the law of tort enables a person who has no contractual relationship with a sole practitioner (or trader) to bring an action against that person. The claimant must be able to show that the practitioner/trader acted in breach of a legally recognised duty of care which was owed to the claimant and that the breach caused the claimant loss or injury. As regards purely financial loss, such a tortuous duty would probably only be owed if the practitioner had accepted responsibility for specific acts or statements to specific persons. In *White* v. *Jones* (1995), a solicitor was instructed to draft a will for his client. The solicitor delayed, and the client died before the will was completed. The two claimants, who should have benefited from the will, received nothing. They recovered damages from the solicitor, even though they were not his clients. See also cases such as *Smith* v. *Eric S Bush* (1990). The courts will not, however, recognise any duty to a potentially large or undefined number of people; see *Caparo Industries plc* v. *Dickman* (1990). These cases are discussed in Chapter 1, and should be referred to again now. Since 1999 it has also been possible for a person who was not a party to the original contract to enforce a term of the contract which expressly provides that he can enforce the term, or that the term purports to confer a benefit upon him (see the Contracts (Rights of Third Parties) Act 1999).

It is becoming increasingly common for the activities of all traders and professionals to be regulated by law. As seen in the chapters dealing with contract law, statute implies terms into contracts for the sale of goods and services and restricts the ability of traders to exclude these terms through such legislation as the Unfair Contract Terms Act 1977. To ensure that traders keep to the rules, bodies such as the Office of Fair Trading are given powers to prosecute offenders. Many professionals are, of course, regulated by their own professional bodies which commonly issue rules to their members relating to professional conduct (see Chapters 3 and 4). In addition, Acts of Parliament and statutory instruments set down rules concerning particular professions. For example, the Insolvency Act 1986 and the Financial Services Act 1996 provide respectively that all insolvency practitioners such as liquidators, and all financial advisers must be 'fit and proper persons' that is, they must be qualified. It is still possible, of course, to come across fraudulent or incompetent traders and professionals, depending on how effectively their activities are policed by the authorities entrusted to enforce the rules.

4.2.2 Partnerships (and some comparisons with companies)

The Partnership Act 1890 sec.1 defines a partnership as 'the relation which subsists between persons carrying on a business in common with a view to profit'. Normally, partnerships (often called 'firms') will be fairly small, but this is not always the case. For example, companies are 'persons' within the above definition, and large companies can therefore be partners (see *Stevenson & Sons Ltd.* v. *AG fr Cartonnagen Industries* (1918), for instance). Some large firms of solicitors have several hundred partners, and are billion pound enterprises with offices throughout the world. Large firms of accountants have many more partners, and are correspondingly even more wealthy and powerful.

No formalities are required to form general partnerships, no documentation and no registration. This is in marked contrast to the documentation and registration requirements for company formation and the formation of Limited Liability Partnerships – see later. In practice, larger firms often do have formal partnership agreements which add to, and vary, the provisions of the Partnership Act. The reason for this is that the Partnership Act 1890 applies to every partnership agreement whether written or oral. Many of the Act's provisions apply, unless they are excluded by the agreement. For example, the Act provides that partners shall share profits equally. In cases where partners are bringing in different amounts of capital or expertise, equal shares may not be appropriate and the partners will need to agree specific profit sharing arrangements. 'Expulsion clauses' provide; a further example. Suppose that A, B and C are in partnership and have no written partnership agreement. C is proving to be a very unsatisfactory partner in that he often fails to turn up for work and when he does turn up, he is rude to customers and is causing the firm to lose money. As there is no written partnership agreement, it would be practically impossible for A and B to expel C. As a result they are left with the choice of dissolving the whole partnership (which means that the business would have to be closed down, all the assets sold and all creditors paid off), or offering C sufficient money to persuade him to leave. This is so because the Partnership Act is silent on the expulsion of partners. It follows that if A, B and C had entered into a written partnership agreement, the lawyer who drafted the agreement could have ensured that an expulsion clause was included to cover the above situation. If so, A and B would have been able to give C notice of expulsion and paid him his share of the partnership. The business could then have carried on without having to be dissolved. Partnership agreements are not open to public inspection, unlike the memorandum and articles of association of a registered company.

For a partnership, the only publicity requirements arise if it chooses to use a 'business name', different from the true surnames, with or without additional names or initials, of all of the partners. There are other permitted additions such as '& Sons', or an 's' at the end of the surnames of all of the partners (Smiths).

If there are several partners (more than three or four usually), they will usually choose a 'firm name'. This may be an business name, for example Mobile Valeting, or it may comprise the names of one or more of the senior partners. Additions such as 'Company' or '& Co.' are allowed by the CA 2006, but *not* 'limited' or 'Ltd' or 'plc'. The firm can then trade in its firm name, and sue or be sued in it; but *all* partners are liable for its debts, and so on (see later). The names of all partners must be shown beside letterheads, except for firms with more than twenty partners, where no names need to be given. Such a firm must display all partners' names at its business premises, and written disclosure must be given on request to those doing business with the firm. Under the CA 2006, artificial names which are misleading offensive or falsely suggest connection with another business are prohibited. In the UK a person may not carry on business under a name which is likely to give the impression that the business is connected with

- Her Majesty's Government;
- The Scottish Administration;
- Her Majesty's Government in Northern Ireland;
- Any local or public authority specified in regulations made by the Secretary of State.

If an application is made for the approval of a particular name the Secretary of State may require the applicant to seek the approval of a specified Government department. (Section 1193 CA 2006.). Breach of these provisions is a criminal offence by each partner; but partnership contracts are valid and the partnership can carry on business, although if the other party to a contract defaults, the contract is unenforceable without leave of the court.

When operating under a firm name, partners must also beware the tort of 'passing-off'. This would occur if their chosen name and the nature of their business was so like those of a competitor that third parties might be deceived. If Mr A and Mr B choose to call their retail shop 'Marks and Spencers', the owners of the well-known Marks and Spencers retail chain could obtain an injunction against A and B by suing under the tort of passing off. The well-known Marks and Spencers could also claim compensation if it could be shown that use of that name by A and B had caused a loss of revenue.

External regulation of a partnership business other than by professional bodies, is virtually non-existent. Apart from the names of partners, no formal general records need be kept, although the Inland Revenue might ask to see accounts. There is nothing comparable to the requirements for annual returns, audits, and so on, for corporate bodies (see later), although there are special requirements for some professional partnerships such as solicitors.

Partnership property belongs to the partners jointly. If more than four partners own or lease partnership land, legal title to the land must be vested in not more than four of the partners who act as trustees (and for practical purposes, at least two); these will usually be senior partners, who hold the land on trust for all the partners.

In theory, a partnership can be dissolved very easily. Unless the partners agree otherwise in advance, it is dissolved by expiration of the time, or completion of the specific task for which it was initially made. If, as is usual, the partnership is entered into for an undefined time, it can be ended by any partner giving notice to all the others. Unless otherwise agreed, every partnership is automatically dissolved by the death or bankruptcy of any partner. All of this can be very inconvenient, as the business would have to be sold and all the creditors paid off. This is reason why these provisions are often excluded or varied by a partnership agreement. Compare the ease with which shares in a company can be transferred without affecting the continuity of the enterprise.

Agency and partnerships

Partners are, in effect, mutual agents. By the Partnership Act s.5, every partner is the agent of the firm and his partners for the purpose of the partnership business. The firm is bound by what he does on its behalf if the act is one for carrying on in the usual way business of the kind carried on by the firm. If the partners try to restrict the usual authority of one of their number, they may still be bound if what he does on their behalf *appears* to be normal. An outsider cannot be expected to know what has occurred inside the partnership. The firm is therefore bound if a partner is acting within his *apparent* authority, even if this involves a breach of his actual instructions. However, the firm will not be bound if the outsider either knows that the partner is exceeding his authority, or does not know or believe him to be a partner; an outsider who is not deceived cannot rely on apparent authority.

If one partner commits a tort or crime in the course of the business, the firm (i.e. his fellow partners) will be liable, similarly, if the act was within the offending partner's actual *or* apparent authority.

Liability of partners for debts of the firm

Each partner may be sued and held liable for the full amount due under any of the firm's contracts. By s.9 of the Partnership Act, partners are liable jointly, and therefore if one partner has to pay the full amount he can recover appropriate shares from his fellow partners – but some of these may no longer be solvent or available. By s.12 the partners are similarly jointly and severally liable for torts for which the firm is responsible. Again, each partner can be individually liable for the full damages awarded against the firm. The gravity of this position can be seen from cases such as *ADT Ltd* v. *BDO Binder Hamlyn* (1995), where a (large) firm of accountants was held liable in tort for damages of £65 million (plus substantial costs). Admittedly, the firm had insured itself against liability, but the actual policy covered much less than this. Any partner could be held personally liable for the full amount.

In this context, the importance of limited liability for company shareholders can hardly be overemphasised, see Section 4.3.2. A shareholder in a limited company is *not* liable for debts of the corporation.

In partnerships, even non-partners can sometimes be personally liable for debts of the firm. This can occur, for example, if a retiring partner fails to adequately publicise his retirement, especially to clients who know him. More generally, *any* person may be personally liable for a debt of the firm if he has by his words, spoken or written, or conduct represented himself as being a partner, or allowed himself to be so represented, and persons who have been deceived have given credit to the firm because they believed him to be a partner (s.14).

By the Limited Partnerships Act 1907, it is possible for some of the partners to have limited liability, but this Act is not much used. Some of the partners (at least one) must have unlimited liability, and the unlimited partner(s) effectively run the firm. Limited partners must not take any active part in management, although they may inspect the accounts. The firm must be registered by filing documents with the Registrar of Companies. The death, insanity or insolvency of a limited partner does not end the partnership. The limited partner simply contributes a stated amount of capital, has no further liability, and takes little further part. It may be thought that the reason limited partnerships have not proved popular lies in the fact that at least one partner must have unlimited liability and be prepared to be fully liable for the firm's debts. Clearly it might be difficult to find someone who was prepared to run the risk of total liability. However, as a limited company is a legal person it is possible for it to be a partner and to be the partner fully responsible for the firms debts and indeed some limited partnerships use a limited company in that manner. The unpopularity of the limited partnership has arisen for other reasons, such as the fact that it is relatively easy to form a limited company and there is now the option, particularly for professional firms of forming a Limited Liability Partnership (see later).

Internal relations of partners

As between themselves, partners are governed by provisions in the Partnership Act, but as mentioned earlier they are free to vary or exclude many of these. Unless otherwise agreed, every partner may take part in management of the partnership business. This contrasts radically with the position in limited companies (which sometimes have millions of members); see later. As between themselves, partners do owe some statutory duties of good faith, whereas shareholders owe few, if any, such duties to each other. The main contrast with companies, however, is the relative ease with which partners can vary their internal relations, as compared with the fairly formal procedures required for changing the memorandum and articles of a company. Moreover, a partnership agreement is private, whereas the company documents are not.

Existence of Partnership – Commencement of Trading

***NLJ Practitioner*, 10 November 2000**
Reproduced by permission of Reed Elsevier (UK) Limited, trading as LexisNexis UK
Khan v. *Miah and others*
House of Lords
Lord Bingham of Cornhill, Lord Steyn, Lord Hoffmann, Lord Clyde and Lord Millett
2 November 2000

There is no rule of law that the parties to a joint venture do not become partners until actual trading commences.

The first and second respondents wished to open a restaurant, and they approached the appellant, K, with a view to interesting him in joining the venture. It was agreed that they would all be partners in the business. They found suitable premises, obtained planning permission for its conversion to a restaurant, took a lease of the premises and agreed to buy the freehold reversion, opened a partnership bank account, arranged to borrow up to £60,000 from the bank towards the purchase of the freehold, commissioned a design, entered into a contract with a firm of builders for the conversion and fitting out of the premises as a restaurant, and contracted for the purchase of equipment and table linen. Nearly all the moneys in the partnership bank account were provided by K. By 25 January 1994, a month before the restaurant was opened, K's relationship with the respondents had broken down, and the latter subsequently carried on the business on their own account, without any settling of accounts with K. In subsequent proceedings, the judge concluded that there had been a partnership between the parties and that K was entitled to a 50 per cent share in it. The Court of Appeal, by a majority, allowed the respondent's appeal, holding that parties to a joint venture did not become partners until actual trading had commenced. K appealed to the House of Lords.

Lord Millett

The majority of the Court of Appeal had considered that it was necessary first to identify the business of the partnership, and then decide whether that business was being carried on by the partners at the material time. They identified the business of the partnership as the carrying on of a restaurant business from the premises, and posed the question: 'Were the . . . parties . . . carrying on a restaurant business at [the premises] prior to 25 January 1994?' So expressed, the question could only be answered in one way. The restaurant was not open for business. Everything that had been done was preparatory to the commencement of trading.

The majority of the Court of Appeal had been guilty of nominalism. They thought that it was necessary, not merely to identify the joint venture into which the parties had agreed to enter, but to give it a particular description, and then to decide whether the parties had commenced to carry on a business of that description.

They described the business which the parties agreed to carry on together as the business of a restaurant, meaning the preparation and serving of meals to customers, and asked themselves whether the restaurant had commenced trading by the relevant date. But that was an impossibly narrow view of the enterprise on which the parties agreed to embark. They did not intend to become partners in an existing business. They did not agree merely to take over and run a restaurant. They agreed to find suitable premises, fit them out as a restaurant and run the restaurant once they had set it up. The acquisition, conversion and fitting out of the premises and the purchase of furniture and equipment were all part of the joint venture, were undertaken with a view of ultimate profit, and formed part of the business which the parties agreed to carry on in partnership together.

There was no rule of law that the parties to a joint venture did not become partners until actual trading commenced. The rule was that persons who agreed to carry on a business activity as a joint venture did not become partners until they actually embarked on the activity in question. It was necessary to identify the venture in order to decide whether the parties had actually embarked upon it, but it was not necessary to attach any particular name to it. Any commercial activity which was capable of being carried on by an individual was capable of being carried on in partnership. Many businesses required a great deal of expenditure to be incurred before trading commences. Films, for example, were commonly (for tax reasons) produced by limited partnerships. The making of a film was a business activity, at least if it was genuinely conducted with a view of profit. But the film rights had to be bought, the script commissioned, locations found, the director, actors and cameramen engaged, and the studio hired, long before the cameras start to roll. The work of finding, acquiring and fitting out a shop or restaurant began long before the premises were open for business and the first customers walked through the door. Such work was undertaken with a view of profit, and might be undertaken as well by partners as by a sole trader.

It did not matter how the enterprise should properly be described. The question was whether they had actually embarked upon the venture on which they had agreed. The mutual rights and obligations of the parties did not depend on whether their relationship broke up the day before or the day after they opened the restaurant, but on whether it broke up before or after they actually transacted any business of the joint venture. The question was not whether the restaurant had commenced trading, but whether the parties had done enough to be found to have commenced the joint enterprise in which they had agreed to engage. Once the judge found that the assets had been acquired, the liabilities incurred and the expenditure laid out in the course of the joint venture and with the authority of all parties, the conclusion inevitably followed.

It followed that the appeal would be allowed.

Lord Bingham of Cornhill, Lord Steyn, Lord Hoffmann and Lord Clyde delivered concurring opinions.

When partners fall out

Kathy Dumbrill, *Solicitors Journal*, 15 December 2000

The impact of a major partnership dispute on a business cannot be understated. It is often said that a partnership is like a marriage. Having worked with both partners and spouses in dispute, in my experience partnership disputes can often be the more acrimonious of the two. I shall leave it to your imagination to picture how explosive the situation can be when the partners in dispute are also married to each other!

In general, the smaller the partnership, the greater the negative impact of a partnership dispute on the business and the more embittered the dispute becomes. This is probably because larger partnerships are more likely to have agreed procedures to deal with circumstances giving rise to disputes. Also, the greater the number of individuals in partnership, the less personal a dispute should become and the more likely it is that a sensible solution can be found by negotiation.

This article is, therefore, particularly aimed at smaller partnerships, or those advising such partnerships. However, many of the issues raised are equally pertinent to larger partnership situations.

Why do disputes arise?

The reasons partners fall out can usually be summarised into three key areas:

(a) an actual or perceived inequality in input to the business linked to inequitable profit-sharing arrangements;

(b) one or more partners drawing too much cash from the business. This is often linked with a downturn in business profitability or cash generation and partners reliant on particular drawings levels to maintain lifestyle;

(c) external factors such as marriage breakdown, illness, financial problems or personality change. In practice these external factors often manifest themselves by (a) or (b) above, that is by affecting the level of partner input or outflow (cash drawings).

Although the solicitor may initially be presented with a client proclaiming that they simply can no longer 'get on' with their fellow business partner, further enquiry will usually establish that one of the key causes outlined above is the root of the problem.

Importance of a partnership agreement

A well-structured partnership agreement is the prime weapon in the armoury against disputes. It enables the partners to agree procedures to be applied if certain potentially contentious situations arise, for example if a partner is unable to work for a long period of time. It also enables the partners to consider and agree how differing input to the partnership should be rewarded.

In the event of any dispute, the partnership agreement enables the route to resolution to be set out. This will encompass the voting requirements for different categories of partnership decision and can often specify how any residual grievances should be dealt with.

Unfortunately, it is not a requirement that there is a formal written agreement before a partnership can commence business. Too few partners seek specialist legal advice when the partnership is formed. Many professional advisers are familiar with the vision of the bright-faced eager new business partners (usually two, three or four in number) unable to see any need whatsoever to have a formal agreement because 'they get on and work so well together'. Sadly, time and the pressure of business can often cloud the rosy spectacles.

If no formal partnership agreement exists then in the event of a partnership dispute, the Partnership Act 1890 (PA 1890) may ultimately decide how it should be resolved. New partners need to understand that the PA 1890 prescribes:

- an equal sharing of profits;
- that majority decisions prevail for 'ordinary' decisions, that in all partners have to agree to admission of new partners or a change in the nature of the partnership business.

Of course, a 'majority decision' is of no use whatsoever in a partnership of two.

However bright-faced and eager a new partner may be, the professional adviser should be able to convince them that equal profit share and majority rule can and do precipitate dispute and dissatisfaction between partners. Partners must be encouraged to think through various possible scenarios, for example long-term illness or unequal input, and to discuss and agree what should happen in these circumstances.

Fundamentally, the individuals involved need to consider whether partnership is the correct medium for their business, as opposed to sole traders sharing resources or a limited company route.

Profit sharing – the 'input' problem

Equality is still the most common form of profit-sharing arrangement in the smaller partnership. This can sometimes work very successfully when all partners trust each other and value their respective inputs into the business. However, it does not take much to upset the equilibrium.

The partners need to consider how differing input might be dealt with. Unfortunately, there is no easy way to define how profits should be shared between partners in different circumstances. In most cases the solution will be a combination of reward based on financial contribution (for example, billing and individual client profitability) and recognition of management and business development input.

The practical problem for the smaller partnership is that non-financial input is difficult to measure. A common solution is for the first tranche of profit to be shared on an equal basis, with a second tranche of profit shared based on relative financial contribution.

A number of benefits are achieved by the potential business partners agreeing together how profit share should be dealt with in the partnership agreement:

- It encourages the partners to accept that, during the life of any partnership, it is quite usual for partners to contribute to the business in different ways and with differing levels of respective input. There is nothing wrong in this provided the reward system is appropriate.

- It forces the prospective partners to sit down together and discuss a difficult issue. If they cannot agree how varying input should be rewarded, this highlights that they should reconsider whether partnership is the correct route for them.
- If a profit share method is agreed by all at the outset, this minimises the likelihood of future dispute.

Overdrawn partners – the 'outflow' problem

Another prime cause of partnership dispute is one or more partners drawing out more from the business than their profit share permits or than their fellow partners. This problem often comes to a head when there are business difficulties and financing problems.

A number of steps can be taken, within the partnership agreement or in the general management of the partnership, to minimise the likelihood of a dispute being triggered by excess drawings:

(1) Set conservative drawings levels for the partners that are linked to profitability. These can use a formula based on anticipated profit levels less taxation and a contingency reserve just in case things go wrong.
(2) Ensure that the partners have regular financial management information so that any possibility of excess drawings can be identified and corrected at the earliest opportunity. Even for the smallest partnership, the level of fees, work and cash received should be monitored at least on a quarterly basis and preferably monthly.
(3) Ensure the partnership retains sufficient funds to meet partners' business taxation liabilities and that these can be paid out of retention of historic profits as opposed to an anticipation of future profits, which may not materialise.
(4) Incorporate interest on partnership capital within the profit sharing arrangements so that the partners with the greater financial interest in the business are appropriately rewarded and overdrawn partners are penalised.

What to do when it all goes wrong

However good the partnership agreement and management style, disputes can still arise. Unfortunately, partnership law has no dispute resolution provisions with the flexibility of the 'unfair prejudice' provisions of ss.459 to 461 of the Companies Act available to shareholders.

Ultimately a partnership dispute will be resolved by a combination of:

- negotiation;
- mediation;
- legal action; or
- dissolution.

However, when it seems inevitable that a dispute will escalate, a number of things can be done to aid a speedy resolution (see box).

Conclusion

Professional advisers will be only too aware that many of the solutions available to resolve a partnership dispute such as legal action or dissolution can also be immensely disruptive and costly to the business. The clear message to those considering setting up in partnership and in existing partnerships must be: prevention is better than cure.

Practice points

- Nip the dispute in the bud – if it is allowed to fester, it will be ten times harder to find any solution that all parties are comfortable with. Partners and their professional advisers should ensure any grievances are aired at the earliest opportunity and discussed in an open fashion.
- Bring in the professionals at an early stage. In particular, most partnership disputes are linked to financial and profitability issues. Advice from an accountant to explain the financial implications is vital. Often the partnership accountants and tax advisers can provide this expert input. However, sometimes a partner may perceive that the partnership accountant is more loyal to one party than another. In this case a neutral adviser acting for both parties can help calm the waters and speed resolution. Early neutral evaluation of the problems is a form of alternative dispute resolution (ADR) that can be particularly useful in these circumstances.
- Keep talking and negotiating and, in the spirit of Lord Woolf, take full advantage of mediation and ADR.
- If dissolution is unavoidable, ensure there is appropriate accountancy advice as regards taxation issues and other complexities such as valuation and assignment of ongoing contracts.

4.2.3 Limited liability partnerships (LLPs)

The Limited Liability Partnerships Act 2000 introduced another potentially important form of business organisation from April 2001. LLPs came about as a result of pressure from professional bodies, and in particular from accountants providing audit services, for the protection of limited liability. Unlike an ordinary partnership, an LLP is a separate legal entity. Outside bodies will contract with the LLP, not with individual partners. Debts will normally be debts of the LLP, not of its members. The property of the body will belong to the LLP, which will continue in existence in spite of any change in its membership. (However, it does seem possible that an individual partner might sometimes be personally liable for a tort which he commits in the course of the business.)

An LLP is entitled to do anything which a natural person can do; there is no need for the 'objects' of the body to be stated as is still required for a company (although it should be noted that the importance of a company's 'objects clause' has lessened vastly now – see Section 4.5.2). As with partnerships, a corporate body can be a member. There is no limit on the number of members.

For an LLP to be incorporated, two documents – an incorporation document and a statement of compliance – must be filed with the Registrar of Companies. The incorporation document must be signed by 'two or more persons associated for carrying on a lawful business with a view to profit'. The document must include the name of the LLP, the address of its registered office, and the names and addresses of the persons who are to be the initial members. The Registrar of Companies keeps the incorporation document, register it and gives a certificate of registration. (There will be detailed provisions for the disqualification of would-be partners whose record renders them unsuitable to act as such; compare the Company Directors' Disqualification Act 1986.)

In return for the limited liability of its members, an LLP will have to submit an annual return and audited accounts to the Registrar of Companies. To administer this and some other matters in the LLP, the incorporation document must also nominate some 'designated members'. These may be all of the partners in a small firm, or a group selected by members in a larger LLP. These are not the same as a board of directors in a limited company, because the designated members will have no general powers of management.

The Registrar of Companies will keep a register of members. When a person becomes or ceases to be a member or a designated member the Registrar must be notified of this; similarly with a change in the name or address of any member.

The Companies Act 2006 (Commencement No. 2, Consequential Amendments, Transitional Provisions and Savings) Order 2007, restores protection to members of LLPs who have been granted confidentiality orders, from having their details open to inspection on the public register.

Internally, an LLP is much more flexible than a company. There is no complex statutory requirement for meetings of members or types of resolution. There is no board of directors. The ways in which the LLPs organise themselves is largely a matter for the partners themselves to agree upon. In a large firm, there will often be a written agreement but this (unlike the Articles of Association of a company) can be confidential and not made public. There are no statutory provisions for the protection of minority partners from the decisions of the majority, see Section 5.8.3 for the situation regarding companies.

Taxation (a subject which will interest members) will be on a partnership basis, with liability falling on partners individually, and not on the LLP as a whole.

Many of the LLPs will be formed by professional practices seeking the protection of limited liability without too many of the internal management constraints imposed on companies.

The Limited Liability Partnerships Act 2000

David Mason, *New Law Journal*, 16 February 2001
Reproduced by permission of Reed Elsevier (UK) Ltd, trading as LexisNexis Butterworths

A young girl travelling in her father's car saw a sign for Coventry. 'What's Coventry for, Daddy', she asked. A similar question might be asked about limited liability partnerships that will become part of the legal landscape from 6 April, 2001.

A cynic, or student, of the evidence submitted by Professor Sikka (of the University of Essex) to the Select Committee for Trade and Industry,[1] might answer that it exists primarily to aid the audit industry in further eroding its liability to its clients and the public generally. Professor Sikka argues that the legislation has been introduced with undue haste to satisfy the large accountancy firms' wish to avoid the consequences of 'mega claims' that might consign them to oblivion.

The Select Committee was critical of the attempt of the DTI officials who gave evidence to it to portray the Limited Liability Partnerships Act 2000 as a 'technical measure to bring British commercial law up to date'. If that was the case, the introduction of an entirely new platform for trade had been unduly delayed. The idea of introducing a form of limited liability partnership, as it then existed in Europe (the partnership *en commandite*), was first considered in 1837 by a commission that received evidence from, among others, John Stuart Mill, who no doubt contributed the utilitarian view, and Charles Babbage (the inventor of the mechanical computer). The commission reached no conclusion. Then, as now, opinion as to the merit and evils of the idea of limiting the liability of partnerships was divided. The inconclusive result of the commission was the Partnership Act 1890, which codified the common law relating to partnership but which introduced no concept of limited liability.

Successive governments have sought to provide the UK economy with the structures necessary to provide a competitive, modern, economy. As the Select Committee said, 'Over the past century there have been a raft of reviews and committees which have looked at company and commercial law, a number of which have touched on unlimited liability and absence of legal liability and absence of legal personality of partnerships.'

The Law Commission and the DTI collaborated in the early 1990s to review the law relating to joint and several liability in partnerships. As part of the overall need to provide modern and effective trading arrangements, to match those in the USA and Europe, the Conservative Government sought a Law Commission review of partnership law. In 1998, the present Government launched a review of company law. The DTI told the Select Committee that the result of the two reviews 'would be read across into the LLP regime'. The Act and its infant can therefore be seen as an interim measure. The Select Committee said that this 'was not an ideal way to proceed'.

Professor Sikka criticised the then Bill for various reasons. He said that it was 'difficult to read'. He is undoubtedly correct. In particular, the Act is a daunting example of legislation by reference. Various provisions of the companies, insolvency and taxation legislation are incorporated by reference in the Act, or in regulations made under the Act. Part of the 1890 partnership legislation is incorporated by regulation. No doubt law publishers will be rushing to provide a user-readable version.

More seriously, Professor Sikka sees the relative speed of implementation, and presumably the separation of the legislation from current reviews, as a panic reaction to pressure by that select circle of massive accountancy firms. Despite having had the right to trade as companies since 1989, accountants have proved reluctant to do so. The Select Committee thought that about 100 firms had incorporated. The profession still wanted limited liability, and two large firms promoted, at considerable expense, a Bill in Jersey. The legislation, limiting access to limited liability partnerships (LLPs) to accountancy firms, became Jersey law in 1996. The accountancy profession was then able, with the threat of offshore incorporation, to persuade, or as Professor Sikka would say, hold to ransom, the British Government into rapidly introducing LLPs into UK law.

Whether, for taxation or other practical reasons, moving offshore was practical or possible for the multinational accountants, and whether any recognisable economic result would have followed, is debatable. In any event, the efforts of the Select Committee, the professional bodies, and the DTI have produced a reasonably workable piece of legislation. Whether to proceed without making LLPs part of a wholly revised system of corporate and unincorporated trading system is debatable. No doubt politicians recognised the pressure on parliamentary time, the fact that Companies Acts do not attract votes, and judged it more likely than not that nothing would ultimately result from the reviews. Meanwhile, most of the States of the USA have LLP legislation, the Jersey law is in place and Germany, a major European competitor, has produced a form of limited liability partnership.

The Act creates 'a new form of legal entity'[2] with 'unlimited capacity'.[3] It may be formed by 'two or more persons associated for carrying on a lawful business with a view to profit'.[4] The Act makes it clear that partners may be corporate bodies.

Externally, the entity created by the Act looks very like a company. Unlike a partnership, it has legal personality. Partners in a conventional partnership contract as agents for the other partners. In an LLP, the contract will be with the LLP. Individual members will have no contractual liability to creditors. The position in tort is less clear. There may be circumstances in which the corporate veil will be lifted when an individual commits a tort. This has been left to the courts to work out. Similar issues were considered in *Williams* v. *Natural Health Foods Ltd*,[5] and it seems likely that an individual partner could be liable in tort.

Internally, the LLP closely resembles a conventional partnership. Relations between the partners are regulated by agreement between the partners, or where there is no agreement, default provisions largely based upon the 1890 Act apply. Partners will be taxed individually as now, and the creation of an LLP is intended to be tax-neutral.

There is no restriction on the type of business that can trade as an LLP. Early versions of the Bill allowed only regulated professions to operate as LLPs. That was considered unfair and unworkable. The Select Committee estimated that there are about 650,000 partnerships in the United Kingdom. Many will be small businesses, often among family members, and it seems unlikely that they will wish to be subject to the restrictions of an LLP.

The regulatory provisions of an LLP resemble a company. An annual return must be filed, with audited accounts, and many of the provisions of the Companies Acts apply. After much deliberation, protection for minorities is excluded. Much of the insolvency legislation applies, as do the provisions on director disqualification.

The main users of the LLP will presumably be professional firms. There is no legal reason why, for instance, dentists and doctors should not practise as LLPs.

Whilst the LLP may be seen as a means of avoiding expensive indemnity insurance and professional regulation, experience of those solicitors and accountants that have incorporated shows that not to be the case. Clients rely as much on the existence of cover as on professional ability when instructing professionals. Professionals will be individually subject to any professional regulations that apply. The professional bodies are unlikely to look kindly upon members who allow an LLP to become insolvent and then leave creditors to recover what they can from the corporate wreckage.

The final form of the regulations are at present unavailable (late January). There is an immense amount of detail to be considered later. Who will use the LLP, and how, is yet to be seen. It may become a relic of legal history, like the Limited Partnership

Act 1907, or a major vehicle for professional practice and trade. Time will tell. Hopefully, the accountancy profession will at last be content now with – four means of practice available to it.

References

1 Fourth Report, 16 February 1999
2 s.1(1)
3 s.1(3)
4 s.2(1)(a)
5 (1998) 1WLR 830

4.3 Corporations

4.3.1 The concept of incorporation

Corporations can come into existence in various ways. In England, the earliest surviving way is by *Royal Charter*. The Charter is issued by the Crown (the government) under the Royal prerogative on the advice of the Privy Council. Today, this form of incorporation is used almost entirely for non-trading bodies, such as the new universities, and professional bodies (including CIMA). The BBC is another example. As the powers of Parliament and the functions of government increased in the last two centuries, it then became common to create corporate bodies by *statute*. Local government authorities are notable examples today.

For businesses, a relatively simpler procedure is possible. Corporate bodies – companies – can be created under the Companies Acts by *registration* with a public official, the Registrar of Companies and, provided that the requirements of the Acts have been met, it is he who issues the certificate of incorporation (see later). The position today is substantially governed by the Companies Act 2006 which consolidates many earlier Acts.

All of the above types of corporation consist in reality of many human beings, who cooperate to form a further artificial person, the corporation. Because in reality the corporation is the activity of a group, it is sometimes called a *corporation aggregate*.

Some types of corporation can consist of only one human being, who is the holder for the time being of a particular office. The Public Trustee, who is a statutory official, is one human person. The *office* of Public Trustees is also a corporation, which owns the property and has the rights associated with that office. Therefore, when one holder of the office dies or retires, there is no need to transfer the property, rights and powers to his successor. The *office* is known as a *corporation sole*.

4.3.2 Some features of corporate personality

Separate legal personality

It will already be apparent that a corporation is *in law* a person in its own right. If Messrs A, B and C form a company, X Ltd, there are now *four* legal persons. X Ltd can sue its own members and be sued by them. It can employ its own members. Its property belongs to X Ltd, not to A, B or C. Its debts are its own, not those of A, B or C. The shareholders own the company, the company owns the assets. Many leading cases involve companies.

In *Salomon* v. *Salomon & Co Ltd* (1897), Mr Salomon formed a company in which, initially, seven people held one share each (as required by the Companies Act 1862 which was in force at the time): the shares were taken by Mr Salomon, his wife and five of his children. Mr Salomon then transferred his footwear business which he valued at some £30,000 to the new company. The company paid him by issuing to him 20,000 ordinary £1 shares and 'owing' him a further £10,000 which was secured over the company's assets by the terms of a debenture (a document which evidences a loan to a company and specifies any security granted). In short, he incorporated his existing business with himself as the main shareholder and a major creditor. Within twelve months the business became insolvent, and the company went into insolvent liquidation owing £10,000 to Mr Salomon and a lot of money to other creditors.

At first the liquidator of Salomon and Co Ltd refused to acknowledge the validity of Mr Salomon's security arguing that, in effect, Mr Salomon and the company were one and the same as he owned 20,001 of the 20,007 issued shares. As a result Mr Salomon had to sue his own company which was now under the control of the liquidator to establish the validity of his security. In fact Mr Salomon lost in every court until the case reached the House of Lords which held that Mr Salomon was entitled to his security. The House came to this conclusion by establishing that Mr Salomon and the company were two separate legal persons at law. In addition nothing fraudulent had happened in this case. The company did owe Mr Salomon £10,000 as part of the purchase price of the footwear business and the fact that he had a debenture which granted him security was properly registered and published so that those dealing with the company were aware of that fact.

When a company goes into insolvent liquidation the liquidator is required to be paid the company's creditors in a particular order. In Mr Salomon's time the holder of a debenture containing a floating charge (like Mr Salomon) had to be paid in full before anything could be paid to the unsecured creditors and the shareholders were last on the list to be paid. As a result of these rules Mr Salomon lost the value of his shares but:

(i) he was not personally liable for the debts which the company could not pay; and
(ii) as a secured creditor, i.e. a debenture holder, he was entitled to be (re)paid the amount owing, £10,000 from the sale of the company's assets in priority to the trade creditors, whose credit was unsecured.

It may be noted that today, following changes introduced by the Enterprise Act 2002, a certain amount of the assets available to floating charge holders has to be set aside for the benefit of any unsecured creditors. That point and fixed and floating charges are explained fully in Chapter 5.

The fact that a company is a separate legal entity also has pitfalls for the unwary. In *Macaura* v. *Northern Assurance Co Ltd* (1925), Mr Macaura formed a company in which he and his nominees held all of the shares. He then transferred his timber business to the company in return for shares in the same way as Mr Salomon had done. However, Mr Macaura continued to maintain insurance on the timber in his own name as if he was the owner of the timber. The timber yard was destroyed by fire, and Mr Macaura attempted to claim on his insurance policy. However, the insurance company refused to meet his claim as he was not the legal owner of the property. It is generally unlawful to insure another person's property, as the holder of the insurance may be tempted to destroy the property and claim on the policy! In law Mr Macaura had tried to insure someone else's property as he had transferred ownership of the timber to the company when he incorporated the business.

Limited liability

It follows naturally from separate legal personality that members of the corporation will have limited liability. The debts of the company (or council or building society or university) are those of the corporation, not those of the members. As a general rule, therefore, shareholders/directors/managers are not liable for the company's debts even if it becomes insolvent and is unable to pay: see *Salomon* v. *Salomon & Co Ltd* (1897) above. There are a few exceptions to this, particularly if the company has been run dishonestly: see Section 4.3.4 But the general rule normally applies.

Describing a company as a limited liability company is something of a misnomer as the ***company's*** liability is not limited in any way. Rather the expression is intended to signify that the liability of the ***members (shareholders)*** is limited. The company is fully liable for its own debts and creditors may pursue their claims against the company and its assets. The use of the term 'limited' in the name of a company is meant to warn outsiders that the liability of its shareholders is limited, that is, limited to the nominal value of the shares they hold. In practice it is quite common for the shareholders of many newly incorporated private companies to not have limited liability. This is so because many private companies are incorporated with insufficient capital to run their businesses. It follows that the company will have to obtain finance from elsewhere, usually in the form of a bank loan, and the bank will insist on the directors personally guaranteeing the company's debt as the company has insufficient assets to stand on its own feet. Only when the company has traded successfully and has sufficient assets to offer security for bank loans and other credit will the lenders proceed without insisting on personal guarantees with the result that they will truly enjoy limited liability.

This is one of the great advantages of corporate status; people are more likely to engage in large-scale or adventurous activity if they know that, so long as they are honest, they will not lose everything if the venture fails. They may lose what they have invested in this venture when (for instance) their shares become valueless; but they do not normally lose personal assets such as their homes and savings.

In this respect, companies differ fundamentally from partnerships, which have no separate legal personality. Each partner is potentially liable for all of the firm's debts. This can have drastic effects on businesses which were not permitted to operate as limited companies; see *ADT* v. *Binder Hamlyn* (1995) earlier.

Perpetual succession

This is another advantage which follows naturally from separate legal personality. As we have seen, the corporation's property belongs to the corporation, not to its members: see the *Macaura* case above. Therefore, when a member dies or transfers his share, there is no need *for the corporation* to transfer any part of its assets. This can be important for all types of corporate bodies. At every election, some local authority councillors will lose their seats and others will be elected instead. It would be quite impracticable to transfer ownership of the council's huge assets from the old members to the new each time. Even more so in a large company, where shares can be bought and sold every minute without any need for the company to alter ownership of the company's property.

The ultra vires rule

At one time the *ultra vires* rule was something of a disadvantage of corporate status, although it only applies to companies to a very limited extent today. A corporate body, being an artificial legal person, only has those powers which the law gives it. A statutory corporation, for example, depends largely on the statute which created it. Therefore, a local authority created for one town normally has no powers over the next town and even within its own boundaries, it can only spend its money for authorised purposes. Anything else would be *ultra vires* (beyond its powers) and therefore invalid. The issues can sometimes cause difficult: in *London Borough of Bromley* v. *Greater London Council* (1982), it was held *ultra vires* for Greater London Council (GLC) to subsidise public transport in the way in which it had done.

Since the Companies Act 1989, the effect of the *ultra vires* rule has been greatly lessened as regards companies, and this will be discussed later (Section 4.5.2).

4.3.3 Different types of companies

Companies registered under the Companies Acts can be classified in various ways.

Classification by limitation of liability

Unlimited companies can be created by registration under the Acts. The company is a separate legal entity and, if it has assets, it will have the benefits arising from separate legal personality when membership changes. But if the company's assets are insufficient to meet its liabilities, all members are liable to contribute without limit towards paying its debts and the cost of liquidation. If the personal resources of present members are insufficient, then ex-members who had left within the last 12 months can be called upon for debts incurred while they were members.

Such companies do have the advantage that they need not have their accounts audited, and need not deliver annual copies to the Registrar of Companies. This exemption does not apply, however, if the unlimited company is a subsidiary or a holding company of a limited one – otherwise, the unlimited company could be used to make nonsense of the disclosure requirements of the Companies Acts.

A company may be registered as unlimited from the outset, with or without share capital. A limited company may be re-registered as unlimited: the Registrar must be sent a prescribed form of assent, signed by or on behalf of all members; a statutory declaration by the directors that the signatories constitute all members; and a copy of the new Memorandum and Articles. Because of the risks, unlimited companies are rare.

In *companies limited by guarantee*, a member must, when he joins, guarantee the company's debts, but only up to a limited amount. There is no statutory minimum, and the guarantee may be for only £1. If the company engages in trading, however, a potential creditor might want a higher guarantee, or possibly a separate guarantee of his own credit to the company. If a guarantee company becomes insolvent, the members must pay the amount of their guarantee towards the company's debts. If this is insufficient, ex-members who had left within the last 12 months could be called upon for their guarantees towards debts incurred while they were members.

A guarantee company does have some of the advantages associated with separate legal personality, and it can sometimes escape having to end its name with the word 'limited' (see later). But it does have the expense of making annual returns to the Registrar, and of having its accounts audited.

It is no longer possible to create a company limited both by shares and by guarantee, although some such companies created before the 2006 Act still exist. Guarantee companies are not very common, and are used substantially for non-trading associations and clubs.

Companies limited by shares comprise the vast majority of companies. The company's capital is divided into 'shares'. Each member holds one or more. Initially, the shares are issued by the company in return for a payment by the member. Each share will have a 'nominal' value of, say, 50p, but a company will often issue its shares at a premium, that is, for more than the nominal value. If 50p shares are issued for £2.50 each, they are issued at a premium of £2. Sometimes a company allows payment by instalments, for example £1 immediately and the remaining £1.50 in one year's time. During this time, the shares are said to be 'partly paid'. The shareholder can be called upon to pay the remaining £1.50 immediately if the company becomes insolvent. But once the remaining £1.50 has been paid, the share is 'fully paid', and the shareholder has no further liability for the company's debts. A share can be sold partly paid, and the above rules apply to the new holder in the same way as they would have done to the old holder had he kept the share.

There are some exceptions to the basic rule that the holder of a fully paid share has no further liability for the company's debts: see the notes in Section 4.3.4. But these are very much exceptions, and the basic rule normally applies.

Public and private companies

Learning Outcome: To explain the differences between public and private companies.

A public company is almost invariably one limited by shares. (A guarantee company with a share capital can be public, but no new companies of this type can now be created.) It must comply with the following requirements of the Companies Act 2006:

1. The Memorandum of Association must specifically state that the company is to be public.
2. The name must end with the words 'public limited company' or the initials 'plc'. Welsh equivalents may be used if the registered office is in Wales.
3. The nominal capital must be at least 'the authorised minimum', currently £50,000.

A private company is one which does not satisfy *all* of these requirements. The vast majority of companies are formed as private and remain so. A private company can later be turned into a public one by satisfying the above requirements and re-registering as public. Some companies are public from the outset. The main differences between public and private companies are:

1. A public limited company's name must end with these words 'public limited company' or the initials 'plc' or Welsh equivalents in Wales.
2. There are no minimum nominal share capital requirements for private companies.
3. A private company can commence business immediately, as soon as it receives its certificate of incorporation (see later). A public company cannot do business until it has received a further certificate from the Registrar under S.761 CA 2006. The Registrar must be satisfied that shares with a nominal value of at least £50,000 have been allotted, with at least one quarter of the nominal value and the whole of any premium paid up. It follows that a public company must have received at least £12,500 in cash or assets before it can start trading. The Registrar must also be given information about preliminary expenses and payments to promoters.
4. A public company must have at least two directors. A private company needs only one.

5. A public company must have at least two shareholders but a private company needs only one. With effect from October 2008, the Companies Act 2006 provides that a public company need only have one member. Public companies are still required to have at least two directors and a qualified company secretary.
6. Only a private company can be unlimited, and a public company cannot be created limited by guarantee.
7. There are special provisions discussed later to lessen the administrative burden on small companies. The provisions for 'small' companies can only apply to private companies.
8. A private company cannot advertise its shares for sale to the public.

Single-member companies

The Companies (Single Member Private Limited Company) Regulations 1992 allow such companies to be formed in the same way as other private limited companies. Only one subscriber to the Memorandum is required and there need be only one share. There must however be two officers, a director and a secretary. Neither of these need hold shares. Existing companies can reduce their membership to one without re-registration, but the register must now state that the remaining shareholder is the only one. Such companies are likely to be very small businesses, or wholly owned subsidiaries of a single corporate shareholder. The law has struggled to fit the single member company into mainstream company law. For example, some provisions require directors to formally disclose their interests in contracts to the other members of the board, for example see S.177 CA 2006. In relation to board meeting, Lightman J in *Neptune (Vehicle Washing Equipment) Ltd* v. *Fitzgerald* (1996) stated: 'The sole director may hold a meeting attended by himself alone or he may hold a meeting attended by someone else, normally the company secretary. When holding the meeting on his own, he must still make the declaration to himself and have the statutory pause for thought, though it may be that the declaration does not have to be read out loud, and he must record that he made the declaration in the minutes.'

This decision has been criticised and it may be that it will not be followed by future courts. However, the court was keen to prevent the single director of this company from benefiting from his wrongdoings by arguing that the board knew what he was doing as he was the only director. The court noted that there was no evidence of disclosure to the board in board minutes so this argument could not stand.

For shareholder meetings, one member present is a quorum. He must provide the company with a written record of resolutions which can be taken in a general meeting, but no notices of meeting or minutes are required. The sole member can pass a written resolution (see later). Single-member companies which fall within the 'small companies' exemptions can escape the filing of reports, and even sometimes the need for an annual audit.

Holding and subsidiary companies

It will already be apparent that one company can hold shares in another. Many large businesses consist of many companies. Although in law each of these companies is a separate person, in reality the members of the 'group' are closely related and (usually) are run as a coherent whole. In this context, a 'holding' company is one which controls another (the 'subsidiary') either by:

(a) being a member of the subsidiary and controlling the composition of the subsidiary's board of directors; or
(b) holding more than half the equity share capital in the subsidiary.

Where the subsidiary itself has similar powers over another company, that other company too is a subsidiary of the holding or 'parent' company.

The relations can be complex but, in general, a subsidiary must not be a member of (i.e. shareholder in) its holding company. However, a company can take over another which *already* holds shares in the parent, and the subsidiary can continue to hold those shares.

Quoted companies

These are public companies whose 'securities' (shares and/or debentures) are 'listed' for buying or selling on a recognised stock exchange. The company must apply to the exchange, and must satisfy the requirements of the exchange as to matters such as disclosure and total value of shares. 'Listing' of their securities is sought, in the main, by the largest public companies.

Community interest companies

Since 2004 it has been possible to form a 'Community Interest Company' for those wishing to establish social enterprises. The company's object must be considered by a reasonable person to be of benefit to the community and any surpluses made by the company should be re-invested for the purposes of the company. Such a company must first be registered as a company limited by guarantee or as a company limited by shares and then apply to the Regulator for community interest company status. These companies may be used as vehicles for community interests such as a local crime prevention group. The company name must end in C.I.C. or Welsh equivalent (C.B.C.).

European companies

Since 8 October 2004 it has been possible to establish a European company ('Societas Europana' (SEs)). This is a public limited company formed under European law rather than the law of an individual member state. The founders must operate a business in at least two member states. For example, an SE could be formed by the merger of two companies operating in different member states. In practice, a number of problems remain with such companies, in particular the fact that the law which governs the SE largely depends upon the country in which it is registered. Rules relating to taxation, employment, insolvency, and so on are still not harmonised across the European Union and such harmonisation is not imminent. It follows that the establishment of such companies is unlikely to prove popular in practice at the present time.

'Small' companies

In general, companies must prepare annual reports and professionally audited accounts, which must then be filed with the Registrar of Companies and be open to public inspection. This can be a burden, and exceptions have therefore been made for 'small' companies. These are companies which have had for the present and previous financial years (or since incorporation) any two of the following: turnover not exceeding £2.8 million; balance sheet assets not exceeding £1.4 million; and on average, not more than 50 employees.

'Small' companies need not file their directors' report or profit and loss account with the Registrar. They need only file a shortened balance sheet, with no details of dividends or directors' remuneration. Most of them must still have their accounts audited, but the accounts of companies with sales of less than £350,000 do not need to be audited.

4.3.4 'Lifting the veil' of incorporation

The rule of separate legal personality can sometimes work injustice, particularly where the shareholders who control a company use its façade to conceal their own wrongdoing. ('Wrongdoing' in this sense means much more than mere *inability* to pay debts.) Both the courts and legislature have therefore, *exceptionally* looked behind the veil of separate personality, and taken account of who the shareholders behind the company really are. The following are some examples.

By the courts

The instances where the courts have lifted the veil of incorporation are difficult to classify. It is not easy to detect any coherent policy: the courts have been prepared to lift the veil in circumstances where justice demands it. These circumstances may be categorised as follows:

(a) In *fraud* or *sham cases* the courts will not allow the corporate form to be used to conceal dishonesty.

Examples

In *Gilford Motor Co. Ltd* v. *Horne* (1933), Horne was an ex-employee/director of the Gilford Motor Co Ltd. Whilst in the company's employ he signed a contract in which he agreed that if he left the company he would not attempt to solicit the company's customers. After leaving the company Mr Horne registered a company and in the name of that company attempted to solicit customers of the Gilford Motor Company. It was held that the company had been established to enable Mr Horne to get around his contract and was a mere sham to cloak his wrong doings. As a result the court granted an injunction against Mr Horne and his company to prevent any further soliciting of the Gilford Motor Company's customers.

In *Jones* v. *Lipman* (1962), the owner of land contracted to sell it to J, but then changed his mind. In order to keep the land, the owner set up a company and sold the land to it. He hoped that, although he personally would have to pay damages to J, the land would still be owned by 'his' company, which was a separate person. The court awarded specific performance against him and the company.

In *Catamaran Cruisers Ltd* v. *Williams* (1994), the court treated the company as a sham in a way which could have operated to the shareholder's advantage. W was employed by Catamaran Ltd. To lessen his tax liability, W formed a company, U Ltd, and Catamaran subcontracted W's work to U Ltd, paying it W's *gross* wages. In reality, W still did the work exactly as before. He worked under the same conditions as other Catamaran employees, even having sick pay and holiday leave. The court held that the company, U Ltd, was a 'subterfuge', and ignored the supposed 'veil' between U Ltd and its main shareholder, W. When Catamaran ended its contract with U Ltd, this was treated as a dismissal of W personally, even though strictly he himself was not an employee. (However, his dismissal was then held to be fair on the facts.)

(b) Courts have been prepared to recognise an *agency relationship* where groups of companies are concerned, though the notion has not gone very far. At no time have the courts regarded companies within the same group as liable for the debts of other companies in the group. In fact, where tax is concerned, the application of agency to groups has operated to the benefit of the companies concerned. A subsidiary which owns and funds (part of) a business has been held to do so as agent for the holding company so that the latter is treated as really running the business for the purposes of this case. In *Smith, Stone & Knight Ltd* v. *Birmingham Corporation* (1939), premises owned by SSK but used by a subsidiary were compulsorily purchased. The owner of the premises was entitled to compensation if it ran the business there itself, but the business seemed to be operated by its subsidiary, a separate person. However, the subsidiary was treated as doing so as agent for SSK and SSK was therefore entitled to compensation.

(c) In some cases, the courts are prepared to treat the group as one economic unit.

Examples

In *DHN Food Distributors Ltd* v. *London Borough of Tower Hamlets (1976)*. By Act of parliament when there has been a compulsory purchase order by a local authority, the authority must pay the market value of the land and compensation for any disruption to business. In this case the holding company was claiming compensation for disruption to business, even though the land purchased was held by one of its subsidiary companies, which, at law was a separate legal person. The court unanimously held that the parent company could recover compensation payments. It seemed to base its decision not upon the agency relationship between the companies but rather on the fact that the companies comprised a single economic unit. This decision has been widely criticised and would be unlikely to be followed today.

However, in *Woolfson* v. *Strathclyde Regional Council* (1978), the House of Lords, in a Scottish appeal, refused to treat the group as an economic unit and questioned it as a basis for lifting the corporate veil.

Perhaps the leading English authority on this point is the case of *Adams* v. *Cape Industries plc and Another* (1991), where the Court of Appeal refused to lift the veil of incorporation and treat the UK parent company, its US subsidiary, and an independent US corporation through which it marketed asbestos in the United States, as a single economic unit. The case concerned claims for damages for injuries sustained by exposure to asbestos dust and it was brought against the UK parent company because its US subsidiary had no assets. The court recognised that Cape's intention in setting up the corporate structure was to enable the sales of asbestos in the United States to be made while eliminating the appearance of any involvement therein of Cape itself. This could reduce its exposure to claims, as well as reducing its liability to taxation. The court said that there was nothing illegal in the defendants using their corporate structure to ensure that future legal liabilities to third parties would fall on another member of the group rather than on the defendants. The refusal of the court to lift the veil of incorporation or to treat the group of companies as a single economic unit meant that the plaintiffs, even if successful in their action against the US subsidiary, would receive no compensation since the subsidiary had no assets. In effect the court held that the Salomon principle is the correct starting point and the corporate veil will only be lifted where the subsidiary is a 'mere façade designed to conceal the true facts.' Presumably that means that *Gilford Motor Company* v. *Horne* above would still be decided the same way if the facts arose today. However in the case of *Adams* v. *Cape Industries plc and Another* there was no 'façade' and the holding company had acted entirely lawfully.

(d) *By EU law* in cases involving competition controls, the European Court of Justice can treat groups of companies as an economic unit (EC Treaty, Art. 86).

(e) *In national emergency cases*, in times of war or other emergency where economic sanctions may be imposed, the courts may have to lift the corporate veil to reveal the nationality of a company. In *Daimler Co Ltd* v. *Continental Tyre and Rubber (GB) Ltd* (1916), C Ltd was registered in England but all shares except one were German-owned. It was treated as German.

(f) The courts have been prepared to lift the veil in cases concerning the *Inland Revenue*. Thus, companies formed to facilitate tax evasion schemes have been treated as shams, and schemes to attract tax benefits between companies within the same group have been exposed.

In *Littlewoods Mail Order Stores Ltd* v. *Commissioners of Inland Revenue* (1969), the court lifted the veil to expose capital asset transfers between associated companies made for the purposes of obtaining capital allowances against tax.

For a review of recent case law on this topic, see the article entitled 'The Veil of Incorporation – Fiction or façade?'

By statute

Groups of companies generally have to produce group accounts which recognise that, although in law each company is a separate person, in reality the group is one business.

The relation between members of a group is recognised for tax purposes, and losses by one company can often be set against profits of another.

For the purposes of statutory employment protection, the transfer of an employee from one company to another *associated* company in the same group does not break the continuity of his employment.

There are many situations in which a director, manager, secretary or other officer of the company can become personally liable for the company's actions. These are not necessarily gaps in the veil between a company and its *members*, because such officers, directors and managers need not be shareholders. However, in practice, they usually do have shares, and the following are some instances:

- If a public company enters into a transaction without a S.761 CA 2006 certificate, and fails to comply with the transaction within 21 days of being called upon to do so, the directors can be personally liable.
- If a director signs a company cheque on which the company's full name does not appear, he is personally liable if the company does not pay – for example if he signs a cheque for ABC Ltd, omitting the word 'limited' (S.1295, Sch16 CA 2006). This rule can also apply to other contractual documents.
- When an insolvent company is wound up, someone who was a director during its last 12 months must not for the next 5 years carry on business in a name too similar to that of the ex-company. If he does so, he can be personally liable for his new company's debts.
- By the Company Directors Disqualification Act 1986, the court can disqualify a person from acting as a director. A person who disobeys such an order can be personally liable for the company's debts while he does so.
- When a company is wound up, the court may make a director, who is guilty of 'wrongful trading' (trading when he should have realised that his insolvent business could not recover), personally liable to contribute. There are wider provisions if a director or manager, and so on have been guilty of 'fraudulent trading' (see Section 5.7).

The Veil of Incorporation – Fiction or Façade?

Georgina Andrews, *Business Law Review*, January 2004, pp. 4–7
Reprinted with the permission of the author and Kluwer Law International

Introduction

The willingness of the courts to piece the corporate veil in cases where the use of the company structure is deemed to be a mere façade is a well-established feature of company law.[1] Identifying what is meant by the term façade is much more difficult.[2] In the recent case of *Trustor AB* v. *Smallbone and Others*[3], Sir Andrew Morritt VC re-examined the circumstances in which the courts may be prepared to lift the veil of incorporation, and determined that channelling funds through a company will not be sufficient to prevent the controller of the company from incurring personal liability in equity for knowing receipt of those funds, where the company is deemed to be a façade. Meanwhile, in *Re North West Holdings plc, Secretary of State for Trade and Industry* v. *Backhouse*[4], the Court of Appeal lifted the veil of incorporation by finding that a director who caused the companies that he controlled to incur costs in opposing winding up petitions without considering whether his actions were in the best interests of the companies and their creditors was personally liable for the costs incurred, despite the absence of any finding of dishonesty on the part of the director.

This article will investigate the willingness of the courts to pierce the corporate veil in cases such as *Trustor* where the corporate structure is deemed to be a façade, and will consider the nature of the 'façade' requirement. The significance of the intentions and motives of the defendant in cases involving the lifting of the corporate veil will be considered, and the differing attitudes of the courts to cases involving the use of the company structure to avoid existing and future liabilities will be explored. The writer will contend that the courts are more willing to lift the veil of incorporation on the grounds that the use of the corporate structure is a façade in cases where the company structure is deliberately used to conceal or avoid existing legal liabilities or to avoid liability for improprieties which are already planned at the time the company structure is procured, since in these cases evidence of the intentions and motivations of the defendant is also evidence that the company structure is being abused from the outset.

The fiction of the veil of incorporation

The principle that a company is an independent legal person is the single most significant principle of company law, famously articulated in the case of *Salomon* v. *Salomon and Co Ltd*.[5] This fundamental principle is based on fiction.[6] It is based on the pretext that the company is an artificial legal person that can be viewed as a distinct being; separate from its creators, directors, and members.[7] However, this principle is not inviolable. Parliament and the courts have proved willing to lift the fictitious veil in a number of circumstances,[8] including where the use of the corporate structure is deemed to be a 'sham' or 'façade'. In *Trustor*, Sir Andrew Morritt VC considered the circumstances that warrant the lifting of the corporate veil and stated that:

> the court is entitled to 'pierce the corporate veil' . . . if the company was used as a device or façade to conceal the true facts thereby avoiding or concealing any liability of those individuals.[9]

Trustor v. Smallbone

The facts leading to the High Court decision in *Trustor* are set out in detail in the Court of Appeal decision in the earlier case of *Trustor AB* v. *Smallbone (No 1)*.[10] In 1997, Mr Smallbone and Lord Moyne were appointed as directors of Trustor AB, a company incorporated in Sweden. Lord Moyne and Mr Smallbone misappropriated some SEK 779 m from *Trustor*. The recipients of the misappropriated funds included Mr Smallbone, and Introcom (International) Ltd, which was a company controlled by a Liechtenstein Trust of which Smallbone was a beneficiary. Some of the funds received by Introcom were applied for the benefit of Smallbone, whilst other funds were paid out to Lord Moyne and to a Mr Thomas Jisander, who in turn made substantial payments to Lord Moyne. Moyne was declared bankrupt in 1998. In 1999, Rimer J made an order for summary judgment against Smallbone in respect of the monies that he had received. Rimer J also dismissed Introcom's appeal against the much larger summary judgment order made against Introcom by Master Bowman. These orders were appealed in 2000, and in determining the appeals, the Court of Appeal indicated that Smallbone's liability was not limited to the amount of the judgment against him, but extended to a joint and several liability with Introcom for the much larger amount for which Introcom had been found liable. The Court of Appeal's judgment against Smallbone was not extended to this larger amount on this occasion because Smallbone's counsel had not had adequate opportunity to deal with some of the relevant points. Hence in 2001 Trustor made a further application to the High Court for the additional relief that had been suggested by the Court of Appeal.

In the High Court application by Trustor before Sir Andrew Morritt VC, Trustor accepted that whilst it was not disputed that the misappropriation of funds from Trustor constituted a breach of duty by Smallbone which gave rise to a liability for compensation, an interim payment order for £1 million against Smallbone on account of compensation was not justified as the amount of the loss was still too uncertain.[11] Hence Trustor's claim for summary judgment against Smallbone was advanced on a restitutionary basis only, as a claim in knowing receipt in respect not only of the funds which Smallbone and his family had personally received from Introcom, but in respect of all of the funds which Introcom had received from Trustor, including the substantial funds paid out to Moyne and Jisander. The claim based in knowing receipt could only succeed if the Court was willing to pierce the veil of incorporation and treat the receipt by Introcom as receipt by Smallbone.

In his judgment, Sir Andrew Morritt VC rejected the contention that the piercing of the veil of incorporation can be justified whenever it is deemed necessary in the interests of justice provided no unconnected third party is involved. This contention was said to be derived from *Re a Company*,[12] however Sir Andrew Morritt VC, found that the decision in *Re a Company* was inconsistent with the Court of Appeals decision in *Adams* v. *Cape Industries plc*,[13] where Slade LJ said:

> the court is not free to disregard the principle of *Salomon* v. *A Salomon & Co Ltd* merely because it considers that justice so requires.[14]

The Vice Chancellor also felt that the proposition that the corporate veil could be pierced where the company was engaged in some impropriety was too widely stated, since companies are often involved in improprieties, and:

> it would make undue inroads into the principle of *Salomon* v. *Salomon & Co Ltd* if an impropriety not linked to the use of the company structure to avoid or conceal liability for that impropriety was enough.[15]

However, Sir Andrew Morritt VC upheld the contention that the court was entitled to pierce the corporate veil where the company was shown to be a façade or sham with no unconnected third party involved. Since Introcom was a device or façade that was used as a vehicle for the receipt of the money of Trustor, the Vice Chancellor concluded that Smallbone was personally liable for knowing receipt of all of the funds that Introcom had received from Trustor.

Was Sir Andrew Morritt VC's decision to allow the corporate veil to be lifted in *Trustor* conceptually necessary? Susan Watson posed this question in her article 'Two Lessons from *Trustor*'[16] and concluded, interestingly, that it was not, stating that:

> What the judge did in essence was to look through the company and the trust structures in order to hold liable the individual who received the actual benefit of the money. The company and the trust structures were merely the conduit through which Smallbone received the funds.[17]

Thus, channelling the funds through the company structure was not sufficient to obstruct the operation of the normal rules of tracing, and hence to defeat the claim for personal liability for knowing receipt.

Whilst this is an accurate reflection of Smallbone's liability in equity for knowing receipt of the funds that were received by Introcom and applied for his benefit, it does not adequately explain the basis of his liability in respect of the substantial funds that were paid out to Moyne and to Thomas Jisander. There is no need to lift the veil of incorporation if the eventual recipient of funds channelled through a company is a defendant who receives the funds in the knowledge that the money has been misappropriated. However, if the funds are channelled to a third party, the only way in which a person other than the eventual recipient can be liable in equity for knowing receipt is if someone else received the funds first.

Liability for knowing receipt

Equitable liability for knowing receipt is a personal liability that arises when the defendant receives money or property that has been procured as a result of a breach of a fiduciary duty. Lord Hoffmann set out the requirements of liability for knowing receipt in the case of *El Anjou* v. *Dollar Land Holdings*.[18] His lordship stated that the claimant must show:

> first, a disposal of his assets in breach of fiduciary duty; secondly, the beneficial receipt by the defendant of assets which are traceable as representing the assets of the [claimant], and thirdly, knowledge on the part of the defendant that the assets received are traceable to a breach of fiduciary duty.

In recent years, the attention of the courts in cases such as *BCCI* v. *Akindele*[19] has focussed on the third requirement of knowledge.[20] In *Trustor*, there was no doubt that Smallbone had appropriated funds in breach of his fiduciary duties as a director. There was also no dispute that he had the requisite knowledge. Smallbone's personal liability for the funds that he and his family personally received from Introcom was therefore not in question. The contentious issue was whether Smallbone was liable for *all* of the funds that Introcom had received from Trustor. The only way in which this liability could be established was if the court was entitled to regard the receipt by Introcom as receipt by Smallbone. Thus, it is submitted, the lifting of the veil of incorporation was in fact required.

Sir Andrew Morritt VC's decision to lift the corporate veil in *Trustor* was based on cases such as *Gilford Motor Co Ltd* v. *Horne* and *Jones v. Lipman*, *Woolfson* v. *Strathclyde Regional Council, Adams* v. *Cape Industries plc, Re: H and others*, and *Gencor ACP Ltd* v. *Dalby*.[21] In these cases, the courts demonstrated that they were willing to lift the veil of incorporation in situations where companies were set up for the purpose of the avoidance of *existing*, as opposed to *future*, legal obligations, or where improprieties were planned at the time the companies were procured. For example, *Gilford Motor Co Ltd* v. *Horne* involved an individual who set up a company as a device to breach an existing contractual obligation (a non-solicitation covenant). Similarly, in *Jones* v. *Lipman* an individual wishing to avoid his personal liability to transfer land to a third party transferred the land to a company that he had acquired solely for that purpose. In *Adams* v. *Cape Industries plc* Slade LJ said:

> we do not accept as a matter of law that the court is entitled to lift the corporate veil as against a defendant company which is the member of a corporate group merely because the corporate structure has been used so as to ensure that the legal liability (if any) in respect of particular *future* activities of the group . . . will fall on another member of the group rather then the defendant company.[22]

It is submitted that this principle, applied in *Adams* in relation to use of the group corporate structure, is equally applicable to cases where the controller of the company is an individual, as opposed to a parent company. Namely, the court is not entitled to lift the corporate veil merely because the corporate structure has been used in an attempt to ensure that legal liability in respect of future activities will fall on the company rather than on the individual.

In *Trustor*, Smallbone gave evidence in person that Introcom had been formed as a vehicle for his remuneration in connection with an earlier scheme that had no connection with Trustor. However, Sir Andrew Morritt VC stated that Smallbone was bound by findings made by the Court of Appeal in *Trustor AB* v. *Smallbone (No 1)* that Introcom was controlled by Smallbone, and that the company was simply a vehicle set up for receiving money from Trustor. Thus the Vice Chancellor found that the potential to explore this evidence was precluded, since the Court of Appeal had already determined this point.

In different circumstances, evidence such as this might be sufficient to prevent the piercing of the corporate veil. Whilst it is appropriate to pierce the corporate veil in cases where the controllers of the company use the company as a device to escape liability for some existing legal obligation, or for some impropriety linked to the company structure which is planned at the time the company is procured, allowing the veil to be pierced on the grounds that the company structure has been used as a façade in cases where legal obligations arise subsequently (provided only that no third party is involved) would render virtually all one-man company directors and shareholders vulnerable to personal claims, and would take away the ability for them to organise their future business activities to limit personal liability. This would extend the principle that the veil can be lifted in cases involving façade or sham much further than envisaged in *Gilford Motor Co Ltd* v. *Horne, Jones* v. *Lipman* or *Adams* v. *Cape Industries plc*.

If the High Court had been able to consider Smallbone's evidence, and had found that Introcom had been formed for legitimate purposes unconnected with the misappropriation of funds from Trustor, a refusal to lift the veil of incorporation would not have prevented Smallbone from being liable in equity for knowing receipt of the funds that he had personally received. It would also not have affected Smallbone's personal liability to compensate Trustor for his breach of duties as a director as soon as it was possible to quantify the extent of the loss suffered. However, it might have defeated the claim for summary judgment against Smallbone based on his restitutionary liability in equity for knowing receipt in respect of the funds paid to Moyne and Jisander.

The significance of motives

In *Adams* v. *Cape Industries plc*, Slade LJ stated:

> whenever a device or sham or cloak is alleged . . . the motive of the alleged perpetrator must be legally relevant . . .[23]

His Lordship went on to recall the significance of the proven motive of the defendant in *Jones* v. *Lipman*. In *Trustor*, the Court was also clearly influenced by the finding of dishonesty on Smallbone's part. The recent case of *Re North West Holdings plc, Secretary of State for Trade and Industry* v. *Backhouse*[24] did not involve the lifting of the corporate veil on the grounds that the company structure had been used as a façade from the outset, however the case provides a further useful insight into the significance which the courts attach to the intentions and motives of the defendant in other cases involving the potential lifting of the corporate veil.

Mr Backhouse owned and controlled two companies that were the subject of winding up petitions. The companies were described in the Court of Appeal as having operated as mere alter egos of Mr Backhouse, as extensions of himself. Backhouse caused the companies to oppose the winding up orders, despite having been advised by counsel that the companies should not resist the orders since they were insolvent. Although Backhouse was not guilty of any conscious dishonesty, he perceived the petitions as an attack on his personal bonafides, and his motivation in causing the companies to resist the petitions was to achieve personal vindication. He had not given adequate consideration to the best interests of the companies and their creditors. Hence the Court of Appeal required Backhouse personally to pay the costs that he had caused his companies to incur in opposing the winding up petitions.

In dismissing the appeal against the orders of Hart J to wind the companies up, the Court of Appeal did not comment on Hart J's rejection of the submission that this amounted to the lifting of the corporate veil. According to Hart J, the relevant question in *Backhouse* amounted to whether sufficiently exceptional circumstances existed to justify the court in ordering a non-party to pay costs, which did not require the corporate veil to be lifted. Since Backhouse had not given any serious consideration to what was in the best interests of the companies and their creditors, and the costs had in fact been expended for Backhouse's individual interests, Hart J held that it would be just for Backhouse to pay the costs personally. The Court of Appeal found that this was a proper exercise of the judge's discretion.

Whilst the *Backhouse* decision may be appropriate on its facts, it is difficult to see how this in truth amounted to anything other then the lifting of the corporate veil.[25] Although the independent existence of the companies was not technically denied, the corporate veil was lifted in the sense that on this occasion the controller of the companies was not allowed to shelter behind the fictional veil of incorporation, and hence avoid personal liability for the costs incurred by the companies. Interestingly, in *Backhouse*, a finding of conscious dishonesty on the part of the controller of a company was not required to justify the lifting of the corporate veil by virtue of the discretion given under s.51 of the Supreme Court Act 1981 to order exceptionally a person not a party to court proceedings to pay the costs of those proceedings. Actions motivated by factors other than the best interests of the companies and their creditors were sufficient.

Why do the courts place so much emphasis on the intentions or motives of the defendant in cases involving the lifting of the corporate veil? The decision to place the interests of the controllers of a company before the interests of the company itself, in addition to constituting a breach of fiduciary duties by the directors of the company,[26] may provide evidence that the corporate structure is being abused. Certainly, in both *Backhouse* and *Trustor*, the defendants' perceived motivations and actions demonstrated their view of their respective companies, not as independent entities, but rather as vehicles through which their own best interests could be best served. In *Backhouse*, the controller of the companies purported to shelter behind the veil of incorporation, but was content to ignore the implications of the existence of the veil, and the interests of those independent entities, when it suited him. This did not result in the lifting of the corporate veil on the grounds of façade, since there was no evidence that the companies had been procured to conceal any existing or planned improprieties, but the veil was lifted on other grounds. Meanwhile, in *Trustor*, the company structure was used simply as a vehicle for Smallbone to receive funds that he had misappropriated from Trustor. This amounted to an abuse of the company structure from the outset, and as no third parties were involved, the corporate veil was lifted on the grounds that the use of the company structure was a façade.

Conclusions

Where a company is procured to enable an individual to avoid liability for some existing legal obligation, or to conceal some planned impropriety linked to the company structure, evidence of the intentions and motives of the controller of the company is also evidence that the use of the company structure is a façade or sham, which is an abuse of the company structure from the outset. In contrast, sheltering behind the fictional veil of incorporation to limit personal liability for future business activities, in the absence of any specific planned impropriety linked to the company structure, is simply legitimate reliance on the principle articulated in *Salomon* v. *Salomon*. In these circumstances, the corporate veil will not be lifted on the grounds that the company structure has been used as a façade, although the veil may be lifted on other grounds if appropriate circumstances arise. The problem that remains for the courts is to ascertain the intentions of the controller, and hence determine whether the controller should benefit from the protection provided by the fictional veil of incorporation, or incur personal liability as a consequence of the façade.

Notes

1 *Gilford Motor Co Ltd* v. *Horne* [1933] Ch 935; *Jones* v. *Lipman* [1962] 1 WLR 832; *Woolfson* v. *Strathclyde Regional Council* [1978] STL 159; *Adams* v. *Cape Industries plc* [1990] 1 Ch 433; *Re: H and others* [1966] 2 BCLC 500; *Gencor ACP Ltd* v. *Dalby* [2000] 2 BCLC 734.

2 Hawke, N & Hargreaves, P 'Corporate Liability: Smoke and Mirrors' ICC LR 2003, 14(2), 75–82.

3 [2001] 3 All ER 987.

4 [2001] EWCA Civ 67, [2001] 1 BCLC 468.

5 [1897] AC 22.

6 See *Trustees of Dartmouth College* v. *Woodward* (1819) 17 US (4 Wheat) 518; *Welton* v. *Saffery* [1897] AC 299.

7 Although subscribers to 'realist' or 'natural entity' theories argue that an association of persons has a real personality which is recognised by incorporation as a company, see Mayson, French & Ryan *Company Law* (20th Edn, 2003) at p. 171.

8 For example, the corporate veil will be lifted under s.4 of the Companies Act 1985 if the minimum member requirements are breached; it will also be lifted under ss.213 and 214 of the Insolvency Act 1986 in cases involving fraudulent or wrongful trading. The Courts will lift the corporate veil in the cases where the company is deemed to be acting as an agent for a third party *Smith, Stone and Knight Ltd* v. *Birmingham Corporation* [1939] 4 All ER 116.

9 N3 *supra* at 22.

10 [2000] 1 All ER 811.
11 This is similar to the House of Lords' decision in *Standard Chartered Bank* v. *Pakistan National Shipping Corpn and others* [2002] UKHL 43, [2003] 1.AC 959, where a director was found to be personally liable in fraud not because he was a director, but because he personally had committed the fraud. Likewise, in *Trustor*, Smallbone was liable for his personal breach of duty.
12 [1985] BCLC 333.
13 [1990] 1 Ch 433.
14 N 13 *supra* at p. 536.
15 N 3 *supra* at 22.
16 (2003) 119 LQR 13.
17 N 16 *supra* at p. 14.
18 [1994] 2 All ER 685, at 700.
19 [2000] 3 WLR 1439.
20 Peter Jaffrey provides an explanation of the knowledge requirement in his article 'The Nature of Knowing Receipt' (2001) *Trust Law International* 15(3), 151.
21 N 1 *supra*.
22 N 13 *supra* at 544, italics added by the author.
23 N 13 *supra* at 540.
24 N 4 *supra*.
25 *Backhouse* is described as a case in which the Court of Appeal was prepared to lift the corporate veil in Hawke, N & Hargreaves, P 'Corporate Liability: Smoke and Mirrors' N 2 *supra*.
26 *Re Smith and Fawcett Ltd* [1942] Ch 304.

4.4 Company registration

Learning Outcome: To explain the distinction between establishing a company by registration and purchasing 'off the shelf'.

4.4.1 Promoters

Those who set out to form a company are called its 'promoters'. They include those who arrange for the documents to be drafted and filed, those who buy for or transfer property to the new company, nominate the first directors, *choose* the company's accountants and solicitors, open its bank accounts and arrange finance and shareholding.

They do not include the independent *providers* of professional services, such as the proposed company's accountants, solicitors or bankers themselves.

Promoters owe stringent fiduciary duties to the company: good faith, care and such skill as they have. Although they are allowed to charge for, or make a profit from, their activities, promoters must disclose this to the company and its shareholders; otherwise they may be made to account for it to the company. When a small private company is formed, the promoters themselves may be the only shareholders and directors, and in this situation, little difficulty should occur. The position may be more complex if there are also new shareholders.

Most of the activities undertaken by promoters will lead at some point to a contract made (purportedly) between an outsider and the company. Promoters should be careful not to enter into such contracts until the company is actually in existence. Pre-incorporation contracts are not enforceable against a company but they may be enforced personally against the promoter himself. Promoters are allowed to charge for their pre-incorporation services but they cannot compel the company to pay them. The company may, however, choose voluntarily to reimburse their expenses.

4.4.2 Registration

The main legal task of the promoters is to file the necessary documents with the Registrar of Companies in Cardiff. These documents are:

- the Memorandum of Association;
- the Articles of Association (not strictly necessary – see later);
- details of the registered office, the first directors and the company secretary (Form G. 10);
- a statutory declaration that the requirements of the Companies Acts have been complied with; (Form 12);
- a small registration fee (currently £20). Company registration agents are able to register a company electronically. Persons wishing to register a company can use the services of such agents and the process can be completed within approximately 4–5 hours.

When the CA 2006 is fully in force there will be a new process of registration. Section 8 introduces a new format for the Memorandum of Association which becomes a record of the initial subscribers and their request to be incorporated. It ceases to have its former prominence as the principal element of a company's constitution. (Scheduled to come into force October 2009.) After that time the company's constitution will effectively consist of a single document – the Articles of Association. The Memorandum, which will be a prescribed form, will simply state that the subscribers wish to form a company and agree to be the members and take at least one share each. It will be delivered to the Registrar with an application for registration, and must state the proposed name, the situation of the registered office (England and Wales; Wales; Scotland or Northern Ireland); whether the members liability is to be limited by shares or guarantee and whether the company is to be public or private. (Section 9 CA 2006). If the company is to have a share capital there must also be a statement of capital and initial shareholdings. (S.10 CA 2006.)

The Memorandum of Association and its clauses

At present this document describes the company's characteristics and affects its relationship with the outside world. Its form is governed by regulations under the Companies Act. There are five compulsory clauses:

1. name;
2. registered office;
3. objects;
4. liability of members;
5. nominal/authorised capital.

Name. The promoters will choose this, but there are some constraints, and the Registrar must refuse to accept some names.

- The name must end with 'limited' (or its abbreviation 'Ltd') if the company is a private one limited by shares, or 'public limited company' ('plc') if it is public. These words or abbreviations must not appear other than at the end. If the company is specifically registered as Welsh, then the Welsh language equivalents ('cyfyngedig', 'cyf', etc.) may be used.
- Exceptionally, a non-profit making *guarantee* company can apply for exemption from ending with 'limited', and so on.
- The name must not be the same (or virtually the same) as that of an existing registered company. In practice it is possible to log on to the companies house website and check the index of names to see whether or not the proposed name is already in use.

In general a company may select any name it wishes. However, the Secretary of State may issue regulations regarding the letters or other characters, signs, symbols and punctuation that may be used in a corporate name. (S.57 CA 2006.)

The use of certain names is prohibited. A name must not be 'offensive' or constitute a criminal offence. The Secretary of State may direct a company to change its name and a failure to comply constitutes a criminal offence. (S.67 CA 2006.) There will be an independent adjudicator who will be able to consider objections from people who argue that a company name is the same as the name of the company in which they have goodwill or is sufficiently similar to suggest a connection. In addition, the members of a company may change its name by passing a special resolution (see later).

In choosing a name, the promoters should also be aware of the law of trade marks, under which another business could prevent the use of a name too like that of itself *or its products*, irrespective of what the Registrar has approved.

Companies trade under corporate names but they may also trade under other, non-corporate, names. For example, ABC Limited may trade under the name 'Simply Blue' a business name. When selecting a business name, care must be taken not to choose one which is already in use, that is, by another undertaking, as either a corporate or a business name – otherwise it may give rise to an action in tort for passing-off: [*Ewing* v. *Buttercup Margarine Co Ltd* (1917)]. Under the Part 41 of the CA 2006, the name of the company must appear on all business documents and be clearly shown at all premises to which the public is likely to have access or where business is transacted.

Registered office. Every company must have one. This is the company's legal home and determines the company's domicile. Writs and other documents can be served on it there, and various registers must be kept there, often available for inspection by shareholders, creditors and/or the public. It need not be at or near any place where the company does business.

The Memorandum need only state the (British) country of registration: Scotland; England and Wales generally; or specifically Wales for Welsh companies. The actual address need only be given on Form G.10 (together with particulars of directors, etc.) which must be delivered with the Memorandum, but it is often also included in the Memorandum.

The address of the registered office may later be changed by the members by an ordinary resolution of which the Registrar is informed. However, an English and/or Welsh company cannot move its registered office to Scotland and vice versa. A new company must be formed in the new country.

Objects clause. This defines (often at great length) the purpose for which the company is set up, and the activities which it proposes to carry out. Its original purpose was to protect shareholders and investors by limiting the ventures for which their investment could be used. Anything outside of this range was *ultra vires* and therefore void. Proposed activities could be stopped in advance by an individual shareholder, and *ultra vires* contracts did not bind the company. In fact, the objects clause was often drafted very widely, so as to give the company as much freedom as possible. Companies can limit or extend their objects by passing a special resolution (75 per cent majority of votes cast) at a general meeting. Private companies can also change their objects by a written resolution approved by 75 per cent of all the shareholders without having to call a meeting.

The potential importance of the objects clause has been lessened by the following changes:

1. Since the Companies Act 1989, s.110, it has been permissible to state simply that the object of the company is to 'carry on business as a general commercial company'. This effectively renders the *ultra vires* doctrine irrelevant so far as trade and business activities are concerned, although any non-business activity might still be affected. However, most existing companies still keep their original objects, and many new companies do not use this 'general commercial' formula.
2. As a result of EU law, the *ultra vires* rule was restricted as regards any transaction decided on by the directors. This became s.35 of the Companies Act 1985. The 1989 Act clarified and extended s.35, so that now 'the validity of an act done by the company shall not be called into question on the ground of lack of capacity by reason of anything in the company's Memorandum'. The law is now contained in Section 31 to 52 of the CA 2006. This will be discussed in more detail later in this chapter.

With effect from October 2009, the Companies Act 2006 provides that all companies will have unlimited objects, unless they choose to restrict them in their Articles of Association. (S.31 CA 2006.). After October 2009, any company registered before then which has restrictions on its objects in the Memorandum will be treated as if those restriction are contained in the company's Article of Association. (Section 28 CA 2006).

Liability clause. This merely states that the liability of members is limited. It need not even state whether the limitation is by shares or by guarantee.

Capital clause. A company limited by shares must state the amount of the share capital with which it is to be registered, and how this will be divided into shares of a fixed amount. This is the company's *authorised* or *nominal* capital, and represents the number of shares which a company can issue. A public company must have an authorised capital of at least £50,000 (see earlier). The authorised capital does not necessarily represent the *amount* of capital which a company can raise, because shares are often issued at a premium, that is, for more than their nominal value. They cannot be issued at a discount. The authorised capital can be increased later by special resolution if, for example, the company wishes to expand.

Association clause. The Memorandum ends with a statement that the subscribers wish to be formed into a company. For public companies, there must be at least two subscribers whose names and addresses appear at the end. Each must take at least one share, and the Memorandum must say how many he should take. Each must sign, and signatures must be witnessed. Private limited companies can now be formed with only one subscriber.

Other clauses. In appropriate cases, some other clauses must be included before the association clause. For example:

- If the company is public, there must be a statement that the company is to be a public one.
- If the company does not wish to submit any Articles of Association, it must provide in its Memorandum that it is adopting Table A; see later.

With effect from October 2009, the Companies Act 2006 provides for a new format of Memorandum of Association which will cease to be the principal document of a company's constitution.

The Articles of Association

These regulate the internal affairs of the company and the position of the members. They cover such matters as meetings, voting and other rights of shareholders, transfer of shares, dividends, the position of directors and their powers of management. Articles must be printed and signed by the subscribers of the Memorandum, and the signatures must be witnessed.

A company need not, however, submit any Articles. It may simply provide in the Memorandum that it is adopting Table A, a model set of Articles published in regulations made under the Companies Act 1985 (or, before the 1985 Act, set out in Schedules to the earlier Companies Acts). Table A has been changed from time to time, and a company which adopts Table A keeps the version existing at the time when it was formed. In any event, the Table A current at the time of incorporation always applies except in so far as it is expressly or impliedly overruled by the company. Most companies do in fact submit their own printed Articles, for example, so as to give greater protection to the directors: see *Bushell* v. *Faith* (1970) (later).

The Articles may later be altered at a general meeting of shareholders by special resolution (75 per cent of votes cast), or by a written resolution agreed to by 75 per cent of all the members in a private company. The alteration must not:

- clash with the Memorandum;
- oblige existing shareholders to take more shares or to provide more capital without their written consent;
- discriminate between members; or take away the rights of any class of shareholders, without approval of the change by a special resolution of shareholders *of that class*;
- be illegal; and
- the alteration must be for the benefit of all shareholders and the company as a whole.

With effect from October 2009, a new simplified model form of articles of association will be available for private companies and a separate form of articles for public companies. The draft version of the new articles of association for private companies can be seen by following the links at the following website www.berr.gov.uk/

Statement of directors, company secretary, and so on – Form G.10

This must be signed by the subscribers of the Memorandum and filed with it. It must give particulars of the first director or directors, with their consent to act. Particulars include information about any other directorships which they have.

The first company secretary must be nominated on this form, with consent to act. A director can serve as company secretary, but only if there is at least one more director; the company must have at least two officers. The secretary is, in effect, responsible for administering the requirements of the Companies Acts, particularly as regards the registers, information and documents which must be kept and made available.

Those named and consenting to act on this form automatically become the first directors and secretary. The address of the registered office must also be given here; see above.

With effect from October 2009, the Companies Act 2006 provides that directors will be able to provide a service address for the public record – rather than the home address.

Statutory declaration

A person named as a director or the company secretary (above), or a solicitor engaged in forming the company, must complete a statutory declaration that the registration requirements of the Companies Acts have been complied with. The Registrar can accept this declaration as sufficient evidence.

The registration fee

This is currently £20.

The certificate of incorporation

On receipt of the above documents and his fee, the Registrar will satisfy himself that the statutory requirements have been met; for example, that the purposes are lawful, that the chosen name is available, that all of the required documents have been submitted and that the Memorandum (and Articles if submitted) are in the proper form, printed, signed and the signatures witnessed.

If he is satisfied, the Registrar must then sign a certificate stating that the company is incorporated, and the company comes into existence on the date given in the certificate. The company's registered number given in the certificate must thenceforth be used in all of the company's official documents and business letters.

A certificate of incorporation is conclusive evidence of the matters which it states. For example, if any future dispute arises over exactly when the company was formed (e.g. over taxation or an allegedly pre-incorporation contract), the date in the certificate is conclusive, even if it is alleged that the Registrar's office accidentally put the wrong date. If the certificate states that the company is public, again this is conclusive evidence that it is public. The company's affairs cannot, therefore, be challenged later by any allegation of irregularities in the registration *procedure*. Exceptionally, however, registration may later be challenged *by the Crown*, through the Attorney General, on grounds that the *objects* were illegal or contrary to public policy: see *Bowman* v. *Secular Society* (1917).

As we have seen, a private company can start its activities immediately from the date of incorporation. A public company must satisfy the further requirements of S.761 CA 2006 before doing business or borrowing money.

4.4.3 'Off-the-shelf' companies

Rather than forming a new company themselves, by registration under the above procedures, those wishing to set up a company may buy one 'ready-made' or 'off-the-shelf' from a firm which deals in formation services. The dealer holds in stock a number of ready-made companies, with generally non-descriptive names and an authorised share capital of, say, £1,000. These companies have been incorporated using members of the dealer's staff as the subscribers of the memorandum and articles and as the first directors and secretary. The companies are available for immediate trading once ownership of the shares has been transferred and the new officers have been appointed. There need be no problem with the objects because the ready-made company will often have the 'carry on business as a general commercial company' objects clause allowed by the Companies Act 1989 (see earlier). So far as the name is concerned, the company can either trade with the existing name, or have the existing name changed to one of the purchaser's choice, subject to availability. Alternatively, the name could be retained and a business name utilised. If required, the dealer will usually arrange for the name to be changed for a fee. The new members may want to change the registered office, but need not do so.

Some advantages have been claimed (often unjustifiably) for buying ready-made companies:

- *Speed.* If the company is required urgently and the forms can be delivered or faxed to the buyer, the company can be obtained in a single day. A certificate of incorporation for a tailor-made company may not be received from Companies House for 8–10 working days after receipt of the requisite documents. However, Companies House now offers a "Same Day Incorporation Service" the registration cost of which is £50.00 and for which the registration documents must be received by Companies House before 15.00 hours. It may be thought that such a service would have rendered the advantage of off the shelf companies obsolete, particularly as they usually cost upwards of £90. However, it must be remembered that in order to take advantage of the Same Day Incorporation Service, the requisite documents must be completed and sent to Companies House. When purchasing off the shelf companies all these documents have already been correctly completed so the promoter is saved the trouble of having to do this him/herself or paying for a lawyer or accountant to complete them.

- *Cost.* An 'off-the-shelf' or ready-made company can be obtained for less than £100, whereas a lawyer or accountant is likely to charge something in the region of £200 plus to register a company. In practice the latter may be cheaper in the long run. The memorandum and articles of an off-the-shelf company are likely to be in a standard format. It may be preferable for the incorporators to pay the extra £100 or so and have a memorandum and articles that is tailor-made for their requirements. If the memorandum or articles or name have to be changed, then these transactions require a special resolution and new documentation to be sent to the registrar of companies. If the business has been carried on under a business name, it is of course possible to continue to use that name. However, to comply with the Business Names Act 1985, the name of the company (the new owner) must be substituted on all business correspondence and stated at all business premises.
- *Administration.* The administration in establishing the company is looked after by the formation dealers, who keep it fairly simple for buyers. However, formation dealers often act as agents in forming newly registered companies as well, and they can keep the procedure for this simple too. The dealer can usually give some advice (without charge) over the availability of new company names sought. They will often also offer to act as a joint company secretary for a while so as to look after early administrative needs.

4.4.4 The company's 'constitution'

Learning Outcome: To explain the purpose and legal status of the Memorandum and Articles of Association.

Effect of the Memorandum and Articles

By the Companies Act 2006, s.33, the Memorandum and Articles, when registered, bind the company and its members as a contract between them. All shareholders, and the company itself, are taken to covenant to observe all of the provisions. This applies not only to those who were members when the company was formed, but also to all current shareholders at any time in the future.

Therefore, any member who breaks his obligations as a member (e.g. by not paying uncalled amounts on his shares) can be sued by the company. Members can also owe duties to each other as members: see *Rayfield* v. *Hands* (1958). And the company can be prevented from denying to a shareholder his rights as a shareholder (e.g. to have his votes accepted at a meeting: *Pender* v. *Lushington* (1877)).

In *Eley* v. *Positive Government Security Life Assurance Co* (1876) the Articles of Association of the company provided that Eley was to be the company's solicitor for life. The company decided to use another solicitor and Eley sued the company for breach of contract under what is now s.33 of the CA 2006. The court stated that the Articles (and Memorandum) of Association of a company are only contractual in respect of *ordinary membership rights*. As this provision in the Articles referred to Eley in his capacity as a solicitor rather than as a shareholder, it was an *outsider right* and not contractual under s.33. It follows that the Memorandum and Articles of Association are only contractual under s.33 in respect of shareholder rights such as the right to vote, the right to receive dividends and the right to attend and vote at company meetings, and so on. If the Articles or Memorandum provide rights or obligations to a person in a capacity other than shareholder, the right is not contractual under s.33, although it may be contractual by the application of the general law. For example, in *Re New British Iron Co Limited ex parte Beckwith* (1898), the articles stated that the directors should be paid remuneration of £1,000 per annum. When the directors (who were also shareholders) were not paid, they sued for breach of contract under what is now s.33. It was held that although the directors could not succeed under s.33 (as this was not a membership right), it was clear that under the ordinary rules of contract they had carried out work for the company and were entitled to payment. How much should they be paid? As the Articles mentioned a figure of £1,000 per annum the court held that that was the amount payable. It follows that if the Articles could not be enforced *directly* under s.33 they were enforceable *indirectly* in that the court in effect transferred the provision in the Articles into the implied contract between the company and the directors.

For a review of recent case law on this topic see the article entitled 'Interpreting corporate constitutions: recent judicial illumination' in the 'Readings' section at the end of this chapter.

After October 2009 the Articles of Association will be the main constitutional document of the company.

Altering the company's constitution

The Memorandum of Association can subsequently be altered. The various compulsory clauses already outlined (company name, etc.) can each be altered in the ways already mentioned in each case. Sometimes, other provisions are included in the Memorandum even though they could simply have been put in the Articles. For example, sometimes a division of the shares into different classes, such as preference and ordinary shares, is made in the Memorandum. Such a non-compulsory provision can be altered by a special resolution (75 per cent of votes cast) or a written resolution (of 75 per cent of all private company members). This is subject to special provisions to protect the rights of each class.

The Articles of Association may be altered by special or written resolution. The resolution and the revised Articles must be filed with the Registrar within 15 days of the date of the resolution. There are, however, important limits on shareholders' powers of alteration:

- There are special protections for class rights.
- The alteration must not contravene any other provisions of the Companies Acts, or contravene a court order under, for example, S.994–999 CA 2006 (Chapter 5). Nor must it be inconsistent with any provision in the Memorandum which, in cases of conflict, prevails.
- An alteration cannot force members to buy more shares or to contribute more to the share capital unwillingly.
- Under the common law an alteration may be amended or cancelled if it discriminates between majority and minority shareholders. It follows that to be valid the alteration

must be made in good faith in the best interests of all the shareholders. This is an objective test and is applied by taking the case of an individual hypothetical member and asking whether his/her rights have been improved by the alteration. If the answer is 'yes', the alteration is valid at common law [*Greenhalgh* v. *Arderne Cinemas Ltd* (1950)].

Examples

In *Brown* v. *British Abrasive Wheel Co Ltd* (1919), the holders of 98 per cent of the issued capital of the company promised to invest further capital in it provided that they were given the right compulsorily to purchase the shares of the minority shareholders. An alteration was proposed to effect this change and the minority sued. The alteration was held invalid, as it was not for the benefit of the company as a whole, only box the majority.

However, in *Shuttleworth* v. *Cox Bros & Co Ltd* (1927), the Articles were altered in a way which allowed the board to sack a particular director. This was held valid because, on the facts, it was in the company's interests to sack the director, who had several times failed to account to the company for money which he had received on its behalf.

Model Memorandum and Articles of Association for a private company limited by shares

(Note that the following applies until October when the CA 2006 is expected to be fully in force. The vast majority of companies were, of course, registered before October 2009 so they will have documents in the form shown below. However, any restrictions on the objects clause in the Memorandum of Association will be treated as if they were contained in the company's Articles of Association. (S28 CA 2006).)

Memorandum of Association of Glitch Limited

Those who set up a company may have any Articles of Association that they wish. However, Table A which is a model form of Articles and its provisions apply unless they are excluded. There is now a new form of Table A for private companies which will apply to all private companies registered after the issue of the new Table A. Any private company may adopt the new Table A by passing a special (or written special) resolution to that effect. Companies registered before the new Table A was issued will, of course, still have Articles related to the old Table A which will remain in force for those companies. You may view the new Table A by following this link www.berr.gov.uk/ Clearly the vast majority of companies were registered before the issue of the new Table A and the following example of a Memorandum and Articles of Association is still relevant to a large number of existing private companies.

1. The name of the company is Glitch Limited.
2. The registered office of the Company is situated in England.
3. The objects for which the Company is established are:
   (a) To carry on the business as a general commercial company;
   (b) To carry on any other business which seems to the Company's directors capable of being conveniently or profitably carried on in connection with that business or calculated directly or indirectly to enhance the value or render more profitable any of the Company's assets;
   (c) To do all such other things which may seem to the Company's directors to be incidental or conducive to the attainment of the objects;
   (d) Without prejudice to the generality of the foregoing, the Company shall have power

- to carry on its business in any part of the world,
- to carry on its business alone or in association with any one or more persons (whether natural or legal) or by any one or more subsidiary companies,
- to pay all expenses of and incidental to its formation and the underwriting, placing or issue of its securities,
- to grant options and other rights over its securities in favour of employees and others,
- to sell, lease or dispose of for cash or for any other consideration the whole or any part of its undertaking and property,
- to draw and accept and negotiate negotiable instruments,
- to borrow money, and guarantee the indebtedness and the performance of the obligations of others (whether or not the Company receives any consideration for or direct or indirect advantage from the giving of any guarantee) and to do so with or without security,
- to give mortgages and other securities on all or any of its assets including uncalled capital,
- to lend and invest its money in such manner as the directors determine,
- to promote other companies,
- to distribute assets in specie to its members.

(e) None of the sub-clauses of this clause and none of the objects therein specified shall be deemed subsidiary or ancillary to any of the objects specified in any other such sub-clause, and the Company shall have as full a power to exercise each and every one of the objects specified in each sub-clause of this clause as though each such sub-clause contained the objects of a separate company.

4. The liability of the members is limited.
5. The share capital of the Company is one hundred pounds divided into one hundred shares of £1 each.

We, the subscribers to this Memorandum of Association, wish to be formed into a company pursuant to this Memorandum of Association, and we agree to take the number of shares in the Company's capital set opposite to our respective names.

Names and addresses of subscribers	No. of shares taken by each subscriber
Name	One
Address	
Name	One
Address	
Dated this (*date*)	
Witness to the signatures:	
Name	
of (*address*)	
(*occupation*)	

Articles of Association of Glitch Limited

Preliminary

1. Except as mentioned in these Articles, the regulations contained in or made applicable by Table A in the Schedule to the Companies (Tables A to F) Regulations 1985 (such table being hereinafter called 'Table A') shall apply to the Company.

2. Where there is any conflict between these regulations and the provisions of Table A applying to the Company by these regulations, these regulations shall prevail.
3. In these articles, 'the Act' means the Companies Act 1985.

Share capital

4. Shares which are comprised in the authorised but unissued share capital of the Company shall be under the control of the Directors who may (subject to ss. 80 and 89 of the Act and to paragraphs (a) and (b) below) allot, grant options over or otherwise dispose of the same, to such persons, on such terms and in such manner as they think fit.
   (a) The Directors are authorised for 5 years from the date on which these articles are adopted to exercise the power of the Company generally and without conditions to allot relevant securities (as defined in s.80 of the Act) up to the amount of the authorised share capital with which the Company is incorporated. The authority hereby given may at any time (subject to the said s.80) be renewed, revoked or varied by ordinary resolution of the Company in general meeting.
   (b) Section 89(1) of the Act (offers to shareholders on pre-emptive basis) shall not apply to the Company.

Transfer of shares

5. In addition to the powers given by regulation 24 of Table A the directors may, in their absolute discretion and without assigning any reason, decline to register any transfer of any share, whether or not it is a fully paid share.

Directors

6. The first directors shall be the persons named in the statement delivered to the Registrar of Companies under s. 10 of the Act.

Powers and duties of directors

7. The directors shall not without the previous sanction of an ordinary resolution of the Company:
   (a) sell or dispose of the Company's business or the shares of any of the Company's subsidiaries or any part of the business or shares or any interest in land or buildings where a substantial part of the Company's business if for the time being carried on;
   (b) acquire any business;
   (c) acquire or dispose of any shares in the Company;
   (d) make any investment whose capital value (whenever payable) exceeds £ ....;
   (e) exercise its borrowing powers in any way which causes or might cause its total borrowings to exceed £ ....; or
   (f) dismiss or engage or alter the terms of employment of any director or any manager whose emoluments are or exceed £ .... per annum.

Secretary

8. The first Secretary of the Company shall be the person named in the statement delivered to the Registrar of Companies under s.10 of the Act.

Interpreting Corporate Constitutions: Recent Judicial Illumination

David Milman, *Sweet & Maxwell's Company Law Newsletter*, 17 November 2003, Issue 20, pp. 1–4

(Please note that the following article remains relevant despite the Companies Act 2006. A number of the section number have now changed but the law has not).

The issue of the interpretation of the constitution of a company has over the years produced a vast quantity of precedent, some of which is contradictory and incapable of reconciliation. This lamentable state of affairs has entertained the intellects of academics, but has done little to improve the reputation of company law with their counterparts in practice. The response of practitioners has been to attempt to circumvent the uncertainties of the law by making extensive use of explicit contractual arrangements external to the formal constitution as such. Although this stratagem has mitigated the inherent difficulties posed by this area of core company law, the problems have not entirely disappeared, as a perusal of recent law reports on the subject will confirm. In more recent times disputes over what were the entitlements of a shareholder have often been raised in the context of unfair prejudice petitions under s.459 of the Companies Act 1985 (now s.994 CA 2006). With the reining back of the concept of 'legitimate expectation' by the House of Lords in *O'Neill* v. *Phillips* [1999] BCC 600; [1999] 1 WLR 1092 by restricting it within the parameters of what had been formally agreed, the focus has again switched back to the need for a close examination of what was explicitly provided for as the basis of the shareholder relationship. Unfortunately, such matters are not always as clear as one would have hoped.

Interpreting articles of association

It is well settled that the courts will resist any attempt to argue that the articles of association are subject to additional implied provisions or indeed that they should be rectified by the courts to reflect an unimplemented understanding between the parties – see *Scott* v. *Frank Scott (London) Ltd* [1940] Ch 794. There are various reasons for this exclusionary approach. The curious nature of the 'statutory contract' created by virtue of s.14 of the Companies Act 1985 (now Section 33 CA 2006) is undoubtedly a significant influence, as is the concern that shareholders may have made investment decisions on the back of what the memorandum and articles expressly stated. Although this rationalisation of investment motivation is suspect in many circumstances, it would be wrong to dismiss such judicial concerns entirely out of hand, particularly in those instances where one is considering a substantial investment in a private company. Thus, in *Bratton Seymour Service Co Ltd* v. *Oxborough* [1992] BCC 471, the Court of Appeal was adamant in its refusal to accept an implied term that members of a company had an obligation to contribute towards expenditure incurred by the company. In so deciding, the Court of Appeal laid great emphasis upon the peculiar nature of the articles as a statutory contract and this justified excluding the normal principles of 'business efficacy' when considering the possibility of implied terms. Other factors influencing the judgment were the existence of explicit statutory procedures to alter the articles (which had not been invoked) and the unequivocal statutory bar on exposing members to additional liability (see s.16 of the Companies Act 1985). In these circumstances the conclusion reached by the court was hardly surprising because, as Sir Christopher Slade put it, otherwise the court would place potential shareholders in limited companies in an 'intolerable position' ([1992] BCC 471 at p. 476).

The point was revisited by Patten J. in a different factual context in *Towcester Racecourse Co Ltd* v. *The Racecourse Association Ltd* [2002] EWHC 2141 (Ch), [2003] 1 BCLC 260. The question the judge was invited to investigate was whether the articles of association of a racecourse association could contractually bind that corporate association by imposing a contractual obligation on it towards its members (individual racecourses) with regard to the exercise of its powers – powers which it had quite properly delegated the exercise of to its directors. Hardly surprisingly, the judge answered this question in the negative and in so doing he based his conclusion on two foundations. First, the judge opined ([2002] EWHC 2141 (Ch) at para. 16, [2003] BCLC 260 at p. 268) that articles of association must be interpreted in accordance with standard principles of contractual interpretation, but by applying this test to the facts of the present case no such enforceable obligation arose. At first sight this interpretative approach may appear to be inconsistent with the aforementioned analysis. But on closer examination it is clear that the judge was restricting his comments to the interpretation of the *express* provisions in the articles. He later reinforced his conclusions by citing with approval the bar on introducing *implied* terms into the articles of association ([2002] EWHC 2141 (Ch) at para. 22, [2003] 1 BCLC 260 at p. 272). The circle is thus squared and the current position perfectly summarised.

Even accepting that there is limited scope for supplementing the scope of the articles of association by the introduction of implied terms, we are still left with trying to attach meaning to what has been explicitly provided for. The problem here, as we have seen, is one of contractual interpretation and the issues arising are not exclusively relevant to company law. The general principles to be applied when interpreting contractual documents (as opposed to seeking rectification thereof) were explained by Lord Hoffmann in *Investors Compensation Scheme Ltd* v. *West Bromwich Building Society* [1998] 1 WLR 896 at p. 913. This statement is to be read in the light of the view that has been expressed that it is acceptable that the articles of association could be interpreted by reference to the context in order to promote business efficacy – see the comments of Jenkins L.J. in *Holmes* v. *Keyes* [1959] Ch 199 at p. 215. Tensions therefore exist in the underlying law. The approach taken by Rimer J. in *Folks Group plc* v. *Alexander* [2002] EWHC 51 (Ch), [2002] 2 BCLC 254 is instructive in this context. Here we were faced with an amendment of the articles of a public listed company and in particular with the interpretation of that amendment. Rimer J. ruled that evidence relating to correspondence between the company and its solicitors was inadmissible as that related to subjective intention but it was acceptable to look at the original form of the articles to ascertain the background to the amendment. Put another way, contractual arrangements are not carried out in a vacuum. Rimer J. was not prepared to accept a construction that would produce an absurd result and therefore he was prepared to indulge in creative interpretation (by the addition of explanatory words into the articles) to produce a sensible construction. He did, however, concede at the end of his judgment:

> I recognise that this approach to the interpretation of art 7(1)(e) may be regarded as close to the limits of what is permissible as a pure exercise of construction, but I have no doubt that a construction of the amended subparagraph with the addition of those five words reflects the true sense of what it is intended to mean.
>
> [2002] EWHC 51 (Ch) at para.22, [2002] 2 BCLC 254 at p. 262.

This general problem of assisting interpretation of the corporate constitution is likely to be revisited in future cases.

The relationship between articles of association and external contracts

The difficulties revealed in cases such as *Bratton* (*supra*) may be circumvented if there is in existence an external contract (for example a contract of service with a director). In *Globalink Telecommunications Ltd* v. *Wilmbury Ltd* [2002] BCC 958, [2002] EWHC 1988 (QB), the issues arising in this context were fully reviewed by Stanley Burnton J. Here a director argued that under the articles of association of his company he was contractually entitled to an indemnity against any costs which might be incurred by him whilst carrying out his directorial duties in connection with legal proceedings relating to the company. This contention was rejected. First, it was well settled that although articles of association could form the basis of a contractual relationship between a company *and its members*, that contract did not extend to a link between the company *and its officers*. Having stated that, the court then conceded that the same result could be achieved if the officer had a separate service contract with the company and the facts showed that the terms of that service contract were extended by the incorporation of provisions found in the articles of association – (see [2002] BCC 958 at p. 965, [2002] EWHC 1988 (Ch) at para.30). In so indicating, the views of Ferris J. in *John* v. *PricewaterhouseCoopers* [2002] 1 WLR 953 at p. 960 were cited by Stanley Burnton J.; Ferris J. himself relied on the old established authority of *Re New British Iron Co; ex parte Beckwith* [1898] 1 Ch 324 as authority for the proposition in question. Unfortunately, for the officer in the case of *Globalink* (*supra*) there was insufficient evidence to support such an incorporation of article provisions into the external contract. In spite of optimistic judicial comments on the potential for such implication, the negative conclusion will, one suspects, be the normal outcome where this insidious line of argument is used because of its tendency to undermine the fundamentals of company law. If article provisions are meant to be incorporated, it is a simple enough matter for this to be done explicitly.

Shareholder agreements

For small private companies shareholder agreements offer a valuable addition to the constitutional regime embodied in the memorandum and articles of association. They have the advantage of relative privacy and cannot (in the absence of provision to the contrary) be modified without unanimous agreement.

The value of such agreements was made apparent in *Russell* v. *Northern Bank Development Corp Ltd* [1992] BCC 578; [1992] 1 WLR 588 where the House of

Lords held that such an agreement, although incapable of fettering the statutory entitlement of a company to increase its share capital, could place curbs on the manner in which members exercised their voting rights within the company when exercising a vote on a capital increase. The practical utility of such an agreement thus received support from the highest court in the land.

The interpretation of a shareholders' agreement was at the fore of the litigation in *Euro Brokers Holdings Ltd* v. *Monecor (London) Ltd* [2003] BCC 573; [2003] EWCA Civ 105. This case concerned the enforceability of a provision in a shareholders' agreement, made in the context of a joint venture company, requiring a member to sell its shares to the other member in defined circumstances. That question turned on whether the triggering event (a purported board decision) was valid or whether it could be regarded as valid by applying the *Duomatic* principle (*Re Duomatic Ltd* [1969] 2 Ch 365) of informal shareholder assent. Both the judge at first instance (Leslie Kosmin QC) and the Court of Appeal (Pill, Waller and Mummery LJJ.) agreed that this pragmatic common law principle could operate in the context of a shareholder agreement. Mummery L.J., commenting on the *Duomatic* principle, stated the position thus:

> It is a sound and sensible principle of company law allowing the members of the company to reach an agreement without the need for strict compliance with formal procedures . . . What matters is the unanimous assent of those who ultimately exercise power over the affairs of the company through their right to attend and vote at a general meeting. It does not matter whether the formal procedures in question are stipulated for in the articles of association, in the Companies Acts or in a separate contract between the members of the company concerned. What matters is that all the members have reached an agreement. If they have, they cannot be heard to say that they are not bound by it because the formal procedure was not followed.
>
> [2003] BCC 573 at p. 584; [2003] EWCA Civ 105 at para.62.

Reform?

As might be expected the policymakers have had something to say about this area of law. The Law Commission in its 1997 Report on *Shareholder Remedies* (Law Comm no.246, Cm 3769) touched upon it, though it was clearly regarded as a side-issue when compared to the more vexed questions raised by the ineffectiveness of derivative actions and by the proliferation of unfair prejudice petitions. Unfortunately, the Law Commission did not feel justified in recommending clarification of the particular issues reviewed in this article. The wording of s.14 of the Companies Act 1985 did not require amendment and on reflection there was no need for a non-exhaustive statutory list of enforceable personal rights under the constitution (para.7.17). To some extent this cautious approach was informed by the view that there were no real difficulties in practice caused in this area of law by the undoubted limitations of the law as it then stood.

What was proposed by the Company Law Review was the merger of the memorandum and articles into a single constitutional document (see *Modern Company Law for a Competitive Economy – Final Report*, para.9.4). The vexed issues of the interpretation of such a document will of course not be resolved by such a welcome simplification in corporate documentation. On this point there was a proposal in the earlier iterations of its work that enforceable rights under the constitution should be itemised (in a non-exclusive fashion) and this then developed into a suggestion that all provisions in the constitution should be freely enforceable by members against the company and other members unless express provision to the contrary was made or in *de minimis* circumstances. Although this approach was persisted with in the *Final Report*, the Company Law Review did acknowledge the real difficulties involved (see paras 7.34 *et seq*.). Earlier tentative suggestions by the Company Law Review that a move should be made away from the contractual interpretation of the memorandum and articles were not pursued (para.7.33) and therefore the courts will continue to play a key interpretative role in the years to come. As far as the *Duomatic* principle was concerned the Company Law Review supported it, and indeed it favoured the proposal that it should be embodied in a new Companies Act consolidation (paras 7.20–7.26), notwithstanding the fact that its consultees had opposed the latter step. This proposal was very much in line with its philosophy of promoting a user-friendly system of regulation for small private companies.

In the follow up government White paper, *Modernising Company Law* (Cm 5553, July 2002), these modest proposals of the Company Law Review were largely supported. Thus the switch to a single constitutional document was agreed as the way forward (para.2.2). Nothing appears to have been said about the scope for enforceability of provisions in the constitution. The White Paper gave strong support to the idea of improving procedures for simpler decision-taking by private companies by extending the written resolution procedure (on this see the article by Lower [2002] 18 *Sweet & Maxwell's Company Law Newsletter* 1) though it resisted the idea of converting the *Duomatic* concession into a formal statutory facility (see paras 2.34 and 2.35). Bearing in mind the delay in introducing statutory reforms in core company law, there is something to be said for leaving the development of this area of the law in the capable hands of the judiciary. In the absence of any immediate prospect for change company law practitioners should take heed of the recent jurisprudence in this area and maintain their efforts both to promote clarity and to ensure that contractual understandings are enforceable. They should note that judges may be prepared to be flexible and take a 'commercial view' but there is no guarantee that such a favourable response will ensue in every case. As always, there is no substitute for good drafting.

Shareholder agreements

It can be seen above therefore that the contractual status of the Memorandum and Articles of Association can be rather problematic. First, it is unclear as to precisely what types of provision will be regarded as having contractual status under s.14. Second, these documents can be changed by majority vote (special resolution, 75 per cent of those members who are present and voting). That means that an individual holding less than 25 per cent of the shares may not be protected by a provision inserted into the Articles for his/her protection. In addition, every company's Memorandum and Articles of Association are open to inspection by the public at large, which means that it is not possible for shareholders to retain privacy in relation to provisions contained in these documents.

For these reasons, lawyers will often recommend the so-called 'shareholder agreements' to potential shareholders in a private company, as they are seen to have the following advantages:

(i) A shareholder agreement is a private document and is not open to inspection by the public.

(ii) A shareholder agreement is a contract, and, like any other contract, can only be altered by unanimous consent of those who have signed it (rather than by 75 per cent of the members as is the case with the Memorandum and Articles).
(iii) As an ordinary contract, the agreement is not subject to s.14 and the uncertainty surrounding what is and what is not a 'membership right'. It follows that all the provisions of the agreement are contractual, subject to the general rules of contract.
(iv) The agreement may contain remedies which may be applied in the event of a breach of the agreement, for example a liquidated damages clause.

Re-registration

It is possible to re-register a private company as a public one at a later date. The decision must be by special or written resolution, and the Memorandum and Articles must be altered. The requirements for capital of a public company must be met, and there are detailed provisions to control payment for shares other than by money. In particular, shares cannot be paid for merely by a promise to do future work for the company. Application for re-registration must be made to the Registrar, signed by a director or the company secretary and accompanied by various documents including the new Memorandum and Articles, audited accounts and a statutory declaration similar to that described above.

It is also possible to re-register a public company as a private one, a private company as an unlimited one and vice versa.

4.5 Corporate capacity to contract

Learning Outcome: To explain the ability of a company to contract.

4.5.1 Pre-incorporation contracts

A contract made on behalf of a company before it is formed is void. The company cannot make contracts because it simply does not exist yet. Therefore, the company cannot sue the other party on it, nor can the other side sue the company.

When the company is formed, it cannot validly ratify contracts made in its name before incorporation: see *Kelner* v. *Baxter* (1866). It follows that if the company wishes to take over the contract, it must enter into a new contract after incorporation.

By the CA 2006 S51 a contract which purports to be made by or on behalf of a company at a time when the company has not yet been formed has effect as a contract made with the person purporting to act for the company or as agent for it. He is therefore personally liable on the contract, and can sue on it personally. This section is 'subject to any agreement to the contrary' and, for example, one of the promoters might seek a clause exempting him from personal liability if other parties to the contract agree.

The legal status of pre-incorporation contracts can cause difficulty, because the promoters may want to borrow money, buy or lease premises and machinery, print stationery, and so on in the company's name before it is formed and without incurring personal liability. They may also want such expenditure to be the company's liability for tax reasons.

There are various possible solutions:

- The obvious one is to start the company well before starting the business or, in the case of a partnership or sole trader turning an existing firm into a company, before transferring the business to the company. This still does not, however, solve problems such as charging the promoters' expenses and/or fees to the company.
- Pre-incorporation contracts can be left as a series of non-binding options or agreements to agree in future. The terms will formally be settled by the company after incorporation. However, the other party might not wish to proceed on this basis, particularly if he is asked to incur expense before incorporation.
- The promoters might make the contracts in their own names, but assign the contracts to the company after incorporation. However, this can only be done with the other party's consent.

The problems of pre-incorporation contracts should not be great where the business is fairly small and the promoters themselves are the only shareholders. The company can then safely be relied upon to make the contracts necessary to indemnify the promoters. If the shareholding is more diverse, the problems may be greater.

4.5.2 The ultra vires doctrine: the company's capacity

We have seen that *ultra vires* applies to corporate bodies generally, but that it has been greatly modified in relation to companies (see earlier). The powers of a company are, in theory, limited to those set out in the objects clause of its Memorandum. Anything done outside of these powers is void: see *Ashbury Railway Carriage & Iron Co.* v. *Riche* (1875). But there have been both practical and legal changes.

Objects clauses are often widely drafted so that things are much less likely to be *ultra vires*. Each paragraph or clause in the objects can contain a separate and main object which can be carried on independently of the others [*Cotman* v. *Brougham* (1918)]. More radically, a company can now register as simply a 'general commercial company' (see earlier).

By the Companies Act 1985, Section 40 CA 2006, 'The validity of an act done by a company shall not be called into question on the ground of lack of capacity by reason of anything in the company's Memorandum.' Moreover, a party to a transaction with the company is not bound to enquire whether it is permitted by the company's Memorandum. Indeed, the company can be bound even if the outsider knew that the proposed transaction was *ultra vires* the objects clause.

Although the validity of an act undertaken cannot be called into question on the grounds of lack of capacity, the directors may have exceeded their authority. Section 40 CA 2006, however, provides that 'In favour of a person dealing with a company in good faith, the power of the board of directors to bind the company or authorise others to do so, shall be deemed to be free of any limitation under the company's constitution.' The section has both internal and external consequences.

Companies registered after October 2009 under the CA 2006 will have no restrictions on their contractual ability unless they choose to have restrictions. If they do they must be included in the Articles of Association.

External consequences

Where a company enters into an *ultra vires* transaction, it has exceeded its objects and its directors, in doing so, have exceeded their authority. However, an outsider dealing with the company is not concerned with the fact that the company has acted outside its objects clause because the effect of Section 40 CA 2006 is to validate the act of the company. And provided he can rely on Section 40 CA 2006, the outsider can enforce the contract against the company even though the directors have exceeded their powers by taking the company into an *ultra vires* transaction. Thus, Section 40 CA 2006 validates the act of the directors.

Internal consequences

The *ultra vires* rule is still important as regards the internal affairs of the company because directors must conduct its affairs in accordance with its Memorandum and Articles of Association. If they exceed their authority, they may be liable to the company for such conduct (see also Section 5.6.3). For example:

(a) Any member, even holding only one share, can seek a court injunction to prevent the directors from making a proposed (future) *ultra vires* transaction. But:
- this cannot stop a transaction which has already been agreed with the outsider;
- it does not apply if the proposed transaction has been approved by a special resolution (75 per cent of votes cast) at a general meeting, or a 75 per cent written resolution without a meeting in a private company;
- a court action for an injunction can be expensive.

(b) If the company makes an *ultra vires* contract and suffers a *loss*, the directors can be liable to the company for damages. However, the members can relieve the directors from liability by special or written resolution.

(c) Certain transactions *between a company and its directors* can be set aside *by the company* if they are *ultra vires* its objects. This applies also to transactions between the company and directors' close family, and transactions with directors, and so on, of a holding company. However, the company might not wish to rescind the transaction.

Thus, companies may no longer raise *ultra vires* as a reason for not being bound by their actions *vis-á-vis* outsiders. Likewise, liquidators cannot refuse to acknowledge corporate debts and contracting parties cannot escape liability. Such parties can now enforce contracts which would previously have been held *ultra vires*.

To summarise, Section 40 CA 2006 ensures that persons dealing with a company are no longer affected by the *ultra vires* doctrine. A company may not plead *ultra vires* but neither may a contracting party raise it as a defence. *Ultra vires*, however, is still relevant as between:

(a) the company, its directors and its members;
(b) the company, its directors and third parties with whom they deal.

Section 40 CA 2006 applies only to a limited extent to companies which are charities, so that if a charity is making a contract for an *ultra vires* purpose, the contract may still be void.

4.5.3 Changing the objects

When the CA 2006 is fully in force, any restrictions on a company's objects contained in its Memorandum of Association will be treated as if they are contained in the company's Articles of Association. (Section 28 CA 2006). If the company wishes to alter those restrictions it will need to pass a special or written resolution to alter the Articles. Until that time the objects remain in the Memorandum of Association which again can be altered by special or written resolution. At present the law enables the holders of 15 per cent of the company's issued share to object to any alteration of the objects clause in the Memorandum. This right to object will disappear when the CA 2006 is fully in force. Application by the objector must be within 21 days of the resolution. The court need not cancel the alteration, but in this event it may order the company to buy back the shares of the applicants, or there may be arrangements for the majority to buy the shares. The Registrar must be notified by the company of any court application.

As mentioned above, with effect from October 2009, the Companies Act 2006 provides that all companies will have unlimited objects, unless they choose to restrict them.

4.6 Advantages and disadvantages of companies limited by shares

Learning Outcome: To explain the main advantages and disadvantages of carrying on business through the medium of company limited by shares.

4.6.1 Advantages

(In practice, those who carry on business through the medium of such a company may enjoy a number of tax advantages, depending on the tax regime in force at any particular time. However, tax considerations are outside the scope of *Business Law* and will be covered in *Business Taxation*.)

The main advantages derive from the separate legal personality of companies (see Section 4.3.2).

- *Limited liability* is the main advantage. A shareholder whose shares are fully paid up is not liable for the debts of the company. If the business is owned by a company, therefore, it becomes much more attractive to entrepreneurs. An entrepreneur is more likely to start a business if he/she knows that potential liability is limited. Equally, people are much more likely to invest money in the business by becoming shareholders later if they know that liability is limited. Both commencement and expansion of the business can benefit. It must be noted, however, that although limited liability is always enjoyed by shareholders in public companies which are quoted on the Stock Exchange, in practice it may not be enjoyed by shareholders in a small private company. Whether the shareholders have limited liability depends on their particular circumstances. Thus, for example, persons who own shares in asset-rich companies may well enjoy limited liability, as the company is itself able to provide security for any borrowing. However, many companies are incorporated under capitalised, many with share capital of less than £100.

Example

X is the sole director and shareholder in X Ltd and holds 100 £1 shares. X wants to borrow £100,000 from the bank on behalf of X Ltd so that the company can purchase a house and rent it out to students. Clearly, the bank will require security for the loan and the company itself is unable to provide any as it only has £100. It follows that if the loan is to proceed, it is likely that the bank will require (i) a charge over the property to be purchased and (ii) a personal guarantee from X that if the company does not repay the loan, he will. (The bank may also possibly require a charge over X's matrimonial home.) It follows that until the loan is repaid, X does not enjoy limited liability, because if the company fails to pay its debts, X can be called upon under his guarantee to pay them.

Assume that the loan is repaid from the rents X Ltd has received from students, and X wishes to repeat the process and buy another house to rent out. Now the company has an asset (the first property) and the bank may be persuaded to make a loan to the company taking security over the company's existing property and the property to be acquired without requiring X to enter into a contract of guarantee. If that is the case, X has now begun to enjoy limited liability.

- *Perpetual succession* indicates that a company, as a separate legal person, lasts for ever until it is wound up by due legal process. If the business is owned by the company it remains the property of the company, whatever happens to ownership of the shares. Investors can come and go, buy shares and sell them, without any change in ownership of the business. This too can help to attract capital.

  A partnership only lasts as long as the agreement lasts, and ownership of the business may change and have to be transferred on the death or retirement of any partner. The assets of an individual practitioner can similarly have to be transferred on his death. All of this can involve complications and expense.
- *Agreement to the transfer of interests* is not needed in public companies. A member who wishes to transfer his shares does not need to obtain the permission of the other shareholders.

  A partner cannot normally transfer his share of the partnership without first obtaining the permission of all the other partners.
- *The number of members permitted* can be a major difference. A company may have a limitless number of members, although a private company must not offer its shares for sale to the public. A large public company may well have many billions of shares. Most trading partnerships are limited to twenty members, and even in the exceptional professional partnerships which are allowed to exceed this limit there are rarely more than a few hundred or so partners.

  The freedom to attract vast numbers of shareholders can be a vital source of finance.
- *Borrowing money* might be easier and/or more convenient for a company than for an unincorporated business, because a company can offer a floating charge over such assets of a particular type as the company might have from time to time. This security leaves the company free to deal with its assets without having to redeem the charge each time. An unincorporated business cannot issue a valid 'floating' charge (see Section 5.4.3).

4.6.2 Disadvantages

- *On formation*, the detailed documents and administration procedures required on registration can deter a small business from forming a company; see Section 4.4.
- *Disclosure requirements* are imposed on companies. A great deal of information about the company and its officers must be kept at the registered office, and most of it must be available for public inspection. Much information must also be sent to the Registrar of Companies and be similarly available. Some disclosure requirements apply even to very small companies.
- *Many administrative requirements* are imposed, for example in preparing and keeping the accounts (which must be audited in all but very small companies) and registers which contain the above information. There are also detailed requirements as to the meetings to be held and the types of resolution which must be used; see later.

Generally, this does not apply to unincorporated businesses. The bureaucracy imposed on companies is largely the price to be paid for potential size, and disclosure provisions give outsiders some safeguard against the company's limited liability, in that they can at least find out who and what they are dealing with.

4.6.3 Other features of companies

- *Taxation*. In practice, the different tax treatment of companies on the one hand and sole traders and partnerships on the other, may be one of the main factors in deciding whether to carry on business in corporate or non-corporate form.
  (a) *Companies*. Companies pay corporation tax on their profits, whether or not they are distributed to the shareholders by way of dividends. Directors are liable to pay income tax and national insurance contributions on salaries and fees paid by the company. The amounts are deducted monthly through the operation of PAYE (pay-as-you-earn). The separate legal personality of the company could be problematic for directors in small private companies, as they could find themselves in effect being subjected to a double charge to national insurance in that both the company as employer and the directors as officers/employees are liable to pay such contributions. On the other hand, dividends extracted by shareholders are not subject to national insurance contributions and the tax payable on them is not due until some 10 months after the income tax year in which they are received. Dividends are also currently taxed at rates below those applicable for employment income. Thus, dividends taking total taxable income up to £34,800 are taxed at 10 per cent and the excess at 32.5 per cent. For employment income the 10% starting rate has been abolished and taxable income up to £34,800 is now taxed at 20% and any excess at 40%. For 2009/10 dividends taking taxable income up to £37,400 are taxed at 10% and the excess at 32.5%.
  (b) *Partnerships and sole traders/practitioners*. Partners and sole traders extract profits from the business in the form of 'drawings'. Drawings are advance payments of profit extracted by the proprietor pending the determination of the annual profit on production of the accounts. Drawings (like dividends above), may be extracted from the business weekly or monthly without any tax being payable on the date of extraction. Rather income tax of the proprietor's share of profits for the year is payable following the determination of final accounts.
- *Management systems* differ. In a company the members elect the directors who are then responsible for the day-to-day management and policy-making of the corporation. The members have no right to intervene in normal management, although they may have some rights in the event of managerial misconduct. They also have the right to remove directors, and to exercise their rights to vote at general meetings.

These divisions of function are inevitable in large companies. In very small companies they may not matter too much if the directors and the shareholders are the same persons.

In a partnership, unless the partnership agreement provides otherwise, all the partners have a right to participate in management.

4.7 The use and procedure of board meetings and general meetings of shareholders

Learning Outcome:	To explain the use and procedure of board meetings and general meeting of shareholders.

Under the Companies Act 2006, every public company must have at least two directors, and every private company at least one. Most companies have more than this. A director need not be a shareholder, and even a single-member company can, therefore, if it wishes, have several directors.

The function of the directors is to manage the company. They must make management decisions on most matters, and ensure that those decisions and the decisions of shareholders are carried out. Their exact powers will be determined by the Articles, for example, Table A reg. 70.

Directors' powers must generally be exercised as a board, acting at board meetings. The actual way in which boards reach their decisions is governed by the Articles of Associators. It follows that the company may adopt any rules that it chooses. Table A permits directors to regulate proceedings at board meetings as they think fit. In practice the chairman of the board will attempt to achieve unanimity. If this is not possible however, and the matter has to be put to the vote, most boards will reach their decisions by simple majority vote. Each director will normally have one vote, apart from the chairman who is often given a casting vote so that a decision can be reached in the event of deadlock. As a *general* rule, individual directors have no authority. However, the board can delegate executive powers to individual directors, usually through service contracts. The board can even appoint a managing director, although it has no need to do so.

The members of a company are its shareholders. They do not, in their capacity of shareholders, take part in the day-to-day management of the company. They do, however, have considerable powers to control the management, and they also have some wider powers. Their powers are exercised through voting on resolutions at general meetings of shareholders (members' meetings). Two types of general meeting are recognised, annual general meetings (AGMs) and general meetings (GMs). Where different classes of share have been created (see Chapter 5) there can also be class meetings for example a meeting of all the preference shareholders. Each of these is discussed below.

The size of the company can be relevant to determine what internal procedures are appropriate. There are complex rules for larger companies, with many millions of shares and the management often widely separated from the share ownership. For smaller 'family' companies, however, these rules can be unnecessary bureaucracy, and important changes have therefore been made. Again, many of the rules can depend on the Articles, and Table A applies unless varied or excluded.

Much of the internal constitutional work of larger companies must be done through meetings. There must be meeting of members (shareholders), where their voting rights can be exercised; and (as we have already seen) there must be board meetings of directors.

4.7.1 Board meetings

The board is the agent of the company and is responsible for management. The board determines the overall policy of the company and leaves the day-to-day management to appointed managers. It follows that boards of directors do not meet every day or week but meet from time to time when the situation demands it. Thus, the board will meet to consider such matters as whether to diversify into another business area, to raise further capital, to make investments, to issue further shares, to change the constitution of the company, to purchase another business, and so on. For some of these matters, the law requires shareholder approval so the board will have to call an GM in order to allow the shareholders to vote on the matter. In the case of a private company, it may not be necessary to call an GM as, in most cases, the law allows a written resolution of the shareholders to be used as an alternative to an ordinary or special resolution of members voted at general meetings.

The powers of directors must generally be exercised as a board, except to the extent that they are validly delegated. The board normally operates at meetings, although it can agree unanimously by each member signing a written resolution without a meeting. Procedure is generally governed by the Articles.

Under Table A, a meeting can be called by any director, and must be called by the company secretary if any director so requires. Reasonable notice must be given to all directors, but not necessarily to those out of the United Kingdom or whose whereabouts are not known. No agenda need be sent. The quorum is presumed to be two, but this may be varied by the directors themselves, as it will be in single-director private companies. There are detailed provisions which prevent a director from voting if he has a personal interest in the matter to be decided. He may still attend and speak, but his presence cannot count towards a quorum on the issue. The board can appoint a chairman, and give him a second 'casting' vote if one should be needed. Otherwise, the rule is generally one vote per director, regardless of shareholding, and decisions are reached by a simple majority. Minutes of board meetings must be kept, and trade available to directors but not to members generally.

If there are an equal number of votes for and against a particular resolution, there is deadlock and the negative view prevails. This means that the proposed resolution is defeated, unless the chairman chooses to exercise his/her casting vote.

Written resolutions by the *directors* to make a decision without a board meeting must not be confused with written resolutions of *shareholders* (members) without a *shareholders' meeting*; see Section 7.3.2.

4.7.2 Meetings of members

Types of meeting

1. *Annual General Meeting (AGM)*. By virtue of S.336 CA 2006 every public company must hold an AGM within 6 months of the end of its accounting reference date. Failure to do so constitutes an offence by every officer of the company who is in default. Members must be given notice that an AGM is to be held and of any resolution which is to be moved at the AGM. Members are entitled to propose a resolution if they alone or together hold at least 5 per cent of the total voting rights. If not at least 100 members who have paid up on average £100 and each have the right to vote may propose a resolution. In either case the company must give notice to all the members of the proposed resolution (ss.338 and 3390 CA 2006).

   Before the enactment of the CA 2006, private companies were required to hold an AGM unless their members unanimously agreed to dispense with this requirement. Following the CA 2006 private companies are not required to hold an AGM unless they wish to do so.

   The AGM is called by the directors who are required to give at least 21 clear days notice to the members. The business ordinarily includes considering the accounts, receiving the directors' and auditors' reports, declaring (or not declaring) a dividend, and election of directors.

2. *General meetings (GM).* A general meeting of shareholders is any meeting other than an AGM. A GM may be called in various ways:
   (a) Under Table A, the *directors* can call an GM whenever they think fit, so long as they give at least 14 days' notice in writing to members. The notice must indicate the purpose of the meeting sufficiently for members to make an informed decision on whether to attend. More detailed notice must be given of some resolutions (see later).
   (b) By S.303 CA 2006 the registered owners of at least one-tenth of such of the paid-up share capital as carries voting rights can give written and signed notice to the registered office requiring the directors to call an GM for a date within 28 days of the notice. Those requiring the meeting must say why they want it. If the directors have done nothing after 21 days, the members themselves can call the meeting at the company's expense. Whoever calls the meeting must give at least 14 days' notice of it to (other) members.
   (c) By S.306 CA 2006, if for any reason it is impracticable for a meeting to be called or conducted properly, the court may order that a meeting be held. The court may act on its own initiative, or on the application of any one director, or any one shareholder who would be entitled to vote at the meeting. Conduct of the meeting can be as the court thinks fit.

Examples

In *Re El Sombrero Ltd* (1958), the majority shareholder could not obtain a meeting because the only other two members would not attend and, under the Articles, the quorum for a meeting was two. The court ordered a 'meeting' of the one majority member (who then used his votes to sack the other two as directors).

In *Re Opera Photographic Ltd* (1989), a 'meeting' of one member was allowed by the court. Here a 51 per cent shareholder wished to remove the only other shareholder from a position as director. The quorum for meetings was two and the minority member had failed to attend meetings where his removal as director was to be voted upon.

   (d) An auditor can require the directors to call an GM on his resignation.
3. *Class meetings.* Members of a particular class of shareholders can hold meetings on matters which only affect that class. Procedure and conduct will depend almost entirely on the company's Articles.

4.8 Resolutions

Learning Outcome: To identify the various types of shareholder resolutions.

Decisions at shareholders' meetings are taken by resolutions upon which the members can vote. There are different sorts of resolution.

1. *An ordinary resolution* is one which can be passed by a simple majority of the votes cast in the meeting. If votes are equal then the resolution is lost unless, perhaps, the Articles give a casting vote to the chairman (which Table A does). Note that on a poll, it is one

vote per share, not one per person; one member with a large shareholding can therefore constitute a majority. Also, on some issues, the Articles may validly give more than one vote to some shares; see *Bushell* v. *Faith* (1970) (Chapter 5). Those who cannot attend the meeting are normally allowed by the Articles to vote by proxy; see later. There need be no seconder unless the Articles require one; Table A does not. Members may move amendments, but only fairly minor ones. This sort of resolution will be used where neither statute, nor company memorandum nor articles require a different type of resolution.

2. *An ordinary resolution of which special notice is required* can be passed by a simple majority at the meeting as above; but notice that it is to be moved must be given to the company at the registered office at least 28 days before the meeting. The company must then notify members, and so on, of the text when it gives notice of the meeting. (Because of this, probably only minor grammatical amendments can be accepted at the meeting.) When the resolution is to remove a director under s.303, there are also detailed procedures allowing the director to defend his position; similarly with resolutions to dismiss or not reappoint an auditor. There must also be special notice to appoint a director aged over 70.
3. *A special resolution* can only be passed by a three-quarters majority of votes (in person or by proxy) cast in the general meeting. Note therefore that a special resolution is a 75 per cent majority vote of members present and voting, and not of the whole of the membership. It follows that in theory, even if a company has several hundred members and only four turn up for the meeting, if three vote in favour, that is a special resolution. This is, of course, subject to quorum provisions in the Articles and subject to a poll being taken, in which case each member who attended the meeting may use one vote for every share he owns. If in the above example where only four members attended the meeting one of the members held 750 shares and the other three only 250 between them, it follows that one person would effectively have passed the special resolution. Moreover, at least 14 days' notice of the meeting, stating the resolution and the intention to move it as a special one, must be given to members. The requirement of a three-quarters majority can be a protection to minorities, and we have seen that special resolutions are demanded by statute for various purposes, such as changes of name, Memorandum or Articles, reducing share capital or creation of reserve capital.
4. *A written resolution*. The law now enables shareholders of private companies to pass resolutions without having to attend a meeting by way of written resolutions. This type of resolution requires the same majority as for ordinary and special resolutions. Thus, 50 per cent plus one must be in favour to pass a written ordinary resolution and 75 per cent must be in favour to pass a written special resolution. However, ordinary and special resolutions passed at general meetings only require a majority and 75 per cent respectively *of those present and voting*. For a valid written ordinary and special resolution the written consent of a majority and 75 per cent respectively *of all the members entitled to vote* must have signed their consent. (See sections 281 to 283 CA 2006.) Each shareholder must sign a written statement of the terms, but not necessarily all on the same piece of paper; a written copy of the terms can be sent to each member. No meeting need be held. In a *private* company, anything which can be done by resolution in a general meeting can be passed by a written resolution without a meeting. There can similarly be written resolutions of all class shareholders without a class meeting. The date of the resolution is that of the last signature. However, written resolutions can *not* be used to remove directors, or to remove auditors, because this would prejudice the statutory rights of directors or auditors to put their case to members.

It is also possible for the directors to pass a resolution by written resolution and thus avoid the need to hold a board meeting. Thus, for example, suppose that following telephone calls or emails between the directors of Exe Ltd it has become obvious that all the directors are in favour of a particular course of action. Rather than hold a formal board meeting the directors may prefer to have a copy of the proposal sent to them in the form of a written resolution which they can all sign and return.

4.9 Calling a meeting

Learning Outcome: To explain the voting rights of directors and shareholders.

1. *Time and place* of meetings is normally fixed by the directors (Table A reg. 37). Directors must exercise their powers in good faith, and must not deliberately make it difficult for members who oppose them to attend.
2. *Notice of meetings*
   (a) The AGM
      - *A public company* must give at least 21 days notice to its members of the AGM. The members may agree to short notice, but this only applies if ALL the members agree.
      - *A private company*, (if it chooses to hold an AGM) must give at least 14 days to its members. Again the AGM may be held on short notice, if a majority in number of the members holding at least 90 per cent of the total votes agree. For example, suppose Wye Ltd has five members, Wye holds 90 per cent of the shares and the other four hold 10 per cent between them. Wye alone cannot agree to short notice without the support of at least another two members.

   (b) General meetings
      - *A public company must give at least 14 days notice. The members can agree to short notice if a majority in number holding at least 95 pre cent of the total voting rights are in favour.*
      - *A private company* must also give at least 14 days notice, but may agree to short notice if a majority in number holding at least 90 per cent of the total voting rights agree.

If notice is sent by post, then Table A treats it as served 48 hours after posting. Again, directors must act in good faith, so that where notices were posted during a postal strike they were not treated as served. The length of notice (see minima earlier) must be in clear days, excluding the day of receipt and the day of the meeting. A company's Articles will specify what details a notice must contain; see also Table A reg. 38. The notice must state the general nature of the business to be carried out. If the meeting is an AGM then the notice must say so. Notice should always be sufficient to enable members to decide whether they should attend. If (as is usual) members can appoint a proxy, the notice should say so. Directors' personal interests must be disclosed.

Generally, where proper notice of a meeting is not given to everyone entitled, resolutions passed at the meeting will be invalid. In *Young* v. *Ladies' Imperial Club Ltd* (1920), a member was not given notice of a meeting because she had already said that she would not be able to attend. The court held that she should nevertheless have been given notice, and that a resolution passed at the meeting was invalid.

Companies can protect themselves against *accidental* errors by a provision in the Articles. Table A reg. 39, for instance, provides that accidental omission to give notice to, or the non-receipt of notice by, any person entitled shall not invalidate proceedings at that meeting. In *Re West Canadian Collieries Ltd* (1962), the inadvertent omission of some address plates when notices were being prepared did not invalidate events at that meeting. Table A would also protect a large company, one of whose many members had changed address without informing the company. However, it only covers inadvertent errors. In *Musselwhite* v. *CH Musselwhite Ltd* (1962), a shareholder had agreed to sell his shares, but the seller's name still appeared on the company's register. The directors, knowing of the agreement to sell, did not send notice to the seller. This was an error of law; the seller was still the owner. The error was not covered by the Articles.

With effect from January 2007 the law has been changed by the Companies Act 2006 in relation to companies communicating electronically with their shareholders. The position now is that, subject to members' consent in general meeting, or to a provision in the company's articles of association, all companies may communicate electronically with their shareholders as a matter of course. Members who object may continue to request paper communications. Companies may also communicate via their websites, but they must give members notice to that effect. Members or debenture holders who have received information or a document in electronic form, can request a hard copy of the document or information. The company must comply with the request, without any charge to the member or debenture holder. Failure to comply with these rules renders the company liable to a default fine (see ss.308, 1143, 1259 and Schedules 4 and 5 of the Companies Act 2006).

In addition all shareholders must be contacted individually and asked if they consent to receiving communications in electronic form. If a shareholder fails to respond within 28 days the company can assume that he consents. If a shareholder refuses to agree to e-communication, the company must wait 12 months before asking him again.

4.9.1 Conduct of meetings

1. *A quorum* of members must be present if the meeting is to be valid, this must be at least two members; the Articles can require more, but not less. One person holding proxy votes for others as well as his own shares is not a 'meeting' (unless by order of the court). There are special provisions for single-member companies; see later.
2. *The Chairman* of the meeting of members will be the chairman of the board of directors, if he is present (under Table A). Otherwise, directors present can choose or be the chairman. Otherwise, the members present can choose one of their number. The chairman must ensure that proceedings at the meeting are properly conducted, that majority and minority shareholders are given reasonable time to contribute to the meeting, that decisions on incidental issues and questions arising are provided and that order is preserved. The chairman does not have a casting vote unless the articles expressly provide such.
3. *Proxies* may be appointed. Every member entitled to attend and vote at a meeting can appoint a proxy (who need not be a member) to do so on his or her behalf. Notice of the meeting should inform members of this right, and proxies can be nominated by notice in writing to the company at least 48 hours before the meeting. The shareholder can instruct his proxy which way to vote. A proxy can speak at meetings of a private company, but not of a public one.

4. *Voting* can initially be by a show of hands at the meeting, in which case the rule is one *person* one vote, and the proxy normally has no vote. However, a poll can be demanded at any time, before or after any show of hands. Under Table A, the following can insist upon a poll: the chairman; or any two members; or a member with at least one-tenth of the total voting rights of members entitled to vote at the meeting; or a member holding voting shares representing at least one-tenth of the total amount paid up on such shares. A proxy has the same rights to demand a poll as the member(s) whom he represents. Even if Table A is varied, there are statutory minimum numbers who can demand a poll. The Articles cannot debar five or more members from validly demanding a poll, for example. In a poll, voting becomes one vote *per share*, and a proxy can exercise the votes of his or her principal. Members and directors *can* vote on matters in which they have an interest, although a director's interests must be declared.

4.9.2 Minutes and filing

1. *Minutes* must be kept of all decisions at general meetings. If signed by the chairman of this or the next meeting, they are *prima facie* evidence, that is they are presumed correct unless proved otherwise. The Articles sometimes make such minutes conclusive evidence, in which case they cannot be proved incorrect. Minutes must be kept at the registered office and be available free of charge to members and auditors.
2. *Filing*. The Registrar of Companies must be given a record of some decisions. For example copies of all special, resolutions must be filed within 15 days. Most ordinary resolutions need not be filed with the Registrar, but there are exceptions such as decisions to increase the authorised/nominal capital.

   As an alternative to filing hard copies, Companies House now allow electronic filing of specified resolutions and documents. Examples are Appointment of a Director/ Secretary (Form 288a); Increase in Nominal Capital (with resolution (Form 123)); Annual Returns (Form 363a). Full information is available if you follow the links from the Companies House website, for example Webfiling and Software filing.

Overview

Company meetings form an important element in the syllabus. Provided here therefore are a model notice calling the annual general meeting of a public company, two notices calling extraordinary general meetings, some model ordinary and special resolutions of general meetings, and some resolutions of board meetings. A further Reading describes a rare external limit on the right of a shareholder to vote as he wishes at meetings.

Blackthorn plc

Notice of annual general meeting

NOTICE IS HEREBY GIVEN that the annual general meeting of Blackthorn plc will be held at .... on .... at 12 noon when the following ordinary business will be transacted:

1. To receive and consider the report of the directors and the statement of accounts for the year ended .... with the directors' and auditor's report thereon.

2. To declare a final dividend on the ordinary shares.
3. To propose the following Directors for election or re-election:
   Mr AJC Thompson.
   Mrs C Eccles.
   Miss S Fraser.
4. To reappoint the Auditors.
5. To fix the remuneration of the Auditors.

And the following special business:
To consider and, if thought fit, to pass the following resolution as a special resolution:

Special resolution
That the regulations contained in the document submitted to this meeting and, for the purpose of identification, signed by the Chairman hereof be approved and adopted as the Articles of Association of the Company in substitution for and to the exclusion of all the existing Articles thereof, such substitution to take effect from the conclusion of this Annual General Meeting.

By order of the Board
.... Secretary

Note
Any member may appoint a proxy or proxies and a form is enclosed for the use of members unable to attend the meeting. A proxy need not be a member of the company. Authorised representatives or corporate members have full voting powers. Completed forms of proxy must be lodged at the address shown on the form not later than 48 hours before the meeting. Members who have lodged proxy forms are not thereby prevented from attending the meeting and voting in person if they wish.

Notice of a general meeting

NOTICE IS HEREBY GIVEN that an General Meeting of .... (the 'Company') will be held at .... on September .... at 11.00 a.m. to consider and, if thought fit, pass the following resolutions of which Resolutions 1 to 4 will be proposed as ordinary resolutions and Resolutions 5 and 6 as special resolutions.

1 Resolution 1 ORDINARY RESOLUTION
THAT:

6 Resolution 6 SPECIAL RESOLUTION
THAT:
the Articles of Association of the Company be and are hereby amended as set out in Schedules A and B to this Notice of General Meeting, such amendments to take effect from the dates set out in such schedules.
By order of the Board,
(Signed)
Company Secretary Registered Office: (address)
(date)

An alteration of the Articles does not need to be at an general meeting. It was included at one here because it was convenient. However, the alteration must be by special resolution. (Remember that if at least 75 per cent of all the shareholders of a private company agree, it is possible to pass a written resolution which would remove the need to have an GM altogether.)

Notice of a general meeting

NOTICE IS HEREBY GIVEN that an General Meeting of the company will be held at .... on .... April .... at 10.00 a.m. for the purposes of considering and, if thought fit, passing the following resolution which will be proposed as an ordinary resolution:
THAT the acquisition of .... by the Company (whether or not through a subsidiary of the Company) as described in the circular to shareholders dated .... be and it is hereby approved and that the Directors or a Committee of the Directors be and they are hereby authorised to complete the same with such modifications, variations, amendments or revisions as are not of a material nature.

On behalf of the Board
(signed)
Company Secretary and General Counsel   Registered Office: (address)

Resolutions

Ordinary resolutions for general meetings

1. *Resolution declaring a final dividend*
   That the recommendation of the Directors as to the amount of the dividend be accepted and accordingly that a final dividend of .... pence per share on the paid-up capital of the company for the year ended .... be declared payable forthwith out of the profits of the company to the holders of ordinary shares on the register of members as at .... in proportion to their respective shareholdings in the company.
2. *Resolution removing a director from office*
   That .... is hereby removed from the office of director of the company. (Note that under Section 168 of the Companies Act 2006, special notice of this resolution must be given in advance to the company. See Section 9.2.5, later.)

Special resolutions for general meetings

Special Resolution
That the name of the company be changed to 'Standpipe Ltd'.

Special Resolution
That the articles contained in the document submitted to this meeting and signed by the chairman for identification purposes be approved and adopted as the Articles of Association of the company in substitution for all the existing Articles of the company.

Resolutions of the board of directors

That .... be elected chairman of the board of directors.

That such accounting records of the company be kept as comply with the requirements of the Companies Act 2006.

That 100 ordinary shares of £1 each numbered .... to .... inclusive, in the capital of the company be hereby allotted to .... of .... and that the secretary be directed to register .... as the holder of such shares.

Shareholder's Freedom to Vote

Stuart Urquhart, *The Company Lawyer Digest*, October 1992
© Sweet & Maxwell Ltd. Reprinted with permission

It is an accepted principle of company law that a shareholder is free to exercise his voting rights in whichever way he chooses and that he owes no duty to the company in doing so. Although there are laws permitting the courts to intervene if there is minority oppression, the position of those holding 10 per cent of the votes acting on their own account would generally be regarded as unassailable. Not so in *Standard Chartered Bank* v. *Walker* (1992) BCLC 603, a case before Vinelott J in the High Court.

An individual shareholder together with a company with which he was associated held ordinary and preference shares which gave them between 5 and 10 per cent of the votes at the extraordinary general meeting of the company in question.

The company was in grave financial difficulty. Resolutions were to be proposed to restructure the company's finances. The proposals were made as a result of extensive negotiations with the financial institutions involved. Vinelott J accepted that one of the fundamental conditions for the continued support of these creditors was the removal of the individual shareholder and a colleague from their offices as non-executive directors. Without this support, the company would collapse. The votes held by the two shareholders could have proved critical to the success or failure of the resolutions.

Unsurprisingly, the individual shareholder was not in favour of a scheme whereby he would be divested of his directorship. Accordingly, the financial institutions sought either a mandatory injunction requiring the shareholders to vote in favour of the resolutions or a negative injunction restraining them from voting against.

Vinelott J considered whether the court could grant injunctive relief in such circumstances.v Counsel for the banks relied upon the court's jurisdiction to grant injunctive relief restraining a person from destroying his assets to the disadvantage of a creditor. The judge agreed that there would be a point beyond which the conduct of a debtor in relation to his property would be so plainly injurious to a creditor that the court would have the power to intervene. He cited the example of a trader who, being heavily in debt, chose to destroy his assets rather than give them to his creditors. In case, the creditor would be entitled to restrain such wilful destruction in order to protect his own interests.

However, any court interference with a shareholder's exercise of his voting rights would run contrary to the principle that he could vote them as he wished. Vinelott J accepted that intervention could only be sanctioned in exceptional circumstances. This case provided such exceptional circumstances.

The evidence clearly showed that the financial institutions would withdraw their support if the resolutions were not passed. As there were no other concrete proposals for saving the company, the court would intervene even though the circumstances in which they were permitted to do so were 'very rare indeed'.

It is interesting to note that the financial institutions also had a charge over other shares in the company. The failure of the resolutions would have rendered this security worthless as the shares would themselves have had no value. Without deciding whether this principle applied to the case, Vinelott J held that there was a jurisdiction to restrain a person from destroying property over which another had a charge. Again, the court would only exercise this jurisdiction in 'rare circumstances'.

A shareholder's free right to exercise his vote at general meetings is therefore not unimpeachable. *Standard Chartered Bank* v. *Walker* shows that the creditor of a company can successfully challenge this right. It remains to be seen how far the court will be prepared to go to find the 'rare circumstances' which allow the creditor such injunctive relief.

It should be borne in mind that this case does not impose any duty towards the company or fellow shareholders. It was the *creditors* who obtained the injunctions.

More importantly, there have for a long time been some exceptions to the old rule that shareholders could exercise their voting rights as they wished. Today, the powers of the company and fellow shareholders to intervene are even more substantial, particularly under the Companies Act 1985 s.459 (now S.994 CA 2006); see Section 9.3.4.

4.9.3 Shareholders' rights and duties

As shown above, the effect of S.33 CA 2006 is that the Memorandum and Articles of a company operate as a contract between the company and its members, and between members themselves. The rights of shareholders are governed by this, and also by the terms upon which the shares were issued. Where Table A reg. 2 applies, a company may issue new shares 'with such rights and restrictions as the company may by ordinary resolution determine' (within the limits of the authorised capital).

The main rights which a share may give are to attend and receive notice of meetings, and to vote on resolutions (see earlier in this chapter); also to receive such dividends as the company may declare. One share can also give rights to inspect many company records, or to appoint a proxy, and so on, see earlier. Groups of shares or shareholders have greater rights, depending upon the size of the group.

The duties which a shareholder owes to his company are very limited. Unlike a director, he owes no general duties of good faith, care or skill. He can normally exercise his powers for whatever reasons he thinks fit. However, there are some constraints, particularly on the abuse of majority rights (see later), and a shareholder's powers are subject to equitable principles which may make it unjust to exercise them in some ways. This is less than a full duty of good faith, but it can be important. It is established that the court can declare invalid an alteration to the Articles which is not made for the benefit of the company as a whole, and when voting on a resolution to alter the Articles, 'the shareholder must proceed on what, in his honest opinion, is for the benefit of the company as a whole' [per Evershed MR in *Greenhalgh* v. *Arderne Cinemas Ltd* (1950)]. In *Clemens* v. *Clemens Bros Ltd* (1976), this type of approach was taken further. A 55 per cent shareholder in a small domestic company used her votes to pass resolutions issuing new shares with the effect (and apparent motive) of increasing her own control. The plaintiff's holding was reduced to less than 25 per cent. The company did not need the extra capital. The court set aside the resolutions.

Variation of the rights of a particular class of shareholder is subject to particular safeguards. For example, where a company's share capital is divided into shares of different classes, the rights of any class can only be varied (a) with the written consent of the holders of three-quarters in nominal value of the issued shares of that class; or (b) by an extraordinary resolution passed at a separate general meeting of the holders of that class. Any further requirements of the terms of issue or the Memorandum or Articles must also be met.

Even if the requirements of the CA 2006 and the company's constitution have been met, a minority can still apply to the court. Holders of not less that 15 per cent of the issued shares of the class, who did not vote for the resolution to vary or assent to it in writing, can apply to the court to have the variation set aside. Application to the court must be within 21 days of the resolution or written consent. One dissentient may acquire written authority from others to act on their behalf. The court may approve or disallow a variation, but not change it.

4.10 Summary

At the end of this chapter, students should make sure that they understand the following:

- the legal position of individual traders and practitioners;
- partnerships: nature, structure and liabilities;
- the concept of incorporation, especially in relation to companies;
- in particular, the concepts of:
  - separate legal personality;
  - limited liability;
  - perpetual succession;
  - *ultra vires;*
- different types of company, especially public/private, single-member and quoted companies;
- lifting the veil of incorporation, both by the courts and by statute;
- the procedure for forming and registering companies, including the advantages and disadvantages of off-the-shelf companies. In particular, students should be familiar with:
  - the position of promoters;
  - registration;
  - Memorandum of Association – including alteration;
  - Articles of Association – including alteration;
  - shareholder agreements;
  - details of directors, and so on;
  - the certificate of incorporation;
- the (remains of) the *ultra vires* doctrine as it affects companies today;
- the advantages and disadvantages of carrying on business through the medium of a company limited by shares.

At the end of this chapter, students should make sure that they understand the following:

- the general legal structure of companies: directors and shareholders;
- board meetings;

- meetings of members – types of meeting:
  - annual general meeting;
  - general meetings;
  - class meetings;
- resolutions at meetings:
  - ordinary (with or without special notice);
  - special;
  - written;
- calling a meeting;
- conduct of meetings, including minutes, and so on.

Revision Questions 4

Question 1 Multiple-choice selection

1.1 Which one of the following is not an example of an artificial legal person?

(A) The chairman of a public company.
(B) The BBC.
(C) A company limited by guarantee.
(D) A private company with only two shareholders.

1.2 DC, who had never been in business before, decided to rent a corner shop and open a food store which he named The *All-Hours Food Mart*. From this information it can be inferred that

(i) *The All-Hours Food Mart* is a legal person.
(ii) *The All-Hours Food Mart* is an unincorporated business.
(iii) DC is a sole trader.
(iv) DC is a director of a private company.

Which of the above are correct?

(A) (i) and (ii) only.
(B) (ii) and (iii) only.
(C) (i), (iii) and (iv) only.
(D) (i), (ii) and (iii) only.

1.3 A partnership is a significant form of business organisation, particularly among providers of professional services such as architects and financial accountants. Which one of the following statements about partnerships is correct?

(A) A partnership is an example of an incorporated business organisation.
(B) A partnership is recognised in law as an artificial legal person.
(C) Partners generally benefit from limited liability for any debts incurred as a result of their business activities.
(D) Professional codes of practice may require members of the profession to trade as partners or as sole traders rather than through companies.

1.4 All the following statements about the formation of a company in the United Kingdom are true *except* one. The *exception* is
(A) The company comes into existence when the Registrar of Companies issues a Certificate of Incorporation.
(B) The company comes into existence when granted a listing by the Stock Exchange.
(C) The Memorandum of Association must be sent to the Registrar of Companies prior to incorporation.
(D) A public company must have a certificate of incorporation and a trading certificate before it can commence business.

1.5 A company wishing to be incorporated must send all except one of the following to the Registrar. The *exception* is
(A) A Memorandum of Association.
(B) Separate articles of Association.
(C) Separate particulars of the first directors.
(D) A separate statutory declaration that the requirements of the Companies Act have been satisfied.

1.6 Which of the following is *incorrect* in relation to company names.
(A) In general, the name of a private or public company must end in 'limited', 'Ltd', 'public limited company' or 'plc' as appropriate.
(B) The name must not be the same as that of an existing company.
(C) The name cannot be changed without the unanimous approval of the shareholders.
(D) The name of the company may be registered as a trade mark.

1.7 Identify the *one* statement relating to Annual General Meetings which is inaccurate:
(A) A private company can decide not to hold an Annual General Meeting.
(B) An Annual General Meeting in a public company must be held within one year of incorporation.
(C) Accounts of a public company must be laid before members for approval at an Annual General Meeting.
(D) Articles of Association can be altered at an Annual General Meeting.

1.8 To dismiss a director under s.168 of the Companies Act 2006 requires
(A) an ordinary resolution with 14 days' notice to the company.
(B) a special resolution with 14 days' notice to the company.
(C) an ordinary resolution with 28 days' notice to the company.
(D) a special resolution with 28 days' notice to the company.

1.9 Identify which type of resolution from the list below cannot be used by a public company:
(A) Ordinary resolution.
(B) Special resolution.
(C) Written resolution.
(D) Ordinary resolution with special notice.

1.10 Which one of the following statements is inaccurate in relation to a shareholders' agreement?

(A) The agreement need not be open to public inspection.
(B) It can validly provide that a particular director will remain a director for life.
(C) It can be enforced simply by means of an action by one shareholder against another.
(D) It can be changed by a simple majority of members.

Question 2

Paul had been in business on his own account for a number of years, acting as a retailer of household goods and furnishings. In April 2002 Paul decided that he would incorporate his business by transferring it to Paul's Furnishings Ltd, a company which he proposed to register as soon as possible. Paul called to see his solicitor (Anne) who arranged for the necessary documents to be sent to the Registrar of Companies. In the meantime Paul notified his suppliers of the change and ordered some new furniture from Luxury Chairs Ltd. Paul signed the order 'Paul, for and on behalf of Paul's Furnishings Ltd'.

Requirements

Delete as appropriate and complete the following:

At law Paul is a .... (1 word) **(2 marks)** of Paul's Furnishings Ltd. The company will not come into existence until Paul receives a .... (3 words) **(2 marks)** from the .... (3 words) **(2 marks)**. Paul has ordered goods on behalf of the company before it has been registered, and has therefore entered into a .... (1 word) **(2 marks)** contract. This contract is enforceable against .... (1 word) **(2 marks)**.

(Total marks = 10)

Question 3

Requirements

Delete as appropriate and complete the following:

In a general partnership the partners are .... (3 words) **(2 marks)** liable for the debts of the company. In contrast when business is carried on through the medium of a company limited by .... (1 word) **(1 mark)**, the .... (1 word) **(2 marks)** is fully liable for any debts contracted rather than the shareholders. A company is a separate .... (1 word) **(1 mark)** at law and if the shareholders have fully paid the amount due on their .... (1 word) **(1 mark)** they cannot be called upon to make any further contribution. The relationship between the company and its shareholders is set down in the company's .... (1 word) **(1 mark)** of Association and the company's contractual ability is contained in the .... (2 words) **(2 marks)** of Association.

(Total marks = 10)

Question 4

A, B, C and D are the only directors and shareholders in ABCD Ltd, each holding 500 ordinary £1 shares.

Requirements

Delete as appropriate and complete the following:

To propose an ordinary resolution .... (1 word) **(1 mark)** days' notice must be given to the shareholders. To pass a special resolution .... (1 word) **(1 mark)** days' notice must be given. If the shareholders wish to change the company's Articles of Association they will need to pass a .... (1 word) **(2 marks)** resolution. This resolution can be passed by the votes of any .... (1 word) **(2 marks)** of the shareholders. Alternatively, the Articles could be changed by a .... (percentage) **(2 marks)** resolution which would require the support of .... (1 word) **(1 mark)** the shareholders.

(Total marks = 9)

Question 5

Requirements

Delete as appropriate and complete the following:

A board meeting may be called by giving .... (1 word) **(2 marks)** notice of the meeting to all the directors. A board usually reaches its decisions by .... (1 word) **(2 marks)** vote. If the directors cannot attend a board meeting it may still make a decision by all the directors signing a .... (1 word) **(2 marks)** resolution. The procedure at board meetings and the voting rights of directors are set down in the company's .... (3 words) **(2 marks)**. Sometimes the law will require the shareholders to support the board's proposals. In that event the board may call .... (2 words) **(2 marks)** on 14 days' notice. **(Total marks = 10)**

Solutions to Revision Questions

4

Solution 1

1.1 Answer: (A)

Human beings are 'natural' legal persons and not 'artificial' legal persons. The chairman of a public company is a human being; hence statement (A) is the answer. All the other statements relate to incorporated organisations which possess an artificial legal personality.

1.2 Answer: (B)

Since DC is commencing business as an unincorporated individual proprietor or sole trader, only (ii) and (iii) of the statements in the question are correct. Being a 'natural person', DC is a legal person, but not his business. Statement (i) is therefore incorrect. And as his business is not a company, DC cannot be a director. Statement (iv) is the therefore also incorrect.

1.3 Answer: (D)

Being unincorporated, a partnership does not possess a personality in law separate from the natural personality of each of the partners. Hence, statements (A) and (B) are incorrect. Statement (C) is also incorrect because most partners do not possess limited liability. This leaves statement (D) as the correct answer: as part of the professional ethic, many (though not all) professional bodies prevent their members from selling their services through the intermediary of a company.

1.4 Answer: (B)

All the statements except (B) are correct. (B) certainly does not apply to private companies which are not allowed by law to market their shares. Many, but not all, public companies apply for a Stock Exchange listing so that a market may be created in their shares. However, even when a public company applies for a Stock Exchange listing, the granting of such a listing does not define when the company comes into existence. (B) is therefore the exception and the correct answer.

1.5 Answer: (B)

A company can simply state in the Memorandum that it will adopt Table A.

1.6 Answer: (C)

(C) is incorrect as although the name may be changed by a written resolution of all the shareholders, it may also be changed by the shareholders passing a special resolution, which is achieved by at least 75 per cent of those present at the meeting voting in favour.

1.7 Answer: (B)

(C) identifies what must be undertaken at the meeting as ordinary business. (D) identifies what also can be carried out at the meeting but as special business, in other words that which is done out of choice rather than necessity. Private companies are now able to dispense with the need to hold this meeting by passing an elective resolution. Some flexibility exists in the time allowed to companies following incorporation before they need to hold the meeting. The maximum period is 18 months, not 1 year.

1.8 Answer: (C)

By s.303 of the Companies Act 1985, removal of a director before the expiry of his term of office requires an ordinary resolution on special notice, and the length of special notice is 28 days. Therefore (A), (B) and (D) are all incorrect.

1.9 Answer: (C)

The written resolution procedure enables private companies only to dispense with the need to hold general meetings. Public and private companies will use the ordinary resolution where the law or the company's articles do not require another form of resolution. The use of special resolution and ordinary resolution with special notice by both private and public companies is determined by statute.

1.10 Answer: (D)

A shareholders' agreement is a *contract* which, like any other contract, can only be changed by *all* of the parties to the contract ('members'). (A) (B) and (C) are all potential advantages of shareholders' agreements.

Solution 2

At law Paul is a *promoter* of Paul's Furnishings Ltd. The company will not come into existence until Paul receives a *Certificate of Incorporation* from the *Registrar of Companies*. Paul has ordered goods on behalf of the company before it has been registered, and has therefore entered into a *pre-incorporation* contract. This contract is enforceable against *Paul*.

Solution 3

In a general partnership the partners are *jointly and severally* liable for the debts of the company. In contrast, when business is carried on through the medium of a company limited by *shares*, the *company* is fully liable for any debts contracted rather than the shareholders. A company is a separate *person* at law and if the shareholders have fully paid the amount due on their *shares* they cannot be called upon to make any further contribution. The relationship between the company and its shareholders is set down in the company's *Articles* of Association and the company's contractual ability is contained in the *Memorandum* of Association.

Solution 4

To propose an ordinary resolution *fourteen* days' notice must be given to the shareholders. To pass a special resolution *fourteen* days' notice must be given. If the shareholders wish to change the company's Article of Association, they will need to pass a *special* resolution. This resolution can be passed by the votes of any *three* of the shareholders. Alternatively, the Articles could be changed by *written* resolution which would require the support of 75 per cent the shareholders.

Solution 5

A board meeting may be called by giving *reasonable* notice of the meeting to all the directors. A board usually reaches its decisions by *majority* vote. If the directors cannot attend a board meeting it may still make a decision by all the directors signing a *written* resolution. The procedure at board meetings and the voting rights of directors are set down in the company's *Articles of Association*. Sometimes the law will require the shareholders to support the board's proposals. In that event the board may call *a general Meeting* on 14 days' notice.

Company Finance and Management

Company Finance and Management

5

Learning Outcomes

After completing this chapter you should be able to:

- explain the nature of different types of share, the procedure for the issue of shares, and acceptable forms of payment;
- explain the maintenance of capital principle and the procedure to increase and reduce share capital; including the repercussions of issuing shares for an improper purpose;
- explain the ability of a company to take secured and unsecured loans, the different types of security and the registration procedure;
- explain the procedure for the appointment, retirement, disqualification and removal of directors and their powers and duties during office;
- explain the rules dealing with the possible imposition of personal liability upon the directors of insolvent companies;
- identify and contrast the rights of shareholders with the board of the company;
- explain the qualifications, powers and duties of the company secretary.

The chapter has been arranged into sections based around the learning outcomes as above.

5.1 Shares and share capital

Learning Outcome:	To explain the nature of different types of share, the procedure for the issue of shares and acceptable forms of payment.

5.1.1 The nature of shares

A share is a bundle of rights and duties which the holder has in relation to the company and his fellow shareholders. These derive principally from the Memorandum and Articles of Association of the company (see S.33 A 2006), and from the terms on which the shares were allotted. The main rights which a share may give today are the rights to attend meetings, to vote on resolutions, and to receive such dividends as the company may declare. Beyond this, a share gives the holder no automatic right to take part in management. In the great majority of companies, which are small and private, the main shareholders and the directors (who are responsible for management) will be the same persons. In large companies the majority of shares are usually held by institutional investors such as the pension funds. Although such shareholders can influence management they are often criticised for not participating more actively in their companies affairs and thus giving the directors too much freedom to run the companies as they see fit. (This is dealt with more fully in Chapter 8, 'Corporate Governance'). Finally it should be noted that their is no *legal* obligation upon any director to own any shares in his/her company as such.

5.1.2 Terminology: meaning of 'share capital'

Companies issue shares to raise capital, usually in the form of cash although shares may be issued in exchange for assets. This is known as non-cash consideration, and public companies particularly are subject to strict rules regarding the valuation of this non-cash consideration.

Capital is the company's funds available for use in the business and represented by its assets. Companies raise their capital usually by way of loan or share capital. In relation to shares the expression 'capital' is used in a variety of ways.

Companies will have *authorised* share capital, *issued* share capital, *called up* share capital, and *paid up* share capital.

- *Authorised share capital.* This is the amount of capital which can be raised by issuing shares, for example 'the company's share capital is £100,000 divided into 100,000 ordinary shares of £1 each.' The amount is selected by those who registered the company and could be of any amount they consider appropriate. As stated this shows the maximum amount which can be raised by issuing shares. If the full amount has been raised, (£100,000 in the above example) the authorised capital may be increased at a later date to facilitate further issues. This would be done by the board resolving to raise further capital by issuing shares and the shareholders passing an ordinary resolution (see later). At present the authorised (or 'nominal') share capital must be shown in the company's Memorandum of Association. When the CA 2006 is fully in force in October 2009, there will no longer be any need for a public or private company to have an authorised share capital although they may if they wish include a restriction in the Articles of Association. After October 2009 a statement of capital and initial shareholdings must be submitted to the Registrar with the application for registration of the company. (Section 10 CA 2006). Thereafter companies will be able to allot shares without having to increase any authorised share capital, although a 'return of allotment' will need to be delivered to Companies House with a statement of capital (Section 555 CA 2006).
- *Issued share capital* refers to that amount of the authorised share capital which is actually issued. It may be part or all of the authorised share capital and represents the company's funding from its members.
- *Called up share capital* is the total amount of money which the directors have 'called up' from members. This arises when shares are not initially required to be paid for in full and the directors will request the outstanding money to be paid at a later date. For example, subscribers may have been required to pay 30p per share on 1,000 £1 shares, with an additional amount of 20p called up by the directors a month later. The total amount called up is then 50p per share. The called up capital of the company will be £500.

- *Paid up share capital* is the amount of called up capital which members have actually paid. Unless any member has not paid for his or her shares when called to do so, the two amounts will be the same.

Example

A, B, C and D decide to register ABCD Ltd.

(i) Pre – October 2009

The promoters of the company will have to submit a number of documents to the Registrar of Companies including a Memorandum of Association which shows the company's authorised share capital. Assume that A, B, C and D decide that the company will have an authorised share capital of £200,000 divided into 200,000 ordinary £1 shares and initially A, B, C and D will subscribe for 10,000 shares each which are to be paid for in full. It follows that the authorised share capital of ABCD Ltd is £200,000, the issued share capital £40,000 and the called up and paid up share capital is £40,000.

(ii) Post – October 2009.

A, B, C and D will still be required to submit a number of documents to the Registrar of Companies including a Memorandum of Association in the prescribed form. That document will simply state (a) that A, B, C and D wish to form a company under the CA 2006 and (b) that they agree to be members and take at least one share each. The Memorandum of Association will not contain any statement of authorised capital but A, B, C and D must submit an additional document, i.e. a 'statement of capital and initial shareholdings' which states:

(a) the total number of shares to be taken on formation; (in this example 40,000);
(b) the aggregate nominal value of those shares (in this example £40,000);
(c) prescribed particulars of the rights attached to those shares (e.g. the right to vote etc); and
(d) the amount to be paid up and the amount (if any) unpaid on each share (in this example £1 to be paid on each £1 share).

5.1.3 Types of shares

Companies may issue a number of different types or classes of shares with varying rights attaching to them. Where a company issues different classes of shares, then the rights attaching to those shares are known as 'class rights' and are only alterable by each particular class. For example, a company could issue ordinary and preference shares. These are different classes of shares each carrying specific rights.

Shares have to be issued with a par (nominal) value attaching to them. Although shares with a par value of £1 are common, shares listed on the stock exchange often have a par value of less than this (say 10p or 25p). There are varieties of shares which can be issued, but companies will normally issue ordinary shares and preference shares.

- *Ordinary shares* usually carry the right to vote but have no fixed dividend. The dividend, if any, will be recommended by the directors and approved by the shareholders at the annual general meeting (AGM). Dividends can only be paid from a company's accumulated realised profits less its accumulated realised losses. Where the company has made a large profit, the dividend will generally be high to keep the shareholders happy and, if the company is a public company, keep the market price of the shares buoyant. Equally, if profits are low then the dividend would reflect this. If the company goes into liquidation and is solvent, that is able to pay its debts in full, the holders of the ordinary shares share in any surplus that there might be after all shareholders have been paid back the par value of the shares. If a company should go into solvent liquidation, the equity shareholders have a right to participate in any surplus which remains after all the creditors have been paid in full.

- *Preference shares*, on the other hand, give their holders the right to receive their dividend in preference to ordinary shareholders, although they do not have an automatic right to a dividend. Whether a dividend is paid is determined in the same way as with the ordinary shareholders, that is a recommendation from the board and approved by the shareholders at the AGM. Instead of a variable dividend, though, these shares carry a fixed rate of dividend, such as 7 per cent. The dividend is presumed to be cumulative unless stated otherwise. This means that if the dividend is unable to be paid in a particular year, it must normally be carried forward and paid the next year before the ordinary dividend, assuming profits allow. If the company goes into liquidation and there is a surplus, the preference shareholders will only get back the par value of the shares, and will not share further in any surplus.

  However, when deciding whether to issue preference shares or not, the directors have a range of choices as they can issue different types of preference shares. If they wish to raise capital for a period of time and then repay it, as an alternative to borrowing they could offer redeemable preference shares. These will be issued for a specified period of time and then bought back by the company at the time agreed. Once bought back, the shares have to be cancelled so they cannot be re-issued (but see 'treasury shares' below).

  In times of high interest rates or the current difficulties associated with obtaining credit/finance, redeemable preference shares may be particularly attractive to companies. This is so because if a company borrows money, interest at the agreed rate must be paid whether or not the company is making a profit. However, dividends to the preference (and ordinary) shareholders are only paid if the company has available profits. At the time of writing these notes the 'credit crunch' is making it particularly difficult for businesses to obtain necessary finance. It may be therefore, that obtaining additional finance from the company's membership is a more attractive proposition than attempting to obtain it by way of bank loans.

  Clearly the share issue must be made attractive to the participating preference shareholders. It is likely therefore that the company will provide an additional return, perhaps in the form of a premium payable on redemption, or allowing the shareholders the right to share in any surplus profits which remain after a certain percentage has been paid to the ordinary shareholders.

  The courts have held that possession of a share certificate is only prima facie evidence of ownership of the shares described in the certificate. It is not conclusive because the share certificate could have been stolen, copied or forged. Conclusive evidence is obtained by looking at the name of the person who has been allotted the shares in the company's register of shareholders.

  It follows that a shareholder will be issued with a share certificate to evidence that he/she has a certain number of shares in the company. *Ownership* of shares, however, depends on the company's register of shareholders.

- *Deferred shares.* The holders of such shares are normally not entitled to any dividend at all unless and until preference shareholders are paid, and then ordinary shareholders receive at least a specified amount or percentage per share. Exact rights will depend on the Articles and terms of issue. Such shares, sometimes called 'management' or 'founders' shares, are uncommon today.
- *Redeemable shares.* As a general rule, a share, once issued by the company and paid for by the shareholder, remains in existence until the company is wound up. The holder of that share can sell it to another holder, but the share itself must continue to exist. It is part of

the share capital of the company, and there have been stringent rules which control the power of a company to reduce its share capital.

In more recent times, these rules have been somewhat relaxed. One such relaxation is that it is possible to issue shares which are stated at the time of issue to be 'redeemable'. These can later be redeemed – bought back by the company – in accordance with the terms of issue.

- *Treasury shares.* These shares were introduced on 1 December 2003 by ss 162A-162G, Companies Act 1985. A public company (PLC), whose shares are listed on the Stock Exchange or traded on AIM, which purchases its own shares out of distributable profits may hold the shares purchased 'in treasury'. This means that the directors may re-issue the shares without the formalities associated with a new issue of shares. The company can hold up to 10 per cent of its shares in treasury shares but cannot exercise any rights in respect of the shares, such as voting, receiving dividends, and so on. The shares are shown on the register as being owned by the company and are treated as part of the PLC's issued share capital. Treasury shares can only be sold for cash.
- *Stock.* If authorised by its Articles, a company may convert paid up shares into 'stock', where the holding of the member is expressed in an amount, rather than in a number of shares each with a nominal value. Stock came into being partly to avoid having to give each share a separate number. Since this is no longer required for fully paid up shares, stock is rarely seen.
- *Class rights.* The rights which attach to shares are known as class rights. Normally, these rights relate to dividends, voting, and the distribution of the company's assets when it is wound up. Different classes of shares have different rights. For example, preference shareholders have the right to receive their dividend before the company pays a dividend to its ordinary shareholders.

Companies with different classes of shares may wish to vary the rights attaching to them. This is not always easy, and the company's Memorandum and Articles have to be examined to see whether they can be varied and by what procedure. Class rights may be attached to a class of shares by:

(a) the Memorandum;
(b) the Articles;
(c) a shareholders' agreement;
(d) a special resolution of the company in general meeting.

For example: in *Re Northern Engineering Industries plc* (1994), the company wished to reduce its capital by paying off all of its preference shares, but the reduction was opposed by a preference shareholder. The Court of Appeal held that, since the company's Articles provided that such a reduction was a variation of class rights, the company must first obtain the consent of the preference shareholders, that is, by an extraordinary resolution passed at a separate meeting of the preference shareholders. Following the Companies Act 2006, extraordinary resolutions no longer exist. Today if class rights are to be varied the most common requirement is that the variation be agreed by a special resolution of the class affected. Thus if the rights of the preference shareholders are to be varied a separate meeting of the preference shareholders would be called and they would be asked to approve the variation by special resolution.

5.2 Issuing shares

5.2.1 Authority to issue shares

The first shareholders will be the subscribers to the Memorandum of Association. Each must take at least one share. Many will take more.

Subsequent shares may be issued by the directors if they have authority to do so. By S.550 CA 2006, such authority can be given in either of two ways:

(i) *By the Articles of Association*. A special article may be included in the company's Articles giving the board the authority to allot the company's shares. This power is not contained in Table A which would have to be amended.

(ii) *By a resolution of the members*. Alternatively, directors may be authorised to allot new shares by the shareholders passing an ordinary or, in the case of a private company, written ordinary resolution.

Whichever method is used, the authority only lasts 5 years and the authority of the directors in all cases will be subject to the following:

(a) The issue must not raise the total shareholding above the company's current nominal/authorised capital (see above). The authorised capital itself may, however, first be raised by the shareholders, by ordinary resolution. In a private company, the written ordinary resolution can be used. The resolution must be filed with the Registrar of Companies together with an amended Memorandum of Association. Remember that after October 2009 companies will no longer need to have an authorised share capital, but alterations of share capital will still have to be notified to the Registrar (see above).

(b) The authority granted to the directors by the Articles or by ordinary resolution may be subject to limits; for example, the directors may only be empowered to issue ordinary shares, not preference shares.

(c) In any event, the authorisation, whether in the Articles or by resolution, must state the maximum number/amount of shares which the directors can issue, and when the authority expires. It cannot generally be given for more than 5 years. Some companies ensure that a resolution authorising the directors to allot new shares is on the agenda at the AGM each year to ensure that it never expires. Prior to the Companies Act 2006, a private company could extend the 5-year period by passing an 'elective' resolution to that effect. However, elective resolutions were abolished by the 2006 Act.

(d) The S.561 CA 2006, gives limited pre-emption rights to existing shareholders if it is proposed to issue new shares for cash to a specific person (human or corporate). The shares must first be offered to existing shareholders in proportion to their existing holdings. It follows, for example, that if Susan holds 10 per cent of the shares in ABC Ltd, she must be offered 10 per cent of the new shares. The aim of the pre-emption rules is to maintain the existing power structure within the company. The terms must be at least as favourable as those available to the specific offeree, and members must be given at least 21 days in which to accept. This can give existing shareholders some statutory protection against new issues which could lessen their control or influence over the company. However, S.561 is limited.

    It does not apply if:

    (i) the new shares are issued for a non-cash payment (as may be the case in a takeover where the shareholders in the target company may be offered shares in the bidding company instead of cash);

(ii) the company, whether public or private, has passed a special resolution under S.570 CA 2006 to disapply S.561;
(iii) the company's Articles provide for the disapplication of S.561; or
(iv) the shareholders 'waive' their pre-emption rights.

Example

ABC Ltd has three shareholders, A, B and C, each holding 25,000 ordinary £1 shares, that is, one-third of the company's issued share capital. The company is in need of further capital and A, the sole director of the company, is proposing to offer 25,000 ordinary £1 shares to D. Clearly, if this share issue goes ahead the effect will be to reduce the voting power of each of A, B and C from one-third to one-quarter. It follows that one-third of the new shares must first be offered to A, B and C unless they agree to disapply their pre-emption rights by passing a special (or written) resolution or they each agree to waive their rights to the new shares.

The Articles may set down increased protection for the shareholders by providing that all new shares must first be offered to the existing members, whether or not they are being issued for a non-cash consideration, for example in exchange for assets. Such a provision may be used by small companies where, for instance, the family shareholders wish to protect their control so that every issue of shares whether for cash or otherwise must first be offered to the existing shareholders.

It is important to distinguish between the statutory pre-emption rights under S.561, which apply when a *company issues* new shares, and the pre-emption rights commonly found in the Articles of private companies, which apply where a *shareholder wishes to transfer his/her shares.* Private companies usually restrict the transfer of shares by members because the people who hold shares in private companies are often members of a family, friends or business associates who do not wish outsiders to come into the company. A typical clause in the Articles may provide, 'Any member who wishes to sell his shares must first offer them to the existing shareholders.' In addition under the Articles, the approval of the directors is normally required before members of private companies can transfer their shares to other existing members or to outsiders.

(e) In a private company, the shares must not be issued for public subscription. An advertisement inviting public applications for shares in a private company would be a criminal offence by the directors.
(f) In addition to these statutory controls, there is a general equitable rule that directors must exercise their powers, including powers to issue shares, for the benefit of the company as a whole, and not, for example, solely as a device for protecting or increasing their own interests in the company, or even for preventing a takeover; see *Hogg* v. *Cramphorn* (1967) in Section 5.8.5.

5.2.2 Finding buyers

Private companies cannot invite the public generally to purchase the company's shares. Rather share capital is obtained from the family, friends or business associates who have decided to combine their resources into a business venture. In the case of private companies, loan capital is usually obtained from a bank.

Public companies however, may indeed raise share capital by inviting members of the public to subscribe for shares. Such companies may also raise loans from the public. In fact there are a number of ways in which public companies may raise share capital. Most public companies aim to be 'listed' in other words to have their shares quoted on a stock exchange, the largest in the UK being the London Stock Exchange which in fact operates two markets, the Stock Exchange and the Alternative Investment Market ('AIM'). However, not all public companies are quoted on the London Stock Exchange or the AIM which require the companies to be listed on either market to be of a certain size and to comply with stringent regulations.

Listing

In order to obtain a listing, on the London Stock Exchange (known as a 'flotation'), a company must be registered as a public company or have re-registered as such. In addition to raising finance, a flotation allows the founders of the business to obtain a public valuation of the business and thus to sell out to new owners if that is desired. The listing of securities is governed by the Financial Services and Markets Act 2000 ('FSMA') and the regulatory authority is the Financial Services Authority which is known as the UK Listing Authority ('UKLA') when acting in this regard. UKLA is responsible for drafting the rules which are designed to provide a level of protection for investors and to maintain the integrity of the Exchange. Conditions which must be satisfied to obtain a listing include (a) the company is properly incorporated and is not a private company; (b) the company has published or filed audited accounts for the previous 3 years; (cc) the company must be able to carry on business at arms length from any shareholder with a controlling interest, which generally means 30% of the voting rights in this context. In addition the company must be applying to have securities listed which (a) are freely transferable; (b) the expected market value of the securities being listed must be at least £700,000 (usually much more); and (c) usually at least 25% of the shares being listed must be distributed to the public. It is also a condition for admission to the official list of any new securities that have not been offered to the public before, that a prospectus in the form and containing the information which has been specified by UKLA. Please note these conditions are not exhaustive but are designed to demonstrate some of the factors involved.

Methods of raising share capital

New issues of shares may be by:

- *Prospectus*. The Prospectus Directive (203/71/EC) specifies that where there is a public offer of shares or a request for admission of securities to trading on a regulated market a prospectus must be issued which contains all the information necessary to enable investors to make an informed choice. A prospectus could be published in a glossy brochure or could be contained in the pages of the financial press. Members of the public respond by applying to purchase shares and the offer is accepted by the company allotting shares into the applicants name. A person induced to purchase securities on the basis of a false or misleading prospectus may have remedies in misrepresentation and under the FSMA 2000.
- *A public offer*. In this case, the public subscribes directly to the company for the shares.
- *A placing*. This where the shares are offered to (placed with) a small number of persons. It could well be that this is the cheapest way of issuing the shares as there are only a small number of persons involved, usually some of the major financial institutions.
- *An offer for sale*. In this case, an issuing house will acquire a company's new issue of shares and then offer them for resale to the public.

Example

The Graham Group plc, for example, which has a large share of the builders' merchants market, particularly in heating, plumbing, sanitaryware and kitchen products, had a placing and offer for sale in March 1994 of 114,638,890 ordinary shares of 50p each at 183p per share (ordinary shares with a par value of 50p and a premium of 133p). JO Hambro Morgan & Company Ltd were acting as sponsor and financial adviser with NatWest Securities Ltd acting as sponsor and underwriter. The underwriter, in effect, guarantees the success of the offer by agreeing, for a fee of course, to take up any shares not taken up by the public.

- *A rights issue*. This involves a company offering shares to its existing members in proportion to their shareholdings. In the first place, directors need authority to allot shares. This will come from the Articles or an ordinary resolution of the company in general meeting. Any ordinary shares which are allotted have to be offered first of all to existing members under s.561 CA 2006 in proportion to the shares they already hold. As stated above the shareholders have what are known as *pre-emption rights*. This gives them first refusal. The reasoning behind this is that if shares were issued directly to non-members, this would have the effect of weakening the voting power of existing members. From the members' point of view, they may be offered the shares at a lower price than the existing market value, although, of course, not less than the par value of the shares. The directors would be wishing to raise capital for some particular project which is beneficial to the company for example to re-equip the company's production lines or possibly to obtain necessary finance not readily available elsewhere, and the existing members, by being given the opportunity to take up these shares, are being given the chance to share in this to a greater extent than their existing shareholding gives them.

  If members do not wish to take up their rights, they may renounce them in favour of some other person. It is possible to disapply these rights in relation to a particular share issue, either through the Articles or by special resolution.

  Private companies can exclude these pre-emption rights permanently, if the members wish to do so, although it must be remembered that private companies must not offer their shares to the public.

  Very occasionally, and most likely in relation to a private company, a minority shareholder may be able to show that an issue of shares is unfairly prejudicial against him as a member, perhaps because it reduces his voting power in the company and there was some implied understanding that this would not happen. This would be done under the Companies Act 2006 s.994, which gives the court wide powers where it can be shown that the conduct complained of is unfairly prejudicial. The court may order that the issue be set aside, or that the shares of the complainant be purchased at a fair price as determined by the court; see Section 5.6.4.

Example

Eurotunnel provided a potent example of the importance of a rights issue when it went to its shareholders for £816m. It also borrowed money from the banking syndicate backing it. This money was needed to fund the project until Eurotunnel generated enough revenue from its passenger and freight services to cover its costs. The total funding of it is now twice the original estimate.

The rights issue enabled shareholders to buy three shares for every five they already held at a price of 265p, which was a large discount on the market price of the existing shares. However, the shareholders needed to exercise patience as it was expected that there will be no dividend pay out until 2004. Raising this amount of capital was expensive, and a number of City institutions were paid £42m to cover underwriting fees (where the underwriters guarantee to purchase any shares not taken up), expenses and general financial advice.

- *A bonus issue.* These arise when a company wishes to capitalise its reserves; or profits. An alternative name is *capitalisation issue.* Thus for example rather than distribute profits of £500,000 to the shareholders by way of dividend, Exe Ltd decided to capitalise those profits and issue 500,000 ordinary £1 bonus shares to its members. It is important to realise that no cash is raised by the company on the issue of these bonus shares, but rather existing profits are transferred to capital account. The existing members are given shares on a pro-rata basis through using the capital reserves of the company. Although the number of shares that a member holds will be increased after this issue, as there are now more shares available the total value of his shareholding is unlikely to have increased.

5.2.3 Factors to take into account when issuing shares

Obviously, when the company's directors are deciding that they need to raise money and are considering doing so through a share issue, they have to take into account:

- the costs involved, and the more people they have to reach the more costly it will be;
- other major share issues that have recently occurred or are occurring, as they will be competing against these to the extent that there is only so much investors' money to go round;
- the price at which the shares are to be offered. If it is too high then they will find that shares are not taken up. If they have had the issue underwritten then the shares not taken up will be purchased by the underwriter.

Conversely, if the share price is too low, they will find themselves inundated with demands for shares exceeding those which they have on offer, involving a costly procedure to return cheques and so on.

- The type of share to issue and the conditions attaching to the shares.
- The expertise within the company relating to share offers and the facility the company has to cope.

In the end, the offer has to be attractive to potential investors, whether existing shareholders or not, otherwise they will not apply for the shares.

5.2.4 Payment for and value of shares

Each share must have a 'nominal' or 'par' value, usually of a small amount (say £1). This will be set out in the capital clause of the Memorandum, and noted on the share certificates. This does not necessarily represent the real value of the share, even when it is first issued, because most shares are allotted and issued at a premium. The main significance of the nominal value is that it represents the *minimum* amount for which the share can be issued, because although shares can be issued at a premium, they cannot be issued at a discount (for less than the nominal value). It follows that the creditors know that the company must receive at least the nominal value. It represents the value comparatively to other shares in the company. It has sometimes been suggested that companies should be allowed to issue no-par-value shares, but this is not permitted in the United kingdom.

Shares are usually issued/allotted by the company at a premium, that is for more than their nominal value. A 50p share may be issued for £2.50, that is, at a premium of £2. (If 50p shares issued earlier by the company have since grown in value, this will only be fair to the earlier shareholders.) See also Section 5.1.3.

A *public* company normally must not allot any shares unless at least one-quarter of its nominal value and the whole of any premium have been paid. The company and any officer in default of this rule commits a criminal offence. A share which is not paid for to this extent can still be validly issued, but the holder is liable to interest on the deficit. Similar rules apply to shares issued at a discount (see above). A *private* company need not demand any immediate payment, although at least the nominal value must be *payable at some point.*

As will be apparent from the above paragraph, a company does not necessarily require full payment immediately for shares which it issues. It may be prepared – within the above rules – to take payment by instalments. When only part of the allotment price has been paid to the company, the shares are said to be 'partly paid'. When the rest has been paid, they are 'fully paid'. The total amount paid by shareholders is the company's 'paid up capital', and any public references in the company's letters and so on to 'capital' must be to this sum. Any amount not yet payable on partly paid shares is the company's 'uncalled capital'.

When a shareholder pays for shares issued to him, the payment is not necessarily in cash. For example, when the partners in an unincorporated business turn it into a registered company, the company will issue shares in return for the transfer to it of the assets, including goodwill, of the partnership. The human beings who were the partners will be issued with shares in the new corporate owner. They may be the main shareholders and/or directors, as in *Salomon* v. *Salomon & Co. Ltd* (1897) (see Section 4.2.2). More complex but similar arrangements can take place in takeovers and mergers between existing companies.

When shares in a *public* company are issued otherwise than for cash, the consideration for the allotment must be independently valued. A report must be made to the company within 6 months before the allotment, and a copy sent to the proposed allottee. Subject to this, in a *private* company for instance, the value of assets transferred to a company is accepted as being subjective. Even if the value is arguably less than the price of the shares, a court would not normally interfere unless fraud were alleged, or unless, perhaps, the assets were alleged to be worth less than the *nominal* value of the shares, so that the shares were being issued at a discount.

Certain things cannot be accepted by a public company in payment for its shares, in particular an undertaking that any person would do work in the future, and any undertaking which might be performed more than 5 years after the allotment. In each case, the allottee remains bound by the undertaking, but must still pay the cash price of the shares.

Once issued, shares can increase or decrease in value. Shareholders can transfer their shares, or some of them, to other persons, human or corporate. Other transactions are possible; for example, shares can be mortgaged or otherwise charged.

5.2.5 The issue of shares for an improper purpose

Learning Outcome:	To explain the repercussions of issuing shares for an improper purpose.

Obviously, shares are usually issued to raise capital. However, when a person purchases a share in a company he/she not only holds an investment in that company but also becomes a member of it and usually has the right to vote. The power to issue shares vests in the directors and the fact that shares carry the right to vote has tempted them, particularly directors of private companies, to issue shares in order to change the power structure within the company. In *Bamford* v. *Bamford* (1969), the directors allotted shares to a company which they knew would vote against a threatened takeover bid. At least one reason was to ensure that the directors remained on the board. It is very common for a company which is taking over another to appoint its own directors and remove the existing board. Although it was accepted that the directors were acting in what they believed to be the best interests of the company, it was held that since the shares were issued for a collateral purpose it was an improper exercise of the directors' powers. The fact is that shares are supposed to be issued to raise capital and not to manipulate the voting power of the existing shareholders. Nevertheless, ratification of the directors' actions by the shareholders other than the company was held to be valid. Again in *Hogg* v. *Cramphorn Ltd* (1967), it was held to be an improper use of the directors' powers when they issued shares with the objective of destroying the voting control of the existing majority. It should be noted that a number of statutory provisions now governs the issue of shares (see Section 5.2.1).

5.3 Variation and maintenance of share capital

> *Learning Outcome*: To explain the maintenance of capital principle and the procedure to increase and reduce share capital.

5.3.1 Variation

So long as the articles of a company with a share capital permit, the 1985 Act s.121 currently provides that it may:

(i) increase its authorised share capital by new shares;
(ii) consolidate all or any of its share capital (e.g. by changing five 20p shares into one £1 share);
(iii) subdivide its shares, or any of them, into shares of a smaller amount (e.g. changing one £1 share into five 20p shares);
(iv) cancel shares which have not been taken or agreed to be taken by anyone, and reduce the company's share capital by the amount of the shares cancelled; this does not for the purposes of the Act, constitute a reduction of share capital (see later).

The powers in s.121 may be exercised by an ordinary resolution of the shareholders in a general meeting or in a private company, by written resolution.

Reduction of share capital cannot be achieved so easily. By s.135 CA 1985, in order to bring about such a reduction:

(i) the company's Articles must so permit;
(ii) a special resolution must approve the reduction; and
(iii) the court must approve the reduction.

This section is an exception to the general maintenance of capital principle of company law, and is discussed in more detail below.

From October 2009 a company will no longer be required to have an authorised share capital, but may have one if it wishes and may restrict any alteration in its Articles. If the company changes its share capital, either by a reduction or an increase, it will be required to deliver a revised statement of capital to the Registrar.

5.3.2 Maintenance of capital

As a basic principle of company law, a limited company's share capital must normally be maintained. The expression 'maintenance of capital' is somewhat misleading, in that it tends to suggest that the company's share capital must be put to one side and kept intact. In fact the expression really means that the company cannot simply give back its share capital to its members. It can and will be actively used to finance the company's business. The maintenance of capital rule only means that, once the share capital has been invested in the company, it must not normally be given back to members until the company is wound up, and even then not unless and until all creditors have been repaid in full.

The capital maintenance rule manifests itself in various ways. As a general rule:

- Shares must not be issued at a discount, that is, for less than their nominal value. This is capital maintenance at the very outset – at least the nominal value must *arrive* at the company.
- No dividends should be paid to shareholders except out of profits, although profits set aside from earlier years can be used if the company is not at present profitable.
- The CA 2006 S.656, requires that an extraordinary meeting of shareholders be held within 56 days of any director in a public company becoming aware that the value of the company's net assets has fallen to half or less of the company's called up share capital. This is intended to give some protection against loss of the *real* value of a company's capital. At the meeting, measures to remedy the situation should be considered (including possible changes of directors).
- A company must not buy its own shares, because to do so would effectively be to pay off those shareholders. This is based on the case of *Trevor* v. *Whitworth* (1887). There are important exceptions to this rule today, and these are discussed below.
- A company must not give financial assistance to help anyone to acquire its shares, or reward anyone for doing so. Again, there are exceptions discussed below.
- A company must not hold its own shares.

The last three of these general rules are discussed more fully below.

5.3.3 A company acquiring its own shares

Generally, companies must not acquire their own shares. There are several objections to this. It offends the maintenance of capital principle. Moreover, it would be absurd if a company could be a member of itself. Further, if they could freely deal in their own shares, companies could create a false market in those shares.

Exceptions to this general prohibition do exist, and these are exceptions to the general maintenance of capital rule.

A valid acquisition can occur in the following ways:

1. Shares can validly be *forfeited* (e.g. for non-payment of calls) or surrendered. In this case, the company must then cancel the shares and diminish the amount of the share capital within 3 years.

2. A company can accept a *gift* of shares, but again it must then cancel them.
3. *Redeemable shares.*

   Public and private companies can, if their Articles authorise them to do so, issue some shares which are specified at the outset, by their terms of issue, to be redeemable. The company may choose, or be made, to buy back these shares from the holders; the terms of issue can make this an option either of the shareholder or of the company. Table A does authorise this. There are restrictions on this power.

   - Not all of a company's shares can be redeemable. There must always be some shares which are irredeemable, although in theory there need only be one.
   - The source of the company's redemption payment must normally be either distributable profits, or the proceeds of a new share issue. In the case of a private company, payment may also be drawn from some other sources (see below).
   - The Articles must set out the terms on which redemption can be made. Either the redemption amount or a formula according to which it is to be calculated must be set out in advance. The Articles must fix a date or period during which the company or shareholder may opt for redemption, or the Articles may provide that the directors may make such a provision before the issue.
   - The redeemed shares must have been fully paid up, and the terms must require that the company repays immediately on redemption. A premium can be charged and be repayable on redeemable shares.
   - Where shares are redeemed from *profits*, the amount by which the company's issued share capital is reduced by the redemption must be transferred from profits to an account called the 'capital redemption reserve', which is shown as a liability in the balance sheet. It must be treated as capital, and this amount must generally not be paid to other shareholders in any way before the company is wound up, although it can be used to fund an issue of new fully paid bonus shares.
   - If repayment is to come from the issue of new shares, the new shares can be issued first, even if this temporarily takes the issued capital above the authorised figure.
   - In a *private* company, the funds to redeem (or purchase – see later) a company's own shares can be drawn partly from other sources. This 'permissible capital payment' (p.c.p.) must be authorised by the Articles (Table A does), and can represent a reduction in capital without a court order.

     There are therefore many safeguards:

     – All distributable profits must be used first, plus the proceeds of any new share issue if one is made. There is however no obligation to issue new shares. If extra is needed, then a p.c.p. may be used. For example, the company may borrow money with which to redeem or buy its own shares, subject to all of these safeguards.
     – The directors must make a statutory declaration that the company will be able to pay its debts both now and during the next year. This must be supported by an auditors' report confirming that the directors' view is reasonable.
     – Within one week after this, the payment must be approved by a special resolution at a general meeting of shareholders (75 per cent of votes cast), or a written special resolution without a meeting. Those whose shares are to be redeemed or bought cannot exercise the votes given by those shares.
     – The company must pay for the shares between 5 and 7 weeks after the resolution. Until then, members or creditors who object can challenge the redemption/purchase by an application to the court, which can confirm or cancel it. Creditors must be informed of their objection rights by an advertisement in the *London Gazette* and a national newspaper.

Shares which have been redeemed are cancelled apart from in the case of the treasury shares (although the company's *authorised* capital is not altered). A return must be made to the Registrar within 28 days, showing the number and nominal value of shares which have been cancelled, and the date of redemption.

If a company breaks an obligation to redeem shares, it is in breach of its contract with the shareholder. He cannot recover damages, but he can obtain an order for specific performance if the company has sufficient distributable profits. He may also obtain an injunction prohibiting payment of any dividend from those profits until his shares have been redeemed. He may also petition for winding-up of the company on just and equitable grounds.

4. *Purchase by a company of its own shares – CA 2006 S.690.*
   The Articles of a public or private company can give it power to buy out shares which were *not* initially issued as redeemable, or to buy redeemable shares early. Table A does give this power. Again, there are several restrictions.
   - A company cannot buy all of its shares; nor can it leave only redeemable shares.
   - The source of funds to purchase shares must generally be either distributable profits, or the proceeds of a new share issue. The Articles of a private company may also permit a 'permissible capital payment' (see above). Table A does authorise this.
   - A special resolution at a general meeting must approve any 'off-market' purchase of unquoted shares before any contract for the purchase is made. This procedure under S.694, is used mainly by private companies. A copy of the proposed contract must be made available for inspection by members, both at the registered office for 15 days before the meeting, and at the meeting itself or attached to a copy of the written resolution which the members are being asked to approve instead of holding a meeting. Otherwise the resolution will be invalid. The holders of shares to be bought must not use any votes given to them by those shares on the resolution. Subject to similar safeguards, the resolution can be a written one in a private company, passed without a meeting by 75 per cent of those entitled to vote.
   - By 701, a quoted public company can authorise itself by ordinary resolution to buy a number of its own shares within specified price bands and time limits (up to 18 months) on the stock market. The ordinary resolution must be registered as if it were a special one.
   - If the shares are bought from distributable profits, the amount by which issued capital is reduced must be transferred to the capital redemption reserve. The rules generally are as for redemption.

   The shares bought are cancelled (apart from treasury shares), and a return must be made to the Registrar.
5. Purchase by a company of its own shares by order of the court
   Various provisions in the Companies Act give the court power to *order* a company to buy the shares (or some of them) of some of its members. For example:
   - A 15 per cent minority of members may object to the alteration of a company's Memorandum. If so, a detailed objection procedure must be followed, during which the court has power (*if* it thinks fit) to require the company to buy the shares of any member, with the consequent reductions in capital and alterations to the Memorandum and Articles (see Chapter 4).
   - Where a special resolution by a public company to be re-registered under as a private one has been passed, a small minority may apply to the court for cancellation of the resolution. At the hearing, the court's order may (if the court thinks fit) include

provision for the purchase by the company of any of its members' shares, with the consequent reduction in capital and alterations in the Memorandum, and so on.

- A single member of a company may apply to the court under S.994 on the ground that the company's affairs are being conducted in a manner which is unfairly prejudicial to him and, possibly, others. The court's order may include provision for the company to buy shares from its shareholder(s), and reduce the company's capital; see later.

In order to fund a purchase or redemption of shares, either distributable profits or the proceeds of an issue of shares introduced for the purpose of raising the necessary funds must be used. If a company fails to provide money as required on a purchase or redemption, the shareholders concerned cannot sue for damages. Their only remedy is a specific performance order, and this will only be introduced if the company is able to fulfil the requirement.

A private company is permitted to use capital on a redemption or purchase of its shares, but only to make up a shortfall between money available, and money required under the agreement. This is known as a permissible capital payment. In order for capital to be used, the Articles must permit this, the company's directors must provide a statutory declaration of solvency, and a special resolution must be passed.

The prescribed procedure contains safeguards for creditors. A notice must be published in the *London Gazette* and any creditor or shareholder who feels prejudiced by the purchase has 5 weeks within which to object.

5.3.4 The reduction of capital

If the Articles so permit, shareholders have a general power to reduce the company's share capital 'subject to confirmation by the court'. Table A does so permit. The power can in theory be used in any way, but three possible uses are specifically given. The company may:

1. extinguish or reduce liability for share capital not fully paid up;
2. cancel paid up share capital which is lost or unrepresented by available assets;
3. off any paid up share capital which is in excess of the company's wants.

As with other reductions of capital, there are many safeguards:

- A special resolution of shareholders is required. Again, companies can use the written special resolution as an alternative.
- Confirmation by the court must be obtained. The court must consider the interests of creditors, existing shareholders, and potential future investors.
- Creditors have a right to object if unpaid capital ceases to be payable, or if shareholders are repaid. Creditors must normally either be paid off or given security in these cases.
- Existing shareholders must be treated fairly. If there are different classes of share, the court will normally expect that they will be affected in the same ways as on a winding-up.

The Companies Act 2006 has enacted major changes in respect of capital reduction for private companies. The changes, which come into effect from October 2009, provide that it is no longer necessary for a company's Articles to authorise any reduction of capital, although they may prohibit or restrict such a reduction. (S641(b) CA 2006). Private companies may then reduce share capital by special resolution supported by a statement of solvency. Conformation by the court will only be necessary in the case of a public company.

5.3.5 Provision by a company of financial assistance for the purchase of its own shares

Currently there is a basic prohibition on companies providing financial assistance for the purchase of their own shares, but exceptions do exist. If the principal purpose of giving the assistance was not for the acquisition and was given in good faith an exception arises; also, if the principal purpose of giving the assistance was for a share acquisition, but was incidental to a larger purpose, and was given in good faith, a further exception can be found.

Section 153(3) Companies Act 1985 identifies a number of other specific exceptions including the payment of dividends, allotment of bonus shares and compliance with any court order.

By s.153(1), a company may give assistance if:

(a) the company's main purpose in giving help is merely 'an incidental part of some larger purpose of the company'; and
(b) the assistance is given in good faith in the interests of the company.

Moreover, if lending money is part of the ordinary business of a company, then the borrower may use the loan (e.g. bank overdraft) to buy shares in the company (bank).

Example

X Limited purchases an asset from Y, who uses the money to purchase shares in X Limited. In this case the main purpose of the company is to acquire the asset from Y, not to give him financial assistance. However, if X Limited purchased the asset at an inflated price to enable Y to purchase its shares, this would not be in good faith in the interests of the company.

Under the present law, a company can make loans to its employees (other than directors) to help them buy shares in itself or a holding company under an employees' share scheme.

A *private* company has wide powers to help potential buyers of its own shares, subject to certain safeguards:

(a) The help must not reduce the company's net assets. Therefore, it must either come from distributable profits (which could have disappeared as dividends) or take the form of a loan (which then replaces the help given as an asset of the company).
(b) The directors must make a statutory declaration stating the nature of the business and of the financial help to be given, and identifying the person(s) receiving the help. It must state that the company is solvent and that the directors believe that it will continue to be solvent for at least the next year. An auditors' report annexed to the directors' declaration must confirm their view.
(c) A special resolution at a general meeting (or 75 per cent written resolution) must then approve the scheme within 1 week after the directors' declaration. There are detailed provisions for at least 10 per cent of shareholders to apply to the court for cancellation of the resolution within the next 28 days.
(d) The financial assistance must not be given until the 28-day objection period has expired; nor more than 8 weeks after the directors' declaration. Clearly if all the shareholders have voted in favour there is no need to wait 28 days for objections.
(e) Copies of the declaration, the auditors' report, and the resolution must be sent to the Registrar of Companies.

One important purpose of these provisions may be to help companies to survive when an important shareholder withdraws, and neither the remaining shareholders nor the management can afford to buy his shares from him from their own resources. They can borrow money from the company itself to keep it alive. They also facilitate management buy-outs.

By s.98, no company shall apply any of its shares or capital money in payment of any commission, discount or allowance to anyone in consideration of his subscribing for shares in the company. Again, however, there are detailed exceptions to this.

With effect from October 2009, the Companies Act 2006 abolishes the restriction on financial assistance in relation to private companies, unless they are subsidiaries of public companies.

5.3.6 A company holding its own shares

In almost all of the situations where a company can validly acquire its own shares, it must then go on to cancel or dispose of them. A company holding its own shares would be particularly susceptible to the objections that a company cannot be a member of itself, and that it should not be in a position to create a false market in the shares.

Treasury shares are a major exception to this rule. However, protection exists in so far as the company cannot exercise the voting or other rights attaching to the shares.

Similarly, as a general rule, a subsidiary company must not be a shareholder in its holding company. Any allotment or transfer of shares in a company to its subsidiary is void. However, a company can validly take over another which already holds shares in the (new) holding company, and the subsidiary can continue to hold those shares.

5.4 Loan capital

Learning Outcome:	To explain the ability of a company to take secured and unsecured loans, the different types of security and the registration procedure.

5.4.1 Whether to borrow

If a company needs to raise more cash then it has three main possibilities:

1. retain profits;
2. issue further shares;
3. borrow the money.

So far as (1) is concerned, the company can only retain profits if the profits have been made, and it sometimes needs more cash at the very times when profits are low. In any event, if it wishes to expand, it will probably need more money than its present profits can provide. Whether a company raises cash by borrowing and issuing debentures, or by a new share issue, can depend on a number of considerations.

If short-term finance is required then the company may choose to raise the money by issuing redeemable shares, for example, on terms that the company will redeem them in 12 months' time at a premium of 10 per cent. At the time of writing interest rates are falling with the result that persons who have savings held in banks or building societies etc are seeing a considerable fall in the rate of return on their capital investments. It follows that an investment in redeemable share which will provide a premium of 10% may be attractive to such persons, although the investment does carry greater risk than holding the money in a bank/building society savings account. Also at the time of writing the banks are the subject of much criticism because of their reluctance to provide loans, particularly loans to business. Raising capital by issuing shares may therefore be advantageous to both the company and the new shareholders in that the company obtains finance and the investors obtain a better return than they would from savings accounts. It should be noted that the company only needs to pay a dividend on the shares if it makes a profit and even then, only if a dividend is recommended by the directors. However, there are also disadvantages for the existing shareholders. For example, if the new holders of the redeemable shares are to be given voting rights, this may affect the power structure within the company. Second, the shares must normally be redeemed out of the distributable profits of the company or the proceeds of a new share issue (see Section 5.3.3).

Borrowing money also has advantages and disadvantages. Disadvantages include the fact that the loan must be repaid according to the contractual obligation on the company, and whether or not the company is making a profit. Second, the lender may require security, thereby resulting in possible restrictions being placed on the ability of the company to freely use its assets, and leading to the possibility of receivership or administration should the company default in repaying the debt.

On the other hand, the company will be able to obtain tax relief on the interest payable under the loan, whereas tax relief is not available on dividends. However, as stated, at the time of writing businesses are suffering because of their inability to obtain loans from banks.

5.4.2 Power to borrow

A trading company probably has implied powers to borrow for the trading purposes set out in its objects. To remove any doubt the objects often also give express borrowing powers. In any event, the powers of the company are much less likely to affect a lender today because of the substantial disappearance of the *ultra vires* rule in recent years.

Exercise of the power to borrow depends largely on the Articles. The board of directors will decide whether or not the company should borrow money. S,40 CA 2006, provides protection to a person dealing with the company in good faith where directors have exceeded their borrowing powers. Moreover, a party to a transaction decided on by the directors is not bound to enquire as to the capacity of the company to enter into it or as to any limitation placed by the Memorandum or Articles on the powers of the directors, and is presumed to have acted in good faith unless the contrary is proved.

5.4.3 Debentures

A debenture is simply a document creating or evidencing the indebtedness arising from a loan to the company. It is theoretically possible for a company to borrow money without any documentary evidence, but where the company is borrowing large amounts, the lender will require documentary evidence and security.

Unsecured debentures

Loans, and therefore debentures, are not necessarily secured by any charge on the property of the company. In a small company, for instance, the creditor may seek a personal guarantee from a director or directors (which, of course, is not a charge on the company's assets), but some security offered by the company might make lenders more willing to advance money, particularly over a long term.

Secured debentures

Debentures secured by fixed charges. A fixed charge has two elements:

1. It is a charge over specific identifiable property, for example the company's land or plant and machinery; and
2. The charge will include some restriction which prevents the company from dealing freely with the asset in the ordinary course of business. For example, in the case of a fixed charge over the company's land, the charge may prevent the company from exercising its power to lease the land without the permission of the lender.

It should be noted that the court will not be bound to recognise a charge as being fixed just because it is so called. The charge must have the above two elements in order to be 'fixed'. The main advantage of a fixed charge is that in the event of the company becoming insolvent, the holder of the charge has priority over all the other creditors of the company, including any 'preferential creditors' (see later).

In practice, most lending is done by the banks. Clearly, it is the banks' interest to have as many assets as possible falling within the ambit of a fixed charge, as the money raised from the sale of those assets will be paid to the bank in priority to every other creditor. Over the years, banks' legal advisers have attempted to place more and more of a company's assets within a fixed as opposed to a floating charge. Most banks have standard form debenture documents which will attempt to impose fixed charges over, for example, freehold and leasehold land, whether owned by the company now or in the future, plant and machinery, shares owned by the company, all contracts of insurance and assurance, all intellectual property and all the company's book debts.

In the case of book debts, the banks have attempted to satisfy the two elements of a fixed charge by first, stating that they are creating a fixed charge over book debts (i.e. identifying the property), and second by stating that the company is required to pay all recovered book debts into its bank account and that the company cannot sell, factor, discount, or otherwise charge or assign the debts without the prior written consent of the bank. The latter requirement is an attempt to satisfy the second element of a fixed charge, by apparently making it so that the company cannot deal freely with the book debts in the ordinary course of business, i.e. the banks permission must be obtained before the recovered book debts can be used.

However, recent case law has decided that if *in reality* the bank is not enforcing its power in the debenture document, and the company for all practical purposes is able to deal freely with its book debts, then the charge is floating rather than fixed. These cases may have serious consequences for the bank, because if the charge is regarded as floating, the money raised from book debts must first be used to pay off preferential creditors and also, under the new rules introduced by the Enterprise Act 2002, if the charge was issued after 15 September 2003 a percentage of the money raised must be made available for the payment of the unsecured creditors.

Debentures secured by floating charges. Companies can also give 'floating' charges, where the loan is charged on other assets such as stock. A floating charge may be defined as an equitable charge on some or all of the present and future property of the company. Thus, the three common characteristics of a floating charge are:

1. it is a charge over a class of assets of a company, present and future;
2. that class is one which, in the ordinary course of the company's business, changes from time to time;

3. by the charge it is contemplated that, until some future step is taken by or on behalf of the chargee (the lender), the company may deal freely with the assets in the ordinary course of its business [*Re Yorkshire Woolcombers Association Ltd* (1903)].

A company may give a lender a floating charge over some or all of its current assets. Such assets may be changing constantly – for example, the company's stock-in-trade will change every time it sells existing stock and buys in new. A floating charge may be said to 'hover' over the assets concerned and it will become attached to them only when the charge crystallises. Once the floating charge crystallises, it becomes a fixed charge over all the items it covers, for example over all the stock in the company's possession on the day the charge crystallised. A charge will crystallise when:

(a) a voluntary winding-up resolution is passed by the company;
(b) a petition is presented for winding up by the court;
(c) the court appoints a receiver;
(d) the creditors appoint a receiver under powers given by the debentures;
(e) any other circumstances arise which, under the terms on which the floating charge was made, will cause it to crystallise (e.g. if the company defaults in payments of interest).

A floating charge does have some disadvantages from a creditor's viewpoint. For example, assets such as stock-in-trade can easily reduce in amount and therefore in value as security. A floating charge has other disadvantages in that it ranks after all of the following if the company is wound up:

(a) The costs and expenses of the winding up.
(b) Fixed charges created before the floating charge. A fixed charge created after the floating charge will also rank higher than the floating charge unless the company has contractually agreed in the debenture document not to create any new charges ranking equally or in priority to the charges already created. Major lenders such as the main banks always insist upon such a term (known as a 'negative pledge clause') being included in the debenture. It should be noted that any new lender is only bound by the clause if given actual notice of it (see Section 5.4.5).
(c) Preferential creditors. If the assets comprised in the floating charge are sold, the proceeds must first be used to pay off the preferential creditors. However, a number of important changes to this area of law have been made by the Enterprise Act 2002 which was enacted on 7 November 2002 and came into force on 15 September 2003. In particular the Act has abolished the preferential status of debts due to the Crown such as the inland taxes payable to Her Majesty's Revenue and Customs, ('HMRC') which are now reduced to the status of unsecured creditors. Following the changes made by the Act the following are the only remaining preferential creditors: (i) contributions to occupational pension schemes; (ii) arrears of employee remuneration; and (iii) coal and steel levies. Although this may appear beneficial to the floating charge holders in that there are now fewer prior claims, the Insolvency Act 1986 (Prescribed Part) Order 2003 which also came into force on 15 September 2003, provides that out of a company's 'net property', that is, the property which would have been available for satisfaction of the claims of floating charge holders before the Order was enacted, the following amounts shall be set aside for the benefit of unsecured creditors:
    1. where the company's net property does not exceed £10,000, 50 per cent of that property.

2. where the company's net property exceeds £10,000 the sum of
   (i) 50 per cent of the first £10,000 and
   (ii) 20 per cent of the property exceeding £10,000 up to a maximum of £600,000.

Example

PQR Ltd is in liquidation. Wye Bank plc has made a loan of £70,000 to PQR Ltd secured by a floating charge over the company's stock. The company's stock has raised £100,000 and there are preferential creditors who are owed £20,000.

The amount available for the floating charge holder is

	£	£
Proceeds from sale of stock	100,000	
Less preferential creditors		20,000
		80,000
'Prescribed part' for unsecured creditors		
50% × 10,000	5,000	
20% × 70,000	14,000	19,000
Available for the floating charge holder		£61,000

It follows that £9,000 is still owed to the bank, which must stand as an unsecured creditor for that amount. This appears to be a tremendous step forward for the rights of the unsecured creditors who, prior to the introduction of these rules, were often left with nothing in a company's liquidation.

(d) A landlord's execution and distress for rent completed before crystallisation.

(e) The interests of a judgment creditor (who has obtained judgment in the court against the company) if, to enforce the judgment, the creditor has had the company's goods seized and sold by the sheriff; similarly if he has obtained a garnishee order over money in the company's bank accounts.

(f) The owners of goods supplied to the company under a hire-purchase agreement (i.e. usually the finance company).

(g) The owners of goods supplied under a contract containing a reservation of title clause (sometimes called a 'Romalpa clause'). In fact, a supplier of goods who is able to rely upon such a clause will obtain priority over all creditors of the company, including those holding fixed charges. The reason for this is that such clauses commonly state words to the effect that '... ownership of the goods supplied does not pass to the buyer until the goods have been paid for.' It follows that if the company fails to pay for the goods, the supplier is entitled by law to recover them as the supplier remains the legal owner of them.

Furthermore, a floating charge may be invalid if it was created within certain periods before either the commencement of a liquidation or the presentation of a petition for an administration order.

The Insolvency Act 1986 s.245 provides that a floating charge may be invalid if:

(a) It was created in favour of a connected person within 2 years of the company becoming insolvent – for example, in favour of a relative of a director of the company.

(b) It was created in favour of any other person within 1 year of the company becoming insolvent. This applies only if, at the time the charge was created, the company was unable to pay its debts as a result of the transaction.

(c) It was created at a time between the presentation of a petition for the making of an administration order and the making of the order.

Example

ABC Ltd had an unsecured overdraft of £10,000 with the Exe Bank plc. The company was in need of further finance and approached the bank for a loan of £20,000. The bank was prepared to lend the additional £20,000 only if the company was prepared to secure the total borrowing of £30,000. The company agreed and issued a debenture containing a fixed charge over the company's land and a floating charge over the company's stock on 1 October 2008. In June 2009, the company was placed in insolvent liquidation. The effect on the Exe Bank plc is as follows:

(i) *The fixed charge*. Assuming that the charge has been correctly registered within 21 days at Companies House and has also been registered at HM Land Registry and is otherwise valid, the bank may sell the land and use the proceeds to discharge the total debt. It follows that the bank may not need to rely on its floating charge.

(ii) *The floating charge*. If for some reason the bank does need to rely on its floating charge, the validity of the charge is affected by Section 245 Insolvency Act 1986 as the charge was issued to a non-connected person (the bank) and the company has gone into liquidation within 12 months of the issue of the debenture. It follows that the floating charge is valid in respect of the new borrowing (the loan of £20,000) but not the overdraft of £10,000 which existed before the debenture was issued. (If the company had survived for more than 12 months, the floating charge would have been valid for the full £30,000.) If the debenture had been issued to a connected person (such as a director), the effective time would have been 24 rather than 12 months.

Despite all these disadvantages, it does give the creditor some protection in a way which is not available for private traders or partnerships, to which the Bills of Sale Acts 1878 and 1882 apply. These Acts, which require the charge on each separate piece of personal property to be separately written and registered, render floating charges impracticable, but do not apply to companies' debts.

5.4.4 Registration of charges

There are detailed provisions in the Companies Acts requiring that registers be kept of charges on the company's property. These are partly to protect purchasers of the property charged, partly to establish priority of claims to the value of the assets charged if the company is insolvent when wound up, and partly to inform/warn those dealing with the company generally.

Registration with the company itself

A company must keep a register of all charges on its property, including floating charges and these charges which do not need to be registered with the Registrar (see below). Any person is entitled, for a suitable fee, to be given a copy of any charge or entry on the register within 10 days of requesting it. Non-compliance is a criminal offence, and performance may be ordered by the court. A company secretary may also keep a register of unsecured debentures, although this is not required.

Registration with the Registrar of Companies (S.860 CA 2006)

When a company creates a charge over its property, it must register particulars of it with the Registrar of Companies. This relates to virtually all charges, fixed and floating, over land, goods, goodwill, book debts, patents, and so on. It does not apply, however, to charges over goods where the creditor is entitled to *possession* of the goods or documents of title to them. It would not, therefore, apply to the lien of an unpaid seller if the company had bought goods but not yet paid for or collected them. Particulars must also be registered if the company buys property which is already, and remains, subject to a charge.

The company *must* send prescribed particulars of the charge to the Registrar within 21 days. If it fails to do so within this time, the company and officers of it, in default, commit a criminal offence and may be fined. Any other person with an interest in the charge *may* send the prescribed particulars, and in practice the creditor will always register the charge himself because the matter is far too important to be left to the officers of the company, who may fail to register the charge with disastrous consequences for the lender.

Once he has registered the charge, the Registrar issues a certificate of registration, which is conclusive evidence that the requirements of the Act as to registration have been complied with. Registration gives constructive notice of the charge to anyone dealing with the company.

If particulars are not delivered at all, then the charge will be void in a subsequent liquidation as a general rule. The creditor will only be paid if there is anything left after the registered secured creditors have been paid. The charge will also be void against a subsequent purchaser of the item charged, or a subsequent chargee of it. However, even a wholly unregistered charge can still have some validity; it can give priority over another wholly unregistered charge although, since both can register late, the second chargee can still obtain priority if he registers first. An unregistered charge can also be valid against a person acquiring an interest in the property, where the acquisition is *expressly* made subject to the charge.

If particulars are delivered late, the charge can be valid against a liquidator or administrator or subsequent purchaser appointed or buying *after* the late registration. However, if the company is already insolvent at the time when particulars are delivered, or becomes insolvent because of this charge, then it will be void if liquidation proceedings begin within 6 months of delivery for a fixed charge, 12 months for a floating charge, or 2 years for a floating charge to a person connected with the company (e.g. director).

If incomplete or partially inaccurate particulars are registered, then rights which should have been disclosed and are not may be void. Properly disclosed rights can still be valid. Moreover, a court can give full effect to the charge if, for example, it is satisfied that unsecured creditors or subsequent purchasers of the thing(s) charged have not been prejudiced. When a floating charge crystallises, this fact too must be notified to the Registrar. The Companies Registry is open to public inspection, and those proposing to deal closely with a company will often have a search made. When a charge ceases to affect a company's property, for example, because the debt has been repaid, the company should send a certificate of discharge to be filed with the Registrar.

Note: The Companies Act 1989 provided for the introduction of a new system of registration. However, the system has not yet been implemented. Lending institutions are opposed to the proposed system and thus it may *never* be implemented.

Registration of land charges

Details of any mortgage or charge over a company's *land* must also be registered with HM Land Registry. This is in addition to the Companies Acts requirements above. An unregistered mortgage is void against a subsequent purchaser (or mortgagee) for value. There are detailed provisions for situations where a floating charge covers or includes a company's land. A prospective buyer of the company's land will search the registers, and normally require that any mortgage be redeemed before he buys.

5.4.5 Priority of charges

Where there are several charges over a company's property, then questions of priority can arise, particularly if the company is insolvent.

Fixed charges generally have priority over floating ones in relation to the property specifically charged. This applies even if the floating charge was created earlier, and properly registered. Therefore, in a winding-up, a fixed chargee may be paid in full before earlier creditors.

Holders of floating charges can be protected to some extent by the terms of issue of their security – that is, by the use of negative pledge clauses. These commonly forbid the company to create any charge ranking equally or in priority to the charges contained in the debenture document regarding the relevant property. This gives the floating charge priority over any subsequent fixed chargee, provided that he had notice of the prohibition when he took his charge. Although registration of a charge gives notice of its existence, it does not provide notice of the terms attached to it unless these are also registered with the charge. Thus the prohibition contained in a negative pledge clause must be registered with the charge to establish notice and ensure that it is effective.

It should be borne in mind that a company can deal freely with assets which are the subject of a floating charge – that is, it can sell them and it can therefore buy and mortgage them. Hence the need for the negative pledge clause.

Floating charges generally rank between themselves in order of creation, provided that they are all properly registered within 21 days. If one of two floating charges is not registered, however, then the registered one will prevail. If neither is registered, then either can be registered late, and the first to do so takes priority. Where one floating charge covers the whole of a company's property, and a later floating charge is created over only some of the assets, the latter generally takes priority over the assets which it does cover; but the rules described above apply if the earlier floating charge expressly forbids further charges.

5.4.6 Debentures and debenture stock

Debentures can take many forms. The main debenture for a small company may be a loan agreement with its bank. This may be unsecured, but for any substantial amount it will normally give the bank some security, such as a floating charge over all the company's undertaking and assets.

A larger business might wish to seek capital from public subscription without having to dilute its share capital. A public company can do this by a prospectus proffering a series of debentures, usually for a fairly small amount each and ranking equally between themselves for sale to the public, or by proffering debenture stock. Buyers will receive a debenture or debenture stock certificate, and can usually sell on their investment to other holders, as with shares. Unlike shares, debentures can be issued at a discount. A private company cannot issue debentures for public subscription.

Usually, a public company will issue debentures or stock through a financial institution such as a bank or insurance company, which will hold legal title to the debentures as trustee for the eventual buyers, and generally carry out the necessary administration. Debentures are often long term, and can even be 'perpetual', in that the company is not bound to repay the loan until the company is wound up (although it usually reserves the *right* to redeem). The contract contained in the terms by which the debentures are issued will give the holders a right to interest payments, usually at stated intervals such as twice per year. A company will usually keep a register of all debenture holders at its registered office, although strictly it is only bound to do so for debentures which are secured.

Trust deed

When debentures are issued by a public company to investors, it is usual for them to be issued under a trust deed. Where the loan stock is to be quoted on the Stock Exchange, the company must, to comply with the requirements of the Stock Exchange, establish a trust for the duration of the loan and appoint trustees to safeguard the interests of the stock-holders. One of the trustees appointed (or the sole trustee) must be a trust corporation (e.g. a bank). This arrangement has the following advantages:

(a) The trustees can take action to protect the interests of the investors – for example, the appointment of a receiver when interest on the loan stock is in arrears.
(b) The company need deal only with the trustees, on matters relevant to the issue – instead of having to deal with large numbers of individual investors.
(c) It facilitates the holding of meetings with investors and the passing of resolutions by those investors.
(d) Any security given by the company to secure the debentures can be vested in the trustees who, where appropriate, can enforce that security on behalf of all the investors.
(e) It satisfies the requirements of the Stock Exchange that the trustees represent the holders of the listed debt securities.

The trust deed will, *inter alia,* specify the amount and terms of issue of the debentures; the date and amount of redemption, including details of any sinking fund established by the company for that purpose; the circumstances in which the security (if any) may be enforced by the trustees – for example, on the company's failure to pay interest on the debentures, or the failure of the company's business.

5.4.7 Rights of debenture holders on default by the company

If the company defaults in paying interest or in repaying the loan, a debenture holder will have a variety of possible remedies, under the terms of issue, at common law, and by statute. For example:

1. He or She can sue the company for the amount due under the terms of the loan agreement.
2. The terms of the debenture will usually give the lender a charge over the company's property and will set out the right of the lender to sell the property in the event of the company defaulting in repaying the debt.
3. He or She may be entitled to appoint a receiver in order to achieve the sale. Any surplus after the debt has been repaid will go to the company.
4. In the absence of express powers, there are various statutory powers to have a receiver appointed and to realise any security.
5. If the assets are substantial (e.g. a floating charge over the entire undertaking), the holder of the floating charge would often be entitled by the terms of the debenture to appoint an administrative receiver. However, following the enactment of the Enterprise Act 2002 this will only apply to floating charges issued before the date when the corporate insolvency provisions in the Enterprise Act 2002 came into force, that is, 15 September 2003. In future a floating charge holder will be entitled to appoint an administrator. An administrator differs from an administrative receiver in that his prime objective is to attempt to ensure the survival of the business for the benefit of all the creditors. An administrative receiver's task was to act in the interest of the debenture holder rather than the creditors as a whole and his task would be finished when he had realised as much as possible for the benefit of the floating charge holder.

The change reflects the new 'rescue culture' under which the government is keen to attempt to ensure the survival of the business wherever possible.

6. Any of this may result in a petition for a winding-up of the company.

   Usually, the holder of a fixed charge will appoint a receiver in relation to the piece of property charged, whereas the holder of a floating charge over the whole or substantially the whole of the company's assets or undertaking may appoint an administrator to take over the running of the entire business. The court will sanction the sale of the property subject to the fixed charge, but only if the net proceeds of the sale, or its open-market value if that is greater, is applied to discharge the sum secured on the property (Insolvency Act 1986, s.43).

A summary of the main changes to this area of law is contained in the article entitled 'Corporate insolvency after the Enterprise Act 2002' in the 'Readings' section at the end of this chapter.

5.4.8 Shares and debentures compared

1. A shareholder is a member of the company, and can normally therefore attend and vote at meetings. A debenture holder is not a member.
2. Debenture interest must be paid, even if the company has current trading losses. Dividends can generally only be paid if (after debenture interest and all other expense has been paid) there are still available profits.
3. Directors and members have a discretion over whether to declare a dividend on shares. Debenture interest is a contractual debt which *must* be paid.
4. Loan interest is deducted before the company's profits are assessed for tax, but dividends paid on shares are payable out of company profits after they have been assessed for tax. The tax laws make it advantageous for the owners of a company to extract profits in the form of dividends as opposed to salaries or loans. This is so because (a) dividends are taxed at a lower starting rate than salaries, and (b) national insurance contributions are payable by the company and the director/employee on salaries, but are not payable on dividends.
5. Shares may well vary substantially in value, according to whether or not the company is successful.
6. Debentures can be repaid while the company still exists; shares, generally, cannot (see 'capital maintenance' earlier).
7. Debenture (loan) capital must be repaid on a winding-up before the shareholders receive anything. Secured debentures will have even earlier claims on the assets given as security.
8. Directors need little or no special authority to borrow money and issue debentures, unlike the detailed authority which may be required to issue further shares.

5.5 Corporate management – directors

Learning Outcome:	To explain the procedure for the appointment, retirement, disqualification and removal of directors.

5.5.1 General requirement

All companies must have directors. Every public company must have at least two directors, and every private company at least one (S.154 CA 2006). Since 6 April 2008 a private company is no longer required to have a company secretary, but may have one if it wishes. The actual numbers of directors will normally depend upon the Articles, which often fix a maximum and minimum between which numbers may fluctuate. Table A, provides for a minimum of two, even for private companies, and no maximum. In all cases there must be at least one natural person (S.155 CA 2006), but Table A, can be varied.

Whatever the provision made when the company was first incorporated, the number of directors can later be changed by the members. This can be by ordinary resolution unless the Articles or Memorandum need to be changed.

'Executive directors' and 'non-executive directors' are terms which express the very different roles which individual directors can play. All directors have non-executive functions: duties to attend board meetings, to advise with due diligence and in good faith, and to take a constructive part in making decisions, are but a few; see later. For some directors, this is the limit of their function (plus possibly giving the support of their name and personal reputation to the company). Other directors may play a more active role; in addition to their general duties, they may also take special responsibility for some aspect of the company's work. There might, for instance, be a works director, or a director of finance, who would have executive responsibilities. However, a company has no duty to have executive directors of any type; the board could, if it so wished, delegate all of its executive functions to employees, although this is probably very uncommon.

A *managing director* is largely an extended example of the executive director. Companies do not need to have a managing director, and some do. On the other hand, in most enterprises it can be convenient (at the least) to have someone who will take executive responsibility for the enterprise as a whole. A director who does this will normally be the managing director, although his formal title need not be that. The board is the agent of the company and individual directors, as such, have no power to contract on behalf of the company. However, the board may delegate authority to a director to contract, and if the board appoints a managing director, he/she will be an agent of the company. Under the rules of agency, if a director appears to an outsider to be the managing director, the company will be bound by his actions, even if he was never formally appointed managing director, see *Freeman and Lockyer* v. *Buckhurst Park Properties Ltd* (1964). The real test is the function which in reality he carries out; the chairman of a board of directors, for instance, will not necessarily be a managing director.

As we have seen, companies can vary widely in size and function. For example, there are small 'family firm' companies with only a few shareholders who may all be directors; and there are larger companies with millions of shares, where membership and management are much more widely separated. Within the limits set by the Acts, companies can make their own management structure by their Memorandum and Articles, but Table A applies unless it has been varied or overruled by express Articles.

5.5.2 Appointment

The first directors are those named as such in the statement which must be filed when the company is formed (Form G.10). They may also be named in the Articles.

Subsequent directors are normally appointed by the members. If Table A applies, this will be by ordinary resolution of shareholders in a general meeting (or unanimous written resolution without a meeting, if so preferred, in a private company).

Temporary or additional directors can, if the Articles so permit, be appointed by the existing board of directors itself. In practice the Articles usually permit the board to co-opt new directors, either to fill a casual vacancy or as an addition to the board. In these circumstances, the director will hold office until the next annual general meeting when the appointment will be confirmed or not as the case may be by the shareholders. The new directors must hold the necessary qualifying shares (if any are required), and the total number of directors must not exceed any maximum set by the Articles. Alternate directors can, if the Articles so permit, be nominated by an individual director (who, perhaps, knows that he will be absent for sometime). Table A does permit this, so long as the rest of the board resolves to accept the nominee. The alternate director has the general powers of the director whom he replaces, and he holds office for as long as the latter would have done. The alternate can be removed under 168 CA 2006 (see later), and the nominating director himself can later remove his alternate.

Life directors can be appointed by the Articles to hold office indefinitely. Nevertheless, they can still be removed by a change to the Articles, or under 168 CA 2006. If they are appointed at the outset, their appointment is only effective if they are also named in Form G.10. If a director is appointed for more than 2 years under a service contract which does not permit the director to be removed by reasonable notice, then the contract must be approved by the shareholders (S.188 CA 2006).

For some purposes of the Companies Acts, a person may be treated as a director without ever having formally been appointed as such (a *de facto* director). By the CA 2006, S.250, the term 'director' includes any person occupying the position of director, by whatever name called. Someone who is effectively in charge of a company, wholly or substantially, can be treated as a director, and cannot escape his responsibilities as such simply by calling himself something such as 'principal' or 'controller' or 'consultant'.

'Shadow directors' are the main type of *de facto* directors. By S.251 CA 2006, a shadow director is 'a person in accordance with whose directions or instructions the directors of the company are accustomed to act'. However, a person is not deemed a shadow director by reason only that the directors act on advice given by him in a professional capacity.

Most of the important provisions of the Companies Acts and of the Insolvency Act 1986 can apply to shadow directors in the same ways as to the formally appointed ones. In particular, their names should be registered as directors, and copies of their service contracts made available for members. A shadow director may be held liable for wrongful trading under the Insolvency Act 1986, and he may be disqualified under the Company Directors Disqualification Act 1986, as if he were a formally appointed director. The provisions of S.172 (duty to have regard to interests of employees), S.188 (approval for directors' long-term contracts of employment), Ss.190–196 (substantial property transactions involving directors) and 197–214 (restrictions on power of companies to lend to directors) can all apply; but for these purposes a body corporate is not to be treated as a shadow director of any of its subsidiaries by reason only that the directors of the subsidiary normally act on the holding company's instructions.

5.5.3 Retirement

Retirement by rotation may be required by the Articles. If Table A applies, all of the directors must retire at the first annual general meeting of the shareholders. The directors can offer themselves for re-election. After this, one-third must retire each year but, again, can be re-elected at the AGM. Directors seeking re-election can use the votes given by their shares to vote for themselves, and the Articles of a fairly small company can lawfully give weighted voting rights (e.g. three votes per share) to a director voting on such an issue [see the case of *Bushell* v. *Faith* (1970)]. In any event, in a fairly small private company, the directors themselves may hold most or all of the shares. If no alternative directors are proposed, Table A provides that the retiring directors are automatically re-elected unless the company specifically resolves otherwise.

To simplify matters, many private companies remove the retirement by rotation provisions of Table A from their Articles.

Retirement by notice is covered by Table A, which allows a director to give written notice to the company that he intends to retire from his position. No fixed length of notice is required, but a reasonable time may be required by any service contract which the director has with the company.

With effect from October 2009, the Companies Act 2006 provides that although corporate directors will still be permitted, at least one director must be a natural person. It is also provided that directors must be at least 16 years old, but there is no upper age limit.

5.5.4 Disqualification of directors

Directors are in a position which they could exploit to their personal advantage. They are also in a position where, particularly in larger companies, the potential for causing loss to a large number of people exists. As a deterrent, and to try to ensure that those who do abuse their position do not have the chance to do it again within a short space of time, the Company Directors' Disqualification Act 1986 contains provisions under which, as the title of the Act suggests, directors may be disqualified by the courts.

Directors may be disqualified for any of the following reasons:

- they are convicted of an indictable offence in connection with company matters – a serious offence triable in the Crown Court, for example theft from a company;
- they have been a director of a company which has gone into insolvent liquidation and the court feel they are largely to blame – they would be regarded as unfit to be a director;
- they have persistently been in breach of the Companies Act regarding filing accounts with the Registrar, sending in the annual return, filing resolutions with the Registrar and so on;
- they are undischarged bankrupt;
- they have been guilty of fraudulent trading – this occurs when the directors have carried on business with the intent to defraud creditors;
- they have been found liable for wrongful trading – this is when a company has gone into insolvent liquidation and the directors either knew or should have known that the company could not avoid going into insolvent liquidation; it is a defence against this if they have taken every step to minimise potential losses to creditors.

Schedule 1 to the Company Directors Disqualification Act 1986 identifies matters that must be considered when looking to the question of whether or not an individual is unfit to act as a director. Misfeasance, breach of duty, misapplication of assets and failure to meet the requirements of the Companies Act 2006 in relation to the preparation, maintenance and dealing with documentation are identified. Schedule 1 also identifies the need, where a company has gone into liquidation, to look at the degree of blame for the liquidation which attaches to directors, and at any failure to meet statutory obligations to be satisfied in the event of liquidation.

Case law also provides assistance in determining conduct which establishes the unfitness of a person to act as a director. In *Re Lo-Line Electric Motors Ltd* (1988) '... ordinary commercial misjudgement' was deemed insufficient to justify a disqualification. In this same case, '... an extreme case of gross negligence or total incompetence ...', it was said, could warrant a disqualification order. Imprudent and improper conduct of a director was said not to justify director disqualification in *Re Bath Glass Ltd* (1988).

Fraudulent and wrongful trading are particularly important for directors when the company has gone into insolvent liquidation. Not only can they be disqualified from acting as directors, but they can also be required by the court to contribute any amount which the court thinks appropriate from their personal wealth to go towards paying off the creditors. In effect, the veil of incorporation is lifted to expose them to liability.

Bankruptcy of a director can effectively disqualify him or her. By the Company Directors Disqualification Act 1986, s.11, it is a criminal offence for an undischarged bankrupt to *act* as a director or liquidator, or to be concerned in managing a company.

The Articles of a company can make further provision for disqualification. If Table A applies, the director loses office if he or she becomes bankrupt, or becomes a mental patient. If he or she misses directors' meetings for at least 6 months without the board's permission, he or she can be removed from office by resolution of the board.

The consequences of disqualification

(a) If a person who is disqualified by some statutory provision continues to act as a directors, he commits a criminal offence.
(b) A person who becomes involved in the management of a company at a time when he is disqualified from acting as a director by a court order, or in breach of the Company Directors Disqualification Act, s.11 (while personally bankrupt), can be personally liable for debts of the company incurred while he is involved (but he might not be worth suing). Indirect involvement, for example, as a management consultant, can be sufficient. A properly qualified director who acts on the orders of one whom he knows to be disqualified can also be personally liable.
(c) Nevertheless, the acts of a disqualified 'director' may still be binding on the company if he has *ostensible* (or *apparent*) authority; see Section 5.6.

5.5.5 Removal

By ordinary resolution under S.168 CA 2006

The shareholders of a company can remove a director or directors at any time by an ordinary resolution at a general meeting. A simple majority of votes cast at the meeting is sufficient. Special notice of the resolution must normally be given to the company at least 28 days before the meeting. The company must forthwith send a copy of the resolution to the director challenged. He can then make representations to the company in writing and, unless these are defamatory, demand that they be circulated to members before the meeting. If the company wrongfully does not circulate them, the director can have them read out at the meeting. The director also has the right to speak at the meeting. The director can exercise the votes which his own shares give to him.

As a general principle, nothing in the Articles can take away the powers given to shareholders by S.168; nor can the exercise of management functions be restricted. Several devices may be tried. Most are unsuccessful:

(a) The Articles may provide that a director is to hold office for life. This is ineffective, as even a life director can be removed under S.168.
(b) The director may have a long-term service contract with the company, which tries to guarantee his position. Legally, this is ineffective; S.168 applies notwithstanding anything in the contract. However, the contract might provide a practical difficulty if it entitles the director to a substantial severance payment.
(c) The board has no duty under the Acts or Table A to put the resolution for removal expressly on the agenda of a meeting. However, the holders of 5 per cent of shares can insist on having the motion on the agenda of an annual general meeting, or 10 per cent for other general meetings, see later.
(d) The board could call a general meeting early, before the 28-day notice for the resolution had expired. This would be ineffective if the meeting was called after the notice was received.
(e) The real limit on S.168 is that a director can vote for himself. In a small private company, the director himself might hold most of the shares, and therefore be irremovable under S.168.
(f) In *Bushell* v. *Faith* (1970), it was held that the Articles of a fairly small company could validly give weighted voting rights to a director on such a resolution (e.g. three votes per share). In this event, a director with only 25 per cent of the shares could be protected.

Under the Articles

A company's Articles may provide other ways in which a director can be removed. For example, Table A allows the board of directors to remove one of its member who fails to attend meetings for 6 months without the board's consent.

5.5.6 Registers and information concerning directors

The company itself must keep a register of directors at its registered office (S.162 CA 2006).

The company's register of directors should contain details of each director such as their name, nationality, business occupation, other directorships and should include a service address. Currently the director's private address has to be stated but this will change when S. 163 of the CA 2006 comes into force in October 2009. At present a director wishing to keep his or her private address confidential must apply to the Registrar of Companies for a 'Confidentiality Order.'

A company will also required to keep a register of director's residential addresses which must be notified to the Registrar of Companies. However, this information, with a few exceptions, will not be disclosed. (See S.240 CA 2006.)

This register must be available for inspection by shareholders (free) and by the public (for a small fee).

The Registrar of Companies must be given the same details of directors on Form G. 10 when the company is formed, and later within 14 days of any change. This is open to public inspection.

A register of directors' interests must be kept by the company, showing directors' interests in the company's shares and debentures. Interests of the director's spouse and infant children must also be shown. Interests of shadow directors must be included. All types of interest must be shown, for example, charges over shares or options to buy. This register too must be open to shareholders and the public.

Copies of directors' service contracts (if any), or terms of employment (if any), must be available to members, normally at the registered office.

5.6 Powers and duties of directors

Learning Outcome: To explain director's powers and duties during office.

5.6.1 Powers of directors

The function of the directors is to manage the company. They must make management decisions on most matters, and they are responsible for ensuring that those decisions and the decisions of shareholders are executed. The exact powers will be determined by the Articles. Table A reg. 70 provides that 'the business of the company shall be managed by the directors, who may exercise all the powers of the company'; detailed powers are then specified.

The division of powers between directors and shareholders is discussed again later. There are some things which, under the Companies Acts, can *only* be done by a resolution of shareholders. The most important of these are changes to the company's name, objects, nominal capital or Articles. Other things *may* be done by shareholders' resolution, such as removal of a director under S.168. Moreover, Table A reg. 70 (if it applies) gives power to shareholders to give *directions* to the board by special resolution in a general meeting.

Exercise of directors' powers must generally be by the board, acting collectively at board meetings. Unless there has been delegation, individual directors have no authority. The Articles will usually fix a quorum (minimum number) of directors which must be present if the meeting is to be valid. The board is usually given power to elect one of its members as chairman of meetings, and decisions are then taken by a majority vote. The Articles often give the chairman a casting vote in the event of a tie. Table A provides that a director cannot validly vote at board meetings on a matter in which he personally has a material interest which might conflict with those of the company, nor may his presence be counted towards a quorum on the issue. There are, however, a number of exceptions to this.

Board resolutions, can, under Table A, be reached without a meeting if a written resolution is signed by all directors. Delegation of powers by the board is authorised by Table A. As we have seen earlier, a managing director and/or other executive directors can validly be appointed if the Articles so permit, with extended powers to decide and execute on behalf of the board.

5.6.2 Limits and controls over the powers of directors

Various common law precedents and statutory provisions aim to prevent abuse of power by the directors. Some transactions are prohibited as criminal offences. Others can only take place if approved by the shareholders. The prohibitions often have the effect of limiting the situations where there is a potential conflict between the personal interests of the director, and his fiduciary duties to the company.

Directors with a personal interest in contracts with the company are affected by S.177. It is the duty of a director of a company who is in any way, directly or indirectly, interested in a contract or proposed contract with the company to declare the nature of his interest at a board meeting. Disclosure to a subcommittee of the board may not be enough. A director who fails to comply with this section is liable to a fine. The contract is usually voidable by the company.

This rule extends to contracts where persons 'connected with' the director have an interest. These include the director's spouse, children under 18, and associated companies in which the director and/or his family have at least a one-fifth share interest.

Property transactions between the company and its own directors are controlled by S.190-196 CA 2006. If a director wishes to buy, sell or deal with a non-cash asset of the 'requisite value' from or to his company, he must first obtain the approval of the shareholders by ordinary resolution. The 'requisite value' is £100,000; or 10 per cent of the company's net assets, subject to a £2,000 minimum. The rule extends to dealings between the company and persons 'connected with' a director (see above).

If approval of the shareholders is not obtained, any directors who made or authorised the transaction must indemnify the company against any loss, and the director or connected person who actually contracted with the company must normally account to it for any profit which he has made. The contract is often voidable by the company.

Directors' service contracts for over 2 years must be approved by ordinary resolution of shareholders; similarly if an existing contract is extended for more than 5 years; see S.188. If Table A applies, a director must not vote on the terms of his own service contract. A copy must be kept at the registered office. The term 'service contract' has now been extended to cover letters of appointment and also contracts for services, for example consultancy contracts.

5.6.3 Loans and quasi loans to directors

The Companies Act 2006 has removed criminal penalties in relation to loans to directors. There is now a general provision whereby any loan to a director must be approved by the shareholders, so long as they are informed of the amount of the loan, the nature of the transaction, its purpose and the extent of the company's liability. (Ss.197–214 CA 2006).

In relation to quasi loans, shareholder approval is only required in the case of public companies. A quasi loan is a payment of a director's debts or expenses on terms that the payment must be repaid by the director. A quasi loan to a connected person, such as the director's spouse, must be approved by the shareholders.

The Companies Act 1985 contained a number of exemptions to the shareholder approval rule. These have been amended as follows:

(a) In the case of a company which makes loans in the ordinary course of its business, such as a bank, there is now no maximum loan.
(b) For loans and quasi loans, the exemption has been increased from £5,000 to £10,000.
(c) For credit transactions, the exemption has been increased from £10,000 to £15,000. A credit transaction is where the company sells, leases or hires land, goods or services to a director on the understanding that payment is to be deferred.
(d) The current exemption in relation to loans to directors to enable them to meet expenses incurred for the company's purposes have also been amended in that there is

no longer a requirement for shareholder approval and the maximum permitted is now £50,000.

(e) A loan to enable a director to defend him/herself against an investigation by a regulatory authority is also exempt.

5.6.4 Duties of directors to the company

The powers of a director are accompanied by responsibilities. The powers are balanced against duties which a director owes to his company, and these are similar but not identical to the duties owed by agents and partners.

Reasonable care and skill must be shown by directors. As with all things 'reasonable', this can vary. Normally, more detailed work and care can be expected of executive directors, and a higher degree of skill from directors who have professional expertise. Directors should certainly attend board meetings as regularly as possible, and they should not rely unquestioningly on information supplied to them by company officers and managers.

- A director must not take an unauthorised benefit for himself from his position as director. This and the next three items are part of a general duty of good faith ('fiduciary' duty) which a director owes to his company. A director has to account to the company for any wrongful benefit which he takes.
- A director must not allow an undisclosed conflict of interest between himself and his company. A director can run his own business in the same field as that of the company, and he can be a director of two or more companies in the same type of business. But if he does so, then he must make full disclosure of his other interests. It is undisclosed conflicts of interest which are unlawful; note also the provisions of the Companies Act and Table A mentioned earlier. Conflicts can occur in many ways: in *Cook* v. *Deeks* (1916), for example, the directors of a building company negotiated a contract as if they were doing so on behalf of the company, but then took the contract in their own names and kept the profit. They had to account to the company for the profit.
- A director has duties of confidentiality as regards company information, similar to the duties owed by an agent to his principal. A director involved in more than one business must take care to observe these duties.
- More generally, when he is acting on behalf of the company, the tests of a director's motives are probably the following. First, the transaction should normally be reasonably incidental to the company's business. Second, it must be in good faith [unlike in *Piercy* v. *Mills* (1920), below]. Third, it should be done for the benefit and prosperity of the company. In *Rolled Steel Products Ltd* v. *British Steel Corporation* (1985), the directors of Rolled Steel decided that the company should guarantee repayment of a loan which BSC had made to someone else. Rolled Steel gained no benefit from the loan or guarantee. This was, therefore, held to be an improper use of the directors' powers and was invalid.

Examples

The following cases illustrates ways in which the above rules have applied in practice.

Reasonable care and skills:

- In *Re City Equitable Fire Insurance Co.* (1925), it was apparently accepted that the non-executive directors were wrong to leave the chairman (who proved dishonest) to run the business virtually unchecked.

- *In Dorchester Finance Co Ltd v. Stebbing* (1977) there were three directors, but only one of them ran the company. There were no board meetings. The other two directors signed blank cheques, rarely visited the business, and took virtually no active part. They were held not to have shown reasonable care. Moreover, since one was a qualified accountant and the other had accountancy experience, they had not made reasonable use of their skills, in that they had not even made them available intermittently at meetings.

Good faith – duty to account:

- *In Boston Deep Sea Fishing and Ice Co. v. Ansell* (1888), the director had to account for undisclosed commission which he personally received from the builders of a new boat for his company, and undisclosed bonuses which he personally received from a company supplying ice. The fact that the donors would not have paid the sums to his company was immaterial. Indeed, the bonus from the company supplying ice was paid to him as a shareholder in that company, and could not have been paid to the Boston company. Nevertheless, these were undisclosed benefits arising in connection with his position as director.
- In *Regal (Hastings) Ltd* v. *Gulliver* (1942), some of the directors of Regal contributed their own money towards setting up a subsidiary of Regal. They took shares in the subsidiary, which was able to buy some cinemas. The directors then sold their shares at a profit. They had to account for this to Regal. It was a personal profit which would not have been made but for their position as directors of Regal. They could have protected themselves by making full disclosure in advance, and seeking consent of the other shareholders; see also statutory provisions such as Sections 317 and 320 today.

Good faith in exercise of powers – share issues:

- In *Piercy* v. *S Mills & Co. Ltd* (1920), the directors issued further shares to themselves and their supporter, not because the company needed the extra money, but in order to prevent the election of rival directors.
- In *Howard Smith Ltd* v. *Ampol Petroleum Ltd* (1974), the directors of M Ltd issued new shares to Smith Ltd in an attempt to deprive Ampol of its majority. In both of these cases the share issue was declared void and set aside. The directors were acting wholly or partly in their own interests.
- In *Hogg* v. *Cramphorn* (1967), the directors issued shares to trustees for employees in an attempt to thwart a takeover. They believed that this was in the company's interests. Nevertheless, the issue by the directors was wrong; their powers were limited to raising capital. What the directors should have done was to call a meeting of members and ask them to agree to the proposals. If members had agreed (which they later did), the directors could have gone ahead with their scheme without being in breach of duty.

For a review of recent case law on this topic, see the article entitled 'Directors' fiduciary duties to shareholders: the Platt and Peskin cases' in the 'Readings' section at the end of this chapter.

With effect from October 2009, the Companies Act 2006 has enacted the following statutory statement of directors' duties which are to be interpreted and applied in the same way as case law.

Statutory statement of directors' duties (ss.170–180 CA 2006)

Note that although this statement is stated to replace common law and equitable rules so that director's duties are now codified, common law and equitable rules are to be used in *interpreting* the statutory duties.

1. Duty to act within their powers

Section 171 provides that directors must

(a) act in accordance with the company's constitution, and
(b) only exercise powers for the purposes for which they are conferred.

The statement at (a) means that if directors ignore the company's Memorandum and/or Articles of Association they have acted in breach of duty. Provision (b) effectively restates the rule that directors must not use their powers for an improper purpose. (See 5.2.5).

2. Duty to promote the success of the company

Section 172 provides that directors must promote the 'success of the company for the benefit of its members.' Previously directors had a general equitable duty to act 'in good faith in the best interests of the company'. Section 172 appears to replace that equitable duty. In complying with this duty directors are required to take account of a number of factors:

(a) the likely consequences of any decision in the long term;
(b) the interests of the company's employees;
(c) the need to foster the company's business relationships with suppliers, customers, and others;
(d) the impact of the company's operations on the community and the environment;
(e) the desirability of the company maintaining a reputation for high standards of business conduct; and
(f) the need to act fairly between members of the company.

Section 172 is said to enshrine the principle of 'enlightened shareholder value'. Directors are required to, for example, balance the short-term requirements of shareholders who are demanding dividends with the long term need of the company to retain profits in order to reinvest and re-equip. Directors no longer owe their duties purely to shareholders, but to a wider group of stakeholders in the form of employees, customers, creditors and the environment generally. It should be noted however, that although directors owe duties to these additional stakeholders, the duties are enforceable by the company, i.e. the legal entity which, in turn, is managed by the directors. Clearly this could lead to breaches of duty not being enforced so the law provides for shareholders to be able to pursue actions against the directors in appropriate circumstances. (See page 256)

3. Duty to exercise independent judgement

Section 173 provides in effect that a director must exercise independent judgment, but that principle is not breached by a director taking advice. Neither is the duty breached if the director acts in accordance with an agreement entered into by the company which restricts the future exercise of the director's discretion; neither is the duty breached if the director acts in manner authorised by the company's constitution.

4. Duty to exercise reasonable care, skill and diligence

Section 174 provides that a director must exercise the same care, skill and diligence that would be used by a reasonably diligent person with the general knowledge, skill and experience that may reasonably be expected of a person carrying out the functions that are being carried out by the director.

This is an objective test, the law is in effect asking would a reasonable person have acted in the same way as the director has acted?

The section goes on to provide a mixture of an objective and subjective test by setting the standard required as that of a reasonable person with the general knowledge, skill and experience that the director has. To apply this element of the test it is necessary to clothe the reasonable person (the objective element) with the actual qualities of the director in question (the subjective element) and ask whether a reasonable person with the knowledge, skill and experience of the director in question would have acted in the way he/she has acted.

The test is similar to that provided by section 214 of the Insolvency Act 1986 which related to 'wrongful trading'.

5. The duty to avoid conflicts of interest

Section 175 provides in effect that a director must not place him/herself in a situation where he has or may have a direct or indirect interest that conflicts with the interests of the company.

If a director places him/herself in such a conflict situation, that is a breach of duty.

However, in the case of a private company, the conflict or potential conflict may be disclosed to the board and, if the board authorises the conflict, no further action would be taken against the director. This is so unless the company's constitution invalidates such means of authorisation, for example by requiring the authorisation to be given by the shareholders. The director in question cannot vote on the matter at board level.

In the case of a public company, the board will only be able to authorise the conflict or potential conflict, if the constitution specifically permits this.

Section 175 must be read in conjunction with Section 182 CA 2006. The latter section deals with the situation where a director has an interest in an existing transaction or arrangement. For example, assume that Exe Ltd is about to enter into a contract with Wye Ltd and Tom is a director of both Exe Ltd and Wye Ltd.

(i) The fact that Tom is a director of both companies is obviously a conflict of interest situation. However, as long as Tom has disclosed the position to the boards of Exe Ltd and Wye Ltd and has received authorisation to be a member of both boards, he has complied with section 175.
(ii) In relation to the contract which is about to be entered into, that is a transaction or arrangement in which Tom has at least an indirect interest. It follows that Tom must disclose his interest to the boards of both companies as required by section 182. Failure to comply with section 182 is an offence which may result in the director being liable to a fine.

6. The duty not to accept benefits from third parties. (Section 176 CA 2006)

This duty is a codification of the previous case law which provided that a director must not accept secret profits. The director cannot accept a benefit paid to him by virtue of the fact that he is a director or in return for doing or not doing anything as a director. No breach of this duty occurs if the benefit cannot 'reasonably be regarded as likely to give rise to a conflict of interests.' (S.176(4) CA 2006.)

It follows that if a director takes a bribe from someone in order to attempt to change company policy in favour of that person, then that would be a breach of section 176. However, the acceptance of a small gift by way of a Christmas present would be likely to fall within the exception in section 176(4).

The consequences of a breach of director's duty (ss.178 and 239 CA 2006)

The CA 2006 does not impose any new consequences for breach of duty, but rather preserves the remedies which existed before the Act. Thus section 178 refers to the civil consequences of a breach by providing that the duties are enforceable in the same way as any other common law or fiduciary duty.

This means that, as a general rule, the company must bring the action against the director in question. This is therefore consistent with the rule in *Foss* v. *Harbottle* (1843). (See 5.8.3.) It follows that the previous difficulties, i.e. the fact that it may be difficult for shareholders to persuade a board to cause the company to take action against a particular director, still remain. The problem becomes particularly acute where it is alleged that the whole board has acted in breach of duty, as the board is unlikely to cause the company to sue themselves!

The CA 2006 has, however, introduced a new procedure in relation to so-called 'derivative' actions which may enable shareholders to take action in appropriate situations. (See 5.8.4.)

Section 239 CA 2006 preserves the previous rules whereby a directors breach of duty may be ratified by an ordinary resolution of the shareholders. If the resolution is written, neither the director nor any connected person is an eligible member. If the resolution is to be passed at a general meeting then the director may vote on the matter in his capacity of shareholder. However, the ratifying resolution is only valid if it would have been passed irrespective of the votes of the director.

5.6.5 Liability of directors to shareholders

As stated above, directors (and the company secretary) owe their duties to the *company*, not to individual shareholders. Therefore, it is only in exceptional circumstances that a director can be liable to legal action by members. Certainly, negligent directors whose conduct causes the value of the shares to fall are not liable to pay damages to the shareholders. Generally, directors will only become personally liable to a shareholder if they make a contract between themselves and the shareholder which is separate from the directors' duties to the company. In *Allen* v. *Hyatt* (1914), some directors made what amounted to an agency agreement with some of the shareholders. The directors took an option on the shares with a view to selling them for the benefit of the shareholders during takeover negotiations. The directors abused this option. They bought the shares for themselves, sold them at a profit, and kept the profit. The directors had to account to the shareholders for this profit, for breach of the agency contract.

Companies Act 2006 S.168, allows shareholders to remove directors, but directors of public companies often have rolling contracts of service, entitling them to large compensation payments if dismissed – a significant disincentive to dismissal. In private companies, the directors are often the majority shareholders. Thus, the main protection for shareholders today is S.994 CA 2006 (unfairly prejudicial conduct) which, arguably renders the use of the rule in *Foss* v. *Harbottle* (1843) and its exceptions largely obsolete. This topic, the case of *Foss* v. *Harbottle* (1843), and minority protection are covered more fully later.

5.7 Liability of directors to the company's creditors

Learning Outcome:	To explain the rules dealing with the possible imposition of personal liability upon the directors of insolvent companies.

As a general rule, directors are not personally liable to the company's creditors or to other outsiders. The debts, etc., are the debts of the company, which is a separate legal person from its members or officers (see Chapter 6). However, there are some exceptional situations where a director may be personally liable to outsiders.

While the company is still operating

In this case the exceptions are few.

(a) If a director claims to make a contract on behalf of the company in circumstances where the company is not bound, the director is personally liable to the other party for breach of warranty of authority. This will not often occur today because, by s.40 CA 2006 Act as amended, the company will almost always be bound by the acts of directors on its behalf.

(b) Under the Company Directors Disqualification Act 1986, if a person who has been disqualified by a court order from acting as a director then disobeys the order, he can be personally liable for company debts while he does so. Similar rules apply to undischarged bankrupts.
(c) By the Insolvency Act 1986, s.216, someone who was a director of an insolvent company during the last 12 months before it was wound up must not without court consent be a director in a new company with a name too similar to that of the old company for the next 5 years. To do so is a criminal offence, and makes him personally liable for the debts of the new ('phoenix') company. Section 216 also applies to unincorporated businesses.
(d) The Memorandum of a limited company may specifically provide that the liability of the directors or managers, or of the managing director, is to be unlimited. This is rare.
(e) Exceptionally, it seems that a director may be vicariously liable for torts committed by the company, if he had had extensive control over the company's conduct in connection with the tortious activity. In *Evans & Sons Ltd* v. *Spritebrand Ltd* (1985), a director was held personally liable for a company's breach of copyright.
(f) If the directors of a very small company seek credit from a large lender (e.g. an overdraft for the company from the bank), the lender may insist that the directors personally guarantee repayment. This is probably the most common situation in which directors will be personally liable.
(g) If an officer or other person signs any bill of exchange, cheque, and so on, or order for money or goods on the company's behalf, in which the company's name is not properly given, then he is personally liable if the company does not pay.

The name must be stated fully and accurately. Officers have several times been held personally liable where the word 'limited' was omitted (although 'ltd' is sufficient, as is 'co' for 'company'). Even the omission of '&', so that 'L & R Agencies Ltd' appeared as 'LR Agencies Ltd' rendered directors who had signed the cheque personally liable: see *Hendon* v. *Adelman* (1973).

In the course of a winding-up

In this case there are further possibilities:

(a) *Fraudulent* trading may occur. By the Insolvency Act 1986, s.213, if it appears in the course of a winding-up that any business has been carried on with intent to defraud creditors, or for any fraudulent purpose, the liquidator may ask the court to declare that persons knowingly party to the fraudulent trading must make such contribution to the company's assets (and therefore indirectly to the creditors) as the court thinks proper. This can take place even if the company was solvent when wound up, and the section applies to managers as well as to directors. Persons guilty of the fraud also commit a criminal offence. In practice, fraudulent trading is very difficult to prove. Fraud is a subjective test, and it must be shown beyond reasonable doubt (which is the criminal standard of proof) that the individual intended to defraud the creditors. For this reason liquidators, who are primarily interested in obtaining a monetary contribution from the wrongdoers, would tend to pursue wrongful rather than fraudulent trading.
(b) *Wrongful* trading was introduced by the Insolvency Act 1986, s.214, because of the difficulty in proving fraud. It is an objective test in that the directors are judged against what they ought to have known rather than what they actually knew. When a company has financial difficulties, and a director knows or ought to conclude that it has no reasonable prospect of recovery, he should take immediate steps to minimise the loss

to creditors. For example, he should apply as soon as possible for a winding-up order. A director who wrongfully carries on trading in these circumstances may be ordered to contribute personally to the company's assets in the eventual liquidation. Unlike s.213 above, wrongful trading only applies to directors, and only if the liquidation is insolvent. In effect the directors lose the benefit of limited liability from the period when they should have known that insolvency was inevitable. In summary form, the following must be established:

(i) Whether the director(s) knew or ought to have known that there was no reasonable prospect of avoiding insolvent liquidation;
(ii) The date which they knew or should have known this;
(iii) Whether they took 'every step' after that date to minimise the loss to the creditors (in which case that is a complete defence); and, if not
(iv) How much they should contribute to the assets of the company.

It follows that neither fraud nor dishonesty needs to be proved, the over-optimistic folly of directors can be enough. In *Re Produce Marketing Consortium Ltd* (1989), two directors insisted on trading after auditors had warned them that the company was insolvent. They were ordered to pay £75,000 with interest in the eventual winding-up. If directors carry on trading when insolvency is inevitable, they are, in effect, using the creditors' money to finance their trade. In practice many liquidators use the threat of the wrongful trading provisions to attempt to extract a contribution from directors who have continued trading in these circumstances.

5.8 Division of powers between directors and shareholders

Learning Outcome:	To identify and contrast the rights of shareholders with the board of the company

The powers of a company are exercised by the board of directors and by members in general meetings. Who can do what depends partly on statute and partly on the Articles.

Some decisions must be *made* by a resolution of shareholders, which will normally involve a general meeting. The most important of these are changes to the company's name, objects, nominal capital or Articles.

Some transactions by the board must specifically be *approved* by a resolution of shareholders, again normally at a general meeting. Examples include property transactions between a company and any of its directors which fall within Ss. 190–196 (see earlier). If Table A applies, the board's recommended dividend is actually declared by the members, normally at a general meeting.

Subject to this, Table A reg. 70 (if it applies) provides that 'subject to the provisions of the Act, the Memorandum and the Articles and to any directions given by *special* resolution, the business of the company shall be managed by the directors who may exercise all of the powers of the company…and a meeting of directors at which a quorum is present may exercise all powers exercisable by the directors'. The board is the agent of the company, not the shareholders. It is the board which has the authority to carry on the day-to-day management of the company and the shareholders cannot interfere unless the Articles permit them to do so. Therefore, a general meeting cannot by ordinary resolution dictate to or overrule the directors in respect of matters entrusted to them by the Articles. To do that it is necessary to have a special resolution if reg. 70 applies, and Table A may be varied to take away even this power. Moreover a special resolution, even one altering the Memorandum or Articles for the future, cannot retrospectively invalidate something which was valid at the time when the board did it.

5.8.1 Duty of the board to report to a general meeting

The boards of public companies have to report annually to their shareholders at an AGM. However, as stated above, private companies are only obliged to do so if they so wish. In respect of each financial year of a company, the directors must lay before the company in general meeting copies of the accounts for that year. These 'accounts' must comprise:

(a) the company's profit and loss account and balance sheet,
(b) the directors' report, and
(c) the auditors' report;
(d) where the company has subsidiaries, it may also have to lay the company's group accounts.

As we have seen, the company's accounts must be prepared and audited each year. Copies must be sent to members and debenture holders at least 21 days before the date of the AGM.

The company must also send a copy of the above documents to the Registrar of Companies.

With effect from October 2009, the Companies Act 2006 provides that private companies must file their annual report within 9 months of the year end and public companies within 6 months. Another change is that auditors will be able to limit their liability to such as is fair and reasonable in the circumstances (with a monetary cap permitted) by agreement with the company and subject to approval by the shareholders. In addition there will be a criminal offence in respect of auditors knowingly or recklessly including materially misleading information in an audit report.

With effect from October 2009, the Companies Act 2006 provides that quoted companies must ensure that they include a 'business review' in the directors' report which includes a commentary on (a) the main trends and factors likely to affect its future business; (b) information about the environment, the employees and social community issues and (c) information about persons who have contractual or other arrangements with the company which are essential to its operations – unless this would be seriously prejudicial to that person or to the public interest. Directors will be liable to the company for misleading statements made in bad faith or recklessly.

5.8.2 Exemption clauses for directors

By ss.532–533 CA 2006, any provision, whether in the Articles or in any contract with the company or elsewhere, which tries to exempt a director, company secretary or auditor from liability which would otherwise attach to him for negligence (e.g. pay the damages). Such a provision can, however, entitle the company to pay the costs of a director (etc.) if the proceedings find him not liable (or not guilty in a criminal case).

5.8.3 Majority rule and minority protection

In *Foss* v. *Harbottle* (1843), two directors sold some of their own land to the company. Minority shareholders tried to sue the directors, alleging that the company had paid far too much. The court refused to hear the action. If the directors had acted wrongfully, it was a wrong against the company. It was therefore for the company to decide whether to sue.

It follows that the rule in *Foss* v. *Harbottle* contains two elements:

(i) If it is alleged that a wrong has been done to the company, the company is the proper claimant. This element is a logical application of the principle that a company is a separate person in its own right. The decision whether to sue or not is a management decision and is, therefore, taken by the directors. In some instances the board may not want the company to sue, for example when the directors are the alleged wrongdoers! In this situation the law provides a means whereby the shareholders may initiate court proceedings on behalf of the company (see later).

(ii) If the act complained of may be ratified by the shareholders in general meeting, then the shareholders will not be permitted to cause the company to sue. This again is a logical rule. If shareholders were allowed to proceed against wrongdoing directors, and the court were to find against the directors, the court's decision could be nullified by the majority of shareholders subsequently ratifying the directors' actions. In cases where the shareholders are entitled to ratify the directors' actions, it is likely that the court will stay any proceedings by minority shareholders and call a general meeting of the company to see whether the majority shareholders do in fact wish to ratify the directors' actions or whether they wish to proceed with the action (*Prudential Assurance* v. *Newman Industries* (No 2) (1982)).

5.8.4 The exceptions to the Rule in *Foss* v. *Harbottle* (1843)

A few exceptions have developed to the rule in *Foss* v. *Harbottle* (1843). These are situations where a minority shareholder can seek a remedy *for the company* for a wrong done to the company (e.g. for breach of a director's duties of good faith to the company).

(a) A minority shareholder, even with only one share, can obtain an injunction to prevent a *proposed* act by the directors which would be *ultra vires* the company. However, this cannot stop a transaction which has already been agreed with an outsider; and it does not apply if the proposed transaction has been approved by a special resolution at a general meeting. Similarly, a minority shareholder can obtain an injunction to restrain the directors from a proposed illegal action which would amount to a criminal offence by the company. Under S.31 of the CA 2006 companies will have unlimited objects unless they choose to restrict them in their Articles of Association.

(b) The court will grant a remedy if the directors or management, in breach of their fiduciary duties to the company, have committed a 'fraud on the minority'. In this context, 'fraud' means grossly inequitable conduct, not necessarily amounting to a criminal offence. The courts have granted remedies where the directors have used their powers deliberately, or dishonestly, or even grossly negligently (note the directors' duties of care) in a manner which benefits themselves personally at the expense of the company.

Examples

In *Cook v. Deeks* (1916), the directors negotiated a contract with an outsider in the normal way, as if they were making it for the company. They then, however, took the contract (and its benefits) in their own names. As majority shareholders, they passed an ordinary resolution declaring that the company had no interest in the transaction. A minority shareholder obtained a court order requiring them to account to the company for their profits.

In *Daniels v. Daniels* (1978), the board of directors, which held most of the shares, sold land belonging to the company to one of the directors. It was alleged that the price paid by the director was a gross undervaluation, possibly less than 10 per cent of its true worth. No dishonesty was alleged. Nevertheless, it was held that a minority shareholder could sue, on the basis that at the very least a sale at this price was a breach of the duties of care and skill which the board owed to the company.

(c) If the board of a company tries to do something, which requires a special resolution (with appropriate notice), without obtaining such a resolution, a simple majority cannot ratify it. To allow this would destroy the whole protection given to minorities by the requirement of a special resolutions, namely that for some matters (e.g. a change of name) only a 75 per cent majority can prevail.

(d) An alteration to the Articles of Association can be attacked by shareholders where they can show that the alteration was not passed *bona fide* for the benefit of a company as a whole. This can be difficult, because the minority must show conduct on the part of the majority which effectively amounts to fraud on the minority; see *Brown* v. *British Abrasive Wheel Co* (1917) and *Shuttleworth* v. *Cox Bros* (1927) in Section 4.3.4

(e) In *Clemens* v. *Clemens Bros. Ltd* (1976), it was held that a majority shareholder *as such*, even if he or she is not a director, can owe duties approaching good faith in certain types of company. In this case, the court set aside a resolution which a majority shareholder had carried by her votes but had done so for an improper motive (i.e.) to confirm a measure designed to reduce further the voting power of a minority shareholder. This action by a minority shareholder was apparently derived from breach by the majority holder of her duty to the company; see also Section 7.4. Most litigants would today bring an action under S.994 (below) in this situation.

In certain circumstances minority shareholders may be able to bring an action on behalf of the company in respect of a wrong done by the directors to the company. This is known as a 'derivative action'. This is to recognise the fact that if the wrongdoers are the directors, then it is unlikely that the directors will cause the company to sue themselves! Sections 260–269 of the CA 2006 have introduced a new procedure with effect from October 2007. Under the new regime a claim may be brought by any member, not only in respect of actions carried out by the board, but also regarding proposed acts or omissions, involving negligence, breach of duty and breach of trust. It is not necessary for the claimant to show that there has been a loss to the company, or a gain by the director(s). The procedure now is for the claimant to apply to the court for permission to continue the claim. If the court does not consider the application to support a prima facie case, then the court may order the action to be discontinued and make any other order it thinks fit. Alternatively, if a prima facie case is established, the claimant may continue the action and the court may order evidence to be provided by the company, adjourn the proceedings and give such directions as it thinks fit. Permission to continue must be refused if the court is satisfied that persons who seek to promote the success of the company would not continue or the act complained of has been authorised or ratified by the company.

5.8.5 Wrongs to members personally

These are not directly affected by the rule in *Foss* v. *Harbottle* (1843). They are based on the CA 2006 s33, under which the Memorandum and Articles form a contract between members. If, therefore, a member contravenes the company's constitution in a way which takes away the rights of another member, the latter can seek a remedy against the offending shareholder(s). Such an action may be 'representative', in that one offended member may sue on behalf of himself and others similarly affected. But it is not 'derivative': the member is complaining of breach of a duty owed *to him*, not to the company. In *Pender* v. *Lushington* (1877), the chairman at a meeting of members refused to accept the votes to which the plaintiff's shares entitled him. The court compelled the directors to record the votes.

5.8.6 Unfairly prejudicial conduct: Companies Act 2006 S.994

The remedy under S.994 is probably the most important of all shareholder remedies. Any member may apply to the court on the ground that the company's affairs are being or have been conducted in a manner which is unfairly prejudicial to the interests of its members generally, or of some section of them, including himself; or that any actual or proposed act or omission would be so prejudicial.

Examples of such unfairly prejudicial conduct would be directors paying themselves excessive salaries, thereby depriving other members of a dividend; issue of shares to directors on unduly advantageous terms; refusal by the board to recommend a dividend for non-voting non-cumulative preference shareholders; refusal to put personal representatives personally on the register of shareholders; unfair removal from the board or other exclusion from management.

The court 'may make such order as it thinks fit for giving relief in respect of the matters complained of'. In particular, the order may:

(a) regulate the conduct of the company's affairs in the future;
(b) restrain the company from doing or continuing to do an act complained of, or require it to do something which has been omitted;
(c) authorise civil proceedings to be brought in the name and on behalf of the company (e.g. in a *Foss* v. *Harbottle* situation);
(d) require the company or other members to buy the petitioner's shares at a fair price or valuation; this has proved a useful remedy.

In *Re HR Harmer Ltd* (1959) (under an earlier statutory provision), the major shareholder was father of the other two directors. He ran the company in an autocratic and high-handed manner, ignoring board decisions, overruling his sons, and offending employees. He was ordered to obey board decisions in the future, and not to interfere in the company except as the board decided. Section 994 is by far the most important of the remedies available to shareholders, and scores of actions have been brought since its introduction. (A recent case example is Citybranch Group Ltd, Gross and others v. Rackind and others [2004] 4 All ER 735).

5.8.7 Winding up on the just and equitable ground: Insolvency Act 1986, s.122(g)

Under this section a shareholder may apply to the court for a winding up order if he/she can demonstrate that it is just and equitable to wind up the company. The shareholder(s) must show that the company is solvent and that they have 'sufficient interest' in the winding up. In other words that they stand to benefit substantially by being able to withdraw their investment after all the company's debts have been repaid. Obviously, making an application for a winding-up order is an extremely drastic step. For that reason, an order will not be granted where the court is of the opinion that some other remedy is available to the petitioners, and that they are acting unreasonably in not pursuing that other remedy (IA 1986, s.125). For example, it may be, in the case of a private company (to which this section is most relevant) that the petitioner has had a major dispute with other members or directors of the company. In these circumstances, it may be just as beneficial for the petitioner to sell his/her shares, but an offer to buy them is being refused to enable the petitioner to take some kind of revenge against the other members/directors. Clearly, in this situation the court will refuse to grant a winding-up order and will expect the petitioners to withdraw their investment by selling their shares rather than liquidating the company.

5.8.8 Other statutory rights and remedies

Many statutory provisions, mentioned at various places in this book, give rights and remedies to minorities of varying sizes. For example, in this chapter we have seen that a minority of 25 per cent plus can protect itself against anything which has to be done by special or extraordinary resolution; 15 per cent of shareholders of a particular class can petition against variation of class rights; one-tenth of registered members can require the directors to call an general meeting; 5 per cent can require the inclusion of a resolution at the next AGM; under Table A, two members may demand a poll; and one member may petition under s.994 above.

5.9 The company secretary

Learning Outcome:	To explain the qualifications, powers and duties of the company secretary.

5.9.1 Appointment

Prior to 6 April 2008 all companies were required to appoint a company secretary. Since that date private companies need not have a company secretary but they may have one if they wish. (S270 CA 2006). Obviously most private companies were registered before 6 April 2008 and may wish to wish continue to have a company secretary. Such companies will have to enter particulars in their register of secretaries and send details of any changes to Companies House in the same way as required by public companies. (S277 CA 2006).

All public companies are required to have a company secretary.

5.9.2 Registration of company secretaries

All companies are required to maintain a register of directors which must keep at the registered office, Public companies and private companies which decide to appoint company secretaries must include details of the company's secretary in the register of directors. The following information must be maintained: For an individual, his present first name and surname and any former name, and his usual residential address; for a corporate secretary, its corporate name and registered or principal office. If there are joint secretaries, this information must be registered for each. The register is open to inspection by members without charge, and by the public for a small fee. With effect from October 2009 company secretaries, like directors, will be able to register a service address which may be stated as the company's registered office (CA 2006 s.277).

5.9.3 Qualifications

The company secretary of a private company need not be qualified. Qualifications for the company secretaries of public companies were introduced in 1980. Section 273 CA 2006 provides that the directors must 'take all reasonable steps to ensure that the secretary or each joint secretary is a person with the requisite knowledge and experience and who:

(a) was the secretary of a public company for at least three of the five years immediately preceding the appointment as secretary;
(b) is a member of one of the following professional bodies:
   (i) The Institute of Chartered Accountants in England and Wales;
   (ii) The Institute of Chartered Accountants in Scotland;
   (iii) The Institute of Chartered Accountants in Ireland;
   (iv) The Association of Certified Accountants;
   (v) The Institute of Chartered Secretaries and Administrators;
   (vi) The Institute of Chartered Management Accountants;
   (vii) The Chartered Institute of Public Finance and Accountancy.

Or

   (i) is qualified in the UK as a barrister, an advocate or a solicitor; or
   (ii) is a person who by holding or having held any other position or being a member of any other body, appears to the directors to be capable of discharging the functions of a secretary.

5.9.4 Functions and status

The function and status of company secretaries have increased over the last century. The secretary is the chief administrative officer of the company, with wide responsibilities. At the very least, he will be present at all meetings of shareholders and of the board of directors. He will be responsible for proper minutes, and will issue notices to members and others. He is responsible for the many registers which a company must keep. He will administer the annual and other returns to the Registrar, and generally carry out the company's legal duties in these respects. He may, and in some cases must by statute, authenticate documents filed with the Registrar. Some statutory provisions can render him criminally liable.

Other functions of the company secretary will vary with the size and complexity of the company. He will not, as such, take part in management. His main role is to provide the administrative support indicated. He may have actual or ostensible authority to make contracts of an administrative nature with outsiders [see *Panorama Developments Ltd* v. *Fidelis Furnishing Fabrics Ltd* (1971)], but generally he will not be able to bind the company contractually.

5.9.5 Removal

Removal of a company secretary can normally be accomplished by the directors; see Table A reg. 99, cited above. A simple majority in a board meeting will suffice.

With effect from October 2009, the Companies Act 2006 provides that private companies are not required to have a company secretary but may choose to have one. Public companies must have a qualified company secretary.

5.10 Summary

At the end of this chapter, students should make sure that they understand the following matters:

- the nature of shares;
- meaning of 'share capital', including authorised, issued, called up and paid up share capital;
- types of share, particularly ordinary, preferred, deferred and redeemable shares;
- class rights;
- issuing shares: authority to issue; finding buyers (e.g. by prospectuses or listing particulars); types of share issue (public offer, placing, etc);
- the issue of shares for an improper purpose;
- variation of share capital;
- maintenance of share capital: general rule; exceptions such as:
  - redeemable shares;
  - purchase by a company of its own shares;
  - reduction of share capital with confirmation of the court or by court order;
  - limits on a company holding its own shares;
- loan capital, including whether to borrow and how to borrow. In particular, students must understand secured and unsecured debentures;
- security for debentures, particularly the difference between fixed charges and floating charges;
- registration of charges;
- priority of charges;
- rights of debenture holders on default by the company;
- trust deeds;
- shares and debentures compared and contrasted.
- directors: company's general requirement; appointment; retirement; disqualification; possible removal; registration and keeping of information about directors;
- duties of directors: to the company; to employees; to report to a general meeting;
- possible liability of directors
  - to the company's creditors,
  - to shareholders,
  - effect of attempted exemption clauses for directors;
- protection of minority shareholders
  - general position: majority rule,
  - 'derivative' actions,
  - wrongs to members personally,
  - Companies Act 2006 s.994 – unfairly prejudicial conduct;
- petition for winding up the company;
- the company secretary: appointment, functions and status, removal.
- the changes made by the Companies Act 2006.

Revision Questions 5

Question 1 Multiple-choice selection

1.1 Ethel is unsure whether to invest in shares or debentures. Which of the following statements is inaccurate?

(A) Debenture holders are members of the company whereas shareholders are not.
(B) Shareholders are members of the company whereas debenture holders are not.
(C) Maintenance of capital rules apply to shares but not to debentures.
(D) Shareholders are controllers of a company while debenture holders are creditors.

1.2 Which of the following statements is untrue?

(A) No company may issue shares at a discount.
(B) A public company may issue shares for an undertaking to do work or perform services.
(C) A company need not require full payment for shares immediately.
(D) When a public company issues shares for a non-cash consideration, such consideration must be independently valued by a person qualified to be the auditor of the company.

1.3 Once a company has raised capital, it must be maintained. In which *one* of the following is it permissible for this principle to be breached?

(A) Purchase by a private company of its own shares.
(B) Purchase by a public company of its own shares.
(C) By a private company when paying a dividend.
(D) By a public company when paying a dividend.

1.4 HIJ Ltd has borrowed money from K Bank plc and has provided security by executing a fixed charge debenture in favour of the bank. A fixed charge is:

(A) a charge over specific company property which prevents the company from dealing freely with the property in the ordinary course of business.
(B) a charge over a class of company assets which enables the company to deal freely with the assets in the ordinary course of business.
(C) a charge over specific company property which enables the company to deal freely with the assets in the ordinary course of business.
(D) a charge over company land enabling the company to deal freely with the land in the ordinary course of business.

1.5 Big plc, a manufacturing company, has just taken over Small plc by buying all of Small plc's shares. At the time of the takeover, Small plc owned 2 % of Big plc's ordinary shares. Can Big plc take any of the following steps?

(A) Let Small plc keep the shares in Big plc.
(B) Buy and retain these shares itself.
(C) Allow Small plc to buy more shares in Big plc on the open market.
(D) Lend money to a director of Big plc to help him to buy the Big plc shares from Small plc for himself.

1.6 Which of the following is correct in relation to 'Treasury Shares'?

(A) All companies which have purchased their own shares may hold them as Treasury Shares.
(B) A listed plc which has purchased its own shares out of distributable profits may hold Treasury Shares.
(C) Shares held as Treasury Shares must be cancelled and cannot be re-issued.
(D) A listed plc may purchase its own shares and hold up to 15% of them as Treasury shares.

1.7 Which of the following statements concerning the role of non-executive directors of public companies is *correct*?

(A) A non-executive director cannot own shares in the company.
(B) A non-executive director inevitably lacks any expertise in the company's main line of business.
(C) A non-executive director may have an important role in determining the pay of the executive directors.
(D) A non-executive director bears no responsibility to the company's shareholders.

1.8 Joe is a director of Abe Ltd, and has been sued by the company on the grounds of having made a secret profit. Which one of the following could *not* arise?

(A) Joe could be ordered to account to the company for the secret profit.
(B) Joe could be dismissed as a director.
(C) The breach of fiduciary duty could be ratified by the company in general meeting.
(D) The articles could validly provide an exemption for directors from liability for breach of duty.

1.9 Which one of the following is correct? The register of directors' interests is open:

(A) Only to other members of the board.
(B) Only to members of the board and to shareholders.
(C) Only to the board, shareholders and debenture holders.
(D) To the public.

1.10 Which one of the following is correct? An application to the court under the Companies Act 2006, s.994, claiming that the company's affairs have been conducted in unfairly prejudicial manner can be made:

(A) By any shareholder, irrespective of the size of his/her/its shareholding.
(B) Only by a member or members holding at least 5 % in number of the company's issued shares.
(C) Only by a creditor or creditors.
(D) Only after an ordinary resolution of shareholders.

1.11 Which one of the following is correct? Where Table A applies, removal of the company secretary in a public company can be done:

(A) By the board of directors by a majority decision.
(B) By the board of directors, but only by a unanimous decision.
(C) By the board, but only after a petition by a member or members holding at least 25 % in number of the company's issued shares.
(D) Only after an ordinary resolution of shareholders of which 28 days' notice has been given to members and the secretary.

1.12 Section 175 (1) of the Companies Act 2006 provides that a director owes a duty to avoid a situation in which he has an interest which conflicts or may conflict with the interests of the company. Bill is a non-executive director of Exe plc and has been offered an investment opportunity in his personal capacity which he wishes to take up. Which of the following is correct?

(A) The duty does not apply to Bill in this situation as the investment opportunity was offered to him personally and not to the company.
(B) The duty does not apply to Bill if Exe plc was not itself in a position to take advantage of the investment opportunity.
(C) The duty can apply to Bill unless he ceases to be a director of Exe plc before taking up the opportunity.
(D) The duty can apply to Bill as the situation can reasonably be regarded as being likely to give rise to a conflict of interest.

Question 2

Requirement

Complete the following sentences:
Under the .... (3 words) **(2 marks)** rule a company cannot return its .... (1 word) **(1 mark)** capital to its members. However, a company may reduce its capital if it has power in its .... (3 words) **(2 marks)** and it passes a .... (1 word) **(2 marks)** resolution and obtains the permission of .... (2 words) **(2 marks)**. In addition, in certain circumstances, a company may purchase or redeem its own shares using its authorised funds which are its .... (2 words) **(2 marks)** or the proceeds of .... (4 words) **(2 marks)**.

(Total marks = 13)

Question 3

B plc obtained a substantial loan from A Bank plc on 1 January 2002. The loan is secured by the following charges, which are set out in the bank's standard form of debenture document:

(i) A charge over the company's freehold land. The company is not free to sell, lease or in any way deal with the land without the bank's express permission.
(ii) A charge over all the company's other assets and undertakings. The company may deal freely with these in the ordinary course of business.

Requirement

Complete the following sentences:
The charge over the land is a .... (1 word) **(2 marks)** charge and the charge over the company's other assets and undertaking is a .... (1 word) **(2 marks)** charge. If the charges were not registered at .... (2 words) **(2 marks)** within .... **(2 marks)** days of the creation of the charges they will be .... (1 word) **(2 marks)** against the liquidator. In addition the charges will need to be registered in the company's .... **(4 words) (2 marks)**. If the company should default in repaying the loan, A Bank plc will be able to appoint an .... (2 words) **(2 marks)** who will be able to take over the company in an attempt to ensure the survival of its business. If the charges had been created after 15 September 2003, A Bank plc would have been required to appoint an ... .(1 word) **(2 marks)**.'

(Total marks = 16)

Question 4

Dee Ltd was incorporated to purchase and resell a large estate. The company had three directors – D, E, and F – who each held one-third of the company's issued share capital.

The Articles of Association of Dee Ltd provided that all three directors had to be present to constitute a quorum and thus a valid board meeting. E and F had to travel abroad on other business, and, although they did not formally appoint D managing director, they agreed he should carry out the day-to-day management of the company in their absence, and that the company should attempt to sell the estate on their return.

While E and F were abroad, D decided to develop the estate, and on behalf of Dee Ltd instructed Gee Ltd, a property development company, to produce a major development plan and to secure the necessary planning consents. Following the return of E and F, Dee Ltd refused to pay Gee Ltd on the ground that D had no authority to engage the latter company. Gee Ltd has now advised Dee Ltd of its intention to initiate court proceedings to recover the amount due.

Requirement

Delete as appropriate and complete the following sentences:
The .... (1 word) **(1 mark)** is the agent of the company. Individual directors have no/also have **(1 mark)** power to contract on behalf of the company unless power has been/irrespective of whether power has been **(1 mark)** delegated by the board. In this case Dee Ltd will/will not **(1 mark)** be liable to Gee Ltd, as D has acted within his apparent authority/without any authority **(1 mark)**. Gee Ltd may/will not **(1 mark)** be entitled to obtain compensation from D personally for breach .... (4 words) **(2 marks)**, a remedy available to a third party where an agent exceeds his authority. E and F have nor power to/may dismiss D **(1 mark)** by passing .... (2 words) **(2 marks)** resolution with .... (1 word) **(1 mark)** notice under section 168 of the Companies Act 2006.

(Total marks = 12)

Question 5

Jane is a member of the board of Retailer Ltd and holds 51 % of the company's issued share capital. The company has a number of shops situated at holiday resorts around the country. One particular shop has traded at a loss for a number of years and the board has decided that it should be sold. The shop has been valued at £120,000 to include the premises and the stock. Jane wishes to buy the shop for her own use and is willing to pay the £120,000 valuation.

Requirement

Complete the following sentences:

As a director Jane owes a .... (1 word) **(1 mark)** duty to the company not to place herself in a conflict of .... (1 word) **(1 mark)** and duty situation. As a result she is required to formally .... (3 words) **(2 marks)** to the board. In addition, as the value of the property being sold to Jane exceeds .... (state the amount) **(1 mark)** this is a '........... (2 words) **(2 marks)** transaction' and it follows that the .... (1 word) **(1 mark)** must approve the sale by passing .... (2 words) **(2 marks)** resolution which requires a simple majority to vote in favour. **(Total marks = 10)**

Solutions to Revision Questions 5

Solution 1

1.1 Answer: (A)

Debenture holders are not members of a company, and shareholders are members. (B), the opposite, is therefore true. (C) is true: maintenance of capital rules are rules to prevent capital being returned to members without the consent of the court, except in the course of a liquidation. (D) is also true: debenture holders are creditors of the company and cannot vote on company resolutions.

1.2 Answer: (B)
(A) is true. This is forbidden, to ensure that the company receives the whole of the nominal value of the issued share capital from shareholders. (B) is the right answer. A public company is *prohibited* from accepting as consideration an obligation to do work or perform services in exchange for shares. (C) is true. (D) is true: this requirement is to make sure that the consideration received by public companies is actually the full worth of the shares.

1.3 Answer: (A)
In all the other instances, capital must be maintained. But a private company is allowed to purchase its own shares out of capital, provided that it is authorised to do so in its articles, and that it first exhausts distributable profits (and any proceeds of a fresh share issue). There are other safeguards to ensure that members and creditors are not prejudiced.

1.4 Answer: (A)
Assets subject to fixed charges (as opposed to floating charges) cannot be dealt with while subject to the charge, except with the consent of the creditor holding the charge. (B) is not correct because the assets subject to a fixed charge cannot be dealt with freely in the course of business. (C) and (D) are likewise incorrect for the same reason.

Assets subject to a fixed charge are identified at the time of creation of the charge, and the assets subject to the charge will not fluctuate over time, unlike a floating charge.

1.5 Answer: (A)
(B) and (C) both contravene the *general* rule that a company (Big plc) must not directly or indirectly own shares in itself. (A) is a statutory exception.

There is a general rule that a company (particularly public) must not give financial assistance for the purchase of its own shares (D).

1.6 Answer: (B)
(A) is incorrect as only listed public limited companies may hold Treasury Shares. (C) is incorrect because Treasury Shares may be re-issued for cash. (D) is incorrect as the limit is 10%.

1.7 Answer: (C)
There is no law which prevents non-executive or independent directors on a company's board from owning shares in the company. And although non-executives may lack expertise in the company's business activities, this is not inevitable. All the directors on the board – executive and non-executive – bear a responsibility to the shareholders who own the business. (A), (B) and (D) are therefore untrue, leaving (C) as the correct answer. An increasingly important function of non-executive directors is to serve on the board's 'remuneration committee' which determines the pay of the executive directors.

1.8 Answer: (D)
Outcome (A) could arise, since this is a remedy for the breach of duty which Joe has committed – *Regal (Hastings) Ltd* v. *Gulliver* (1967). Outcome B could also arise, since a director can always be dismissed by rules under s.168 of the Companies Act 2006, whatever else the articles may provide. Outcome (C) is possible, provided the act was not done in bad faith. Outcome (D) could not arise, because by s.310 of the Companies Act 1985 such a provision would be void.

1.9 Answer: (D)
The register is available to all of the others, (A), (B) and (C), but not *only* to them. They are therefore incorrect.

1.10 Answer: (A)
The actual shareholding of the member is irrelevant, therefore (B) and (D) are incorrect. Further, the section provides protection to minority shareholders, not creditors, therefore (C) is inaccurate.

1.11 Answer: (A)
A company secretary is normally appointed by the directors of a company and is an employee. As such, no shareholder involvement in the removal is necessary. (C) and (D) are therefore inaccurate. A board of directors usually makes decisions on a majority vote and that is applicable here. (B) is therefore incorrect.

1.12 Answer: (D)
The duty can apply to Bill as the investment opportunity may be such that it involves a competitor of Exe plc or it may require Bill to give of his time which should be available to Exe plc.

✓ Solution 2

Under the *maintenance of capital* rule a company cannot return its *share* capital to its members. However, a company may reduce its capital if it has power in its *Articles of Association* and it passes a *special* resolution and obtains the permission of *the court.* In addition, in certain circumstances a company may purchase or redeem its own shares using its authorised funds which are its *distributable profits* or the proceeds of *a new share issue.*

Solution 3

The charge over the land is a *fixed* charge and the charge over the company's other assets and undertaking is a *floating* charge. If the charges were not registered at *Companies House* within *21* days of the creation of the charges they will be *void* against the liquidator. In addition the charges will need to be registered in the company's *register of debenture holders.* If the company should default in repaying the loan, A Bank plc will be able to appoint an *administrative receiver* who will be able to take over the company in an attempt to ensure the survival of the business. If the charges had been created after 15 September 2003, A Bank plc would have been required to appoint an *administrator.*

Solution 4

The *board* is the agent of the company. Individual directors *have no* power to contract on behalf of the company *unless power has been* delegated by the board. In this case Dee Ltd *will* be liable to Gee Ltd, as (D) has acted *within his apparent authority.* Gee Ltd *may* be entitled to obtain compensation from (D) personally for breach *of warranty of authority,* a remedy available to a third party where an agent exceeds his authority. (E) and (F) *may* dismiss (D) by passing an *ordinary* resolution with *special* notice under Section 168 of the Companies Act 2006.

Solution 5

As a director Jane owes a *statutory* duty to the company not to place herself in a conflict of *interest* and duty situation. As a result she is required to formally *declare her interest* to the board. In addition, as the value of the property being sold to Jane exceeds £100,000 this is a '*substantial property* transaction', and it follows that the *shareholders* must approve the sale by passing *an ordinary* resolution which requires a simple majority to vote in favour.

6

Ethics and Business

Ethics and Business

Learning Outcomes

After completing this chapter, you should be able to:

- explain the need for a framework of laws, regulations and standards in business and their application;
- identify the difference between rules-based and framework approaches to ethics;
- explain the nature of ethics and its application to business and the accountancy profession;
- explain the reasons why CIMA and IFAC each have a 'Code of Ethics for Professional Accountants';
- identify key concepts of independence, scepticism, accountability and social responsibility;
- apply the values and attitudes that provide professional accountants with a commitment to act in public interest and with social responsibility;
- identify the need for continual personal improvement and life-long learning based on an understanding of virtues of reliability, timeliness, courtesy and respect;
- explain the ethical principles of integrity, objectivity, professional competence, due care and confidentiality.

6.1 Why ethics are important

Learning Outcome: Apply the values and attitudes that provide professional accountants with a commitment to act in the public interest and with social responsibility.

A management accountant's role is to provide the crucial information that forms the basis of decision-making within an organisation. If work is undertaken badly or in bad faith there can be wide-ranging consequences. Unethical behaviour can affect not only the accountant (perhaps resulting in disciplinary action against the employee or by CIMA), but may also affect the jobs, financial viability and business efficacy of an organisation in which the accountant works. Management Accountants in the public sector are also dealing with tax-payer's money which, if poorly stewarded, might be wasted or misused.

The current world financial crisis once again shows the relationship between those who manage and account for finance and social responsibility. Increasingly, there is global pressure to add tougher ethical regulation to existing regimes. This was evidenced by proposals by the International Federation of Accountants in 2007 to add tougher restrictions and even fee-setting to the International Code. This pre-dates the current economic crisis which highlighted complex investment instruments and practices such as fair-value accounting. Inevitably, there will be growing political pressure on governments to make law to regulate financial practices.

Legal and disciplinary frameworks do provide an effective means of challenging serious wrong-doing. They can provide deterrents to bad practice, through punishment and censure and remedies for some of the damage that results, for example by means of compensation. However, these means of controlling behaviour set the threshold for what amounts to unacceptable accounting practice at a fairly high level. The reasons for this is that punishing or imposing a financial obligation on an individual through law should only be done where it is necessary and where there is an objective proof of wrong-doing.

Thus, relying solely on the law and disciplinary frameworks to 'police' accounting ethics is not the most desirable way of preventing and detecting undesirable practices. Moreover, even when they are deployed, they are not always very effective. The sophistication required to prove that financial judgements have been made in bad faith or negligently, and the time and the cost involved in finding and managing evidence is considerable. This explains the comparatively low level of successful legal and disciplinary action reported.

Nevertheless, the effectiveness of any system of accounting needs to be based on the impartial and sound judgement being exercised by the accountant. This means that professionalism and ethical behaviour are vital to the role itself. The very word 'accountant' tells the story. An accountant is there to say things as they are, to present variances, activities and so on as objectively as possible, so that managers can make decisions based on real information. Any factors which influence an accountant in such a way as to jeopardise the objectivity of the accounts they produce will distort internal judgements about the management of the organisation.

Because there are always choices in the way in which accounting information is prepared and presented, and because of the close working relationship between managers, whose performance is measured or reflected in accounting reports, there are numerous temptations to present a particular bias and many other factors that might influence the professional judgement of management accountants. The exercise of good judgement is a fundamental attribute of a competent accountant. An example of such a problem was highlighted during a CIMA roadshow (reported by Danielle Cohen in the May 2007 issue of *Financial Management*):

> [The accountant] CI has been the finance director of his company – a clothing retailer – for ten years. He's responsible for the financial accounts and has identified some slow-moving stock that's over nine months old, which would usually be written down. The shareholders are trying to sell the firm and the managing director (the majority shareholder) has told him that it's not necessary to write down the stock this time. CI is sure that this is because the managing director wants to inflate the stock valuation. The managing director has found a prospective buyer and has indicated to CI that, if the deal is done, all employees will keep their jobs and CI will receive a pay rise.

In this real life example, as well as the pressure from the manager on the accountant to comply, there appears to be moral value in doing the wrong thing (saving people's jobs) as well as a personal incentive of a pay rise. However, misrepresenting the value of stock would be a threat to the integrity of the accountant, and also threatens the financial viability of the enterprise in the longer term. Resolving these issues is sometimes taxing and complex. Often it is simply a question of accepting that there is a right way to act and a wrong way. Understanding the standards for professional behaviour and also having the skills to identify where difficult questions of ethical conflict arise and how to address them are both areas of required professional knowledge.

In order to help the management accountant in his or her day-to-day role, CIMA has followed the approach of many professions in preparing a Code of Ethics, which seeks to help management accountants identify common areas where ethical pressures may exist; the sort of pressures which might compromise independent and sound decision-making. The Code is there to help the accountant analyse those situations and provide a recommended course of action for their resolution.

The ability to identify, explain and resolve or address ethical problems is now regarded as being a core competence that the student of management accounting needs to have a firm grasp of. It is now explicitly tested by CIMA in order to satisfy the profession of the student's suitability to practice. For the member of CIMA, departure from ethical standards is a disciplinary matter.

So what then do we mean by ethics? The ethics of a profession can be simply the description of the prevailing standards of ethical behaviour. It would be a matter of fact to see whether CIMA members behave in an ethical way. There is some evidence to suggest that CIMA members do view their behaviour as informed by ethical standards. A recent survey of members by CIMA and IBE showed that over half of the accountants (59%) saying they contribute to their organisations' ethical performance, with 73% believing that ethical performance will become a formal part of their role in the next few years. The majority of those surveyed said that they contribute to the ethics of the company by 'upholding their professional code of ethics', 'ensuring the integrity of management information' and 'leading by example'. Such a view would suggest that the ethics of accounting, at least as far as CIMA is concerned, is increasingly healthy and that ethics are increasingly part of the role.

However, the purpose of this syllabus is not to determine how well accountants do perform the ethical dimension of their roles, but for the student to discover, learn and be committed to determining what their behaviour should be, Ethics reflect principles and ideals of behaviour that ought to be adhered to, rather than merely describing and conforming to current professional practice. In short, just because everybody bends the rules *in practice*, does not mean that they *should* do so. The concern of the CIMA Code of practice on ethics is to reflect how the profession ought to behave in the future and how its professionalism can be improved or maintained.

Ethics is therefore a matter of what we ought to do. 'Ethics' is often used interchangeably with the term 'morals.' However, there is an important difference between them. Both concern questioning what is the right thing to do in a problem situation. Morals resolve problems with reference to the individual's personal belief system about what might be right or wrong. They are linked to the safety valve of personal conscience, and may additionally be linked to religious or other convictions.

Personal, religious, political or other morality is not directly relevant to a system of professional ethics. While all effective systems of professional ethics have a significant overlap with moral systems, just because an individual believes a course of action to be morally wrong does not mean that it is ethically wrong. Equally, you may consider an act to be morally justifiable or even desirable, but it may not accord with the ethics of your profession.

In the preceding example, the finance director might feel that he has a moral duty to keep his colleagues employed and sees nothing wrong at all with enjoying a personal benefit from doing so. However, following his own conscience at the expense of professional standards would nonetheless amount to a breach of professional ethics.

Another example might be where a management accountant is aware of confidential figures relating to the performance of an area under threat of redundancy. They are also aware of the amount of money being spent on corporate hospitality. Morally, that accountant may think it is reprehensible that the organisation is making people redundant while their senior directors are enjoying lavish perks. A person might feel that it is their moral duty to make this known. However, that would certainly be a breach of confidentiality, which would be breach of professional ethics (as well as breach of the terms of employment).

This doesn't mean that ethical rules are a substitute for moral action. An individual is always free to protest against management acts they feel are immoral, can resign or do whatever their conscience dictates, however there is likely to be a professional consequence. Moreover, an accountant who resigns may feel that they are no longer morally compromised, but may leave the professional issue unresolved and this may be no different in ethical terms than turning a blind eye. Acting in accordance with your conscience is often the harder route than swallowing your conscience. Acting in accordance with the ethics of your profession does not arrogate to you the claim to be personally right, but also gives you the objective claim that you are following the standards of your profession and, as such the law will accord additional protection if you protest against actions by your employer that you feel are unethical.

Indeed it is relatively unusual for there to be a conflict between moral judgement and professional ethical duty. Sometimes they go hand in hand. More often, however the situations that give rise to ethical difficulties are ones that simply do not give rise to moral objection as well; they may be morally ambiguous or indeed they may seem to be the normal type of problem that you face from day to day which you perceive as being morally neutral. It used to be thought that you could identify ethical conflicts if you felt the pricking of your conscience, but conscience is not a sure fire way of detecting ethical problems.

But what is 'ethics', if it is not a question of moral behaviour? Simply, ethics could be stated as answering the question, 'what can *I* **do** for the *best*?' There are three key elements here.

1. 'I', because ethics are about your individual professional responsibility to act (as opposed to your liability if you get caught);
2. 'do', because ethics are about practical courses of action in the real world where things are not always about what you do but how you do them;
3. 'best', because ethics are not about doing what is right or wrong, but often involve making choices between courses of action, both of which might be unpalatable or give rise to problems.

Thus the CIMA Code of Ethics and the IFAC Code, which it substantially reflects, aim to (a) identify the nature of the personal responsibility that the management accountant takes on as part of the price for getting a reasonable salary and status; (b) provide guidance on how to identify the practical situations where particular care might need to be taken because of the ethical pitfalls involved; (c) provide general guidance on how to address those difficult questions.

Ethical reasoning is difficult because it involves practical reasoning, judgement and an invariable sense of professional values. Unlike most professional practices, it is not something that you can learn through practice, largely because significant ethical problems come up rarely and they don't get any easier to deal with. They do become easier to spot and avoid and you do become more confident in the steps you have to follow to find a resolution.

However, solving ethical problems is a bit like being blindfolded and then turned around and around. The first problem is to get a sense of direction. Most ethical systems start off with the idea that because ethics are doing things for the best, a person does need to have some motivation to do whatever the best is.

The famous philosopher and founder of most modern ethical thinking, Emmanuel Kant, called this 'the good will.' You cannot solve ethical problems unless you start off with the motivation to do what is right, rather than simply doing what is convenient, personally gratifying or picking a solution at random. Being well-meaning provides a motivation, but the accountant needs more than the desire to be good.

However, indications are that although those who are attracted to accounting tend to be positively disposed towards ethical conduct, the traditional focus of the work and the effect of training are to desensitise accountants to ethical issues. The result is that 'the tendency of the evidence is to suggest, that accountants occupy the middle ground or lean towards amoral tendencies.' (Freeman, 1996). Kant's starting point of 'the good will' is nonetheless crucial to ethical behaviour. Without a positive motivation to do what is right, any ethical code is worthless.

An older and even more fundamentally important philosopher, Aristotle, suggested that the foundations of good ethical reasoning are laid by cultivating in people fundamental virtues. Essentially, if people value and practise honesty, integrity and openness, not only will they want to do what is best, but they will have the fundamental ethical compass. The CIMA Code of Ethics starts with this same approach.

In order to make sound ethical judgements that will form the basis of robust business information, an accountant needs to have a 'professional attitude' which displays 'professional attributes.' Subscribing and internalising professional values is at the heart of ethical decision-making in accounting.

Example

Imagine you are faced with a choice between either presenting information that may compromise your manager's-claims to super-efficiency in his section or obscuring the facts.

- If your motivation when preparing a report is simply to earn money for yourself and to please your manager, you will be tempted to obscure the facts.
- If your motivation is to be honest, transparent and act with integrity, you will be driven in the other direction.

Values and personal attributes are decisive in this case, as in many cases. This is why, in addition to the framework approach to ethical behaviour, the CIMA Code starts out with statements about the essential attributes of a professional accountant.

These are laid out in Section 100.4.

Fundamental Principles

100.4 A professional accountant is required to comply with the following fundamental principles:

(a) Integrity

A professional accountant should be straightforward and honest in all professional and business relationships.

(b) Objectivity

A professional accountant should not allow bias, conflict of interest or undue influence of others to override professional or business judgements.

(c) Professional Competence and Due Care

A professional accountant has a continuing duty to maintain professional knowledge and skill at the level required to ensure that a client or employer receives competent professional service based on current developments in practice, legislation and techniques. A professional accountant should act diligently and in accordance with applicable technical and professional standards when providing professional services.

(d) Confidentiality

A professional accountant should respect the confidentiality of information acquired as a result of professional and business relationships, and should not disclose any such information to third parties without proper and specific authority unless there is a legal or professional right or duty to disclose. Confidential information acquired as a result of professional and business relationships should not be used for the personal advantage of the professional accountant or third parties.

(e) Professional Behaviour

A professional accountant should comply with relevant laws and regulations and should avoid any action that discredits the profession.

By 'fundamental' it is meant that these form the very foundations of reasoning and professional practice. The accountant should therefore not only know them, but use them as tools of reasoning and decision-making when judging their own work and that of fellow-professionals. Alongside checking the technical competence of a piece of work, the management accountant should ask, for example 'am I being objective and impartial in the way I am presenting these figures?'

Because they are fundamental, they merit further, deeper explanation, which you will find later on in this chapter. However, to sum up: CIMA has produced a Code of Ethics that states the fundamental values that accountants should work by, and a framework by which they can put these into practice in challenging practical situations, where there may be more than one course of action which may have undesirable consequences. For the time being, we need to understand the different tools available for regulating ethical behaviour.

6.2 Regulations, legislation, guidelines, codes and other standards: what do they all mean?

Learning Outcome:	Explain the need for a framework of laws, regulations and standards in business and their application.

Earlier, in section 6.1, it was pointed out that external policing of mandatory obligations is not always the most effective way of regulating professional behaviour. It certainly is not the most effective way of promoting best practice, since legislation and legal rules tend to provide sanctions for those who dip below minimum standards of acceptable behaviour, rather than laying down normal standards for professional behaviour or a framework for improving and promoting the best standards in the profession.

However, there is a complex relationship between legal and ethical duties because often they are dealing with different consequences of the same behaviour or more or less serious examples of behaviour that are to be discouraged. Thus, management accounting ethics can be regarded as being controlled and directed by a variety of means with a variety of consequences for a variety of purposes.

The following table indicates the broad differences in the approaches. Note that each does different things and that they are overlapping. It is not simply a case that breach of the criminal law is more serious than breach of ethical guidance.

The combination of legal frameworks, regulations, guidelines and standards for business provide guidance on a whole range of behaviours. They exist for individuals, and collective bodies to adhere to, and are a means of engendering public confidence in the profession, as well as making it beneficial in economic and social terms. These standards are administered through and by regulatory bodies (often policing duties laid down for the profession by Acts of Parliament), and the accountancy profession (which sets its own standards in addition to statutory duties).

In the United Kingdom, the ethical lead for financial reporting has been taken by the Financial Reporting Council (FRC). The FRC is the United Kingdom's independent regulator for corporate reporting and governance, with the aim of promoting confidence in these areas.

Two further bodies forming part of the FRC are the Professional Oversight Board (POB) and the Audit Practices Board (APB). Each has a number of stated objectives, but they include an oversight and review function on ethical matters.

1. *The Professional Oversight Board for Accountancy*
   In relation to the regulation of the accountancy profession, the Board intends to achieve its aims by:
   - Reviewing the regulatory activities of the professional accountancy bodies in relation to their members, including education, training, continuing professional development, standards, ethical matters (except those which are the responsibility of the APB), professional conduct and discipline, registration and monitoring, including making recommendations on how these activities might be improved.

   www.frc.org.uk/poba/about/

Different approaches to controlling ethical behaviour

Approach	Deals with	Created by	Format	Enforced by	Consequence	Purpose
Criminal law (e.g. fraud laws)	Direct and serious threat to the public or to public administration	National authorities through Parliament or court	Acts of Parliament, Principles in court cases	Police, Statutory, regulators	Fine, Imprisonment, Confiscation of assests	To deter, protect and stigmatise
Civil law (e.g. professional negligence laws)	Damage or loss caused to other members of society Failure to comply with legal duties that have been voluntarily assumed (e.g. breaking a contract)	National authorities through Parliament of court	Acts of Parliament, Principles in court cases	Lawsuits initiated by injured parties	Compensation, Compulsion to comply with legal obligations and enforceable agreements	To undo damage or to compensate where someone has not met their legal obligations to other private members of society
Regulations	Anything where further detail of actual practice needs to be spelled out	National authorities through Parliament, regulatory bodies or professional bodies	Rules made under powers stated in Acts of Parliament	Regulatory body or professional body	Anything from fine, through compensation to professional disciplinary hearing	To provide detailed rules of practice specific to a particular activity
Codes of practice	Guidance on how to undertake tasks as a practitioner	Regulatory or professional bodies	Guidance, rules, examples and principles	Regulatory or professional body or self-enforced	Disciplinary or development	To provide working guidance on how to perform tasks

2. *The Auditing Practices Board*
   The Board intends to achieve its aims by:
   - Establishing Auditing Standards which set out the basic principles and essential procedures with which external auditors in the United Kingdom and the Republic of Ireland are required to comply;
   - Issuing guidance on the application of Auditing Standards in particular circumstances and industries, and by providing timely guidance on new and emerging issues;
   - Establishing Standards and related guidance for accountants providing assurance services;
   - Establishing Ethical Standards in relation to the independence, objectivity and integrity of external auditors and those providing assurance services;
   - Taking an appropriate role in the development of statutes, regulations and accounting standards which affect the conduct of auditing and assurance services, both domestically and internationally;
   - Contributing to efforts to advance public understanding of the roles and responsibilities of external auditors and the providers of assurance services, including the sponsorship of research.

   www.frc.org.uk/apb/about/aims.cfm

   In addition to the FRC and those forming the FRC there is also the International Federation of Accountants.
3. *The International Federation of Accountants*
   The International Federation of Accountants (IFAC) reviews the profession worldwide and in June 2005 published a Code of Ethics.
   - This Code of Ethics establishes ethical requirements for professional accountants.

   www.ifac.org

The framework of laws, regulations and standards are applied to the accountancy profession by the bodies mentioned above, and through matters brought to their attention by professional firms. They test the efficacy of the framework through consultation with interested parties (professional firms and others) and review the professional accountancy bodies' practices.

The CIMA Code of Ethics takes what is called a 'framework-based' approach. What is meant by this is that it does not simply provide a list of 'thou shallt not' commands, but rather provides steps to identify, explain and problem-solve. It is an acceptance that just saying what you should not do in general theory is not always very helpful when dealing with immediate practical problems. The Framework Approach is common in the accounting profession because it helps practitioners, rather than merely directing them.

There are two categories of framework. The first is legally binding and therefore is mandatory on all governed by them to comply. The second is voluntary in nature, where it is good or best practice to follow the guidelines/standards and to adhere to them as well. Either way, the professional accountant needs to know and understand them all.

While breach of an ethical framework may not, of itself, give rise to a legal consequence, it may be taken as evidence of something more serious, such as negligence in failing to comply with standards to be expected of a reasonably competent professional.

A further source of guidelines and standards with which the professional accountant must be aware is the working practices pertaining to their place of employment (perhaps embodied in an Office Manual or Approved Procedures). A majority of large corporate entities and a number of smaller companies now have codes of ethics giving guidance to company personnel as to expected levels of behaviour of their staff.

6.3 Isn't ethics simply a question of knowing the rules and sticking to them?

> *Learning Outcome*: Explain the nature of ethics and its application, identifying the difference between rules-based and framework approaches to ethics.

In law, there is a distinction sometimes made between 'formal' and 'actual' compliance. Formal compliance means following the letter of the law, staying just inside it, but doing no more than the minimum required to keep out of trouble. Actual compliance means seeking to achieve the underlying purpose, which often means going beyond the minimum necessary.

There has been a change in public and private attitudes to the performance of duties over the last 25 years that has moved against the idea of just doing what you can get away with towards continually striving to do the right thing. It is mirrored in the changes in management accounting trends from variance accounting, through activity-based to lean accounting. In management, it is reflected in the idea of performance management, rather than the management of labour. In public life, it is reflected in the change from a culture of trust and deference to those with authority, to a requirement for standards in public life and accountability.

The management accountant finds him or herself pushed by all three strands. Trends in management accounting look towards a more transparent approach to representing the life cycle of accounts. As an employee, the accountant is not there just to do a job and go home, but to do it well and continually improve. Ultimately, whether or not the accountant is employed in the public sector, the role of the accountant is to perform a public function in providing the truthful and independent account of finances that will be the basis of judgements by owners, shareholders, regulators, the government and so on.

The publicly employed accountant is explicitly subject to the 'The Seven Principles of Public Life' issued by the 'Committee of Standards in Public Life', which arose out of the perceived crisis in public ethics of the 1990s in the United Kingdom. They are reflected to a great extent in the professional standards for all accountants.

Selflessness
Holders of public office should act solely in terms of the public interest. They should not do so in order to gain financial or other benefits for themselves, their family or their friends.

Integrity
Holders of public office should not place themselves under any financial or other obligation to outside individuals or organisations that might seek to influence them in the performance of their official duties.

Objectivity
In carrying out public business, including making public appointments, awarding contracts, or recommending individuals for rewards and benefits, holders of public office should make choices on merit.

Accountability
Holders of public office are accountable for their decisions and actions to the public and must submit themselves to whatever scrutiny is appropriate to their office.

Openness
Holders of public office should be as open as possible about all the decisions and actions that they take. They should give reasons for their decisions and restrict information only when the wider public interest clearly demands.

Honesty
Holders of public office have a duty to declare any private interests relating to their public duties and to take steps to resolve any conflicts arising in a way that protects the public interest.

Leadership
Holders of public office should promote and support these principles by leadership and example.

Given the trends towards less trust and more desire for accountability, it is therefore of little surprise that management accountants are now expected to do more than merely follow the rules.

Rules tend to be characterised by three things:

1. In theory, you are either inside a rule (compliant) or have broken it. This sometimes provides a harsh divide which is often more about the precise interpretation of the rule than the human activity it regulates;
2. Because of these attempts to make sharp distinctions in rules (so people know where the boundaries of self-preservation lie), there is always argument about the precise meaning of rules;
3. Rules require enforcement by an objective party to decide on things like interpretation and to ensure that breach of the rule has a consequence.

These factors make rules expensive, the source of contention and inflexible. Moreover, in ethics, rules seldom are capable of encompassing the rather difficult questions about behaviour that are involved, without becoming incredibly complicated. The Code-based approach blends the mandatory requirement to take account of the Code with a principles or values-based approach.

This approach is illustrated well by the way in which the following extract from the CIMA 'Code of Ethics' discusses threats and safeguards regarding compliance.

100.12 Safeguards created by the profession, legislation or regulation include, but are not restricted to:

- Educational, training and experience requirements for entry into the profession.
- Continuing professional development requirements.
- Corporate governance regulations.
- Professional standards.
- Professional or regulatory monitoring and disciplinary procedures.
- External review by a legally empowered third party of the reports, returns, communications or information produced by a professional accountant.

100.13 Parts B and C of this Code, respectively, discuss safeguards in the work environment for professional accountants in public practice and those in business.

100.14 Certain safeguards may increase the likelihood of identifying or deterring unethical behaviour. Such safeguards, which may be created by the accounting profession, legislation, regulation or an employing organisation include, but are not restricted to:

- Effective, well publicised complaints systems operated by the employing organisation, the profession or a regulator, which enable colleagues and members of the public to draw attention to unprofessional or unethical behaviour.
- An explicitly stated duty to report breaches of ethical requirements.

100.15 The nature of the safeguards to be applied will vary depending on the circumstances. In exercising professional judgement, a professional accountant should consider what a reasonable and informed third party, having knowledge of all relevant information, including the significance of the threat and the safeguards applied, would conclude to be unacceptable.

Thus, because rules are not particularly effective on their own, and because the profession would rather operate on the basis of trust and professional reputation than be policed by some other body, a framework approach to ethics aimed at helping the individual accountants to 'self-police' or more accurately to 'self-regulate' has been put forward. Self-regulation is at the heart of the reason for following a framework approach.

But self-regulation is based upon trust. That accountants are acting in the interests of all concerned is no longer a given. The choice in ensuring that accountants are compliant is stark. They can evince standards that show evidently that they are trustworthy and work with integrity, in which case they are likely to be trusted. They can be open and involve stakeholders voluntarily so that trust is further engendered. They can build a reputation for 'doing the right thing.' The aim of framework approaches is to encourage trust and confidence because professionals are acting professionally.

The failure of accountants to act ethically and the failure of the accounting profession and its leaders to have in place an effective means of prevention of unethical practices is leading to a trend internationally, whereby accountants have to demonstrate that they are working in accordance with good practice and ultimately are subject to rules, the breach of which results in the imposition of penalties.

This journey has been reinforced by many corporate scandals over the years, of which the recent banking collapses are only the latest. These have undermined the faith that the public have in financial institutions and indeed the whole ethos of the market-based economy. In the United Kingdom, there were scandals such as Maxwell, Polly Peck, Barings and BA in the 1990s. In the United States, in the early years of the twenty-first century, there have been such scandals as Enron, WorldCom and Tyco. In Europe, during the same period there was Parmalat and Ahold, whilst in the Far East there was Daewoo and Mitsubishi Motors. There have been many other instances worldwide where individuals have lived by double standards which has not made public news. In nearly all instances, though, the misapplication or ignoring of ethical values has been at the root of the scandal.

Such scandals provide a learning opportunity for others by helping to identify where a conflict of interest can lead to, or how an uncorrected mis-statement can lead, and how the misuse of privileged information and the exercise of undue influence can disadvantage vulnerable customers and clients. The scandals also emphasise the importance of managing non-financial impacts.

Having clear ethical values will set the cultural tone of a company, particularly where they are embedded. To do so needs leadership and example from the top, and guidance and training for all staff on expected behaviours. Through doing this, the values will become part of the company's DNA. This is then a backdrop for all its business. The strategy for business growth is set in this light, as are the company's corporate responsibility policies. There is clear evidence, most recently reflected by research by Microsoft, that companies with a clear sense of ethical direction are ones that will ride out the recession and

A professional body has an overriding commitment as a Chartered Institute in the United Kingdom to protect the public interest. It, therefore, has agreed an ethics code based on principles and ethics as specific guidance for members in business and practice as to 'how they will behave in carrying out their role.' This leads to reinforcing the culture and behaviour expectations of everyone working in the profession. It is on this that reputations are built and trust engendered. Compliance is a mechanism for reporting to others how the profession is measuring up to those expectations.

This can be demonstrated in the following table, contrasting the characteristics of a compliance-driven framework versus one primarily driven by values, principles and ethics.

Feature	Ethics	Compliance (Rules)
Objective	Prevention	Detection
Approach	Principles based	Law based
Motivation	Values driven	Fear driven
Standards	Implicit	Explicit
Measure	Principles (values)	Rules
Choices	Judgement	Obedience/disobedience
Enforceability	Discretionary	Mandatory

An example of applying the different approaches above would be a company which has a strong rules-based culture, where individuals clearly have a sense of what they can and cannot do (letter of the law, black and white, mandatory, explicit) and what will happen if they do not (fear-driven, requires obedience, mandatory). However, if an employee is faced with a situation not covered by the 'rule book' they will be required to use their own judgement as to what to do. In most instances, the decision they take will be the right one but any potential for the wrong decision being made will be reduced if the employee has guiding values and principles which will underpin that difficult decision-making. So, an ethical framework of guidance is likely to be more wide-ranging in its applicability than a fully rules-based one.

A key aspect of compliance is measurement in addition to 'ticking boxes' that all is well. This, of course, is difficult with ethical issues which tend not to be conveniently black and white. There is therefore a need to develop and use proxy indicators by those assuring themselves that individuals are acting in a proper fashion.

In a wider context, the same is true in the public and private sectors, where organisations equally, as though they were individuals, seek to build trust with their employees, customers, suppliers, shareholders and all others who have a legitimate interest in how they perform.

But the essential question remains: Is trust better engendered by principled behaviour based on 'doing it because it is the right thing to do' or because the individual, the company or the public body has to?

6.4 The CIMA and IFAC 'Codes of Ethics for Professional Accountants'

Learning Outcome: Explain the reasons why CIMA and IFAC each have a 'Code of Ethics for Professional Accountants'.

It should be clear from the discussion above that the professions themselves have a responsibility in taking a lead and that if they fail to provide robust and comprehensive guidance, the government may be tempted to step in with a more stringent rule-based approach (as happened in the Financial Services sector).

In June 2005, IFAC published their Code of Ethics for Professional Accountants which was prepared by the Ethics Committee of the International Federation of Accountants. That Committee was charged with developing and issuing *high-quality ethical standards and other pronouncements for professional accountants around the world*. This reflected what has been seen as a growing crisis of confidence in accounting ethics internationally, following financial scandals with global implications.

In 2006, the CIMA 'Code of Ethics for Professional Accountants' was launched, Based on IFAC's Code for Professional Accountants, reflecting the contribution CIMA made to the preparation of the IFAC Code. The CIMA Code reflects the standards CIMA expects of its members and students. It is aligned with global standards across the profession.

CIMA has its own Code reflecting its status as a Chartered Institute and as a basis for any complaints or cases under CIMA's disciplinary procedures. It follows very closely the IFAC Code and in places is identical. However, the guidance on the resolution of ethical problems must be followed, as must the reflection of values.

This does not give rise to a tick-list per se, because the requirements of the Code are to continually practice in a certain way, rather than to do particular things or follow a specific process. It sets out aspirations and standards of general behaviour and attitude for the professions, in consequence of which it still has more in common with guidance principles than rules.

The Code itself is split into three parts with a list of definitions at the end:

Part A – General Applications of the Code

This covers an introduction and the fundamental principles of integrity, objectivity, professional competence and due care, confidentiality and professional behaviour.

Part B – Professional Accountants in Public Practice

This covers particular issues identified as being of relevance to accountants in public practice such as professional appointment, conflicts of interest, second opinions, fees and other types of remuneration, marketing professional services, gifts and hospitality, custody of client assets, objectivity in all services and independence in assurance engagements.

Part C – Professional Accountants in Business

This covers issues such as potential conflicts, preparation and reporting of information, acting with sufficient expertise, financial interests and inducements.

The Code establishes ethical requirements for professional accountants and applies to all member firms or bodies of IFAC. Any such firm or body *may not apply less stringent standards than those stated in this Code.*

There is an override, should any firm or body be prohibited by law or regulation in complying with any parts of the Code. The expectation is that all parts of IFAC Code will be complied with otherwise. Professional accountants need to familiarise themselves with any differences if there are any, but to comply with the more sstringent requirements and guidance unless prohibited.

6.5 Personal development and life-long learning

Learning Outcome:	Identify the need for continual personal improvement and life-long learning based on an understanding of virtues of reliability, timeliness, courtesy and respect.

Every professional person has a duty in maintaining their role of acting in public interest by keeping themselves up to date professionally, that is technically as well developing their competencies to be better informed. It is also essential in a dynamic area of practice, where failure to keep oneself aware of developments may fundamentally undermine basic professional competence and leave the accountant open to accusations of negligence.

This has grown in importance as the pace of change develops and the role of the professional accountant grows more complex. It is now regarded as one of the fundamental principles in the CIMA 'Code of Ethics' (see Appendix for the complete code), where *the professional accountant has the duty to maintain professional knowledge and skill at the level required to ensure that a client or employer receives competent professional service based on current developments in practice, legislation and techniques.*

The concept of competent professional service is thus based not only on attaining professional competence but also in maintaining it. This requires a continuing awareness of up-to-date developments in the profession. This can be met through continuing professional development. CIMA has developed the CIMA Professional Development framework which addresses both the requirements on members and the institute regarding CPD, and the ways in which CIMA is supporting members in their professional development.

For example, the public expectation is that all accountants are 'up to speed all the time' which requires commitment from all those in the profession. This is because the issues a professional faces do change over time. For instance, given the rapid advance in technology, returns may be filed electronically putting greater emphasis on professional review. In matters of security of customer/client data, where confidential information is transferred via e-mail, there is always the potential for that information to be corrupted if the computer system does not have up-to-date firewall and virus protection and so forth.

In areas of public service, there are increasing developments in the way in which information is made available to the public and in transparent costing processes. Similarly, in the private sector, the way in which data and private commercial and financial information is constantly evolving as are the means by which this is regulated.

6.5.1 Personal qualities

Members of the profession need, or need to develop, certain qualities and virtues in order to meet the expectations of CIMA and the public, served in the wider context. In upholding the highest standards of ethical behaviour, members are contributing to the promotion of the integrity of CIMA's qualification and supporting CIMA's purpose.

The underlying reason has been explained earlier, in the context of 'virtue ethics'. The professional attitude being encouraged provides the ethical compass and personal motivation to act in accordance with the values of the profession and to make ethically sound decisions in everyday practice.

The particular qualities and virtues sought are reliability, responsibility, timeliness, courtesy and respect. These are taken from International Education Standard for Accountants, published by IFAC *Values, Ethics & Attitudes*.

Reliability

This is the concept of being able to be trusted by others and to be dependable through the ability to deliver what and when it has been agreed with another. It is linked to the idea of providing a consistent approach to work, both in quality and in dependability. It is fairly clear that an unreliable accountant would almost certainly also be falling short of other basic standards of professional competence.

Responsibility

This is the concept of being accountable for one's actions and decisions. This also entails an individual's assumption of authority for making decisions. A responsible accountant addresses the decision-making processes that he needs to engage with and is willing and able to personally answer for those decisions. A management accountant is in a position of responsibility because he is being employed for his expertise in making professional judgements and will need to be able to explain and answer for their exercise to colleagues who may or may not share that expertise.

Timeliness

This is the concept of delivering in a timely manner without delay and meeting the expectations of others. The practical implications of poor time-keeping are self-evident, however there is a further reflection of the ethics of diligence in addressing tasks and responsibility in prioritising and managing work.

Courtesy

This is the virtue of demonstrating politeness and good manners towards others. While respect for clients and others is regarded as appropriate and professional, the increasing seriousness with which unacceptable forms of address (racist, sexist, homophobic and the like) are being tackled by law mean that it underpins a more fundamental set of societal values.

Respect

This is the virtue demonstrating an attitude of esteem, deference, regard or admiration of others in dealing with them, especially where their attitudes might differ. It is not to be mistaken for undue deference, merely that the accountant should listen to others, take account of their views and ideas, and if for no other reason then these may provide a broader base for making informed judgements.

Like a number of these qualities, it is easy to see reasons why respect might be practically useful and help avoid problems that might lead to sanction or censure, but the utility of respecting people is not the reason why you should respect them; it is not simply a case of respecting those who you think might have something useful to say, like each of these qualities they are aspects of professionalism to be cultivated for their own sake.

6.6 Ethical principles

The CIMA 'Code of Ethics' identifies five fundamental principles in Section 100.4: (see Appendix for the full code)

Learning Outcome:	Explain the ethical principles of integrity, objectivity, professional competence and due care, confidentiality and professional behaviour.

Fundamental Principles

A professional accountant is required to comply with the following fundamental principles:

1. Integrity
2. Objectivity
3. Professional competence and due care
4. Confidentiality
5. Professional behaviour.

6.6.1 Integrity

Integrity is a holistic term implying other values too. So, in addition to being straightforward and honest in all professional and business relationships, this principle implies fair dealing and truthfulness. It particularly relates to reporting where a false or misleading statement might be made, or provided without care or attention, or a report might omit information, or be obscure and dense such that the report becomes misleading.

Integrity also denotes an attitude of personal and professional consistency in the way in which the accountant acts. It may be denoted by things as simple as the way in which the accountant interacts with different people. If he or she shows an inclusive and open attitude to one colleague and is formal and distant with another, it may lead to the inference that he or she nurtures a professional bias. This would certainly undermine the perception of the individual's integrity. Similarly, if an individual is willing to compromise principles and values that he or the profession espouses, in order to avoid conflict or challenge, then this too would be the sort of inconsistency that may give rise to questions about integrity.

6.6.2 Objectivity

Objectivity is contrasted with subjectivity. Subjective decisions are taken from the point of view of the individual concerned, taking into account the things that matter to them. These considerations might be friendship, loyalty or the instinct for self-preservation. While these subjective considerations are vital to making life go on, they have no place in professional decision-making. The management accountant should assemble all the relevant information available, account for what is not available (rather than guessing), and base decisions only on that data and the guiding principles of the profession.

This is of course easier said than done, because in the exercise of professional judgement, personal decision-making is the key. The accountant needs to be ever-vigilant, questioning himself whether other factors, such as self-interest or personal preference, are guiding a decision. Objective decision-making is the true value of the accountant within the management process, but it will frequently expose the accountant to difficult situations because others may not always like what they hear or appreciate a dispassionate analysis of a situation.

It is important for students and members to avoid putting themselves in positions where they or their work could become compromised. This might be through bias, conflicts of interest or through the undue influence of others. In these types of situations, an individual's objectivity may be impaired.

The sorts of situation that could arise are numerous, from forming an illicit relationship that may cause embarrassment, to accepting lavish hospitality which is later used to influence behaviour. It is impracticable to define and prescribe all such situations, but students need to be aware of, and resist, any such potential compromises on their objectivity.

If a threat to objectivity is identified, safeguards should be considered and applied to eliminate or reduce the threat to an acceptable level. Such safeguards could include withdrawing from the engagement, introducing more supervision into the process, terminating the relationship giving rise to the threat, and discussing the issue with the higher management and those reviewing the governance of the client relationship.

6.6.3 Professional competence and due care

Professional competence implies knowledge, skill, diligent delivery and an awareness of all the relevant issues in performing tasks. The professional is expected to maintain the competence and their capabilities to act responsibly at all times through continuing professional development.

There is also an expectation of acting diligently, which encompasses acting in accordance with the requirements of an assignment carefully, thoroughly and on a timely basis. Due care covers the wider responsibility the professional accountant has to ensure that those working under their authority have the necessary skills and capabilities to do so, and in particular have the professional capacity and appropriate training and supervision.

In accordance with the other principles and virtues expected of a professional accountant, they should ensure that clients or employers are aware of limitations inherent in services being provided to them so as to avoid the misinterpretation of an expression of opinion as an assertion of fact.

6.6.4 Confidentiality

The professional accountant is bound by the principle of confidentiality in all that they do unless required by law, professional right or duty to disclose. Such confidentiality covers disclosing information outside the firm or employing organisation and using information for personal or third party gain. Confidentiality extends to situations in a social environment too, where the professional accountant should be alert to the possibility of inadvertent disclosure to a close friend or family member.

Confidentiality also extends after the end of a relationship between a professional accountant and a client or employer. The professional accountant may use prior experience but not prior information gained in a previous role. In the Code, in Section 140.7, instances are explained when it would be appropriate to disclose confidential information, such as the requirement to produce documents as evidence in the course of legal proceedings.

The following are circumstances where professional accountants are or may be required to disclose confidential information or when such disclosure may be appropriate:

(a) Disclosure is permitted by law and is authorised by the client or the employer;

An example of this might be personal data. Personal data held by an accountant (for example, bank details of an individual) is covered by the Data Protection Act 1998. This gives rise to particular responsibility on the accountant to maintain that data accurately and not to disclose it, except for the purposes it was disclosed. There are, however, some exceptions. One important one is that the person to whom that data pertains may have been given an authorisation for disclosure to third parties for marketing purposes. This would still need authorisation by the employer, but falls within the category of permissible disclosure.

(b) Disclosure is required by law, for example:

(i) Production of documents or other provision of evidence in the course of legal proceedings – Numerous pieces of legislation allow investigative bodies, ranging from the Inland Revenue through to the police, the power to gain access to documents in the process of investigation. Strictly speaking, such access is limited to circumstances where the investigating agency has specific authorisation by a court, normally in the form of a warrant. In such circumstances, there is a duty to disclose which overrides any others.

(ii) Disclosure to the appropriate public authorities of infringements of the law that come to light – accountants are under some professional and ethical responsibility to disclose information which they believe tend to show illegal activity. This is a problematic area because such disclosures frequently run in the face of what an employer considers to be a duty of trust and confidence. A misplaced belief that an employer is doing wrong, which leads to an unauthorised disclosure will often end up as an acrimonious employment dispute.

The Public Interest Disclosure Act in the United Kingdom provides a means by which these two issues can be balanced. The accountant should first draw their manager's attention to the wrongdoing, or if it is inappropriate in the circumstances, a senior manager's attention may be drawn to it. If there is no adequate response or there is serious malfeasance which the accountant believes may be 'covered up', they may alert a professional body or an agency such as the police. Going to press is a risky and inadvisable course of action and carries with it few of the protections that are offered to those disclosing to professional bodies. In such circumstances, it is advisable to contact CIMA's Ethics Support Line.[1] Uk members and students of CIMA can contact the whistleblowing Advice the for advice on whether and how to make a public interest disclosure. CIMA's Ethics Helpline can help any member or student facing an ethical conflict.

(c) There is a professional duty or right to disclose, when not prohibited by law:

(i) To comply with the quality review of a member body or professional body;
(ii) To respond to an inquiry or investigation by a member body or regulatory body;
(iii) To protect the professional interests of a professional accountant in legal proceedings; or
(iv) To comply with technical standards and ethics requirements.

All these examples in (c), above, relate to the regulation and disciplinary functions of CIMA and the profession more generally. It is important that disclosures are not only those necessary for the achievement of purpose of the inquiry but that they also cover all relevant aspects of the subject matter being inquired into. Partial disclosure is tantamount to deception and may give rise to disciplinary or legal penalties or consequences.

Disclosure is generally a question of professional discretion, as much as the application of rules. In identifying whether confidential information can be disclosed, it is necessary to consider whether any parties would be harmed by such disclosure, whether all relevant information is known and substantiated, and the type of disclosure and to whom it is to be made. Once again, being well-intended when disclosing or not disclosing is part of the pavement to perdition.

6.6.5 Professional behaviour

Every professional accountant needs to be mindful that their behaviour will not bring the profession and CIMA into disrepute. The profession defines this as including *actions which a reasonable and informed third party, having knowledge of all relevant information, would conclude negatively affects the good reputation of the profession.*

It is to be remembered as Benjamin Franklin once said 'Glass, china and reputations are easily cracked and never well mended'. It is a constant challenge to management to maintain a good reputation. Without it, an organisation be it a professional body, a company or public sector body will become demoralised. Staff will not take pleasure in their work, the better qualified and able ones will leave and a downward spiral may develop. In addition, customers may be lost, the ability to raise finance made more difficult, and perhaps the 'licence to operate' from society also lost with many other consequences too.

6.7 Concepts of independence, accountability and responsibility

Learning Outcome:	Identify key concepts of independence, accountability and social responsibility.

6.7.1 Independence

It is in the public interest, and required in CIMA's 'Code of Ethics' that members of assurance engagement teams and their firms (and when applicable extended network firms too) be independent of the assurance clients.

There are two key attributes to independence used in connection with the assurance engagement:

1. *Of mind*

It is required that the professional accountant has a state of mind that permits a conclusion to be expressed without being affected by influences that would compromise their professional judgement. This allows the individual to act with integrity and exercise objectivity and professional scepticism. Bias is an insidious thing, and sometimes we are not fully aware of the influencing factors on our mind. Second opinions of close judgement calls can often help, but the accountant is ultimately responsible for his or her decisions. Keeping a clear, professional attitude and focusing on objective information, rather than over-relying on intuitions is a useful means of maintaining some independence of mind.

2. *In appearance*

This is a test reliant on the view that a reasonable and informed third party would conclude that a member of the assurance team's integrity, objectivity or professional scepticism was compromised if significant facts and circumstances were avoided or overlooked. The accountant often exercises judgements that have impacts on people's jobs, pay and progression. It is therefore of paramount importance that the exercise of professional judgement not only be just, but manifestly and undoubtedly be seen to be so.

It is impossible to define all situations where independence might be compromised, so it is in the public interest to prepare a conceptual framework requiring firms and member of assurance teams to identify, evaluate and address threats to independence. This can be based on identifying relationships between all the parties. For any threats so identified, safeguards can be introduced to eliminate or significantly reduce them to an acceptable level.

6.7.2 Accountability

The concept of accountability is that of the professional accountant being responsible to someone and for some thing or an action, and being able to explain those actions. It is an important aspect of the profession and of leadership in the wider business environment.

It is acknowledged that the professional accountant through CIMA, as a Chartered Institute, is accountable to the public in performing a public interest duty. That accountability is monitored by the FRC in the United Kingdom through the Professional Oversight Board for Accountancy (POBA) and the Accounting Standards Board (ASB).

Accountability is also to every client and employer too for whom the professional accountant is providing services. If that accountability fails then the client or employer can seek redress through complaint or disciplinary procedures.

6.7.3 Social responsibility

The professional accountant has a wider role in fulfilling their public duty, which is to be aware of their social or corporate responsibility. This is their role within the community, be it defined as their profession, their firm or place of work, where their place of work or home is located or howsoever the individual cares to define community.

Corporate Responsibility (CR) is the outward manifestation of an ethical policy. CR policies state the nature of the interaction between the company and its stakeholder base, employees, customers, suppliers and so forth (see Section 7.1.5). These CR policies need to be factored into risk management, which the better companies will report on in their reporting, internally and externally.

Many companies now prepare Social or Corporate Responsibility Reports for their shareholders and stakeholders. There are new methodologies developing to monitor non-financial impacts. Some CR activities can be measured, such as environmental impact, where a company can relatively easily evaluate its carbon footprint. But, evaluating ethical behaviour is more difficult and proxy indicators, such as staff turnover, may need to be used.

Typically, this is in relation to stakeholders listed as shareholders, employees, customers, suppliers and the wider community, to whom the company pays taxes and with whom it has a relationship as part of society. In upholding the principles of CIMA's 'Code of Ethics', the individual has a social responsibility to behave with integrity, courtesy, respect and with due care.

Revision Questions

Question 1

1.1 Which statement is true?

(A) Professional accountants are expected to have regard to the public interest in performing their duties.
(B) Professional accountants are not expected to have regard to the public interest in performing their duties.

1.2 Are these statements true or false?

(A) The Auditing Practices Board (APB) reviews the regulatory activities of the professional accounting bodies.
(B) The Professional Oversight Board for Accountancy (POB) is part of the Financial Reporting Council (FRC).
(C) 'The Seven Principles of Public Life' govern all professional accountants.
(D) The CIMA 'Code of Ethics' includes reference to how a professional accountant can raise a concern about unprofessional or unethical behaviour.

1.3 Which statement is true?

(A) Ethical values describe what an entity does, not how it does business.
(B) Ethical values describe how entity does its business, not what it does.

1.4 Are these statements true or false?

(A) An ethically based code is based on principles.
(B) A Compliance based code is a rules-based framework.
(C) A characteristic of a compliance based code is that it takes a tick box approach.
(D) A characteristic of an unethically based code is obeying the spirit of the law.
(E) Compliance with legislation is mandatory.
(F) Ethics is mandatory.

1.5 Which statement is true?

In order to provide competent professional service, CIMA requires an accountant to

(A) Attain professional competence.
(B) Attain and maintain professional competence.

1.6 Which statement is true?

(A) The five qualities and virtues sought by CIMA are reliability, accountability, fairness, responsibility and timeliness.
(B) The five qualities and virtues sought by CIMA are reliability, responsibility, timeliness, courtesy and respect.

1.7 Which statement is true?

(A) The professional accountant is not bound by the principles of confidentiality after the end of the relationship with a client or employer.
(B) The professional accountant is bound by the principles of confidentiality after the end of the relationship with a client or employer.

1.8 Which statement is true?

(A) Professional accountants are expected to exercise professional scepticism.
(B) Professional accountants are not expected to exercise professional scepticism.

1.9 Which statement is true?

(A) The IFAC code is mandatory for all member firms or bodies of IFAC.
(B) The IFAC code is a guide for all member firms or bodies of IFAC.

Questions 1.10–1.12 are reflective questions and should be discussed or thought over. Answers to these have not been provided.

1.10 Consider your work and, separately, everyday life. In what circumstances do you find the following compromised

(A) Objectivity.
(B) Courtesy.
(C) Confidentiality.
(D) The Appearance of Independence.
(E) Timeliness.

1.11 In relation to 2, above, consider whether each is because of:

(A) Something you have done.
(B) Something you have failed to do.
(C) Something you believe in.
(D) Something outside your control.
(E) Something you could have aided had your attitude to the situation been different.

1.12 Drawing on the discussions above, consider how and whether application of the ethical principles outlined might help you identify problems, and whether they might help you avoid them if you put them into practice.

Solutions to Revision Questions

Solution 1

1.1 Answer: (A)

Professional accountants, whether practicing in public or private practice have a leadership role and are expected to behave and act in the public interest. This is laid down in the Royal Chater which governs CIMA – the *Chartered Institute of Management Accountants.*

1.2 (A) False. The Professional Oversight Board for Accountancy reviews the regulatory activities of the professional accountancy bodies.
(B) True.
(C) False. The Seven Principles of Public Life apply to all holders of public office.
(D) True.

1.3 Answer: (B)

Ethical values describe how an entity does its business, not what it does.

1.4 (A) True.
(B) True.
(C) False. A characteristic of compliance is detection.
(D) True.
(E) True. Compliance with the law is mandatory.
(F) False. Ethics involves judgement as to behaviour.

1.5 Answer (B)

The concept of competent professional service is based not only on attaining professional competence but also in maintaining it.

1.6 Answer (B)

The five qualities and virtues by CIMA – reliability, responsibility, timeliness, courtesy and respect.

1.7 Answer (B)

The professional accountant continues to be bound by the principle of confidentiality.

1.8 Answer (A)

Professional accountants are expected to demonstrate independence of mind and exercise objectivity and professional scepticism.

1.9 Answer (A)

The IFAC code establishes ethical requirements for professional accountants and applies to all member firms or bodies of IFAC.

7

Ethical Conflict

Ethical Conflict

7

Learning Outcomes

After completing this chapter you should be able to:

- explain the relationship between ethics, governance, the law and social responsibility;
- describe the consequences of unethical behaviour to the individual, the profession and society;
- identify situations where ethical dilemmas and conflicts of interest occur and how they can be resolved.

7.1 The relationship between ethics, governance, the law and social responsibility

Learning Outcome:	Explain the relationship between ethics, governance, the law and social responsibility.

7.1.1 Ethical Codes vs Legislation

If the question of ethics is 'what to do for the best?' then the next natural question is 'why should I take responsibility for deciding what to do?' In effect, a key issue for all accountants is the linked questions of who should take responsibility for doing the right things and who picks up the pieces when it all goes wrong.

If there are problems of global or national significance that arise from a systematic failure, which in turn pressurises the individual into facing unpleasant choices, shouldn't the government or the profession step in to deal with the problem? The answer has to be 'yes.' This is why some aspects of professional conduct are regulated not by the profession, but by law. If the problem is too big or the temptations are too great or the professional body is too weak, then the law steps in. A classic example of this was the tightening of insider dealing laws in the 1980s; because of the signal failure of financial authorities to control their employees' use of advantageous privileged information.

Laws do not, of themselves, help you out of general ethical problems. For example, you might feel that it is unethical to obey an immoral law. However, such difficulties do not arise in management accounting. If there is a conflict between a professional duty, such as confidentiality, and statute law, the CIMA Code explicitly states that the law is to be preferred. In the hierarchy of obligations, law overrides everything.

7.1.2 Ethical Codes vs Contracts

But what about other legal obligations? Surely the contract you sign with your employer is a legal obligation and the contracts with clients have legal effects? Of course this is true. However, voluntarily assumed legal obligations are exactly that. You have made a choice to enter into tat obligation. You have a choice not to comply with a contractual obligation and take instead the penalty for breach of that contract. This might be the appropriate course of action when performing the contract would bring you into serious breach of the CIMA Code.

An example of where you might break with a contractual duty is where your employer instructed you to act in a way that is professionally unacceptable. Another might be where you are directed to follow a corporate policy that was devised to apply to general situations, but which you feel is inappropriate in a particular context because there are special ethical considerations.

From a purely ethical standpoint, if you are confronted by a choice of breach of professional ethics and a breach of your contract of employment, you are ultimately supposed to favour your profession over your employer.

This is easier said than done. Nobody wishes to directly confront the person who pays their wages, and refusal to do your job because of ethical conflict can sound very much like being uncooperative, idealistic, unrealistic or ill-disciplined. There is some small comfort to be had here. An employer who victimises a professional because of the professional's sense of duty to their profession and public is likely to be given little time by an Employment Tribunal, should you need to challenge them or should they dismiss you! The law will not enforce obligations that are unconscionable or contrary to public policy (the enforcement of a contract to force someone to breach their professional duty would easily fall into this category), but legal rights ultimately rely on the Employment Tribunal to enforce, rather than good faith.

However, most people consider that a problem that gets them into court is already a bigger problem than they wish to take on. Spotting the ethical problems before they turn into personal nightmares or planning to avoid them in the first place is obviously the most desirable course of action.

A different, but possibly equally difficult situation arises when you are expected to do something which is part of a contract with an outside client. Often, the management accountant has no direct relationship with the client. However, the repercussions of refusing to act in a certain way on your employer's client relationships can be considerable. Often, clients will simply take their business elsewhere, if they feel that your employer will not accommodate them. It may not cause a direct confrontation between you and your employer, but if clients won't work with your employer because of you, there is always the chance that you may feel that it is you who will be the first in line for redundancy!

Often, you will be trying to do the right thing, not for you, but for someone else. Resolving ethical conflict seldom has much more reward to the individual than the feeling that you know you have done the right thing. However, the accountant is not on his or her own. CIMA provides support for individuals faced with ethical conflict situations and the law 'helps' accountants and employers to make the right choice, often by imposing personal liability for the individual who acts unprofessionally or forces another to do so.

7.1.3 Corporate governance and responsibility

Life is getting easier for the ethical professional. Much more pressure is being directed at employers to subscribe to ethical values and practice at an corporate level. There is greater willingness to use the word 'ethics' within the context of business, which perhaps a few years ago was not the case. The 'ethical consumer' and the impact of corporate scandals have redirected corporate attentions to how they operate on an organisational level.

Increasingly, professional bodies, firms, companies and other types of organisations are producing values-based codes and building values into their corporate strategies. The first and foremost reason is that by stating its values, it is setting the tone of the business. It clearly states the standard expected of employees and it encourages a sense of pride and loyalty. It has great marketing value as well. The terms 'corporate responsibility' and 'social responsibility' have ceased to be words of challenge by external critics of corporate practice and have become part of mainstream management thinking. In this context, these organisational values are often ones that the professional can hitch his or her own ethical standards to in order to avoid the immediate conflict with employers.

Corporate values are important for giving guidance to staff about what the expectations an employer has of them with regard to their behaviour. They seek to ensure a consistency of conduct across the entity, including conduct that relates to personal probity and professionalism. This in turn underpins the risk management strategies of organisations. Consistent conduct will reduce the risk of someone behaving inappropriately and the organisation potentially suffering a 'hit' to its reputation and credibility. Such codes are often voluntary and will be monitored through a variety of means, such as assurance, audit, through employee surveys, development and performance reviews, exit interviews and so forth.

'Governance' on its own is a term in common use in many types of organisations, from companies to charities, schools, local authorities and the National Health Service in the United Kingdom. In the United Kingdom, it was developed by the Committee on the Financial Aspects of Corporate Governance in 1992 (the Cadbury Report) with a code of best practice attached. It was aimed at listed companies but looked especially at standards of corporate behaviour. It also referred to ethics.

Taken from the Committee on the Financial Aspects of Corporate Governance 1992 (the Cadbury Report). 'It is important that all employees should know what standards of conduct are expected of them. We regard it as good practice for boards of directors to draw up codes of ethics or statements of business practice and to publish them both internally and externally.'

Governance has come to denote the generic way that an organisation is run, with particular emphasis on accountability, integrity and in many instances risk management. There are clear lines of responsibility for ethics that lead directly to Board level, with corresponding penalties for Board members for malfeasance. It is not surprising therefore that ethical compromises are counted as risk factors in an increasing number of organisations.

'Social Responsibility' is another newly popular term in management. It refers to how an organisation manages its relationships in the wider community. The range of issues is broad and encompasses many aspects of the current political agenda. For instance: How 'green' is the organisation? How much recycling of waste and paper is undertaken? Is low energy lighting used in the offices? Does the organisation support the local community in providing mentors or reading assistants at the local school, for instance? There are many possibilities.

It has long been accepted that all organisations have responsibilities beyond their shareholders or paymasters. Nowadays, the broader community has been reclassified as potential stakeholders or groups to whom a corporation might owe responsibilities.

Many organisations seek to express their social responsibility policies by identifying their stakeholders, those people or bodies who have either a financial or interested/influential relationship with the entity. It is now seen as part of good governance to have such policies.

An organisation has two types of stakeholder. The first are those with a financial relationship with the body, if anything were to happen to that entity then these groups would suffer. This group includes the shareholders, the employees, customers and suppliers, and the community in the sense that the company pays its taxes to support the community, both at local and national level.

The second group are those with an interest in how the organisation behaves. They may actually have an influence (greater than the financial stakeholders at times) over the entity. This group includes the media, non-governmental organisations (NGOs), activist groups, competitors and even the regulator (unless it has power to set prices, when it becomes a financial stakeholder).

The corporate and social responsibility agenda means that adherence to the ethics of the professions that support the business and the more general promotion of professionalism in the workplace is of paramount importance in the determination of the culture of organisations.

All policies for governance and social responsibility are ultimately rooted in the organisation's values and code of ethics.

There is a separate issue when an organisation spends its money; guided by issues other than pure profit and loss, which is usually referred to as its corporate social responsibility policy. Typically, there will be policies as to how communities are supported in which it operates, and a list of charities it will support.

In both respects though, the organisation needs to tie these policies back to its core values. If it does not, they may not be sustainable if there is a downturn in income and it has to make difficult decisions about continuing to support its community work and charities.

Ultimately, employers are coming round to building their own infrastructure of ethics, codes of ethics to give guidance to members, staff and employees to reduce the risk of problematic occurrences happening.

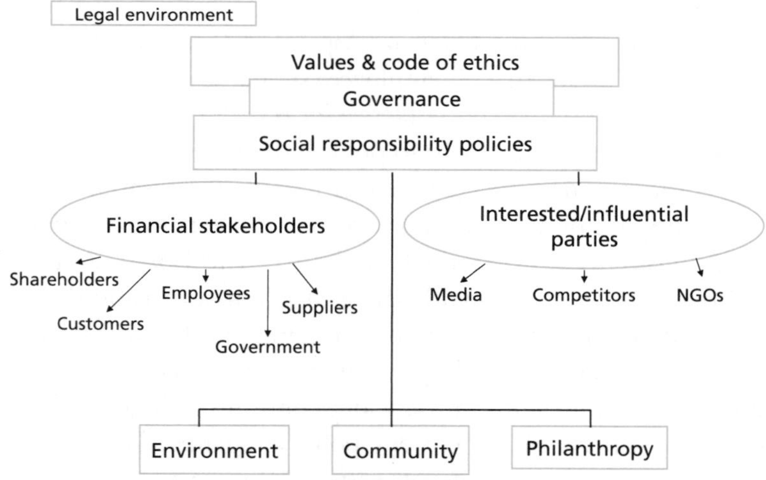

Figure 7.1 Interrelationship between ethics, governance, law and social responsibility in an organization

Source: Institute of Business Ethics

Three things are essential in developing an effective ethics programme.

1. The first need is active leadership from the top. Not only should a senior member of the organisation's board act as a champion, but organisations should encourage all senior executives to lead by example.
2. Secondly, that champion needs to get buy-in, which can be best done through consultation, information and encouraging transparency of decision-making.
3. Thirdly, there needs to be a programme of training everyone covered by the code to embed the message.

The message is a simple one: the corporation's code of ethics expresses the values by which people are expected to behave and to assist them in dealing with dilemmas which emerge day to day in the course of business activities. These dilemmas are the tests of individual responses to carrying out the spirit of the code. To quote Carly Fiorina in 2003, the then CEO of Hewlett Packard: 'it is doing the right thing when no-one is watching'. Codes amplify what is the 'right thing' and help to reduce instances of unethical behaviour.

7.2 Unethical behaviour

Learning Outcome:	Describe the consequences on unethical behaviour to the individual, the profession and the society.

Strictly speaking ethical reasoning should not be consequentialist reasoning. This means that the question, 'but what will happen to me?' is not a relevant one when trying to work out what is the right thing to do. There is not really a whole lot of difference between not doing something you ought to do professionally because someone will pay you less if you do it and doing something you ought not to do because someone offers to pay you more. Either way the motive for your action is your financial interest, rather than doing the right thing. Yet, most people would see the former (protecting job security) as an understandable lack of courage, whereas the former (acting on inducement) would be regarded as corruption. Ethically and morally, there is little difference, except the latter is the result of the development of an anti-corruption culture in this country over a series of several centuries. What happens to you as an individual is actually the last consideration that the accountant should be thinking about.

Considering objective social consequences, e.g. what will happen to society or the profession may however be relevant, provided that does not overwhelm the underpinning values that are the basis of the CIMA Code. For example, revealing a systematic widespread fraud that has not been countered by professional standards may be catastrophic for confidence in the profession, but it is still ethically the duty of the accountant not to cover it up. One might argue that it can never be in the interest of the profession to hide its weaknesses, but then that is also one of those things that is easier to say than to subscribe to.

However, human beings are not perfect. Compliance with professional ethics is likely to be greater when that behaviour is encouraged, or when unethical behaviour is punished.

The personal consequences of unethical behaviour can be dire, as typically it will entail a loss of reputation. For the individual, a loss of reputation may result in loss of earning potential, job, professional status, position in the community and so forth. For a professional body, a significant loss of reputation, if it were brought into disrepute, would undermine its credibility and, ultimately, potentially its loss of Chartered Institute status. For a corporation, loss of public confidence is likely to result in the failure and dissolution of the organisation.

These are dire consequences and there are many gradations in between, for instance when the Barings Bank scandal in the United Kingdom happened, the individual went to jail but the Bank was 'saved' as it was purchased by ING Bank. In the Maxwell case, the Mirror Group survived, though Polly Peck did not survive the scandals that were linked to its chief executive. Worldcom survived and reinvented itself but Arthur Andersen did not.

In the wider context, when such unethical behaviour is identified there is a greater damage, as trust is undermined not only in the people and organisations directly affected but also in similar bodies or institutions on the fear that they also may be targeted or affected by scandal. This is the trust that society bears for its organisations.

Often however, the true economic and human consequences of unethical behaviour are diffuse and hard to pinpoint. Like a lot of 'victimless crimes', the indirect global effects of one person who is discourteous, slow and unreliable might be minimal, but the impact on the profession of a few thousand practitioners who are like that can be considerable, as the legal profession would have to acknowledge.

7.3 Ethical dilemmas and conflicts of interest

Learning Outcome: Identity situations where ethical dilemmas and conflicts of interest occur and how they can be resolved.

7.3.1 Introduction

There is an expectation in wider society that professional accountants have a leadership role in ensuring that companies, institutions, public bodies and all types of organisations where they work will behave ethically in carrying out their activities. Demonstrating such leadership by example can be achieved only if the individual professional concerned is sensitive enough to spot and to tackle ethical dilemmas. Without an 'inner guide' to ethical behaviour an individual may easily trip up.

For instance, a leader who fails to follow company procedures by deciding to appoint a friend to the board of the company is vulnerable to accusations of a conflict of interest if the appointment fails, or if there is a lack of transparency in making the appointment in the first instance. Governance procedures can add rigour to the appointment process, but it should be natural instinct to realise that business cannot be run without a core ethical values.

All individuals need to be able to recognise an ethical dilemma and deal with it appropriately. Pressures challenge personal integrity as well as business skills, which is why ethical acumen is an essential ingredient for a professional accountant.

7.3.2 Identifying ethical dilemmas

In identifying ethical dilemmas, it is important to understand how they arise. Figure 7.2 represents the tensions that can exist between differing sources of values: society, through the legislative process; individuals, through their personal values, professional bodies and the norms they set; and companies themselves, which lay down codes of ethics for their staff to follow.

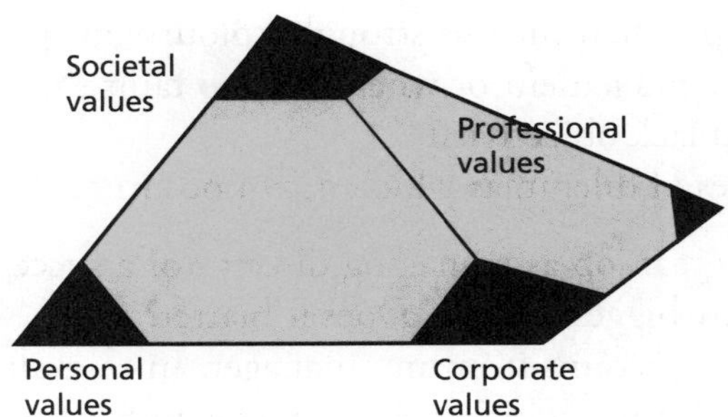

Figure 7.2 Where ethical dilemmas arise

Individuals will recognise the tensions along the baseline if they are asked to condone the behaviour by their company which they feel to be wrong or inappropriate. If the tension is too great, they will leave the company. Before doing so, however, they may try to speak up, to voice their concerns. An example is where an employee is asked to 'overlook' improprieties carried out by their company, which would be counter to their professional code.

There are also tensions between corporate values and the values of society. If companies or individuals are deemed by society to be behaving or conducting their business inappropriately, then laws will be introduced to enforce minimum levels of behaviour. Such laws are wide ranging in order to cover the wide ranging activities of a business from employment practices to disposal of products in an environmentally friendly way, to banning cartels and unfair competitive activities and fraud, and the prevention of bribery and corruption.

Moves towards an ever-increasing body of business-related law represent a breakdown of trust by society in individuals, companies and professionals. Criminal Law is then introduced on the basis that 'if you don't behave, we'll introduce a law to make you do so'. The corollary is better enforced self-regulation in order to stamp out bad practice. This encourages companies to act with a higher standard of behaviour rather than the minimum level of behaviour set by law. Organisations therefore need to pay attention to society's agenda, if only to protect themselves from more legislation.

Ethical dilemmas arise in many guises within an organisation – from those related to strategy and policy as faced by those running the organisation to those faced by middle managers or individuals in the course of their work. Dilemmas can occur at all levels.

How to identify an ethical dilemma

The boundaries of right and wrong as defined in the Criminal Law are clear. However, behaving ethically or choosing how one wants to undertake business and achieve business goals is discretionary. Therefore, companies, as represented by the board, may or may not choose to encourage ethical behaviour by their staff.

Dilemmas arise when the boundaries of right and wrong are not clear; when an individual is faced with two options – the choice between making a better choice, or the least wrong. The individual must choose what to do. What makes ethical decisions hard is that they often are such unpalatable choices.

It is clear that what is not an ethical dilemma is when there is a choice between what is good for me and what is prescribed by professional standards. Doing what I want for my own reasons is not a professional choice but a personal preference, and therefore has no place in ethical reasoning.

Personal compromises include when friendships, families, loyalties and affiliations to organisations, political and other belief systems are involved. None of these are relevant to decision-making, except when they so strongly colour your perceptions that they make you incapable of objective judgement or where they so taint the outside perception of you that others think that you lack objectivity.

Here are some examples of dilemmas which might occur:

- My wife has just got a great job as managing director of a successful business, which also happens to be one of my biggest clients. Does it matter?
- I have taken over a new account from my manager. In re-evaluating their work, I have come across a significant error, which nobody seems to have picked up on. I don't want to jeopardise my relationship with my manager. What should I do?
- I have had a client for many years who has always taken me for dinner after his year end to celebrate and say thank you. This year he says he's done rather well so he's offered to take me golfing for the weekend in St Andrews. Should I accept?
- Our firm has taken out an advert in the local paper to promote our services. However, it says that we are experts in tax and none of the partners have that expertise. I feel uncomfortable, but what can I do?
- Our firm is being taken over and there is talk of redundancies being made. I've been asked to review the accounting policies and see if I could 'make things look more favourable'; it was implied that my job would depend upon it. What should I do?
- I'm tendering for new business, and I bumped into the current accountants at a conference. They said they wouldn't be re-tendering for the business because of 'certain difficulties' with the client, but when pressed said that the information was confidential. What should I do?

In response to each of these instances, the CIMA Code gives guidance on how to avoid conflicts of interest and threats to independence, and how to deal with confidential issues.

By working through the code, you will find definitive answers to how you should address these problems.

The design of the Code is to systematically lay out the potential areas of conflict or breach and help individuals work through them. In that context, it is perhaps unwise to paraphrase various courses of action. Instead, it is reiterated that the real problems arise when there are two or more unpalatable choices. The professional should always:

- Take his own preferences out of the equation (think objectively);
- Seek guidance from the Code of Practice and CIMA (act professionally);
- Reflect on the situation, what brought it about and its consequences (continue to learn and develop).

7.3.3 Conflicts of interest

Individuals can often find that they face a conflict of interest between their professional and business lives. In such instances, it is important to follow guidelines laid down in the Code of Ethics. Some instances are obvious, others are subtle so the individual needs to be sensitive in spotting them.

Example Conflicts of Interest

Steve is the Management Accountant at the Head Office of EnviroServices Group. One of his best friends, Dan, works in another part of the group. They've been friends since university, their wives are also great friends and their families have been on holiday together once or twice. Steve and Dan often talk about work when their wives aren't listening, keeping each other abreast of developments in the respective parts of the group, although neither of them puts pressure on the other to divulge any sensitive information.

Restructuring is taking place throughout EnviroServices. Steve is a member of an internal working party mandated to ensure that the internal communications policies and practices of the group fully support the changes that will take place in the course of the restructuring. As a member of the working party, Steve is privy to plans for the restructuring. This is price-sensitive information available only to a few people apart from top management. This includes information about the proposed selling off of one part of the group, which is no longer seen as core business. It is the part of the group where Dan works.

There are bound to be redundancies, especially at Dan's middle manager level. When Steve and Dan had last got together, he'd been talking about moving his house, taking on a substantial new mortgage in the process, in order to be able to send his daughter to a special school for children with learning disabilities.

In training, the following three questions would be asked:

1. What is the ethics issue?
2. What are the options to resolve this issue?
3. What would you do?

Conflicts of interest are not wrong in themselves, but they do become a problem when a professional continues to engage in a course of action being, aware of that conflict. When you think you may have a conflict of interest, it is always a sensible idea to declare it. It is normal that an individual will withdraw from a course of dealing when a conflict arises.

7.3.4 Resolving ethical dilemmas

A professional accountant may be called upon to resolve a dilemma in the application of the CIMA Code of Ethics' Fundamental Principles. Guidance is given in the Code in Sections 100.17–100.21.

Ethical Conflict Resolution

100.16

In evaluating compliance with the fundamental principles, a professional accountant may be required to resolve a conflict in the application of fundamental principles.

100.17

When initiating either a formal or informal conflict resolution process, a professional accountant should consider the following, either individually or together with others, as part of the resolution process:

(a) Relevant facts;
(b) Ethical issues involved;
(c) Fundamental principles related to the matter in question;
(d) Established internal procedures;
(e) Alternative courses of action.

Having considered these issues, a professional accountant should determine the appropriate course of action that is consistent with the fundamental principles identified. The professional accountant should also weigh the consequences of each possible course of action. If the matter remains unresolved, the professional accountant should consult with other appropriate persons within the firm* or employing organisation for help in obtaining resolution.

100.18
Where a matter involves a conflict with, or within, an organisation, a professional accountant should also consider consulting with those charged with governance of the organisation, such as the board of directors or the audit committee.

100.19
It may be in the best interests of the professional accountant to document the substance of the issue and details of any discussions held or decisions taken, concerning that issue.

100.20
If a significant conflict cannot be resolved, a professional accountant may wish to obtain professional advice from the relevant professional body or legal advisors, and thereby obtain guidance on ethical issues without breaching confidentiality. For example, a professional accountant may have encountered a fraud, the reporting of which could breach the professional accountant's responsibility to respect confidentiality. The professional accountant should consider obtaining legal advice to determine whether there is a requirement to report.

100.21
If, after exhausting all relevant possibilities, the ethical conflict remains unresolved, a professional accountant should, where possible, refuse to remain associated with the matter creating the conflict. The professional accountant may determine that, in the circumstances, it is appropriate to withdraw from the engagement team or specific assignment, or to resign altogether from the engagement, the firm or the employing organisation.

In essence, the resolution process entails several stages of investigation. First, the relevant facts need to be established and the ethical issues identified. The issue has to be tested against the Fundamental Principles. As a practical matter, the resolution process entails several stages of investigation.

- The relevant facts need to be established.
- The ethical issues are identified.
- Test the issue against the Fundamental Principles and Code of Ethics.

Once the relevant facts have been ascertained, then a course of action will need to be identified. Options would include:

(a) Do nothing
Sometimes it is impossible to ascertain or verify facts, for example when there is a dispute over matters discussed in a telephone call between two parties. In such an instance, it may not be possible to adjudicate, so nothing can be done.

(b) Avoidance
Where a dispute has arisen in which both parties are at fault, for instance, it might be prudent to separate them by introducing an intermediary through whom they will work thereby avoiding direct contact between the parties.

(c) Modifying behaviours
Sometimes it will be necessary to suggest that individuals modify or adjust their behaviours towards others. This is often the case where innocent banter in the office has been misinterpreted by other staff members.

(d) Arbitration
In difficult and complex situations, the professional accountant might wish to seek the advice or assistance of a professional mediator. This might happen where the allegations are of a more serious nature, such as bullying and harassment of one colleague by another but there is no third party corroboration of it.

In preparation for handling investigations, internal procedures for handling such dilemmas need to have been established so they can be referred to. During the course of such investigations, the professional accountant may well need to refer or discuss the issue with others within the organisation. All investigations should be documented in case any subsequent action has to be taken, as should all conversations held in connection with the issue.

Where there is a requirement to report, such as in cases of suspected or identified fraud, the professional accountant should obtain legal advice.

In many organisations, the procedures laid down for resolving ethical issues will refer to three initial tests for an ethical decision.

- *Transparency*:
  Do I mind who knows about my decision? Can I openly defend my stance?
- *Effect*:
  Have I identified whom the decision affects or hurts? Have I taken everything into account, including mitigating circumstances?
- *Fairness*:
  Will my decisions be judged by others to be fair?

Ethical dilemmas may be raised with a professional accountant through a number of routes:

(i) directly through an enquiry
(ii) via an in-house speak-up/help/whistleblower line
(iii) from an external customer, supplier or other agent to the organisation
(iv) anonymously.

In each case, the same rigorous process should be applied to ensure a consistent approach and consistent application of CIMA's Code of Ethics.

Ultimately, the existence of CIMA and the management accountant's subscription to their Code of Ethics and to their membership entitles the individual to support and guidance in resolving ethics. While confidentiality means details cannot be discussed, ethical conflicts are really matters of principle. The outside objective viewpoint can often highlight what is really at stake and produce an analysis which might not be what we want to hear, but nonetheless provides a clear and definitive resolution to the problem.

Revision Questions 7

Question 1

1.1 Which statements are true or false?

(A) Codes of ethics are voluntary.
(B) Governance refers to a how an organisation is run.
(C) Social responsibility refers to a company's relationship with its shareholders.

1.2 Which statement is true?

(A) Unethical behaviour will lead to financial loss.
(B) Unethical behaviour may lead to financial loss.

1.3 Which statements are true or false?

(A) Dilemmas arise when the boundaries of right and wrong are not clear.
(B) Conflicts of interest only arise in business life.
(C) The CIMA 'Code of Ethics' does not include guidance on how to resolve an ethical dilemma.

Solutions to Revision Questions

Solution 1

1.1 (A) True. A company may require its employees to comply with its code of ethics as part of the employees' contract of employment, but it is a voluntary decision of a company to set up a code of ethics initially.

(B) True. This is the generic manner in which the term *governance* is used.

(C) False. A company's social responsibility is a wider responsibility to ALL stakeholders of the company, not just the shareholders.

1.2 Answer: (B)

Unethical behaviour may have consequences when it is highlighted. Those consequences may include loss of reputation and ultimately financial loss. Not all unethical behaviour is highlighted.

1.3 (A) True.

(B) False. A conflict of interest can arise in many situations, in business life, between professional and private life and so forth.

(C) False. Guidance is given in Sections 100.17–100.21 in CIMA's 'Code of Ethics'.

Corporate Governance

Corporate Governance

8

Learning Outcomes

On completion of their studies, students should be able to:

- define corporate governance;
- explain the interaction of corporate governance with business ethics and company law;
- describe the history of corporate governance internationally;
- explain the effects of corporate governance on directors' behaviour and their duties of care and skill;
- explain different board structures, the role of the board and corporate governance issues;
- describe the types of policies and procedures that best-practice companies introduce;
- explain the regulatory governance framework for companies.

8.1 Introduction

As you have seen, companies have always been subject to quite strict regulation. Thus, there are detailed requirements in relation to company formation, corporate administration and corporate finance (see Chapter 4 and 5). Despite all this regulation, a number of issues have continued to cause considerable unrest and political controversy. The main concerns have centered on the apparent lack of effective control of directors of public listed companies, which have manifested themselves in perceived excessive remuneration packages and mismanagement leading to a number of high-profile corporate collapses. Public listed companies employ thousands of employees and are the recipients of billions of pounds in investment by individuals and institutional investors such as pension funds. It follows that all governments, in the United Kingdom, in Europe and throughout the world, consider it crucial that public confidence in such companies is maintained. The attempts to effectively control the remuneration of directors and the activities of directors in their management of public companies so as to avoid high-profile scandals are known as 'corporate governance'. At the time of writing this revision of Chapter 8 US President Barack Obama has described as "shameful" reports that employees in financial companies in New York had collected an estimated $18.4 billion (£12.9 billion) in bonuses last year. This information has become known at a time when billions of dollars of American taxpayers' money is being injected into the American banking system in an attempt to recapitalise the banks so that money is available for loans to businesses and consumers in the current recessionary times. Mr Obama continued: 'It is shameful, and part of what we are going to need is for the folks on Wall Street who are asking for help to show some restraint and show some discipline and show some sense of responsibility.' It can be seen therefore, that excessive remuneration remains an urgent issue of the day and, despite all the attempts at regulation, the President is reduced to appealing to those concerned to show restraint. However, it must be noted that corporate governance is not static, but rather develops to meet the issues of the day. Another urgent issue of the day is climate change and the effect of corporate activities upon the environment now falls to be included within the ambit of corporate governance.

8.2 What is corporate governance?

Learning Outcome: To define corporate governance.

The term 'corporate governance' is neither defined by legislation nor has it been defined by the courts. As Farrar notes in his text book on company law, 'corporate governance is a term which has been much in vogue in the last 10 years. It suffers, nevertheless, from a lack of precision.' The Cadbury Committee defined corporate governance in its Report on the Financial Aspects of Corporate Governance (see below) as 'the system by which companies are directed and controlled'.

Corporate governance is primarily concerned with the effective control, business efficacy and accountability of the management of public listed companies for the benefit of stakeholders. 'Stakeholders' in this context means all those who are affected directly or indirectly by a company's activities. It follows that the expression includes directors, shareholders, investors, subsidiaries, joint venture partners, employees, customers, communities, local neighbourhoods, suppliers, and the environment. As stated corporate governance is predominantly concerned with the management of public listed companies which, of course, are the most important in terms of size and economic impact. It does, however, also impact to a lesser degree upon private companies. An alternate way of describing corporate governance is to say that it is broadly concerned with the interaction between, on the one hand, the management of listed companies and the desire of directors to produce wealth for themselves and the shareholders and, on the other hand, the impact of management structures and decision-making on stakeholders as described above.

8.3 Governance, ethics and company law

Learning Outcome: Explain the interaction of corporate governance with business ethics and company law.

Clearly, there is an overlap between business ethics, company law and corporate governance. Company law is made up of ethical principles and standards of behaviour which legislators and the courts have thought it right and proper to enshrine within the law of the land. Thus, for example, company law provides that directors owe a number of statutory duties including the duties to promote the success of the company under S. 172 CA 2006, to avoid conflicts of interest under S175 CA 2006 and not to accept benefits from third parties under S176 CA 2006. It may be questioned therefore, if the law is so stringent, why has it proved necessary to have an additional body of rules and standards known as corporate governance? Why is it that the law has not prevented directors from paying themselves excessive salaries and/or involving their companies in major scandals? The answer lies in the fact that, in many instances, the law provides for internal regulation of the activities of directors by (i) requiring directors to fully disclose their dealings to the shareholders and (ii) by giving the shareholders the power to regulate the activities of the directors through their control of the company's constitution and, of course, by giving the shareholders the ultimate power, of appointing and dismissing the directors. The shareholders are the owners of the company and for many years it was thought appropriate to leave internal regulation to them. Thus, Section 168 of the Companies Act 2006 provides in effect that directors may be dismissed for any reason by a majority vote of the shareholders.

Why then does the law need to be supplemented? The short answer is that quite clearly these rules have not proved watertight, and in a number of high-profile instances directors have been able to circumvent the law. In general, this has happened for the following main reasons. First, persons and institutions who invest in shares in public limited companies mainly do so in order to achieve good capital growth, a good return on their investment in the form of dividends or a combination of the two. If that is what the investor is receiving, then he is less likely to be interested in the way that the company is being managed. In any event, the investors, particularly institutional investors, will be likely to have invested in a large number of companies throughout the world. It appears unrealistic in the extreme therefore, to suppose that fund managers will have the time to actively participate in the internal affairs of all the companies in which they invest. Despite this, some commentators note that 'shareholder activism' by institutional investors is now 'a bigger part of the corporate scene than it was, say 20 years ago'. (See Gower and Davies Principles of Modern Company Law, 7th edition 2003 at page 338.) However, even Gower notes that institutional investors may simply sell their shares or accept a takeover offer if that would prove to be a better alternative to spending time and money attempting to influence an under-performing board. However, both the Company Law Review and Myner's Report of 2001 concluded that intervention by institutional investors was less than it should be in the interests of their clients and of British business in general.

Secondly, shares in public companies are potentially held by hundreds or even thousands of shareholders. It follows that shareholders in any particular company tend to be a disparate body, not united by any common objectives other than good returns on their investments. Such a group is likely to be difficult to organise behind a coherent policy and thus in a poor position to take on a relatively small powerful group like a board of directors. Even the ultimate power to remove directors may be difficult to use in practice. For example, it may be that the shareholders are concerned that if the market becomes aware of internal conflict within the company, that may have a detrimental effect on the share price. Additionally it may be that dismissing directors can be expensive in the extreme. Many directors of public companies would be entitled to large compensation payments in the event of their removal.

These are just some of the factors which may compromise the ability of shareholders to effectively regulate the activities of board of directors. These factors are often not present in the case of private companies. This is so because the directors and shareholders of private companies are often one and the same and may commonly be tied together by family relationships. In any event, unlike the shareholders of public companies, they will know each other personally and are likely to be more interested in the long-term success or otherwise of the company. Other factors and the measures taken to provide effective regulation are discussed in more detail below.

Morality and ethical behaviour are also enshrined in the criminal law. For example, as it is considered wrong and unethical that directors and other insiders should be able to benefit from inside information, it has been made a criminal offence for them to benefit from inside knowledge by making a profit or avoiding a loss in connection with share dealings under 'insider dealing' legislation. (See Part V of the Criminal Justice Act 1993.) Despite the fact that insider dealing is a criminal offence, there seems little doubt that it still goes on. Like any other branch of the criminal law, its effectiveness or otherwise depends upon a number of factors, including how well the law has been drafted and the efficiency of those who police it. As Gower notes: 'It is difficult to make a wholly accurate assessment of the extent of the use of the criminal process in this area but the figures for the numbers of prosecutions and convictions initiated by the DTI are not encouraging.' (Gower and Davies Principles of Modern Company Law, 7th edition 2003 at page 775.)

As seen in Chapter 6, business ethics are modern-day principles of morality and behaviour which are considered appropriate but which have not been afforded the force of law. The principles considered in that chapter relate directly to the work of accountants. Thus, in the recent scandal involving Enron, auditors were criticised for being less than independent, in that their accountancy firms also had contracts with the company to provide other accounting services. This was considered inappropriate in that it could possibly compromise the integrity of the accountant's role as independent auditors. To put it bluntly, it might be in the auditors' financial interests to give the company a clean bill of health so that the company will continue to contract with them. If the auditors' proved too troublesome the board of the company may seek to use other auditors, thereby causing a potential loss of income for the firm in post. To counter these types of criticisms, the APB, for example, establishes auditing standards and issues guidance and so on to ensure that auditors operate within strict guidelines and ethical principles. Chapter 7 largely relates to the work of professionals, in particular professional accountants. Although the expression 'corporate governance' takes in the role of accountants, in this chapter we are largely concentrating on governance issues which affect the supervision and control of boards of directors of public companies.

As will be seen below, what has come to be regarded as corporate governance is, at present, largely contained in the 'Combined Code' which contains codes of best practice which do not have the force of law. The Combined Code is described in Gower and Davies' Principles of Modern Company Law (seventh edition) as 'soft law' in that it is 'only a disclosure obligation'.

Thus UK-registered listed companies must disclose in their annual report the extent to which they have complied with the Combined Code in the last 12 months and to give reasons, if any, for their non-compliance. Gower goes on to explain that although the Code is largely enforced through the Stock Exchange Listing Rules, this so-called 'comply or explain' principle means that a company can fully comply with the listing rules by reporting that it has not complied with the Code at all, so long as it gives reasons for its failure to do so! If a company should follow this practice, whether any action is taken against the board is entirely a matter for the shareholders and 'not for the Financial Services Authority ('FSA') or for any other government body' (ibid.). Such practice would, of course, leave the company vulnerable to adverse publicity and criticism by regulatory bodies such as the FSA and the Stock Exchange. It is likely therefore that pressure will be brought to bear to ensure that all companies comply with the letter and the spirit of the Code. Clearly, in light of the current banking crisis and the resultant criticism of the way banks are regulated, much work remains to be done. Companies are well aware, however, that if the Code is seen to be widely ignored, it may result in the removal of the effectively voluntary nature of the Code, and its replacement with a compulsory regime backed up by legislation, something that the City is keen to avoid.

8.4 The history of corporate governance internationally

Learning Outcome: To describe the history of corporate governance internationally.

Although not described as such, until relatively recently, corporate governance has been in existence as long as it has been possible to form limited companies. The main cause of concern historically has arisen because of the consequences of the separation of ownership and control of companies. As mentioned above at law, for both public and private companies, the board of directors is subject to the overall control of the shareholders who are the owners of the company. Thus, if a majority of shareholders vote in favour of such a resolution, a director may be dismissed for any reason whatsoever. (See Section 168 Companies Act 2006.) In private companies, there is no strict separation of ownership and control of the company. The directors themselves often own the majority of shares, and their interests as shareholders are intricately connected with their interests as directors.

In practice, it is public companies which are listed on international stock exchanges which are the main players in the world economy and which are therefore, the main targets of corporate governance. In public companies, there is a clear distinction between those who control the company (the board) and those who own it (the shareholders). The latter came to be seen as a group not concerned with controlling management, but interested only in the return on their investment in the form of dividends and/or capital growth. Even if they were intent on taking an active interest in the running of the company, the fact that they were a widely dispersed, disparate group militated against their ability to organise and dispense effective control.

(i) **The United States**

Writing in the United States in the 1930s, Berle and Means noted that:

> The shift of powers from the individual to the controlling management combined with the shift from the interests of the individual to those of the group have so changed the position of the stockholder that the current conception with regard to him must be radically revised. (The stockholder) becomes simply a supplier of capital on terms less definite than those customarily given or demanded by bondholders; and the thinking about his position must be qualified by the realization that he is, in a highly modified sense, not dissimilar in kind from the bondholder or lender of money (The Modern Corporation and Private Property 1932).

A major development since the work by Berle and Means has been the growth of the institutional investor both in the United States and United Kingdom. Although the directors of public companies may well own shares in the company, the vast majority of the shares, on an average some 60 per cent, are owned by institutional investors such as the pension funds and insurance companies. Originally, the criticism of fund managers was that they too were only interested in shares as investments rather than as shareholders as such. It followed that even though they were seen to hold considerable power it was said that if they become aware of any likely problem with the company, they were more likely to offload the investment as soon as possible rather than involve themselves in controlling management. Today, fund managers are under legal obligations to actively manage investments on behalf of their clients and are more likely than before to take an active interest in the way companies are managed.

Despite this development, problems have continued to arise in relation to the effective control of the directors of public listed companies. In more recent times, corporate governance issues arose first in the United States in the 1980s when company boards adopted protective measures to ward off what they considered to be undesirable takeover bids. Some shareholders, particularly institutional investors, saw this as being against their interests and, as they had a legal obligation to manage their assets, they began to take more interest in how the companies in which they invested were managed. This in turn led to the activities and practices of companies and their managers being brought to the attention of the public at large by the media. The recent collapse of Enron and WorldCom in the United States has given renewed impetus to governments to take action in order to restore public confidence in the corporate sector.

Enron's problems came about because of unsustainable growth which had to be financed through increased borrowing. Following an investigation by the Securities and Exchange Commission, it became clear that in order to hide its excessive borrowing and thus maintain confidence in its stock, Enron effectively created a number of subsidiaries, each a legal entity in its own right, for the purpose of keeping Enron's borrowing off its balance sheet and thus maintaining its creditworthiness. In December 2001, Enron filed for protection under Chapter 11 of the United States Bankruptcy Code with debts of approximately £3 billion. The investigation has also revealed that the persons primarily responsible for Enron's fraud and subsequent collapse were the directors, chief executives and the company's auditors. To date there have been guilty pleas in relation to fraud, money laundering and insider dealing by Enron executives and a plea of guilty to obstructing justice by destroying Enron-related documents by Arthur Anderson's lead Enron auditor. As may be imagined, the collapse of such a large corporation as Enron and the criminal activities revealed have led to renewed attention being given to the effectiveness of corporate governance measures. The Sarbanes-Oxley Act was passed in July 2002 seeking to protect investors by improving the accuracy of corporate disclosure and reporting procedures and increasing corporate openness.

In addition, it had become clear that in many cases the relationship between corporations and their auditors was far too close. Auditors are required to carry out their work independently of the interests of the company's board or senior executives and to provide a check for the benefit of the shareholders. However, in true 'he who pays the piper calls the tune' style the auditors of Enron had conspired with the company in attempts to remove excessive debt from the Enron accounts. In practice, the independence of the auditors was compromised by the fact that they also received fees from the company for acting as financial consultants. As a result, the Sarbanes-Oxley

Act created the Public Company Accounting Oversight Board which is charged with the task of policing the auditing of public companies in the United States. All auditors of public companies must be registered with the board which is required to set up quality assurance procedures, ethics and independent standards to which auditors are required to adhere. The Act also prohibits auditors from providing certain audit and non-audit services to the companies for which they act. In addition, the Act requires the separate disclosure of the fees received by auditors for audit and all other fees. It follows that the independence of the scrutineers is now also subject to scrutiny!

(ii) **Europe**

In 2003, the European Commission announced that it did not believe it necessary to formulate a separate code of European corporate governance. Rather such matters could safely be left to individual member states. However, it did see the need for a common approach to be taken in regard to fundamental governance issues throughout the European Union. These are to be developed overtime through the issue of Directives. Thus such matters as the greater involvement in management of independent non-executive directors, more information regarding directors' remuneration and greater disclosure of and access to other financial information should form the basis of the corporate governance of all EU member states.

In furtherance of this common approach, the European Union established an EU Corporate Governance Forum in October 2004. The forum has 15 members representing various stakeholders from across the European Union and its overall objective is to 'co-ordinate corporate governance efforts of member states' (DTI publication 'Promoting Competitiveness: The UK approach to EU company Law and corporate governance').

(iii) **The United Kingdom**

In the United Kingdom, there have been a number of scandals involving the likes of Guinness and Robert Maxwell and these highlighted the continuing ability of directors to involve public companies in mismanagement. Clearly the success or otherwise of public companies is crucial both to the United Kingdom and the global economy. High-profile company collapses do not only impact on those directly involved, such as the shareholders, creditors, suppliers and customers of the company (so-called 'stakeholders'), but also have an impact worldwide, in that they create a lack of confidence on the part of investors. These scandals and high-profile company collapses made it clear that effective control of the directors of public companies was not being carried out by the shareholders, with the result that governments and regulators have had to look to other means for effective control mechanisms.

Corporate governance of public listed companies was the subject of the following reports prepared for the Stock Exchange in the 1990s.

(a) **The Cadbury Committee Report 1992**

The Cadbury Committee was set up by the Financial Reporting Council, the London Stock Exchange and the accountancy professions in 1991. The Cadbury Committee Report was published in 1992 and recommended that the boards of public companies should be required to comply with a code of best practice as a condition of continuing to be listed on the Stock Exchange. Listed companies were required to include a statement in their annual reports confirming that they had complied with the code or, where appropriate, detailing instances of non-compliance and the reasons for it. The code recommended:

(i) Independent non-executive directors should be appointed to the boards of listed companies.
(ii) The appointment of all executive directors should be vetted by a nomination committee made up of the company's non-executive directors.
(iii) Executive directors should not be offered service contracts for more than 3 years, unless approved by the shareholders in a general meeting.
(iv) The remuneration packages of executive directors should be agreed by a remuneration committee, wholly or mainly comprising non-executive directors.
(v) An audit committee consisting of a majority of non-executive directors should be established to oversee the company's finances.
(vi) In order to promote the independent nature of the board the same person should not act as both chief executive and chairman.

(b) **The Greenbury Committee Report 1995**
Despite the introduction of the code of practice as recommended by the Cadbury Committee, the issue of the excessive remuneration of directors of listed companies became a political embarrassment for the government of the day, following the privatisation of the nationalised utility companies such as the Gas Board. As a result, the Greenbury Report contained a new code of best practice for the directors of public listed companies as follows:

(i) The remuneration committee should consider the interests of both the shareholders and the directors when determining the level of directors' remuneration.
(ii) Directors should never be given discounted share options and annual bonuses should not be pensionable.
(iii) Any long-term incentive schemes to be offered to directors should first be approved by the shareholders.
(iv) Executive directors' service contracts should not provide notice periods exceeding 1 year.
(v) The remuneration committee should prepare an annual report to be included in the annual accounts and placed before the shareholders. The report should contain a statement that full consideration has been given to the Greenbury code and should explain any instances of non-compliance.

With effect from December 1995, the recommendations of the Greenbury Report were incorporated within the Stock Exchange listing rules apart from those relating to share options, long-term incentive schemes and pension entitlement. It follows that compliance with the Report became a necessary prerequisite to obtaining a listing.

(c) **The Hampel Committee Report 1998**
This report was published on 28 January 1998. The report seeks to give effect to and, where necessary, add to the work done by the Cadbury and Greenbury committees. The conclusions of the Hampel Report which primarily related to public listed companies were as follows:

(i) Executive and non-executive directors should owe the same corporate duties and should be provided with more information and instruction as to their responsibilities.
(ii) Executive directors should have the necessary experience to be able to understand the nature and extent of the interests of the company for which they are acting.

(iii) The majority of non-executive directors should be independent and make up at least one-third of the board.
(iv) One person should not occupy the role of Chairman and Chief Executive.
(v) All companies should have nomination committees for recommending new board appointments. Directors should be obliged to seek re-election every 3 years.
(vi) The remuneration of executive directors should not be excessive and should be based upon the recommendations of a remuneration committee made up entirely of non-executive directors.
(vii) Directors's contracts should not exceed 12 months.

On 25 June 1998, the London Stock Exchange published a general code of good practice ('The Combined Code') which was based upon the Hampel Report. The code became compulsory for all listed companies after 31 December 1998. Although it did not have the force of law, non-compliance could lead to the imposition of a fine by the London Stock Exchange and potentially lead to a refusal to list.

(d) **The Turnbull Report**
The Turnbull Report was published in 1999. The report concluded that the board of directors should include within its responsibilities:

(i) An evaluation of the likely risks and categories of risk facing the company;
(ii) Ensuring that effective safeguards and internal controls were put in place to prevent or reduce risk;
(iii) Internal controls including an annual assessment of risk should be made transparent.

(e) **The Higgs Report and the Revised Combined Code 2003.**
The Higgs Report was a response to the collapse of the giant American corporation, Enron (see above). The main thrust of the report was to emphasise collective board responsibility. So far as board structures were concerned, Higgs rejected the French and German models and preferred the existing unitary structure. Higgs also proposed the much greater involvement of non-executive directors as may be seen from the review of the Revised Combined Code below.

(f) The Smith Report on Audit Committees 2003.
Sir Robert Smith, Chairman of the Weir Group plc and a member of the FRC was asked to prepare a report on the role and responsibilities of audit committees. He stated that his report and recommendations would build on current best practice. It was intended to reinforce the independence of the auditor and raise British corporate governance standards and help to maintain the UK's position among the leaders in the field.

8.5 The effect of corporate governance on directors' behaviour and their duties of care and skill

Learning Outcome:	Explain the effects of corporate governance on directors' behaviour and their duties of care and skill.

You have seen in Chapter 5 that the management of companies is vested in the directors, who are also subject to considerable regulation and legal requirements in relation to their powers and duties.

Directors' powers and duties can be determined by reference to the company's constitution, that is the Memorandum of Association, Articles of Association and the shareholder agreement (if any – private companies only). In addition, they may be derived from individual contracts of service (executive directors) and contracts for services (non-executive directors), the Companies Acts and case law.

Directors' owe statutory duties contained in the Companies Act 2006. One of the duties is to 'promote the success of the company.' (Section 172 CA 2006). This duty has replaced the former equitable duty to act in good faith in the best interests of the company. Nonetheless the new statutory duties must be interpreted in the light of previous common law and equitable principles. Another duty requires directors (a) to act in accordance with the company's constitution and (b) to only exercise powers for the purposes for which they are conferred. This means that if directors ignore the company's Memorandum and/or Articles of Association they have acted in breach of duty. In addition part (b) effectively restates the rule that directors must not use their powers for an improper purpose. It follows, for example, that even if the board of a target company considers itself to be more suited to manage that company than a board which would be appointed following a successful takeover bid, that does not justify the issue of shares to supporters of the target company board so as to enable them to outvote those in favour of the bid. This is so even though the directors had the legal right to issue shares (*Hogg* v. *Cramphorn* [1967] Ch 254). In addition, a director may be held to have acted in breach of his statutory duty where it is obvious that he could not have been acting in the best interests of the company. For example, a director in poor health entered into a new service contract with his company and one of the terms provided that a generous pension should be paid to his widow in the event of his death. The director died shortly after entering into the agreement and it became clear that he had not disclosed the poor state of his health to the company. It was held that the director had acted in the interests of his wife rather than of the company as a whole (Re W & M Roith Ltd [1967] 1 WLR 432). Further examples of fiduciary duties may be seen in Chapter 5.

As also considered in Chapter 5, directors also a duty to exercise reasonable care, skill and diligence. Section 174 CA 2006 provides that a director must exercise the same care, skill and diligence that would be used by a reasonably diligent person with the general knowledge, skill and experience that may reasonably be expected of a person carrying out the functions that are being carried out by the director. This is a change from the previous common law which did not seek to judge the director by reference to the skills etc of a reasonable person. The important change lies in the inclusion of the expression 'reasonably diligent person' as it follows that the director is imputed with the general knowledge, skill and experience that may reasonably be expected of the holder of the position in question. If a director's standard, of care should fall below that which could be expected of a reasonably diligent person, then the director could no longer rely on his/her own inadequacies to argue that he/she did not breach the duty of care. In short, today a director's behaviour is judged against an objective standard, that is that of the reasonably diligent person, rather than against his/her own standards. The duty is now comparable with that set down by statute, that is in Section 214 of the Insolvency Act 1986 which relates to 'wrongful trading'. A director owes the above duty of care to the company, that is the shareholders as a body. The duty is enforceable by the company, that is the legal entity.

The duty of care is largely concerned with expressing the standard of behaviour expected of directors when they are carrying out their duties of management. Thus, the duty enables the shareholders to proceed against a negligent director; for example, where his negligent actions have caused loss to the company. The rules and standards which make up corporate governance are aimed at a much wider audience than just the shareholders. As mentioned above, the rules are intended to benefit 'stakeholders', that is all those who are affected directly or indirectly by a company's activities. It follows that the expression includes directors, shareholders, investors, subsidiaries, joint venture partners, employees, customers, communities, local neighbourhoods, suppliers and the environment. It can be seen, therefore, that (a) the law setting down the duty of care and (b) the rules and standards which make up corporate governance have different aims. Corporate governance is much wider than the duty of care. A director could act in breach of the duty of care and yet could still be complying with the principles of corporate governance. The corporate governance role of the board is discussed in Section 8.6.

8.6 Board structures

Learning Outcome:	Explain different board structures, the role of the board and corporate governance issues.

1. **Board Structures**

   (a) **Board structures in the United Kingdom**
   The following is largely derived from the Institute of Directors. In the United Kingdom, boards are usually '**unitary**'. This means that there is one board which is responsible for management and governance. Tricker (1996) classified unitary board structures into the following three groups:

   (i) *The all-executive board.* This structure is commonly found in private and subsidiary companies. All the directors have a managerial role. The main criticism of such a board is that the directors appear to be monitoring and supervising their own performance.

   (ii) *The majority executive board.* This structure is more sophisticated than (i) above and comprises a mixture of executive and non-executive directors. Such a board structure would tend to be found in a company that has been in existence for some time. An executive director is effectively an employee of the company and operates under a contract of service. Non-executive directors are not employees but operate under a contract for services. They often provide additional expertise or are appointed as nominees by investors of loan or share capital.

   (iii) *The majority non-executive board.* This structure is found in some UK companies but is more commonly found in public companies in Australia and the United States.

   There are no rules as to maximum or minimum numbers of directors. The role of executive directors at board level can give rise to problems because of the so-called 'two hat syndrome'. In other words, the executive directors are responsible for both management and governance. According to the Institute of Directors: 'This can give rise to some conflicts and complexities about what hat the director is wearing at a particular time. That is why the role of director needs to be clearly differentiated from that of the executive and the board meetings need to concentrate on governance issues – NOT management tasks.'

(b) **Board structures in France**
In general, there are three types of board structures in France:

(i) Unitary boards (Conseil D'administration) with a combined Chairman and Chief Executive Officer (President Directeur General (PDG)). The roles may now be separated.
(ii) Unitary boards with separate functions for the Chairman and Chief Executive Officer.
(iii) Two-tier boards comprising a supervisory board (Conseil De Surveillance) with a Chairman and a management committee (Directoire) with a Chief Executive Officer (Directeur General).

A board must have at least three and not more than eighteen directors. In listed companies at least two-thirds of the board must be non-executive directors.

(c) **Board structures in Germany**
In Germany, **the two-tier board structure** is used in many limited liability companies (GmbH) and all joint stock companies (AG). The two-tier board structure comprises:

(i) A Supervisory Board that supervises the management of the company (Aufsichstrat); and
(ii) A Management Board that manages the company (Vorstand)

The Supervisory Board must have at least 20 members who are elected by the shareholders. A major distinction between UK boards and German boards is the fact that in Germany employees are represented at board level. In many cases, the shareholders elect two-thirds of the board and the employees (and trade unions) one-third. In AG companies which employ 2000 or more, the employees elect one-half of the board and the shareholders the other half. The Chairman of the Supervisory Board is elected by the shareholders and usually has a casting vote.

The members of the Management Board are usually appointed for 5 years and are appointed, advised, supervised and dismissed by the Supervisory Board. The largest public listed companies have between five and ten members and the smaller companies three to five members.

The Management Board, as the name suggests, is responsible for independently managing the company, and undertakes to increase the value of the enterprise. It reports to the Supervisory Board in respect of business policy and future strategy; profitability; the state of the business and transactions which have a material impact upon profitability or liquidity. The Management Board:

- prepares resolutions;
- submits annual financial statements to the general meeting;
- ensures that the company complies with all applicable laws and regulations.

Both the Supervisory and the Management Boards report on the company's corporate governance in the annual report.

(d) **Board structures in the United States**
Boards are generally unitary in structure. For large public companies, the trend is towards the appointment of more independent outside directors in a similar way to the increase in importance of independent non-executive directors in the UK.

2. **The Role of the Board**
   According to the Combined Code (2003):

   > 'The board's role is to provide entrepreneurial leadership of the company within a framework of prudent and effective controls which enables risk to be assessed and managed. The board should set the company's strategic aims, ensure that the necessary financial and human resources are in place for the company to meet its objectives and review management performance. The board should set the company's values and standards and ensure that its obligations to its shareholders and others are understood and met.'

   It follows that the board is responsible for the policy and direction of the company. Although executive power is vested in the board as a whole, in practice the board delegates executive authority to the Chief Executive Officer (or Managing Director). The board retains overall responsibility for management, however, and must monitor, intervene and even dismiss the managing director if necessary.

3. **Corporate Governance Issues**
   The main corporate governance issue appears to have centred around the underlying purpose of corporate governance. Initially, it was thought that corporate governance related purely to devices for increasing shareholder value, that is purely in financial terms. Following a number of major scandals both in the United Kingdom and abroad, it has become clear that it is also to be understood in terms of Corporate Social Responsibility (CSR). In other words, a company's corporate governance obligation is not restricted to economic and financial matters but also includes social and environmental matters. Critics argue that compliance with corporate governance adds more red tape to the running of a business, with the result that it is required to spend more and more time complying with regulatory matters to the detriment of its profit-making activities. Supporters, on the other hand, point to increasing evidence that compliance with social responsibility increases rather than decreases company performance.

8.7 Best practice – policies and procedure

Learning Outcome: Describe the types of policies and procedures that best-practice companies introduce.

Obviously, best practice is intricately tied up with the size and resources of the company in question. For listed companies, the most important issues of best practice are contained in the Revised Combined Code. The Combined Code was first issued in 1998 and has been updated at regular intervals since then. At present two versions are in effect. (i) the 2006 edition, which applies to accounting periods beginning on or after 1 November 2006; and (ii) the June 2008 edition which applies to accounting periods beginning on or after 29 June 2008.

The June 2008 edition incorporates changes made following a review of the impact and effectiveness of the Code held during 2007. The changes:

(a) remove the restriction on an individual chairing more than one FTSE 100 company; and
(b) for listed companies outside the FTSE 350, allow the company chairman to sit on the audit committee where he or she was considered independent on appointment.

The June 2008 edition of the Code took effect at the same time as new FSA Corporate Governance Rules implementing EU requirements relating to corporate governance statements and audit committees.

The Revised Combined Code sets out principles designed to:

- encourage shareholders, non-executive directors and auditors to accept their legal responsibilities and scrutinise the stewardship of companies, and
- impose adequate checks and balances on executive directors without unduly restricting the enterprise side of governance (Institute of Directors).

The Revised Combined Code, including the June 2006 and June 2008 revisions, can be seen in full on the FRC website at www.frc.org.uk/CORPORATE/COMBINEDCODE.

The main provisions of the Revised Combined Code may be summarised as follows:

(i) The Board.

- Every company should be headed by an effective board which is collectively responsible for the success of the company. Non-executive directors should scrutinise the performance of management and constructively challenge and help develop proposals on strategy. The board should meet regularly; there should be a formal schedule of matters reserved for its decision; the annual report should contain a statement of how the board operates including which types of decisions are taken by the board and which are delegated to management.
- The annual report should identify the chairman, deputy chairman, the chief executive, the senior independent director and the chairmen of the nomination, audit and remuneration committees.
- The chairman should hold meetings with the non-executive directors without the executives present. The senior independent director should meet at least once a year with the non-executives without the chairman present to appraise the chairman's performance.
- Concerns regarding the running of the company which cannot be resolved should be minuted; any non-executive director who resigns should provide a written statement to the chairman for circulation to the board if he/she has any such concerns.
- The company should arrange appropriate insurance cover in respect of legal action against its directors.

(ii) The chairman and chief executive.

- There should be a clear division of responsibilities between the running of the board and the running of the business. No individual should have unfettered decision-making power.
- The chairman leads the board, sets the agenda, should ensure the directors are fully informed, should ensure effective communication with the shareholders and facilitate the effective contribution of non-executive directors and constructive relations between non-executive and executive directors.
- The roles of chairman and chief executive should be clearly established and should not be exercised by the same individual. The chairman should meet the independence criteria set out under 'Board balance and independence' below. A chief executive should not normally go on to be the chairman of the same company. If he does, the board should consult major shareholders and should set out its reasons at the time of appointment and in the annual report.

(iii) Board balance and independence.

- Balance. The board should include a balance of executive and independent non-executive directors so that no individual or small group can dominate the board.
- Except for smaller companies, (i.e. those below the FTSE 350) at least half of the board as a whole should be made up of independent non-executive directors. The primary function of non-executive directors is to give an independent judgement on issues of strategy, performance, resources, appointments and standards of conduct. A person who has been an employee of the company in the previous 5 years, had a material business relationship with the company in the previous 3 years, or who has served on the board for more than 9 years should not be regarded as independent.
- The board should appoint one of the independent non-executive directors to be the 'senior independent director' available to the shareholders.

(iv) Appointments to the board.

- There should be a formal, rigorous and transparent procedure for the appointment of new directors to the board.
- Appointments should be on merit and appointees should have sufficient time available to devote to the job, particularly in the case of the chairman.
- The nominations committee should lead the process for appointments by evaluating the balance of skills knowledge and experience on the board and make recommendations to the board. A majority of members of the nominations committee should be independent non-executive directors. The committee should prepare a job specification for the appointment of a chairman. The former advice that no individual should be the chairman of two FTSE 100 companies was removed by the June 2008 changes to the June 2008 Combine Code. The Code now requires disclosure to the board of 'a chairman's other significant commitments before appointment' and inclusion in the annual report.
- Terms and conditions of appointment of non-executive directors should be available for inspection by any person at the company's registered office.
- The board should not agree to a full time executive director taking on more than one non-executive directorship of a FTSE 100 company.
- A separate section of the annual report should describe the work of the nominations committee.

(v) Information and professional development.

- All directors should receive induction on joining the board and should regularly refresh their skills and knowledge. The board should be provided with the necessary information to enable it to discharge its duties.
- The chairman is responsible for making sure that management provide the necessary information for the board and directors update their professional skills.
- The board should appoint a competent company secretary to be responsible to the board for ensuring that good information flows within the board, its committees and between senior management and non-executive directors.
- The company secretary is responsible for advising the board through the chairman on all corporate governance matters.
- The chairman should ensure that all directors have access to independent legal advice at the company's expense where they judge it necessary to discharge their responsibilities as directors.

- All directors should have access to the company secretary who is responsible to the board for making sure that board procedures are complied with.
- The appointment and removal of the company secretary should be a matter for the board as a whole.

(vi) Performance evaluation.

- The board should undertake a formal and rigorous annual evaluation of its own performance and that of its committees and individual directors and state in the annual report how this was conducted. The chairman should act on the results of the evaluation and, where appropriate, propose new members be appointed or seek the resignation of directors.

(vii) Re-election.

- All directors should be subject to election by the shareholders at the first AGM after their appointment and to re-election at 3-year intervals thereafter.
- Non-executive directors should be appointed on specific terms. Any term beyond 6 years (2 × 3 year terms) should be subject to particularly rigorous review. Non-executive directors may serve for longer than 9 years subject to annual re-election.

(viii) Remuneration.

- Levels of remuneration should be sufficient to attract, retain and motivate directors but they should not be paid more than is necessary for this purpose. A significant proportion of executive directors remuneration should be performance linked.
- Levels of remuneration should be determined by the remunerations committee.
- Executive share options should not be offered at a discount save as permitted by the Listing Rules.
- Remuneration of non-executive directors should not normally include share options without shareholder approval.

(ix) Service contracts and compensation.

- Notice periods should normally be set at 1 year or less. The aim should be to avoid rewarding poor performance and reduce compensation for termination of office to reflect obligations to mitigate loss.

(x) Procedure.

- There should be a formal and transparent procedure for developing policy on executive pay. No director should be involved in deciding his/her own remuneration.
- The remuneration committee should consist of at least 3 (smaller companies 2) independent non-executive directors who consult with the chairman and/or chief executive about the proposals for remuneration and set the level of remuneration, including pension rights and compensation payments, for all executive directors and the chairman.
- The chairman should ensure that the company maintains contacts as required with principal shareholders about remuneration.
- The board, or where required by the Articles of Association the shareholders, should determine the remuneration of the non-executive directors.
- Shareholders should be invited to approve all new long-term incentive schemes.

(xi) Financial reporting.

- The board should provide a balanced and understandable assessment of the company's position and prospects.

- The directors should report that the company is a going concern with supporting assumptions or qualifications as necessary.
- There should be a statement by the auditors about their reporting responsibilities.

(xii) Internal control.

- The board should maintain a sound system of internal control to safeguard shareholders' investments and the company's assets.
- The board should conduct an annual review of the effectiveness of the group's system of internal controls.

(xiii) Audit committees and auditors.

- The board should establish an audit committee made up of at least 3 (smaller companies 2) independent non-executive directors, at least one of whom should have recent and relevant financial experience. The June 2008 changes to the Code provide that in smaller companies the company chairman may be a member of but not chair the committee in addition to the independent non-executive directors, as long as he/she was considered independent on appointment.
- The role and responsibilities of the audit committee should be set out in writing and include, monitoring the integrity of financial statements of the company; reviewing the internal controls; recommend appointments, re-appointments and removals of the external auditor; reviewing the external auditors independence and develop and implement policy relating to engaging the auditor on non-audit services taking account of relevant ethical guidance.
- The annual report should explain to shareholders how the auditor maintains objectivity and independence if he provides non-audit services.

(xiv) Relations with shareholders.

- The board is responsible for making sure that there is a satisfactory dialogue with shareholders.
- The board should keep in touch with shareholder opinion in whatever ways are practical and effective.
- The annual report should state the steps taken to develop an understanding of shareholder opinion.

(xv) Constructive use of the AGM.

- The board should use the AGM to communicate with investors and encourage participation.
- Shareholders should vote on separate resolutions regarding the report and accounts.
- The company should publish the result of each vote, i.e. the number for, against, proxy votes and shares in which the vote directed to be withheld.
- The chairman of the audit, remuneration and nomination committees should be available to answer questions.
- Shareholders should be provided with at least 20 working days notice of the AGM.

(xvi) Institutional shareholders.

- Institutional shareholders should enter into a dialogue with companies based on mutual understanding of objectives.
- Institutional shareholders should apply the principles set out in 'The Responsibilities of Institutional Shareholders and Agents – Statement of Principles' (available at www.investmentuk.org/news/research/2005/topic/corporate_governance/isc0905.pdf)

- Institutional shareholders have a responsibility to make considered use of their votes.
- They should be encouraged to participate more in the affairs of the company so that their views are known to the board. They should be fully informed of the steps taken by the board to ensure compliance with governance issues.
- Major shareholders should attend AGMs where appropriate and practicable.

Schedules to the June 2006 Combined Code contain the following:

- Schedule A: Provisions on the design of performance related remuneration.
- Schedule B: Guidance on liability of non-executive directors: care, skill and diligence.
- Schedule C: Disclosure of corporate governance arrangements.

As stated above the full Combined Code and the Schedules may be viewed online at www.frc.org.uk/CORPORATE/COMBINEDCODE.

8.8 The Regulatory Governance Framework for UK Companies

Learning Outcome: Explain the regulatory governance framework for companies.

The regulatory governance framework for UK companies consists of a combination of law (statutes, statutory instruments and case law) and codes of practice.

(i) **The law**

The main UK statutes are the Companies Act 2006 ('The Act') the Company Directors Disqualification Act 1986 ('CDDA'), the Insolvency Act 1986 ('IA') and the Financial Services and Markets Act 2000. The Act contains the rules which regulate the registration, administration and operation of companies, including obligations placed upon directors, rules relating to loan and equity finance and the publication of financial information such as the accounts and annual returns. For example, Part 30 of the 2006 Act is headed 'Protection of Members Against Unfair Prejudice' and includes both civil sanctions to ensure that directors comply with its provisions. The Act contains 1,300 Sections and 16 schedules. The Insolvency Act 1986 (as amended by the Enterprise Act 2002 and supplemented by the Insolvency Rules which are contained in a statutory instrument) provides for individual and corporate insolvency, including methods of liquidation and alternatives such as administration orders. Other Acts provide for particular types of behaviour, such as the Criminal Justice Act 1993 which contains the rules relating to 'insider dealing'.

In addition, there is a growing body of European legislation which seeks to harmonise aspects of company law throughout the European Union. Examples are Council Directive 2004/25 on takeover bids and Council Directive 2004/109 on transparency requirements in relation to companies which are listed on a regulated stock exchange. The Stock Exchange Listing Regulations 1984 implemented three EU Directives in addition to the Exchange's existing listing rule. A company wishing to be admitted to the Official List of the Stock Exchange must first comply with the Stock Exchanges' requirements as to admission and disclosure, and thereafter the listing rules of the Financial Services Authority to regulate the listing of securities.

The Stock Exchange website states as follows:

> All companies are subject to Company Law, but publicly listed companies have to abide by additional regulations called the 'Listing Rules'. These were traditionally set by the Stock Exchange itself but are now administered by the Financial Services Authority (FSA) and effectively have the force of law.
>
> The Listing Rules dictate such matters as the contents of the prospectus on an IPO, and on-going obligations such as the disclosure of price sensitive information, and communications on new share offers, rights issues, and potential or actual takeover bids for the company. The Combined Code on Corporate Governance is also now the responsibility of the FSA but is more advisory.
>
> Go to the FSA web site at www.fsa.gov.uk for more information.
>
> A note on our response in June 2006 to the FSA consultation on the EU Transparency Directive and the UK Listing Rules is present in FSA_Listing_Rules_June2006.
>
> A note on our submission to the proposed changes to the Listing Rules for Investment Companies made in February 2007 is present in Listing_Rules_CP06_21 – a press release on this subject is present at Press038_ListingRules

Rules relating to the interaction of the shareholders and the board are contained in a company's articles of association. Table A is a model form of articles and its provisions apply unless they have been excluded. In practice, most companies adopt Table A either wholly or partly. In addition to all this statute law, there is an ever-expanding body of case law which develops as the courts seek to interpret and apply the statutes.

(ii) **Codes of practice**

For the reasons explained above, the law is supplemented by a number of codes of practice. The most important of these for the purposes of this chapter is the Revised Combined Code 2008 which is discussed in detail at paragraph 8.7. Other codes of practice also directly concern corporate governance such as the City Code on Takeovers and Mergers. As seen in Chapter 6, codes of practice are also produced by the professional bodies, in particular the CIMA Code of Ethics and Fundamental Principles which are discussed in detail in that chapter.

8.9 Summary

At the end of this chapter, students should make sure that they understand the following:

- how corporate governance interacts with the law and ethics;
- the history of corporate governance in the United Kingdom and overseas;
- the distinction between director's duties and corporate governance;
- know the different types of board structure;
- know what constitutes best practice according to the Revised Combined Code;
- be able to describe the regulatory governance framework for companies in the United Kingdom.

Revision Questions

Question 1

1.1 Which of the following is *correct*?

(A) It is criminal offence for listed companies to fail to comply with the Revised Combined Code.
(B) A listed public company has complied with the Combined Code if it produces a report explaining why it has not implemented its recommendations.
(C) The Combined Code has no status and may be ignored by all companies.
(D) A public company may be sued for breach of statutory duty if it fails to comply with the Combined Code.

1.2 To which of the following does a director owe duties of care and skill?

(i) The public at large.
(ii) The company's creditors.
(iii) The shareholders.

(A) (i) only.
(B) (ii) only.
(C) (i) and (iii) only.
(D) (iii) only.

1.3 Which of the following are not represented at board level in the United Kingdom?

(i) Creditors.
(ii) Shareholders.
(iii) Employees.

(A) (i) only.
(B) (i) and (ii) only.
(C) (iii) only.
(D) (i) and (iii) only.

1.4 Which of the following types of committee are not recommended by the Combined Code?

(A) Planning Committee.
(B) Nominations Committee.
(C) Remuneration Committee.
(D) Audit Committee.

1.5 Which of the following are examples of unitary board structures?

(i) An all-executive board.
(ii) A majority executive board.
(iii) A majority non-executive board.

(A) (i) only.
(B) (i) and (ii) only.
(C) (ii) and (iii)only.
(D) (i), (ii) and (iii).

1.6 Which of the following was a change made to the Combined Code by the June 2008 changes?

(A) A non-executive director may be appointed for 9 years subject to annual re-election.
(B) An individual may be the chairman of more than one FTSE 100 company.
(C) The roles of chairman and chief executive should not be exercised by the same individual.
(D) The person to be the chairman should be recommended by the nomination committee.

Solutions to Revision Questions

Solution 1

1.1 Answer: (B)
The Combined Code 2003 is not contained in any statute. The code is effectively a 'comply or explain' code. It follows that a company which explains why it has not taken up the recommendations of the Code would nonetheless be complying with it.

1.2 Answer: (D)
Directors' owe duties of care and skill to the shareholders as a body. The duty is enforceable by the company. Although the duties are not owed to the company's creditors, if the company should become insolvent then directors would owe fiduciary duties of good faith to creditors. Directors do not owe duties of care to the public at large.

1.3 Answer: (D)
In the United Kingdom, directors are mainly concerned with the short- and long-term interests of the company's owners, that is the shareholders. In Germany, up to one-third of the board may be elected by the employees. In the United Kingdom, directors must take account of the interests of employees, but the latter are not represented as such.

1.4 Answer: (A)
The Combined Code recommends the use of board committees made up wholly or mainly of non-executive directors. Audit, remuneration and nominations committees are recommended, but not planning committees.

1.5 Answer: (D)
In the United Kingdom, companies generally utilise the unitary board system. The examples given, that is an all-executive board, a majority executive board and a majority non-executive board, are all types of unitary boards.

1.6 Answer: (B)
Prior to June 2008 the Code provided that 'no individual should be appointed to a second chairmanship of a FTSE 100 company.' A, C and D are correct – but were not changed in June 2008.

Appendix 1
CIMA Code of Ethics for Professional Accountants

Appendix 1 CIMA Code of Ethics for Professional Accountants

CIMA Preface

As chartered management accountants, CIMA members (and registered students) throughout the world have a duty to observe the highest standards of conduct and integrity, and to uphold the good standing and reputation of the profession. They must also refrain from any conduct which might discredit the profession. Members and students must have regard to these guidelines irrespective of their field of activity, of their contract of employment or of any other professional memberships they may hold.

CIMA upholds the aims and principles of equal opportunities and fundamental human rights worldwide, including the handling of personal information. The Institute promotes the highest ethical and business standards, and encourages its members to be good and responsible professionals. Good ethical behaviour may be above that required by the law. In a highly competitive, complex business world, it is essential that CIMA members sustain their integrity and remember the trust and confidence which is placed on them by whoever relies on their objectivity and professionalism. Members must avoid actions or situations which are inconsistent with their professional obligations. They should also be guided not merely by the terms but by the spirit of this Code.

CIMA members should conduct themselves with courtesy and consideration towards all with whom they have professional dealings and should not behave in a manner which could be considered offensive or discriminatory.

To ensure that CIMA members protect the good standing and reputation of the profession, members must report the fact to the Institute if they are convicted or disqualified from acting as an officer of a company, or if they are subject to any sanction resulting from disciplinary action taken by another professional body.

CIMA has adopted the following Code of Ethics. This Code is based on the **IFAC*** Code of Ethics, issued in June 2005, that was developed with the help of input from CIMA and the global accountancy profession. If a member cannot resolve an ethical issue by following this Code or by consulting the ethics information on CIMA's website or CIMA's 'Best Practice' advice, he or she should seek legal advice as to both his or her legal rights and any obligations he or she may have. The CIMA Charter, Bye-laws and Regulations give definitive rules on many matters.

NB All references to 'professional accountants' in this Code should be taken to refer, as appropriate, to CIMA members or registered students.

Part A: General Application of the Code

***See Definitions.**

Section 100

Introduction and Fundamental Principles

100.1 A distinguishing mark of the accountancy profession is its acceptance of the responsibility to act in the public interest. Therefore, a **professional accountant's*** responsibility is not exclusively to satisfy the needs of an individual client or employer. In acting in the public interest, a professional accountant should observe and comply with the ethical requirements of this Code.

100.2 This Code is in three parts. Part A establishes the fundamental principles of professional ethics for professional accountants and provides a conceptual framework for applying those principles. The conceptual framework provides guidance on fundamental ethical principles. Professional accountants are required to apply this conceptual framework to identify threats to compliance with the fundamental principles, to evaluate their significance and, if such threats are other than **clearly insignificant***, to apply safeguards to eliminate them or reduce them to an acceptable level such that compliance with the fundamental principles is not compromised.

100.3 Parts B and C illustrate how the conceptual framework is to be applied in specific situations. It provides examples of safeguards that may be appropriate to address threats to compliance with the fundamental principles and also provides examples of situations where safeguards are not available to address the threats, and consequently the activity or relationship creating the threats should be avoided. Part B applies to **professional accountants in public practice***. Part C applies to **professional accountants in business***. Professional accountants in public practice may also find the guidance in Part C relevant to their particular circumstances.

Fundamental Principles

100.4 A professional accountant is required to comply with the following fundamental principles:

(a) *Integrity*
A professional accountant should be straightforward and honest in all professional and business relationships.

(b) *Objectivity*
A professional accountant should not allow bias, conflict of interest or undue influence of others to override professional or business judgments.

(c) *Professional Competence and Due Care*
A professional accountant has a continuing duty to maintain professional knowledge and skill at the level required to ensure that a client or employer receives competent professional service based on current developments in practice, legislation and techniques. A professional accountant should act diligently and in accordance with applicable technical and professional standards when providing professional services.

***See Definitions.**

(d) *Confidentiality*
A professional accountant should respect the confidentiality of information acquired as a result of professional and business relationships and should not disclose any such information to third parties without proper and specific authority unless there is a legal or professional right or duty to disclose. Confidential information acquired as a result of professional and business relationships should not be used for the personal advantage of the professional accountant or third parties.

(e) *Professional Behaviour*
A professional accountant should comply with relevant laws and regulations and should avoid any action that discredits the profession.

Each of these fundamental principles is discussed in more detail in Sections 110–150.

Conceptual Framework Approach

100.5 The circumstances in which professional accountants operate may give rise to specific threats to compliance with the fundamental principles. It is impossible to define every situation that creates such threats and specify the appropriate mitigating action. In addition, the nature of engagements and work assignments may differ and consequently different threats may exist, requiring the application of different safeguards. A conceptual framework that requires a professional accountant to identify, evaluate and address threats to compliance with the fundamental principles, rather than merely comply with a set of specific rules which may be arbitrary, is, therefore, in the public interest. This Code provides a framework to assist a professional accountant to identify, evaluate and respond to threats to compliance with the fundamental principles. If identified threats are other than clearly insignificant, a professional accountant should, where appropriate, apply safeguards to eliminate the threats or reduce them to an acceptable level, such that compliance with the fundamental principles is not compromised.

100.6 A professional accountant has an obligation to evaluate any threats to compliance with the fundamental principles when the professional accountant knows, or could reasonably be expected to know, of circumstances or relationships that may compromise compliance with the fundamental principles.

100.7 A professional accountant should take qualitative as well as quantitative factors into account when considering the significance of a threat. If a professional accountant cannot implement appropriate safeguards, the professional accountant should decline or discontinue the specific professional service involved, or where necessary resign from the client (in the case of a professional accountant in public practice) or the employing organization (in the case of a professional accountant in business).

100.8 A professional accountant may inadvertently violate a provision of this Code. Such an inadvertent violation, depending on the nature and significance of the matter, may not compromise compliance with the fundamental principles provided, once the violation is discovered, the violation is corrected promptly and any necessary safeguards are applied.

100.9 Parts B and C of this Code include examples that are intended to illustrate how the conceptual framework is to be applied. The examples are not intended to be, nor should they be interpreted as, an exhaustive list of all circumstances experienced by a professional accountant that may create threats to compliance with the fundamental principles. Consequently, it is not sufficient for a professional accountant merely to comply with the examples presented; rather, the framework should be applied to the particular circumstances encountered by the professional accountant.

Threats and Safeguards

100.10 Compliance with the fundamental principles may potentially be threatened by a broad range of circumstances. Many threats fall into the following categories:

(a) Self-interest threats, which may occur as a result of the financial or other interests of a professional accountant, or of an immediate or **close family*** member;
(b) Self-review threats, which may occur when a previous judgment needs to be re-evaluated by the professional accountant responsible for that judgment;
(c) Advocacy threats, which may occur when a professional accountant promotes a position or opinion to the point that subsequent objectivity may be compromised;
(d) Familiarity threats, which may occur when, because of a close relationship, a professional accountant becomes too sympathetic to the interests of others; and
(e) Intimidation threats, which may occur when a professional accountant may be deterred from acting objectively by threats, actual or perceived.

Parts B and C of this Code, respectively, provide examples of circumstances that may create these categories of threat for professional accountants in public practice and professional accountants in business. Professional accountants in public practice may also find the guidance in Part C relevant to their particular circumstances.

100.11 Safeguards that may eliminate or reduce such threats to an acceptable level fall into two broad categories:

(a) Safeguards created by the profession, legislation or regulation; and
(b) Safeguards in the work environment.

100.12 Safeguards created by the profession, legislation or regulation include, but are not restricted to:

- Educational, training and experience requirements for entry into the profession.
- Continuing professional development requirements.
- Corporate governance regulations.
- Professional standards.
- Professional or regulatory monitoring and disciplinary procedures.
- External review by a legally empowered third party of the reports, returns, communications or information produced by a professional accountant.

100.13 Parts B and C of this Code, respectively, discuss safeguards in the work environment for professional accountants in public practice and those in business.

***See Definitions.**

100.14 Certain safeguards may increase the likelihood of identifying or deterring unethical behaviour. Such safeguards, which may be created by the accounting profession, legislation, regulation or an employing organization include, but are not restricted to:

- Effective, well publicized complaints systems operated by the employing organization, the profession or a regulator, which enable colleagues, employers and members of the public to draw attention to unprofessional or unethical behaviour.
- An explicitly stated duty to report breaches of ethical requirements.

100.15 The nature of the safeguards to be applied will vary depending on the circumstances. In exercising professional judgment, a professional accountant should consider what a reasonable and informed third party, having knowledge of all relevant information, including the significance of the threat and the safeguards applied, would conclude to be unacceptable.

Ethical Conflict Resolution

100.16 In evaluating compliance with the fundamental principles, a professional accountant may be required to resolve a conflict in the application of fundamental principles.

100.17 When initiating either a formal or informal conflict resolution process, a professional accountant should consider the following, either individually or together with others, as part of the resolution process:

(a) Relevant facts;
(b) Ethical issues involved;
(c) Fundamental principles related to the matter in question;
(d) Established internal procedures; and
(e) Alternative courses of action.

Having considered these issues, a professional accountant should determine the appropriate course of action that is consistent with the fundamental principles identified. The professional accountant should also weigh the consequences of each possible course of action. If the matter remains unresolved, the professional accountant should consult with other appropriate persons within the **firm*** or employing organization for help in obtaining resolution.

100.18 Where a matter involves a conflict with, or within, an organization, a professional accountant should also consider consulting with those charged with governance of the organization, such as the board of directors or the audit committee.

100.19 It may be in the best interests of the professional accountant to document the substance of the issue and details of any discussions held or decisions taken, concerning that issue.

100.20 If a significant conflict cannot be resolved, a professional accountant may wish to obtain professional advice from the relevant professional body or legal advisors, and thereby obtain guidance on ethical issues without breaching confidentiality. For example, a professional accountant may have encountered a fraud, the reporting of which could breach the professional accountant's responsibility to respect confidentiality. The professional accountant should consider obtaining legal advice to determine whether there is a requirement to report.

***See Definitions.**

100.21 If, after exhausting all relevant possibilities, the ethical conflict remains unresolved, a professional accountant should, where possible, refuse to remain associated with the matter creating the conflict. The professional accountant may determine that, in the circumstances, it is appropriate to withdraw from the **engagement team*** or specific assignment, or to resign altogether from the engagement, the firm or the employing organization.

Section 110

Integrity

110.1 The principle of integrity imposes an obligation on all professional accountants to be straightforward and honest in professional and business relationships. Integrity also implies fair dealing and truthfulness.

110.2 A professional accountant should not be associated with reports, returns, communications or other information where they believe that the information:

(a) Contains a materially false or misleading statement;
(b) Contains statements or information furnished recklessly; or
(c) Omits or obscures information required to be included where such omission or obscurity would be misleading.

A professional accountant will not be considered to be in breach of paragraph 110.2, if the professional accountant provides a modified report in respect of a matter contained in paragraph 110.2.

Section 120

Objectivity

120.1 The principle of objectivity imposes an obligation on all professional accountants not to compromise their professional or business judgment because of bias, conflict of interest or the undue influence of others.

120.2 A professional accountant may be exposed to situations that may impair objectivity. It is impracticable to define and prescribe all such situations. Relationships that bias or unduly influence the professional judgment of the professional accountant should be avoided.

Section 130

Professional Competence and Due Care

130.1 The principle of professional competence and due care imposes the following obligations on professional accountants:

(a) To maintain professional knowledge and skill at the level required to ensure that clients or employers receive competent professional service; and
(b) To act diligently in accordance with applicable technical and professional standards when providing **professional services***.

***See Definitions.**

130.2 Competent professional service requires the exercise of sound judgment in applying professional knowledge and skill in the performance of such service. Professional competence may be divided into two separate phases:

(a) Attainment of professional competence; and
(b) Maintenance of professional competence.

130.3 The maintenance of professional competence requires a continuing awareness and an understanding of relevant technical, professional and business developments. Continuing professional development develops and maintains the capabilities to enable a professional accountant to perform competently within the professional environments.

130.4 Diligence encompasses the responsibility to act in accordance with the requirements of an assignment, carefully, thoroughly and on a timely basis.

130.5 A professional accountant should take steps to ensure that those working under the professional accountant's authority in a professional capacity have appropriate training and supervision.

130.6 Where appropriate, a professional accountant should make clients, employers or other users of the professional services aware of limitations inherent in the services to avoid the misinterpretation of an expression of opinion as an assertion of fact.

Section 140

Confidentiality

140.1 The principle of confidentiality imposes an obligation on professional accountants to refrain from:

(a) Disclosing outside the firm or employing organization confidential information acquired as a result of professional and business relationships without proper and specific authority, or unless there is a legal or professional right or duty to disclose; and
(b) Using confidential information acquired as a result of professional and business relationships to their personal advantage or the advantage of third parties.

140.2 A professional accountant should maintain confidentiality even in a social environment. The professional accountant should be alert to the possibility of inadvertent disclosure, particularly in circumstances involving long association with a business associate or a close or **immediate family*** member.

140.3 A professional accountant should also maintain confidentiality of information disclosed by a prospective client or employer.

140.4 A professional accountant should also consider the need to maintain confidentiality of information within the firm or employing organization.

140.5 A professional accountant should take all reasonable steps to ensure that staff under the professional accountant's control and persons from whom advice and assistance are obtained respect the professional accountant's duty of confidentiality.

140.6 The need to comply with the principle of confidentiality continues even after the end of relationships between a professional accountant and a client or employer. When

---

***See Definitions.**

a professional accountant changes employment or acquires a new client, the professional accountant is entitled to use prior experience. The professional accountant should not, however, use or disclose any confidential information either acquired or received as a result of a professional or business relationship.

140.7 The following are circumstances where professional accountants are or may be required to disclose confidential information or when such disclosure may be appropriate:

(a) Disclosure is permitted by law and is authorized by the client or the employer;
(b) Disclosure is required by law, for example:
  (i) Production of documents or other provision of evidence in the course of legal proceedings; or
  (ii) Disclosure to the appropriate public authorities of infringements of the law that come to light; and
(c) There is a professional duty or right to disclose, when not prohibited by law:
  (i) To comply with the quality review of a member body or professional body;
  (ii) To respond to an inquiry or investigation by a member body or regulatory body;
  (iii) To protect the professional interests of a professional accountant in legal proceedings; or
  (iv) To comply with technical standards and ethics requirements.

140.8 In deciding whether to disclose confidential information, professional accountants should consider the following points:

(a) Whether the interests of all parties, including third parties whose interests may be affected, could be harmed if the client or employer consents to the disclosure of information by the professional accountant;
(b) Whether all the relevant information is known and substantiated, to the extent it is practicable; when the situation involves unsubstantiated facts, incomplete information or unsubstantiated conclusions, professional judgment should be used in determining the type of disclosure to be made, if any; and
(c) The type of communication that is expected and to whom it is addressed; in particular, professional accountants should be satisfied that the parties to whom the communication is addressed are appropriate recipients.

Section 150

Professional Behaviour

150.1 The principle of professional behaviour imposes an obligation on professional accountants to comply with relevant laws and regulations and avoid any action that may bring discredit to the profession. This includes actions which a reasonable and informed third party, having knowledge of all relevant information, would conclude negatively affects the good reputation of the profession.

150.2 In marketing and promoting themselves and their work, professional accountants should not bring the profession into disrepute. Professional accountants should be honest and truthful and should not:

(a) Make exaggerated claims for the services they are able to offer, the qualifications they possess, or experience they have gained; or
(b) Make disparaging references or unsubstantiated comparisons to the work of others.

Part B: Professional Accountants in Public Practice

Section 200

Introduction

200.1 This Part of the Code illustrates how the conceptual framework contained in Part A is to be applied by the professional accountants in public practice. The examples in the following sections are not intended to be, nor should they be interpreted as, an exhaustive list of all circumstances experienced by a professional accountant in public practice that may create threats to compliance with the principles. Consequently, it is not sufficient for a professional accountant in public practice merely to comply with the examples presented; rather, the framework should be applied to the particular circumstances faced.

200.2 A professional accountant in public practice should not engage in any business, occupation or activity that impairs or might impair integrity, objectivity or the good reputation of the profession and as a result would be incompatible with the rendering of professional services.

Threats and Safeguards

200.3 Compliance with the fundamental principles may potentially be threatened by a broad range of circumstances. Many threats fall into the following categories:

(a) Self-interest;
(b) Self-review;
(c) Advocacy;
(d) Familiarity; and
(e) Intimidation.

These threats are discussed more fully in Part A of this Code.

The nature and significance of the threats may differ depending on whether they arise in relation to the provision of services to a **financial statement audit client***, a non-financial statement audit **assurance client*** or a non-assurance client.

***See Definitions.**

200.4 Examples of circumstances that may create self-interest threats for a professional accountant in public practice include, but are not limited to:

- A **financial interest*** in a client or jointly holding a financial interest with a client.
- Undue dependence on total fees from a client.
- Having a close business relationship with a client.
- Concern about the possibility of losing a client.
- Potential employment with a client.
- **Contingent fees*** relating to an **assurance engagement***.
- A loan to or from an assurance client or any of its directors or officers.

200.5 Examples of circumstances that may create self-review threats include, but are not limited to:

- The discovery of a significant error during a re-evaluation of the work of the professional accountant in public practice.
- Reporting on the operation of financial systems after being involved in their design or implementation.
- Having prepared the original data used to generate records that are the subject matter of the engagement.
- A member of the **assurance team*** being, or having recently been, a **director or officer*** of that client.
- A member of the assurance team being, or having recently been, employed by the client in a position to exert direct and significant influence over the subject matter of the engagement.
- Performing a service for a client that directly affects the subject matter of the assurance engagement.

200.6 Examples of circumstances that may create advocacy threats include, but are not limited to:

- Promoting shares in a **listed entity***, when that entity is a financial statement audit client.
- Acting as an advocate on behalf of an assurance client in litigation or disputes with third parties.

200.7 Examples of circumstances that may create familiarity threats include, but are not limited to:

- A member of the engagement team having a close or immediate family relationship with a director or officer of the client.
- A member of the engagement team having a close or immediate family relationship with an employee of the client who is in a position to exert direct and significant influence over the subject matter of the engagement.
- A former partner of the firm being a director or officer of the client or an employee in a position to exert direct and significant influence over the subject matter of the engagement.
- Accepting gifts or preferential treatment from a client, unless the value is clearly insignificant.
- Long association of a senior member of the personnel of the assurance team with the assurance client.

***See Definitions.**

200.8 Examples of circumstances that may create intimidation threats include, but are not limited to:

- Being threatened with dismissal or replacement in relation to a client engagement.
- Being threatened with litigation.
- Being pressured to reduce inappropriately the extent of work performed in order to reduce fees.

200.9 A professional accountant in public practice may also find that specific circumstances give rise to unique threats to compliance with one or more of the fundamental principles. Such unique threats obviously cannot be categorized. In either professional or business relationships, a professional accountant in public practice should always be on the alert for such circumstances and threats.

200.10 Safeguards that may eliminate or reduce threats to an acceptable level fall into two broad categories:

(a) Safeguards created by the profession, legislation or regulation; and
(b) Safeguards in the work environment.

Examples of safeguards created by the profession, legislation or regulation are described in paragraph 100.12 of Part A of this Code.

200.11 In the work environment, the relevant safeguards will vary depending on the circumstances. Work environment safeguards comprise firm-wide safeguards and engagement-specific safeguards. A professional accountant in public practice should exercise judgment to determine how to best deal with an identified threat. In exercising this judgment, a professional accountant in public practice should consider what a reasonable and informed third party, having knowledge of all relevant information, including the significance of the threat and the safeguards applied, would reasonably conclude to be acceptable. This consideration will be affected by matters such as the significance of the threat, the nature of the engagement and the structure of the firm.

200.12 Firm-wide safeguards in the work environment may include:

- Leadership of the firm that stresses the importance of compliance with the fundamental principles.
- Leadership of the firm that establishes the expectation that members of an assurance team will act in the public interest.
- Policies and procedures to implement and monitor quality control of engagements.
- Documented policies regarding the identification of threats to compliance with the fundamental principles, the evaluation of the significance of these threats and the identification and the application of safeguards to eliminate or reduce the threats, other than those that are clearly insignificant, to an acceptable level.
- For firms that perform assurance engagements, documented **independence*** policies regarding the identification of threats to independence, the evaluation of the significance of these threats and the evaluation and application of safeguards to eliminate or reduce the threats, other than those that are clearly insignificant, to an acceptable level.

***See Definitions.**

- Documented internal policies and procedures requiring compliance with the fundamental principles.
- Policies and procedures that will enable the identification of interests or relationships between the firm or members of engagement teams and clients.
- Policies and procedures to monitor and, if necessary, manage the reliance on revenue received from a single client.
- Using different partners and engagement teams with separate reporting lines for the provision of non-assurance services to an assurance client.
- Policies and procedures to prohibit individuals who are not members of an engagement team from inappropriately influencing the outcome of the engagement.
- Timely communication of a firm's policies and procedures, including any changes to them, to all partners and professional staff, and appropriate training and education on such policies and procedures.
- Designating a member of senior management to be responsible for overseeing the adequate functioning of the firm's quality control system.
- Advising partners and professional staff of those assurance clients and related entities from which they must be independent.
- A disciplinary mechanism to promote compliance with policies and procedures.
- Published policies and procedures to encourage and empower staff to communicate to senior levels within the firm any issue relating to compliance with the fundamental principles that concerns them.

200.13 Engagement-specific safeguards in the work environment may include:

- Involving an additional professional accountant to review the work done or otherwise advise as necessary.
- Consulting an independent third party, such as a committee of independent directors, a professional regulatory body or another professional accountant.
- Discussing ethical issues with those charged with governance of the client.
- Disclosing to those charged with governance of the client the nature of services provided and extent of fees charged.
- Involving another firm to perform or re-perform part of the engagement.
- Rotating senior assurance team personnel.

200.14 Depending on the nature of the engagement, a professional accountant in public practice may also be able to rely on safeguards that the client has implemented. However, it is not possible to rely solely on such safeguards to reduce threats to an acceptable level.

200.15 Safeguards within the client's systems and procedures may include:

- When a client appoints a firm in public practice to perform an engagement, persons other than the management ratify or approve the appointment.
- The client has competent employees with experience and seniority to make managerial decisions.
- The client has implemented internal procedures that ensure objective choices in commissioning non-assurance engagements.
- The client has a corporate governance structure that provides appropriate oversight and communications regarding the firm's services.

Section 210

Professional Appointment

Client Acceptance

210.1 Before accepting a new client relationship, a professional accountant in public practice should consider whether acceptance would create any threats to compliance with the fundamental principles. Potential threats to integrity or professional behaviour may be created from, for example, questionable issues associated with the client (its owners, management and activities).

210.2 Client issues that, if known, could threaten compliance with the fundamental principles include, for example, client involvement in illegal activities (such as money laundering), dishonesty or questionable financial reporting practices.

210.3 The significance of any threats should be evaluated. If identified threats are other than clearly insignificant, safeguards should be considered and applied as necessary to eliminate them or reduce them to an acceptable level.

210.4 Appropriate safeguards may include obtaining knowledge and understanding of the client, its owners, managers and those responsible for its governance and business activities, or securing the client's commitment to improve corporate governance practices or internal controls.

210.5 Where it is not possible to reduce the threats to an acceptable level, a professional accountant in public practice should decline to enter into the client relationship.

210.6 Acceptance decisions should be periodically reviewed for recurring client engagements.

Engagement Acceptance

210.7 A professional accountant in public practice should agree to provide only those services that the professional accountant in public practice is competent to perform. Before accepting a specific client engagement, a professional accountant in public practice should consider whether acceptance would create any threats to compliance with the fundamental principles. For example, a self-interest threat to professional competence and due care is created if the engagement team does not possess, or cannot acquire, the competencies necessary to properly carry out the engagement.

210.8 A professional accountant in public practice should evaluate the significance of identified threats and, if they are other than clearly insignificant, safeguards should be applied as necessary to eliminate them or reduce them to an acceptable level. Such safeguards may include:

- Acquiring an appropriate understanding of the nature of the client's business, the complexity of its operations, the specific requirements of the engagement and the purpose, nature and scope of the work to be performed.
- Acquiring knowledge of relevant industries or subject matters.
- Possessing or obtaining experience with relevant regulatory or reporting requirements.
- Assigning sufficient staff with the necessary competencies.
- Using experts where necessary.

- Agreeing on a realistic time frame for the performance of the engagement.
- Complying with quality control policies and procedures designed to provide reasonable assurance that specific engagements are accepted only when they can be performed competently.

210.9 When a professional accountant in public practice intends to rely on the advice or work of an expert, the professional accountant in public practice should evaluate whether such reliance is warranted. The professional accountant in public practice should consider factors such as reputation, expertise, resources available and applicable professional and ethical standards. Such information may be gained from prior association with the expert or from consulting others.

Changes in a Professional Appointment

210.10 A professional accountant in public practice who is asked to replace another professional accountant in public practice, or who is considering tendering for an engagement currently held by another professional accountant in public practice, should determine whether there are any professional or other reasons, such as circumstances that threaten compliance with the fundamental principles, for not accepting the engagement. For example, there may be a threat to professional competence and due care if a professional accountant in public practice accepts the engagement before knowing all the pertinent facts.

210.11 The significance of the threats should be evaluated. Depending on the nature of the engagement, this may require direct communication with the **existing accountant***
to establish the facts and circumstances behind the proposed changes so that the professional accountant in public practice can decide whether it would be appropriate to accept the engagement. For example, the apparent reasons for the change in appointment may not fully reflect the facts and may indicate disagreements with the existing accountant that may influence the decision as to whether to accept the appointment.

210.12 An existing accountant is bound by confidentiality. The extent to which the professional accountant in public practice can and should discuss the affairs of a client with a proposed accountant will depend on the nature of the engagement and on:

(a) Whether the client's permission to do so has been obtained; or
(b) The legal or ethical requirements relating to such communications and disclosure, which may vary by jurisdiction.

210.13 In the absence of specific instructions by the client, an existing accountant should not ordinarily volunteer information about the client's affairs. Circumstances where it may be appropriate to disclose confidential information are set out in Section 140 of Part A of this Code.

210.14 If identified threats are other than clearly insignificant, safeguards should be considered and applied as necessary to eliminate them or reduce them to an acceptable level.

***See Definitions.**

210.15 Such safeguards may include:

- Discussing the client's affairs fully and freely with the existing accountant;
- Asking the existing accountant to provide known information on any facts or circumstances, that, in the existing accountant's opinion, the proposed accountant should be aware of before deciding whether to accept the engagement;
- When replying to requests to submit tenders, stating in the tender that, before accepting the engagement, contact with the existing accountant will be requested so that inquiries may be made as to whether there are any professional or other reasons why the appointment should not be accepted.

210.16 A professional accountant in public practice will ordinarily need to obtain the client's permission, preferably in writing, to initiate discussion with an existing accountant. Once that permission is obtained, the existing accountant should comply with relevant legal and other regulations governing such requests. Where the existing accountant provides information, it should be provided honestly and unambiguously. If the proposed accountant is unable to communicate with the existing accountant, the proposed accountant should try to obtain information about any possible threats by other means such as through inquiries of third parties or background investigations on senior management or those charged with governance of the client.

210.17 Where the threats cannot be eliminated or reduced to an acceptable level through the application of safeguards, a professional accountant in public practice should, unless there is satisfaction as to necessary facts by other means, decline the engagement.

210.18 A professional accountant in public practice may be asked to undertake work that is complementary or additional to the work of the existing accountant. Such circumstances may give rise to potential threats to professional competence and due care resulting from, for example, a lack of or incomplete information. Safeguards against such threats include notifying the existing accountant of the proposed work, which would give the existing accountant the opportunity to provide any relevant information needed for the proper conduct of the work.

Section 220

Conflicts of Interest

220.1 A professional accountant in public practice should take reasonable steps to identify circumstances that could pose a conflict of interest. Such circumstances may give rise to threats to compliance with the fundamental principles. For example, a threat to objectivity may be created when a professional accountant in public practice competes directly with a client or has a joint venture or similar arrangement with a major competitor of a client. A threat to objectivity or confidentiality may also be created when a professional accountant in public practice performs services for clients whose interests are in conflict, or the clients are in dispute with each other in relation to the matter or transaction in question.

220.2 A professional accountant in public practice should evaluate the significance of any threats. Evaluation includes considering, before accepting or continuing a client relationship or specific engagement, whether the professional accountant in public practice has any business interests, or relationships with the client or a third party that could give rise to threats. If threats are other than clearly insignificant, safeguards should be considered and applied as necessary to eliminate them or reduce them to an acceptable level.

220.3 Depending upon the circumstances giving rise to the conflict, safeguards should ordinarily include the professional accountant in public practice:

(a) Notifying the client of the firm's business interest or activities that may represent a conflict of interest, and obtaining their consent to act in such circumstances; or
(b) Notifying all known relevant parties that the professional accountant in public practice is acting for two or more parties in respect of a matter where their respective interests are in conflict, and obtaining their consent to so act; or
(c) Notifying the client that the professional accountant in public practice does not act exclusively for any one client in the provision of proposed services (for example, in a particular market sector or with respect to a specific service) and obtaining their consent to so act.

220.4 The following additional safeguards should also be considered:

(a) The use of separate engagement teams; and
(b) Procedures to prevent access to information (e.g., strict physical separation of such teams, confidential and secure data filing); and
(c) Clear guidelines for members of the engagement team on issues of security and confidentiality; and
(d) The use of confidentiality agreements signed by employees and partners of the firm; and
(e) Regular review of the application of safeguards by a senior individual not involved with relevant client engagements.

220.5 Where a conflict of interest poses a threat to one or more of the fundamental principles, including objectivity, confidentiality or professional behaviour, that cannot be eliminated or reduced to an acceptable level through the application of safeguards, the professional accountant in public practice should conclude that it is not appropriate to accept a specific engagement or that resignation from one or more conflicting engagements is required.

220.6 Where a professional accountant in public practice has requested consent from a client to act for another party (which may or may not be an existing client) in respect of a matter where the respective interests are in conflict and that consent has been refused by the client, then they must not continue to act for one of the parties in the matter giving rise to the conflict of interest.

Section 230

Second Opinions

230.1 Situations where a professional accountant in public practice is asked to provide a second opinion on the application of accounting, auditing, reporting or other standards or principles to specific circumstances or transactions by or on behalf of a company or an entity that is not an existing client may give rise to threats to compliance with the fundamental principles. For example, there may be a threat to professional competence and due care in circumstances where the second opinion is not based on the same set of facts that were made available to the existing accountant, or is based on inadequate evidence. The significance of the threat will depend on the circumstances of the request and all the other available facts and assumptions relevant to the expression of a professional judgment.

230.2 When asked to provide such an opinion, a professional accountant in public practice should evaluate the significance of the threats and, if they are other than clearly insignificant, safeguards should be considered and applied as necessary to eliminate them or reduce them to an acceptable level. Such safeguards may include seeking client permission to contact the existing accountant, describing the limitations surrounding any opinion in communications with the client and providing the existing accountant with a copy of the opinion.

230.3 If the company or entity seeking the opinion will not permit communication with the existing accountant, a professional accountant in public practice should consider whether, taking all the circumstances into account, it is appropriate to provide the opinion sought.

Section 240

Fees and Other Types of Remuneration

240.1 When entering into negotiations regarding professional services, a professional accountant in public practice may quote whatever fee deemed to be appropriate. The fact that one professional accountant in public practice may quote a fee lower than another is not in itself unethical. Nevertheless, there may be threats to compliance with the fundamental principles arising from the level of fees quoted. For example, a self-interest threat to professional competence and due care is created if the fee quoted is so low that it may be difficult to perform the engagement in accordance with applicable technical and professional standards for that price.

240.2 The significance of such threats will depend on factors such as the level of fee quoted and the services to which it applies. In view of these potential threats, safeguards should be considered and applied as necessary to eliminate them or reduce them to an acceptable level. Safeguards which may be adopted include:

- Making the client aware of the terms of the engagement and, in particular, the basis on which fees are charged and which services are covered by the quoted fee.
- Assigning appropriate time and qualified staff to the task.

240.3 Contingent fees are widely used for certain types of non-assurance engagements[1]. They may, however, give rise to threats to compliance with the fundamental principles in certain circumstances. They may give rise to a self-interest threat to objectivity. The significance of such threats will depend on factors including:

- The nature of the engagement.
- The range of possible fee amounts.
- The basis for determining the fee.
- Whether the outcome or result of the transaction is to be reviewed by an independent third party.

---

[1]Contingent fees for non-assurance services provided to assurance client are discussed in Section 290 of this part of the Code.

240.4 The significance of such threats should be evaluated and, if they are other than clearly insignificant, safeguards should be considered and applied as necessary to eliminate or reduce them to an acceptable level. Such safeguards may include:

- An advance written agreement with the client as to the basis of remuneration.
- Disclosure to intended users of the work performed by the professional accountant in public practice and the basis of remuneration.
- Quality control policies and procedures.
- Review by an objective third party of the work performed by the professional accountant in public practice.

240.5 In certain circumstances, a professional accountant in public practice may receive a referral fee or commission relating to a client. For example, where the professional accountant in public practice does not provide the specific service required, a fee may be received for referring a continuing client to another professional accountant in public practice or other expert. A professional accountant in public practice may receive a commission from a third party (e.g., a software vendor) in connection with the sale of goods or services to a client. Accepting such a referral fee or commission may give rise to self-interest threats to objectivity and professional competence and due care.

240.6 A professional accountant in public practice may also pay a referral fee to obtain a client, for example where the client continues as a client of another professional accountant in public practice but requires specialist services not offered by the existing accountant. The payment of such a referral fee may also create a self-interest threat to objectivity and professional competence and due care.

240.7 A professional accountant in public practice should not pay or receive a referral fee or commission, unless the professional accountant in public practice has established safeguards to eliminate the threats or reduce them to an acceptable level. Such safeguards may include:

- Disclosing to the client any arrangements to pay a referral fee to another professional accountant for the work referred.
- Disclosing to the client any arrangements to receive a referral fee for referring the client to another professional accountant in public practice.
- Obtaining advance agreement from the client for commission arrangements in connection with the sale by a third party of goods or services to the client.

240.8 A professional accountant in public practice may purchase all or part of another firm on the basis that payments will be made to individuals formerly owning the firm or to their heirs or estates. Such payments are not regarded as commissions or referral fees for the purpose of paragraphs 240.5–240.7 above.

Section 250

Marketing Professional Services

250.1 When a professional accountant in public practice solicits new work through **advertising*** or other forms of marketing, there may be potential threats to compliance with the fundamental

***See Definitions.**

principles. For example, a self-interest threat to compliance with the principle of professional behaviour is created if services, achievements or products are marketed in a way that is inconsistent with that principle.

250.2 A professional accountant in public practice should not bring the profession into disrepute when marketing professional services. The professional accountant in public practice should be honest and truthful and should not:

- Make exaggerated claims for services offers, qualifications possessed or experience gained; or
- Make disparaging references to unsubstantiated comparisons to the work of another. If the professional accountant in public practice is in doubt whether a proposed form of advertising or marketing is appropriate, the professional accountant in public practice should consult with the relevant professional body.

Section 260

Gifts and Hospitality

260.1 A professional accountant in public practice, or an immediate or close family member, may be offered gifts and hospitality from a client. Such an offer ordinarily gives rise to threats to compliance with the fundamental principles. For example, self-interest threats to objectivity may be created if a gift from a client is accepted; intimidation threats to objectivity may result from the possibility of such offers being made public.

260.2 The significance of such threats will depend on the nature, value and intent behind the offer. Where gifts or hospitality which a reasonable and informed third party, having knowledge of all relevant information, would consider clearly insignificant are made, a professional accountant in public practice may conclude that the offer is made in the normal course of business without the specific intent to influence decision making or to obtain information. In such cases, the professional accountant in public practice may generally conclude that there is no significant threat to compliance with the fundamental principles.

260.3 If evaluated threats are other than clearly insignificant, a professional accountant in public practice should not accept such an offer.

Section 270

Custody of Client Assets

270.1 A professional accountant in public practice should not assume custody of client monies or other assets unless permitted to do so by law and, if so, in compliance with any additional legal duties imposed on a professional accountant in public practice holding such assets.

270.2 The holding of client assets creates threats to compliance with the fundamental principles; for example, there is a self-interest threat to professional behaviour and may be a self-interest threat to objectivity arising from holding client assets. To safeguard against such threats, a professional accountant in public practice entrusted with money (or other assets) belonging to others should:

(a) Keep such assets separately from personal or firm assets;
(b) Use such assets only for the purpose for which they are intended;
(c) At all times, be ready to account for those assets, and any income, dividends or gains generated, to any persons entitled to such accounting; and
(d) Comply with all relevant laws and regulations relevant to the holding of and accounting for such assets.

270.3 In addition, professional accountants in public practice should be aware of threats to compliance with the fundamental principles through association with such assets, for example if the assets were found to derive from illegal activities, such as money laundering. As part of client and engagement acceptance procedures for such services, professional accountants in public practice should make appropriate enquiries about the source of such assets and should consider their legal and regulatory obligations. They may also consider seeking legal advice.

Section 280

Objectivity – All Services

280.1 A professional accountant in public practice should consider when providing any professional service whether there are threats to compliance with the fundamental principle of objectivity resulting from having interests in, or relationships with, a client or directors, officers or employees. For example, a familiarity threat to objectivity may be created from a family or close personal or business relationship.

280.2 A professional accountant in public practice who provides an assurance service is required to be independent of the assurance client. Independence of mind and in appearance is necessary to enable the professional accountant in public practice to express a conclusion, and be seen to express a conclusion, without bias, conflict of interest or undue influence of others. Section 290 provides specific guidance on independence requirements for professional accountants in public practice when performing an assurance engagement.

280.3 The existence of threats to objectivity when providing any professional service will depend upon the particular circumstances of the engagement and the nature of the work that the professional accountant in public practice is performing.

280.4 A professional accountant in public practice should evaluate the significance of identified threats and, if they are other than clearly insignificant, safeguards should be considered and applied as necessary to eliminate them or reduce them to an acceptable level. Such safeguards may include:

- Withdrawing from the engagement team.
- Supervisory procedures.
- Terminating the financial or business relationship giving rise to the threat.
- Discussing the issue with higher levels of management within the firm.
- Discussing the issue with those charged with governance of the client.

Section 290

Independence – Assurance Engagements

290.1 In the case of an assurance engagement, it is in the public interest and, therefore, required by this Code of Ethics, that members of **assurance teams**,* firms and, when applicable, **network firms*** be independent of assurance clients.

290.2 Assurance engagements are designed to enhance intended users' degree of confidence about the outcome of the evaluation or measurement of a subject matter against criteria. The International Framework for Assurance Engagements (the Framework) issued by the International Auditing and Assurance Standards Board describes the elements and objectives of an assurance engagement, and identifies engagements to which International Standards on Auditing (ISAs), International Standards on Review Engagements (ISREs) and International Standards on Assurance Engagements (ISAEs) apply. For a description of the elements and objectives of an assurance engagement, reference should be made to the Assurance Framework.

290.3 As further explained in the Assurance Framework, in an assurance engagement the professional accountant in public practice expresses a conclusion designed to enhance the degree of confidence of the intended users other than the responsible party about the outcome of the evaluation or measurement of a subject matter against criteria.

290.4 The outcome of the evaluation or measurement of a subject matter is the information that results from applying the criteria to the subject matter. The term 'subject matter information' is used to mean the outcome of the evaluation or measurement of subject matter. For example:

- The recognition, measurement, presentation and disclosure represented in the **financial statements*** (subject matter information) result from applying a financial reporting framework for recognition, measurement, presentation and disclosure, such as International Financial Reporting Standards, (criteria) to an entity's financial position, financial performance and cash flows (subject matter).
- An assertion about the effectiveness of internal control (subject matter information) results from applying a framework for evaluating the effectiveness of internal control, such as COSO or CoCo, (criteria) to internal control, a process (subject matter).

290.5 Assurance engagements may be assertion-based or direct reporting. In either case, they involve three separate parties: a public accountant in public practice, a responsible party and intended users.

290.6 In an assertion-based assurance engagement, which includes a **financial statement audit engagement***, the evaluation or measurement of the subject matter is performed by the responsible party, and the subject matter information is in the form of an assertion by the responsible party that is made available to the intended users.

290.7 In a direct reporting assurance engagement, the professional accountant in public practice either directly performs the evaluation or measurement of the subject matter, or

---

***See Definitions.**

obtains a representation from the responsible party that has performed the evaluation or measurement that is not available to the intended users. The subject matter information is provided to the intended users in the assurance report.

290.8 Independence requires:

Independence of Mind

The state of mind that permits the expression of a conclusion without being affected by influences that compromise professional judgment, allowing an individual to act with integrity, and exercise objectivity and professional scepticism.

Independence in Appearance

The avoidance of facts and circumstances that are so significant that a reasonable and informed third party, having knowledge of all relevant information, including safeguards applied, would reasonably conclude that a firm's, or a member of the assurance team's, integrity, objectivity or professional scepticism had been compromised.

290.9 The use of the word 'independence' on its own may create misunderstandings. Standing alone, the word may lead observers to suppose that a person exercising professional judgment ought to be free from all economic, financial and other relationships. This is impossible, as every member of society has relationships with others. Therefore, the significance of economic, financial and other relationships should also be evaluated in the light of what a reasonable and informed third party having knowledge of all relevant information would reasonably conclude to be unacceptable.

290.10 Many different circumstances, or combination of circumstances, may be relevant and accordingly it is impossible to define every situation that creates threats to independence and specify the appropriate mitigating action that should be taken. In addition, the nature of assurance engagements may differ and consequently different threats may exist, requiring the application of different safeguards. A conceptual framework that requires firms and members of assurance teams to identify, evaluate and address threats to independence, rather than merely comply with a set of specific rules which may be arbitrary, is, therefore, in the public interest.

A Conceptual Approach to Independence

290.11 Members of assurance teams, firms and network firms are required to apply the conceptual framework contained in Section 100 to the particular circumstances under consideration. In addition to identifying relationships between the firm, network firms, members of the assurance team and the assurance client, consideration should be given to whether relationships between individuals outside of the assurance team and the assurance client create threats to independence.

290.12 The examples presented in this section are intended to illustrate the application of the conceptual framework and are not intended to be, nor should they be interpreted as, an exhaustive list of all circumstances that may create threats to independence. Consequently, it is not sufficient for a member of an assurance team, a firm or a network firm merely to comply with the examples presented, rather they should apply the framework to the particular circumstances they face.

290.13 The nature of the threats to independence and the applicable safeguards necessary to eliminate the threats or reduce them to an acceptable level differ depending on the characteristics of the individual assurance engagement: whether it is a financial statement, audit engagement or another type of assurance engagement; and in the latter case, the purpose, subject matter information and intended users of the report. A firm should, therefore, evaluate the relevant circumstances, the nature of the assurance engagement and the threats to independence in deciding whether it is appropriate to accept or continue an engagement, as well as the nature of the safeguards required and whether a particular individual should be a member of the assurance team.

Assertion-based Assurance Engagements

Financial Statement Audit Engagements

290.14 Financial statement audit engagements are relevant to a wide range of potential users; consequently, in addition to independence of mind, independence in appearance is of particular significance. Accordingly, for financial statement audit clients, the members of the assurance team, the firm and network firms are required to be independent of the financial statement audit client. Such independence requirements include prohibitions regarding certain relationships between members of the assurance team and directors, officers and employees of the client in a position to exert direct and significant influence over the subject matter information (the financial statements). Also, consideration should be given to whether threats to independence are created by relationships with employees of the client in a position to exert direct and significant influence over the subject matter (the financial position, financial performance and cash flows).

Other Assertion-based Assurance Engagements

290.15 In an assertion-based assurance engagement, where the client is not a financial statement audit client, the members of the assurance team and the firm are required to be independent of the assurance client (the responsible party, which is responsible for the subject matter information and may be responsible for the subject matter). Such independence requirements include prohibitions regarding certain relationships between members of the assurance team and directors, officers and employees of the client in a position to exert direct and significant influence over the subject matter information. Also, consideration should be given to whether threats to independence are created by relationships with employees of the client in a position to exert direct and significant influence over the subject matter of the engagement. Consideration should also be given to any threats that the firm has reason to believe may be created by network firm interests and relationships.

290.16 In the majority of assertion-based assurance engagements that are not financial statement audit engagements, the responsible party is responsible for the subject matter information and the subject matter. However, in some engagements the responsible party may not be responsible for the subject matter. For example, when a professional accountant in public practice is engaged to perform an assurance engagement regarding a report that an environmental consultant has prepared about a company's sustainability practices for distribution to intended users, the environmental consultant is the responsible party for the subject matter information but the company is responsible for the subject matter (the sustainability practices).

290.17 In those assertion-based assurance engagements that are not financial statement audit engagements, where the responsible party is responsible for the subject matter information but not the subject matter, the members of the assurance team and the firm are required to be independent of the party responsible for the subject matter information (the assurance client). In addition, consideration should be given to any threats the firm has reason to believe may be created by interests and relationships between a member of the assurance team, the firm, a network firm and the party responsible for the subject matter.

Direct Reporting Assurance Engagements

290.18 In a direct reporting assurance engagement, the members of the assurance team and the firm are required to be independent of the assurance client (the party responsible for the subject matter).

Restricted Use Reports

290.19 In the case of an assurance report in respect of a non-financial statement audit client expressly restricted for use by identified users, the users of the report are considered to be knowledgeable as to the purpose, subject matter information and limitations of the report through their participation in establishing the nature and scope of the firm's instructions to deliver the services, including the criteria against which the subject matter are to be evaluated or measured. This knowledge and the enhanced ability of the firm to communicate about safeguards with all users of the report increase the effectiveness of safeguards to independence in appearance. These circumstances may be taken into account by the firm in evaluating the threats to independence and considering the applicable safeguards necessary to eliminate the threats or reduce them to an acceptable level. At a minimum, it will be necessary to apply the provisions of this section in evaluating the independence of members of the assurance team and their immediate and close family. Further, if the firm had a material financial interest, whether direct or indirect, in the assurance client, the self-interest threat created would be so significant that no safeguard could reduce the threat to an acceptable level. Limited consideration of any threats created by network firm interests and relationships may be sufficient.

Multiple Responsible Parties

290.20 In some assurance engagements, whether assertion-based or direct reporting, that are not financial statement audit engagements, there might be several responsible parties. In such engagements, in determining whether it is necessary to apply the provisions in this section to each responsible party, the firm may take into account whether an interest or relationship between the firm, or a member of the assurance team, and a particular responsible party would create a threat to independence that is other than clearly insignificant in the context of the subject matter information.

This will take into account factors such as:

- The materiality of the subject matter information (or the subject matter) for which the particular responsible party is responsible; and
- The degree of public interest associated with the engagement.

If the firm determines that the threat to independence created by any such interest or relationship with a particular responsible party would be clearly insignificant it may not be necessary to apply all of the provisions of this section to that responsible party.

Other Considerations

290.21 The threats and safeguards identified in this section are generally discussed in the context of interests or relationships between the firm, network firms, members of the assurance team and the assurance client. In the case of a financial statement audit client that is a listed entity, the firm and any network firms are required to consider the interests and relationships that involve that client's related entities. Ideally, those entities and the interests and relationships should be identified in advance. For all other assurance clients, when the assurance team has reason to believe that a **related entity*** of such an assurance client is relevant to the evaluation of the firm's independence of the client, the assurance team should consider that related entity when evaluating independence and applying appropriate safeguards.

290.22 The evaluation of threats to independence and subsequent action should be supported by evidence obtained before accepting the engagement and while it is being performed. The obligation to make such an evaluation and take action arises when a firm, a network firm or a member of the assurance team knows, or could reasonably be expected to know, of circumstances or relationships that might compromise independence. There may be occasions when the firm, a network firm or an individual inadvertently violates this section. If such an inadvertent violation occurs, it would generally not compromise independence with respect to an assurance client provided the firm has appropriate quality control policies and procedures in place to promote independence and, once discovered, the violation is corrected promptly and any necessary safeguards are applied.

290.23 Throughout this section, reference is made to significant and clearly insignificant threats in the evaluation of independence. In considering the significance of any particular matter, qualitative as well as quantitative factors should be taken into account. A matter should be considered clearly insignificant only if it is deemed to be both trivial and inconsequential.

Objective and Structure of this Section

290.24 The objective of this section is to assist firms and members of assurance teams in:

(a) Identifying threats to independence;
(b) Evaluating whether these threats are clearly insignificant; and
(c) In cases where the threats are not clearly insignificant, identifying and applying appropriate safeguards to eliminate or reduce the threats to an acceptable level.

Consideration should always be given to what a reasonable and informed third party having knowledge of all relevant information, including safeguards applied, would reasonably conclude to be unacceptable. In situations where no safeguards are available to reduce the threat to an acceptable level, the only possible actions are to eliminate the activities or interest creating the threat, or to refuse to accept or continue the assurance engagement.

***See Definitions.**

290.25 This section concludes with some examples of how this conceptual approach to independence is to be applied to specific circumstances and relationships. The examples discuss threats to independence that may be created by specific circumstances and relationships (paragraphs 290.100 onwards). Professional judgment is used to determine the appropriate safeguards to eliminate threats to independence or to reduce them to an acceptable level. In certain examples, the threats to independence are so significant that the only possible actions are to eliminate the activities or interest creating the threat, or to refuse to accept or continue the assurance engagement. In other examples, the threat can be eliminated or reduced to an acceptable level by the application of safeguards. The examples are not intended to be all-inclusive.

290.26 Certain examples in this section indicate how the framework is to be applied to a financial statements audit engagement for a listed entity. When a member body chooses not to differentiate between listed entities and other entities, the examples that relate to financial statement audit engagements for listed entities should be considered to apply to all financial statement audit engagements.

290.27 When threats to independence that are not clearly insignificant are identified, and the firm decides to accept or continue the assurance engagement, the decision should be documented. The documentation should include a description of the threats identified and the safeguards applied to eliminate or reduce the threats to an acceptable level.

290.28 The evaluation of the significance of any threats to independence and the safeguards necessary to reduce any threats to an acceptable level, takes into account the public interest. Certain entities may be of significant public interest because, as a result of their business, their size or their corporate status they have a wide range of stakeholders. Examples of such entities may include listed companies, credit institutions, insurance companies, and pension funds. Because of the strong public interest in the financial statements of listed entities, certain paragraphs in this section deal with additional matters that are relevant to the financial statement audit of listed entities. Consideration should be given to the application of the framework in relation to the financial statement audit of listed entities to other financial statement audit clients that may be of significant public interest.

290.29 Audit committees can have an important corporate governance role when they are independent of client management, and can assist the Board of Directors in satisfying themselves that a firm is independent in carrying out its audit role. There should be regular communications between the firm and the audit committee (or other governance body if there is no audit committee) of listed entities regarding relationships and other matters that might, in the firm's opinion, reasonably be thought to bear on independence.

290.30 Firms should establish policies and procedures relating to independence communications with audit committees, or others charged with governance of the client. In the case of the financial statement audit of listed entities, the firm should communicate orally and in writing at least annually, all relationships and other matters between the firm, network firms and the financial statement audit client that in the firm's professional judgment may reasonably be thought to bear on independence. Matters to be communicated will vary in each circumstance and should be decided by the firm, but should generally address the relevant matters set out in this section.

Engagement Period

290.31 The members of the assurance team and the firm should be independent of the assurance client during the period of the assurance engagement. The period of the engagement starts when the assurance team begins to perform assurance services and ends when the assurance report is issued, except when the assurance engagement is of a recurring nature. If the assurance engagement is expected to recur, the period of the assurance engagement ends with the notification by either party that the professional relationship has terminated or the issuance of the final assurance report, whichever is later.

290.32 In the case of a financial statement audit engagement, the engagement period includes the period covered by the financial statements reported on by the firm. When an entity becomes a financial statement audit client during or after the period covered by the financial statements that the firm will report on, the firm should consider whether any threats to independence may be created by:

- Financial or business relationships with the audit client during or after the period covered by the financial statements, but prior to the acceptance of the financial statement audit engagement; or
- Previous services provided to the audit client.

Similarly, in the case of an assurance engagement that is not a financial statement audit engagement, the firm should consider whether any financial or business relationships or previous services may create threats to independence.

290.33 If a non-assurance service was provided to the financial statement audit client during or after the period covered by the financial statements but before the commencement of professional services in connection with the financial statement audit and the service would be prohibited during the period of the audit engagement, consideration should be given to the threats to independence, if any, arising from the service. If the threat is other than clearly insignificant, safeguards should be considered and applied as necessary to reduce the threat to an acceptable level. Such safeguards may include:

- Discussing independence issues related to the provision of the non-assurance service with those charged with governance of the client, such as the audit committee;
- Obtaining the client's acknowledgement of responsibility for the results of the non-assurance service;
- Precluding personnel who provided the non-assurance service from participating in the financial statement audit engagement; and
- Engaging another firm to review the results of the non-assurance service or having another firm re-perform the non-assurance service to the extent necessary to enable it to take responsibility for the service.

290.34 A non-assurance service provided to a non-listed financial statement audit client will not impair the firm's independence when the client becomes a listed entity provided:

(a) The previous non-assurance service was permissible under this section for nonlisted financial statement audit clients;
(b) The service will be terminated within a reasonable period of time of the client becoming a listed entity, if they are impermissible under this section for financial statement audit clients that are listed entities; and
(c) The firm has implemented appropriate safeguards to eliminate any threats to independence arising from the previous service or reduce them to an acceptable level.

Application of Framework to Specific Situations

CONTENTS

Introduction

290.100 The following examples describe specific circumstances and relationships that may create threats to independence. The examples describe the potential threats created and the safeguards that may be appropriate to eliminate the threats or reduce them to an acceptable level in each circumstance. The examples are not all inclusive. In practice, the firm, network firms and the members of the assurance team will be required to assess the implications of similar, but different, circumstances and relationships and to determine whether safeguards, including the safeguards in paragraphs 200.12 through to 200.15, can be applied to satisfactorily address the threats to independence.

290.101 Some of the examples deal with financial statement audit clients while others deal with assurance engagements for clients that are not financial statement audit clients. The examples illustrate how safeguards should be applied to fulfil the requirement for the members of the assurance team, the firm and network firms to be independent of a financial statement audit client, and for the members of the assurance team and the firm to be independent of an assurance client that is not a financial statement audit client. The examples do not include assurance reports to a non-financial statement audit client expressly restricted for use by identified users. As stated in paragraph 290.19 for such engagements, members of the assurance team and their immediate and close family are required to be independent of the assurance client. Further, the firm should not have a material financial interest, direct or indirect, in the assurance client.

290.102 The examples illustrate how the framework applies to financial statement audit clients and other assurance clients. The examples should be read in conjunction with paragraphs 290.20 which explain that, in the majority of assurance engagements, there is one responsible party and that responsible party comprises the assurance client. However, in some assurance engagements there are two responsible parties. In such circumstances, consideration should be given to any threats the firm has reason to believe may be created by interests and relationships between a member of the assurance team, the firm, a network firm and the party responsible for the subject matter.

290.103 Interpretation 2005–01 to this section provides further guidance on the application of the independence requirements contained in this section to assurance engagements that are not financial statement audit engagements.

Financial Interests

290.104 A financial interest in an assurance client may create a self-interest threat. In evaluating the significance of the threat, and the appropriate safeguards to be applied to eliminate the threat or reduce it to an acceptable level, it is necessary to examine the nature of the financial interest. This includes an evaluation of the role of the person holding the financial interest, the materiality of the financial interest and the type of financial interest (direct or indirect).

290.105 When evaluating the type of financial interest, consideration should be given to the fact that financial interests range from those where the individual has no control over the investment vehicle or the financial interest held (e.g., a mutual fund, unit trust or similar intermediary vehicle) to those where the individual has control over the financial interest (e.g., as a trustee) or is able to influence investment decisions. In evaluating the significance of any threat to independence, it is important to consider the degree of control or influence that can be exercised over the intermediary, the financial interest held, or its investment strategy. When control exists, the financial interest should be considered direct. Conversely, when the holder of the financial interest has no ability to exercise such control the financial interest should be considered indirect.

Provisions Applicable to All Assurance Clients

290.106 If a member of the assurance team, or their immediate family member, has a **direct financial interest***, or a material **indirect financial interest***, in the assurance client, the self-interest threat created would be so significant that the only safeguards available to eliminate the threat or reduce it to an acceptable level would be to:

(a) Dispose of the direct financial interest prior to the individual becoming a member of the assurance team;
(b) Dispose of the indirect financial interest in total or dispose of a sufficient amount of it so that the remaining interest is no longer material prior to the individual becoming a member of the assurance team; or
(c) Remove the member of the assurance team from the assurance engagement.

290.107 If a member of the assurance team, or their immediate family member receives, by way of, for example, an inheritance, gift or, as a result of a merger, a direct financial interest or a material indirect financial interest in the assurance client, a self-interest threat would be created. The following safeguards should be applied to eliminate the threat or reduce it to an acceptable level:

(a) Disposing of the financial interest at the earliest practical date; or
(b) Removing the member of the assurance team from the assurance engagement.

During the period prior to disposal of the financial interest or the removal of the individual from the assurance team, consideration should be given to whether additional safeguards are necessary to reduce the threat to an acceptable level. Such safeguards might include:

- Discussing the matter with those charged with governance, such as the audit committee; or
- Involving an additional professional accountant to review the work done, or otherwise advise as necessary.

290.108 When a member of the assurance team knows that his or her close family member has a direct financial interest or a material indirect financial interest in the assurance client, a self-interest threat may be created. In evaluating the significance of any threat, consideration should be given to the nature of the relationship between the member of the assurance team and the close family member and the materiality of the financial interest. Once the significance of the threat has been evaluated, safeguards should be considered and applied as necessary. Such safeguards might include:

- The close family member disposing of all or a sufficient portion of the financial interest at the earliest practical date;
- Discussing the matter with those charged with governance, such as the audit committee;

***See Definitions.**

- Involving an additional professional accountant who did not take part in the assurance engagement to review the work done by the member of the assurance team with the close family relationship or otherwise advise as necessary; or
- Removing the individual from the assurance engagement.

290.109 When a firm or a member of the assurance team holds a direct financial interest or a material indirect financial interest in the assurance client as a trustee, a self-interest threat may be created by the possible influence of the trust over the assurance client. Accordingly, such an interest should only be held when:

(a) The member of the assurance team, an immediate family member of the member of the assurance team, and the firm are not beneficiaries of the trust;
(b) The interest held by the trust in the assurance client is not material to the trust;
(c) The trust is not able to exercise significant influence over the assurance client; and
(d) The member of the assurance team or the firm does not have significant influence over any investment decision involving a financial interest in the assurance client.

290.110 Consideration should be given to whether a self-interest threat may be created by the financial interests of individuals outside of the assurance team and their immediate and close family members. Such individuals would include:

- Partners, and their immediate family members, who are not members of the assurance team;
- Partners and managerial employees who provide non-assurance services to the assurance client; and
- Individuals who have a close personal relationship with a member of the assurance team.

Whether the interests held by such individuals may create a self-interest threat will depend upon factors such as:

- The firm's organizational, operating and reporting structure; and
- The nature of the relationship between the individual and the member of the assurance team.

The significance of the threat should be evaluated and, if the threat is other than clearly insignificant, safeguards should be considered and applied as necessary to reduce the threat to an acceptable level. Such safeguards might include:

- Where appropriate, policies to restrict people from holding such interests;
- Discussing the matter with those charged with governance, such as the audit committee; or
- Involving an additional professional accountant who did not take part in the assurance engagement to review the work done or otherwise advise as necessary.

290.111 An inadvertent violation of this section as it relates to a financial interest in an assurance client would not impair the independence of the firm, the network firm or a member of the assurance team when:

(a) The firm, and the network firm, have established policies and procedures that require all professionals to report promptly to the firm any breaches resulting from the purchase, inheritance or other acquisition of a financial interest in the assurance client;
(b) The firm, and the network firm, promptly notify the professional that the financial interest should be disposed of; and
(c) The disposal occurs at the earliest practical date after identification of the issue, or the professional is removed from the assurance team.

290.112 When an inadvertent violation of this section relating to a financial interest in an assurance client has occurred, the firm should consider whether any safeguards should be applied. Such safeguards might include:

- Involving an additional professional accountant who did not take part in the assurance engagement to review the work done by the member of the assurance team; or
- Excluding the individual from any substantive decision-making concerning the assurance engagement.

Provisions Applicable to Financial Statement Audit Clients

290.113 If a firm, or a network firm, has a direct financial interest in a financial statement audit client of the firm the self-interest threat created would be so significant that no safeguard could reduce the threat to an acceptable level. Consequently, disposal of the financial interest would be the only action appropriate to permit the firm to perform the engagement.

290.114 If a firm, or a network firm, has a material indirect financial interest in a financial statement audit client of the firm, a self-interest threat is also created. The only actions appropriate to permit the firm to perform the engagement would be for the firm, or the network firm, either to dispose of the indirect interest in total or to dispose of a sufficient amount of it so that the remaining interest is no longer material.

290.115 If a firm, or a network firm, has a material financial interest in an entity that has a controlling interest in a financial statement audit client, the self-interest threat created would be so significant that no safeguard could reduce the threat to an acceptable level. The only actions appropriate to permit the firm to perform the engagement would be for the firm, or the network firm, either to dispose of the financial interest in total or to dispose of a sufficient amount of it so that the remaining interest is no longer material.

290.116 If the retirement benefit plan of a firm, or network firm, has a financial interest in a financial statement audit client, a self-interest threat may be created. Accordingly, the significance of any such threat created should be evaluated and, if the threat is other than clearly insignificant, safeguards should be considered and applied as necessary to eliminate the threat or reduce it to an acceptable level.

290.117 If other partners, including partners who do not perform assurance engagements, or their immediate family, in the **office*** in which the **engagement partner*** practices in connection with the financial statement audit hold a direct financial interest or a material indirect financial interest in that audit client, the self-interest threat created would be so significant that no safeguard could reduce the threat to an acceptable level. Accordingly, such partners or their immediate family should not hold any such financial interests in such an audit client.

290.118 The office in which the engagement partner practices in connection with the financial statement audit is not necessarily the office to which that partner is assigned. Accordingly, when the engagement partner is located in a different office from that of the

---

***See Definitions.**

other members of the assurance team, judgment should be used to determine in which office the partner practices in connection with that audit.

290.119 If other partners and managerial employees who provide non-assurance services to the financial statement audit client, except those whose involvement is clearly insignificant, or their immediate family, hold a direct financial interest or a material indirect financial interest in the audit client, the self-interest threat created would be so significant that no safeguard could reduce the threat to an acceptable level. Accordingly, such personnel or their immediate family should not hold any such financial interests in such an audit client.

290.120 A financial interest in a financial statement audit client that is held by an immediate family member of

(a) a partner located in the office in which the engagement partner practices in connection with the audit, or
(b) a partner or managerial employee who provides non-assurance services to the audit client is not considered to create an unacceptable threat provided it is received as a result of their employment rights (e.g. pension rights or share options) and, where necessary, appropriate safeguards are applied to reduce any threat to independence to an acceptable level.

290.121 A self-interest threat may be created if the firm, or the network firm, or a member of the assurance team has an interest in an entity and a financial statement audit client, or a director, officer or controlling owner thereof also has an investment in that entity. Independence is not compromised with respect to the audit client if the respective interests of the firm, the network firm, or member of the assurance team, and the audit client, or director, officer or controlling owner thereof are both immaterial and the audit client cannot exercise significant influence over the entity. If an interest is material to either the firm, the network firm or the audit client, and the audit client can exercise significant influence over the entity, no safeguards are available to reduce the threat to an acceptable level and the firm, or the network firm, should either dispose of the interest or decline the audit engagement. Any member of the assurance team with such a material interest should either:

(a) Dispose of the interest;
(b) Dispose of a sufficient amount of the interest so that the remaining interest is no longer material; or
(c) Withdraw from the audit.

Provisions Applicable to Non-Financial Statement Audit Assurance Clients

290.122 If a firm has a direct financial interest in an assurance client that is not a financial statement audit client the self-interest threat created would be so significant that no safeguard could reduce the threat to an acceptable level. Consequently, disposal of the financial interest would be the only action appropriate to permit the firm to perform the engagement.

290.123 If a firm has a material indirect financial interest in an assurance client that is not a financial statement audit client, a self-interest threat is also created. The only action appropriate to permit the firm to perform the engagement would be for the firm to either dispose of the indirect interest in total or to dispose of a sufficient amount of it so that the remaining interest is no longer material.

290.124 If a firm has a material financial interest in an entity that has a controlling interest in an assurance client that is not a financial statement audit client, the self-interest threat created would be so significant that no safeguard could reduce the threat to an acceptable level. The only action appropriate to permit the firm to perform the engagement would be for the firm either to dispose of the financial interest in total or to dispose of a sufficient amount of it so that the remaining interest is no longer material.

290.125 When a restricted use report for an assurance engagement that is not a financial statement audit engagement is issued, exceptions to the provisions in paragraphs 290.106 through to 290.110 and 290.122 through to 290.124 are set out in 290.19.

Loans and Guarantees

290.126 A loan or a guarantee of a loan to the firm from an assurance client that is a bank or a similar institution would not create a threat to independence provided the loan, or guarantee, is made under normal lending procedures, terms and requirements and the loan is immaterial to both the firm and the assurance client. If the loan is material to the assurance client or the firm it may be possible, through the application of safeguards, to reduce the self-interest threat created to an acceptable level. Such safeguards might include involving an additional professional accountant from outside the firm, or network firm, to review the work performed.

290.127 A loan or a guarantee of a loan from an assurance client that is a bank or a similar institution to a member of the assurance team or their immediate family would not create a threat to independence provided the loan, or guarantee, is made under normal lending procedures, terms and requirements. Examples of such loans include home mortgages, bank overdrafts, car loans and credit card balances.

290.128 Similarly, deposits made by, or brokerage accounts of, a firm or a member of the assurance team with an assurance client that is a bank, broker or similar institution would not create a threat to independence provided the deposit or account is held under normal commercial terms.

290.129 If the firm, or a member of the assurance team, makes a loan to an assurance client, that is not a bank or similar institution, or guarantees such an assurance client's borrowing, the self-interest threat created would be so significant that no safeguard could reduce the threat to an acceptable level, unless the loan or guarantee is immaterial to both the firm or the member of the assurance team and the assurance client.

290.130 Similarly, if the firm or a member of the assurance team accepts a loan from, or has borrowing guaranteed by, an assurance client that is not a bank or similar institution, the self-interest threat created would be so significant that no safeguard could reduce the threat to an acceptable level, unless the loan or guarantee is immaterial to both the firm or the member of the assurance team and the assurance client.

290.131 The examples in paragraphs 290.126 through to 290.130 relate to loans and guarantees between the firm and an assurance client. In the case of a financial statement audit engagement, the provisions should be applied to the firm, all network firms and the audit client.

Close Business Relationships with Assurance Clients

290.132 A close business relationship between a firm or a member of the assurance team and the assurance client or its management, or between the firm, a network firm and a financial statement audit client, will involve a commercial or common financial interest and may create self-interest and intimidation threats. The following are examples of such relationships:

- Having a material financial interest in a joint venture with the assurance client or a controlling owner, director, officer or other individual who performs senior managerial functions for that client.
- Arrangements to combine one or more services or products of the firm with one or more services or products of the assurance client and to market the package with reference to both parties.
- Distribution or marketing arrangements under which the firm acts as a distributor or marketer of the assurance client's products or services, or the assurance client acts as the distributor or marketer of the products or services of the firm.

In the case of a financial statement audit client, unless the financial interest is immaterial and the relationship is clearly insignificant to the firm, the network firm and the audit client, no safeguards could reduce the threat to an acceptable level. In the case of an assurance client that is not a financial statement audit client, unless the financial interest is immaterial and the relationship is clearly insignificant to the firm and the assurance client, no safeguards could reduce the threat to an acceptable level. Consequently, in both these circumstances the only possible courses of action are to:

(a) Terminate the business relationship;
(b) Reduce the magnitude of the relationship so that the financial interest is immaterial and the relationship is clearly insignificant; or
(c) Refuse to perform the assurance engagement.

Unless any such financial interest is immaterial and the relationship is clearly insignificant to the member of the assurance team, the only appropriate safeguard would be to remove the individual from the assurance team.

290.133 In the case of a financial statement audit client, business relationships involving an interest held by the firm, a network firm or a member of the assurance team or their immediate family in a closely held entity when the audit client or a director or officer of the audit client, or any group thereof, also has an interest in that entity, do not create threats to independence provided:

(a) The relationship is clearly insignificant to the firm, the network firm and the audit client;
(b) The interest held is immaterial to the investor, or group of investors; and
(c) The interest does not give the investor, or group of investors, the ability to control the closely held entity.

290.134 The purchase of goods and services from an assurance client by the firm (or from a financial statement audit client by a network firm) or a member of the assurance team would not generally create a threat to independence provided the transaction is in the normal course of business and on an arm's length basis. However, such transactions may be of a nature or magnitude so as to create a self-interest threat. If the threat created is other than clearly insignificant, safeguards should be considered and applied as necessary to reduce the threat to an acceptable level. Such safeguards might include:

- Eliminating or reducing the magnitude of the transaction;
- Removing the individual from the assurance team; or
- Discussing the issue with those charged with governance, such as the audit committee.

Family and Personal Relationships

290.135 Family and personal relationships between a member of the assurance team and a director, an officer or certain employees, depending on their role, of the assurance client, may create self-interest, familiarity or intimidation threats. It is impracticable to attempt to describe in detail the significance of the threats that such relationships may create. The significance will depend upon a number of factors including the individual's responsibilities on the assurance engagement, the closeness of the relationship and the role of the family member or other individual within the assurance client. Consequently, there is a wide spectrum of circumstances that will need to be evaluated and safeguards to be applied to reduce the threat to an acceptable level.

290.136 When an immediate family member of a member of the assurance team is a director, an officer or an employee of the assurance client in a position to exert direct and significant influence over the subject matter information of the assurance engagement, or was in such a position during any period covered by the engagement, the threats to independence can only be reduced to an acceptable level by removing the individual from the assurance team. The closeness of the relationship is such that no other safeguard could reduce the threat to independence to an acceptable level. If application of this safeguard is not used, the only course of action is to withdraw from the assurance engagement. For example, in the case of an audit of financial statements, if the spouse of a member of the assurance team is an employee in a position to exert direct and significant influence over the preparation of the audit client's accounting records or financial statements, the threat to independence could only be reduced to an acceptable level by removing the individual from the assurance team.

290.137 When an immediate family member of a member of the assurance team is an employee in a position to exert direct and significant influence over the subject matter of the engagement, threats to independence may be created. The significance of the threats will depend on factors such as:

- The position the immediate family member holds with the client; and
- The role of the professional on the assurance team.

The significance of the threat should be evaluated and, if the threat is other than clearly insignificant, safeguards should be considered and applied as necessary to reduce the threat to an acceptable level. Such safeguards might include:

- Removing the individual from the assurance team;
- Where possible, structuring the responsibilities of the assurance team so that the professional does not deal with matters that are within the responsibility of the immediate family member; or
- Policies and procedures to empower staff to communicate to senior levels within the firm any issue of independence and objectivity that concerns them.

290.138 When a close family member of a member of the assurance team is a director, an officer, or an employee of the assurance client in a position to exert direct and significant influence over the subject matter information of the assurance engagement, threats to independence may be created. The significance of the threats will depend on factors such as:

- The position the close family member holds with the client; and
- The role of the professional on the assurance team.

The significance of the threat should be evaluated and, if the threat is other than clearly insignificant, safeguards should be considered and applied as necessary to reduce the threat to an acceptable level. Such safeguards might include:

- Removing the individual from the assurance team;
- Where possible, structuring the responsibilities of the assurance team so that the professional does not deal with matters that are within the responsibility of the close family member; or
- Policies and procedures to empower staff to communicate to senior levels within the firm any issue of independence and objectivity that concerns them.

290.139 In addition, self-interest, familiarity or intimidation threats may be created when a person who is other than an immediate or close family member of a member of the assurance team has a close relationship with the member of the assurance team and is a director, an officer or an employee of the assurance client in a position to exert direct and significant influence over the subject matter information of the assurance engagement. Therefore, members of the assurance team are responsible for identifying any such persons and for consulting in accordance with firm procedures. The evaluation of the significance of any threat created and the safeguards appropriate to eliminate the threat or reduce it to an acceptable level will include considering matters such as the closeness of the relationship and the role of the individual within the assurance client.

290.140 Consideration should be given to whether self-interest, familiarity or intimidation threats may be created by a personal or family relationship between a partner or an employee of the firm who is not a member of the assurance team and a director, an officer or an employee of the assurance client in a position to exert direct and significant influence over the subject matter information of the assurance engagement. Therefore, partners and employees of the firm are responsible for identifying any such relationships and for consulting in accordance with firm procedures. The evaluation of the significance of any threat created and the safeguards appropriate to eliminate the threat or reduce it to an acceptable level will include considering matters such as the closeness of the relationship, the interaction of the firm professional with the assurance team, the position held within the firm, and the role of the individual within the assurance client.

290.141 An inadvertent violation of this section as it relates to family and personal relationships would not impair the independence of a firm or a member of the assurance team when:

(a) The firm has established policies and procedures that require all professionals to report promptly to the firm any breaches resulting from changes in the employment status of their immediate or close family members or other personal relationships that create threats to independence;
(b) Either the responsibilities of the assurance team are re-structured so that the professional does not deal with matters that are within the responsibility of the person with

whom he or she is related or has a personal relationship, or, if this is not possible, the firm promptly removes the professional from the assurance engagement; and

(c) Additional care is given to reviewing the work of the professional.

290.142 When an inadvertent violation of this section relating to family and personal relationships has occurred, the firm should consider whether any safeguards should be applied. Such safeguards might include:

- Involving an additional professional accountant who did not take part in the assurance engagement to review the work done by the member of the assurance team; or
- Excluding the individual from any substantive decision-making concerning the assurance engagement.

Employment with Assurance Clients

290.143 A firm or a member of the assurance team's independence may be threatened if a director, an officer or an employee of the assurance client in a position to exert direct and significant influence over the subject matter information of the assurance engagement has been a member of the assurance team or partner of the firm. Such circumstances may create self-interest, familiarity and intimidation threats, particularly when significant connections remain between the individual and his or her former firm. Similarly, a member of the assurance team's independence may be threatened when an individual participates in the assurance engagement knowing, or having reason to believe, that he or she is to, or may, join the assurance client some time in the future.

290.144 If a member of the assurance team, partner or former partner of the firm has joined the assurance client, the significance of the self-interest, familiarity or intimidation threats created will depend upon the following factors:

(a) The position the individual has taken with the assurance client.
(b) The amount of any involvement the individual will have with the assurance team.
(c) The length of time that has passed since the individual was a member of the assurance team or firm.
(d) The former position of the individual within the assurance team or firm.

The significance of the threat should be evaluated and, if the threat is other than clearly insignificant, safeguards should be considered and applied as necessary to reduce the threat to an acceptable level. Such safeguards might include:

- Considering the appropriateness or necessity of modifying the assurance plan for the assurance engagement;
- Assigning an assurance team to the subsequent assurance engagement that is of sufficient experience in relation to the individual who has joined the assurance client;
- Involving an additional professional accountant who was not a member of the assurance team to review the work done or otherwise advise as necessary; or
- Quality control review of the assurance engagement.

In all cases, all of the following safeguards are necessary to reduce the threat to an acceptable level:

(a) The individual concerned is not entitled to any benefits or payments from the firm unless these are made in accordance with fixed pre-determined arrangements. In addition, any amount owed to the individual should not be of such significance to threaten the firm's independence.

(b) The individual does not continue to participate or appear to participate in the firm's business or professional activities.

290.145 A self-interest threat is created when a member of the assurance team participates in the assurance engagement while knowing, or having reason to believe, that he or she is to, or may, join the assurance client some time in the future. This threat can be reduced to an acceptable level by the application of all of the following safeguards:

(a) Policies and procedures to require the individual to notify the firm when entering serious employment negotiations with the assurance client.
(b) Removal of the individual from the assurance engagement.

In addition, consideration should be given to performing an independent review of any significant judgments made by that individual while on the engagement.

Recent Service with Assurance Clients

290.146 To have a former officer, director or employee of the assurance client serve as a member of the assurance team may create self-interest, self-review and familiarity threats. This would be particularly true when a member of the assurance team has to report on, for example, subject matter information he or she had prepared or elements of the financial statements he or she had valued while with the assurance client.

290.147 If, during the period covered by the assurance report, a member of the assurance team had served as an officer or director of the assurance client, or had been an employee in a position to exert direct and significant influence over the subject matter information of the assurance engagement, the threat created would be so significant that no safeguard could reduce the threat to an acceptable level. Consequently, such individuals should not be assigned to the assurance team.

290.148 If, prior to the period covered by the assurance report, a member of the assurance team had served as an officer or director of the assurance client, or had been an employee in a position to exert direct and significant influence over the subject matter information of the assurance engagement, this may create self-interest, self-review and familiarity threats. For example, such threats would be created if a decision made or work performed by the individual in the prior period, while employed by the assurance client, is to be evaluated in the current period as part of the current assurance engagement. The significance of the threats will depend upon factors such as:

- The position the individual held with the assurance client;
- The length of time that has passed since the individual left the assurance client; and
- The role the individual plays on the assurance team.

The significance of the threat should be evaluated and, if the threat is other than clearly insignificant, safeguards should be considered and applied as necessary to reduce the threat to an acceptable level. Such safeguards might include:

- Involving an additional professional accountant to review the work done by the individual as part of the assurance team or otherwise advise as necessary; or
- Discussing the issue with those charged with governance, such as the audit committee.

Serving as an Officer or Director on the Board of Assurance Clients

290.149 If a partner or employee of the firm serves as an officer or as a director on the board of an assurance client the self-review and self-interest threats created would be so significant that no safeguard could reduce the threats to an acceptable level. In the case of a financial statement audit engagement, if a partner or employee of a network firm were to serve as an officer or as a director on the board of the audit client, the threats created would be so significant that no safeguard could reduce the threats to an acceptable level. Consequently, if such an individual were to accept such a position the only course of action is to refuse to perform, or to withdraw from the assurance engagement.

290.150 The position of Company Secretary has different implications in different jurisdictions. The duties may range from administrative duties such as personnel management and the maintenance of company records and registers, to duties as diverse as ensuring that the company complies with regulations or providing advice on corporate governance matters. Generally, this position is seen to imply a close degree of association with the entity and may create self-review and advocacy threats.

290.151 If a partner or employee of the firm or a network firm serves as Company Secretary for a financial statement audit client, the self-review and advocacy threats created would generally be so significant, that no safeguard could reduce the threat to an acceptable level. When the practice is specifically permitted under local law, professional rules or practice, the duties and functions undertaken should be limited to those of a routine and formal administrative nature such as the preparation of minutes and maintenance of statutory returns.

290.152 Routine administrative services to support a company secretarial function or advisory work in relation to company secretarial administration matters is generally not perceived to impair independence, provided client management makes all relevant decisions.

Long Association of Senior Personnel with Assurance Clients

General Provisions

290.153 Using the same senior personnel on an assurance engagement over a long period of time may create a familiarity threat. The significance of the threat will depend upon factors such as:

- The length of time that the individual has been a member of the assurance team;
- The role of the individual on the assurance team;
- The structure of the firm; and
- The nature of the assurance engagement.

The significance of the threat should be evaluated and, if the threat is other than clearly insignificant, safeguards should be considered and applied to reduce the threat to an acceptable level. Such safeguards might include:

- Rotating the senior personnel off the assurance team;

- Involving an additional professional accountant who was not a member of the assurance team to review the work done by the senior personnel or otherwise advise as necessary; or
- Independent internal quality reviews.

Financial Statement Audit Clients That are Listed Entities[2]

290.154 Using the same engagement partner or the same individual responsible for the **engagement quality control review*** on a financial statement audit over a prolonged period may create a familiarity threat. This threat is particularly relevant in the context of the financial statement audit of a listed entity and safeguards should be applied in such situations to reduce such threat to an acceptable level. Accordingly, in respect of the financial statement audit of listed entities:

(a) The engagement partner and the individual responsible for the engagement quality control review should be rotated after serving in either capacity, or a combination thereof, for a pre-defined period, normally no more than seven years; and
(b) Such an individual rotating after a pre-defined period should not participate in the audit engagement until a further period of time, normally two years, has elapsed.

290.155 When a financial statement audit client becomes a listed entity the length of time the engagement partner or the individual responsible for the engagement quality control review has served the audit client in that capacity should be considered in determining when the individual should be rotated. However, the person may continue to serve as the engagement partner or as the individual responsible for the engagement quality control review for two additional years before rotating off the engagement.

290.156 While the engagement partner and the individual responsible for the engagement quality control review should be rotated after such a pre-defined period, some degree of flexibility over timing of rotation may be necessary in certain circumstances. Examples of such circumstances include:

- Situations when the person's continuity is especially important to the financial statement audit client, for example when there will be major changes to the audit client's structure that would otherwise coincide with the rotation of the person's; and
- Situations when, due to the size of the firm, rotation is not possible or does not constitute an appropriate safeguard.

In all such circumstances, when the person is not rotated after such a pre-defined period equivalent safeguards should be applied to reduce any threats to an acceptable level.

290.157 When a firm has only a few people with the necessary knowledge and experience to serve as engagement partner or individual responsible for the engagement quality control review on a financial statement audit client that is a listed entity, rotation may not be an appropriate safeguard. In these circumstances, the firm should apply other safeguards to reduce the threat to an acceptable level. Such safeguards would include involving an additional professional accountant who was not otherwise associated with the assurance team

---

[2]See also interpretation 2003–02 on page 54.
***See Definitions.**

to review the work done or otherwise advise as necessary. This individual could be someone from outside the firm or someone within the firm who was not otherwise associated with the assurance team.

Provision of Non-assurance Services to Assurance Clients[3]

290.158 Firms have traditionally provided to their assurance clients a range of non-assurance services that are consistent with their skills and expertise. Assurance clients value the benefits that they derive from having these firms, which have a good understanding of the business, bring their knowledge and skill to bear in other areas. Furthermore, the provision of such non-assurance services will often result in the assurance team obtaining information regarding the assurance client's business and operations that is helpful in relation to the assurance engagement. The greater the knowledge of the assurance client's business, the better the assurance team will understand the assurance client's procedures and controls, and the business and financial risks that it faces. The provision of non-assurance services may, however, create threats to the independence of the firm, a network firm or the members of the assurance team, particularly with respect to perceived threats to independence. Consequently, it is necessary to evaluate the significance of any threat created by the provision of such services. In some cases, it may be possible to eliminate or reduce the threat created by application of safeguards. In other cases, no safeguards are available to reduce the threat to an acceptable level.

290.159 The following activities would generally create self-interest or self-review threats that are so significant that only avoidance of the activity or refusal to perform the assurance engagement would reduce the threats to an acceptable level:

- Authorizing, executing or consummating a transaction, or otherwise exercising authority on behalf of the assurance client, or having the authority to do so.
- Determining which recommendation of the firm should be implemented.
- Reporting, in a management role, to those charged with governance.

290.160 The examples set out in paragraphs 290.166 through to 290.205 are addressed in the context of the provision of non-assurance services to an assurance client. The potential threats to independence will most frequently arise when a non-assurance service is provided to a financial statement audit client. The financial statements of an entity provide financial information about a broad range of transactions and events that have affected the entity. The subject matter information of other assurance services, however, may be limited in nature. Threats to independence, however, may also arise when a firm provides a non-assurance service related to the subject matter information of a non-financial statement audit assurance engagement. In such cases, consideration should be given to the significance of the firm's involvement with the subject matter information of the engagement, whether any self-review threats are created and whether any threats to independence could be reduced to an acceptable level by application of safeguards, or whether the engagement should be declined. When the non-assurance service is not related to the subject matter information of the non-financial statement audit assurance engagement, the threats to independence will generally be clearly insignificant.

[3]See also interpretation 2003–01 on page 54.

290.161 The following activities may also create self-review or self-interest threats:

- Having custody of an assurance client's assets.
- Supervising assurance client employees in the performance of their normal recurring activities.
- Preparing source documents or originating data, in electronic or other form, evidencing the occurrence of a transaction (for example, purchase orders, payroll time records, and customer orders).

The significance of any threat created should be evaluated and, if the threat is other than clearly insignificant, safeguards should be considered and applied as necessary to eliminate the threat or reduce it to an acceptable level. Such safeguards might include:

- Making arrangements so that personnel providing such services do not participate in the assurance engagement;
- Involving an additional professional accountant to advise on the potential impact of the activities on the independence of the firm and the assurance team; or
- Other relevant safeguards set out in national regulations.

290.162 New developments in business, the evolution of financial markets, rapid changes in information technology, and the consequences for management and control, make it impossible to draw up an all-inclusive list of all situations when providing non-assurance services to an assurance client might create threats to independence and of the different safeguards that might eliminate these threats or reduce them to an acceptable level. In general, however, a firm may provide services beyond the assurance engagement provided any threats to independence have been reduced to an acceptable level.

290.163 The following safeguards may be particularly relevant in reducing to an acceptable level threats created by the provision of non-assurance services to assurance clients:

- Policies and procedures to prohibit professional staff from making management decisions for the assurance client, or assuming responsibility for such decisions.
- Discussing independence issues related to the provision of non-assurance services with those charged with governance, such as the audit committee.
- Policies within the assurance client regarding the oversight responsibility for provision of non-assurance services by the firm.
- Involving an additional professional accountant to advise on the potential impact of the non-assurance engagement on the independence of the member of the assurance team and the firm.
- Involving an additional professional accountant outside of the firm to provide assurance on a discrete aspect of the assurance engagement.
- Obtaining the assurance client's acknowledgement of responsibility for the results of the work performed by the firm.
- Disclosing to those charged with governance, such as the audit committee, the nature and extent of fees charged.
- Making arrangements so that personnel providing non-assurance services do not participate in the assurance engagement.

290.164 Before the firm accepts an engagement to provide a non-assurance service to an assurance client, consideration should be given to whether the provision of such a service would create a threat to independence. In situations where a threat created is other than clearly insignificant, the non-assurance engagement should be declined unless appropriate safeguards can be applied to eliminate the threat or reduce it to an acceptable level.

290.165 The provision of certain non-assurance services to financial statement audit clients may create threats to independence so significant that no safeguard could eliminate the threat or reduce it to an acceptable level. However, the provision of such services to a related entity, division or discrete financial statement item of such clients may be permissible when any threats to the firm's independence have been reduced to an acceptable level by arrangements for that related entity, division or discrete financial statement item to be audited by another firm or when another firm reperforms the non-assurance service to the extent necessary to enable it to take responsibility for that service.

Preparing Accounting Records and Financial Statements

290.166 Assisting a financial statement audit client in matters such as preparing accounting records or financial statements may create a self-review threat when the financial statements are subsequently audited by the firm.

290.167 It is the responsibility of financial statement audit client management to ensure that accounting records are kept and financial statements are prepared, although they may request the firm to provide assistance. If the firm's, or network firm's, personnel providing such assistance make management decisions, the self-review threat created cannot be reduced to an acceptable level by any safeguards. Consequently, personnel should not make such decisions. Examples of such managerial decisions include:

- Determining or changing journal entries, or the classifications of accounts or transaction or other accounting records without obtaining the approval of the financial statement audit client;
- Authorizing or approving transactions; and
- Preparing source documents or originating data (including decisions on valuation assumptions), or making changes to such documents or data.

290.168 The audit process involves extensive dialogue between the firm and management of the financial statement audit client. During this process, management requests and receives significant input regarding such matters as accounting principles and financial statement disclosure, the appropriateness of controls and the methods used in determining the stated amounts of assets and liabilities. Technical assistance of this nature and advice on accounting principles for financial statement audit clients are an appropriate means to promote the fair presentation of the financial statements. The provision of such advice does not generally threaten the firm's independence. Similarly, the financial statement audit process may involve assisting an audit client in resolving account reconciliation problems, analyzing and accumulating information for regulatory reporting, assisting in the preparation of consolidated financial statements (including the translation of local statutory accounts to comply with group accounting policies and the transition to a different reporting framework such as International Financial Reporting Standards), drafting disclosure items, proposing adjusting journal entries and providing assistance and advice in the preparation of local statutory accounts of subsidiary entities. These services are considered to be a normal part of the audit process and do not, under normal circumstances, threaten independence.

General Provisions

290.169 The examples in paragraphs 290.170 through 290.173 indicate that self-review threats may be created if the firm is involved in the preparation of accounting records or financial statements and those financial statements are subsequently the subject matter information of an audit engagement of the firm. This notion may be equally applicable in situations when the subject matter information of the assurance engagement are not financial statements. For example, a self-review threat would be created if the firm developed and prepared prospective financial information and subsequently provided assurance on this prospective financial information. Consequently, the firm should evaluate the significance of any self-review threat created by the provision of such services. If the self-review threat is other than clearly insignificant, safeguards should be considered and applied as necessary to reduce the threat to an acceptable level.

Financial Statements Audit Clients that are Not Listed Entities

290.170 The firm, or a network firm, may provide a financial statement audit client that is not a listed entity with accounting and bookkeeping services, including payroll services, of a routine or mechanical nature, provided any self-review threat created is reduced to an acceptable level. Examples of such services include:

- Recording transactions for which the audit client has determined or approved the appropriate account classification;
- Posting coded transactions to the audit client's general ledger;
- Preparing financial statements based on information in the trial balance; and
- Posting the audit client approved entries to the trial balance.

The significance of any threat created should be evaluated and, if the threat is other than clearly insignificant, safeguards should be considered and applied as necessary to reduce the threat to an acceptable level. Such safeguards might include:

- Making arrangements so that such services are not performed by a member of the assurance team;
- Implementing policies and procedures to prohibit the individual providing such services from making any managerial decisions on behalf of the audit client;
- Requiring the source data for the accounting entries to be originated by the audit client;
- Requiring the underlying assumptions to be originated and approved by the audit client; or
- Obtaining audit client approval for any proposed journal entries or other changes affecting the financial statements.

Financial Statement Audit Clients that are Listed Entities

290.171 The provision of accounting and bookkeeping services, including payroll services and the preparation of financial statements or financial information which forms the basis of the financial statements on which the audit report is provided, on behalf of a financial statement audit client that is a listed entity, may impair the independence of the firm or network firm, or at least give the appearance of impairing independence. Accordingly, no safeguard other than the prohibition of such services, except in emergency situations and when the services fall within the statutory audit mandate, could reduce the threat created to an acceptable level. Therefore, a firm or a network firm should not, with the limited exceptions below, provide such services to a listed entity that is a financial statement audit client.

290.172 The provision of accounting and bookkeeping services of a routine or mechanical nature to divisions or subsidiaries of a financial statement audit client that is a listed entity would not be seen as impairing independence with respect to the audit client, provided that the following conditions are met:

(a) The services do not involve the exercise of judgment.
(b) The divisions or subsidiaries for which the service is provided are collectively immaterial to the audit client, or the services provided are collectively immaterial to the division or subsidiary.
(c) The fees to the firm, or network firm, from such services are collectively clearly insignificant.

If such services are provided, all of the following safeguards should be applied:

(a) The firm, or network firm, should not assume any managerial role nor make any managerial decisions.
(b) The audit client should accept responsibility for the results of the work.
(c) Personnel providing the services should not participate in the audit.

Emergency Situations

290.173 The provision of accounting and bookkeeping services to financial statement audit clients in emergency or other unusual situations, when it is impractical for the audit client to make other arrangements, would not be considered to pose an unacceptable threat to independence provided:

(a) The firm, or network firm, does not assume any managerial role or make any managerial decisions;
(b) The audit client accepts responsibility for the results of the work; and
(c) Personnel providing the services are not members of the assurance team.

Valuation Services

290.174 A valuation comprises the making of assumptions with regard to future developments, the application of certain methodologies and techniques, and the combination of both in order to compute a certain value, or range of values, for an asset, a liability or for a business as a whole.

290.175 A self-review threat may be created when a firm or network firm performs a valuation for a financial statement audit client that is to be incorporated into the client's financial statements.

290.176 If the valuation service involves the valuation of matters material to the financial statements and a significant degree of subjectivity, the self-review threat created cannot be reduced to an acceptable level by the application of any safeguard. Accordingly, such valuation services should not be provided or, alternatively, the only course of action would be to withdraw from the financial statement audit engagement.

290.177 Performing valuation services for a financial statement audit client that are neither separately, nor in the aggregate, material to the financial statements, or that do not involve a significant degree of subjectivity, may create a self-review threat that could be reduced to an acceptable level by the application of safeguards. Such safeguards might include:

- Involving an additional professional accountant who was not a member of the assurance team to review the work done or otherwise advise as necessary;
- Confirming with the audit client their understanding of the underlying assumptions of the valuation and the methodology to be used and obtaining approval for their use;
- Obtaining the audit client's acknowledgement of responsibility for the results of the work performed by the firm; and
- Making arrangements so that personnel providing such services do not participate in the audit engagement.

In determining whether the above safeguards would be effective, consideration should be given to the following matters:

(a) The extent of the audit client's knowledge, experience and ability to evaluate the issues concerned, and the extent of their involvement in determining and approving significant matters of judgment.
(b) The degree to which established methodologies and professional guidelines are applied when performing a particular valuation service.
(c) For valuations involving standard or established methodologies, the degree of subjectivity inherent in the item concerned.
(d) The reliability and extent of the underlying data.
(e) The degree of dependence on future events of a nature which could create significant volatility inherent in the amounts involved.
(f) The extent and clarity of the disclosures in the financial statements.

290.178 When a firm, or a network firm, performs a valuation service for a financial statement audit client for the purposes of making a filing or return to a tax authority, computing an amount of tax due by the client, or for the purpose of tax planning, this would not create a significant threat to independence because such valuations are generally subject to external review, for example by a tax authority.

290.179 When the firm performs a valuation that forms part of the subject matter information of an assurance engagement that is not a financial statement audit engagement, the firm should consider any self-review threats. If the threat is other than clearly insignificant, safeguards should be considered and applied as necessary to eliminate the threat or reduce it to an acceptable level.

Provision of Taxation Services to Financial Statement Audit Clients

290.180 In many jurisdictions, the firm may be asked to provide taxation services to a financial statement audit client. Taxation services comprise a broad range of services, including compliance, planning, provision of formal taxation opinions and assistance in the resolution of tax disputes. Such assignments are generally not seen to create threats to independence.

Provision of Internal Audit Services to Financial Statement Audit Clients

290.181 A self-review threat may be created when a firm, or network firm, provides internal audit services to a financial statement audit client. Internal audit services may comprise an extension of the firm's audit service beyond requirements of generally accepted auditing standards, assistance in the performance of a client's internal audit activities or outsourcing of the activities. In evaluating any threats to independence, the nature of the service will need to be considered. For this purpose, internal audit services do not include operational internal audit services unrelated to the internal accounting controls, financial systems or financial statements.

290.182 Services involving an extension of the procedures required to conduct a financial statement audit in accordance with International Standards on Auditing would not be considered to impair independence with respect to the audit client provided that the firm's or network firm's personnel do not act or appear to act in a capacity equivalent to a member of audit client management.

290.183 When the firm, or a network firm, provides assistance in the performance of a financial statement audit client's internal audit activities or undertakes the outsourcing of some of the activities, any self-review threat created may be reduced to an acceptable level by ensuring that there is a clear separation between the management and control of the internal audit by client management and the internal audit activities themselves.

290.184 Performing a significant portion of the financial statement audit client's internal audit activities may create a self-review threat and a firm, or network firm, should consider the threats and proceed with caution before taking on such activities. Appropriate safeguards should be put in place and the firm, or network firm, should, in particular, ensure that the audit client acknowledges its responsibilities for establishing, maintaining and monitoring the system of internal controls.

290.185 Safeguards that should be applied in all circumstances to reduce any threats created to an acceptable level include ensuring that:

(a) The audit client is responsible for internal audit activities and acknowledges its responsibility for establishing, maintaining and monitoring the system of internal controls;
(b) The audit client designates a competent employee, preferably within senior management, to be responsible for internal audit activities;
(c) The audit client, the audit committee or supervisory body approves the scope, risk and frequency of internal audit work;
(d) The audit client is responsible for evaluating and determining which recommendations of the firm should be implemented;
(e) The audit client evaluates the adequacy of the internal audit procedures performed and the findings resulting from the performance of those procedures by, among other things, obtaining and acting on reports from the firm; and
(f) The findings and recommendations resulting from the internal audit activities are reported appropriately to the audit committee or supervisory body.

290.186 Consideration should also be given to whether such non-assurance services should be provided only by personnel not involved in the financial statement audit engagement and with different reporting lines within the firm.

Provision of IT Systems Services to Financial Statement Audit Clients

290.187 The provision of services by a firm or network firm to a financial statement audit client that involves the design and implementation of financial information technology systems that are used to generate information forming part of a client's financial statements may create a self-review threat.

290.188 The self-review threat is likely to be too significant to allow the provision of such services to a financial statement audit client unless appropriate safeguards are put in place ensuring that:

(a) The audit client acknowledges its responsibility for establishing and monitoring a system of internal controls;
(b) The audit client designates a competent employee, preferably within senior management, with the responsibility to make all management decisions with respect to the design and implementation of the hardware or software system;
(c) The audit client makes all management decisions with respect to the design and implementation process;
(d) The audit client evaluates the adequacy and results of the design and implementation of the system; and
(e) The audit client is responsible for the operation of the system (hardware or software) and the data used or generated by the system.

290.189 Consideration should also be given to whether such non-assurance services should be provided only by personnel not involved in the financial statement audit engagement and with different reporting lines within the firm.

290.190 The provision of services by a firm, or network firm, to a financial statement audit client which involves either the design or the implementation of financial information technology systems that are used to generate information forming part of a client's financial statements may also create a self-review threat. The significance of the threat, if any, should be evaluated and, if the threat is other than clearly insignificant, safeguards should be considered and applied as necessary to eliminate the threat or reduce it to an acceptable level.

290.191 The provision of services in connection with the assessment, design and implementation of internal accounting controls and risk management controls are not considered to create a threat to independence provided that the firm's or network firm's personnel do not perform management functions.

Temporary Staff Assignments to Financial Statement Audit Clients

290.192 The lending of staff by a firm, or network firm, to a financial statement audit client may create a self-review threat when the individual is in a position to influence the preparation of a client's accounts or financial statements. In practice, such assistance may be given (particularly in emergency situations) but only on the understanding that the firm's or network firm's personnel will not be involved in:

(a) Making management decisions;
(b) Approving or signing agreements or other similar documents; or
(c) Exercising discretionary authority to commit the client.

Each situation should be carefully analyzed to identify whether any threats are created and whether appropriate safeguards should be implemented. Safeguards that should be applied in all circumstances to reduce any threats to an acceptable level include:

- The staff providing the assistance should not be given audit responsibility for any function or activity that they performed or supervised during their temporary staff assignment; and
- The audit client should acknowledge its responsibility for directing and supervising the activities of the firm's, or network firm's, personnel.

Provision of Litigation Support Services to Financial Statement Audit Clients

290.193 Litigation support services may include activities such as acting as an expert witness, calculating estimated damages or other amounts that might become receivable or payable as the result of litigation or other legal dispute, and assistance with document management and retrieval in relation to a dispute or litigation.

290.194 A self-review threat may be created when the litigation support services provided to a financial statement audit client include the estimation of the possible outcome and thereby affects the amounts or disclosures to be reflected in the financial statements. The significance of any threat created will depend upon factors such as:

- The materiality of the amounts involved;
- The degree of subjectivity inherent in the matter concerned; and
- The nature of the engagement.

The firm, or network firm, should evaluate the significance of any threat created and, if the threat is other than clearly insignificant, safeguards should be considered and applied as necessary to eliminate the threat or reduce it to an acceptable level. Such safeguards might include:

- Policies and procedures to prohibit individuals assisting the audit client from making managerial decisions on behalf of the client;
- Using professionals who are not members of the assurance team to perform the service; or
- The involvement of others, such as independent experts.

290.195 If the role undertaken by the firm or network firm involved making managerial decisions on behalf of the financial statement audit client, then the threats created could not be reduced to an acceptable level by the application of any safeguard. Therefore, the firm or network firm should not perform this type of service for an audit client.

Provision of Legal Services to Financial Statement Audit Clients

290.196 Legal services are defined as any services for which the person providing the services must either be admitted to practice before the Courts of the jurisdiction in which such services are to be provided, or have the required legal training to practice law. Legal services encompass a wide and diversified range of areas including both corporate and commercial services to clients, such as contract support, litigation, mergers and acquisition advice and support and the provision of assistance to clients' internal legal departments. The provision of legal services by a firm, or network firm, to an entity that is a financial statement audit client may create both self-review and advocacy threats.

290.197 Threats to independence need to be considered depending on the nature of the service to be provided, whether the service provider is separate from the assurance team and the materiality of any matter in relation to the entities' financial statements. The safeguards set out in paragraph 290.162 may be appropriate in reducing any threats to independence to an acceptable level. In circumstances when the threat to independence cannot be reduced to an acceptable level, the only available action is to decline to provide such services or withdraw from the financial statement audit engagement.

290.198 The provision of legal services to a financial statement audit client which involves matters that would not be expected to have a material effect on the financial statements are not considered to create an unacceptable threat to independence.

290.199 There is a distinction between advocacy and advice. Legal services to support a financial statement audit client in the execution of a transaction (e.g. contract support, legal advice, legal due diligence and restructuring) may create self-review threats; however, safeguards may be available to reduce these threats to an acceptable level. Such a service would not generally impair independence, provided that:

(a) Members of the assurance team are not involved in providing the service; and
(b) In relation to the advice provided, the audit client makes the ultimate decision or, in relation to the transactions, the service involves the execution of what has been decided by the audit client.

290.200 Acting for a financial statement audit client in the resolution of a dispute or litigation in such circumstances, when the amounts involved are material in relation to the financial statements of the audit client, would create advocacy and self-review threats so significant that no safeguard could reduce the threat to an acceptable level. Therefore, the firm should not perform this type of service for a financial statement audit client.

290.201 When a firm is asked to act in an advocacy role for a financial statement audit client in the resolution of a dispute or litigation in circumstances when the amounts involved are not material to the financial statements of the audit client, the firm should evaluate the significance of any advocacy and self-review threats created and, if the threat is other than clearly insignificant, safeguards should be considered and applied as necessary to eliminate the threat or reduce it to an acceptable level. Such safeguards might include:

- Policies and procedures to prohibit individuals assisting the audit client from making managerial decisions on behalf of the client; or
- Using professionals who are not members of the assurance team to perform the service.

290.202 The appointment of a partner or an employee of the firm or network firm as General Counsel for legal affairs to a financial statement audit client would create self-review and advocacy threats that are so significant that no safeguards could reduce the threats to an acceptable level. The position of General Counsel is generally a senior management position with broad responsibility for the legal affairs of a company and consequently, no member of the firm or network firm should accept such an appointment for a financial statement audit client.

Recruiting Senior Management

290.203 The recruitment of senior management for an assurance client, such as those in a position to affect the subject matter information of the assurance engagement, may create current or future self-interest, familiarity and intimidation threats. The significance of the threat will depend upon factors such as:

- The role of the person to be recruited; and
- The nature of the assistance sought.

The firm could generally provide such services as reviewing the professional qualifications of a number of applicants and provide advice on their suitability for the post. In addition, the firm could generally produce a short-list of candidates for interview, provided it has been drawn up using criteria specified by the assurance client. The significance of the threat created should be evaluated and, if the threat is other than clearly insignificant, safeguards should be considered and applied as necessary to reduce the threat to an acceptable level. In all cases, the firm should not make management decisions and the decision as to whom to hire should be left to the client.

Corporate Finance and Similar Activities

290.204 The provision of corporate finance services, advice or assistance to an assurance client may create advocacy and self-review threats. In the case of certain corporate finance services, the independence threats created would be so significant that no safeguards could be applied to reduce the threats to an acceptable level. For example, promoting, dealing in, or underwriting of an assurance client's shares is not compatible with providing assurance services. Moreover, committing the assurance client to the terms of a transaction or consummating a transaction on behalf of the client would create a threat to independence so significant that no safeguard could reduce the threat to an acceptable level. In the case of a financial statement audit client the provision of those corporate finance services referred to above by a firm or a network firm would create a threat to independence so significant that no safeguard could reduce the threat to an acceptable level.

290.205 Other corporate finance services may create advocacy or self-review threats; however, safeguards may be available to reduce these threats to an acceptable level. Examples of such services include assisting a client in developing corporate strategies, assisting in identifying or introducing a client to possible sources of capital that meet the client specifications or criteria, and providing structuring advice and assisting a client in analyzing the accounting effects of proposed transactions. Safeguards that should be considered include:

- Policies and procedures to prohibit individuals assisting the assurance client from making managerial decisions on behalf of the client;
- Using professionals who are not members of the assurance team to provide the services; and
- Ensuring the firm does not commit the assurance client to the terms of any transaction or consummate a transaction on behalf of the client.

Fees and Pricing

Fees – Relative Size

290.206 When the total fees generated by an assurance client represent a large proportion of a firm's total fees, the dependence on that client or client group and concern about the possibility of losing the client may create a self-interest threat. The significance of the threat will depend upon factors such as:

- The structure of the firm; and
- Whether the firm is well established or newly created.

The significance of the threat should be evaluated and, if the threat is other than clearly insignificant, safeguards should be considered and applied as necessary to reduce the threat to an acceptable level. Such safeguards might include:

- Discussing the extent and nature of fees charged with the audit committee, or others charged with governance;
- Taking steps to reduce dependency on the client;
- External quality control reviews; and
- Consulting a third party, such as a professional regulatory body or another professional accountant.

290.207 A self-interest threat may also be created when the fees generated by the assurance client represent a large proportion of the revenue of an individual partner. The significance of the threat should be evaluated and, if the threat is other than clearly insignificant, safeguards should be considered and applied as necessary to reduce the threat to an acceptable level. Such safeguards might include:

- Policies and procedures to monitor and implement quality control of assurance engagements; and
- Involving an additional professional accountant who was not a member of the assurance team to review the work done or otherwise advise as necessary.

Fees – Overdue

290.208 A self-interest threat may be created if fees due from an assurance client for professional services remain unpaid for a long time, especially if a significant part is not paid before the issue of the assurance report for the following year. Generally, the payment of such fees should be required before the report is issued. The following safeguards may be applicable:

- Discussing the level of outstanding fees with the audit committee, or others charged with governance.
- Involving an additional professional accountant who did not take part in the assurance engagement to provide advice or review the work performed.

The firm should also consider whether the overdue fees might be regarded as being equivalent to a loan to the client and whether, because of the significance of the overdue fees, it is appropriate for the firm to be re-appointed.

Pricing

290.209 When a firm obtains an assurance engagement at a significantly lower fee level than that charged by the predecessor firm, or quoted by other firms, the self-interest threat created will not be reduced to an acceptable level unless;

(a) The firm is able to demonstrate that appropriate time and qualified staff are assigned to the task; and
(b) All applicable assurance standards, guidelines and quality control procedures are being complied with.

Contingent Fees

290.210 Contingent fees are fees calculated on a predetermined basis relating to the outcome or result of a transaction or the result of the work performed. For the purposes of this section, fees are not regarded as being contingent if a court or other public authority has established them.

290.211 A contingent fee charged by a firm in respect of an assurance engagement creates self-interest and advocacy threats that cannot be reduced to an acceptable level by the application of any safeguard. Accordingly, a firm should not enter into any fee arrangement for an assurance engagement under which the amount of the fee is contingent on the result of the assurance work or on items that are the subject matter information of the assurance engagement.

290.212 A contingent fee charged by a firm in respect of a non-assurance service provided to an assurance client may also create self-interest and advocacy threats. If the amount of the fee for a non-assurance engagement was agreed to, or contemplated, during an assurance engagement and was contingent on the result of that assurance engagement, the threats could not be reduced to an acceptable level by the application of any safeguard. Accordingly, the only acceptable action is not to accept such arrangements. For other types of contingent fee arrangements, the significance of the threats created will depend on factors such as:

- The range of possible fee amounts;
- The degree of variability;
- The basis on which the fee is to be determined;
- Whether the outcome or result of the transaction is to be reviewed by an independent third party; and
- The effect of the event or transaction on the assurance engagement.

The significance of the threats should be evaluated and, if the threats are other than clearly insignificant, safeguards should be considered and applied as necessary to reduce the threats to an acceptable level. Such safeguards might include:

- Disclosing to the audit committee, or others charged with governance, the extent and nature of fees charged;
- Review or determination of the final fee by an unrelated third party; or
- Quality and control policies and procedures.

Gifts and Hospitality

290.213 Accepting gifts or hospitality from an assurance client may create self-interest and familiarity threats. When a firm or a member of the assurance team accepts gifts or hospitality, unless the value is clearly insignificant, the threats to independence cannot be reduced to an acceptable level by the application of any safeguard. Consequently, a firm or a member of the assurance team should not accept such gifts or hospitality.

Actual or Threatened Litigation

290.214 When litigation takes place, or appears likely, between the firm or a member of the assurance team and the assurance client, a self-interest or intimidation threat may be created. The relationship between client management and the members of the assurance team must be characterized by complete candour and full disclosure regarding all aspects of a client's business operations. The firm and the client's management may be placed in adversarial positions by litigation, affecting management's willingness to make complete disclosures, and the firm may face a self-interest threat. The significance of the threat created will depend upon such factors as:

- The materiality of the litigation;
- The nature of the assurance engagement; and
- Whether the litigation relates to a prior assurance engagement.

Once the significance of the threat has been evaluated the following safeguards should be applied, if necessary, to reduce the threats to an acceptable level:

(a) Disclosing to the audit committee, or others charged with governance, the extent and nature of the litigation;
(b) If the litigation involves a member of the assurance team, removing that individual from the assurance team; or
(c) Involving an additional professional accountant in the firm who was not a member of the assurance team to review the work done or otherwise advise as necessary.

If such safeguards do not reduce the threat to an appropriate level, the only appropriate action is to withdraw from, or refuse to accept, the assurance engagement.

Section 290 Interpretations

NB These interpretations are not part of the CIMA Code of Ethics, but are intended as guidance only. These interpretations are directed towards the application of the *CIMA Code of Ethics* to the topics of the specific queries received. Those subject to the regulations of other authoritative bodies, such as the US Securities and Exchange Commission, may wish to consult with them for their positions on these matters.

Interpretation 2003–01

The provision of non-assurance services to assurance clients

The *CIMA Code of Ethics* addresses the issue of the provision of non-assurance services to assurance clients in paragraphs 290.158–290.205 inclusive. The Code does not currently include any transitional provisions relating to the requirements set out in these paragraphs, however it is appropriate to allow a transitional period of one year, during which existing contracts to provide non-assurance services for assurance clients may be completed if additional safeguards are put in place to reduce any threat to independence to an insignificant level. This transitional period commences from the date of implementation of the Code for members of CIMA.

Interpretation 2003–02

Lead engagement partner rotation for audit clients that are listed entities

The *CIMA Code of Ethics* addresses the issue of engagement partner rotation for financial statement audit clients that are listed entities in paragraphs 290.154–290.157. The paragraphs state that in the financial statement audit of a listed entity, the engagement partner should be rotated after serving in that capacity for a pre-defined period, normally no more than seven years. They also state that some degree of flexibility in the timing of rotation may be necessary in certain circumstances. The implementation (or early adoption) of this Code constitutes an example of a circumstance in which some degree of flexibility over timing of rotation may be necessary.

The Code does not currently include any transitional provisions relating to these requirements. It is appropriate to allow a transitional period of two years. Consequently, on implementation or early adoption of this Code, while the length of time the engagement partner has served the financial statement audit client in that capacity should be considered in determining when rotation should occur, the partner may continue to serve as the engagement partner for two additional years from the date of implementation (or early adoption) before rotating off the engagement. In such circumstances, the additional requirements of paragraph 290.157 to apply equivalent safeguards in order to reduce any threats to an acceptable level should be followed.

Interpretation 2005–01

Application of Section 290 to assurance engagements that are not financial statement audit engagements

This interpretation provides guidance on the application of the independence requirements contained in Section 290 to assurance engagements that are not financial statement audit engagements. This interpretation focuses on the application issues that are particular to assurance engagements that are not financial statement audit engagements. There are other matters noted in Section 290 that are relevant in the consideration of independence requirements for all assurance engagements. For example, paragraph 290.15 states that consideration should be given to any threats the firm has reason to believe may be created by network firms' interests and relationships. Similarly, paragraph 290.21 states that for assurance clients, that are other than listed entity financial statement audit clients, when the assurance team has reason to believe that a related entity of such an assurance client is relevant to the evaluation of the firm's independence of the client, the assurance team should consider that related entity when evaluating independence and applying appropriate safeguards. These matters are not specifically addressed in this interpretation. The International Framework for Assurance Engagements issued by the IAASB (page 178 of the 2005 Handbook, found at www.ifac.org/Members/DownLoads/2005 IAASB handBook.pdf) states that in an assurance engagement, the professional accountant in public practice expresses a conclusion designed to enhance the degree of confidence of the intended users other than the responsible party about the outcome of the evaluation or measurement of a subject matter against criteria.

Assertion-based Assurance Engagements

In an assertion-based assurance engagement, the evaluation or measurement of the subject matter is performed by the responsible party, and the subject matter information is in the form of an assertion by the responsible party that is made available to the intended users. In an assertion-based assurance engagement independence is required from the responsible party, which is responsible for the subject matter information and may be responsible for the subject matter.

In those assertion-based assurance engagements where the responsible party is responsible for the subject matter information but not the subject matter, independence is required from the responsible party. In addition, consideration should be given to any threats the firm has reason to believe may be created by interests and relationships between a member of the assurance team, the firm, a network firm and the party responsible for the subject matter.

Direct Reporting Assurance Engagements

In a direct reporting assurance engagement, the professional accountant in public practice either directly performs the evaluation or measurement of the subject matter, or obtains a representation from the responsible party that has performed the evaluation or measurement that is not available to the intended users. The subject matter information is provided to the intended users in the assurance report.

In a direct reporting assurance engagement, independence is required from the responsible party, which is responsible for the subject matter.

Multiple Responsible Parties

In both assertion-based assurance engagements and direct reporting assurance engagements there may be several responsible parties. For example, a public accountant in public practice may be asked to provide assurance on the monthly circulation statistics of a number of independently owned newspapers. The assignment could be an assertion based assurance engagement, where each newspaper measures its circulation and the statistics are presented in an assertion that is available to the intended users. Alternatively, the assignment could be a direct reporting assurance engagement, where there is no assertion and there may or may not be a written representation from the newspapers.

In such engagements, when determining whether it is necessary to apply the provisions in Section 290 to each responsible party, the firm may take into account whether an interest or relationship between the firm, or a member of the assurance team, and a particular responsible party would create a threat to independence that is other than clearly insignificant in the context of the subject matter information. This will take into account:

- The materiality of the subject matter information (or the subject matter) for which the particular responsible party is responsible; and
- The degree of public interest that is associated with the engagement.

If the firm determines that the threat to independence created by any such relationships with a particular responsible party would be clearly insignificant, it may not be necessary to apply all of the provisions of this section to that responsible party.

The following example has been developed to demonstrate the application of Section 290. It is assumed that the client is not also a financial statement audit client of the firm, or a network firm.

A firm is engaged to provide assurance on the total proven oil reserves of 10 independent companies. Each company has conducted geographical and engineering surveys to determine their reserves (subject matter). There are established criteria to determine when a reserve may be considered to be proven, which the professional accountant in public practice determines to be a suitable criteria for the engagement.

The proven reserves for each company as at December 31, 20X0 were as follows:

	Proven oil reserves thousands barrels
Company 1	5,200
Company 2	725
Company 3	3,260
Company 4	15,000
Company 5	6,700
Company 6	39,126
Company 7	345
Company 8	175
Company 9	24,135
Company 10	9,635
TOTAL	**104,301**

The engagement could be structured in differing ways:

Assertion based engagements

A1 Each company measures its reserves and provides an assertion to the firm and to intended users.

A2 An entity other than the companies measures the reserves and provides an assertion to the firm and to intended users.

Direct reporting engagements

D1 Each company measures the reserves and provides the firm with a written representation that measures its reserves against the established criteria for measuring proven reserves. The representation is not available to the intended users.

D2 The firm directly measures the reserves of some of the companies.

Application of approach

A1 Each company measures its reserves and provides an assertion to the firm and to intended users.

There are several responsible parties in this engagement (companies 1–10). When determining whether it is necessary to apply the independence provisions to all of the companies, the firm may take into account whether an interest or relationship with a particular company would create a threat to independence that is other than clearly insignificant. This will take into account factors such as:

- The materiality of the company's proven reserves in relation to the total reserves to be reported on; and
- The degree of public interest associated with the engagement. (paragraph 290.20).

For example, Company 8 accounts for 0.16 per cent of the total reserves, therefore a business relationship or interest with the Company 8 would create less of a threat than a similar relationship with Company 6, which accounts for approximately 37.5 per cent of the reserves.

Having determined those companies to which the independence requirements apply, the assurance team and the firm are required to be independent of those responsible parties which would be considered to be the assurance client (paragraph 290.20).

A2 An entity other than the companies measures the reserves and provides an assertion to the firm and to intended users.

The firm would be required to be independent of the entity that measures the reserves and provides an assertion to the firm and to intended users (paragraph 290.17). That entity is not responsible for the subject matter and so consideration should be given to any threats the firm has reason to believe may be created by interests/relationships with the party responsible for the subject matter (paragraph 290.17). There are several parties responsible for subject matter in this engagement (companies 1–10) As discussed in example A1 above, the firm may take into account whether an interest or relationship with a particular company would create a threat to independence that is other than clearly insignificant.

D1 Each company provides the firm with a representation that measures its reserves against the established criteria for measuring proven reserves. The representation is not available to the intended users.

There are several responsible parties in this engagement (companies 1–10). When determining whether it is necessary to apply the independence provisions to all of the companies, the firm may take into account whether an interest or relationship with a particular company would create a threat to independence that is other than clearly insignificant. This will take into account factors such as:

- The materiality of the company's proven reserves in relation to the total reserves to be reported on; and
- The degree of public interest associated with the engagement. (paragraph 290.20).

For example, Company 8 accounts for 0.16 per cent of the reserves, therefore a business relationship or interest with the Company 8 would create less of a threat than a similar relationship with Company 6 that accounts for approximately 37.5 per cent of the reserves.

Having determined those companies to which the independence requirements apply, the assurance team and the firm are required to be independent of those responsible parties which would be considered to be the assurance client (paragraph 290.20).

D2 The firm directly measures the reserves of some of the companies

The application is the same as in example D1.

Part C: Professional Accountants in Business

Section 300

Introduction

300.1 This Part of the Code illustrates how the conceptual framework contained in Part A is to be applied by professional accountants in business.

300.2 Investors, creditors, employers and other sectors of the business community, as well as governments and the public at large, all may rely on the work of professional accountants in business. Professional accountants in business may be solely or jointly responsible for the preparation and reporting of financial and other information, which both their employing organizations and third parties may rely on. They may also be responsible for providing effective financial management and competent advice on a variety of business-related matters.

300.3 A professional accountant in business may be a salaried employee, a partner, director (whether executive or non-executive), an owner-manager, a volunteer or another working for one or more employing organizations. The legal form of the relationship with the employing organization, if any, has no bearing on the ethical responsibilities incumbent on the professional accountant in business.

300.4 A professional accountant in business has a responsibility to further the legitimate aims of their employing organization. This Code does not seek to hinder a professional accountant in business from properly fulfilling that responsibility, but considers circumstances in which conflicts may be created with the absolute duty to comply with the fundamental principles.

300.5 A professional accountant in business often holds a senior position within an organization. The more senior the position, the greater will be the ability and opportunity to influence events, practices and attitudes. A professional accountant in business is expected, therefore, to encourage an ethics-based culture in an employing organization that emphasizes the importance that senior management places on ethical behaviour.

300.6 The examples presented in the following sections are intended to illustrate how the conceptual framework is to be applied and are not intended to be, nor should they be interpreted as, an exhaustive list of all circumstances experienced by a professional accountant in business that may create threats to compliance with the principles. Consequently, it is not sufficient for a professional accountant in business merely to comply with the examples; rather, the framework should be applied to the particular circumstances faced.

Threats and Safeguards

300.7 Compliance with the fundamental principles may potentially be threatened by a broad range of circumstances. Many threats fall into the following categories:

(a) Self-interest;
(b) Self-review;
(c) Advocacy;
(d) Familiarity; and
(e) Intimidation

These threats are discussed further in Part A of this Code.

300.8 Examples of circumstances that may create self-interest threats for a professional accountant in business include, but are not limited to:

- Financial interests, loans or guarantees.
- Incentive compensation arrangements.
- Inappropriate personal use of corporate assets.
- Concern over employment security.
- Commercial pressure from outside the employing organization.

300.9 Circumstances that may create self-review threats include, but are not limited to, business decisions or data being subject to review and justification by the same professional accountant in business responsible for making those decisions or preparing that data.

300.10 When furthering the legitimate goals and objectives of their employing organizations, professional accountants in business may promote the organization's position, provided any statements made are neither false nor misleading. Such actions generally would not create an advocacy threat.

300.11 Examples of circumstances that may create familiarity threats include, but are not limited to:

- A professional accountant in business, in a position to influence financial or non-financial reporting or business decisions, having an immediate or close family member who is in a position to benefit from that influence.
- Long association with business contacts influencing business decisions.
- Acceptance of a gift or preferential treatment, unless the value is clearly insignificant.

300.12 Examples of circumstances that may create intimidation threats include, but are not limited to:

- Threat of dismissal or replacement of the professional accountant in business or a close or immediate family member over a disagreement about the application of an accounting principle or the way in which financial information is to be reported.
- A dominant personality attempting to influence the decision-making process, for example with regard to the awarding of contracts or the application of an accounting principle.

300.13 Professional accountants in business may also find that specific circumstances give rise to unique threats to compliance with one or more of the fundamental principles. Such unique threats obviously cannot be categorized. In all professional and business relationships, professional accountants in business should always be on the alert for such circumstances and threats.

300.14 Safeguards that may eliminate or reduce to an acceptable level the threats faced by professional accountants in business fall into two broad categories:

(a) Safeguards created by the profession, legislation or regulation; and
(b) Safeguards in the work environment.

300.15 Examples of safeguards created by the profession, legislation or regulation are detailed in paragraph 1.17 of Part A of this Code.

300.16 Safeguards in the work environment include, but are not restricted to:

- The employing organization's systems of corporate oversight or other oversight structures.
- The employing organization's ethics and conduct programs.
- Recruitment procedures in the employing organization emphasizing the importance of employing high calibre competent staff.
- Strong internal controls.
- Appropriate disciplinary processes.
- Leadership that stresses the importance of ethical behaviour and the expectation that employees will act in an ethical manner.
- Policies and procedures to implement and monitor the quality of employee performance.
- Timely communication of the employing organization's policies and procedures, including any changes to them, to all employees and appropriate training and education on such policies and procedures.
- Policies and procedures to empower and encourage employees to communicate to senior levels within the employing organization any ethical issues that concern them without fear of retribution.
- Consultation with another appropriate professional accountant.

300.17 In circumstances where a professional accountant in business believes that unethical behaviours or actions by others will continue to occur within the employing organization, the professional accountant in business should consider seeking legal advice. In those extreme situations where all available safeguards have been exhausted and it is not possible to reduce the threat to an acceptable level, a professional accountant in business may conclude that it is appropriate to resign from the employing organization.

Section 310

Potential Conflicts

310.1 A professional accountant in business has a professional obligation to comply with the fundamental principles. There may be times, however, when their responsibilities to an employing organization and the professional obligations to comply with the fundamental principles are in conflict. Ordinarily, a professional accountant in business should support the legitimate and ethical objectives established by the employer and the rules and procedures drawn up in support of those objectives. Nevertheless, where compliance with the fundamental principles is threatened, a professional accountant in business must consider a response to the circumstances.

310.2 As a consequence of responsibilities to an employing organization, a professional accountant in business may be under pressure to act or behave in ways that could directly or indirectly threaten compliance with the fundamental principles. Such pressure may be explicit or implicit; it may come from a supervisor, manager, director or another individual within the employing organization. A professional accountant in business may face pressure to:

- Act contrary to law or regulation.
- Act contrary to technical or professional standards.
- Facilitate unethical or illegal earnings management strategies.

- Lie to, or otherwise intentionally mislead (including misleading by remaining silent) others, in particular:
  - The auditors of the employing organization; or
  - Regulators.
- Issue, or otherwise be associated with, a financial or non-financial report that materially misrepresents the facts, including statements in connection with, for example:
  - The financial statements;
  - Tax compliance;
  - Legal compliance; or
  - Reports required by securities regulators.

310.3 The significance of threats arising from such pressures, such as intimidation threats, should be evaluated and, if they are other than clearly insignificant, safeguards should be considered and applied as necessary to eliminate them or reduce them to an acceptable level. Such safeguards may include:

- Obtaining advice where appropriate from within the employing organization, an independent professional advisor or a relevant professional body.
- The existence of a formal dispute resolution process within the employing organization.
- Seeking legal advice.

Section 320

Preparation and Reporting of Information

320.1 Professional accountants in business are often involved in the preparation and reporting of information that may either be made public or used by others inside or outside the employing organization. Such information may include financial or management information, for example forecasts and budgets, financial statements, management discussion and analysis, and the management letter of representation provided to the auditors as part of an audit of financial statements. A professional accountant in business should prepare or present such information fairly, honestly and in accordance with relevant professional standards so that the information will be understood in its context.

320.2 A professional accountant in business who has responsibility for the preparation or approval of the general purpose financial statements of an employing organization should ensure that those financial statements are presented in accordance with the applicable financial reporting standards.

320.3 A professional accountant in business should maintain information for which the professional accountant in business is responsible in a manner that:

(a) Describes clearly the true nature of business transactions, assets or liabilities;
(b) Classifies and records information in a timely and proper manner; and
(c) Represents the facts accurately and completely in all material respects.

320.4 Threats to compliance with the fundamental principles, for example self-interest or intimidation threats to objectivity or professional competence and due care, may be created where a professional accountant in business may be pressured (either externally or by the possibility of personal gain) to become associated with misleading information or to become associated with misleading information through the actions of others.

320.5 The significance of such threats will depend on factors such as the source of the pressure and the degree to which the information is, or may be, misleading. The significance of the threats should be evaluated and, if they are other than clearly insignificant, safeguards should be considered and applied as necessary to eliminate them or reduce them to an acceptable level. Such safeguards may include consultation with superiors within the employing organization, for example the audit committee or other body responsible for governance, or with a relevant professional body.

320.6 Where it is not possible to reduce the threat to an acceptable level, a professional accountant in business should refuse to remain associated with information they consider is or may be misleading. Should the professional accountant in business be aware that the issuance of misleading information is either significant or persistent, the professional accountant in business should consider informing appropriate authorities in line with the guidance in Section 140. The professional accountant in business may also wish to seek legal advice or resign.

Section 330

Acting with Sufficient Expertise

330.1 The fundamental principle of professional competence and due care requires that a professional accountant in business should only undertake significant tasks for which the professional accountant in business has, or can obtain, sufficient specific training or experience. A professional accountant in business should not intentionally mislead an employer as to the level of expertise or experience possessed, nor should a professional accountant in business fail to seek appropriate expert advice and assistance when required.

330.2 Circumstances that threaten the ability of a professional accountant in business to perform duties with the appropriate degree of professional competence and due care include:

- Insufficient time for properly performing or completing the relevant duties.
- Incomplete, restricted or otherwise inadequate information for performing the duties properly.
- Insufficient experience, training and/or education.
- Inadequate resources for the proper performance of the duties.

330.3 The significance of such threats will depend on factors such as the extent to which the professional accountant in business is working with others, relative seniority in the business and the level of supervision and review applied to the work. The significance of the threats should be evaluated and, if they are other than clearly insignificant, safeguards should be considered and applied as necessary to eliminate them or reduce them to an acceptable level. Safeguards that may be considered include:

- Obtaining additional advice or training.
- Ensuring that there is adequate time available for performing the relevant duties.

- Obtaining assistance from someone with the necessary expertise.
- Consulting, where appropriate, with:
  - Superiors within the employing organization;
  - Independent experts; or
  - A relevant professional body.

330.4 Where threats cannot be eliminated or reduced to an acceptable level, professional accountants in business should consider whether to refuse to perform the duties in question. If the professional accountant in business determines that refusal is appropriate, the reasons for doing so should be clearly communicated.

Section 340

Financial Interests

340.1 Professional accountants in business may have financial interests, or may know of financial interests of immediate or close family members that could, in certain circumstances, give rise to threats to compliance with the fundamental principles. For example, self-interest threats to objectivity or confidentiality may be created through the existence of the motive and opportunity to manipulate price sensitive information in order to gain financially. Examples of circumstances that may create self-interest threats include, but are not limited to, situations where the professional accountant in business or an immediate or close family member:

- Holds a direct or indirect financial interest in the employing organization and the value of that financial interest could be directly affected by decisions made by the professional accountant in business;
- Is eligible for a profit related bonus and the value of that bonus could be directly affected by decisions made by the professional accountant in business;
- Holds, directly or indirectly, share options in the employing organization, the value of which could be directly affected by decisions made by the professional accountant in business;
- Holds, directly or indirectly, share options in the employing organization which are, or will soon be, eligible for conversion; or
- May qualify for share options in the employing organization or performance related bonuses if certain targets are achieved.

340.2 In evaluating the significance of such a threat, and the appropriate safeguards to be applied to eliminate the threat or reduce it to an acceptable level, professional accountants in business must examine the nature of the financial interest. This includes an evaluation of the significance of the financial interest and whether it is direct or indirect. Clearly, what constitutes a significant or valuable stake in an organization will vary from individual to individual, depending on personal circumstances.

340.3 If threats are other than clearly insignificant, safeguards should be considered and applied as necessary to eliminate or reduce them to an acceptable level. Such safeguards may include:

- Policies and procedures for a committee independent of management to determine the level of form of remuneration of senior management.

- Disclosure of all relevant interests, and of any plans to trade in relevant shares to those charged with the governance of the employing organization, in accordance with any internal policies.
- Consultation, where appropriate, with superiors within the employing organization.
- Consultation, where appropriate, with those charged with the governance of the employing organization or relevant professional bodies.
- Internal and external audit procedures.
- Up-to-date education on ethical issues and the legal restrictions and other regulations around potential insider trading.

340.4 A professional accountant in business should neither manipulate information nor use confidential information for personal gain.

Section 350

Inducements

Receiving Offers

350.1 A professional accountant in business or an immediate or close family member may be offered an inducement. Inducements may take various forms, including gifts, hospitality, preferential treatment and inappropriate appeals to friendship or loyalty.

350.2 Offers of inducements may create threats to compliance with the fundamental principles. When a professional accountant in business or an immediate or close family member is offered an inducement, the situation should be carefully considered. Self-interest threats to objectivity or confidentiality are created where an inducement is made in an attempt to unduly influence actions or decisions, encourage illegal or dishonest behaviour or obtain confidential information. Intimidation threats to objectivity or confidentiality are created if such an inducement is accepted and it is followed by threats to make that offer public and damage the reputation of either the professional accountant in business or an immediate or close family member.

350.3 The significance of such threats will depend on the nature, value and intent behind the offer. If a reasonable and informed third party, having knowledge of all relevant information, would consider the inducement insignificant and not intended to encourage unethical behaviour, then a professional accountant in business may conclude that the offer is made in the normal course of business and may generally conclude that there is no significant threat to compliance with the fundamental principles.

350.4 If evaluated threats are other than clearly insignificant, safeguards should be considered and applied as necessary to eliminate them or reduce them to an acceptable level. When the threats cannot be eliminated or reduced to an acceptable level through the application of safeguards, a professional accountant in business should not accept the inducement. As the real or apparent threats to compliance with the fundamental principles do not merely arise from acceptance of an inducement but, sometimes, merely from the fact of the offer having been made, additional safeguards should be adopted. A professional accountant in business should assess the risk associated with all such offers and consider whether the following actions should be taken:

(a) Where such offers have been made, immediately inform higher levels of management or those charged with governance of the employing organization;
(b) Inform third parties of the offer – for example, a professional body or the employer of the individual who made the offer; a professional accountant in business should, however, consider seeking legal advice before taking such a step; and
(c) Advise immediate or close family members of relevant threats and safeguards where they are potentially in positions that might result in offers of inducements, for example as a result of their employment situation; and
(d) Inform higher levels of management or those charged with governance of the employing organization where immediate or close family members are employed by competitors or potential suppliers of that organization.

Making Offers

350.5 A professional accountant in business may be in a situation where he or she is expected to, or is under other pressure to, offer inducements to subordinate the judgment of another individual or organization, influence a decision-making process or obtain confidential information.

350.6 Such pressure may come from within the employing organization, for example from a colleague or superior. It may also come from an external individual or organization suggesting actions or business decisions that would be advantageous to the employing organization possibly influencing the professional accountant in business improperly.

350.7 A professional accountant in business should not offer an inducement to improperly influence professional judgment of a third party.

350.8 Where the pressure to offer such an ethical inducement comes from within the employing organization, the professional accountant should follow the principles and guidance regarding ethical conflict resolution set out in Part A of this Code.

Definitions

In this Code of Ethics for Professional Accountants the following expressions have the following meanings assigned to them:

Advertising

The communication to the public of information as to the services or skills provided by professional accountants in public practice with a view to procuring professional business.

Assurance client

The responsible party, that is the person (or persons) who:

(a) In a direct reporting engagement, is responsible for the subject matter; or
(b) In an assertion-based engagement, is responsible for the subject matter information and may be responsible for the subject matter.

(For an assurance client, that is a financial statement audit client, see the definition of financial statement audit client.)

Assurance engagement

An engagement in which a professional accountant in public practice expresses a conclusion designed to enhance the degree of confidence of the intended users other than the responsible party about the outcome of the evaluation or measurement of a subject matter against criteria.

(For guidance on assurance engagements, see the International Framework for Assurance Engagements issued by the International Auditing and Assurance Standards Board, which describes the elements and objectives of an assurance engagement and identifies engagements to which International Standards on Auditing (ISAs), International Standards on Review Engagements (ISREs) and International Standards on Assurance Engagements (ISAEs) apply.)

Assurance team

(a) All members of the engagement team for the assurance engagement;
(b) All others within a firm who can directly influence the outcome of the assurance engagement, including:
  (i) those who recommend the compensation of, or who provide direct supervisory, management or other oversight of the assurance engagement partner in connection with the performance of the assurance engagement. For the purposes of a financial statement audit engagement, this includes those at all successively senior levels above the engagement partner through the firm's chief executive;
  (ii) those who provide consultation regarding technical or industry specific issues, transactions or events for the assurance engagement; and
  (iii) those who provide quality control for the assurance engagement, including those who perform the engagement quality control review for the assurance engagement; and
(c) For the purposes of a financial statement audit client, all those within a network firm who can directly influence the outcome of the financial statement audit engagement.

Clearly insignificant

A matter that is deemed to be both trivial and inconsequential.

Close family

A parent, child or sibling, who is not an immediate family member.

Contingent fee

A fee calculated on a predetermined basis relating to the outcome or result of a transaction or the result of the work performed. A fee that is established by a court or other public authority is not a contingent fee.

Direct financial interest

A financial interest:

- Owned directly by and under the control of an individual or entity (including those managed on a discretionary basis by others); or
- Beneficially owned through a collective investment vehicle, estate, trust or other intermediary over which the individual or entity has control.

Director or officer

Those charged with the governance of an entity, regardless of their title, which may vary from country to country.

Engagement partner

The partner or other person in the firm who is responsible for the engagement and its performance, and for the report that is issued on behalf of the firm, and who, where required, has the appropriate authority from a professional, legal or regulatory body.

Engagement quality control review

A process designed to provide an objective evaluation, before the report is issued, of the significant judgments the engagement team made and the conclusions they reached in formulating the report.

Engagement team

All personnel performing an engagement, including any experts contracted by the firm in connection with that engagement.

Existing accountant

A professional accountant in public practice currently holding an audit appointment or carrying out accounting, taxation, consulting or similar professional services for a client.

Financial interest

An interest in an equity or other security, debenture, loan or other debt instrument of an entity, including rights and obligations to acquire such an interest and derivatives directly related to such interest.

Financial statements

The balance sheets, income statements or profit and loss accounts, statements of changes in financial position (which may be presented in a variety of ways, for example as a statement of cash flows or a statement of fund flows), notes and other statements and explanatory material which are identified as being part of the financial statements.

Financial statement audit client

An entity in respect of which a firm conducts a financial statement audit engagement. When the client is a listed entity, the term financial statement audit client will always include its related entities.

Financial statement audit engagement

A reasonable assurance engagement in which a professional accountant in public practice expresses an opinion whether financial statements are prepared in all material respects in accordance with an identified financial reporting framework, such as an engagement conducted in accordance with International Standards on Auditing. This includes a Statutory Audit, which is a financial statement audit required by legislation or other regulation.

Firm

(a) A sole practitioner, partnership or corporation of professional accountants;
(b) An entity that controls such parties; and
(c) An entity controlled by such parties.

IFAC

International Federation of Accountants (the global organization for the accountancy profession).

Immediate family

A spouse (or equivalent) or dependant.

Independence is:

(a) Independence of mind – the state of mind that permits the provision of an opinion without being affected by influences that compromise professional judgment, allowing an individual to act with integrity, and exercise objectivity and professional judgment
(b) Independence in appearance – the avoidance of facts and circumstances that are so significant that a reasonable and informed third party, having knowledge of all relevant information, including any safeguards applied, would reasonably conclude a firm's, or a member of the assurance team's, integrity, objectivity or professional scepticism had been compromised.

Indirect financial interest

A financial interest beneficially owned through a collective investment vehicle, estate, trust or other intermediary over which the individual or entity has no control.

Listed entity

An entity whose shares, stock or debt are quoted or listed on a recognized stock exchange, or are marketed under the regulations of a recognized stock exchange or other equivalent body.

Network firm

An entity under common control, ownership or management with the firm or any entity that a reasonable and informed third party having knowledge of all relevant information would reasonably conclude as being part of the firm nationally or internationally.

Office

A distinct sub-group, whether organized on geographical or practice lines.

Professional accountant

An individual who is a member or registered student of CIMA.

Professional accountant in business

A professional accountant employed or engaged in an executive or non-executive capacity in such areas as commerce, industry, service, the public sector, education, the not for profit sector, regulatory bodies or professional bodies, or a professional accountant contracted by such entities.

Professional accountant in public practice

A professional accountant, irrespective of functional classification (e.g. audit, tax or consulting) in a firm that provides professional services. This term is also used to refer to a firm of professional accountants in public practice.

Professional Services

Services requiring accountancy or related skills performed by a professional accountant, including accounting, auditing, taxation, management consulting and financial management services.

Related entity

An entity that has any of the following relationships with the client:

(a) An entity that has direct or indirect control over the client, provided the client is material to such entity;
(b) An entity with a direct financial interest in the client, provided that such entity has significant influence over the client and the interest in the client is material to such entity;
(c) An entity over which the client has direct or indirect control;
(d) An entity in which the client, or an entity related to the client under (c) above, has a direct financial interest that gives it significant influence over such entity and the interest is material to the client and its related entity in (c); and

An entity which is under common control with the client (hereinafter a 'sister entity'), provided the sister entity and the client are both material to the entity that controls both the client and sister entity.

Index

References are to paragraph number. Int = Interpretation

Preparing for the Assessment

Preparing for the Assessment

Revision technique

The first thing to say about revision is that it is an addition to your initial studies, not a substitute for them. In other words, do not coast along early in your course in the hope of catching up during the revision phase. On the contrary, you should be studying and revising concurrently from the outset. At the end of each week, and at the end of each month, get into the habit of summarising the material you have covered to refresh your memory of it.

As with your initial studies, planning is important to maximise the value of your revision work. You need to balance the demands for study, professional work, family life and other commitments. To make this work, you will need to think carefully about how to make best use of your time.

Begin as before by comparing the estimated hours you will need to devote to revision with the hours available to you in the weeks leading up to the examination. Prepare a written schedule setting out the areas you intend to cover during particular weeks, and break that down further into topics for each day's revision. To help focus on the key areas try to establish:

- which areas you are weakest on, so that you can concentrate on the topics where effort is particularly needed;
- which areas are especially significant for the assessment – the topics that are tested frequently.

Do not forget the need for relaxation, and for family commitments. Sustained intellectual effort is only possible for limited periods, and must be broken up at intervals by lighter activities. And do not continue your revision timetable right up to the moment when you enter the exam hall: you should aim to stop work a day or even 2 days before the exam. Beyond this point, the most you should attempt is an occasional brief look at your notes to refresh your memory.

By the time you begin your revision you should already have settled into a fixed work pattern: a regular time of day for doing the work, a particular location where you sit, particular equipment that you assemble before you begin and so on. If this is not already a matter of routine for you, think carefully about it now in the last vital weeks before the assessment.

You should have notes summarising the main points of each topic you have covered. Begin each session by reading through the relevant notes and trying to commit the important points to memory.

Usually, this will be just your starting point. Unless the area is one where you already feel very confident, you will need to track back from your notes to the relevant chapter(s) in the Study System. This will refresh your memory on points not covered by your notes and fill in the detail that inevitably gets lost in the process of summarisation.

When you think you have understood and memorised the main principles and techniques, attempt an exam-standard question. At this stage of your studies, you should normally be expecting to complete such questions in something close to the actual time allocation allowed in the exam. After completing your effort, check the solution provided and add to your notes any extra points it reveals.

As the assessment approaches, consider the following list of techniques and make use of those that work for you:

(i) Summarise your notes into a more concise form, perhaps on index cards that you can carry with you for revision on the way into work.
(ii) Go through your notes with a highlighter pen, marking key concepts and definitions.
(iii) Summarise the main points in a key area by producing a wordlist, mind map or other mnemonic device.
(iv) For topics which you have found difficult, rework questions that you have already attempted, and compare your answers in detail with those provided in the Study System.
(v) Rework questions you attempted earlier in your studies with a view to producing more 'polished' answers and to completing them within the time limits.

Format of the assessment

Structure of the paper

Fundamentals of Ethics, Governance and Business Law is a Certificate Level subject and examination is by computer-based assessment ('CBA') only. Candidates are required to answer 75 objective test questions within 2 hours.

Objective test questions are used. The most common type is 'multiple choice', which requires you to select the correct answer from a number of possible alternatives. Other types of objective questions may be used and examples of possible questions are included in this chapter.

Assessment by CBA enables CIMA to access the whole syllabus, and the number of questions on each topic is selected according to 'study weightings' (see below).

Allocation of time

Many of the candidates who have failed law and other assessments in the past have done so because of poor assessment technique. It follows that it is crucial for candidates to adhere strictly to the time available for answering each question. Once that time has expired, the candidates should proceed to the next question, and return to any unfinished questions, if time allows after completion of the paper as a whole.

Each topic within the syllabus is given a weighting, so that students are aware of the percentage of time that they should spend studying individual topics. In general, the assessment will attempt to reflect those study weightings as closely as possible in the selection of questions.

The current syllabus weightings are as follows:

- Ethics and Business – 15%
- Ethical Conflict – 10%
- Corporate Governance – 10%
- Comparison of English Law with Alternative Legal Systems – 10%
- The Law of Contract – 20%
- The Law of Employment – 10%
- Company Administration and Finance – 25%

Revision Questions

Learning Outcome	*Question number*
Comparison of English Law with Alternative Legal Systems (10%)	
(1) Explain the manner in which behaviour within society is regulated by the civil and the criminal law	1.1, 1.2, 1.5
(2) Identify and explain the sources of English law	1.3, 1.4
(3) Illustrate the operation of the doctrine of precedent by reference to the essential elements of the tort of negligence, and its application to professional advisers	1.5, 1.14
(4) Compare the elements of alternative legal systems, Sharia law and the role of international legal regulations	1.6, 1.7, 1.8, 1.9
The Law of Contract (20%)	
(1) Identify the essential elements of a valid simple contract and situations where the law requires the contract to be in a particular form	1.6, 1.7, 3(a)
(2) Explain how the law determines whether negotiating parties have reached agreement, and the role of consideration in making that agreement enforceable	1.8, 1.9, 2,3(b)(c)
(3) Explain when the parties will be regarded as intending the agreement to be legally binding, and how an agreement may be avoided because of misrepresentations	1.37, 1.10, 1.11
(4) Explain how the contents and the terms of a contract are established and the possible repercussions of no-performance	7(a)(b)(c), 1.13
(5) Explain how the law controls the use of unfair terms in respect of both consumer and non-consumer business agreements	1.12, 8(a)(b)
(6) Explain what the law regards as performance of the contract, and valid and invalid reasons for non-performance	1.15
(7) Explain the type of breach necessary to cause contractual breakdown and the remedies which are available for serious and minor breaches of contract	1.38, 1.16
The Law of Employment (10%)	
(1) Explain the difference between employees and independent contractors and how the contents of a contract of employment are established	1.18, 12(a)(b), 1.20, 1.21
(2) Explain the distinction between unfair and wrongful dismissal	12(c)
(3) Demonstrate an awareness of how employers and employees are affected by health and safety legislation, including the consequences of a failure to comply	1.19
Company Formation (15%)	
(1) Explain the essential characteristics of the different forms of business organisations	4(a)(b)(c)
(2) Explain the concept and practical effect of corporate personality	1.23
(3) Explain the differences between public and private companies	1.22
(4) Explain the distinction between establishing a company by registration and purchasing 'off the shelf'	9(a)
(5) Explain the purpose and legal status of the memorandum and articles of association	1.24, 1.25, 6(b)(d), 14
(6) Explain the ability of a company to contract	1.31, 14
(7) Explain the main advantages and disadvantages of carrying on business through the medium of a company limited by shares	1.39
Corporate Administration (10%)	
(1) Explain the use and procedure of board meetings and general meetings of shareholders	1.26, 16
(2) Explain the voting rights of directors and shareholders	1.29, 10(a)(b), 13, 15
(3) Identify the various types of shareholder resolutions	1.27

Corporate Finance (10%)

(1) Explain the nature of a share and the essential characteristics of the different types of share	1.40
(2) Explain the procedure for the issue of shares, and the acceptable forms of payment	1.30
(3) Explain the legal repercussions of issuing shares for an improper purpose	1.41
(4) Explain the maintenance of capital principle and the exceptions to the principle	1.28
(5) Explain the procedure to increase and reduce share capital	6(a)
(6) Explain the ability of a company to take secured and unsecured loans, the different types of security and the registration procedure	1.42

Corporate Management (15%)

(1) Explain the procedure for the appointment, retirement, disqualification and removal of directors	6(c), 9(c)
(2) Identify the powers and duties owed by directors to the company, shareholders, creditors and employees	1.33, 5(a)(b)(c)
(3) Explain the rules dealing with the possible imposition of personal liability upon the directors of insolvent companies	1.34
(4) Identify and contrast the rights of shareholders with the Board of a company	1.32, 11(a)(b)(c)
(5) Explain the qualifications, powers and duties of the company secretary	1.35

Ethics and Business (15%)

(1) Apply the values and attitudes that provide professional accountants with a commitment to act in the public interest and with social responsibility	1.47
(2) Explain the need for a framework of laws, regulations and standards in business and their application	1.48
(3) Explain the nature of ethics and its application, identifying the difference between rules-based and framework approaches to ethics	1.49
(4) Identify the need for continual personal improvement and life-long learning based on an understanding of virtues of reliability, timeliness, courtesy and respect	1.50
(5) Explain the ethical principles of integrity, objectivity, professional competence, due care and confidentiality	1.51
(6) Identify key concepts of independence, accountability and social responsibility	1.52
(7) Explain the reasons why CIMA and IFAC each have a 'Code of Ethics for Professional Accountants'	1.53

Ethical Conflict (10%)

(1) Explain the relationship between ethics, governance, the law and social responsibility	1.54
(2) Describe the consequences on unethical behaviour to the individual, the profession and society	1.55
(3) Identify situations where ethical dilemmas and conflicts of interest occur and how they can be resolved	1.56

? **Question 1** Multiple-choice selection

1.1 In England and Wales, which court can make judgements which are binding on all the other courts?

(A) The High Court.
(B) The Queen's Bench Division.
(C) The House of Lords.
(D) The Court of Appeal.

1.2 Which *one* of the following must a Bill receive if it is to become an Act of Parliament?

(A) The Assent of the Government.
(B) The Assent of the Prime Minister.
(C) The Royal Assent.
(D) The Assent of the High Court.

1.3 Which of the following is the primary source of European Union Law?

(A) Regulations.
(B) Treaties.
(C) Directives.
(D) Decisions.

1.4 Which *one* of the following European Union (EU) items will automatically become part of English law?

(A) Directive.
(B) Regulation.
(C) A resolution of the elected EU Parliament.
(D) A decision of the Council of Ministers.

1.5 How many countries joined the European Union on the 1st January 2007?

(A) Two.
(B) Five.
(C) Eight.
(D) Ten.

1.6 In which country within the European Union are judges appointed at the beginning of their legal careers?

(A) Belgium.
(B) France.
(C) Poland.
(D) Cyprus.

1.7 Which *one* of the following is not in the five categories of action recognised as the 'Five Pillars of Islam'?

(A) Permissible.
(B) Meritorious.
(C) Reprehensible.
(D) Tolerated.

1.8 Law is developed in the United States through the common law with decisions of the courts establishing precedents in all states except one. Which one state provides the exception?

(A) Louisiana.
(B) Minnesota.
(C) Texas.
(D) Ohio.

1.9 Manufacturer Ltd (M) makes machines. It sells one of its machines to Factory Ltd (F), which then uses it. Six months later, the machine explodes because of a defect, injuring F's accountant (X) who was visiting the premises. X had been advised to wear a safety helmet, but had not done so. X now seeks damages from M. Which of the following statements is accurate?

(A) M is not liable once it has sold the machine. X must sue F.
(B) M will not be liable because X was not wearing a helmet. The injury is X's fault.
(C) M will be liable unless M can prove that it was not negligent, but M will have a partial defence.
(D) M may be liable if X can prove that M was negligent, but damages against M may be reduced.

1.10 Which of the following is not an essential element of a valid simple contract?

(A) The contract must be in writing.
(B) The parties must be in agreement.
(C) Each party must provide consideration.
(D) Each party must intend legal relations.

1.11 Which *one* of the following must be evidenced by a deed rather than merely be evidenced in writing?

(A) a contract of marine insurance.
(B) an assignment of a debt.
(C) a promise given for no consideration.
(D) a transfer of shares.

1.12 Which of the following is a valid contract?

(A) S agrees in writing to sell goods to B 'at a price to be agreed'.
(B) S offers a car to B for £5,000. B offers £4,750. S rejects this. B therefore agrees to S's original price of £5,000.
(C) S offers his car to B and promises to keep the offer open for a week. B accepts 2 days later, but finds that S has now sold the car elsewhere.
(D) On Monday, S offers his car to B and promises to keep the offer open until Thursday. On Wednesday, B sends an e-mail accepting the offer, but S does not read this until Friday.

1.13 Only one of the following promises is binding. Which one?

(A) Arthur promises to sell a painting to X for £20. He learns before X collects it that the painting is worth £1,000.
(B) B is owed £500 by Y, who is now in a financial difficulty. B therefore promises to take £400 in full payment.
(C) Mrs C returns from the hospital to find that a student neighbour has, unasked, cut her lawn. In gratitude, Mrs C promises the student £20.
(D) D promises to allow the village fete to use his field without charge.

1.14 S sells some old furniture, claiming that the items 'had been is S's family for five generations'. The buyer (B) therefore believes that they are genuine antiques. In fact, some are bogus and had been bought by S's father (unknown to S). When B discovers the truth shortly after the sale, he wants to return all of the goods and recover his price. Is it likely that he can do so?

(A) Yes.
(B) Not unless he can prove that S has been fraudulent.
(C) Not unless he can prove that S has been negligent.
(D) No, because S is not a dealer.

1.15 On the facts in Question 1.8, does the buyer always have a right to damages?

(A) Yes.
(B) Not unless he can prove that S has been fraudulent.
(C) Not unless he can prove that S has been negligent.
(D) Not if S can prove that he believed with reasonable cause that his statements were true.

1.16 In a contract for the sale of goods between a business and a consumer, any attempt to exclude the terms implied by the Sale of Goods Act 1979 as to the quality of goods is:

(A) void.
(B) void unless reasonable.
(C) voidable at the option of the consumer.
(D) valid if the consumer is given written notice of the clause.

1.17 D Ltd has broken one of the terms of its contract with E Ltd. If that term is a warranty, which of the following is correct?

(A) E Ltd may treat the contract with D Ltd as repudiated.
(B) E Ltd can avoid the contract and recover damages.
(C) E Ltd is entitled to sue for damages only.
(D) E Ltd is entitled to sue for damages or to treat the contract as repudiated.

1.18 Which of the following statements about professional practitioners is true?

(A) A practitioner can be allowed to act for both the seller and buyer in a transaction with the knowledge and consent of both, so long as there is no dispute over price or terms.
(B) An inexperienced practitioner owes his clients lower duties of care and skill than experienced ones.
(C) A firm of accountants can always act for both sides in a dispute, as long as one office of the firm acts for one side, and the other office for the other.
(D) A broker engaged to sell his client's shares can secretly buy them himself so long as he pays the price sought by the seller.

1.19 In each of the following contracts, one party gives an excuse for non-performance. Which excuse(s) may be valid?

(A) In this contract, A Ltd refuses to go on because the price of materials has doubled since the contract, and he can now only operate at a loss.
(B) In this case a customer, who buys a tin of food from a retailer, becomes ill because the contents are infected. The retailer denies liability because, as he points out, he bought the sealed tin from the manufacturer, and could not open it to check the contents.
(C) In this contract, C Ltd points out that the proposed acts are contrary to an EC regulation made after the contract.
(D) In this case, D Ltd performs the contract carelessly, and its customer is ill. D Ltd relies on a clause in the contract exempting it from all liability for illness arising from its products.

1.20 Which of the following will *not* be awarded for breach of contract?

(A) Personal injury damages.
(B) Damages for loss of profit on another contract.
(C) Damages for distress.
(D) Deterrent damages to discourage such conduct in the future.

1.21 A right to rescind must be exercised within:

(A) A reasonable time.
(B) Six months.
(C) Three years.
(D) Six years.

1.22 Which of the following types of remedy will not be awarded in employment contracts?

(A) Damages.
(B) Specific performance.
(C) An injunction.
(D) Rescission.

1.23 Which of the following duties does an employer owe?

(A) To provide a reasonably safe system of work.
(B) To insure against possible civil liability to employees.
(C) To ensure that all employees use the safety equipment provided.
(D) To pay fines imposed for breach of the Management of Health and Safety at Work Regulations 1999.

1.24 Which of the following rights do women employees have?

(A) Terms of employment as favourable as those of a man, like work of equal value.
(B) Not to be dismissed because of pregnancy.
(C) One year's post-natal maternity leave.
(D) The same retirement and private pension rights as men in that employment.

1.25 In a contract of employment, which of the following can *not* be restrained after the contract ends?

(A) Future employment specified in the contract by a restraint of trade clause.
(B) Use of specified confidential information.
(C) Disclosure of specified trade secrets.
(D) Use of special skills acquired during the employment.

1.26 Which of the following statements is or are *true* about a private company?

(i) A private company is a company which does not qualify under the Companies Acts to be a public company.
(ii) A private company is an incorporated business.
(iii) A private company must have at least two directors.
(iv) The shareholders of a private company cannot benefit from limited liability.

(A) (i) and (ii) only
(B) (ii) and (iii) only
(C) (i), (iii) and (iv) only
(D) (i), (ii) and (iii) only.

1.27 Which *one* of the following statements about the formation of a company in the United Kingdom is *correct*?

(A) A company comes into existence when the promoters send a Certificate of Incorporation to Companies House.
(B) After the formation of a company, Articles of Association must be submitted to the Registrar of Companies.
(C) After receiving a Certificate of Incorporation, a private company must issue a Prospectus to people who may wish to buy shares in the company.
(D) A Memorandum of Association must be included with the application to form a company submitted to the Registrar of Companies.

1.28 All the following statements relate to a company's Memorandum of Association. Which of the statements is *correct*?

(A) The Memorandum of Association sets out the internal regulations governing the conduct of the company.
(B) The Memorandum of Association is registered with the Registrar of Companies after the Registrar has issued a Certificate of Incorporation.
(C) The Memorandum of Association is required for a public company but not for a private company.
(D) The Memorandum of Association must state that the subscribers wish to form a company under the Companies Act 2006, agree to be members and take at least one share each.

1.29 Which *one* of the following statements, which all relate to a company's Articles of Association, is *incorrect?*

(A) The Articles of Association sets out the internal regulations of the company.
(B) The Articles of Association may be submitted to the Registrar of Companies in the process of company formation.
(C) The Articles of Association contain ordinary membership rights which are contractual.
(D) The Articles of Association must state the authorised share capital of the company.

1.30 In certain circumstances, a general meeting will be valid even if called without proper notice. Which *one* of the following does not validate such a meeting?

(A) For an AGM, validation agreed to by all the members who are entitled to attend and vote.
(B) For a GM of a private company, validation agreed to by a majority entitled to attend and vote, who together hold at least 90 per cent in nominal value of the shares.
(C) For a GM of a private company, a provision in the Articles of Association validating meetings accidentally called with incorrect notice.
(D) For a GM of a private company, validation agreed to by 75 per cent of members present and voting as authorised by a special resolution.

1.31 A written special resolution may be passed by

(A) 75% of those present and voting at a GM.
(B) 75% of all members entitled to attend and vote at a GM.
(C) 51% of those present and voting at a GM.
(D) 51% of all members entitled to attend and vote at a GM.

1.32 In relation to the funding of a purchase of its own shares by a private company, which *one* of the following statements is incorrect?

(A) The company may use distributable profits.
(B) The company may use the proceeds of a new share issue.
(C) The company may use capital.
(D) The company may use directors' loans.

1.33 Which *one* of the following statements is accurate?

(A) Shareholders and debenture holders are members of a company.
(B) Shareholders and debenture holders have voting rights at general meetings.
(C) Shareholders and debenture holders are entitled to receive a copy of the annual accounts.
(D) Maintenance of capital rules apply to both shares and debentures.

1.34 A public company with a stock market listing is about to make a new issue of £1 ordinary shares. Which *one* of the following statements is true?

(A) The new shares will provide an example of loan capital.
(B) The shares may only be traded on the stock market at a price of £1.
(C) Some of the new shares might be offered to directors of the company in a share option scheme.
(D) The shares can be redeemed at a guaranteed value when they mature at a future date.

1.35 Which of the following is *not* correct?

(A) The board of directors is the agent of a company.
(B) If the board of directors exceeds its powers, the company cannot be held liable on a contract with a third party.
(C) Individual directors cannot contract on behalf of the company unless authorised by the company.
(D) The board of directors may delegate authority to a managing director who may contract on behalf of the company.

1.36 A director of a private company has committed a breach of statutory duty. Which of the following statements is inaccurate?

(A) If the director is a majority shareholder he or she cannot waive his or her breach of duty.
(B) A statement in the company articles exempting directors from liability for breach of duty will be valid.
(C) The director cannot be criminally liable for the breach.
(D) The members can pass a resolution in the general meeting waiving the breach of duty.

1.37 If the minority members of a company believe that the company has been managed in a way that prejudices them unfairly, which of the following courses of action is not available to them?

(A) The minority can obtain the permission of the court to pursue a derivative action against the wrongdoers.
(B) The minority can petition the court for the liquidation of the company.
(C) Where a wrong is done to a minority within a company, the minority can always sue the wrongdoers.
(D) The minority can seek a court order for the purchase of their shares by the company or by another member.

1.38 Allestab Ltd has gone into insolvent liquidation. Which *one* of the following statements is correct?

(A) Because of limited liability the members can never be personally liable.
(B) The directors cannot be personally liable for the insolvency because they are merely agents of the company.
(C) Statute law identifies instances where directors and members can be made personally liable on the insolvent liquidation of the company.
(D) Wrongful trading is a criminal offence.

1.39 Which *one* of the following statements is incorrect?

(A) The company secretary to a private company need not be qualified.
(B) A company secretary can never contractually bind his company.
(C) A sole director cannot also be a company secretary.
(D) A company secretary can be removed by the company's directors.

1.40 Which of the following statements is correct?

(A) A professional adviser can be liable to pay damages in contract but not in tort.
(B) A professional adviser can be liable to pay damages in tort but not contract.
(C) A professional adviser cannot be liable to pay damages in either contract or tort.
(D) A professional adviser may be liable to pay damages in contract or tort.

1.41 Which of the following statements is correct?

(i) If one party had made an offer and the other has accepted it a contract has been formed.
(ii) If an agreement is 'binding in honour only' it is not contractual.
(iii) To be contractual, parties must intend the agreement to be legally binding.

(A) (i) only.
(B) (i) and (ii) only.
(C) (ii) and (iii) only.
(D) (iii) only.

1.42 Which of the following statements is correct?

(i) The courts are bound by what the parties call a particular term.
(ii) If a term is a condition, in the event of a breach the innocent party may be entitled to repudiate the contract and claim damages.
(iii) If a broken term is a warranty, the innocent party may be entitled to repudiate the contract but cannot claim damages.

(A) (i) only.
(B) (ii) only.
(C) (ii) and (iii) only.
(D) (iii) only.

1.43 Which of the following statements is correct?

(A) The company's liability for its debts is limited.
(B) The directors' liability to pay the company's debts is unlimited.
(C) The shareholders liability to pay the company's debts is limited.
(D) The company secretary's liability to pay the company's debt is unlimited.

1.44 Redeemable preference shares entitle the holder

(i) to be paid a dividend before ordinary shareholders.
(ii) to have the shares purchased by the company as agreed by the terms of issue.
(iii) to be paid the capital value of the shares before creditors in the event of liquidation.

(A) (i) only.
(B) (i) and (ii) only.
(C) (ii) and (iii) only.
(D) (iii) only.

1.45 Which of the following is correct?

(A) If the board issues shares to a director to enable him to outvote a shareholder resolution to dismiss him, the share issue is voidable.
(B) If the board issues shares to a director to enable him to outvote a shareholder resolution to dismiss him, the share issue is void.
(C) If the board issues shares to a director to enable him to outvote a shareholder resolution to dismiss him, the share issue is valid.
(D) If the board issues shares to a director to enable him to outvote a shareholder resolution to dismiss him, the share issue is valid but unenforceable.

1.46 Which of the following statements is correct in relation to fixed charges?

(i) A fixed charge holder has priority over all other creditors.
(ii) A fixed charge is void unless registered at Companies House within 21 days of its issue.
(iii) If the fixed charge includes a charge over land, the charge must be registered at HM Land Registry.

(A) (i) only.
(B) (i) and (ii) only.
(C) (ii) and (iii) only.
(D) (i), (ii) and (iii).

1.47 Which of the following would *not* help accountants to act in the public interest and with social responsibility?

(A) Staying up to date with developments in business and accounting.
(B) Defining long-term career objectives.
(C) Abiding by the CIMA Code of Ethics for Professional Accountants.
(D) Acting with integrity.

1.48 Which of the following is *not* true of ethical guidelines and standards?

(A) Ethical guidelines and standards encourage good practice.
(B) Accountants are required by law to follow ethical guidelines and standards.
(C) CIMA members must adhere to CIMA's Code of Ethics.
(D) CIMA members must adhere to the International Federation of Accountant's (IFAC) Code of Ethics.

1.49 Which of the following is *not* the case?

(A) The CIMA Code of Ethics takes an ethically based approach.
(B) The IFAC Code of Ethics takes a compliance-based approach.
(C) Company codes of ethics can take an ethically based or a compliance-based approach.
(D) Codes of ethics are often based on core values or principles.

1.50 Which of the following is *not* the case? Professional accountants must keep themselves up to date professionally because:

(A) Accountants have a duty to maintain professional knowledge and skill.
(B) Accountants have a duty to provide a client or employer with competent professional service.
(C) It is a requirement of the CIMA Code of Ethics.
(D) It is a requirement of the Seven Principles of Public Life.

1.51 One of your colleagues has provided information that you believe he knows to be misleading. If you are correct, this violates CIMA's fundamental principle of:

(A) Integrity.
(B) Objectivity.
(C) Professional competence and due care.
(D) Confidentiality.

1.52 The two key attributes to independence when used in connection with the assurance engagement are independence

(A) Of mind and in appearance.
(B) Of belief and in appearance.
(C) Of mind and of belief.
(D) None of the above.

1.53 CIMA has a Code of Ethics for Professional Accountants because the code

(A) Provides evidence that accountants behave ethically at all times.
(B) Provides a basis for complaints or cases under CIMA's disciplinary procedures.
(C) Tells stakeholders what is required of them in terms of behaviour.
(D) Focuses on providing members with information on what is and is not required of them by law.

1.54 Which of the following is true about the relationship between ethics, governance, law and social responsibility in an organisation?

(A) Ethics and governance are mutually exclusive.
(B) Ethics is mandatory, social responsibility is discretionary.
(C) Social responsibility policies need to be consistent with a company's values and code of ethics.
(D) Legislation is designed to be compatible with an organisation's code of ethics.

1.55 Your company has a strict and well-publicised anti-bullying policy. One of your colleagues is found to have been making his assistant's life a misery. She insists that the assistant stays at work until very late each evening, calls him lazy and threatens to fire him if his work is ever less than perfect. The least likely consequence for your colleague would involve:

(A) Praise from the chief executive for getting the best from her staff.
(B) Investigation by the company's internal complaints team.
(C) A severe reprimand.
(D) Dismissal.

1.56 Ethical dilemmas can arise due to conflict between which of the following sets of values?

(A) Personal and professional values.
(B) Professional and corporate values.
(C) Corporate and personal values.
(D) All of the above.

1.57 Who is entitled to enforce a breach of duty against a director?

(i) Any person who has suffered loss because of the breach.
(ii) The company.
(iii) Any shareholder.

(A) (i) only.
(B) (i) and (ii) only.
(C) (ii) only.
(D) (ii) and (iii) only.

1.58 A 'two-tier board' comprises

(A) A Quality Assurance Board and a Management Board.
(B) A Supervisory Board and an Employee Representation Board.
(C) An Executive Board and a Management Board.
(D) A Management Board and a Supervisory Board.

1.59 Which of the following is correct in relation to the Combined Code 2003?

(A) The Code gives rise to civil but not criminal liability.
(B) A failure to comply with the Code may result in a finding of 'wrongful trading' on the part of the directors.
(C) The Code requires disclosure of the extent to which it has been complied with.
(D) Acting in ignorance of the Code may result in a director being disqualified from acting as a director.

? Question 2

On 1 September 2008, Andrew wrote to Edward offering to sell him a Speedy Photocopier at a price of £4,000, for delivery on 1 December 2008. In an accompanying letter, Andrew stated that the offer was subject to his standard conditions of sale, a copy of which was included. These conditions included a currency fluctuation clause, enabling Andrew to increase the price to compensate for any fall in the value of sterling.

Edward replied on 5 September, ordering a machine for delivery on 1 December and enclosing his own conditions of purchase. These conditions stated that all purchases were subject to specific terms, which did not include a currency fluctuation clause.

No further correspondence was entered into until 1 December, when Andrew delivered the machine to Edward, together with an invoice for £4,500. In an accompanying note he stated: 'We regret that owing to a fall in the value of sterling, it has been necessary to increase the price to £4,500.' Edward is now refusing to pay the increased price.

Requirement

Delete as appropriate and complete the following:

Andrew's letter of 1 September 2008 amounted to an .... (1 word) **(2 marks)** at law. Edward's reply on 5 September constituted a .... (2 words) **(1 mark)** at law. By delivering the machine to Edward on 1 December Andrew appears to have .... (1 word) **(2 marks)** Edward's .... (2 words) **(1 mark)**. It follows that Andrew .... (1 word) **(1 mark)** increase the price to £4,500 and was subject to .... (1 word) **(1 mark)** terms and conditions. **(Total marks = 8)**

Question 3

Seller wrote to Buyer on 1 February 2008 offering to sell various items of plant and machinery for £20,000. The letter included the following statement:

Notice in writing of your acceptance of this offer must be received by the Sales Director by 14 February 2008.

Buyer decided to accept the offer and posted his acceptance on 8 February 2008. In addition, Buyer telephoned Seller and asked to speak to the Sales Director. Unfortunately, he was out of the office, so Buyer left a message with his secretary to the effect that he wanted to accept the offer.

Buyer has since discovered that the Sales Director of Seller never received the letter of acceptance and that the secretary forgot to tell him of Buyer's telephone call. As a result, the plant and machinery has been sold to Exe Ltd.

Requirements

(a) Complete the following:

For a valid simple contract there are a number of essential elements. First the parties must be in agreement, which is demonstrated by the presence of an .... (1 word) **(1 mark)** and an .... (1 word) **(1 mark)**. Second, the parties must provide .... (1 word) **(1 mark)** which means that each party must provide something of value. Third, the parties must have legal intent. In this case, legal intent would be .... (1 word) **(2 marks)**, as this is a commercial transaction. **(5 marks)**

(b) Complete the following:

Where it is clear that the post may be used as the means of acceptance, the normal rule is that the acceptance is complete as soon as it is .... (1 word) **(2 marks)**. However, because in this case Seller has asked for .... (3 words) **(2 marks)**, that has the effect of cancelling the post rule. **(4 marks)**

(c) Delete as appropriate:
In this case, there .... (1 word) **(2 marks)** a contract between Buyer and Seller. Exe Ltd .... (1 word) **(2 marks)** entitled to retain the plant and machinery. **(4 marks)** **(Total marks = 13)**

Question 4

Charles and Cynthia have both been operating separate businesses on their own account as suppliers of office services. They have been considering combining their resources, which will allow them to save on rent for business premises and other overheads. They are unsure whether to form a partnership, or to form a private company limited by shares in which they would each hold 50 per cent of the shares, and be the only directors.

Requirements

(a) Delete as appropriate and complete the following:
A general partnership may be established by .... (1 word) **(1 mark),** whereas a private company limited by shares is formed by .... (1 word) **(1 mark)**. **(2 marks)**

(b) Delete as appropriate and complete the following:
Apart from in limited liabily partnerships, partners are .... (3 words) **(2 marks)** liable for the debts of the partnership. Liability for the company's debts rests with the .... (1 word) **(2 marks)**. **(4 marks)**

(c) Delete as appropriate and complete the following:
The board is the agent of the company whereas .... (1 word) **(2 marks)** partner is able to contract on behalf of the partnership. A partner cannot be expelled unless there is an express power to expel in the partnership agreement. In contrast, any director may be dismissed by .... (1 word) **(2 marks)** resolution. **(4 marks)**
(Total marks = 10)

Question 5

Max is the chief executive and Anne the Managing Director of Large plc ('Large'). The two directors enjoy considerable power and, in effect, control the board. Recently, Max and Anne caused Large to acquire the assets of Target Ltd, in return for a payment of £5 m and the assumption by Large of the liabilities of Target Ltd. The acquisition was approved by the shareholders of Large at a general meeting of the company called for that purpose.

Investor plc owns 12 per cent of the shares in Large and has now discovered that Max and Anne, held a substantial shareholding in Target Ltd at the time of the acquisition. Furthermore, Investor plc now believes that Max and Anne caused Large plc to overpay by up to £1 m, in order to benefit themselves as shareholders in Target plc.

Requirements

(a) Complete the following:
As directors of Large, Max and Anne owe .... (1 word) **(2 marks)** duties to act in a way that they consider in good faith will promote the success of the company for the benefit of the members as a whole. As part of that duty they must .... (1 word) **(1 mark)** their interests in any contract involving Large to the .... (1 word) **(1 mark)** and the .... (1 word) **(1 mark)**. **(5 marks)**

(b) Complete the following:
Max and Anne owe their duties to the employees and .... (1 word) **(1 mark)** but not to individual .... (1 word) **(1 mark)**. Under the Rule in *Foss* v. *Harbottle* (1843), where it is alleged that a wrong has been done to the company then it is the .... (1 word) **(1 mark)** which should sue. **(3 marks)**

(c) Delete as appropriate and complete the following:
Investor plc .... (1 word) **(1 mark)** sue the directors for breach of directors' duty. As Investor plc holds more than .... (1 word) per cent **(2 marks)** of the shares in Large, it will be able to demand the calling of a .... (1 word) meeting **(2 marks)** at which the shareholders may decide by .... (1 word) **(2 marks)** resolution whether to ratify Max and Anne's actions, dismiss them or whether other proceedings should be taken against them. Max and Anne can be required to hand back any secret profits they have made to the .... (1 word) **(1 mark)**. **(8 marks)**

(Total marks = 16)

? Question 6

Alan, Brian, Clare and Donna have each agreed to invest £250,000 in share capital in Retail Ltd, a company to be established to carry on the business of retailing clothing. The company is to have an authorised share capital of £1 m. The four parties have also agreed the following conditions:

(i) The company shall neither increase its authorised share capital nor diversify into any other business without the unanimous agreement of the shareholders.
(ii) Each is to be appointed an executive director of the company for life.
(iii) The company shall purchase at least £40,000 of clothing from Alan's wholesale clothing business each year and shall be entitled to 10 per cent discount on the normal wholesale price.

Requirement

(a) Delete as appropriate and complete the following:
At present a company's authorised capital is stated in its .... (1 word) **(1 mark)** of Association. The capital may be increased by .... (1 word) **(2 marks)** resolution or .... (2 words) **(1 mark)** resolution of the .... (1 word) **(1 mark)**. Following the introduction of the Companies Act 2006 new companies must/need not have an authorised capital. **(1 mark)** **(6 marks)**.

(b) Complete the following:
Under the current law, if the objects clause of Retail Ltd contains a statement that the company shall carry on business as a .... (3 words) **(2 marks)**, then the company will have the authority to carry on any business. Even if the object is restricted to retailing, the company may change its objects by .... (1 word) **(2 marks)** resolution. **(4 marks)**

(c) Delete as appropriate and complete the following:
Even if each of the shareholders is to be made a director for life, any one of them may be removed by .... (1 word) **(2 marks)** resolution with .... (1 word) **(1 mark)** notice, irrespective of anything in the Articles of Association. **(3 marks)**

(d) Delete as appropriate:
If the agreement to purchase supplies from Alan's clothing business is stated in the Articles of Association he .... (2 words) **(1 mark)** be protected as the other three shareholders .... (1 word) **(1 mark)** the power to alter the Articles. The purchase agreement amounts to a membership/non-membership **(1 mark)** right, and, as such is/is not **(1 mark)** contractual under section 33 of the Companies Act 2006. **(4 marks)**

(Total marks = 17)

Question 7

David purchased a motor car from Slowly Motors Ltd. for £400. David had inspected the car that was old and needed new tyres and work carried out on the brakes. Beyond this, in order to get an MOT certificate for the vehicle, a fault with the steering system had to be rectified. David was aware of the repairs that needed to be done, but underestimated the seriousness of the steering system problem.

On discovering the cost of repairs needed, which far exceeded that anticipated by David he wrote to Slowly Motors Ltd. stating he would return the car to them and demanding the return of the £400 he paid for the car.

Requirements

(a) Complete the following:
Beyond the .... (1 word) **(2 marks)** terms of a contract agreed by the contracting parties, in some instances .... (1 word) **(2 marks)** terms can also apply. The Sale of Goods Act 1979 (as amended in 1994) identifies such contract terms as .... (1 word) **(2 marks)** rather than terms which are peripheral to the main contract obligations and regarded as .... (1 word) **(2 marks)**. **(8 marks)**

(b) Complete the following:
This Act contains provision that where a sale is made .... (5 words) **(2 marks)**, the goods shall be of .... (1 word) **(2 marks)** quality. Also, the goods shall be .... (1 word) **(2 marks)**, fit for .... (1 word) **(1 mark)**. **(7 marks)**

(c) Complete the following:
A buyer will not be able to rely upon this legislative protection if they have .... (1 word) **(1 mark)** the goods before purchase, and the defect .... (3 words) **(1 mark)** detected, or the seller .... (2 words) **(1 mark)** the defect. **(3 marks)**

(Total marks = 18)

Question 8

Alice and Ben decide to have a weekend break by the sea. On arrival at Crumpton on Sea they obtained overnight accommodation at the Dribble Hotel, an hotel at which they had stayed on a number of previous occasions. On checking into the hotel they registered as guests. They signed a form without reading it, which contained a statement that '... the hotel accepted no liability for any loss of, or damage to property of hotel residents occurring in the hotel'. This same statement was on a notice in Ben and Alice's hotel room.

On returning to the hotel in the evening prior to dinner, Alice went to their room and discovered that her watch, which Ben had recently given her as a birthday present, had been stolen. Alice and Ben seek to obtain compensation for the loss from the hotel.

Requirements

(a) Complete the following:
To be effective, an exemption clause must generally be communicated .... (4 words) **(2 marks)**. If the wording of such a clause is .... (1 word) **(2 marks)**, it will be interpreted against the party wishing to rely on it. **(4 marks)**

(b) Delete as applicable:
Ben and Alice signed the register but did not read the exclusion clause. On this basis, the exclusion clause .... (1 word) **(2 marks)** effective. The fact that they had previously stayed at the hotel .... (1 word) **(2 marks)** relevant in determining the applicability of the exemption clause. **(4 marks)**

(Total marks = 8)

Question 9

Julie and Derek who are married have built up a confectionery business and are now thinking of developing the business further as a registered company. They wish to form the company themselves and then retain, entirely management and control of the company.

Requirements

(a) Complete the following:
To form a company certain documentation must be prepared and filed with Companies House. While the .... (1 word) **(2 marks)** of Association must be registered, the .... (1 word) **(2 marks)** of Association, which deals with the .... (2 words) **(2 marks)** of the company, need not. **(6 marks)**

(b) Complete the following:
Shareholders are the .... (1 word) **(2 marks)** of a company while directors are the .... (1 word) **(2 marks)**. **(4 marks)**

(c) Delete as applicable and complete the following:
Julie and Derek can be the only shareholders and directors of the company. The position of company secretary .... (1 word) **(2 marks)** also be held by one of them. However, a .... (2 words) **(2 marks)** cannot also be company secretary. On company formation, details of the directors and company secretary .... (1 word) **(2 marks)** entered on the same document for forwarding to Companies House. **(6 marks)**

(Total marks = 16)

Question 10

Hugh, Barney, Jane and Christine are all directors and equal shareholders in Quarnked Limited. The company is profitable and they wish to minimise so far as is possible the need for formality in holding meetings for the purpose of making decisions. Hugh and Christine devote a lot of time to the company affairs and tend to make decisions informally, and both Barney and Jane are happy to be involved to a minimal extent.

Requirements

(a) Delete as appropriate and complete the following:
It .... (2 words) **(2 marks)** necessary for any Annual General Meetings or .... (1 word) **(2 marks)** Meetings to be held by a private company. The .... (1 word) **(2 marks)** resolution procedure is only available to the private company. **(6 marks)**

(b) Complete the following:
At a meeting attended by all the members of Quarnked Ltd, any three of them, having collectively 75 per cent of the votes, could pass an .... (1 word) **(2 marks)** resolution or a .... (1 word) **(2 marks)** resolution. In order to pass a written resolution any .... (1 word) **(2 marks)** of the shareholders would have to vote in support. **(6 marks)**

(Total marks = 12)

Question 11

Kevin, a minority shareholder in Talkfastactfast Ltd. believes that Syd and Alf, two directors in the company, have improperly achieved personal benefit in acting as directors and also been guilty of fraud, in that they deliberately deceived shareholders about their conduct and intended objectives. At a General Meeting of the company, Kevin puts his hand up to vote, but he is ignored and his votes are not recorded. He is aggrieved by this and also wishes to pursue an action against Syd and Alf.

Requirements

(a) Delete as appropriate and complete the following:
The rule in *Foss* v. *Harbottle* supports the notion where a wrong has been done to the company that .... (2 words) **(2 marks)** is the proper claimant. Kevin can successfully pursue a .... (1 word) **(2 marks)** action on a claim of fraud. He .... (1 word) **(2 marks)** succeed in an action against the directors even if fraud is not proved. **(6 marks)**

(b) Complete the following:
As Kevin's votes were not recorded at the General Meeting of the company he could successfully pursue a .... (1 word) **(2 marks)** action. Such an action will have its base in s.14, Companies Act 1985 under which the Memorandum and .... (1 word) **(2 marks)** form a .... (1 word) **(2 marks)** between members. **(6 marks)**

(c) Complete the following:
Kevin .... (1 word) **(2 marks)** successfully pursue a claim under s.459, Companies Act 1985 on the grounds of .... (3 words) **(2 marks)**. **(4 marks)**

(Total marks = 16)

Question 12

P Ltd. Employs 500 employees. In 2004, it advertised for a marketing adviser and Q was recruited. When Q was appointed, it was agreed between him and P Ltd that Q would be responsible for payment of his own income tax and national insurance contributions, that he would work the agreed hours each week whenever he chose, and that he could work for other employers so long as they were not competitors of P Ltd.

During 2007, P Ltd. became dissatisfied with Q's work and in November 2007 the decision was made to reduce the importance of Q's work and to reduce his remuneration accordingly. In December 2007, Q resigned from P Ltd. and sought compensation for unfair dismissal. P Ltd. claimed that Q was not entitled to compensation on this ground.

Requirements

(a) Complete the following:
An employee is employed under a contract .... (2 words) **(2 marks)** while an independent contractor is employed under a contract .... (2 words) **(2 marks)**.
(4 marks)

(b) Complete the following:
Tests are used in determining whether a person is an employee or contractor. The .... (1 word) **(2 marks)** test relates to an employer's right to determine what the worker does and how to do it. The .... (1 word) **(2 marks)** test, also known as the .... (1 word) **(2 marks)** test, applies particularly to professional people. More generally used today is the wider .... (2 words) **(2 marks)** test, also known as the .... (1 word) **(2 marks)** test. **(10 marks)**

(c) Complete the following:
While Q has resigned and is claiming unfair dismissal, it may be valid to say that Q is in a position of .... (1 word) **(2 marks)** dismissal. **(2 marks)**
(Total marks = 16)

Question 13

Tony agreed to sell his business to Gaagga Ltd. As part of this agreement, Tony was to acquire 24 per cent of the issued share capital of Gaagga Ltd, and he was to have first option to buy back his business if Gaagga Ltd ever wished to sell. The articles of association of Gaagga Ltd were altered to take account of these factors.

The articles contained a clause requiring the company's directors to purchase equally amongst them at fair value any shares which a member wished to sell. The 76 per cent of shares not acquired by Tony were held by the directors of the company. All the directors were also members.

Eventually, Gaagga Ltd wished to sell Tony's business and Tony attempted to enforce his right to buy the business back. Further, Tony now wants to sell his 24 per cent shares in the company and looks to the directors to purchase them.

Requirements

Articles of association deal with the .... (1 word) **(2 marks)** affairs of a company and at the general meeting can be altered on the passing of a .... (1 word) **(2 marks)** resolution. A private company can alternatively use a .... (1 word) **(2 marks)** resolution requiring approval of .... (number) **(2 marks)** per cent of the members to alter its articles. Articles bind the company and its members as a .... (1 word) **(2 marks)**. Rights provided in the Articles which are not directly enforceable can be transferred by a court into an .... (1 word) **(2 marks)** contract. An alteration of the Articles cannot take away rights of any class of shareholders unless approved by a .... (1 word) **(2 marks)** resolution of that class. Tony .... (1 word) **(2 marks)** compel the directors to purchase his shareholding. **(Total marks = 16)**

Question 14

Wellquar Ltd is a small private company registered in 1998 and having six members. The company was formed with the object of growing and selling flowers to the public. The board agrees that manufacturing greeting cards and selling them to the public would be more profitable. At a GM the members passed a resolution providing that the objects clause of the company be amended to take account of this new pursuit. The resolution was passed with 85 per cent support. However, a minority shareholder who did not receive notice of the meeting is challenging the validity of the alteration.

Requirements

A company objects clause is found in a document called the .... (3 words) **(2 marks)**. Following the CA 2006 the clause is deemed to be in the company's Articles of Association. At the general meeting a .... (1 word) **(2 marks)** resolution requiring a minimum .... (2 words) **(2 marks)** per cent support is needed to alter a companys objects clause. An outsider .... (1 word) **(2 marks)** enforce a contract against a company even if the transaction is outside the objects clause of the company. A GM requires a minimum notice of .... (1 word) **(2 marks)**, days whilst a special resolution now requires .... (1 word) **(2 marks)** days minimum notice to members. The minimum number of members required for a private company is .... (1 word) **(2 marks)**.
(Total marks = 14)

Question 15

The chairman of Quarteer plc asks you to advise him on a number of matters relating to the forthcoming AGM. Specific information required is to be provided through completing the following statement.

Requirements

A minimum of .... (2 words) **(2 marks)** days' notice of an AGM must be given to the members. An AGM must be held within a maximum period of .... (1 word) **(2 marks)** months following the company's accounting reference date. Following a vote with a show of hands a .... (1 word) **(2 marks)** vote may take place with the actual shares with votes attached determining the voting power of members. Where a member is unable to attend an AGM they may use a .... (1 word) **(2 marks)** vote. At an AGM, ordinarily the business dealt with will include receiving the directors' report and the .... (1 word) **(2 marks)** report. **(Total marks = 10)**

Question 16

Hugh, Ken and David formed a company in which each of them held one of the three issued shares. It was further agreed that each of them should be a director of the company. Following a disagreement Ken and David removed Hugh from his position as a director. The Articles provide that if a director is removed from the company the other members must purchase his share at fair value. Ken and David refuse to purchase Hugh's share.

Requirements

Hugh could seek a winding up order on the ground it is .... (3 words) **(3 marks)**. The ground for an action under Sec 994 of the Companies Act 2006 is .... (3 words) **(3 marks)**. On a section 994 Companies Act 2006 action, the court may make such order .... (4 words) **(2 marks)** for giving relief. Specific remedies can include authorising .... (1 word) **(2 marks)** proceedings. The rule in *Foss* v. *Harbottle* provides that the .... (1 word) **(2 marks)** is usually the proper claimant. An exception to the *Foss* v. *Harbottle* rule where fraud is established is described as a .... (1 word) **(2 marks)** action, whilst a minority member bringing a claim for breach of contract against the company would pursue a .... (1 word) **(2 marks)** action.

(Total marks = 10)

Question 17

Your best friend from school days has asked you to tender for audit work. You are keen to assist as his company is successful and looks as though it will continue to be so. Not only could it become a valuable client but it could help you to make the new client target that your firm has set you. From an ethical as well as a business perspective, what is the most appropriate action for you to take?

(A) Tender for the work.
(B) Ask a colleague to handle the client.
(C) Suggest to your friend another firm is approached instead.
(D) Suggest to your friend another firm is approached to create a competitive tender.

Question 18

The company you work for is having financial difficulties and many jobs, including yours, are under threat. You have been asked to review the accounting policies to see if a change could help ease the presentation of the financial situation, particularly in the reports made monthly to the bank. From an ethical perspective, what is the most appropriate action for you to take?

(A) Do as requested.
(B) Go sick.
(C) Seek advice from your professional body.
(D) Do as requested and seek advice afterwards.

Question 19

You are the professional accountant managing the head office accounts function. Another head office department is the treasury function, and for control reasons, you are a password holder for their computer systems. At a recent office party, you struck up a relationship with a junior dealer from the treasury. The relationship is blossoming and has become close. From an ethical perspective, what is the most appropriate action for you to take?

(A) Ignore the situation, as the relationship might not last.
(B) Tell your boss.
(C) Suggest new password system controls, but without explaining why.
(D) End the relationship.

Question 20

You have just joined an entertainments company as a professional accountant. There is a generous gifts and hospitality budget which your boss says you have access to, as well. Just as the external audit is about to commence, he suggests that you offer to take the auditors to Cheltenham for a days' racing. From an ethical perspective, what is the most appropriate action for you to take?

(A) Do as your boss suggests.
(B) Claim you are busy.
(C) Query with your boss his suggestions.
(D) Claim you are allergic to horses.

Question 21

You have been hired as a professional accountant as a deputy to the Finance Director. Shortly after joining the company the Finance Director leaves and you are promoted. You are pleased but realise that you perhaps do not have sufficient expertise in certain areas to take on this responsibility. From an ethical perspective, what is the most appropriate action for you to take?

(A) Talk to the boss about the situation.
(B) Undertake a self-study course.
(C) Seek another job before being 'found out'.
(D) Do nothing.

Solutions to Revision Questions

Solution 1

1.1 Answer: (C)

The text makes it plain that decisions of the House of Lords are binding on the Court of Appeal and the High Court and that the House of Lords is the highest court in the United Kingdom. The Queen's Bench Division is not mentioned in the text and can be treated as irrelevant.

1.2 Answer: (C)

Although (A) and (B) may have some *de facto* relevance for *some* bills (i.e. Government ones), they are not legal/constitutional requirements. (D) is irrelevant.

1.3 Answer: (B)

Regulations, directives and decisions are all sources of European Union law, however, they are secondary sources. Treaties are the only primary source of European Union law.

1.4 Answer: (B)

A directive (A) must be enacted by UK legislation. (C) and (D) are only influential.

1.5 Answer: (A)

On the 1st January 2007, two states joined the European Union bringing the membership up to 27 independent states.

1.6 Answer: (B)

An interesting distinction between France and the other identified members of the European Union is the appointment of individuals to the position of judges at the beginning of their legal careers.

1.7 Answer: (D)

The Five Pillars of Islam are – Obligatory, Meritorious, Permissible, Reprehensible and Forbidden. The correct answer is therefore Tolerated.

1.8 Answer: (A)

Law has developed in the United States through the Common Law, and all states except Louisiana have a common law system with the decisions of the courts establishing precedent.

1.9 Answer: (D)

M can be liable in tort long after the sale; therefore (A) is wrong. X's failure to wear the helmet is at the most contributory negligence; therefore (B) is wrong. The onus of proof normally lies on the claimant; therefore (C) is almost certainly wrong; (*res ipsa loquitur* would not apply here). In (D) damages might be reduced for contributory negligence.

1.10 Answer: (A)

Most valid simple contracts can be made orally, although exceptionally writing may be required by statute for certain special types of contract (e.g. to sell land).

1.11 Answer: (C)

In order to create a legally binding contract, both parties to the agreement must provide consideration. Where a promise in isolation is made that is not enforceable unless it is evidenced in a deed. Marine insurance contracts, assignments of debts and share transfers must all be evidenced in writing, however a formally prepared deed is not required.

1.12 Answer: (C)

In (A) no agreement has been reached yet. In (B), S's initial offer ended when B made a counteroffer; B can therefore no longer accept S's offer. In (D), S's offer lapsed on Thursday. B's 'acceptance' is only made when it is actually communicated to S on Friday, which is too late; (the 'posting rule' does not apply to electronic communications such as e-mail). In (C), B has accepted before learning of any intended revocation by S.

1.13 Answer: (A)

There is no consideration for B's promise to release Y from part of the debt (B). Mrs C's promise is only for past consideration. D's promise too is gratuitous. In (A), Arthur has made a bad bargain, but it is at least a bargain.

1.14 Answer: (A)

B seems to have been induced to enter the contract by S's misrepresentation. B therefore has a right to rescind the contract, so long as he does so reasonably promptly. He need not prove fraud (B) or negligence (C); there can be rescission even for innocent misrepresentation. (D) is irrelevant here.

1.15 Answer: (D)

There is no right to damages for innocent misrepresentation, therefore (A) is wrong. However, there is no need for the claimant to *prove* fraud or negligence; therefore (B) and (C) are wrong. On the other hand, S can escape liability *for damages* if he can, in effect, prove his own innocence; see Misrepresentation Act 1967, s.2(1).

1.16 Answer: (A)

This is by virtue of the Unfair Contract Terms Act 1977, which makes exclusions of all these implied terms in the Sale of Goods Act 1979 void, where the buyer is a consumer.

1.17 Answer: (C)

If a term is a warranty, E Ltd cannot rescind the contract but can only claim damages. Thus, (A) and (B) are incorrect. (D) is also incorrect because repudiation is the act of the party who by words or actions indicates that he does not intend to honour his obligations. In this case, E Ltd on the facts has not repudiated the contract – rather, D Ltd has done so. In any event, E Ltd cannot rescind the contract, as stated above, but can only claim damages.

1.18 Answer: (A)

A practitioner can act for both seller and buyer with the full knowledge and consent of both. (B) is incorrect because any practitioner must show the skills professed. (C) is incorrect in a dispute because no one can be sure that even a 'Chinese wall' within the firm will prevent a conflict of interest and the communication of information which one side does not wish the other to have. (D) is incorrect because there is a secret conflict of interest; could the broker have obtained an even better price elsewhere? In any event, he owes full duties of disclosure to his client.

1.19 Answer: only (C)

The fact that A Ltd will lose money is no excuse for breach of contract (A). A dealer's duties for the quality of his goods are strict, so (B) is no defence. The exemption clause relied upon in (D) is void under the Unfair Contract Terms Act. The contract in (C) is discharged by frustration, which is a valid reason for non-performance.

1.20 Answer: (D)

Damages for breach of contract are awarded to compensate the victim, not to punish the wrongdoer or to deter others. Damages can, where appropriate, be awarded for (A), (B) and (C).

1.21 Answer: (A)

As an equitable remedy, a right to rescind must be exercised within a time which, on the particular facts, appears to the court to be reasonable. There is no fixed time limit.

1.22 Answer: (B)

An employee cannot legally be physically forced to work. Specific performance cannot legally be awarded against him, and therefore will not be awarded in his favour either. All of the other remedies can, where appropriate, be awarded in employment contracts.

1.23 Answer: all except (C)

There are situations where it is sufficient to supply safety equipment to experienced employees, who know why and how to use it, without constant supervision that it is being used.

1.24 Answer: all except (C)

A woman's contract of employment may give her the right to maternity leave of that length, but she has no right to demand it.

1.25 Answer: (D)

All of the others, (A), (B) and (C), can where appropriate be restrained by the employer even after the employment has ended. Special skills, however, belong to the employee alone.

1.26 Answer: (A)

Only the first two statements are correct. Statement (i) provides the core definition of a private company, while statement (ii) centres on the fact that *all* companies, private and public, are incorporated businesses. Private companies only need one director, so statement (iii) is incorrect, as is statement (iv). A standard benefit cited for a sole trader forming a private company is to gain the benefits of limited liability.

1.27 Answer: (D)

Statements (A), (B) and (C) are muddled and hence incorrect. A Certificate of Incorporation is issued by the Registrar of Companies. Table A may be adopted. Otherwise, Articles must be submitted in the application. Public companies rather than private companies must issue a prospectus. This leaves (D) as the correct answer: the Memorandum of Association is the other document (besides the Articles of Association) which must be included in the application to form a company.

1.28 Answer: (D)

Again Statements (A), (B) and (C) are muddled and hence wrong. Statement (A) confuses a Memorandum of Association with a company's Articles of Association. Both documents must be submitted to the Registrar of Companies in the application before a Certificate of Incorporation is issued. Statement (B) is therefore incorrect. Because an application to form any company, private as well as public, must include a Memorandum of Association, Statement (C) is wrong. The correct answer, Statement (D), describes the information which must now be included in a Memorandum of Association.

1.29 Answer: (D)

As the document setting out internal details of the company at the time of company formation, the Articles of Association gives details of the number of the company's directors and the shareholders' voting rights. Companies are no longer required to have an authorised share capital, hence (D) is incorrect.

1.30 Answer: (D)

A special resolution cannot validate a meeting held without proper notice so (D) is the answer. A, B and C are correct.

1.31 Answer: (B)

Following the Companies Act 2006, a written special resolution may be passed by 75% of those entitled to attend and vote at a GM.

1.32 Answer: (D)

Generally, on a private company acquiring its own shares, it is distributable profits and the proceeds of a new share issue which can be used. However, in addition, a private company can use capital where the required statutory procedure is followed. Director loans cannot be used for the purpose of funding an acquisition by a company of its own shares.

1.33 Answer: (C)

Shareholders are members of a company but debenture holders are not. (A) is therefore inaccurate. General meetings are meetings to which shareholders have a right to attend and vote. Debenture holders do not have the right to attend or vote at such meetings. Shareholders may acquire non-voting shares and so have no right to vote at such meetings. (B) is inaccurate. The maintenance of capital rules apply in relation to members only. Both shareholders and debenture holders are entitled to receive annual accounts. (C) is therefore the correct answer.

1.34 Answer: (C)

This question tests understanding of share option schemes, since statement (C) is the correct answer. Statement (A) confuses shares with corporate bonds or debentures and is therefore wrong. Statement (B) also invites confusion of a share's market price with its 'par' value. Ordinary shares are irredeemable and never mature; hence statement (D) is incorrect.

1.35 Answer: (B)

The company can be held liable on a contract with a third party, where the directors have exceeded their powers by virtue of the operation of ss.35 and 35A of the Companies Act 1985.

(A) is correct, as the board of directors is the principal agent of the company. (C) is correct because the board of directors contracts in the company name collectively, or collectively authorises others to do so, including authorising individual directors to contract. For the same reason (D) is also correct, in that the board of directors can authorise a managing director to contract on behalf of the company.

1.36 Answer: (B)

Directors owe statutory duties to the members as a whole. The members can therefore if they wish ratify the directors' conduct or waive the breach of duty. Prior to the Companies Act 2006, a director is was a majority shareholder could waive his own breach. That is no longer the case. (B) is inaccurate and therefore the answer, all the other statements are correct.

1.37 Answer: (C)

(A) is true. This can be done under ss.994-996 of the Companies Act 2006. (B) is also true; this can be done on the 'just and equitable' ground in s.122 (1)(g) of the Insolvency Act 1986. (C) is untrue and therefore the correct answer. The minority cannot do this unless it is an exception to the case of *Foss* v. *Harbottle* (1843), where the minority can persue the new 'derivative' action with the authority of the court.

1.38 Answer: (C)

On the insolvent liquidation of a company, both members and directors can be personally liable. Even though a company is a separate legal entity and limited liability is recognised, members can be liable for fraudulent trading. Equally, it is correct to recognise that directors are agents of the company; however, liability for wrongful trading or fraudulent trading can arise. A and B are therefore incorrect. Wrongful trading can be distinguished from fraudulent trading in that the former is not a criminal offence. The difficulty in establishing criminal intent, required with fraudulent trading, is not necessary in order to establish wrongful trading. (D) is therefore incorrect. The correct answer is (C). Particular reference can be made to ss.213 and 214 of the Insolvency Act 1986 which indeed identify fraudulent and wrongful trading.

1.39 Answer: (B)

The need to be qualified now applies to the company secretary of a public company, not a private company, so (A) is correct. While a director can also be a company secretary, a sole director cannot. Further, directors do generally, have the power to remove a company secretary. (C) and (D) are therefore correct. Generally, a company secretary cannot contractually bind his company; however, an exception exists where the contract is of an administrative nature: note the *Fidelis* case. It is wrong therefore to say that a company secretary can never contractually bind his company. (B) is the incorrect statement.

1.40 Answer: (D)

A professional adviser may be liable in contract to his client if he breaks the terms of his contract. H may also be liable to a third party in tort if that person can establish that the adviser owed him a duty of care, broke that duty, and damage or injury resulted.

1.41 Answer: (C)

The acceptance of an offer results in an agreement. It is not a contract, however, until the other essential elements are in place. If an agreement is 'binding in honour only' the parties are stating that there is no legal intent in which case there cannot be a contract.

1.42 Answer: (B)

The courts are not bound by what the parties have called the terms, but determine the status of the term according to rules of law. Breach of a warranty entitles the innocent party to damages only.

1.43 Answer: (C)

A shareholder's liability for the debts of the company are limited to the amount if any due on his/her shares.

1.44 Answer: (B)

Creditors are always paid in priority to shareholders, whether preferential or ordinary.

1.45 Answer: (A)

On the face of it the shares have been issued for an improper purpose. However, the shareholders may ratify the issue by special resolution.

1.46 Answer: (D)

All the statements are correct.

1.47 Answer: (B)

Although B would help an accountant with his or her career, it would not necessarily have any impact on acting in the public interest.

1.48 Answer: (B)

Ethical guidelines and standards encourage good practice but are not required by law. CIMA requires its members to adhere to its Code of Ethics and CIMA members, as accountants, must also adhere to the IFAC Code of Ethics.

1.49 Answer: (B)

The CIMA and IFAC codes both take an ethically based approach.

1.50 Answer: (D)

This is not a requirement of the Seven Principles of Public Life, which apply only to public sector employees in the United Kingdom.

1.51 Answer: (A)

CIMA defines its fundamental principle of integrity as an accountant being straight-forward and honest in all professional and business relationships.

1.52 Answer: (A)

The two key attributes are independence of mind – being able to make objective conclusions – and in appearance – being seen to be independent.

1.53 Answer: (B)

A code can encourage good behaviour, but cannot guarantee it. CIMA's code tells accountants – not stakeholders – what is required of them in terms of behaviour and it focuses on ethical rather than legal information.

1.54 Answer: (C)

Ethics and governance are interrelated; ethics and social responsibility are both discretionary and codes of ethics must be compatible with legislation, rather than legislation being designed around codes of ethics.

1.55 Answer: (A)

The least likely scenario is for the chief executive to applaud your colleague's bullying behaviour.

1.56 Answer: (D)

Conflicts can arise in any of these situations.

1.57 Answer: (C)

(ii) is incorrect as the law states that statutory duties are owed to the shareholders as a body but not individual shareholders. (i) is incorrect as loss could be suffered by persons other than the body of shareholders.

1.58 Answer: (D)

A two-tier board comprises a management board to carry out the policy and management and a Supervisory Board which includes, for example, employee representation.

1.59 Answer: (C)

At present, the Code gives rise to neither civil nor criminal liability and wrongful trading is actionable where directors cause the company to continue trading where insolvency appears inevitable.

Solution 2

Andrew's letter of 1 September 2008 amounted to an *offer* at law. Edward's reply on 5 September constituted *a counter offer* at law. By delivering the machine to Edward on 1 December Andrew appears to have *accepted* Edward's *counter offer.* It follows that Andrew *cannot* increase the price to £4,500 and was subject to *Edward's* terms and conditions.

Solution 3

(a) For a valid simple contract there are a number of essential elements. First, the parties must be in agreement, which is demonstrated by the presence of an *offer* and an *acceptance.* Second, the parties must provide *consideration* which means that each party must provide something of value. Third, the parties must have legal intent. In this case, legal intent would be *presumed* as this is a commercial transaction.

(b) Where it is clear that the post may be used as the means of acceptance, the normal rule is that the acceptance is complete as soon as it is *posted.* However, because in this case Seller has asked for *notice in writing* that has the effect of cancelling the post rule.

(c) In this case, there *isn't* a contract between Buyer and Seller. Exe Ltd *is* entitled to retain the plant and machinery.

Solution 4

(a) A general partnership may be established by *conduct* whereas a private company limited by shares is formed by *registration.*

(b) Apart from in limited liabily partnership, partners are *jointly and severally* liable for the debts of the partnership. Liability for the company's debts rests with the *company.*

(c) The board is the agent of the company whereas *every* partner is able to contract on behalf of the partnership. A partner cannot be expelled unless there is an express power to expel in the partnership agreement. In contrast, any director may be dismissed by *ordinary* resolution *irrespective of* what is stated in the company's Articles of Association.

Solution 5

(a) As directors of Large, Max and Anne owe *statutory* (1 word) **(2 marks)** duties to act in a way that they consider, in good faith, will promote the success of the company for the benefit of the members as a whole. As part of that duty they must *disclose* (1 word) **(1 mark)** their interests in any contract involving Large to the *board* (1 word) **(1 mark)** and the *shareholders* (1 word) **(1 mark)**. **(5 marks)**

(b) Max and Anne owe their duties to the employees and *shareholders* (1 word) **(1 mark)** but not to individual *shareholders* (1 word) **(1 mark)**. Under the Rule in *Foss* v. *Harbottle* (1843), where it is alleged that a wrong has been done to the company then it is the *company* (1 word) **(1 mark)** which should sue. **(3 marks)**

(c) Investor plc *cannot* (1 word) **(1 mark)** sue the directors for breach of directors' duty. As Investor plc holds more than *ten* (1 word) per cent **(2 marks)** of the shares in Large, it will be able to demand the calling of a *general* (1 word) meeting **(2 marks)** at which the shareholders may decide by *ordinary* (1 word) **(2 marks)** resolution whether to ratify Max and Anne's actions, dismiss them or whether other proceedings should be taken against them. Max and Anne can be required to hand back any secret profits they have made to the *company (*1 word) **(1 mark)**. **(8 marks)**

(Total marks = 16)

Solution 6

(a) At present a company's authorised capital is stated in its *Memorandum* of Association. The capital may be increased by *ordinary* resolution or *written* resolution of the *shareholders.* Following the introduction of the Companies Act 2006 new companies *need not* have an authorised capital.

(b) Under the current law if the objects clause of Retail Ltd contains a statement that the company shall carry on business as a *general commercial company*, then the company will have the authority to carry on any business. Even if the object is restricted to retailing, the company may change its objects by *special* resolution.

(c) Even if each of the shareholders is to be made a director for life, any one of them may be removed by *ordinary* resolution with *special* notice, irrespective of anything in the Articles of Association.

(d) If the agreement to purchase supplies from Alan's clothing business is stated in the Articles of Association, he *will not* be protected as the other three shareholders *have* the power to alter the Articles. The purchase agreement amounts to a *non membership* right, and, as such, i*s not* contractual under section 33 of the Companies Act 2006.

Solution 7

(a) Beyond the *express* terms of a contract agreed by the contracting parties, in some instances *implied* terms can also apply. The Sale of Goods Act 1979 (as amended in 1994) identifies such contract terms as *conditions*, rather than terms which are peripheral to the main contract obligations and regarded as *warranties.*

(b) This Act contains provision that where a sale is made *in the course of business,* the goods shall be of *satisfactory* quality. Also, the goods shall be *reasonably* fit for *purpose.*

(c) A buyer will not be able to rely on this protection if they have *inspected* the goods before purchase, and the defect *should have been* detected, or the seller *made known* the defect.

Solution 8

(a) To be effective, an exemption clause must be communicated *prior to contract creation.* If the wording of such a clause is *ambiguous*, it will be interpreted against the party wishing to rely on it.

(b) Ben and Alice signed the register but did not read the exclusion clause. On this basis, the exclusion clause *is* effective. The fact that they had previously stayed at the hotel *is* relevant in determining the applicability of the exclusion clause.

Solution 9

(a) To form a company, certain documentation must be prepared and filed with Companies House. While the *Memorandum* of Association must be registered, the *Articles* of Association, which deals with the *internal affairs* of the company need not.

(b) Shareholders are the *controllers* of a company while directors are the *managers.*

(c) Julie and Derek can be the only shareholders and directors of the company. The position of company secretary *can* also be held by one of them. However, a *sole director* cannot also be company secretary. On company formation, details of the directors and company secretary *are* entered on the same document for forwarding to Companies House.

Solution 10

(a) It *is not* necessary for any Annual General Meetings or *General* Meetings to be held by a private company. The *written* resolution procedure is only available to a private company.

(b) At a meeting attended by all the members of Quarnked Ltd. any three of them, having collectively 75 per cent of the votes could pass an *ordinary* resolution, or a *special* resolution. In order to pass a written resolution, any *three* of the shareholders would have to vote in support.

Solution 11

(a) The rule in *Foss* v. *Harbottle* supports the notion where a wrong has been done to the company that *the company* is a proper claimant. Kevin can successfully pursue a *derivative* action on a claim of fraud. He *could* succeed in an action against the directors even if fraud is not proved.

(b) As Kevin's votes were not recorded at the General Meeting of the company, he could successfully pursue a *representative* action. Such an action will have its base in s.14, Companies Act 1985 under which the Memorandum and *Articles* form a *contract* between members.

(c) Kevin *may* successfully pursue a claim under s.459, Companies Act 1985 on the grounds of *unfairly prejudicial conduct.*

Solution 12

(a) An employee is employed under a contract *of service* while an independent contractor is employed under a contract *for services.*
(b) Tests are used in determining whether a person is an employee or contractor. The *control* test relates to an employer's right to determine what the worker does and how to do it. The *organisation* test, also known as the *integration* test, applies particularly to professional people. More generally used today is the wider *economic reality* test, also known as the *multiple* test.
(c) While Q has resigned and is claiming unfair dismissal, it may be valid to say that Q is in a position of *constructive* dismissal.

Solution 13

Tony agreed to sell his business to Gaagga Ltd As part of this agreement, Tony was to acquire 24 per cent of the issued share capital of Gaagga Ltd and he was to have first option to buy back his business if Gaagaa Ltd ever wished to sell. The articles of association of Gaagga Ltd were altered to take account of these factors.

The articles contained a clause requiring the company's directors to purchase equally amongst them at fair value any shares which a member wished to sell. The 76 per cent of shares not acquired by Tony were held by the director of the company. All the directors were also members.

Eventually, Gaagga Ltd wished to sell Tony's business and Tony attempted to enforce his right to buy the business back. Further, Tony now wants to sell his 24 per cent shares in the company and looks to the directors to purchase them.

Articles of association deal with the *internal* affairs of a company and at general meeting can be altered on the passing of a *special* resolution. A private company can alternatively use a *written* resolution requiring approval of 75 per cent of the members to alter its articles. Articles bind the company and its members as a *contract.* Rights provided in Articles which are not directly enforceable can be transferred by a court into an *implied* contract. An article alteration cannot take away rights of any class of shareholders unless approved by a *special* resolution of that class. Tony *can* compel the directors to purchase his shareholding.

Solution 14

Wellquar Ltd is a small private company having six members and formed with the object of growing and selling flowers to the public. The board agree that manufacturing greeting cards and selling them to the public would be more profitable. The members at an EGM passed a resolution providing that the objects clause of the company be amended to take account of this new pursuit. The resolution was passed with 85 per cent support. However, a minority shareholder who did not receive notice of the meeting is challenging the validity of the article alteration.

A company objects clause is found in a document called the *Memorandum of Association.* Following the CA 2006 the clause is deemed to be in the company's Articles of Association. At the general meeting, a *special* resolution requiring a minimum *seventy-five* per cent support is needed to alter a company objects clause. An outsider *can* enforce a contract against a company even if the transaction is beyond the powers of the company. A GM requires a minimum notice of *fourteen* days, whilst a special resolution now requires *fourteen* days minimum notice to members. The minimum number of members required for a private company is *one.*

Solution 15

The chairman of Quarteer plc asks you to advise him on a number of matters relating to the forthcoming AGM. Specific information required is to be provided through completing the following statements.

A minimum of *twenty-one* days notice of an AGM must be given to the members. An AGM must be held within a maximum period of *six* months following the company's accounting reference date. Following a vote with a show of hands a *poll* vote may take place with the actual shares with votes attaching determining the voting power of members. Where a member is unable to attend An AGM they may use a *proxy* vote. At an AGM, ordinarily the business dealt with will include receiving the directors' report and the *auditors'* report.

Solution 16

Hugh, Ken and David formed a company in which each of them held one of the three issued shares. It was further agreed that each of them should be a director of the company. Following a disagreement, Ken and David removed Hugh from his position as a director. The articles provide that if ever a director is removed from the company the other members must purchase his share at fair value. Ken and David refuse to purchase Hugh's share.

Hugh could seek a winding up order on the ground it is *just and equitable.* The ground for an action under Sec. 994 of the Companies Act 2006 is *unfairly prejudicial conduct.* On a Sec. 994 of the Companies Act 2006 action, the court may make such order *as it thinks fit* for giving relief. Specific remedies can include authorising *civil* proceedings. The rule in *Foss* v. *Harbottle* provides that the *company* is usually the proper claimant. An exception to the *Foss* v. *Harbottle* rule where fraud is established is described as a *derivative action,* whilst a minority member bringing a claim for breach of contract against the company would pursue a *personal* action.

Solution 17

(B) Professional accountants need to demonstrate independence of mind and appearance, so you should declare the potential conflict of interest and ask a colleague to handle the client. For the sake of completeness, you could also suggest that a competitive tender process should be followed.

Solution 18

(C) Undertaking a review of accounting policies is a legitimate exercise. However, if the request is made based on the clear intent that such changes might be used to mislead others, you should seek guidance from your professional body. If such an intent was not clear, then D would be a better answer, but if subsequently management wished to adopt 'more flattering' policies then you should seek advice before agreeing to affect the changes.

Solution 19

(B) You should inform your boss and suggest the password control system is changed. Even if the relationship does not last, your boss will continue to trust your judgement because of your openness about the situation. To not tell might lead to one or other of you being dismissed under suspicion of potential collusion or fraud.

Solution 20

(C) In this instance, you should query your boss' suggestion on the basis of the timing of the entertainment as it might be interpreted as an inducement to the auditors. You could suggest it would be easier and more enjoyable to do this after the audit has been completed.

Solution 21

(A) You should have the confidence to speak to your boss about this and request support or training to gain the necessary skills and experience to undertake the job asked of you.

Mock Assessment 1

Mock Assessment 1

Certificate Level

Fundamentals of Ethics, Corporate Governance and Business Law

Instructions: attempt all 75 questions

Time allowed 2 hours

Do not turn the page until you are ready to attempt the examination under timed conditions.

Questions

Question 1

Which *one* of the following is *correct*?

(A) The House of Lords has a discretion in applying English Law or European Law.
(B) The House of Lords must apply European Law where it contradicts English Law.
(C) The House of Lords can apply English Law even if it contradicts European Law.
(D) The House of Lords must obtain approval to apply European Law where it contradicts English Law.

Question 2

Which *one* of the following courts has *no* criminal jurisdiction?

(A) Divisional court of the Queens Bench Division.
(B) County Court.
(C) Magistrates Court.
(D) Crown Court.

Question 3

With judicial precedent, subject to the hierarchy of the courts, previous court decisions should be followed. However, it can be possible to avoid following precedent.

Which *one* of the following is *incorrect* in relation to avoidance of precedent?

(A) A higher court can overrule a lower court decision.
(B) Any court can distinguish the facts from those of an earlier decision.
(C) Any court can reverse the decision of a previous court.
(D) Any court need not apply an obiter dicta statement of an earlier court.

Question 4

In relation to establishing a claim of negligence, which *one* of the following is *incorrect*?

(A) There must be sufficient proximity between the wrongdoer and the injured party.
(B) The standard of care required is that expected by the reasonable person.
(C) The same level of care is owed both to adults and children.
(D) The level of care to be shown varies with the level of seriousness of the likely consequences of breach of duty.

Question 5

Which *one* of the following is *correct*?

(A) A professional adviser can be liable to both the client who employs them and any other parties who they know will rely on information provided.

(B) A professional adviser can be liable to anyone who relies on information they provide.
(C) A professional adviser will be liable in negligence but not contract for any negligent advice provided.
(D) A professional adviser cannot be liable where the only form of damage resulting from negligent advice given is financial loss.

Question 6

The standard of proof to be satisfied in

(i) criminal actions
(ii) civil action is

(A) Beyond reasonable doubt for (i) and (ii).
(B) On a balance of probabilities for (i) and (ii).
(C) Beyond reasonable doubt for (i) and on a balance of probabilities for (ii).
(D) On a balance of probabilities for (i) and beyond reasonable doubt for (ii).

Question 7

Common Law developed from which one of the following?

(A) Equity.
(B) Custom.
(C) Decisions of the Court of Chancery.
(D) Judicial precedent.

Question 8

Where a dispute involves issues of European Law the matter must be referred to the European Court by which of the following English courts?

(A) All.
(B) All the courts below the House of Lords.
(C) Only the House of Lords.
(D) Only the Court of Appeal and the House of Lords.

Question 9

Which one of the following contracts would not be presumed to be legally binding?

(A) One or both contracting parties were a business or company.
(B) The contract was a collective agreement between employers and trade unions relating to terms of employment.
(C) The contract is of a clearly commercial nature.
(D) The contract involved money and this was a factor of significance.

Question 10

In which one of the following instances will misrepresentation generally not be recognised?

(A) The contract contains half-truths.
(B) In a contract of the utmost good faith, full disclosure is not made.
(C) Information ceases to be accurate because of changed circumstances.
(D) A party fails to disclose material facts.

Question 11

In which one of the following instances will a term not be incorporated into a contract?

(A) Where a party signs the contract containing the term, whether they have read it or not.
(B) Where the term is an exclusion clause implied under the Unfair Contract Terms Act 1977.
(C) Where there is a course of dealing between the parties.
(D) Where reasonable notice of the term is given but a contracting party remains unaware of its existence.

Question 12

Liability in contract can never be excluded for which one of the following?

(A) Death or physical injury.
(B) The implied conditions under the Sale of Goods Act 1979.
(C) Financial loss.
(D) Guarantees of goods given by manufacturers.

Question 13

The following advertisement appeared in a farming magazine.
'Plough for sale. Little used, very good condition £1,000.'
How would this statement be defined at law?

(A) Advertising puff.
(B) Offer to sell.
(C) Invitation to treat.
(D) Invitation to buy.

Question 14

An offer was made by A to sell goods on the 1st April for £2,000. B the offeree telephoned A on the 5th April offering to pay £1,800 for the goods. On the 8th April, A offered to sell the goods to C for £1,900, and C accepted this offer on the same day. On the 7th April, B sent a letter to A which was received on the 10th April agreeing to pay the £2,000, the asked price for the goods.

(A) There is a contract between A and B created on the 7th April.
(B) There is a contract between A and B created on the 10th April.

(C) There is a contract between A and C.
(D) There is no contract created.

Question 15

A coat was displayed in a shop window with a price tag attached which read £10. The price tag should have read £100. X who saw this went into the shop and demanded the coat for £10.

Which *one* of the following is *correct*?

(A) As the window display is an offer, X can demand the coat at £10.
(B) The window display is merely an invitation to treat and the shopkeeper does not have to sell the coat to X.
(C) The shopkeeper can refuse to sell the coat for £10, but cannot refuse to sell the coat to X for £100 if X was prepared to pay this sum.
(D) The shopkeeper would be bound to sell the coat to any customer prepared to pay this £100.

Question 16

Which *one* of the following is *incorrect*?

(A) A contract term can be implied by a court on the ground of business efficacy.
(B) A contract term can be implied by statute.
(C) A contract term can be implied by a court on the basis of fairness between the parties.
(D) A contract term can be implied by a court on the basis of trade custom.

Question 17

Which *one* of the following statements is *incorrect*?

(A) Statute provides an implied term in sale of goods contracts that the goods are of satisfactory quality.
(B) Statute provides an implied term in sale of goods contracts that the goods supplied must correspond with description.
(C) Statute provides that failure to supply goods of satisfactory quality in a sale of goods contract constitutes breach of condition.
(D) Statute provides that failure to provide goods in a sale of goods contract that correspond with description amounts to a breach of warranty.

Question 18

Which *one* of the following statements is *correct*?

(A) In a contract, a breach of a condition will result in the contract being terminated.
(B) In a contract, a breach of a condition is a breach of a term of fundamental importance to the contract.
(C) In a contract, a breach of warranty entitles the innocent party to terminate the contract.
(D) In a contract, a breach of warranty can terminate a contract, but only on the basis of equity.

Question 19

Which *one* of the following is *incorrect*?

(A) Exclusion clauses attempting to exclude liability for death or injury are void.
(B) Statutory implied conditions giving consumers protection in sale of goods contracts can be excluded so long as the exclusion clause is reasonable.
(C) Where the wording of an exclusion clause is ambiguous it will be interpreted against the party seeking to rely on it.
(D) An unfair term does not bind a consumer but the contract may continue.

Question 20

A contract will be discharged as a result of a frustrating event occurring.

Which one of the following will not bring about discharge of a contract?

(A) Performance becomes radically different from that anticipated.
(B) Performance becomes more expensive and difficult than anticipated.
(C) Physical impossibility of performance due to accidental destruction of subject matter.
(D) If the contract is dependent on a future event which does not occur.

Question 21

X has contracted with Y to paint a portrait of Y's daughter. Y has for a considerable time wanted X to paint the portrait and is very disappointed when X having started the work states that he is not prepared to complete the painting.

Which of the following remedies is appropriate in these circumstances?

(A) Damages.
(B) Rescission.
(C) Specific performance.
(D) Injunction.

Question 22

Which of the following statements is *incorrect* in relation to the determining of damages payable on breach of contract?

(A) The purpose of providing damages is to compensate the injured party.
(B) Quantifying damages is determining the actual amount of the award to be made to the injured party.
(C) The remoteness of damage issue is determined by considering the amount of damages the injured party reasonably expects on the basis of the contract breach and damages suffered.
(D) An innocent party has a duty to mitigate their loss.

Question 23

An employer must provide a written statement of particulars to an employee within what period from the commencement of the employment?

(A) Within 1 week.
(B) Within 1 month.
(C) Within 2 months.
(D) Within 6 weeks.

Question 24

In order to determine whether or not a party is an employee or an independent contractor a number of tests have been devised.

Which *one* of the following is *not* a recognised test?

(A) Organisation test.
(B) Control test.
(C) Multiple test.
(D) Supply and demand test.

Question 25

Which *one* of the following statements is *incorrect*?

(A) An employer is normally liable for wrongs committed by employees.
(B) An independent contractor has no statutory protection in respect of sick pay.
(C) An independent contractor has no preferential rights over other creditors on the insolvency of the employer.
(D) Employees and independent contractors are prohibited from delegating work to others.

Question 26

Which *one* of the following is *incorrect*?

(A) A limited liability partnership has legal personality.
(B) A minimum of two parties are required to form a limited liability partnership.
(C) Partners in a limited liability partnership cannot be corporate bodies.
(D) Individual members of a limited liability partnership will have no contractual liability to creditors of the partnership.

Question 27

In relation to a private limited company, which *one* of the following is *correct*?

(A) Annual General Meetings must be held.
(B) Articles of Association must be filed with a Registrar when seeking registration of the company.
(C) The company will have perpetual succession.
(D) Directors of the company would never be liable to company creditors.

Question 28

Which *one* of the following statements is *incorrect* in relation to a public limited company?

(A) A company must have a minimum issued share capital of £50,000.
(B) The company cannot issue only redeemable shares.
(C) The company must have a certificate of incorporation and a trading certificate before it can validly commence business.
(D) The company must have at least two members.

Question 29

Which *one* of the following is *incorrect*?

(A) Members of a company can ratify any *ultra vires* act of its directors.
(B) Any member can seek an order preventing a company from carrying out an act not specifically permitted in its objects clause.
(C) Where an objects clause provides that a company can carry on business as a 'general commercial company', the company can validly carry out any lawful transaction.
(D) Where a director acts ultra vires on behalf of a company, the transaction will be void unless it is ratified by the members.

Question 30

Which *one* of the following is *correct* in relation to an alteration of articles of association.

(A) Class rights can be altered.
(B) Shareholder liability can be increased.
(C) Members must pass an ordinary resolution.
(D) The alteration must be *bona fide* and in the best interests of every member.

Question 31

Which *one* of the following can be achieved by a public company only with court approval, in addition to a resolution of the members being passed?

(A) Change of company name.
(B) Increase of share capital.
(C) Reduction of share capital.
(D) Change of the situation of the company registered office.

Question 32

Which *one* of the following is *correct*?

(A) A private company can issue only redeemable shares.
(B) A private and a public company can issue only redeemable shares.

(C) A public company can issue redeemable preference shares.
(D) A private company cannot issue redeemable preference shares.

Question 33

Which of the following is *not* correct in relation to a reduction of capital by a public company?

(A) The company must have authority to reduce capital in its Articles of Association.
(B) A special resolution must be passed.
(C) A court order approving the reduction must be obtained.
(D) The company may be ordered to add the words 'and reduced' after its name.

Question 34

Which *one* of the following is *incorrect*?

(A) A private company can accept non-cash consideration in the return for shares without the need to have the consideration valued.
(B) A public company can accept consideration in a contract of allotment of shares of less than market value so long as it is at least the same as the nominal value of the shares.
(C) A public company can only accept money as consideration on an allotment of shares.
(D) If a private company has an authorised share capital it may be increased by passing a resolution.

Question 35

Which of the following is *incorrect* in relation to authorised capital?

(A) A public company is required to have an authorised capital.
(B) A private company is no longer required to have an authorised capital.
(C) When a private company issues further shares a statement of capital must be sent to the Registrar.
(D) When a public company issues further shares a statement of capital must be sent to the Registrar.

Question 36

In relation to a company purchasing its own shares, which *one* of the following is *correct*?

(A) Capital can be used by both private and public companies.
(B) Capital cannot be used by either private or public companies.
(C) Public companies only can use capital to satisfy some of the debt.
(D) Private companies only can use capital to satisfy some of the debt.

Question 37

In relation to a company providing financial assistance for the acquisition of its own shares, after the Companies Act 2006 is in force, which *one* of the following is *correct*?

(A) A private company may provide financial assistance for the purchase of its own shares so long as it follows the correct procedure.
(B) A bank cannot provide financial assistance for an acquisition of shares in the bank itself.
(C) A private company is not subject to restrictions when providing financial assistance.
(D) A public company cannot provide assistance to employees by providing loans which are used to purchase shares in the company.

Question 38

Following the enactment of the Companies Act 2006, which *one* of the following statements is *incorrect*?

(A) A private company must have a secretary but he/she does not need to be qualified.
(B) A private company can have only one member who is also the only director.
(C) A sole member is distinct from the company at law.
(D) A public company must have at least two directors.

Question 39

A minority of members can give written, signed notice to the directors requiring them to hold a General Meeting.

Which *one* of the following is the *correct* minimum shareholding this minority must have?

(A) 5%.
(B) 10%.
(C) 15%.
(D) 25%.

Question 40

Which *one* of the following is *incorrect* in relation to the use of an ordinary resolution with special notice?

(A) It must be used for the removal of a director.
(B) It must be used for the removal of the company secretary.
(C) It must be used for the removal of a director aged over 70 years.
(D) It must be used for the removal of a director over the age of 16 years.

Question 41

In relation to directors, which *one* of the following statements is *incorrect*?

(A) A director is an agent of the company.
(B) A director is an officer of the company.

(C) A company has a duty to have executive directors.
(D) A shadow director is the main type of *de facto* director.

Question 42

Directors do not owe a duty to which *one* of the following?

(A) Members individually.
(B) Members as a body.
(C) The Public at large.
(D) Employees.

Question 43

Where a director is guilty of wrongful trading which *one* of the following is a possible consequence for the individual?

(A) Being required to contribute to the assets of the company in liquidation.
(B) A possible fine.
(C) Imprisonment.
(D) Being subject to an equitable remedy.

Question 44

Which *one* of the following is *incorrect* where a director is in breach of statutory duty?

(A) The members cannot pass a resolution ratifying what has been done.
(B) If the director in breach is also a member, he cannot vote in support of the ratification.
(C) Articles cannot exempt directors from liability for breach of duty.
(D) A director in breach can be liable to account for any secret profit obtained.

Question 45

Alan, Barbara and Clive are the only members of Beeceedee Ltd with equal shareholdings. They are also the only directors of the company. Relations between the three parties have in the past been good. However, now, Alan and Barbara always vote against Clive at board meetings and are not prepared to listen to Clive's views. Further, on numerous occasions Alan and Barbara have refused to attend meetings. The quorum for board meetings and members meetings is two. Clive is unhappy generally with the way in which the company is now being run and wishes to petition for a winding up order.

Which *one* of the following is the appropriate action to obtain a winding up order?

(A) A derivative action.
(B) An action on the basis of unfairly prejudicial conduct.
(C) An action on the just and equitable ground.
(D) A representative action.

Question 46

Secs 994–996 of the Companies Act 2006 identifies a number of remedies which can be introduced by a court where an action for unfairly prejudicial conduct is brought.

Which *one* of the following is *not* a remedy identified in this section?

(A) An order regulating company affairs in the future.
(B) Authorising criminal proceedings to be brought in the name of and on behalf of the company.
(C) Authorising civil proceedings to be brought in the name of and on behalf of the company.
(D) Requiring the company to buy the petitioner's shares at fair value.

Question 47

Which *one* of the following is *incorrect* in relation to the company secretary?

(A) They can never contract on behalf of the company.
(B) Qualification requirements attach to a company secretary of a public company but not a private company.
(C) Details of the company secretary are entered in the same register as that used to register director details.
(D) Some statutory provisions can render the company secretary criminally liable.

Question 48

Corporate governance measures are primarily for the benefit of 'stakeholders'. Who are stakeholders in this context?

(A) All those directly or indirectly affected by the company's activities.
(B) All those directly affected by the company's activities.
(C) The shareholders.
(D) All those indirectly affected by the company's activities.

Question 49

To which type of company is the Combined Code primarily directed?

(A) All companies.
(B) All public companies.
(C) All private and public companies.
(D) All listed public companies.

Question 50

Which of the following is *not* a recommendation of the Combined Code?

(A) A board audit committee should be established.
(B) The roles of Chairman and Managing Director should be combined.
(C) At least one-half of the board should be made up of independent non-executive directors.
(D) All directors should attend the AGM.

Question 51

The two-tier board structure comprises a Supervisory Board and what other organ?

(A) A board representing the employees.
(B) A board majority of non-executive directors.
(C) An all-executive board.
(D) A management board.

Question 52

What is the most commonly used procedure adopted by the European Union for the creation of law?

(A) Consultation.
(B) Codecision.
(C) Assent.
(D) Accord.

Question 53

The European Union is at present made up of how many states?

(A) 18.
(B) 22.
(C) 27.
(D) 28.

Question 54

In which one of the following countries are individuals appointed judges at the beginning of their legal careers?

(A) Germany.
(B) France.
(C) Denmark.
(D) Italy.

Question 55

In the United States of America, all states with one exception have a common law system with court decisions establishing precedent. Which state is the exception?

(A) Ohio.
(B) Missouri.
(C) Louisianna.
(D) Texas.

Question 56

Hong Kong and Macau on transferring sovereignty to China did not change their legal systems. They continue to adopt the legal systems of England and which other country?

(A) Australia.
(B) France.
(C) Spain.
(D) Portugal.

Question 57

Which of the following is not an accurate description of what a company's code of ethics is likely to achieve?

(A) It tells employees what is expected of them in terms of behaviour.
(B) It explains the approach and outlook of the organisation.
(C) It encourages employees to take a consistent approach to ethical issues.
(D) It eliminates the need for legislation.

Question 58

In which country does legislation legally require professional accountants to speak up if they find themselves in a situation where they might not be able to comply with relevant legal, regulatory or standards frameworks?

(A) Italy.
(B) the United States.
(C) Germany.
(D) Japan.

Question 59

Which of the following actions by a company would not encourage employees to speak up if they encounter potentially serious cases of unprofessional or unethical behavior?

(A) Introduce an employee helpline for ethics-related queries.
(B) State in the company's code of ethics that employees have a duty to speak up.
(C) Stress the importance of employees working together to meet ambitious sales targets.
(D) Develop a culture where it is safe and acceptable for employees to raise concerns.

Question 60

Which of the following is not an ethical value?

(A) Tolerance.
(B) Truthfulness.
(C) Training.
(D) Transparency.

Question 61

Which of the following does not specifically relate to business ethics?

(A) The financial viability of a business.
(B) The behaviour of the business and its employees.
(C) How a business conducts its relationships with its stakeholders.
(D) How a company does business, rather than what it does.

Question 62

Which of the following is not one of the five personal qualities that CIMA expects of its members?

(A) Reliability.
(B) Respect.
(C) Responsibility.
(D) Reflection.

Question 63

While reviewing the work of one of your colleagues, you discover that he has made some extremely serious mistakes. When you discuss this with him, it becomes clear that he does not have the understanding of financial matters that he requires to be a competent accountant. This violates CIMA's fundamental principle of:

(A) Integrity.
(B) Objectivity.
(C) Professional competence and due care.
(D) Confidentiality.

Question 64

You are working abroad and find yourself in a situation where a particular element of the country's legislation is in conflict with the IFAC Code of Ethics. In this situation, you should:

(A) Obey the law because it is mandatory to comply with legislation.
(B) Obey the ethics code because it is internationally binding.
(C) Obey the law because you have a public duty to uphold the law, but not to uphold ethics.
(D) Obey the ethics code because it is a requirement of your profession.

Question 65

Which of the following relates specifically to accountability?

(A) Taking responsibility for one's work and conclusions.
(B) Maintaining clear records that provide evidence to back up conclusions.
(C) Being answerable to queries in relation to one's work.
(D) All of the above.

Question 66

Which of the following relates to an ethical issue?

(A) Moving into a larger office as part of a plan to expand your business.
(B) Introducing a new monthly reporting process to maximise efficiency.
(C) Introducing a new IT system to ensure confidentiality of customer information.
(D) Recruiting a new finance director.

Question 67

Which of the following would be of the least help in developing an effective corporate ethics programme?

(A) Having a chairman and chief executive who champion ethics at every opportunity.
(B) Providing copies of the company's code of ethics to trusted personnel only to avoid the document falling into the hands of competitors.
(C) Incorporating ethical issues into new employee induction programmes.
(D) Talking to the company's key stakeholders about the social and environmental issues they believe to be important.

Question 68

In tackling ethical dilemmas, which of the following would not help you to find a solution?

(A) Establishing the facts and the ethical issues involved.
(B) Referring to the CIMA and/or your company's code of ethics.
(C) Following an established internal procedure.
(D) Choosing to postpone tackling the issue due to pressure of deadlines.

Question 69

One of your colleagues has just been passed over for promotion for the third time. She shows you evidence that only a small number of women have ever been promoted to positions of seniority within your company. This, she says, is an issue of:

(A) Harassment.
(B) Discrimination.
(C) Conflict of interest.
(D) Bribery and corruption.

Question 70

Which of the following is not an ethical issue for a bank?

(A) Providing accurate information about terms and conditions when advertising interest rates for customer loans.
(B) Launching a premium account service for customers who are willing to pay a monthly charge for improved service.
(C) Money laundering.
(D) Disabled access to bank branches.

Question 71

Which of the following ethical issues is most likely to be affected by new developments in information technology?

(A) Data protection.
(B) Gifts and hospitality.
(C) Harassment.
(D) Health and safety.

Question 72

Parliament has delegated wide powers to government ministers within their own departments. These ministers and their civil service departments are given the task of making rules and regulations within the guidelines of the enabling Acts. What is the usual form of these rules and regulations?

(A) Bye-laws.
(B) Legislative Instruments.
(C) Orders in Council.
(D) Statutory Instruments.

Question 73

There are several sources of European Union Law. Which of the following are directly applicable and automatically become law in member states?

(A) Treaties only.
(B) Treaties and Regulations only.
(C) Treaties, Regulations and Directives only.
(D) Treaties, Regulations, Directives and Decisions.

Question 74

In contract law, a misrepresentation is which *one* of the following?

(A) An untrue statement of fact or opinion which induces another to contract.
(B) An untrue statement of fact, opinion or intention which induces another to contract.
(C) An untrue statement of fact which induces another to contract.
(D) An untrue statement of fact or intention which induces another to contract.

Question 75

Which of the following would *not* be a useful test for an ethical dilemma? Imagine how you would feel if your decision was splashed across the front pages of a newspaper?

(A) Whether your family would think what you have done is fair to everyone concerned?
(B) Whether your decision would make you more popular in the office?
(C) Whether you think you will be able to live with your decision?

Solutions

Solution 1
(B)

Solution 2
(B)

Solution 3
(C)

Solution 4
(C)

Solution 5
(A)

Solution 6
(C)

Solution 7
(B)

Solution 8
(C)

Solution 9
(B)

Solution 10
(D)

Solution 11
(B)

Solution 12
(A)

Solution 13
(C)

Solution 14
(C)

Solution 15
(B)

Solution 16
(C)

Solution 17
(D)

Solution 18
(B)

Solution 19
(B)

Solution 20
(B)

Solution 21
(C)

Solution 22
(C)

Solution 23
(C)

Solution 24
(D)

Solution 25
(D)

Solution 26
(C)

Solution 27
(C)

Solution 28
(A)

Solution 29
(D)

Solution 30
(A)

Solution 31
(C)

Solution 32
(C)

Solution 33
(A)

Solution 34
(C)

Solution 35
(A)

Solution 36
(D)

Solution 37
(C)

Solution 38
(A)

Solution 39
(B)

Solution 40
(B)

Solution 41
(C)

Solution 42
(C)

Solution 43
(A)

Solution 44
(A)

Solution 45
(C)

Solution 46
(B)

Solution 47
(A)

Solution 48
(A)

Solution 49
(D)

Solution 50
(B)

Solution 51
(D)

Solution 52
(B)

Solution 53
(C)

Solution 54
(B)

Solution 55
(C)

Solution 56
(D)

Solution 57
(D)

Solution 58
(B)

Solution 59
(C)

Solution 60
(C)

Solution 61
(A)

Solution 62
(D)

Solution 63
(C)

Solution 64
(A)

Solution 65
(D)

Solution 66
(C)

Solution 67
(B)

Solution 68
(D)

Solution 69
(B)

Solution 70
(B)

Solution 71
(A)

Solution 72
(D)

Solution 73
(B)

Solution 74
(C)

Solution 75
(C)

Mock Assessment 2

Mock Assessment 2

Certificate Level

Fundamentals of Ethics, Corporate Governance and Business Law

Instructions: attempt all 75 questions

Time allowed 2 hours

Do not turn the page until you are ready to attempt the examination under timed conditions.

Questions

Question 1

Which division of the High Court hears disputes in contract and tort?

(A) The Chancery Division.
(B) The Commercial Division.
(C) The Queen's Bench Division.
(D) The Family Division.

Question 2

Which *one* of the following statements is *incorrect*?

(A) The House of Lords is not bound by its own previous decisions.
(B) The Court of Appeal is not bound by its own previous decisions.
(C) The High Court is not bound by its own previous decisions.
(D) The County Court is not bound by its own previous decisions.

Question 3

In negligence actions on exceptional occasions, the courts reverse the burden of proof and require the defendant to prove no breach of duty of care occurred. What are the requirements for this reversing of the burden of proof to occur?

(i) The harm would not happen if proper care were taken.
(ii) The defendant alleges contributory negligence on the part of the plaintiff.
(iii) The defendant was in control of the situation.
(iv) The only apparent explanation for what has occurred is breach of duty by the defendant.

(A) (i), (ii) and (iv).
(B) (i), (iii) and (iv).
(C) (i), (ii) and (iii).
(D) (ii), (iii) and (iv).

Question 4

Which *one* of the following is a frequently used method of creating law used by the European Union?

(A) Codecision.
(B) Assent.
(C) Accord.
(D) Confirmation.

Question 5

Today, law in France is mainly created by the legislative body and so is codified. Which *one* of the following areas is not codified in France?

(A) Contract.
(B) Company Law.
(C) Family Law.
(D) Tort.

Question 6

Which *one* of the following is an influence that has contributed to the development of the legal system of Denmark?

(A) Roman Law.
(B) The Code *Civile* from France.
(C) German jurisprudence.
(D) English constitutional theory.

Question 7

In China, more than 800,000 mediation committees function in rural and urban areas. Which *one* of the following correctly identifies by percentage the extent to which these committees deal with civil disputes?

(A) Over 60%.
(B) Over 70%.
(C) Over 80%.
(D) Over 90%.

Question 8

Which *one* of the following correctly identifies the Institution(s) of the European Union that pass new laws?

(A) The European Parliament and the Council of the European Union.
(B) The Council of the European Union and the European Commission.
(C) The European Parliament and the European Commission.
(D) The European Commission alone.

Question 9

Equity as a source of English Law was developed by which court?

(A) The Exchequer Court.
(B) The House of Lords.

(C) The Court of Chancery.
(D) The Kings Bench Court.

Question 10

Which *one* of the following is not a form of delegated legislation?

(A) Bye-laws.
(B) Requisitional orders.
(C) Statutory Instruments.
(D) Orders on Council.

Question 11

A promise in isolation cannot be sued upon, however a promise will be respected at law on the basis of promissory estoppel. Which *one* of the following is not a requirement for promissory estoppel to apply?

(A) The promise must be based on an already existing contract.
(B) The promise is the basis upon which the court action is commenced.
(C) The promissor intends the promise to be acted upon.
(D) The promisee does act in reliance on the promise.

Question 12

A specific performance order will rarely be granted in relation to which *one* of the following?

(A) A commercial transaction.
(B) To a minor.
(C) An employment contract.
(D) A building contract.

Question 13

Which *one* of the following is *incorrect*?

(A) A promise to provide consideration in return for consideration already provided by another is not good consideration.
(B) A promise to perform an existing obligation to the promise is not good consideration.
(C) A promise to perform an existing obligation to a third party is not good consideration.
(D) A promise to perform an existing public duty is not good consideration.

Question 14

In which *one* of the following situations will a binding contract be recognised?

(A) Where a collective agreement between employers and trade unions regarding terms of employment exists.
(B) Where an agreement exists but only one vital term remains to be settled.

(C) Where an option to renew a lease exists 'at a market rent'.
(D) Where an option to renew a lease exists 'at such rental as may be agreed between the parties'.

Question 15

Misrepresentation is defined as a false statement of fact which induces another party to contract. Misrepresentation can however be found not in that communicated, but in that which is not communicated. Which *one* of the following does not as a general rule constitute misrepresentation?

(A) Failure to disclose full material facts in a contract of the utmost good faith.
(B) Failure to communicate changed circumstances.
(C) Failure to communicate fully relevant information, although that which is communicated is accurate.
(D) Failure to disclose facts where it is known by the silent party that the other is deceiving himself.

Question 16

Rescission is an equitable remedy, and so will not be granted if the court believes that to do so would be unfair. Which *one* of the following is *correct* in relation to the granting of rescission as a remedy?

(A) Rescission becomes effective once the court order is made.
(B) Rescission must be exercised reasonably promptly.
(C) Rescission can be awarded under s. 2(1) Misrepresentation Act 1967.
(D) Rescission can be awarded under s. 2(2) Misrepresentation Act 1967 in addition to the remedy of damages.

Question 17

Express terms can be incorporated into a contract in a number of ways. Which one of the following is not an acceptable method of such incorporation?

(A) Actual notice.
(B) Reasonable notice.
(C) Signature.
(D) Policy.

Question 18

Which *one* of the following sections of the Sale of Goods Act 1979 (as amended) provides that there is an implied condition that goods must correspond with their description?

(A) Section 12.
(B) Section 13.
(C) Section 14.
(D) Section 15.

Question 19

An exemption clause in a contract will be interpreted *contra proferentem*. On this basis, which *one* of the following statements is *incorrect*?

(A) An exemption clause, where it is clear, will not be upheld if the contract breach is of a serious nature.
(B) An exemption clause stating that warranties are excluded will not be interpreted as including conditions also.
(C) A clause providing that 'nothing in this agreement' shall make the contracting party liable would be restricted to contract law and so not include a tortuous claim.
(D) A clause which is ambiguous will be interpreted against the party seeking to rely on the clause.

Question 20

A breach of condition is a serious breach of contract that gives the innocent party the right to end the contract. However, this right is subject to certain rights and obligations. Which *one* of the following is an applicable right/obligation?

(A) The right must be exercised reasonably promptly.
(B) If the innocent party 'affirms' the contract, the right to terminate is then lost.
(C) If the innocent party 'affirms' where a breach of condition has occurred, this reduces the contractual obligations that need to be satisfied by the innocent party.
(D) If the right to terminate the contract is exercised, the innocent party need perform no further contractual obligations.

Question 21

A 'reservation of title' clause or *Romalpa* clause can be used to protect a seller of goods. Which *one* of the following does not correctly identify a protective feature arising through the use of this type of clause?

(A) The seller remains owner until full payment for the goods is made.
(B) The seller can recover the goods rather than become an unsecured creditor if the buyer becomes insolvent.
(C) The seller is protected by the clause, even if the goods are mixed with other goods.
(D) The seller has a claim in breach of contract where only part payment is made.

Question 22

When deciding upon damages payable on breach of contract, the courts consider the remoteness of the damage. In determining whether or not the loss or damage is too remote, which *one* of the following is not accurate?

(A) Loss recognised is that which may reasonably have been in the contemplation of both parties at the time of contracting.
(B) Where the type of loss suffered is foreseeable, the loss is recoverable irrespective of its extent.

(C) Damages will be awarded for loss that is considered as fairly and reasonably arising naturally.
(D) Damages will be awarded for loss arising in the usual course of things from the breach.

Question 23

When deciding upon the measure of damages payable in contract, which *one* of the following is accurate?

(A) Damages will never be awarded for speculative profits which might have accrued.
(B) Damages will never be awarded in relation to the possible loss of future profits.
(C) Damages will always be awarded for loss of profits suffered when the contract ends.
(D) Damages will always be awarded where some loss has definitely been suffered but it is difficult to assess the extent of the loss.

Question 24

Which *one* of the following statements relating to contract claims and the relevance of contributory negligence is inaccurate?

(A) A party buying goods from a dealer cannot be guilty of contributory negligence for not checking the goods.
(B) A claimant in a contract action cannot be liable for contributory negligence.
(C) A party cannot be liable for contributory negligence in a fraud action.
(D) A party will not be liable for contributory negligence where the action is based on a failure to satisfy an obligation that is strict.

Question 25

For a deed to be valid, certain requirements must be satisfied. Which *one* of the following is not a requirement for a valid deed to be prepared?

(A) It must be signed.
(B) It must be witnessed.
(C) It must be sealed.
(D) It must be delivered.

Question 26

Employers owe certain implied duties to employees. In which *one* of the following instances, does a duty to provide work not exist?

(A) Where the employee's remuneration depends upon the work done.
(B) Where the employee needs work to maintain reputation.
(C) Where the employee needs work to maintain familiarity with technical change.
(D) Where the employee is participating in an ongoing staff training programme.

Question 27

Some grounds for unfair dismissal are deemed to be automatically unfair whilst other reasons may be presumed unfair, but the employer has the opportunity of successfully opposing the claim. In which *one* of the following instances will it not always be deemed a basis for recognised automatic unfair dismissal?

(A) Where an employee brings a court action against the employer in good faith to enforce a statutory right, where no right in fact exists.
(B) Where an employee is selected for redundancy contrary to an agreed arrangement or custom, without good reason.
(C) Where an employee fails to comply with orders on the basis of valid health and safety grounds.
(D) Where an employee is pregnant.

Question 28

Where a dismissed employee claims wrongful dismissal, which *one* of the following is *incorrect*?

(A) The claim can be based on dismissal without proper notice.
(B) The claim will be brought to court, not tribunal.
(C) The claim will essentially be for breach of contract.
(D) The claimant has a duty to mitigate loss by seeking other employment.

Question 29

Which *one* of the following is *incorrect* in relation to a Limited Liability Partnership ('LLP')?

(A) Partners of an LLP are agents of the LLP.
(B) Most LLPs are professional forms.
(C) An LLP must have at least two designated members.
(D) The Limited Liability Partnerships Act 2000 imposes a formal management structure on all LLPs.

Question 30

Which *one* of the following is *incorrect* in relation to a private company limited by shares?

(A) A private company limited by shares is fully liable for its debts and obligations.
(B) In the case of a single member company, the shareholder cannot also act as the sole director.
(C) A private company is a separate legal person distinct from its shareholders.
(D) The board is the agent of the company.

Question 31

Which *one* of the following is *correct* in relation to a public company limited by shares?

(A) The company must have at least one director.
(B) All public limited companies are listed on a stock exchange.

(C) The company must have a qualified company secretary.
(D) The company can commence trading as soon as it receives a certificate of incorporation.

Question 32

Which *one* of the following statement is *correct* in relation to company contracts?

(A) A third party who has acted in good faith can enforce *ultra vires* contracts against the company.
(B) A company may enter into any contract irrespective of its constitution.
(C) A company may not amend its ability to contract by placing restrictions in its Articles of Association.
(D) Shareholders cannot prevent a company from entering into an ultra vires contract.

Question 33

Which *one* of the following statements is *correct* in relation to the articles of association?

(A) A company may change its articles by the directors passing a special resolution.
(B) All provisions in the articles of association are contractual.
(C) Articles of association are private documents.
(D) In the event of any conflict between the memorandum and articles of association, the memorandum prevails.

Question 34

Which *one* of the following is *incorrect* in relation to petitions for a winding up order?

(A) In the event of a petition by a shareholder on the 'just and equitable' ground, an order can be made against a solvent or insolvent company.
(B) A company is deemed to be unable to pay its debts if the court is satisfied that that is the case.
(C) The company may petition for a winding up order against itself by passing a special resolution.
(D) Once a company is wound up, its name is deleted from the register at Companies House.

Question 35

Following the enactment of the Companies Act 2006, which *one* of the following statements is *correct* in relation to the Memorandum of Association?

(A) The Memorandum of Association contains the name of the company.
(B) The Memorandum of Association contains a statement that the subscribers wish to form a company.
(C) The Memorandum of Association must specify the authorised share capital of the company.
(D) If the company is public, the Memorandum of Association must state that to be the case.

Question 36

The Companies Act 2006 is scheduled to be completely in force by which date?

(A) April 2007.
(B) October 2007.
(C) April 2008.
(D) October 2009.

Question 37

Who is able to register a company by submitting the required documents in electronic form?

(A) Persons who are the proposed directors of the company.
(B) Persons who are promoting the company.
(C) Persons who act as company registration agents.
(D) Persons who are the proposed subscribers to the memorandum.

Question 38

Which *one* of the following is *not* required to be stated on all websites, business letters and order forms by the Companies Act 2006?

(A) The nature of the company's business.
(B) The name of the company.
(C) The company's registered number.
(D) The address of the company's registered office.

Question 39

Which of the following must be carried out to take advantage of the provisions in the Companies Act 2006 which facilitate electronic communications with shareholders as a matter of course?

(A) A board resolution authorising electronic communication.
(B) An amendment to the articles of association authorising electronic communication.
(C) An amendment to the Memorandum of Association authorising electronic communication.
(D) An announcement on the company's website stating that future communications with shareholders will be in electronic form.

Question 40

Which *one* of the following statements is *incorrect*?

(A) A private company must first offer any new shares for cash to the existing shareholders.
(B) A public company must first offer any new shares for cash to the existing shareholders.

(C) A private company may issue shares for a non-cash consideration and must have that consideration valued.
(D) A public company may issue shares for a non-cash consideration and must have that consideration valued.

Question 41

Which of the following resolutions may be passed by a private company in place of other resolutions?

(A) An ordinary resolution with special notice.
(B) A written resolution.
(C) A ordinary resolution passed at an AGM.
(D) A special resolution.

Question 42

An auditor may be removed by ordinary resolution with special notice. What is special notice?

(A) 28 days notice to the shareholders.
(B) 28 days notice to the directors.
(C) 28 days notice to the company.
(D) 28 days notice to the auditor.

Question 43

Which *one* of the following statements regarding the Rule in *Foss* v. *Harbottle* (1843) is *incorrect*?

(A) The case sets down a rule of procedure.
(B) Where there has been a wrong to the company, it is for the company to decide on the appropriate action.
(C) Where the act complained of can be ratified by the members, the minority cannot maintain an action.
(D) Minority shareholders are entitled to sue in the company's name if the act complained of was carried out by the directors.

Question 44

Which *one* of the following statements is *not* an exception to the Rule in *Foss* v. *Harbottle* (1843)?

(A) Where the rights of individual shareholders have been infringed.
(B) Where the company acts on a resolution which has not been properly passed.
(C) Where there has been fraud on the minority.
(D) Where there has been an issue of shares designed to reduce the voting power of the minority.

Question 45

Which *one* of the following is a business name?

(A) Jack Wilson Ltd.
(B) High Street Computers.
(C) Enterprise plc.
(D) Morrisey LLP.

Question 46

A, B and C are about to set up in business as a general partnership. In the absence of agreement to the contrary, how will the law presume that they are to share profits?

(A) One third each.
(B) According to the proportion in which they have invested capital.
(C) According to the hours that each of them will work in the business.
(D) According to age and expertise.

Question 47

What is meant by the expression 'lifting the veil of incorporation'?

(A) The company is treated as if it were fully liable for all its debts.
(B) The shareholders are treated as though they were carrying on business in partnership.
(C) The directors are treated as partners and are fully liable for the company's debts.
(D) The company is treated as if it were not a separate person at law.

Question 48

Which *one* of the following statements is *incorrect* regarding a company's registered office?

(A) The registered office is the postal address of the company.
(B) The registered office is the place where the company maintains its statutory registers.
(C) The registered office must be a place where the company carries on business.
(D) The address of the registered office may be changed by ordinary resolution of the shareholders.

Question 49

Which *one* of the following statements is *correct* in relation to contracts entered into on behalf of a private company limited by shares before it has been registered?

(A) The contract is enforceable against the company after registration.
(B) The contract is void against the company.

(C) The contract may be ratified by the directors after registration.
(D) The contract cannot be enforced against anyone if it was entered into in the name of the unregistered company.

Question 50

Which *one* of the following has an implied power to borrow money?

(A) A private company.
(B) An investment company.
(C) A public company.
(D) A trading company.

Question 51

Place the following reasons for following an ethical code of conduct in order of importance, with the most important first:

(i) To prevent personal professional liability from arising.
(ii) To safeguard the reputation of the Accounting Profession.
(iii) Because it is a good thing to do.
(iv) To avoid the need for government regulation.

(A) (ii), (i), (iv), (iii)
(B) (iii), (ii), (i), (iv)
(C) (iv), (iii), (ii), (i)
(D) (i), (iv), (iii), (ii)

Question 52

Which of the following statements most accurately expresses different approaches to ethical regulations?

(A) Breaches of ethics have less serious consequences than breaches of the criminal law.
(B) Ethical frameworks let the individual decide about how they should act in particular situations.
(C) Regulations provide a 'thou shallt not' approach to behaviour, whereas framework approaches encourage positive behaviour in support of ethical conduct.
(D) The framework approach is best suited to practical problem-solving in ethics.

Question 53

Which statement is the most accurate of the statements?

(A) Laws can never be broken, even if they breach ethics.
(B) Ethical breaches always have to be justified, even if they result from the breach of a law.
(C) Legal breaches often result in ethical breaches.
(D) Ethical breaches often result in legal breaches.

Question 54

Why do we need codes of professional ethics?

(A) To resolve disputes.
(B) To punish bad accountants.
(C) To protect the reputation of the profession.
(D) To improve the quality of service to the public.

Question 55

Which is a *correct* statement?

(A) The IFAC Codes of conduct deal with accountants working internationally, while CIMA only applies to business done in Britain.
(B) The CIMA Code is inferior to IFAC's Code.
(C) The IFAC Code reflects the standards laid down by CIMA.
(D) The IFAC Code is reflected in the CIMA Code.

Question 56

Which is the best explanation of independence within the meaning of the CIMA Code?

(A) Independence means thinking for yourself as an accountant.
(B) Independence means the absence of bias.
(C) Independence means the profession is not subject to political direction.
(D) Independence means not always doing what your client tells you to do.

Question 57

Which is the best explanation of social responsibility?

(A) Social responsibility means the accountant is responsible to all of society equally.
(B) Social responsibility means that the accountant should do additional things to support social initiatives.
(C) Social responsibility means that the accountant has to be squeaky clean in his or her social as well as professional life.
(D) Social responsibility means that the accountant should always be aware of the broader social consequences of his actions.

Question 58

Which of these is a good indicator of accountability:

(A) Having regular reviews with your line manager to explain how you are working.
(B) Keeping accurate records in an orderly way.
(C) Always explaining your decisions when you make them.
(D) Being an able accountant.

Question 59

What is acting in the public interest?

(A) Making available information that is of interest to the public.
(B) Deciding what might be in the public interest to make known, even where it may compromise your client, employer and profession.
(C) Always having the idea that doing your job well is relied upon by the public.
(D) Acting as if you are always subject to public scrutiny.

Question 60

Why should an accountant continually develop?

(A) Because management accounting changes so fast that you need to keep up with it to stay marketable for employment.
(B) Because continual development means that the client always gets a better service every time he or she uses your services.
(C) Because professional competence rests on checking what you do know, adding to knowledge and skills and challenging habitual working practices.
(D) Because management accounting needs to reflect the evolving climate in business and finance.

Question 61

In which of the following cases would it be appropriate to disclose information:

(A) Whenever asked to by the boss.
(B) Whenever asked for by a court.
(C) Whenever asked for by a client.
(D) Whenever asked for by an auditor.

Question 62

You have an impossibly tight deadline to meet in preparing a report which is very important to your senior management, but time is running out. Should you:

(A) Work all night to complete it for the following morning?
(B) Do what you can and make your excuses when it comes in incomplete?
(C) Explain to your managers that you cannot meet the deadline they have imposed?
(D) Ask a friend to help you get it done in time?

Question 63

A colleague no longer feels he can work with a member of the management team of your company. He feels that the person is always pressing him to do things in a compromising way. Do you:

(A) Take the work from him, intending to stand up to the manager when she tries it on you?
(B) Report her to personnel for bullying your colleague?

(C) Talk to her to explain that she is making things difficult for your friend?
(D) Give your colleague a copy of the CIMA Code and their web address and wish him good luck in dealing with a difficult problem.

Question 64

A project that your manager is keen on looks set to have problems showing a profit in the first year. Thereafter, it is projected to make a healthy margin. You are aware of the way in which the system has gaps, which could hide the weak performance in the first year and could be disguised, and your manager asks you what they are and whether you can implement them. Do you:

(A) Tell him that the company systems do not permit any variance from the accounting method that would show up the weakness?
(B) Say that you know how to help him, but you can't because you don't think it's right to give false information?
(C) Prepare the financial reports in the way he requests, but get him to send you an e-mail confirming he asked you for this unrepresentative report?
(D) Do what he says, because he's the client?

Question 65

Which of these is *correct*? The importance of the ethical rule is to be judged by the:

(A) cost of breach to the individual bound by that rule.
(B) social consequences for breach of the rule.
(C) impact on the profession of the rule.
(D) the context within which it is applied.

Question 66

Which is a *correct* statement about CIMA's Code of ethics:

(A) It covers all ethical eventualities.
(B) It covers the main situations in practice that are likely to give rise to ethical problems.
(C) It gives the general principles to guide behaviour, rather than any specific guidance on how to act in particular circumstances.
(D) It can only be understood if read in conjunction with the IFAC Code.

Question 67

What is ethical conduct for a CIMA accountant?

(A) Doing what you think is right for society.
(B) Thinking that what you are doing is socially right.
(C) Thinking about the social consequences of what you do before you do it.
(D) Doing things that you believe comply with the CIMA Code.

Question 68

Which *one* of the following statements is *incorrect* in relation to corporate governance?

(A) Corporate governance is primarily concerned with the effective control business efficacy and accountability of the management of public listed companies.
(B) Corporate governance does not affect private companies.
(C) Corporate governance is intended to benefit stakeholders.
(D) The term 'stakeholders' is wider than shareholders and employees.

Question 69

Which *one* of the following statements is *incorrect* in relation to the interaction of corporate governance with business ethics and company law?

(A) Corporate governance is primarily concerned with the effective control business efficacy and accountability of the management of public listed companies.
(B) Corporate governance does not affect private companies.
(C) Corporate governance business ethics and company law are made up of entirely separate principles.
(D) The term 'stakeholders' is wider than shareholders and employees.

Question 70

In Gower and Davies' Principles of Modern Company Law (seventh edition), the Combined Code is referred to as 'soft law.' What did the authors mean by this expression?

(A) The Combined Code contains principles which, if broken, may give rise to civil liability only.
(B) The Combined Code contains principles which, if broken, are punishable by relatively small fines.
(C) The Combined Code contains principles which, if broken, only oblige the board to disclose the reasons for the breach.
(D) The Combined Code contains principles which, if broken, have no consequences whatsoever.

Question 71

In the event of any breach of the Combined Code, who will decide whether any further action is taken against the directors?

(A) The Financial Services Authority.
(B) The Stock Exchange.
(C) The Department of Trade and Industry.
(D) The shareholders.

Question 72

In the United States, the Sarbanes-Oakley Act was passed in 2002 following the major scandal after the collapse of the giant American corporation, Enron. Which of the following is *incorrect* in relation to the Sarbanes-Oakley Act ('the Act')?

(A) The Act created the Public Company Accounting Oversight Board ('PCAOB').
(B) The Act requires all auditors of public companies to be registered with the PCAOB.
(C) The Act requires the separate disclosure of the fees received by auditors for audit and all other fees.
(D) The Act requires directors to be professionally qualified to act as directors of public companies.

Question 73

The two-tier board structure comprises a Management Board and what other organ?

(A) An Employee Representation Board.
(B) A Government Representation Board.
(C) A Non-Executive Board.
(D) A Supervisory Board.

Question 74

Which of the following is not a recommendation of the Combined Code?

(A) Only persons who have industrial experience should be recruited as non-executive directors.
(B) At least half the board should be made up of non-executive directors.
(C) All directors should attend the AGM.
(D) Institutional shareholders should be encouraged to participate more fully in the company's affairs.

Question 75

Which of the following is not part of the regulatory governance framework for companies?

(A) The Companies Act 2006.
(B) The Sarbanes-Oakley Act 2002.
(C) The Combined Code 2003.
(D) The Stock Exchange Listing Regulations 1984.

Solutions

Solution 1
(C)

Solution 2
(B)

Solution 3
(B)

Solution 4
(A)

Solution 5
(D)

Solution 6
(C)

Solution 7
(D)

Solution 8
(A)

Solution 9
(C)

Solution 10
(B)

Solution 11
(B)

Solution 12
(A)

Solution 13
(C)

Solution 14
(C)

Solution 15
(D)

Solution 16
(B)

Solution 17
(D)

Solution 18
(B)

Solution 19
(A)

Solution 20
(B)

Solution 21
(C)

Solution 22
(B)

Solution 23
(A)

Solution 24
(B)

Solution 25
(C)

Solution 26
(D)

Solution 27
(D)

Solution 28
(B)

Solution 29
(D)

Solution 30
(B)

Solution 31
(C)

Solution 32
(A)

Solution 33
(D)

Solution 34
(A)

Solution 35
(B)

Solution 36
(D)

Solution 37
(C)

Solution 38
(A)

Solution 39
(B)

Solution 40
(B)

Solution 41
(B)

Solution 42
(C)

Solution 43
(D)

Solution 44
(A)

Solution 45
(B)

Solution 46
(A)

Solution 47
(D)

Solution 48
(C)

Solution 49
(B)

Solution 50
(A)

Solution 51
(B)

Solution 52
(D)

Solution 53
(A)

Solution 54
(D)

Solution 55
(D)

Solution 56
(A)

Solution 57
(D)

Solution 58
(C)

Solution 59
(C)

Solution 60
(C)

Solution 61
(C)

Solution 62
(B)

Solution 63
(B)

Solution 64
(B)

Solution 65
(D)

Solution 66
(A)

Solution 67
(D)

Solution 68
(B)

Solution 69
(C)

Solution 70
(C)

Solution 71
(D)

Solution 72
(A)

Solution 73
(D)

Solution 74
(A)

Solution 75
(B)

Index

Index